D1466494

PATTERNS IN MODERN DRAMA

PATTERNS IN

IBSEN

CHEKHOV

GALSWORTHY

O'NEILL

KELLY

THURBER

NUGENT

HELLMAN

New

PUBLISHED BY

MODERN DRAMA

Lodwick Hartley

HEAD OF THE DEPARTMENT OF ENGLISH

Arthur Ladu

PROFESSOR OF ENGLISH

NORTH CAROLINA STATE COLLEGE

York

PRENTICE-HALL, INC.

O F THIS COLLECTION of plays the primary purpose is to provide for college students on the freshman and sophomore levels the texts of seven plays that are well established in the repertory of the contemporary theater, that are representative of the main currents in drama from Ibsen to the present day, and that will furnish incentive to discussion of the patterns and ideas giving chief vitality to the twentieth-century theater.

The teeming activity of the European and American theater in the first half of this century has produced plays of bewildering variety. For this reason, any collection attempting to make a historical treatment of modern drama could hardly confine itself to as few plays as this volume contains. Moreover, the principle of selection would have to be markedly different. In the following collection the development of modern drama as a whole and the complicated web of interrelation between Continental and American drama can merely be suggested. The strictly "experimental" aspects of the modern theater have had to be excluded almost entirely. Nevertheless, the plays presented here should lay the foundation for further study of modern drama by providing for the student who is not already widely acquainted with literature of the stage an opportunity to study some of the basic dramatic forms that can be most profitably treated and most easily understood.

On the assumption that the student who has seen and read relatively few plays will be attracted first by the feelings and ideas expressed in the drama rather than by anything so abstract as form, an effort has been made to select as many plays as possible that will stimulate discussion. Ibsen's ideas of political liberalism, Miss Hellman's presentation of an aspect of capitalism, the opinion of Messrs. Thurber and Nugent concerning the intelligence quotient of the college-bred American, Galsworthy's treatment of the difficulties of humanitarianism—all suggest lively issues. On the other hand, problems in characterization and in the conflicts of wills and emotions are amply provided for in the plays of Chekhov, O'Neill, and Kelly. The variety of the selection should enable the student to perceive the proper balance between the drama of ideas and the drama in which human emotions and feelings furnish the predominating element.

Out of an appreciation of drama for itself should develop an appreciation of form. The evolution of a good amateur critic will come chiefly through the intelligent guidance of the teacher, who will develop the necessary criteria for judging between the good and the poor play. A brief introduction has been included as a college primer of criticism. At best, it can be little more than an outline, providing only the most elementary tools for discussing plays. Its main purpose is to provide the student with a few simple definitions and a small critical vocabulary. The dangers of using labels should not be minimized; and the student should be constantly warned to avoid critical cant which is usually a substitute for any thinking at all. He should, therefore, be encouraged to go beyond the introduction for further reading and discussions that will give him a more trustworthy grasp of the major criteria of judgment.

Each play has been provided with a chronology of the author and with an introduction in which an effort has been made to discuss the significance of the play and its author in modern drama. Brief critical bibliographies are appended as guides to further reading.

Acknowledgment is hereby made to the Walter H. Baker Company for permission to use a translation of *An Enemy of the People;* to Charles Scribner's Sons for permission to use a translation of *Uncle Vanya* and the text of *The Pigeon;* to Random House for permission to reprint *The Emperor Jones, The Little Foxes,* and *The Male Animal;* and to Little, Brown and Company for permission to reprint *Craig's Wife.*

The authors wish to acknowledge the assistance of Mrs. Katherine Alston Edsall, of the D. H. Hill Library at North Carolina State College, and that of Mrs. Nell Joslin Styron, whose help in research, in criticism, and in secretarial matters has been of great value.

CONTENTS

PATTERNS IN MODERN DRAMA

I. WHAT IS DRAMA?

THE ETYMOLOGY of the word *drama,* which is derived from the Greek verb *dran* meaning *to do* or *to act,* is important in determining its meaning. Basically, drama involves the presentation of a situation or the telling of a story in terms of some kind of physical *action,* whether it be that of savages dancing around a totem pole, that of strolling players presenting their "interludes" in innyards of sixteenth-century England, or that of a sophisticated group of actors performing a comedy by Noel Coward in a theater just off Broadway. Usually this action is visible physical action on a stage, although radio drama in our own time has been able to accomplish its purpose entirely through sound, and moving pictures have substituted for the limitations of the stage the unlimited potentialities of the screen. Since the basic means of presenting life on the stage is through the spoken words of the actors as well as through pantomime and other forms of physical movement, perhaps we should say that *a drama tells a story by means of dialogue and action.*

It will hardly be appropriate to discuss here at length the easily recognizable and the universal phenomenon called *dramatic instinct*— that desire of human beings, primitive and civilized, to represent action or to impersonate. Its most elementary manifestations are apparent in tribal ceremonials of primitive peoples and in the games and "make-believe" of children. No one, it is true, will want to call a totem-pole dance or a game of cops and robbers drama in the sense in which we usually employ the term; but even these simple forms illustrate the fundamental conception of drama as an *objective representation of action* in which actors assume characters other than their own and engage in "make-believe."

If we seek a definition of drama from professional playwrights and critics, we shall find conflicting opinions. For example, the French critic Brunetière, writing in the eighteen nineties, saw drama as essen-

1

tially "the will of man in conflict with the mysterious powers or natural forces which limit and belittle us." Other critics have felt that Brunetière's emphasis on conflict and struggle is too limited. At one point in his career, Maeterlinck urged the neglect of the external phenomena of life for the attempt to present spiritual and emotional undercurrents or "soul states." In this sort of approach drama may be meaningful action entirely without conflict. William Archer found his most satisfactory approach to drama through crisis (embodying the idea of turn or reversal) rather than through conflict, which he regards as only one of the most important elements, rather than as the sole distinguishing element, of drama. By Archer's definition a play is a "more or less rapidly developing crisis in destiny or circumstances, and a dramatic scene is a crisis within a crisis, clearly furthering the ultimate event."

Since Maeterlinck's approach chiefly involves a type of plotless or "static" play that he himself developed and later abandoned, the need for reconcilement lies chiefly between the theories of Brunetière and those of Archer. A possible compromise is found in the position that whereas obvious or heroic conflict and struggle are not essential, drama does involve some sort of opposition of two forces, external or internal, conscious or subliminal, tangible or intangible—an opposition often emphasized and made effective by crisis. Many plays will have a definite development or motion in one direction and a turn or reversal of this motion that gives significance to the whole. However, even though the action of a play may be slight and though it may end inconclusively, this action will usually develop to the point at which two lines of thought, of physical force, or of feeling either meet or stand out against one another in significant contrast. The fact that a play ends inconclusively obviously does not mean that forces within it have not been revealed in opposition. Actually, inconclusion may be conclusion enough.

To examine specific plays, AN ENEMY OF THE PEOPLE and THE PIGEON embody very obvious opposition and even clashes of ideas and ideals. But whereas in the first the clash of forces has a definite outcome, in the second the outcome is inconclusive. Again, the conflict of personalities and wills in THE LITTLE FOXES is a salient feature of the play. This conflict is no less strong for being less obvious in UNCLE VANYA, the deliberate movement of which is in sharp contrast to the vigorous movement of THE LITTLE FOXES. In THE EMPEROR JONES the opposition exists on two levels: the external, in which the hero struggles with a group for his life; and the internal, in which he struggles with a force within himself.

An analysis of only a few plays will suggest that the opposition or conflict of forces in the drama may fall into many patterns. The two forces may be represented by two human beings, one human being and a particular social group, two groups of human beings, one human being and society at large, a human being and Fate or God, a human being and the forces within himself, or a human being and the forces of nature or environment. It is possible that more than one conflict or opposition may be involved in a play, but usually there is only one of real significance.

Though we shall be concerned with conflict in the main lines of dramatic action in the play, our interest in contrast both as a distinguishing quality of drama and as a structural device will be even more pervading. The thoughtful student will want to perceive how the dramatist contrasts character with character, mood with mood, tempo with tempo in achieving his total pattern.

II. TYPES OF PLAYS

Of every play we may ask three basic questions: Does it give chief emphasis to fullness and intensity of characterization or does it depend upon action for its appeal? Is its intent serious or is it humorous? Does it end unhappily or does it end happily? If we could assume that all plays adhered to type, we might divide them all, according to emphasis, intent, and conclusion, into two general categories: tragedy and comedy. In actual practice, however, plays do not always fall neatly even into general categories. The blending of comedy and tragedy, the possibilities of countless nuances between the two, and the various ways of handling characters and action have all tended to create such an infinite variety of forms that classification may seem ridiculous. Nevertheless, the fundamental concepts of tragedy and comedy remain as valuable guides.

Tragedy is the most serious type of drama. Though no definition of the term is entirely safe, in general it connotes that type of play which deals with the somber and serious aspects of life, places its emphasis on characterization, and ends unhappily—often in the death of

3

the leading character. If we conceive of drama in terms of the opposition of two forces, which we shall call positive and negative, we
may think of tragedy as ending with the defeat of the positive force.
(The character representing the positive force is often referred to as
the *protagonist*, and the opposing force or obstacle is designated as the
antagonist.) So conceived, tragedy may have death as a typical but
not as an absolutely necessary ingredient. The defeat of the hero, it
may easily be seen, may be more poignant if he continues to live than
if he dies at the end of the play.

Since tragedy concentrates, not merely on characterization, but
most often on a single character, there may be certain qualifications
that we shall expect the tragic character to possess. He cannot be a
weakling or a creature of complete depravity. Even a man of impeccable goodness is not usually an acceptable tragic hero. The tragic
character is more often a human being with sufficient strength and
worth to command our sympathy and respect but with some "flaw"
or weakness capable of setting in motion a chain of events that, through
the operations of the laws of cause and effect, will eventually bring
about his destruction. The weak or helpless character who is subjected to misfortune is pathetic rather than tragic.

The Greek playwrights, who wrote with a definite religious sense,
conceived of the tragic hero as violating the will of the gods in some
way that would ultimately bring about his pursuit and death by an
avenging Nemesis. So, in the main, Greek tragedy presents the struggle of man with Fate or Destiny. The Elizabethans, with the Renais-
sance emphasis on man as a free agent, were less concerned with man's
struggle with God or the gods. Rather did their tragedies pit man
against man, and man against the forces inside himself. Modern
drama, with its heightened consciousness of man not as an individual
but as a part of society, has often placed emphasis on the struggle between man and forces in his environment and heredity. The conception of tragedy has also changed; it now comprehends not the fall of
a great man but the defeat of the common man.

But whatever form the objective struggle takes, the important consideration is always what goes on *inside* the tragic character. It is
essentially a contest in which he stands alone against the universe and
in which his destiny—as well as the destiny of mankind, which he
symbolizes—is involved. With this idea in mind, one may make a
broad philosophical distinction between comedy and tragedy that will

go beyond such a technical consideration as a happy or an unhappy ending. Comedy in its purest form becomes an intellectual instrument shaping a criticism of life: its manners, its customs, its institutions, its attitudes. Tragedy apprehends emotionally and is far deeper and broader in scope, for it is concerned, not with the surface manifestations of life, but with the moral order of the universe and the destiny of man.

Great tragedy has the effect of arousing in the spectator the emotions of fear and pity and of inducing in him a sense of awe, giving him as it does so a vision of moral order and law and an insight into human striving and suffering. As Aristotle puts it, tragedy not only arouses the emotions of fear and pity, but it offers an opportunity for a *catharsis* or a purging of these emotions. For these reasons, tragedy is a very lofty form of art and is difficult to achieve.

On a somewhat lower plane is *melodrama,* which is related to tragedy in the type of material used. Melodrama, however, differs from tragedy in the treatment of that material; and it does not of necessity end unhappily. Often the words *melodrama* and *melodramatic* are used to indicate dramatic action that is tawdrily affected or strained in the direction of violence or sentimentality. Such a concept of the terms does an injustice to many plays to which they should rightly be applied. More broadly, melodrama is that type of serious play in which the action tends to become of greater importance than the characterization and in which the excitement produced by the plot tends to take precedence over the seriousness of the theme. In a melodrama either the problem may be of insufficient weight to give the action significance beyond its purely theatrical interest, or the action and characters may be of insufficient worth to lend significance to the problem. Reducing the matter to the simplest terms, one may say that melodrama differs most significantly from tragedy in its emphasis upon action rather than upon characterization and theme.

Returning to our idea of opposing forces in a play, we may conceive of a comedy as a play in which the protagonist or the positive force triumphs. Naturally, a comedy does not have to be light and humorous throughout. It may involve serious action and the complications may even be potentially grim. Unlike a tragedy, which usually concentrates on one character, a comedy may develop several characters of equal importance.

The Greeks kept comedy and tragedy distinct. The Elizabethans, on the other hand, assumed great freedom in mixing them. The greatest of Shakespeare's tragedies, for example, may introduce comic scenes as a means of achieving momentary relief from dramatic tension; and such a comedy as Shakespeare's THE MERCHANT OF VENICE is so full of serious possibilities that up to its very conclusion the action might have been tragic. The modern play, in its attempt to reveal the complete panorama of life, may present such a mixture of the humorous and the serious that neither *comedy* nor *tragedy* will seem an apt term to apply to it. Moreover, as we have seen, it may be inconclusive in its action and, consequently, may present far greater problems of classification than the Elizabethan play, in which almost every character is either married or buried in the last act.

It is easy to see how in some plays in which the conclusion is neither strictly comic nor tragic, the serious elements may greatly overbalance the humorous ones. In such instances, some critics have chosen a term like *problem play* as a compromise. The term *comedy of ideas* is also used for a play involving the discussion of serious ideas.

Comedy into which no very serious element intrudes may achieve a high quality. It is particularly entertaining when it takes the form of the *comedy of manners,* the type of play in which the *mores* of society provide the elements of humor. It may also be very amusing in the *folk comedy,* which has been very popular in recent years, and in which folkways perform the same function that etiquette and social convention do in the comedy of manners. When a comedy is not concerned primarily with characterization, and when it gets its effect chiefly by presenting a series of amusing situations or speeches, it is called *farce.* Like a good melodrama, a good *farce* may be an extremely skillful piece of writing. If its situations degenerate into rough and tumble with little wit or logic, it may become *low comedy* or *slapstick.* On the other hand, it may be colored by satire and may become an instrument of brilliant wit. But the highest and most civilized type of comedy is that in which a significant problem—moral, social, or otherwise—is embodied in characters whose development provides the central interest.

Application of these basic categories to the dramas included in this book should provoke interesting discussion. One may immediately observe that contemporary plays on serious themes are by no means so much concerned with the moral responsibility of the hero for his destruction as Greek and Elizabethan tragedies are. As a result, the hero often becomes of more importance as a symbol in the total meaning of the play than as an individual struggling against great universal forces, and a question may arise as to whether a truly tragic effect is attained. AN ENEMY OF THE PEOPLE, for example, plainly has a tragic outcome. But one may well ask whether the medical reformer defeated by the selfish public is not more important as the embodiment of a limited social idea than he is as an individual representing mankind. A similar question may be asked in regard to UNCLE VANYA, in which the tragedy of the character who gives his name to the play is only an aspect of the total tragic effect of the play. One may also ask whether THE EMPEROR JONES is not rather a penetrating and exciting psychological study of a limited aspect of human experience than a profound comment on universal human aspiration and struggle. These and many other questions may be involved in reaching conclusions about the conception of tragedy in the drama of our own day. The line of demarcation between the pathetic and the tragic is not always a clear one, and revisions in definitions may be necessary. Such considerations will lead the serious student to a more intensive study of the meaning of tragedy.

Though THE LITTLE FOXES ends with the triumph of the central character, it is hardly a comedy. The character of Regina is of such depravity that, even though she had been defeated in her struggle, she could not have been regarded as a tragic heroine. No one can fail to see that the gripping action and brilliant interplay of wits and characters are the genius of the play. The most satisfactory classification for THE LITTLE FOXES is that of melodrama, debatable though the classification may be.

In calling THE PIGEON a "fantasy," Galsworthy warns us that he is going to be as whimsical as he pleases. At the same time, his play is not a mere *jeu d'esprit* for an evening's entertainment in the theater. Its ideas are serious. Though it ends inconclusively, the ending is certainly not unhappy. One will have no difficulty in classifying it as a comedy, and—since it is full of discussion of its central theme—a comedy of ideas.

Though THE MALE ANIMAL is shot through with satire, and though it makes pertinent comments on modern living, its gaiety and boisterousness is in marked contrast to the relatively quiet and deliberate development of THE PIGEON. THE MALE ANIMAL may, therefore, be safely classified as a farce.

If we were forced to choose between the labels comedy and tragedy for CRAIG'S WIFE, we should be confronted with a real difficulty.

7

The play is throughout a serious character study, and its outcome is not exactly happy. Unlike THE LITTLE FOXES, it is not characterized by melodramatic violence and briskness of action. It is hardly tragic, for when in the end we find the heroine alone in the possession of the material things for which she has sacrificed all human values, we can have little sympathy for her. The somberness of this outcome makes the play fit ill among comedies. We may, therefore, compromise by calling it a problem play.

III. THE DRAMATIST'S APPROACH

AFTER we have examined a play to determine whether its intent is humorous or serious, whether its conclusion is happy or unhappy, and whether it emphasizes action or characterization, we must consider still another very significant aspect of the dramatist's use of his material. Though the presentation of life through action is the aim of the dramatist, methods of achieving the dramatic effect may vary widely.

The Greeks regarded drama as an "imitation" of life. A contemporary playwright, however, has pointed out that the duty of the dramatist is not so much to bring life to the stage as it is to bring the stage to life. The two points of view are not incompatible.

What every dramatist is required to do is to create the *illusion of reality*. By no means is he chained inexorably to reality itself. In fact, he may present life on the stage, not as it actually is, but as it might be or should be. Instead of presenting life so that the appeal of the presentation is from its reasonableness, the playwright may make a highly imaginative projection. The play may deal with faraway places, unusual characters, and extraordinary action. Its world may be the world of imagination or the world of dreams. It may take us to the remote past or to the distant future.

In general, the approach which departs from everyday experience to present the exotic, the idyllic, the remote, or the unusual is said to be *romantic*, and the obligation of the dramatist is not so much to convince the audience of the actual truth of his presentation as it is to win from the audience a "willing suspension of disbelief." *Realistic* drama, on the other hand, attempts to present types of people and action that are familiar to us. Though the best realistic plays emphasize characterization rather than action, the realistic approach does not rule out complicated plotting. At the same time, its characters and situations are more nearly acceptable to the reason than are the characters and situations of the romantic play. It may be concluded, then, that whereas the realistic dramatist is more definitely obligated than the romantic dramatist to make a presentation of life as it is actually lived, the former operates with extensive freedom regarding the way in which he selects, arranges, interprets, and criticizes the details of life that he presents.

Naturalistic drama, which has attained wide popularity in our century, attempts to intensify realism and to make what is presented on the stage more scientific and more nearly acceptable to man's reasoning powers. Unlike the realist, who may color his material with his own feelings, the naturalistic dramatist must emancipate himself from his emotions. Sympathy for characters or classes of society must not betray him into pleading their case. He must be coldly objective. He does not condemn, judge, or praise; he observes and describes, giving as nearly photographic a rendering of reality as possible. To tell the *truth* about his characters is his sole object, not to decide what they ought to do or what ought to be done to them. He acknowledges one law, that of cause and effect, and his aim is to show human life to be the product of material causes acting according to natural law. Under such a theory, the naturalistic dramatist must abandon some of the best established dramatic devices. Complicated plotting can hardly exist in naturalistic drama, for such action is not often enough a real part of life. In all respects, the playwright tries to make the pattern of the play appear to lie in life itself rather than in the playwright's mind.

A play like Maeterlinck's PELLÉAS AND MÉLISANDE may be selected as a classic example of the romantic approach. In it the playwright, Maeterlinck, makes little concession to life as it is lived in his own day. The time-setting is in the indefinite past, the very distant past; and the place-setting is in a misty kingdom of medieval romance. The characterization and the action belong to poetry rather than to life. Ibsen, on the other hand, is writing about people and problems of his own day in AN ENEMY OF THE PEOPLE. He embarks on the dramatic presentation of an idea, selecting his characters from contemporary life and arranging his details so that his purpose will be fulfilled. Chekhov also deals with his own contemporaries in UNCLE VANYA, but he is less

9

concerned than Ibsen is to select and arrange characters and action to point up his theme. He is scientific and objective rather than judicial.

Though romanticism, realism, and naturalism are three basic approaches to dramatic materials, evidences of overlapping are not infrequent. There are also approaches that are not distinct in themselves but are related in some way to the basic ones. *Symbolism* is an example. The use of symbols is a part of all imaginative writing. Indeed, in almost every product of art, outward appearances stand for or suggest something inward, spiritual, or intangible. The concrete thing is, therefore, regarded as a symbol. When the method of using concrete things to suggest spiritual or otherwise intangible values is made the primary objective of the dramatic presentation, we usually speak of the method as being symbolistic. Since a great many symbolistic plays treat unusual characters and situations, it may seem that symbolism is more closely related to romanticism than to realism or naturalism. On the other hand, it is possible to achieve symbolistic drama, as Maeterlinck does in THE INTRUDER, by employing such simple and bare situations that the symbolism seems to be an extension of the naturalistic method.

Symbolism is concerned with abstract ideas; so also is *expressionism*. Expressionism grows out of a desire to transcend the physical limitations of realism and naturalism. Whereas naturalism has a tendency to be objective and sociological, expressionism tends to be subjective and psychological. It is concerned with the presentation of inner states rather than with outer reality, and it may show how outward things are distorted by the inner eye. In fact, the expressionistic dramatist assumes the right to distort any or all of his media (lighting, acting, scenery) so that they assume other than their ordinary functions for the most effective expression of his ideas. He may alternate fantasy and reality at will. In expressionistic drama the action is usually episodic, and it may move on several different planes at once. Characters may be types, personified abstractions, automata, live puppets, or pure creations of the imagination. A play like THE EMPEROR JONES, with its gripping dramatization of atavistic fears, is an excellent example of the expressionistic play in which the greatest part is a projection of the hero's mind. There are many other kinds of expressionistic plays. O'Neill's THE HAIRY APE and Čapek's R.U.R. may be cited as widely varying examples.

IV. CHARACTERIZATION

ALONG the way, something has already been said about character-ization, but it is hardly possible to overstress its importance, not only in the drama, but in fiction of all sorts. If one thinks back over the great plays and novels one has read, one will readily see that characters of fiction can remain in the mind long after plots are forgotten. In fact, Hamlet, Becky Sharp, Natty Bumppo, and Cyrano de Bergerac often have a reality more vivid than that of people whom we have actually known and observed.

With a few exceptions, all playwrights attempt to create for pres-entation on the stage flesh-and-blood characters who act according to motives and impulses understandable to any intelligent observer of life. The skilled artist, as we have already suggested, can present extraordi-nary people acting under extraordinary circumstances and still be con-vincing. There is no particular formula for winning the credence of a reader or of a spectator. But when we say that a character in a play is "unconvincing," we do not mean that the playwright has failed in his creation because he has presented a character outside our usual range of observation and comprehension. We mean rather that he has failed to make the character act according to certain laws of cause and effect that the writer himself may have established. It is easy to see that we do not actually judge Uncle Vanya, Jones, and Regina Hubbard by the same standards. Any one of them would be completely out of place in the "world" of the other. At the same time, each of them may be perfectly credible in his own "world."

The novelist has a few more resources of characterization than has the playwright. For example, if the former chooses he may devote a great deal of space to direct description of the character. (The great-est masters of fiction, however, prefer less prejudicial methods.) The playwright on the other hand has to rely chiefly on his two mainstays: action and dialogue. Naturally, his most important method of char-acterization is through what his characters themselves do and say. He may also use the device of letting characters talk about one another. Under the influence of modern psychology and psychoanalysis, some dramatists reveal their characters by allowing them to speak their in-nermost thoughts (a device at least as old as the asides and soliloquies

11

of Elizabethan drama) or by making an objective representation of the processes of their subconscious minds.

Most often only the really important characters of a play are fully presented or developed. The minor characters play a role similar to that of the chorus in Greek tragedy, commenting on the main characters and the action and in general giving continuity to the play. But the clever playwright shows his genius by delineating his subordinate characters with telling vividness in the few strokes allowed him. Shakespeare is, of course, the classic example of supreme genius in creating minor characters of striking reality and individuality. A playwright who is slovenly in writing his "bit" parts is likely to miss greatness.

The English novelist Mr. E. M. Forster has made a distinction between characters in novels that is applicable to characters in plays as well. Most characters, according to his idea, are either "flat" or "round." "Flat" characters, constructed around one idea or quality, tend to be types and sometimes even caricatures. They are like the "humours" of Elizabethan drama—characters constructed under the theory that every human being has some predominating "humour" or passion that shapes him. "Round" characters have more of a three-dimensional quality, in that their actions are not unerringly predictable according to a pre-established pattern, and in that they are capable of change, growth, and development. Undoubtedly, there are great masterpieces of "flat" portraiture in the drama as well as in the novel; and one should not discount the value of the two-dimensional presentation unless it tends toward superficiality; however, the greatest examples of character portrayal present their subjects in the round.

Like the painter, the playwright is concerned with an interpretation of life rather than with a mere reproduction of it. Therefore, even in achieving a "round" characterization he may emphasize whatever features in his delineation will best serve his purpose. Even a distortion may be valuable in achieving his effect. On the other hand, he may feel that truth to reality necessitates a minimum of distortion and "slanting"; thus he may aim rather at fullness, subtlety, and penetration.

Dr. Stockmann, in AN ENEMY OF THE PEOPLE, is an excellent example of full-length portraiture purposefully done, yet without an obvious suggestion of slanting. Mrs. Craig, of CRAIG'S WIFE, is also a full-length portrait, though the slanting is considerably more obvious. A comparison between the "roundness" of Ibsen's portrait and the relative "flatness" of Kelly's should be profitable. The characters in THE LITTLE FOXES are etched with acid, and those of THE MALE ANIMAL are drawn with the broad, distorted lines of caricature.

V. PLOT AND STRUCTURE

IN TALKING about such things as conflict and contrast, we have necessarily been concerned with pattern and with plot. Plot in the drama is, of course, exactly what it is in the novel or the short story. A simple narrative records a series of events in which time sequence is the most important structural principle. For example, we might write of a trip to the beach or a hike in the mountains in such a way that the details themselves would be interesting. At the same time no single detail in the story might be directly dependent for its interest or effectiveness on any of the preceding details. Plot, on the other hand, involves a relationship of events according to some causal scheme. In other words, if, in a straight narrative, events A, B, C, and D are quite independent of one another, in a story with a plot, B occurs because A has occurred; C occurs because A and B have occurred; and so on. Moreover, in the plotted narrative, events A, B, C, and D lead ultimately to some final event X that enables us to see all the rest of the preceding events in a new light.

Some plays may impress us as being tightly plotted; that is, they present a series of closely interrelated situations or circumstances that become progressively involved until a point is reached at which there is some solution or resolution of the complications by unexpected means. Other plays may seem to be collections of situations so loosely connected that they do not constitute a plot at all. Again, some plays are full of movement and physical action, whereas others seem almost completely static. A favorite device of a playwright like Shaw, for example, is to assemble a group of characters on the stage and to allow them to engage in conversation for most of the duration of the play. One of Maeterlinck's one-act plays has little more action than that involved in a conversation of a family seated around a table. Although at one point in UNCLE VANYA there is a vigorous bit of stage business, throughout most of the play little "happens" in the most commonly

13

accepted meaning of the word. In THE PIGEON, too, though we have a presentation of several facets of a problem through several characters, there is not much action, and there is no resolution of the problem.

Yet there is in all these seemingly "plotless" plays an underlying movement toward a goal. Though all the scenes may not move directly toward the culmination, a close examination will reveal that there is a continuous line of connection between all the moments of the play from beginning to end and that all the various contrasts employed in the play are brought together at last in one meaningful pattern.

Regardless of whether the play is obviously plotted or not, the continuous line of connection should be so firmly maintained that no event comes as a complete surprise. Underlying preparation should be fully perceptible for each "surprise"—at least, *after* the event is revealed. The really competent playwright uses coincidences sparingly if at all and strictly avoids *deus ex machina* endings—that is, endings in which some force outside the normal expectancy of events is brought in to effect a solution or to save a situation.

The most conventional kind of plot construction is that in which the action is allowed, step by step, to develop complications which are resolved before the end of the play. When such a plan is used, the play may fall into easily recognizable divisions. First, there will be the *exposition,* which introduces the characters and gives the general background of the play. Then at some point—usually called the *generating circumstance* or the *incentive moment*—the complications will be set in motion. The resulting movement is designated as the *rising action* or the *complication.* The point at which the action definitely turns and at which the forces that finally determine the conclusion become definitely perceptible is called the *crisis.* From the crisis to the end of the play, the action may be called the *falling action* or the *resolution.* The French word *dénouement,* meaning literally "the unravelling," is frequently used to indicate the final revelation or occurrence that clarifies the nature and outcome of a plot. *Climax* is an ambiguous term, often confused with *crisis.* It is safest to allow it to refer only to the point of keenest interest in the play.

A second type of construction is represented in the play that begins with a situation in which some significant or terrible involvement is already present. The play then develops by unfolding action. Of this method, often that of Greek tragedies, the OEDIPUS REX of Sophocles is the finest example. When the play opens, we learn that the city of Thebes is being ravaged by a terrible plague. An oracle warns that there will be no relief from the pestilence until the murderer of Laius, a former ruler, is punished. Oedipus, the present king, utters a strong imprecation on the culprit. The unfolding of the plot reveals the horrible truth that Oedipus himself was the unwitting murderer of his father and that he is married to his mother. In modern drama a classic example of the use of the "unfolding" method is found in Ibsen's GHOSTS. THE EMPEROR JONES also suggests this method, in that the elements of the final catastrophe are strongly presented in the first scene, and in that the rest of the play involves the inexorable consummation of the catastrophe. The device is also popular in contemporary plays dealing with murder mysteries.

A third technique is the loose or episodic method of handling the story. This method has been regularly employed in historical plays, from those of Shakespeare to the present day. But its use is by no means confined to any one type of play. It is regularly employed by dramatists who are more concerned with characterization, mood, theme, or truth to life than with tight plotting. The naturalists, the symbolists, and the expressionists are likely to disregard most of the conventions of plotting in attaining their objectives.

If the playwright follows most of the common conventions, he will divide his play into three, four, or five acts and will assign a distinct function to each act. For all practical purposes each act may be a little play in itself, with crisis and climax. In turn each act may be composed of several scenes. If a play is so constructed, the curtain becomes an invaluable piece of equipment for pointing the action and giving significance to the act as a whole. But many contemporary dramatists in their efforts to depict the flow of life regard such construction as extremely artificial. Sometimes a playwright does not drop his curtain at all. Often he blanks out the stage before the curtain comes down. And when he does make a necessary break in his action, he does so not to round out a scene or to point up the action but rather to indicate the passing of time or merely to give his audience a necessary breathing spell. Though his play may be composed of many scenes and though some of the scenes may be little plays in themselves, the effect of the whole is of supreme importance; and the play is held together, not by cleverness of plotting, but by the dominating character, mood, or idea.

Though THE EMPEROR JONES is regarded as a one-act play, its abandonment of conventional structure for purposes of revealing inner states of mind has become fairly typical of many full-length contemporary plays. In one sense, the play seems almost plotless. In striking contrast is THE LITTLE FOXES, which is ingeniously plotted, and in which tensions are built up and broken down until the final climax comes with great power. Each curtain deftly snaps the tautness of emotion that the act has built up, and we are ready to proceed logically with the action in the next act. A clear and fairly simple progression from the relatively conventional structure of a realistic play to the more casual structure of the naturalistic play may be seen by comparing AN ENEMY OF THE PEOPLE and UNCLE VANYA.

The three methods of construction described above are merely the basic ones. Subordinate and related devices, as well as combinations of methods, are numberless. One of the most commonly used is the "throw-back," in which, with obvious similarities to the "unfolding" method, the climax or the conclusion is presented first and the antecedent action is reconstructed in the main body of the play. Another device almost equally popular is the circular plot—ingeniously used by Galsworthy in THE PIGEON—in which the play ends in a mood or situation similar to that with which it began.

VI. SETTING

THE SETTING of a play may be regarded merely as the place where the action occurs. On the other hand, it may be interpreted more broadly to mean the summation of many of the external forces influencing the characters. To state the matter differently, the setting may be either the background against which the characters move or it may be an organic part of the play. It is entirely possible that the characteristics of a place should so obtrude upon the action of a play or so definitely determine the course of events that the setting might actually become an element of first importance.

In actual production the physical equipment of the stage may be a highly important factor in creating the total effect of a play. For hundreds of years, however, such physical equipment played a relatively unimportant part in the drama. If the medieval players had an opening in the floor of their pageant wagon to represent the entrance to Hell, their needs of staging might be fairly well satisfied. The Elizabethan playwright, knowing that he had only a little more stage equipment at his command, depended upon the evocative power of language to create in the minds of the spectators the mood, atmosphere, and other perquisites of setting.

The contemporary playwright, conscious as he is of the importance and influence of environment in human action, is often inclined to pay a great deal of attention to setting. As a result, he frequently goes into detailed description in the text of his play so that his exact effects may be achieved. On the other hand, though many contemporary plays require such realistic stage sets that the reproduction is scarcely distinguishable from the actuality, there are those playwrights who have sought to simulate the conditions under which more primitive drama was presented by using a bare stage with a minimum of properties. This is the device used some years ago by Thornton Wilder in OUR TOWN and more recently by Maxwell Anderson in JOAN OF LORRAINE. Both plays have been very successful in appealing to the imagination of their audiences chiefly through the media of dialogue and pantomime. Such experiments are stimulating. Moreover, the playwright who is able to make the suggestive power of language do the work of actual scenery is a master of no mean talent. At the same time, there is no reason why a playwright should not use all the media of the stage at his command. The effectiveness of a play like THE EMPEROR JONES is legitimately achieved through the full use of lighting, scenic, and sound effects.

VII. THEME

THE SUM TOTAL of what a play has to say may be called its *theme*. It is also possible to regard the theme as the basic and informing idea of a play. If the play is deliberately directed toward promoting a specific program of action or giving a "message," we may say that it has a *thesis*. When Galsworthy, for example, attempts to effect legal and penal reforms in plays like JUSTICE and THE SILVER BOX, he emphasizes his basic idea much more strongly than most playwrights do.

A theme does not have to be a thesis, nor does it have to be a moral

17

—though it may have moral implications enough. Nor is the theme always something that can be accurately summarized in a sentence or two. A Shakespearean comedy—AS YOU LIKE IT, for example—might suggest several themes. There is hardly one that would sum it up. And what is the theme of UNCLE VANYA? Just as Shakespeare was primarily concerned with writing a brilliant comedy full of wit, music, and poetry, Chekhov was primarily concerned with presenting a segment of life as accurately as he could. So the plays of both dramatists are shaped by so definite an intention that the absence of a single theme is certainly not to be regarded as a dramatic defect. If we tried hard enough, we might evolve one statement for each that would tie together all its elements. But if a predominating theme is not apparent, perhaps we should not waste time in trying too hard to find one that can be stated with complete definiteness.

AN ENEMY OF THE PEOPLE presents an entirely different situation. The whole play is constructed around an immediately apparent theme, and the conclusion is definite enough. Dr. Stockmann, who wishes to expose the pollution of the waters in the municipal baths of his city, is opposed and defeated by those to whom the revelation of the truth would mean a loss of money. He inveighs against the "compact majority" and comes to the conclusion that the majority is always wrong. Apart from the interest that the play gains from characterization and dramatic conflict, additional interest and significance comes from its presentation of a most provocative idea.

Like AN ENEMY OF THE PEOPLE, THE LITTLE FOXES and THE MALE ANIMAL suggest their themes in their titles. In the first Miss Hellman is concerned with pointing out the vulpine appetites of a class of individuals that she regards as being condoned, if not actually nurtured, by our economic system. One may, of course, wonder whether the indictment is strictly fair, and whether, indeed, the theme is of as much importance as the absorbing action. But the idea dominating the play is glaringly clear. Messrs. Thurber and Nugent are also concerned with the animal-like traits of human beings. Though they look on the self-styled *homo sapiens* of our age with more humor and less revulsion than Miss Hellman, at the same time they point incisively to the frequently ridiculous performances of products of the American system of education. As satirists, the playwrights assume great freedom in distorting their characters and other elements of their medium to make their point. The play is so written that it provides hilarious

18

entertainment, but the theme is never really obscured by the merriment.

It happens that in THE PIGEON Galsworthy, also, uses an animal metaphor to suggest his theme. As a later discussion will reveal, the theme of a play by Galsworthy is more likely to be stated in the form of a question than in that of a declarative sentence. Galsworthy's device of presenting a problem in dramatic form without any attempt to solve the problem is a characteristic of his plays that is almost unique. CRAIG'S WIFE offers an interesting contrast to THE PIGEON. Instead of being concerned with a social problem, it is concerned with a problem of character. Instead of leaving the reader or playgoer with a question in his mind, the playwright unswervingly reveals the inevitable results of selfishness and materialism in the individual. In fact, as one contemporary critic has put it, he adheres "almost fanatically" to his single theme of the "good housekeeper" who deliberately sacrifices everything else in her life, including her husband's love, in order to keep in impeccable order a house that she mistakenly regards as a home.

Markedly unlike the plays that we have just discussed, however, is THE EMPEROR JONES. The informing principle of this play may be stated more accurately in terms of mood or psychological approach than in terms of philosophical ideas. For example, one would hardly want to regard THE EMPEROR JONES as merely turning on a theme of "vaulting ambition, which o'erleaps itself."

The great popularity of Ibsen and Shaw has had a tendency to make us look for intellectual content in modern drama. Thus, in the minds of many, the pre-eminence of the drama of ideas has been established. It is very true that in our own century the stage has become increasingly important as an instrument of social criticism and even of political propaganda. We are certainly justified in looking upon the dramatist as a thinker and in seeking from the stage, not only entertainment and a broadening of our understanding of life, but also stimulation to our thinking on moral, social, political, and even religious problems. At the same time, we should not forget two supremely important elements of the drama that should lift it above the mere pamphlet or sermon and should make it significant for all time rather than for a particular period: namely, imagination and literary form.

VIII. READER VERSUS PLAYGOER

IT SHOULD BE perfectly clear that plays are intended to be seen, not read. It is also obvious that many plays that are effective on the stage do not read well and that some plays that read well do not play well. The critic who contends that the text of a play is little more than a blueprint has a good argument on his side. All the instrumentalities of the theater, including an audience, may be necessary to make a play a vital, living thing. Nevertheless, although the final test of a play must come through seeing it produced on a stage, the reading of plays has for centuries provided pleasure and profit. Therefore, the approach to the drama through reading needs no apologies.

Certain difficulties, it is true, are involved in reading a play. When one is in the theater, most of the job of interpreting the play is done for one by the actors, the stage designers, and the electricians. In the production of many plays very little is left to the imagination of the audience. But the reader must design his own stage sets, arrange his own lighting effects, costume his own actors, and put them through all their paces of pantomime and vocal inflection. Indeed, reading a play offers a challenge to the imagination. Fortunately, it is a challenge that can easily be met with a little patience and practice.

HENRIK IBSEN

1828 Born on March 20, in Skien, Norway, son of well-to-do parents.

1836 Failure of father's business. Family impoverished.

1843 Supported himself as apprentice
to to apothecary. Wrote poetry.
1850 Studied painting.

1850 Attended University lectures at Christiania. First play, CATALINA. Ibsen associated with radical and illegal labor agitation.

1852 Stage manager at Norwegian Theatre in Bergen. Secured position through influence of the noted violinist, Ole Bull. Studied dra-
to matic technique for a few weeks in Denmark and Germany. Wrote romantic plays based on
1857 Norwegian history and folklore.

1857 Director of Norwegian Theatre in Christiania. Continued his-
to torical plays. Financial failure of
1862 theater, 1862.

1858 Married.

1862 Collected Norwegian folklore on University appropriation. Danish-Prussian War.

1863 Christiania. Poverty. Wrote poetry and LOVE'S COMEDY—his "first
to great drama of indignation." Bitterly attacked, especially by
1864 conservatives.

1864 Lived in Rome. Bitter toward Norway because of reception of his plays, and failure of Norway to aid Denmark in Danish-Prus-
to sian War. Stayed briefly in dif-

ferent Italian cities. Imagination and taste greatly stimulated by Italian art. Published THE PRETENDERS, 1864; BRAND, 1866;
1868 PEER GYNT, 1867.

1868 Lived in Dresden. Traveled in Germany. Brief journeys to Sweden, Denmark, Norway, Paris, and
to Egypt. THE LEAGUE OF YOUTH, 1869, procured hostility of many former liberal supporters. Published EMPEROR AND GALILEAN,
1875 1873.

1875 Lived in Munich. European fame established. Published PIL-
to LARS OF SOCIETY, first of "social
1878 dramas," 1877.

1878 Rome. Brief stays in other Italian cities and in Germany. Published A DOLL'S HOUSE, 1879; GHOSTS,
to "the most bitterly reviled play of all time," 1881; ENEMY OF THE PEOPLE, 1882; THE WILD DUCK,
1885 1884.

1885 Munich. Visited Norway and
to Denmark. Published ROSMERS-
1891 HOLM, 1886.

1887 Triumphant performance of GHOSTS in Berlin. Ibsen acclaimed by the Germans as a "Germanic" writer. Published THE LADY FROM THE SEA, 1888; HEDDA GABLER, 1890.

1891 Permanent return to Norway. Found former public hostility re-
to placed by admiration. Lived in Christiania. Published THE MAS-
1892 TER BUILDER, 1892.

22

1892 *Marked interest in symbolism con-*
      tinued through following plays:
to   LITTLE EYOLF, *1894;* JOHN GABRIEL
      BORKMAN, *1896;* WHEN WE DEAD
1906 AWAKEN, *1899.*

1906 *Died in Christiania, May 23.*
      Ceremonious public funeral.
      "The ruling men of Norway had
      a daemon among them and they
      buried a grandee."

↩

Wᴴᴱᴺ *Ibsen began his dramatic career in the latter half of the nineteenth century, the popular play of the European stage was designed to entertain the middle class. This aim it achieved by flattering their vanity, by confirming their ideas, and by giving them a feeling of complacent security through approval of their social and domestic conventions. All these qualities Ibsen rejected. He tried, not to entertain, but to enlighten; to disturb, rather than flatter; and to show that the conventional beliefs on which men had felt they could rest as on eternal truth were not only insecure, but perniciously false. He made of the theater, says T. H. Dickinson, an instrument "of serious research into contemporary values." It was this achievement that made Ibsen's influence on modern drama greater than that of any other writer.*

The customary division of Ibsen's dramatic career into three periods is convenient if we remember that during none of these periods did the dramatist remain static, and that at the end of none of them was his change from the past abrupt or complete. The plays of the first period extend from CATALINA *to* EMPEROR AND GALILEAN. *The earliest of these plays were youthful experiments in which Ibsen attempted to dignify and popularize the native Norwegian history and folklore that had been submerged by the influence of the Danish culture imposed upon Norway. The later plays of the period show the rapid maturing of the author's mind. In* LOVE'S COMEDY *and* THE LEAGUE OF YOUTH *Ibsen shows the satirical power that distinguishes the work of his second period. Besides these two satires, he created poetic dramas in which the characters and action represent philosophical ideas. Of these plays Hermann Bahr remarks that Ibsen's senses were Norwegian, but his intellect was European. Although Brand and Peer Gynt move in a Norwegian setting, they belong to no history but that of humanity. The dramas to which they gave their names stand among the author's greatest literary achievements, but they are not among his most successful plays.*

It was mainly the plays of the second period, extending from PIL-

23

LARS OF SOCIETY *through* ROSMERSHOLM, *that established Ibsen's fame as a dramatist. These plays are a series of realistic dramas presenting man in conflict with society. Society Ibsen judged entirely by its influence on individual personality, the fullest development of which was always for him the highest good. With social movements and organizations he had little sympathy. When* A DOLL'S HOUSE *was acclaimed by feminist organizations, Ibsen said he did not know what the "woman's rights" movement was—it was humanity he wished to liberate. To liberate it he demanded freedom of the individual to maintain the integrity of his personality despite social pressure, a demand which, expressed in his slogan, "Truth and Freedom," is inherent in every play of his second period. Representative of this period, in our collection, is the play* AN ENEMY OF THE PEOPLE.

For the writing of GHOSTS *Ibsen had been subjected to abuse unsurpassed in the history of the theater. Most disappointing to him was the failure to support him of those whom he described as "the most cowardly among the cowards . . . the so-called liberals." The timidity of these self-styled liberals Ibsen had already satirized in* THE LEAGUE OF YOUTH; *their censure of* A DOLL'S HOUSE *had angered him; for their apostasy after* GHOSTS, *he arraigned them in* AN ENEMY OF THE PEOPLE. *Although Dr. Stockmann's personal characteristics differ from Ibsen's, the doctor represents Ibsen himself, fighting Ibsen's battle against the liberal majority. In a letter written to a friend not long before the appearance of the play, Stockmann's major discovery had already been stated by Ibsen as his own conclusion: "'The minority is always right'; of course, I am not thinking of that minority of stagnationists who are outstripped by the large middle party, which among us is called the liberal; but I mean that minority which takes the lead where the majority has not yet arrived. I mean that the man is right who is most closely in league with the future."*

The play is an attack, not on liberal ideas, but on those who, using the phraseology of liberalism in behalf of a party or class, are at the same time intolerant of any individual who disregards their code. "Liberation," Ibsen had written, "consists in securing for individuals the right to free themselves, each according to his need"; and the tyranny of a "liberal" group which would coerce this right of individual ...ion he held as baneful as any other tyranny. Thus Hovstad, the ...ate liberal, is a more formidable opponent for Dr. Stockmann than ...onservative Burgomaster. Besides, the right of the individual

to be free from the dictates of the majority is the more imperative because the majority is always wrong—wrong, not only on account of the
self-interest and hypocrisy of its members, but because of the nature of
truth itself. For truths, Dr. Stockmann finds, are not eternal. When
they are new, they are sound; but by the time a party has adopted them,
they are sound no longer. Pulsating life and new truth are in the hands
of the few who stand "at the outposts; so far in advance that the compact majority has not yet reached them." The theme of the play is the
worth and right of these few—or of the strong man alone—who, distinguished by intellect and will, are known by their contemporaries as
"enemies of the people."

The stage popularity of the play has been due in part to the uni-
versality of its theme. For in city, club, and college the intolerance of
self-styled liberals toward nonconformist individuals is still identical
with that exposed by Ibsen. And the individualist who defies them
likewise seems eternal. "For it is the nature of idealism not to learn
from the experience of others," says Otto Heller; "that is why the
Stockmann family never dies out." But it is not alone from the theme
that the play derives its effect. Written more rapidly than any of
Ibsen's other prose dramas, it has in place of their deliberate polish an
unrestrained vigor that they have not. Its boldly-drawn characters are
alive with the mocking indignation of the author. When in 1928 the
play was revived by Walter Hampden on the New York stage, its power
was impressive. In comparison, said one critic, every other play on
Broadway is "flaccid, sentimental, superficial, and weak."

In the final period of his career, often called the period of symbolism, Ibsen showed less interest in the conflict of the individual with society and more in the creation of "human beings and human destinies."
To suggest the subtleties of character, he relied increasingly on symbolism. The use of symbols, it is true, was not new to him; we find them
throughout his social dramas, but in the earlier plays the symbols are
so connected with real objects that they do not seem unnatural. But
in Ibsen's later plays the symbols are not always subordinated to reality.
They seem at times to have a life and meaning of their own. In 1891
Ibsen listened to the young writer Knut Hamsun attack the older realists, Ibsen among them, for confining themselves to the surface of life
and neglecting the inarticulate depths of the subconscious. From that
time Ibsen's work became more introspective. Faced with the difficulty of representing psychological states that are not expressed in any

25

natural way because their possessors are not themselves aware of them, Ibsen resorted to symbolism so extreme as to make some of his latest work vague and confusing. But if the last four plays lack the quality of their predecessors, they yet have power. Beyond the symbols was still the earnest effort to solve what Halvdan Koht has called Ibsen's great problem—"how man's soul could erect and preserve its freedom."

❧

BIBLIOGRAPHICAL NOTE

The best English versions of Ibsen's works are THE COLLECTED WORKS OF HENRIK IBSEN, *Entirely Revised and Edited by William Archer*, 13 vols. (New York: Charles Scribner's Sons, 1906-1912); LETTERS OF HENRIK IBSEN, *translated by J. Laurvik and M. Morison.* (New York: Fox, Duffield & Company, 1905). *The following valuable studies are generally available: Halvdan Koht,* THE LIFE OF IBSEN, 2 vols. (New York: W. W. Norton & Company, Inc., 1931) —*a critical biography of exceptional merit, published first in Norwegian in 1928-1929; Edmund Gosse,* HENRIK IBSEN. (New York: Charles Scribner's Sons, 1926); G. B. Shaw, THE QUINTESSENCE OF IBSENISM. (New York: Brentano's, 1913); Georg Brandes, "Henrik Ibsen," in CREATIVE SPIRITS OF THE NINETEENTH CENTURY. (New York: J. Y. Crowell Company, 1923); J. G. Huneker, chapter on Ibsen in EGOISTS: A BOOK OF SUPERMEN. (New York: Charles Scribner's Sons, 1932); M. J.

Moses, HENRIK IBSEN: THE MAN AND HIS PLAYS. (New York: Little, Brown & Company, 1908)—*contains bibliography;* H. J. Weigand, THE MODERN IBSEN: A RECONSIDERATION. (New York: Henry Holt & Company, Inc., 1925); Otto Heller, HENRIK IBSEN: PLAYS AND PROBLEMS. (Boston: Houghton Mifflin Company, 1912); B. W. Downs, IBSEN: THE INTELLECTUAL BACKGROUND. (New York: The Macmillan Company, 1947); I. T. E. Firkins, HENRIK IBSEN: A BIBLIOGRAPHY. (New York: H. W. Wilson Company, 1921). *A notable adverse criticism of Ibsen may be found in Max Nordau, "Ibsenism," Book III, Chapter IV, in* DEGENERATION. (New York: D. Appleton Company, 1895). *Of the innumerable articles on Ibsen referred to in periodical indexes, many are of little importance. Of merit, however, are articles by C. H. Herford, W. D. Howells, Henry James, Maurice Maeterlinck, Arthur Symons, and Emile Faguet.*

26

An Enemy of the People

CHARACTERS

DOCTOR THOMAS STOCKMANN, *medical officer of the Baths.*
MRS. STOCKMANN, *his wife.*
PETRA, *their daughter, a teacher.*
EJLIF ⎱ *their sons, aged thirteen*
MORTEN ⎰ *and ten respectively.*
PETER STOCKMANN, *the doctor's elder brother, Burgomaster and*

Prefect of Police, Chairman of the Board of Directors, etc.
MORTEN KIIL, *master tanner, Mrs. Stockmann's foster-father.*
HOVSTAD, *editor of the "People's Messenger."*
BILLING, *on the staff.*
HORSTER, *a ship's captain.*
ASLAKSEN, *a printer.*

Townsfolk present at the meeting: all sorts and conditions of men, some women, and a crowd of school-boys.

SCENE: *A town on the south coast of Norway.*

❦

ACT I

Evening. DR. STOCKMANN'S *sitting-room; with simple but cheerful furniture and decorations. In the wall to the right are two doors, the first leading to the Doctor's study, the second to an ante-room. In the opposite wall, facing the ante-room door, a door leading to the other rooms. Near the middle of this wall stands the stove, and further towards the foreground a sofa, with looking-glass above it, and in front of it an oval table with a cover. On the table a lighted lamp, with a shade. In the back wall an open door leading to the dining-room. In the latter is seen a dinner-table, with a lamp on it.* BILLING *is seated at the table, a serviette under his chin.* MRS. STOCKMANN *stands by the*

Reprinted by permission of Walter H. Baker Company, Boston.

27

table and hands him a great plate of roast beef. The other seats round the table are empty; the table is in some disorder, as at the end of a meal.

MRS. STOCKMANN: Well, if you're an hour late, Mr. Billing, you must put up with a cold supper.

BILLING (*eating*): That's excellent, delicious!

MRS. STOCKMANN: You know how Stockmann keeps to regular meal hours——

BILLING: It's all right. Indeed, I think it tastes better when I can sit down like this and eat all by myself, and undisturbed.

MRS. STOCKMANN: Well, if you are satisfied I—— Surely there's Hovstad coming too!

BILLING: Very likely.

[*Enter* BURGOMASTER STOCKMANN, *wearing an overcoat and an official gold-laced cap, and carrying a stick.*]

BURGOMASTER: Good evening, sister-in-law.

MRS. STOCKMANN (*coming into the sitting-room*): What, you! Good evening. It is very nice of you to look in.

BURGOMASTER: I was just passing, and so—— (*Looks towards dining-room.*) Ah! I see you've still got company.

MRS. STOCKMANN (*rather awkwardly*): Oh, no! Not at all; it is quite by chance. (*Hurriedly.*) Won't you come in and have something?

BURGOMASTER: I? No, thanks. God forbid I should eat anything hot in the evening; that wouldn't suit *my* digestion.

MRS. STOCKMANN: Oh! just this once——

BURGOMASTER: No, no. Much obliged to you. I stick to tea and bread and butter. That's more wholesome in the long run—and rather more economical, too.

MRS. STOCKMANN (*smiling*): Now, you musn't think Thomas and I are mere spendthrifts.

BURGOMASTER: You're not, sister-in-law; far be it from me to say that. (*Pointing to doctor's study.*) Perhaps he's not at home?

MRS. STOCKMANN: No, he's gone for a short stroll after supper—with the boys.

BURGOMASTER: Good gracious! Is that healthy? (*Listening.*) There he is.

MRS. STOCKMANN: No, that's not he. (*A knock.*) Come in! (*Enter* HOVSTAD, *the editor, from the ante-room.*) Ah! it's Mr. Hovstad, who——

HOVSTAD: Yes, you must excuse me, but I was delayed at the print-

28

er's. Good evening, Burgomaster.

BURGOMASTER (*bowing rather stiffly*): Mr. Hovstad! I suppose you've come on business?

HOVSTAD: Partly. About something for the paper.

BURGOMASTER: So I supposed. I hear my brother is an extremely prolific contributor to the *People's Messenger.*

HOVSTAD: Yes, he writes for the *Messenger* when he has some truths to speak upon one thing or another.

MRS. STOCKMANN (*to* HOVSTAD): But won't you—— (*Points to dining-room.*)

BURGOMASTER: God forbid I should blame him for writing for the class of readers from whom he expects most appreciation. And, personally, I've no reason to bear your paper any ill-will, Mr. Hovstad.

HOVSTAD: No, I should think not.

BURGOMASTER: On the whole, there's a great deal of toleration in this town. There's much public spirit here. And that's because we have one common interest which unites us all in one undertaking that equally concerns all right-thinking citizens.

HOVSTAD: Yes—the Baths.

BURGOMASTER: Just so. We have our magnificent new Baths. Yes! The Baths will be the center of life in this town, Mr. Hovstad, without doubt.

MRS. STOCKMANN: That's just what Thomas says.

BURGOMASTER: How extraordinary the development of our town has been even within the last few years. Money has circulated among the people, there is life and movement. Houses and ground-rents have risen in value.

HOVSTAD: And the difficulty of getting work is decreasing.

BURGOMASTER: And the poor-rates have been most satisfactorily lessened for the possessing class, and will be still further reduced if only we have a really fine summer this year—and plenty of visitors —lots of invalids, who'll give the Baths a reputation.

HOVSTAD: And I hear there's every prospect of that.

BURGOMASTER: Things look most promising. Every day inquiries about apartments and so forth come flowing in.

HOVSTAD: Then the doctor's essay is very opportune.

BURGOMASTER: Has he been writing something again?

HOVSTAD: It's something he wrote in the winter; recommending the Baths, and describing the advantageous sanitary conditions

29

of our town. But at the time I didn't use it.

BURGOMASTER: Ha! I suppose there was some little hitch!

HOVSTAD: Not at all. But I thought it would be better to wait till the spring, for people are beginning to get ready now for their summer holidays.

BURGOMASTER: You're right, quite right, Mr. Hovstad.

MRS. STOCKMANN: Yes, Thomas is really indefatigable where the Baths are concerned.

BURGOMASTER: Why, of course, he's one of the staff.

HOVSTAD: Yes, he was really their creator.

BURGOMASTER: Was he? I occasionally hear that certain persons are of that opinion. But I should say I too have a modest share in that undertaking.

MRS. STOCKMANN: Yes, that's what Thomas is always saying.

HOVSTAD: Who wants to deny it, Burgomaster? You set the thing going, and put it on a practical footing. Everybody knows that I only meant that the idea originally was the doctor's.

BURGOMASTER: Yes, certainly my brother has had ideas in his time —worse luck! But when anything is to be set going, we want men of another stamp, Mr. Hovstad. And I should have expected that in this house at least.

MRS. STOCKMANN: But, my dear brother-in-law——

HOVSTAD: Burgomaster, how can you——

MRS. STOCKMANN: Do come in and take something, Mr. Hovstad; my husband is sure to be in directly.

HOVSTAD: Thanks; just a mouthful, perhaps.

[*He goes into the dining-room.*]

BURGOMASTER (*speaking in a low voice*): It's extraordinary that people who spring directly from the peasant-class never get rid of a want of tact.

MRS. STOCKMANN: But why should you care? Can't you and Thomas share the honor as brothers?

BURGOMASTER: Yes, one would suppose so; but it seems a share of the honor isn't enough for some persons.

MRS. STOCKMANN: How ridiculous! You and Thomas always get on so well together. There, I think I hear him.

[*Goes to the door of the anteroom.*]

DR. STOCKMANN (*laughing without*): Here's a visitor for you, Katrine. Isn't it jolly here? Come in, Captain Horster. Hang your coat up there. Oh! you don't even wear an overcoat? Fancy, Katrine, I caught him on the street, and I could hardly get him to come along. (CAPTAIN HORSTER *enters.*) In with you, boys. They're famished again! Come on, captain; you must have some of our beef.

[*He forces* HORSTER *into the dining-room.* EJLIF *and* MORTEN *also join.*]

MRS. STOCKMANN: But, Thomas, haven't you seen——

DR. STOCKMANN (*turning round in the doorway*): Oh! is that you, Peter? (*Goes up to him and holds out his hand.*) Now, this is splendid.

BURGOMASTER: Unfortunately, I must be off directly——

DR. STOCKMANN: Nonsense! We'll have some toddy in a minute. You haven't forgotten the toddy, Katrine?

MRS. STOCKMANN: Of course not; the water's boiling.

[*She goes into the dining-room.*]

BURGOMASTER: Toddy, too——!

DR. STOCKMANN: Yes; sit down, and you will see how cozy we shall be.

BURGOMASTER: Thanks; I never join in a drinking bout.

DR. STOCKMANN: But this isn't a drinking-bout.

BURGOMASTER: It seems to me —— (*Looks towards the dining-room.*) It's wonderful how they can get through all that food.

DR. STOCKMANN (*rubbing his hands*): Yes, doesn't it do one good to see young people eat? Always hungry! They must eat!

They need strength! It's they who have to stir up the ferment for the after-time, Peter.

BURGOMASTER: May I ask what there is to be "stirred up," as you call it?

DR. STOCKMANN: Well, you'll have to ask the young people that when the time comes. *We* shall not see it, of course. Two old fogies like us——

BURGOMASTER: There, there. Surely that's a very extraordinary expression to use——

DR. STOCKMANN: Ah! you musn't mind what I say, Peter. For you must know I am so glad and content. I feel so unspeakably happy in the midst of all this growing, germinating life. After all, what a glorious time we do live in. It is as if a new world were springing up around us.

BURGOMASTER: Do you really think so?

DR. STOCKMANN: Well, of course, you can't see this as clearly as I do. You've spent all your life in this place, and so your perceptions have been dulled. But I, who had to live up there in that small hole in the north all those years, hardly ever seeing a soul to speak a stimulating word to me—all this affects me as if I were carried to the midst of a crowded city——

BURGOMASTER: H'm! City——

DR. STOCKMANN: Oh! I know well enough that the conditions of life are small enough compared with many other towns. But here is life, growth, an infinity of things to work for and to strive for; and that is the main point. (*Calling.*) Katrine, haven't there been any letters?

MRS. STOCKMANN (*in the dining-room*): No, none at all.

DR. STOCKMANN: And then, the comfortable income, Peter! That's something a man learns to appreciate when he has starved as we have——

BURGOMASTER: Good heavens!
——

DR. STOCKMANN: Oh yes! you can imagine that we were hard put to it up there. And now we can live like lords! To-day, for example, we had roast beef for dinner, and what's more, we've had some for supper, too. Won't you have some! Come along— just look at it, anyhow.

BURGOMASTER: No, no; certainly not.

DR. STOCKMANN: Well, then, look here. Do you see that fine tablecloth?

BURGOMASTER: Yes, I've noticed it already.

DR. STOCKMANN: And we've some nice lamps, too. Do you see? Katrine has bought them all out of her savings. And it all helps to make a house so homelike. Doesn't it? Come over here. No, no, no, not there! So

—yes—do you see how the light streams down—I do really think it looks very nice. Eh?

BURGOMASTER: Yes, when one can afford such luxuries.

DR. STOCKMANN: Oh! yes, I can afford it now. Katrine says I earn nearly as much as we spend.

BURGOMASTER: Yes—nearly!

DR. STOCKMANN: Besides, a man of science must live in some style. I'm certain a sheriff spends much more a year than I do.

BURGOMASTER: Yes, I dare say! A member of the superior magistracy!

DR. STOCKMANN: Yes, even a mere merchant! Such a fellow spends many times as much.

BURGOMASTER: Well, that is unavoidable in his position.

DR. STOCKMANN: For the rest, I really don't spend anything unnecessarily, Peter. But I can't deny myself the delight of having people about me. I must have them. I, so long isolated, it is a necessity of life for me to see the young, brave, determined, free-thinking, strenuous men gathered around me—and that they are, all of them, sitting there and eating so heartily. I should like you to know more of Hovstad——

BURGOMASTER: Ah, Hovstad! He was telling me that he is going to give another essay of yours.

DR. STOCKMANN: An essay of mine?

BURGOMASTER: Yes, about the Baths. An article written in the winter——

DR. STOCKMANN: Oh! that one—yes. But I don't want that to appear just now.

BURGOMASTER: Why not? This is the very time for it.

DR. STOCKMANN: Well, you may be right, under ordinary circumstances——

[*Crosses the room.*]

BURGOMASTER: And what's unusual in the circumstances now?

DR. STOCKMANN (*standing still*): Peter, I can't tell you yet—not this evening, at all events. The circumstances may turn out to be very unusual. On the other hand, there may be nothing at all. Very likely it's only my fancy.

BURGOMASTER: Upon my word, you're very enigmatical. Is there anything in the wind? Anything I'm to be kept in the dark about? I should think that I, who am chairman——

DR. STOCKMANN: And I should think that I—— There! don't let's tear one another's hair, Peter.

BURGOMASTER: God forbid! I am not in the habit of "tearing hair," as you express it. But I must absolutely insist that everything concerning the Baths shall be carried on in a business-like manner, and under proper authority. I can't consent to the follow-ing of devious and underhand ways.

DR. STOCKMANN: And am I in the habit of following devious and underhand ways?

BURGOMASTER: Anyhow, you've an ingrained propensity for going your own way. And that in a well-ordered community is almost as dangerous. The individual must submit himself to the whole community, or, to speak more correctly, bow to the authority that watches over the welfare of all.

DR. STOCKMANN: Maybe. But what the devil has that to do with me?

BURGOMASTER: Well, it's just this, my dear Thomas, that it seems you won't learn. But take care; you'll have to pay for it one of these days. Now, I've warned you. Good-by.

DR. STOCKMANN: Are you quite mad? You're altogether on the wrong tack.

BURGOMASTER: I'm not in the habit of being *that*. And I must beg that you will—— (*Bowing towards the dining-room.*) Good-by, sister-in-law; good-by gentlemen. (*Exit.*)

MRS. STOCKMANN (*entering the room*): Is he gone?

DR. STOCKMANN: Yes, and in an awful rage, too.

MRS. STOCKMANN: But, dear Thomas, now what have you been up to again?

DR. STOCKMANN: Nothing at all. Surely he can't expect me to account for everything—beforehand.

MRS. STOCKMANN: And what are you to account to him for?

DR. STOCKMANN: H'm. Never mind about that, Katrine. It's very odd that there are no letters. [HOVSTAD, BILLING and HORSTER *have risen from table and come into the room.* EJLIF *and* MORTEN *enter soon after.*]

BILLING: Ah! God bless me! After a good meal one feels a new man.

HOVSTAD: The Burgomaster didn't seem in the best of tempers to-day.

DR. STOCKMANN: That's his stomach. He has a very poor digestion.

HOVSTAD: It's more especially us of the *Messenger* that he can't stomach.

MRS. STOCKMANN: I thought you got on with him well enough.

HOVSTAD: Oh, yes! But now we've only a truce.

BILLING: That's so. That word quite sums up the situation.

DR. STOCKMANN: We must bear in mind that Peter is a bachelor, poor devil! He has no home to be happy in, only business, business. And then that cursed weak tea, that's about all he takes. Now, then, put chairs round the table boys! Katrine, aren't we to have that punch soon?

MRS. STOCKMANN: I'm just getting it.

DR. STOCKMANN: And you, Captain Horster, sit down by me on the sofa. So rare a guest as you —— Be seated, gentlemen. [*The men sit round the table,* MRS. STOCKMANN *brings in a tray with kettle, glasses, water-bottles, etc.*]

MRS. STOCKMANN: There you are! Here's arrak, and this is rum, and this is cognac. Now, help yourselves.

DR. STOCKMANN (*taking a glass*): So we will! And now out with the cigars. Ejlif, you know where the box is. And you, Morten, may fetch my pipe. (*The boys go to the room right.*) I have a suspicion Ejlif cribs a cigar now and then, but I pretend not to notice it. (*Calls.*) And my skull-cap, Morten. Katrine, can't you tell him where I left it? Ah! he's got it. Now, friends, help yourselves. You know I stick to my pipe—this one has been on many a stormy journey with me up there in the north. (*They touch glasses.*) Your health! There's nothing like sitting here, warm and sheltered.

MRS. STOCKMANN (*who sits knitting*): When do you sail, Captain Horster?

HORSTER: I hope I shall have everything straight by next week.

MRS. STOCKMANN: And you're going to America?

HORSTER: Yes, that's my intention.

BILLING: But then you won't be able to take part in the election of the new council.

HORSTER: Is there to be a new election here?

BILLING: Didn't you know?

HORSTER: No, I don't bother about things of that sort.

BILLING: But I suppose you take an interest in public affairs.

HORSTER: No, I don't understand anything about them.

BILLING: Still one ought to make use of one's vote.

HORSTER: Even those who don't understand anything about it?

BILLING: Understand? Now, what do you mean by that? Society is like a ship; every man must help in the steering.

HORSTER: That may be all right on shore, but at sea it would not do at all.

HOVSTAD: It is very remarkable how little most seafaring folk care about public matters.

BILLING: Most extraordinary.

DR. STOCKMANN: Seafaring folk are like birds of passage; they feel at home both in the south and in the north. So the rest of us have to be all the more energetic, Mr. Hovstad. Will there be anything of public interest in the *People's Messenger* to-morrow?

HOVSTAD: Nothing of local interest. But the day after to-morrow I'm thinking of using your paper——

DR. STOCKMANN: Yes—damn it all, I say, you'll have to hold that over.

HOVSTAD: Really? And we'd just got room for it. I should say, too, that this was the very time for it——

DR. STOCKMANN: Yes, yes, you may be right, but you'll have to hold it over all the same. I'll explain to you by-and-by——

[PETRA *enters with hat and cloak on, with a number of exercise books under her arm.*]

PETRA: Good evening!

DR. STOCKMANN: Good evening, Petra! Is that you?

[*They all bow.* PETRA *puts cloak on a chair by the door.*]

PETRA: Here you all are, enjoying yourselves, while I've been out slaving!

DR. STOCKMANN: Well, then, you come and enjoy yourself too.

BILLING: May I mix you a little——

PETRA (*coming towards the table*): Thanks, I'll help myself— you always make it too strong. But, by-the-way, father, I've a letter for you.

[*Goes to the chair where her things are lying.*]

DR. STOCKMANN: A letter! From whom?

35

PETRA: I got it from the post-man just as I was going out——

DR. STOCKMANN: And you only bring it me now?

PETRA: I really hadn't time to run up again. Forgive me, father —here it is.

DR. STOCKMANN (*taking letter*): Let me see, let me see, child. Yes; all right!

MRS. STOCKMANN: It is *the* one you've been expecting so, Thomas.

DR. STOCKMANN: Yes, it is. Now, I must go to my room at once. Where shall I find a light, Katrine? Is there a lamp in the other room?

MRS. STOCKMANN: Yes—the lamp is lit. It's on the writing-table.

DR. STOCKMANN: Excuse me one moment.

[*He goes to room* R. *and closes the door.*]

PETRA: What can it be, mother?

MRS. STOCKMANN: I don't know. For the last few days he has been always on the look-out for the postman.

BILLING: Probably a country pa-tient.

PETRA: Poor father! He really works too hard. (*Mixes her toddy.*) Ah! that'll be good.

HOVSTAD: Have you been teach-ing in the night-school as well to-day?

PETRA: Two hours.

BILLING: And in the morning four hours at the Institute——

PETRA: Five hours.

MRS. STOCKMANN: And I see you've some exercises to correct this evening.

PETRA: Yes, quite a heap of them.

HORSTER: You've enough to do, it seems to me.

PETRA: Yes; but that's a good thing. One is so delightfully tired after it.

BILLING: Do you really think that?

PETRA: Yes, for then one sleeps so well.

MORTEN: I say, Petra, you must be a very great sinner.

PETRA: A sinner!

MORTEN: Yes, if you work so hard. Mr. Rörlund says work is a punishment for our sins.

EJLIF: Bosh! You are a child to believe such stuff as that.

MRS. STOCKMANN: Come, come, Ejlif.

BILLING (*laughing*): No! that's too rich!

HOVSTAD: Would you like to work so hard, Morten?

MORTEN: No, I shouldn't.

HOVSTAD: Yes; but what will you turn out then?

MORTEN: I should like to be a Viking.

EJLIF: But then you'd have to be a heathen.

MORTEN: Then I'd be a heathen.

BILLING: There I agree with you, Morten. I say just the same.

MRS. STOCKMANN (*making a sign to him*): No, no, Mr. Billing, you don't.

BILLING: God bless me! I should. I'm a heathen, and I'm proud of it. You'll see we shall all be heathens soon.

MORTEN: And shall we be able to do anything we like then?

BILLING: Well, you see, Morten——

MRS. STOCKMANN: Now, run away, boys; I'm sure you've some lessons to prepare for to-morrow.

EJLIF: I may stay just a little longer.

MRS. STOCKMANN: No, not you either. Now be off; both of you. [*The boys say good-night and go.*]

HOVSTAD: Do you think it does the boys any harm to hear these things?

MRS. STOCKMANN: Well, I don't know; but I don't like it.

PETRA: But, mother, I think that's ridiculous of you.

MRS. STOCKMANN: Maybe! But I don't like it—here, at home.

PETRA: There's so much falseness both at home and at school. At home you mustn't speak, and at school you have to stand there and lie to the children.

HORSTER: You have to lie?

PETRA: Yes; don't you know that we have to teach many and many a thing we don't believe ourselves.

BILLING: Yes, we know that well enough.

PETRA: If only I could afford it I'd start a school myself, and things should be very different there.

BILLING: Ah! as to means——

HORSTER: If you are really thinking of doing that, Miss Stockmann, I shall be delighted to let you have a room at my place. My big old house is nearly empty; there's a large dining-room on the ground floor——

PETRA (*laughing*): Yes, yes, thank you—but nothing will come of it.

HOVSTAD: Oh, no! Miss Petra will yet come over to the journalists, I fancy. By-the-way, have you done anything at the English novel you promised to translate for us?——

PETRA: Not yet. But you shall have it in good time.

DR. STOCKMANN (*flourishing the letter*): Here's some news, I think, will wake up the town!

BILLING: News?

MRS. STOCKMANN: What news?

DR. STOCKMANN: A great discovery, Katrine.

HOVSTAD: What?

MRS. STOCKMANN: Made by you?

DR. STOCKMANN: Yes—by me! (*Walks up and down.*) Now, let them come as usual, and say these are fads and crack-brained fancies. But they'll not dare to. Ha! ha! I know they won't.

PETRA: Father, do tell us what it is.

DR. STOCKMANN: Well, well, give me time, and you shall hear all about it. If only Peter were here now! There, you see how we men can go about and form judgments like blind moles——

HOVSTAD: What do you mean, doctor?

DR. STOCKMANN: Is it not the general opinion that the town is healthy?

HOVSTAD: Of course.

DR. STOCKMANN: Indeed, a quite exceptionally healthy place, worthy to be recommended in the warmest manner to our fellowmen, both the sick and the whole——

MRS. STOCKMANN: My dear Thomas——

DR. STOCKMANN: And we've recommended and belauded it too. I have written again and again, both in the *Messenger* and in pamphlets——

HOVSTAD: Yes, and what then?

DR. STOCKMANN: These Baths, that we have called the pulse of the town, the living nerves of the town—and the devil knows what else——

BILLING: "The town's palpitating heart"—it was thus that in one inspired moment I allowed myself to——

DR. STOCKMANN: Ah, yes! that also! But do you know what in reality these mighty, magnificent, belauded Baths—that have cost so much money—do you know what they are?

HOVSTAD: No, what are they?

MRS. STOCKMANN: Why, what are they?

DR. STOCKMANN: The whole place is a pest-house.

PETRA: The Baths, father?

MRS. STOCKMANN (*at the same time*): Our Baths!

HOVSTAD (*also at the same time*): But, doctor——!

BILLING: Oh! it's incredible.

DR. STOCKMANN: The whole place, I tell you, is a whited sepulchre; noxious in the highest degree. All that filth up there in the mill dale, with its horrible stench, taints the water in the feed-pipes of the Baths; and the same damned muck oozes out on the shore——

HOVSTAD: Where the sea Baths are?

DR. STOCKMANN: There.

HOVSTAD: But how are you so certain of all this, doctor?

DR. STOCKMANN: I have investigated the conditions as conscientiously as possible. This long time I have had my doubts about it. Last year we had some extraordinary cases of illness—both typhoid and gastric attacks——

MRS. STOCKMANN: Yes, I remember.

38

DR. STOCKMANN: At the time we thought the visitors had brought the infection with them; but since —last winter—I came to another conclusion. So I set about examining the water as well as I could.

MRS. STOCKMANN: It was this you were working so hard at!

DR. STOCKMANN: Yes, you may well say I've worked, Katrine. But here, you know, I hadn't the necessary scientific appliances, so I sent both our drinking and seawater to the university for an exact analysis by a chemist.

HOVSTAD: And you have now received it?

DR. STOCKMANN (showing letter): Here it is. And it proves beyond dispute the presence of organic matter in the water—millions of infusoria. It is absolutely injurious to health, whether used internally or externally.

MRS. STOCKMANN: What a blessing you found it out in time.

DR. STOCKMANN: Yes, you may well say that.

HOVSTAD: And what do you intend to do now, doctor?

DR. STOCKMANN: Why, set things right, of course.

HOVSTAD: Do you think that can be done?

DR. STOCKMANN: It must be done. Else the whole Baths are useless, ruined. But there's no need for that. I'm quite clear as to what will have to be done.

MRS. STOCKMANN: But my dear Thomas, that you should have kept all this so secret!

DR. STOCKMANN: Would you have had me rush all over the town and chatter about it before I was quite certain. No thanks! I'm not so mad as that.

PETRA: But us at home——

DR. STOCKMANN: Not one word to a living soul. But to-morrow you may run in to the Badger.

MRS. STOCKMANN: Oh! Thomas!

DR. STOCKMANN: Well, well, to your grandfather. He'll have something to wonder at now, the old fellow. He thinks I'm not all right in my head—yes, and there are plenty of others who think the same, I've noticed. But now the good folk will see—now they *will* see! (*Walks up and down rubbing his hands.*) What a stir there'll be in the town, Katrine. You can't imagine what it will be! All the water-pipes will have to be relaid.

HOVSTAD (*rising*): All the water-pipes?

DR. STOCKMANN: Why, of course. They've been laid too low down; they must be moved up to higher ground.

PETRA: So, after all you are right.

DR. STOCKMANN: Yes, do you remember, Petra? I wrote against it when they began building them. But then no one would listen to me. Now, be sure, I'll speak straight out, for, of course, I have written a report to the directors. It has been lying there ready a whole week; I've only been waiting for this letter. But now they shall have it at once. See! Four closely written sheets. And the letter shall go too. A newspaper, Katrine! Get me something to wrap them up in. There—that's it. Give it to——to—— (*Stamps.*) What the devil's her name? Well, give it to the girl, and tell her to take it at once to the Burgomaster. [MRS. STOCKMANN *goes out with packet through the dining-room.*]

PETRA: What do you think Uncle Peter will say, father?

DR. STOCKMANN: What should he say? He'll be delighted that so important a fact has been discovered, I fancy.

HOVSTAD: I suppose you'll let me write a short notice about your discovery for the *Messenger.*

DR. STOCKMANN: Yes, I should be really obliged to you.

HOVSTAD: It is very desirable. The sooner the public know about it the better.

DR. STOCKMANN: Yes, so it is.

MRS. STOCKMANN (*returning*): She's gone with it.

BILLING: God bless me, doctor, you're the greatest man in the town.

DR. STOCKMANN: Oh, bosh!

Why, after all, I've done no more than my duty. I've been lucky in digging for treasures; that's all; but all the same——

BILLING: Hovstad, don't you think the town ought to give Dr. Stockmann a torch-light procession?

HOVSTAD: I shall certainly see to it.

BILLING: And I'll talk it over with Aslaksen.

DR. STOCKMANN: No, dear friends. Let all such clap-trap alone. I won't hear of anything of the sort. And if the directors want to give me a higher salary, I won't take it. I tell you, Katrine, I will not take it.

MRS. STOCKMANN: And you will be right, Thomas.

PETRA (*raising her glass*): Your health, father.

HOVSTAD and BILLING: Your health, your health, doctor!

HORSTER: I wish you much joy of your discovery.

DR. STOCKMANN: Thanks, thanks, my good friends. I am so heartily glad—ah! it is in truth a blessing to know in one's own mind that one has deserved well of his native town and his fellow-citizens. Hurrah? Katrine!

[*He seizes her with both hands, and whirls her round with him.* MRS. STOCKMANN *screams and struggles. A*

burst of laughter, applause
and cheers for the doctor.

The boys thrust their heads
in at the door.]

ACT II

The same. The door of the dining-room is closed. Morning.
MRS. STOCKMANN *enters from dining-room with a sealed letter in her*
hand, and goes to the room right first entrance, and peeps in.

MRS. STOCKMANN: Are you there, Thomas?

DR. STOCKMANN (*within*): Yes, I've just got back. (*Enters.*) What is it?

MRS. STOCKMANN: A letter from your brother.

DR. STOCKMANN: Ah! let's see. (*Opens envelope and reads.*) "The inclosed MS. remitted here-with—— (*Reads on, muttering.*) H'm——

MRS. STOCKMANN: Well, what does he say?

DR. STOCKMANN (*putting paper in his pocket*): Nothing; he only writes that he'll come up himself about midday.

MRS. STOCKMANN: Then you must for once remember to stay at home.

DR. STOCKMANN: Oh! I can do that well enough, for I've finished my morning's work.

MRS. STOCKMANN: I am very curious to know how he takes it.

DR. STOCKMANN: You'll see he won't be overpleased that I, and not he himself, have made the discovery.

MRS. STOCKMANN: Yes, aren't you afraid of that, too?

DR. STOCKMANN: No; at bottom you may be sure he'll be glad. But still—Peter is so damnably afraid that others besides himself should do anything for the good of the town.

MRS. STOCKMANN: Do you know, Thomas, you ought to be kind, and share the honors with him. Couldn't you say it was he that put you on the track——

DR. STOCKMANN: Yes, gladly, for aught I care, if only I can set matters straighter, I——

[*Old* MORTEN KIIL *peeps in through*
the further door, looks round
inquiringly, and speaks slyly.]

MORTEN KIIL: Is it—is it true?

MRS. STOCKMANN: Father, is that you?

DR. STOCKMANN: Hallo! Father-in-law, good morning, good morning.

MRS. STOCKMANN: But do come in.

MORTEN KIIL: Yes, if it's true; if not, I'm off again.

DR. STOCKMANN: If what is true?

41

MORTEN KIIL: That ridiculous story about the waterworks. Now, is it true?

DR. STOCKMANN: Why, of course it is. But how did you come to hear of *that?*

MORTEN KIIL *(coming in)*: Petra flew in on her way to school——

DR. STOCKMANN: No; did she though?

MORTEN KIIL: Ay, ay—and she told me—I thought she was only trying to make game of me; but that is not like Petra either.

DR. STOCKMANN: No, indeed; how could you think that?

MORTEN KIIL: Ah! one should never trust anybody. You can be made a fool of before you know it. So it is true after all?

DR. STOCKMANN: Most certainly it is. Now just sit down, father-in-law. And isn't it a real blessing for the town?

MORTEN KIIL *(suppressing his laughter)*: Blessing for the town?

DR. STOCKMANN: Yes, that I made the discovery at such a favorable time——

MORTEN KIIL *(as before)*: Yes, yes, yes; but I never would have believed you could have played your very own brother such a trick.

DR. STOCKMANN: Such a trick!

MRS. STOCKMANN: But really, dear father——

MORTEN KIIL *(resting his hands and chin on the top of his stick and winking slyly at the doctor)*: Now, what is it all about? Isn't it this way, that some animal has got into the water-pipes?

DR. STOCKMANN: Yes; infusorial animals.

MORTEN KIIL: And a good many of them have got in, Petra says; quite an enormous number.

DR. STOCKMANN: Certainly. There may be hundreds of thousands.

MORTEN KIIL: But no one can see them. Isn't that so?

DR. STOCKMANN: True; no one can see them.

MORTEN KIIL: I'll be damned if that isn't the best thing I've heard from you.

DR. STOCKMANN: What do you mean?

MORTEN KIIL: But you'll never be able to make the Burgomaster believe anything of the sort.

DR. STOCKMANN: Well, that remains to be seen.

MORTEN KIIL: Do you really think he'll be so foolish?

DR. STOCKMANN: I hope the whole town will be so foolish.

MORTEN KIIL: The whole town. Well, that may be. But it serves them right; much good may it do them. They wanted to be so much cleverer than we old fellows. They chivvied me out of the chairmanship of the Board. Yes; I tell you they chivvied me out like a dog, that they did. But now it's their turn. Only you keep the game up with them, Stockmann.

DR. STOCKMANN: Yes; but, father-in-law——

MORTEN KIIL: Keep it up, I say. If you can make the Burgomaster and his friends pay through the nose, I'll give a hundred crowns straight away for the poor.

DR. STOCKMANN: Now, that would be good of you.

MORTEN KIIL: Yes. I've not got much to throw away, as you know; but if you do that, I'll give the poor fifty crowns at Christmas.

[*Enter* HOVSTAD *from ante-room.*]

HOVSTAD: Good morning! Oh! I beg your pardon——

DR. STOCKMANN: Not at all. Come in, come in.

MORTEN KIIL: He! Is he in it, too?

HOVSTAD: What do you mean?

DR. STOCKMANN: Yes, of course, he's in it.

MORTEN KIIL: I might have known it! It must be put into the papers. Ah! you're the right sort, Stockmann. Let them have it. Now I'm off.

DR. STOCKMANN: Oh, no! Stop a little longer, father-in-law.

MORTEN KIIL: No, I'm off now. Play them as many tricks as you can; I'll see you don't lose by it. [*Exit.* MRS. STOCKMANN *goes off with him.*]

DR. STOCKMANN (*laughing*): Only think! That old fellow won't believe a word about that affair of the water-works.

HOVSTAD: Was that what he ——?

DR. STOCKMANN: Yes; that was what we were talking about. And maybe you've come to do the same.

HOVSTAD: Yes. Have you a moment to spare, doctor?

DR. STOCKMANN: As many as you like, old man.

HOVSTAD: Have you heard anything from the Burgomaster?

DR. STOCKMANN: Not yet. He'll be here presently.

HOVSTAD: I've been thinking over the matter since last evening.

DR. STOCKMANN: Well——?

HOVSTAD: To you, as a doctor and a man of science, this business of the water-works is an isolated affair. I fancy it hasn't occurred to you that a good many other things are connected with it.

DR. STOCKMANN: Yes—how? Let's sit down, old fellow. No— there, on the sofa.

[HOVSTAD *sits on sofa; the doctor on an easy chair on the other side of the table.*]

DR. STOCKMANN: Well, so you think——?

HOVSTAD: You said yesterday that the bad water is caused by impurities in the soil——

DR. STOCKMANN: Yes, undoubtedly, it is caused by that poisonous swamp up in the mill dale.

HOVSTAD: Excuse me, doctor, but I think it is caused by quite another swamp.

DR. STOCKMANN: What sort of a swamp may that be?

HOVSTAD: The swamp our whole municipal life stands and rots in.

DR. STOCKMANN: Mr. Hovstad, whatever have you got hold of now?

HOVSTAD: All the affairs of the town have little by little come into the hands of a set of bureaucrats.

DR. STOCKMANN: Come, now, they're not all bureaucrats.

HOVSTAD: No; but those who are not are their friends and adherents. They are all wealthy men, the bearers of distinguished names in the town; it is they who control and govern us.

DR. STOCKMANN: But they are men of ability and shrewdness.

HOVSTAD: Did they show their ability and shrewdness when they laid down the water-pipes where they are?

DR. STOCKMANN: No; that was, of course, very stupid of them. But that'll be set right now.

HOVSTAD: Do you think it will be done so smoothly?

DR. STOCKMANN: Well, smoothly or not smoothly, it'll have to be done.

HOVSTAD: Yes, if the press takes it up.

DR. STOCKMANN: Not at all necessary, my dear fellow; I'm sure my brother——

HOVSTAD: Excuse me, doctor, but I want you to know that I think of taking up the matter.

DR. STOCKMANN: In the paper?

HOVSTAD: Yes. When I took over the *People's Messenger,* I determined I would break up this ring of obstinate old blockheads who hold everything in their hands.

DR. STOCKMANN: But you yourself told me what it all ended in. You nearly ruined the paper.

HOVSTAD: Yes, we had to draw in our horns then, that's true enough. For there was the danger that the Baths wouldn't be started if these men were thrown out. But now matters are different, and now we can do without these gentry.

DR. STOCKMANN: Do without them, yes; but still we owe them much.

HOVSTAD: Which shall be paid to the full. But a journalist of such democratic opinions as mine can't let such an opportunity as this slip through his fingers. He must explode the fable of the infallibility of our rulers. Such stuff as this must be got rid of, like every other superstition.

DR. STOCKMANN: I agree with

you there, Mr. Hovstad, with all my heart. If it is a superstition, away with it.

HOVSTAD: Now, I should be sorry to deal too harshly with the Burgomaster, as he is your brother. But I know you think with me—the truth before all other considerations.

DR. STOCKMANN: Why, of course. But—but——

HOVSTAD: You mustn't think ill of me. I am neither more obstinate nor more ambitious than most men.

DR. STOCKMANN: But, my dear fellow, who says you are?

HOVSTAD: I come from humble folk, as you know, and I have had occasion to see what is wanted by the lower classes of society. And this is, that they should have a share in the direction of public affairs, doctor. *This* develops power and knowledge and self-respect——

DR. STOCKMANN: I understand that perfectly.

HOVSTAD: Yes, and I think a journalist assumes an immense responsibility when he neglects an opportunity of aiding the masses, the poor, the oppressed. I know well enough that the upper classes will call this stirring up the people, and so forth, but they can do as they please, if only my conscience is clear, I——

DR. STOCKMANN: Just so, just so,

dear Mr. Hovstad. But still—deuce take it—(*a knock at the door*). Come in!

[*Enter* ASLAKSEN, *the printer, at the door of the ante-room. He is humbly but neatly dressed in black, wearing a white, slightly crumpled neckerchief, and carrying gloves and a felt hat.*]

ASLAKSEN: I beg your pardon, doctor, for making so bold——

DR. STOCKMANN: Hallo! if it isn't Printer Aslaksen!

ASLAKSEN: Yes, it is, doctor.

HOVSTAD (*getting up*): Do you want me, Aslaksen?

ASLAKSEN: No, I don't. I didn't know I should meet you here. No, it was for the doctor himself——

DR. STOCKMANN: Well, what can I do for you?

ASLAKSEN: Is what I've heard from Mr. Billing true—that the doctor is thinking of getting us better water-works?

DR. STOCKMANN: Yes, for the Baths.

ASLAKSEN: Oh! yes, I know that. So I came to say that I'll back up the affair with all my might.

HOVSTAD (*to the doctor*): You see!

DR. STOCKMANN: I'm sure I thank you heartily, but——

ASLAKSEN: For it might do you no harm to have us middle-class men at your back. We now form

45

a compact majority in the town— when we really make up our minds to. And it's always as well, doctor, to have the majority with you.

DR. STOCKMANN: That is undoubtedly true, but I can't conceive that any special preparation will be necessary. I think that in so clear and straightforward a matter——

ASLAKSEN: Yes. But all the same, it can do no harm; for I know the local authorities so well. The people in power are not very much inclined to adopt suggestions coming from others. And so I think it wouldn't be amiss if we made some sort of a demonstration.

HOVSTAD: I think so too.

DR. STOCKMANN: Demonstrate, say you? But what do you want to demonstrate about?

ASLAKSEN: Of course with great moderation, doctor. I am always in favor of moderation; for moderation is a citizen's first virtue—at least those are my sentiments.

DR. STOCKMANN: We all know that about you, Aslaksen.

ASLAKSEN: Yes, I think I may claim that much. And this affair of the water-works is so very important for us small middle-class men. The Baths bid fair to become a kind of little gold-mine for the town. And it is through the Baths that the whole lot of us are going to get our living, especially we householders. And so we shall gladly support the Baths all we can. So, as I am chairman of the Householders' Association——

DR. STOCKMANN: Well?

ASLAKSEN: And as I am agent for the Moderation Society—of course you know, doctor, that I work on behalf of moderation?

DR. STOCKMANN: To be sure, to be sure.

ASLAKSEN: So I naturally meet a great many people. And as I am known to be a temperate and law-abiding citizen, as the doctor himself well knows, I have a certain amount of influence in the town, a position of some authority— though I say it that shouldn't.

DR. STOCKMANN: I know that very well, Mr. Aslaksen.

ASLAKSEN: Well, so you see it would be easy for me to get up an address, if it came to a pinch.

DR. STOCKMANN: An address?

ASLAKSEN: Yes, a kind of vote of thanks to you, from the citizens of the town, for bringing to light a matter of such importance to the whole community. It goes without staying that it will have to be drawn up with befitting moderation, so that the authorities and persons of position may not be set against it. And if only we are careful about that, no one can take offense, I think.

HOVSTAD: Well, even if they didn't like it particularly——

ASLAKSEN: No, no, no; nothing to offend those in authority, Mr. Hovstad. No opposition to people who stand in such close relation to us; I've never gone in for that in my life; no good ever comes of it either. But no one can object to the thoughtful, free expression of a citizen's opinion.

DR. STOCKMANN (*shaking his hand*): I can't tell you, dear Mr. Aslaksen, how heartily it delights me to find so much support among my fellow-citizens. I am so happy —so happy! Look here! Won't you take a drop of sherry? Eh?

ASLAKSEN: No, thank you; I never take any kind of spirituous drink.

DR. STOCKMANN: Well, then, a glass of beer—what say you to that?

ASLAKSEN: Thanks; not that either, doctor. I never take anything so early in the day. But now I'll be off to town, and talk with the householders, and prepare public opinion.

DR. STOCKMANN: Now, that is extremely good of you, Mr. Aslaksen; but I can't really get into my head that all these preparations are necessary; I think the matter will go of itself.

ASLAKSEN: Officials are always very slow, doctor—God forbid I

should say this by way of accusation——

HOVSTAD: To-morrow we'll stir them up in the paper, Aslaksen.

ASLAKSEN: But no violence, Mr. Hovstad. Proceed with moderation, or you'll do nothing with them. You take my advice, for I have gained experience in the school of life. And now I'll say good morning to the doctor. You know, now, that we small middle-class men, anyhow, stand behind you like a rock. You have the compact majority on your side, doctor.

DR. STOCKMANN: Many thanks, my dear Mr. Aslaksen. (*Holds out his hand.*) Good-by, good-by.

ASLAKSEN: Are you coming to the printing-office, Mr. Hovstad?

HOVSTAD: I'll come on presently. I've something to see to first.

ASLAKSEN: All right.

[*Bows and goes.* DR. STOCKMANN *accompanies him into the ante-room.*]

HOVSTAD (*as the doctor reënters*): Well, what do you say to that, doctor? Don't you think it is high time we weeded out and got rid of all this apathy and vacillation and cowardice?

DR. STOCKMANN: Are you speaking of Aslaksen?

HOVSTAD: Yes, I am. He is one of those who are in the swamp, though he's a good enough fellow in other things. And so are most

47

of the people here; they're forever seesawing and oscillating from one side to the other, and what with scruples and doubts, they never dare to advance a step.

DR. STOCKMANN: Yes, but Aslaksen seems to me so thoroughly well-intentioned.

HOVSTAD: There is one thing I value more highly; that is to stand your ground as a trusty and self-reliant man.

DR. STOCKMANN: There I am quite with you.

HOVSTAD: That's why I am going to seize the opportunity now to see if I can't stir up the well-intentioned among them for once. The worship of authority must be rooted up in this town. This immense, inexcusable blunder of the water-works should be enough to open the eyes of every voter.

DR. STOCKMANN: Very well! If you think it is for the good of the community, so let it be; but not till I've spoken to my brother.

HOVSTAD: Anyhow, I'll be getting ready a leader in the meanwhile. And if the Burgomaster won't go in for it——

DR. STOCKMANN: But how can you imagine such a thing?

HOVSTAD: It can be imagined well enough. And then——

DR. STOCKMANN: Well, then, I promise you; look here—then you may print my paper—put it in just as it is.

HOVSTAD: May I, really? Is that a promise?

DR. STOCKMANN (*handing him MS.*): There it is; take it with you. It can do no harm for you to read it; and then tell me what you think of it.

HOVSTAD: Thanks, thanks; I shall do so willingly. And now good-by, doctor.

DR. STOCKMANN: Good-by, good-by. Yes, you'll see it will all go smoothly, Mr. Hovstad, so smoothly.

HOVSTAD: H'm! We shall see. [*Bows. Exit through ante-room.*]

DR. STOCKMANN: Katrine! Hallo! you back, Petra?

PETRA (*entering*): Yes, I've just got back from school.

MRS. STOCKMANN (*entering*): Hasn't he been here yet?

DR. STOCKMANN: Peter? No; but I've been having a long talk with Hovstad. He is quite overwhelmed at my discovery. For, you see, it is much further reaching than I thought at first. And so he has placed his paper at my disposal if occasion requires.

MRS. STOCKMANN: But do you think you will need it?

DR. STOCKMANN: Not I! But all the same, one is proud to think that the free, independent press is on one's side. Just think! I've also had a visit from the director of the Householders' Association.

48

MRS. STOCKMANN: Really! And what did he want?

DR. STOCKMANN: To offer me support, too. Every one of them will stand by me if there should be any unpleasantness. Katrine, do you know what I have behind me?

MRS. STOCKMANN: Behind you? No. What have you behind you?

DR. STOCKMANN: The compact majority!

MRS. STOCKMANN: Oh! Is that good for you, Thomas?

DR. STOCKMANN: Yes, indeed; I should think it was good! (*Rubbing his hands as he walks up and down.*) Ah! by Jove! what a delight it is to be in such fraternal union with one's fellow-citizens!

PETRA: And to do so much good, and be so helpful, father.

DR. STOCKMANN: And to do it, into the bargain, for one's native town!

MRS. STOCKMANN: There's the bell.

DR. STOCKMANN: That must be he. (*Knock at the door.*) Come in!

[*Enter* BURGOMASTER STOCKMANN *from the ante-room.*]

BURGOMASTER: Good morning.

DR. STOCKMANN: I'm glad to see you, Peter.

MRS. STOCKMANN: Good morning, brother-in-law. How are you?

BURGOMASTER: Oh, thanks, so, so. (*To the doctor.*) Yesterday

evening, after office hours, I received a dissertation from you concerning the condition of the water connected with the Baths.

DR. STOCKMANN: Yes. Have you read it?

BURGOMASTER: I have.

DR. STOCKMANN: And what do you think of the affair?

BURGOMASTER: H'm——

MRS. STOCKMANN: Come, Petra. [*She and* PETRA *go into the room, left.*]

BURGOMASTER (*after a pause*): Was it really necessary to make all those investigations behind my back?

DR. STOCKMANN: Yes, till I was absolutely certain I——

BURGOMASTER: And so you are certain now?

DR. STOCKMANN: Yes, and I suppose it has convinced you, too.

BURGOMASTER: Is it your intention to submit this statement to the board of directors as an official document?

DR. STOCKMANN: Of course. Why, something must be done in the matter, and that promptly.

BURGOMASTER: After your wont, brother, you use very strong expressions in your statement. Why, you actually say that what we offer our visitors is a persistent poison!

DR. STOCKMANN: But, Peter, can it be called anything else? Only think—poisonous water both in-

49

ternally and externally! And that for poor sick folk who come to us in good faith, and who pay us heavily to heal them.

BURGOMASTER: And from this you come to the conclusion that we must build a sewer which will carry off all the supposed impurities from the Miller's Dale, and re-lay all the water-pipes.

DR. STOCKMANN: Yes. Can you suggest any other alternative?— I know of none.

BURGOMASTER: I looked in at the town engineer's this morning, and so—half in jest—I brought up the subject of these alterations as of a matter we might, possibly, have to take into consideration at some future time.

DR. STOCKMANN: Possibly at some future time!

BURGOMASTER: He smiled at my apparent extravagance—naturally. Have you taken the trouble to reflect upon what these proposed alterations would cost? From the information I have received, these expenses would most likely run up to several hundred thousand crowns!

DR. STOCKMANN: So much as that?

BURGOMASTER: Yes. But the worst is to come. The work would take at least two years.

DR. STOCKMANN: Two years; do you mean to say two whole years?

BURGOMASTER: At least. And what are we to do in the meanwhile with the Baths? Are we to close them? For that is what it would come to. Besides, do you believe anyone would come here if the rumor got abroad that the water is injurious to health?

DR. STOCKMANN: But, Peter, you know it is injurious.

BURGOMASTER: And all this now, just now, when the Baths are beginning to do well. Neighboring towns, too, have some idea of establishing baths. Don't you see that they would at once set to work to divert the full stream of visitors to themselves? It's beyond a doubt! And we should be left stranded! We should probably have to give up the whole costly undertaking; and so you would have ruined your native town.

DR. STOCKMANN: I—ruined!

BURGOMASTER: It is only through the Baths that the town has any future worth speaking of. You surely know that as well as I do.

DR. STOCKMANN: But what do you think should be done?

BURGOMASTER: Your statement has not succeeded in convincing me that the condition of the water at the Baths is as serious as you represent.

DR. STOCKMANN: I tell you it is, if anything, worse—or will be in the summer, when the hot weather sets in.

BURGOMASTER: The existing supply of water for the Baths is once for all a fact, and must naturally be treated as such. But probably the directors, at some future time, will not be indisposed to take into their consideration whether, by making certain pecuniary sacrifices, it may not be possible to introduce some improvements.

DR. STOCKMANN: And do you imagine I could agree for a moment to such a deception?

BURGOMASTER: Deception?

DR. STOCKMANN: Yes, it would be a deception—a fraud, a lie; an absolute crime against the public, against all society.

BURGOMASTER: I have not, as I have already remarked, been able to attain the conviction that there is really any such imminent danger.

DR. STOCKMANN: You have—you must have. My demonstration was so plainly true and right. Of that I am sure! And you know that perfectly, Peter, only you don't admit it. It was you who insisted that both the Baths and the water-works should be laid out where they now are; and it is *that*, it is that damned blunder which you won't confess. Pshaw! Do you think I don't see through you?

BURGOMASTER: And even if that were so? If, perhaps, I do watch over my reputation with some anxiety, I do it for the good of the town. Without moral authority I can not guide and direct affairs in such a manner as I deem necessary for the welfare of the whole community. Therefore—and on various other grounds—it is of great moment to me that your statement should not be submitted to the board of directors. It must be kept back for the good of all. Later on I will bring up the matter for discussion, and we will do the best we can quietly; but nothing whatever, not a single word, of this unfortunate business must be made public.

DR. STOCKMANN: But it can't be prevented now, my dear Peter.

BURGOMASTER: It must and shall be prevented.

DR. STOCKMANN: It can't be, I tell you; far too many people know about it already.

BURGOMASTER: Know about it! Who? Surely not those fellows on the *People's Messenger*, who——

DR. STOCKMANN: Oh, yes! They know, too. The liberal, independent press will take good care you do your duty.

BURGOMASTER (*after a short pause*): You are an extremely reckless man, Thomas. Haven't you reflected what the consequences of this may be to yourself?

DR. STOCKMANN: Consequences? —Consequences to me?

51

BURGOMASTER: Yes—to you and yours.

DR. STOCKMANN: What the devil do you mean?

BURGOMASTER: I believe I have at all times conducted myself towards you as a useful and helpful brother.

DR. STOCKMANN: Yes, you have, and I thank you for it.

BURGOMASTER: I ask for nothing. To some extent I had to do this—for my own sake. I always hoped I should be able to keep you within certain bounds if I helped to improve your pecuniary position.

DR. STOCKMANN: What! So it was only for your own sake——?

BURGOMASTER: To some extent, I say. It is painful for a man in an official position when his nearest relative goes and compromises himself time after time.

DR. STOCKMANN: And you think I do that?

BURGOMASTER: Yes, unfortunately, you do, without yourself knowing it. Yours is a turbulent, pugnacious, rebellious spirit. And then you have an unhappy propensity for rushing into print upon every possible and impossible matter. You no sooner hit upon an idea than you must write at once some newspaper article or a whole pamphlet about it.

DR. STOCKMANN: Yes, but isn't it a citizen's duty, whenever he has a new idea, to communicate it to the public.

BURGOMASTER: Pshaw! The public doesn't need new ideas. The public is best served by the good old recognized ideas that they have already.

DR. STOCKMANN: And you say that thus bluntly——?

BURGOMASTER: Yes, I must speak to you frankly for once. Until now I have tried to avoid it, as I know how irritable you are; but now I am bound to speak certain truths to you, Thomas. You have no conception how much you injure yourself by your rashness. You complain of the authorities, aye, of the government itself—you even revile them and maintain you've been slighted, persecuted. But what else can you expect, firebrand that you are.

DR. STOCKMANN: What next! So I'm a firebrand, too, am I?

BURGOMASTER: Yes, Thomas, you are an extremely difficult man to work with. I know it from experience. You set yourself above all considerations; you seem quite to forget that it is I whom you have to thank for your position here as medical officer of the Baths.

DR. STOCKMANN: I had a right to it! I, and no one else! I was the first to discover that the town might become a flourishing waterplace. I was the only one who saw it then. For years I stood alone struggling for this idea of mine, and I wrote and wrote——

BURGOMASTER: No doubt. But then the right time hadn't come. Of course, in that out-of-the-world hole of yours, you were not in a position to judge of that. As soon as the propitious moment came I —and others—took the matter in hand——

DR. STOCKMANN: Yes, and you bungled the whole of my splendid plan. Oh! we see now what shining lights you were.

BURGOMASTER: In my opinion we are now seeing that you again need some outlet for your pugnacity. You want to fly in the face of your superiors—and that's an old habit of yours. You can't endure any authority over you; you look jealously upon anyone who has a higher official post than yourself; you regard him as a personal enemy, and then it's all one to you what kind of a weapon you use against him; one is as good as another. But now I have called your attention to this, to the great interests at stake for the town, and consequently for me also. And therefore I tell you, Thomas, that I am inexorable in the demand I am about to make of you!

DR. STOCKMANN: And what is this demand?

BURGOMASTER: As you have been so garrulous in talking about this unpleasant business to outsiders, although it should have been kept an official secret, of course it can't be hushed up. All sorts of rumors will be spread everywhere, and the evil-disposed among us will swell these rumors with all sorts of additions. It will, therefore, be necessary for you to meet these rumors.

DR. STOCKMANN: I? How? I don't understand you.

BURGOMASTER: We venture to expect that after further investigation you will come to the conclusion that the affair is not nearly so dangerous or serious as you had, at the first moment, imagined.

DR. STOCKMANN: Ah! ha! So you expect that!

BURGOMASTER: Furthermore, we shall expect you to have confidence in the Board of Directors, and to express your belief that they will thoroughly and conscientiously carry out all measures for the removal of every shortcoming.

DR. STOCKMANN: Yes; but you'll never be able to do that as long as you go on tinkering and patching. I tell you that, Peter, and it is my deepest, most sincere conviction.

BURGOMASTER: As an official, you've no right to have any individual conviction.

DR. STOCKMANN (*starting*): No right to any——

BURGOMASTER: As official, I say. In your private capacity, good gracious, that's another matter. But as a subordinate servant of the Baths, you've no right to express any conviction at issue with that of your superiors.

DR. STOCKMANN: That is going too far! I, a doctor, a man of science, have no right to——

BURGOMASTER: The matter in question is not a purely scientific one; it is a complex affair; it is both a technical and an economic matter.

DR. STOCKMANN: Pshaw! What's that to me? What the devil do I care! I will be free to speak out upon any subject on earth.

BURGOMASTER: As you please. But not a word about the Baths—we forbid that.

DR. STOCKMANN (*shouting*): You forbid! you!—such fellows——

BURGOMASTER: *I* forbid you that —*I*, your chief; and when I forbid you anything, you'll have to obey.

DR. STOCKMANN (*controlling himself*): Peter, really, if you weren't my brother——

[PETRA *throws open the door.*]

PETRA: Father, you shall not submit to this!

[MRS. STOCKMANN *following her.*]

MRS. STOCKMANN: Petra, Petra!

BURGOMASTER: Ah! so we've been listening!

MRS. STOCKMANN: You spoke so loud; we couldn't help——

PETRA: Yes, I did stand there and listen.

BURGOMASTER: Well, on the whole, I'm glad——

DR. STOCKMANN: You spoke to me of forbidding and obeying——

BURGOMASTER: You forced me to speak to you in that tone.

DR. STOCKMANN: And have I, in a public declaration, to give myself the lie?

BURGOMASTER: We consider it absolutely necessary that you should issue a statement in the terms I have requested.

DR. STOCKMANN: And if I don't obey?

BURGOMASTER: Then we shall ourselves put forth a statement to reassure the public.

DR. STOCKMANN: Well and good. Then I'll write against you. I hold to my opinion. I shall prove that *I* am right, and you wrong. And what will you say to that?

BURGOMASTER: I shall then be unable to prevent your dismissal.

DR. STOCKMANN: What——

PETRA: Father! Dismissal!

MRS. STOCKMANN: Dismissal!

BURGOMASTER: Your dismissal from the Baths. I shall be obliged to urge that notice be given you at once, in order to dissociate you from everything concerning the Baths.

DR. STOCKMANN: And you would dare to do that!

BURGOMASTER: It is you yourself who play the daring game.

PETRA: Uncle, such treatment of

a man like father is shameful.

MRS. STOCKMANN: Do be quiet, Petra.

BURGOMASTER: Ah, ah! We already allow ourselves to express an opinion. Of course! (*To Mrs. Stockmann.*) Sister-in-law, apparently you're the most sensible person in the house. Use all your influence with your husband; try to make him realize all this will bring with it, both for his family——

DR. STOCKMANN: My family concerns only myself.

BURGOMASTER: ——Both for his family, I say, and the town in which he lives.

DR. STOCKMANN: It is I who have the real good of the town at heart. I want to lay bare the evils that, sooner or later, must come to light. Ah! You shall yet see that I love my native town.

BURGOMASTER: You, who, in your blind obstinacy, want to cut off the town's chief source of prosperity.

DR. STOCKMANN: The source is poisoned, man! Are you mad? We live by trafficking in filth and garbage. The whole of our developing social life is rooted in a lie!

BURGOMASTER: Idle fancies—or something worse. The man who makes such offensive insinuations against his own native place must be an enemy of the people.

DR. STOCKMANN (*going towards him*): And you dare to——

MRS. STOCKMANN (*throwing herself between them*): Thomas!

PETRA (*seizing her father's arm*): Oh! hush, father.

BURGOMASTER: I will not expose myself to physical violence. You are warned now. Reflect upon what is due to yourself and to your family. Good-by.

[*Exit.*]

DR. STOCKMANN: And I must bear such treatment! In my own house. Katrine! What do you think of it?

MRS. STOCKMANN: Indeed, it is a shame and an insult, Thomas——

PETRA: If only I could give it to uncle——

DR. STOCKMANN: It is my own fault. I ought to have rebelled against them long ago—have shown my teeth—and made them feel them! And so he called me an enemy of the people. Me! I will not bear this; by heaven, I will not!

MRS. STOCKMANN: But, dear Thomas, after all, your brother has the power——

DR. STOCKMANN: Yes, but I have the right!

MRS. STOCKMANN: Ah, yes, right, right! What is the good of being right when you haven't any might?

PETRA: Oh, mother! how can you talk so?

DR. STOCKMANN: What! No good in a free society to have right on your side? You are absurd, Katrine. And besides, haven't I the free and independent press with me? The compact majority behind me? That's might enough, I should think!

MRS. STOCKMANN: But, good Heavens! Thomas, you're surely not thinking of——

DR. STOCKMANN: What am I not thinking of?

MRS. STOCKMANN: Of setting yourself up against your brother, I mean.

DR. STOCKMANN: What the devil would you have me do, if I didn't stick to what is right and true?

· PETRA: Yes, I too would like to know that?

MRS. STOCKMANN: But that will be of no earthly use. If they won't they won't.

DR. STOCKMANN: Ho, ho! Katrine, just wait awhile and you'll see I shall yet get the best of the battle.

MRS. STOCKMANN: Yes, you'll fight them—but you'll get your dismissal; that's what will happen.

DR. STOCKMANN: Well, then, I shall at any rate have done my duty towards the public, towards society. I to be called an enemy of the people.

MRS. STOCKMANN: But, towards your family, Thomas? To us here at home? Don't you think your duty is to those for whom you should provide?

PETRA: Ah! mother, do not always think first and foremost of us.

MRS. STOCKMANN: Yes, it's all very well for you to talk; if need be you can stand alone. But think of the boys, Thomas, and think a little of yourself too, and of me——

DR. STOCKMANN: But, really, you're quite mad, Katrine. Should I be such a miserable coward as to humble myself to Peter and his damned crew? Should I ever again in all my life have another happy hour?

MRS. STOCKMANN: That I can not say; but God preserve us from the happiness we shall all of us have if you remain obstinate. Then you would again be without a livelihood, without any regular income. I think we had enough of that in the old days. Remember them, Thomas; think of what it all means.

DR. STOCKMANN (*struggling with himself and clenching his hands*): And such threats this officemonger dares utter to a free and honest man! Isn't it horrible, Katrine?

MRS. STOCKMANN: Yes; that he is behaving badly to you is certainly true. But, good God! there is so much injustice to which we must submit here on earth! Here are the boys. Look at them!

What is to become of them? Oh! no, no, you can not find it in your heart——

[EJLIF *and* MORTEN *with school-books have entered meanwhile.*]

DR. STOCKMANN: The boys! (*Suddenly stands still firmly and decidedly.*) Never, though the whole earth should crumble, will I bend my neck beneath the yoke.

[*Goes towards his room.*]

MRS. STOCKMANN: Thomas, what are you going to do?

DR. STOCKMANN: I want to have the right to look into my boys' eyes when they are grown men.

[*Exit into room.*]

MRS. STOCKMANN (*bursts into tears*): Ah! God help and comfort us all!

PETRA: Father is brave! He will not give in!

[*The boys ask wonderingly what it all means;* PETRA *signs to them to be quiet.*]

ACT III

The editor's room, People's Messenger. *In the flat at the back a door left; to the right another door with glass panes, through which can be seen the printing-room. Another door right of the stage. In the middle of the room a large table covered with papers, newspapers and books. Lower down left, a window, and by it a writing desk and high chair. A few arm-chairs around the table; some others along the walls. The room is dingy and cheerless, the furniture shabby, the arm-chairs dirty and torn. Within the printing-room are seen a few compositors; farther within, a hand-press at work.* HOVSTAD, *the editor, is seated at the writing-desk. Presently* BILLING *enters from the right with the doctor's manuscript in his hand.*

BILLING: Well, I must say!——

HOVSTAD (*writing*): Have you read it through?

BILLING: Yes, I should think I had.

HOVSTAD: Don't you think the doctor comes out strong?

BILLING: Strong! God bless me! he is crushing, that's what he is. Every word falls like a lever—I mean like the blow of a sledge-hammer.

HOVSTAD: Yes, but these folk don't fall at the first blow.

BILLING: True enough, but we'll keep on hammering away, blow after blow, till the whole lot of aristocrats come crashing down. As I sat in there reading that, I seemed to hear the revolution thundering afar.

HOVSTAD: Sh! Don't let Aslaksen hear anything of that sort.

BILLING (*in a lower voice*): As-

57

laksen is a weak-kneed, cowardly fellow, who hasn't any manhood about him. But this time surely you'll insist on having your own way. H'm? You'll print the doctor's paper?

HOVSTAD: Yes, if only the Burgomaster doesn't give way I——

BILLING: That would be damned unpleasant.

HOVSTAD: Well, whatever happens, fortunately we can turn the situation to our account. If the Burgomaster won't agree to the doctor's proposal, he'll have all the small middle-class against him —all the Householders' Association, and the rest of them. And if he does agree to it, he'll fall out with the whole crew of big shareholders in the Baths, who, until now, have been his main support——

BILLING: Ah! yes, yes; for it's certain they'll have to fork out a pretty heavy sum——

HOVSTAD: You may take your oath of that. And then, don't you see, the ring will be broken up, and we shall day by day show the public that the Burgomaster is utterly unfit in all respects, and that all positions of trust in the town, the whole municipal government, must be placed in the hands of persons of liberal ideas.

BILLING: God bless me, but that's strikingly true. I see it, I see it. We are on the eve of a revolution!

[*A knock at the door.*]

HOVSTAD: Sh—(*calls.*) Come in! (DR. STOCKMANN *enters from flat left,* HOVSTAD *going towards him.*) Ah! here's the doctor. Well?

DR. STOCKMANN: Print away, Mr. Hovstad.

HOVSTAD: Is it to go in just as it is?

BILLING: Hurrah!

DR. STOCKMANN: Print away, I tell you. Of course it is to go in as it is. Since they will have it so, they shall! Now, there'll be war in the town, Mr. Billing!

BILLING: War to the knife is what I want—to the knife, to the death, doctor!

DR. STOCKMANN: This article is only the beginning. My head's already full of plans for four or five other articles. But where do you stow away Aslaksen?

BILLING (*calling into the printing-room*): Aslaksen! just come here a moment.

HOVSTAD: Did you say four or five more articles? On the same subject?

DR. STOCKMANN: Heaven forbid, my dear fellow. No; they deal with quite different matters. But they all arise out of the waterworks and the sewers. One thing leads to another, you know. It is like beginning to shake an old house, exactly the same.

BILLING: God bless me, that's true! And you can never do any good till you've pulled down the whole rubbish.

ASLAKSEN (*enters from printing-room*): Pulled down! Surely the doctor is not thinking of pulling down the Baths?

HOVSTAD: Not at all! Don't be alarmed.

DR. STOCKMANN: No, we were talking of something quite different. Well, what do you think of my article, Mr. Hovstad?

HOVSTAD: I think it is simply a masterpiece——

DR. STOCKMANN: Yes, isn't it? That does please me; that does please me.

HOVSTAD: It is so clear and to the point. One doesn't in the least need to be a specialist in order to understand the reasoning. I am sure every intelligent, honest man will be on your side.

ASLAKSEN: And let us hope all the prudent ones, too.

BILLING: Both the prudent and imprudent—indeed, I think well-nigh the whole town.

ASLAKSEN: Well, then, we may venture to print it.

DR. STOCKMANN: I should think you could!

HOVSTAD: It shall go in to-morrow.

DR. STOCKMANN: Yes, plague take it, not one day must be lost. Look here, Aslaksen, this is what I wanted you for. You, person-ally, must take charge of the MS.

ASLAKSEN: Certainly, I will.

DR. STOCKMANN: Be as careful as if it were gold. No printers' er-rors, every word is important. I'll look in again, presently; then I can make any small corrections. Ah! I can't say how I long to see the thing in print—to hurl it forth——

BILLING: To hurl it—yes, like a thunderbolt!

DR. STOCKMANN: And to submit it to the judgment of every intelli-gent fellow-citizen. Ah! you've no idea what I've had to put up with to-day. I've been threatened with all sorts of things. I was to be robbed of my most inalienable rights as a man.

BILLING: What! Your rights as a man!

DR. STOCKMANN: I was to be humbled, made a coward of, was to set my personal gain above my deepest, holiest convictions——

BILLING: God bless me! that is really too bad.

HOVSTAD: Well, just what was to be expected from that quarter.

DR. STOCKMANN: But they'll get the worst of it, I can promise them. Henceforth, every day I'll throw myself into the breach in the *Messenger;* bombard them with one article after another——

ASLAKSEN: Yes, but look here ——

BILLING: Hurrah! There'll be

59

war, there'll be war!

DR. STOCKMANN: I will smite them to the earth. I will crush them, level all their entrenchments to the ground before the eyes of all right-thinking men. I'll do it.

ASLAKSEN: But all the same be reasonable, doctor; proceed with moderation——

BILLING: Not at all, not at all; don't spare for dynamite.

DR. STOCKMANN (*going on imperturbably*): For, remember that henceforth it is not merely a question of water-works and sewers. No, the whole of society must be cleansed, disinfected——

BILLING: There sounded the word of salvation!

DR. STOCKMANN: All the old bunglers must be got rid of, you understand. And that in every department! Such endless vistas have opened out before me to-day. It was not all clear to me until now, but now I will right everything. It is the young, vigorous banner-bearers we must seek, my friends; we must have new captains for all the outposts.

BILLING: Hear, hear!

DR. STOCKMANN: And if only we hold together all will go so smoothly, so smoothly. The whole revolution will be only like the launching of a ship. Don't you think so?

HOVSTAD: For my part, I believe we have now every prospect of placing our municipal affairs in the hands of those to whom they rightly belong.

ASLAKSEN: And if only we proceed with moderation, I really don't think there can be any danger.

DR. STOCKMANN: Who the devil cares whether there's danger or not? What I do I do in the name of truth and for conscience sake.

HOVSTAD: You are a man deserving of support, doctor.

ASLAKSEN: Yes, that's certain. The doctor is a true friend to the town; he is a sincere friend of society.

BILLING: God bless me! Dr. Stockmann is a friend of the people, Aslaksen.

ASLAKSEN: I think the Householders' Association will soon adopt that expression.

DR. STOCKMANN (*shaking their hands, deeply moved*): Thanks, thanks, my dear, faithful friends, it does me good to hear you. My fine brother called me something very different just now. I'll pay him back with interest, though! But I must be off now to see a poor devil. I'll look in again, as I said. Be sure and take good care of the MS., Mr. Aslaksen, and on no account leave out any of my notes of exclamation! Rather put in a few more. Well, good-by for the present; good-by, good-by.

[*Mutual salutations while they accompany him to the door.*]

[*Exit.*]

HOVSTAD: He'll be of invaluable service to us.

ASLAKSEN: Yes, so long as he confines himself to the Baths. But if he goes further it might not be advisable to go with him.

HOVSTAD: H'm! Well, that depends——

BILLING: You are always so damned afraid, Aslaksen.

ASLAKSEN: Afraid? Yes, when it is a question of attacking local magnates, I am afraid, Mr. Billing; that, let me tell you, I have learnt in the school of experience. But go for higher politics, attack the government itself, and you'll see if I'm afraid.

BILLING: Oh! no; but that's where you contradict yourself.

ASLAKSEN: The fact is I am a conscientious man. If you attack governments you at least do society no harm, for the men attacked don't care a hang about it, you see; they stay where they are. But *local* authorities *can* be turned out, and thus a lot of know-nothings come to the front, and do no end of harm both to householders and others.

HOVSTAD: But the education of citizens by self-government

—what do you think of *that?*

ASLAKSEN: When a man has anything to look after he can't think of everything, Mr. Hovstad.

HOVSTAD: Then I hope I may never have anything to look after.

BILLING: Hear, hear!

ASLAKSEN (*smiling*): H'm! (*Pointing to desk.*) Governor Stensgaard * sat in that editor's chair before you.

BILLING: Pooh! A turncoat like that!

HOVSTAD: I'm no weather-cock —and never will be.

ASLAKSEN: A politician must not swear to anything on earth, Mr. Hovstad. And as to you, Mr. Billing, you ought to take in a reef or two one of these days, since you're running for the post of secretary to the magistracy.

BILLING: I——

HOVSTAD: Are you really, Billing?

BILLING: Well, yes—but, deuce take it, you know, I'm only doing so to annoy these wiseacres.

ASLAKSEN: Well, that doesn't concern me. But if I am called cowardly and inconsistent I should like to point out this: Printer Aslaksen's past is open to everyone's inspection. I have not changed at all, except that I am perhaps more moderate. My heart

---

* This is the only case in which Ibsen introduces persons who have appeared in earlier plays. Aslaksen figures in DE UNGES FORBUND (THE YOUNG MEN'S LEAGUE), of which play Stensgaard is the central character.

still belongs to the people, but I do not deny that my reason inclines somewhat towards the authorities—at least to the local authorities.

[*Exit into printing-room.*]

BILLING: Don't you think we ought to get rid of him, Hovstad?

HOVSTAD: Do you know of anyone else that'll advance money for the paper and printing?

BILLING: It's a damned nuisance not having the necessary capital.

HOVSTAD (*sitting down by desk*): Yes, if we only had that——

BILLING: Suppose you applied to Dr. Stockmann?

HOVSTAD: What would be the good? He has nothing himself.

BILLING: No; but he has a good man behind him—old Morten Kiil—the "badger," as they call him.

HOVSTAD (*writing*): Are you so sure he has anything?

BILLING: Yes; God bless me, I know it for certain. And part of it will certainly go to Stockmann's family. He is sure to think of providing for them—anyhow, for the children.

HOVSTAD: Are you counting on *that?*

BILLING: Counting? Of course I don't count upon anything.

HOVSTAD: You're right there! And that post of secretary you shouldn't in the least count upon;

for I can assure you you won't get it.

BILLING: Do you think I don't know that as well as you? Indeed, I'm glad I shall not get it. Such a rebuff fires one's courage —gives one a fresh supply of gall, and one needs that in a god-forsaken place like this, where any excitement is so rare.

HOVSTAD: Yes, yes.

BILLING: Well—they'll soon hear of me! Now I'll go and draw up the appeal to the Householders' Association.

[*Exit into room R.*]

HOVSTAD (*sitting by desk, gnawing his pen, says slowly*): H'm! Yes, that'll do. (*A knock at the door.*) Come in. (PETRA *enters from the door* L. *in flat.* HOVSTAD *rising.*) What! Is it you? Here?

PETRA: Yes; please excuse me——

HOVSTAD: Won't you sit down?

PETRA: No, thanks; I must be off again directly.

HOVSTAD: I suppose it's something your father——

PETRA: No. I've come on my own account. (*Takes a book from the pocket of her cloak.*) Here's that English story.

HOVSTAD: Why have you brought it back?

PETRA: I won't translate it.

HOVSTAD: But you promised so faithfully——

PETRA: Yes; but then I hadn't read it. And no doubt you've not read it either.

HOVSTAD: No; you know I can't read English, but——

PETRA: Exactly; and that's why I wanted to tell you that you must find something else. (*Putting book on table.*) This can't possibly go into the *Messenger.*

HOVSTAD: Why not?

PETRA: Because it is in direct contradiction to your own opinions.

HOVSTAD: Well, but for the sake of the cause——

PETRA: You don't understand me yet. It is all about a supernatural power that looks after the so-called good people here on earth, and turns all things to their advantage at last, and all the bad people are punished.

HOVSTAD: Yes, but that's very fine. It's the very thing the public like.

PETRA: And would you supply the public with such stuff? Why, you don't believe one word of it yourself. You know well enough that things don't really happen like that.

HOVSTAD: You're right there; but an editor can't always do as he likes. He often has to yield to public opinion in small matters. After all, politics is the chief thing

in life—at any rate for a newspaper; and if I want the people to follow me along the path of emancipation and progress, I musn't scare them away. If they find such a moral story down in the cellar,* they're much more willing to stand what is printed above it —they feel themselves safer.

PETRA: For shame! You wouldn't be such a hypocrite, and weave a web to ensnare your readers. You are not a spider.

HOVSTAD: Thanks for your good opinion of me. No. That's Billing's idea, not mine.

PETRA: Billing's!

HOVSTAD: Yes. At least he said so the other day. It was Billing who was so anxious to get the story into the paper; I don't even know the book.

PETRA: But how Billing, with his advanced views——

HOVSTAD: Well, Billing is many-sided. He's running for the post of secretary to the magistracy, I hear.

PETRA: I don't believe that, Hovstad. How could he condescend to such a thing?

HOVSTAD: Well, that you must ask him.

PETRA: I could never have thought that of Billing.

HOVSTAD: No? Does that come as a revelation to you?

---

* The reference is to the continental plan; the feuilleton is separated from the main body of the page by a line.

PETRA: Yes. And yet—perhaps not. Ah! I don't know.

HOVSTAD: We journalists aren't worth much, Miss Petra.

PETRA: Do you really think that?

HOVSTAD: I think so, sometimes.

PETRA: Yes, in the little everyday squabbles—that I can understand. But now that you have taken up a great cause——

HOVSTAD: You mean that affair of your father's.

PETRA: Exactly. But now I should think you must feel yourself worth more than the common herd.

HOVSTAD: Yes, to-day I do feel something of that sort.

PETRA: Yes, don't you feel that? Ah! it is a glorious career you have chosen. Thus to clear the way for despised truths and new ideas—to stand forth fearlessly on the side of a wronged man——

HOVSTAD: Especially when this wronged man is—h'm!—I hardly know how to put it.

PETRA: You mean when he is so true and honest.

HOVSTAD (*in a low voice*): I mean when he is your father——

PETRA (*as if she had received a blow*): *That?*

HOVSTAD: Yes, Petra—Miss Petra.

PETRA: So *that* is what you think of first and foremost? Not the cause itself? Not the truth? Not

father's big, warm heart?

HOVSTAD: Yes, of course, that as well.

PETRA: No, thank you; you've just let the cat out of the bag, Mr. Hovstad. Now I shall never trust you again in anything.

HOVSTAD: Can you reproach me because it is chiefly for your sake?

PETRA: What I am angry with you for is that you have not acted honestly towards my father. You told him it was only the truth and the good of the community you cared about. You have fooled both father and me. You are not the man you pretend to be. And I shall never forgive you—never!

HOVSTAD: You should not say that so hardly, Miss Petra—not now.

PETRA: Why not now?

HOVSTAD: Because your father can't do without my help.

PETRA (*looking scornfully at him*): And that is what you are! Oh, shame!

HOVSTAD: No, no. I spoke thoughtlessly. You must not believe that.

PETRA: I know what to believe. Good-by.

[ASLAKSEN *enters from printing-room, hurriedly and mysteriously.*]

ASLAKSEN: Plague take it, Mr. Hovstad. (*Seeing* PETRA.) Sh! that's awkward.

PETRA: Well, there's the book.

64

You must give it to someone else. [*Going towards main door.*]

HOVSTAD (*following her*): But, Miss Petra——

PETRA: Good-by.

[*Exit.*]

ASLAKSEN: I say, Mr. Hovstad!

HOVSTAD: Well, what is it?

ASLAKSEN: The Burgomaster is out there, in the printing-office.

HOVSTAD: The Burgomaster?

ASLAKSEN: Yes. He wants to speak to you; he came in by the back door—he didn't want to be seen.

HOVSTAD: What's the meaning of this? Don't go. I will myself —— (*Goes towards printing-room, opens the door, and bows as the Burgomaster enters.*) Take care, Aslaksen, that——

ASLAKSEN: I understand.

[*Exit into printing-room.*]

BURGOMASTER: You didn't expect to see me here, Mr. Hovstad.

HOVSTAD: No, I can't say I did.

BURGOMASTER: Why, you've arranged everything most comfortably here; quite charming.

HOVSTAD: Oh!

BURGOMASTER: And I've come, without any sort of notice, to occupy your time.

HOVSTAD: You are very welcome; I am quite at your service. Let me take your cap and stick. (*He does so.*) And won't you sit down?

BURGOMASTER: Thanks. I have been much—very much annoyed to-day, Mr. Hovstad.

HOVSTAD: Indeed? Oh, yes! With all your various duties, Burgomaster——

BURGOMASTER: To-day I've been worried by the doctor.

HOVSTAD: You don't say so? The doctor?

BURGOMASTER: He's been writing a sort of statement to the directors concerning certain supposed shortcomings of the Baths.

HOVSTAD: No, has he really?

BURGOMASTER: Yes; hasn't he told you? I thought he said——

HOVSTAD: Oh, yes, so he did. He said something about it.

ASLAKSEN (*from the office*): Wherever is the MS.——?

HOVSTAD: H'm? There it is on the desk.

ASLAKSEN: All right.

BURGOMASTER: Why, that is it——

ASLAKSEN: Yes, that's the doctor's paper, Burgomaster.

HOVSTAD: Oh! was *that* what you were speaking of?

BURGOMASTER: The very same. What do you think of it?

HOVSTAD: I'm not a professional man, and I've only glanced at it.

BURGOMASTER: And yet you are going to print it?

HOVSTAD: I can't very well refuse so distinguished a man——

ASLAKSEN: I have nothing to do with the editing of the paper, Burgomaster.

BURGOMASTER: Of course not.

ASLAKSEN: I merely print whatever comes into my hands.

BURGOMASTER: That's as it should be.

ASLAKSEN: So I must——

BURGOMASTER: No, stay one moment, Mr. Aslaksen. With your permission, Mr. Hovstad——

HOVSTAD: By all means, Burgomaster.

BURGOMASTER: You are a discreet and thoughtful man, Mr. Aslaksen.

ASLAKSEN: I'm glad to hear you say so, Burgomaster.

BURGOMASTER: And a man of considerable influence.

ASLAKSEN: Chiefly among the small middle-class.

BURGOMASTER: The small taxpayers are the most numerous—here as everywhere.

ASLAKSEN: That's true enough.

BURGOMASTER: But I do not doubt that you know what the feeling of most of them is. Isn't that so?

ASLAKSEN: Yes, I think I may say that I do, Burgomaster.

BURGOMASTER: Well—if there is such a praiseworthy spirit of self-sacrifice among the less wealthy citizens of the town, I——

ASLAKSEN: How so?

HOVSTAD: Self-sacrifice?

BURGOMASTER: It is an excellent sign of public spirit—a most ex-

cellent sign. I was near saying I should not have expected it. But, of course, you know public feeling better than I do.

ASLAKSEN: Yes, but, Burgomaster——

BURGOMASTER: And assuredly it is no small sacrifice that the town is about to make.

HOVSTAD: The town?

ASLAKSEN: But I don't understand—it's about the Baths——

BURGOMASTER: According to a preliminary estimate, the alterations considered necessary by the doctor will come to several hundred thousand crowns.

ASLAKSEN: That's a large sum; but——

BURGOMASTER: Of course we shall be obliged to raise a municipal loan.

HOVSTAD (rising): You don't mean to say that the town——

ASLAKSEN: To be paid out of the rates? Out of the needy pockets of the small middle-class?

BURGOMASTER: Yes, my excellent Mr. Aslaksen, where should the funds come from?

ASLAKSEN: That's the business of the shareholders who own the Baths.

BURGOMASTER: The shareholders of the Baths are not in a position to go to further expense.

ASLAKSEN: Are you quite sure of that, Burgomaster?

BURGOMASTER: I have assured

myself on the matter. So that if these extensive alterations are to be made, the town itself will have to bear the costs.

ASLAKSEN: Oh, damn it all!— I beg your pardon!—but this is quite another matter, Mr. Hovstad.

HOVSTAD: Yes, it certainly is.

BURGOMASTER: The worst of it is, that we shall be obliged to close the establishment for some two years.

HOVSTAD: To close it? To close it completely?

ASLAKSEN: For two years!

BURGOMASTER: Yes, the work will require that time at least.

ASLAKSEN: But damn it all! we can't stand that, Burgomaster. What are we householders to live on meanwhile?

BURGOMASTER: Unfortunately, that's extremely difficult to say, Mr. Aslaksen. But what would you have us do? Do you think a single visitor will come here if we go about trying to persuade them into fancying the waters are poisoned, and that we are living on a pest ground, and the whole town——

ASLAKSEN: And it is all nothing but fancy?

BURGOMASTER: With the best intentions of the world, I've not been able to convince myself that it is anything else.

ASLAKSEN: But then it is quite inexcusable of Dr. Stockmann— I beg your pardon, Burgomaster, but——

BURGOMASTER: You are, unhappily, only speaking the truth, Mr. Aslaksen. Unfortunately, my brother has always been a headstrong man.

ASLAKSEN: And yet you are willing to support him in such a matter, Mr. Hovstad!

HOVSTAD: But who could possibly have imagined that——

BURGOMASTER: I have drawn up a short statement of the facts, as they appear from a sober-minded point of view. And in it I have hinted that various unavoidable drawbacks may be remedied by measures compatible with the finances of the Baths.

HOVSTAD: Have you the paper with you, Burgomaster?

BURGOMASTER: Yes; I brought it with me in case you——

ASLAKSEN (*quickly*): Damn it, there he is!

BURGOMASTER: Who? My brother?

HOVSTAD: Where, where?

ASLAKSEN: He's coming through the printing-room.

BURGOMASTER: What a nuisance! I should not like to meet him here, and yet there are several things I want to talk to you about.

HOVSTAD (*pointing to the door L.*): Go in there for a moment.

BURGOMASTER: But——?

67

HOVSTAD: You'll only find Billing there.

ASLAKSEN: Quick, quick, Burgomaster, he's just coming.

BURGOMASTER: Very well. But see that you get rid of him quickly. [*Exit door* L., *which* ASLAKSEN *opens, bowing.*]

HOVSTAD: Be busy doing something, Aslaksen.

[*He sits down and writes.*]

DR. STOCKMANN (*entering from printing-room*): Here I am, back again!

HOVSTAD (*writing*): Already, doctor? Make haste, Aslaksen. We've no time to lose to-day.

DR. STOCKMANN (*to* ASLAKSEN): No proofs yet, I hear.

ASLAKSEN (*without turning round*): No; how could you think there would be?

DR. STOCKMANN: Of course not; but you surely understand that I am impatient. I can have no rest or peace until I see the thing in print.

HOVSTAD: H'm! It'll take a good hour yet. Don't you think so, Aslaksen?

ASLAKSEN: I am almost afraid it will.

DR. STOCKMANN: All right, all right, my good friends; then I'll look in again. I don't mind coming twice on such an errand. So great a cause—the welfare of the whole town; upon my word, this is no time to be idle. (*Just going,*

but stops and comes back.) Oh! look here, there's one other thing I must talk to you about.

HOVSTAD: Excuse me. Wouldn't some other time——

DR. STOCKMANN: I can tell you in two words. You see it's only this. When people read my statement in the paper to-morrow, and find I've spent the whole winter silently working for the good of the town——

HOVSTAD: Yes; but, doctor——

DR. STOCKMANN: I know what you would say. You don't think it was a damned bit more than my duty—my simple duty as a citizen. Of course I know that, just as well as you do. But you see, my fellow-citizens—good Lord! the kindly creatures think so much of me——

ASLAKSEN: Yes, your fellow-citizens did think very highly of you till to-day, doctor.

DR. STOCKMANN: And that's exactly what I'm afraid of, that— *this* is what I wanted to say: when all this comes to them—especially to the poorer class—as a summons to take the affairs of the town into their own hands for the future——

HOVSTAD (*rising*): H'm, doctor, I will not conceal from you——

DR. STOCKMANN: Aha! I thought there was something abrewing! But I won't hear of it. If they're going to get up anything——

HOVSTAD: How so?

DR. STOCKMANN: Well, anything of any sort, a procession with banners, or a banquet, or a subscription for a testimonial—or whatever it may be, you must give me your solemn promise to put a stop to it. And you too, Mr. Aslaksen; do you hear?

HOVSTAD: Excuse me, doctor; we might as well tell you the whole truth first, as last——

[*Enter* MRS. STOCKMANN.]

MRS. STOCKMANN: Ah! just as I thought!

HOVSTAD: Hallo! Your wife, too?

DR. STOCKMANN: What the devil have you come here for, Katrine?

MRS. STOCKMANN: I should think you must know well enough what I've come for.

HOVSTAD: Won't you sit down? Or can——?

MRS. STOCKMANN: Thanks; please do not trouble. And you mustn't be vexed with me for coming here to fetch Stockmann, for you must bear in mind I'm the mother of three children.

DR. STOCKMANN: Stuff and nonsense! We all know that well enough!

MRS. STOCKMANN: It doesn't look as if you were thinking very much about your wife and children to-day, or you'd not be so ready to plunge us all into misfortune.

DR. STOCKMANN: Are you quite mad, Katrine? Mustn't a man with a wife and children proclaim the truth, do his utmost to be a useful and active citizen, do his duty by the town he lives in?

MRS. STOCKMANN: Everything in moderation, Thomas.

ASLAKSEN: That's just what I say. Moderation in all things.

MRS. STOCKMANN: And you are wronging us, Mr. Hovstad, when you entice my husband away from his house and home, and befool him with all this business.

HOVSTAD: I am not aware I have befooled any one in——

DR. STOCKMANN: Befool! Do you think I should let myself be made a fool of?

MRS. STOCKMANN: Yes, but you do. I know well that you are the cleverest man in the town, but you so easily allow yourself to be taken in, Thomas. (*To* HOVSTAD.) And only think, he will lose his post at the Baths if you print what he has written.

ASLAKSEN: What!

HOVSTAD: Yes, but you know, doctor——

DR. STOCKMANN (*laughing*): Ha, ha! just let them try! No, no, my dear, they daren't do it! I've the compact majority behind me, you see.

MRS. STOCKMANN: That's just the misfortune that you have such an awful thing behind you.

DR. STOCKMANN: Nonsense, Katrine; you get home and see after

69

the house, and let me take care of society. How can you be so afraid when I am so confident and happy. (*Rubbing his hands and walking up and down.*) Truth and the people must win the day; that you may be sure. Ah! I see the independent citizens gathering together as in triumphant host! (*Stopping by chair.*) Why, what the devil is that?

ASLAKSEN (*looking at it*): Oh, Lord!

HOVSTAD (*the same*): H'm!

DR. STOCKMANN: Why, here's the top-knot of authority!

[*He takes the Burgomaster's official cap carefully between the tips of his fingers and holds it up.*]

MRS. STOCKMANN: The Burgomaster's cap!

DR. STOCKMANN: And here's the staff of office, too! But how the deuce did they——

HOVSTAD: Well then——

DR. STOCKMANN: Ah! I understand. He's been here to talk you over. Ha! ha! He brought his pigs to the wrong market! And when he caught sight of me in the printing-room (*bursts out laughing*) he took to his heels, Mr. Aslaksen?

ASLAKSEN (*hurriedly*): Exactly; he took to his heels, doctor.

DR. STOCKMANN: Took to his heels without his stick and—— Fiddle, faddle! Peter didn't make

off without his belongings. But what the devil have you done with him? Ah!—in there, of course. Now you shall see, Katrine!

MRS. STOCKMANN: Thomas, I beg you——!

ASLAKSEN: Take care, doctor!

[DR. STOCKMANN *has put the* BURGOMASTER'S *cap on and taken his stick; then he goes up, throws open the door, and makes a military salute. The* BURGOMASTER *enters, red with anger. Behind him enters* BILLING.]

BURGOMASTER: What is the meaning of this folly?

DR. STOCKMANN: Be respectful, my good Peter. Now, it is I who am the highest authority in the town.

[*He struts up and down.*]

MRS. STOCKMANN (*almost crying*): But really, Thomas——!

BURGOMASTER: Give me my cap and stick!

DR. STOCKMANN: If you are the chief of police, I am the Burgomaster. I am master of the whole town, I tell you!

BURGOMASTER: Put down my cap, I say. Remember it is the official cap.

DR. STOCKMANN: Pish! Do you think the awakening leonine people will allow themselves to be scared by an official cap? For you will see, we are going to have a revolution in the town to-morrow.

You threatened to dismiss me, but now I dismiss you—dismiss you from all your offices of trust. You think I can not do it?—Oh, yes, I can! I have the irresistible force of society with me. Hovstad and Billing will thunder forth in the *People's Messenger*, and Printer Aslaksen will come forward at the head of the whole Householders' Association——

ASLAKSEN: I shall not, doctor.

DR. STOCKMANN: Surely you will——

BURGOMASTER: Ah ha! Perhaps Mr. Hovstad is going to join the agitation?

HOVSTAD: No, Burgomaster.

ASLAKSEN: No, Mr. Hovstad isn't such a fool as to ruin both himself and the paper for the sake of a fancy.

DR. STOCKMANN (*looking about him*): What does all this mean?

HOVSTAD: You have represented your case in a false light, doctor; and therefore I am not able to give you my support.

BILLING: And after what the Burgomaster has been so kind as to tell me in there, I——

DR. STOCKMANN: In a false light! Charge me with that, if you will, only print my paper; I am man enough to stand by it.

HOVSTAD: I shall not print it. I can not, and will not, and dare not print it.

DR. STOCKMANN: You dare not?

What nonsense! You're editor, and I suppose it is the editor that directs his paper.

ASLAKSEN: No, it's the readers, doctor.

BILLING: Luckily, it is.

ASLAKSEN: It is public opinion, the enlightened people, the householders, and all the rest. It is they who direct a paper.

DR. STOCKMANN (*quietly*): And all these powers I have against me?

ASLAKSEN: Yes, you have. It would be absolute ruin for the townspeople if your paper were printed.

DR. STOCKMANN: So!

BURGOMASTER: My hat and stick. (DR. STOCKMANN *takes off the cap and lays it on the table. The* BURGOMASTER *takes them both.*) Your magisterial authority has come to an untimely end.

DR. STOCKMANN: The end is not yet. So it is quite impossible to print my paper in the *Messenger*.

HOVSTAD: Quite impossible; and for the sake of your family——

MRS. STOCKMANN: Oh! please leave his family out of the question, Mr. Hovstad.

BURGOMASTER (*takes a manuscript from his jacket*): This will be sufficient to enlighten the public, if you will print this: it is an authentic statement. Thanks.

HOVSTAD (*taking MS.*): Good! I'll see it is inserted at once.

71

DR. STOCKMANN: And not mine! You imagine you can silence me and the truth! But it won't be as easy as you think. Mr. Aslaksen, will you be good enough to print my MS. at once as a pamphlet—at my own cost—on my own responsibility. I'll take five hundred copies—no, I'll have six hundred.

ASLAKSEN: No. If you offered me its weight in gold I should not dare to lend my press to such a purpose, doctor. I must not, for the sake of public opinion. And you'll not get that printed anywhere in the whole town.

DR. STOCKMANN: Then give it me back.

HOVSTAD (handing him MS.): By all means.

DR. STOCKMANN: It shall be made public all the same. I'll read it at a mass meeting; all my fellow-citizens shall hear the voice of truth!

BURGOMASTER: There's not a society in the whole town that would let you their premises for such a purpose.

ASLAKSEN: Not a single one, I am certain.

BILLING: No, God bless me, I should think not!

MRS. STOCKMANN: That would be too shameful! But why are all these men against you?

DR. STOCKMANN (angrily): Ah! I'll tell you. It is because in this town all the men are old women —like you. They all think only of their families, and not of the general good.

MRS. STOCKMANN: Then I will show them how an—an old woman can be a man, for once in a way. For now I will stand by you, Thomas.

DR. STOCKMANN: Bravely said, Katrine! For on my soul the truth will out. If I can't make them let any hall, I'll hire a drum, and I'll march through the town with it; and I'll read my paper at every street corner.

BURGOMASTER: Surely you're not such an arrant fool as all that?

DR. STOCKMANN: I am.

ASLAKSEN: There's not a single man in the whole town who would go with you.

BILLING: No, God bless me, that there isn't.

MRS. STOCKMANN: Do not give in, Thomas. I will send the boys with you.

DR. STOCKMANN: That's a splendid idea!

MRS. STOCKMANN: Morten will be so pleased to go; Ejlif will go too—he too.

DR. STOCKMANN: Yes, and so will Petra. And you yourself, Katrine!

MRS. STOCKMANN: No, no, not I. But I'll stand at the window and watch you—that I will do gladly.

DR. STOCKMANN (throwing his arms about her and kissing her): Thanks, thanks. Now, my good sirs, we are ready for the fight! Now, we'll see if cowardice can close the mouth of a patriot who labors only for the common weal.

[*He and his wife go out together through door L., in flat.*]

BURGOMASTER (*shaking his head doubtfully*): Now he's sent her mad too!

ACT IV

A large old-fashioned room in CAPTAIN HORSTER's *house. An open folding-door in the background leads to an ante-room. Three windows, left. About the middle of the opposite wall is a small platform seat and on it a small table, two candles, a bottle of water, and a bell. The rest of the room is lighted by sconces placed between the windows. Left, near the front of the stage, is a table with a light on it, and by it a chair. In front to the right, a door, and near it a few chairs. Large meeting of all classes of townsfolk. In the crowd are a few women and school-boys. More and more people stream in, until the room is quite full.*

FIRST CITIZEN (*to another standing near him*): So you're here, too, Lamstad?

SECOND CITIZEN: I always go to every meeting.

A BYSTANDER: I suppose you've brought your whistle?

SECOND CITIZEN: Of course I have; haven't you?

THIRD CITIZEN: Rather. And Skipper Evensen said he should bring a great big horn.

SECOND CITIZEN: What a fellow that Evensen is. (*Laughter among the groups of citizens.*)

FOURTH CITIZEN (*joining them*): I say, what's it all about? What's going on here to-night?

SECOND CITIZEN: Why, it's Dr. Stockmann who is going to give a lecture against the Burgomaster.

FOURTH CITIZEN: But the Burgomaster's his brother.

FIRST CITIZEN: That doesn't matter. Dr. Stockmann isn't afraid, he isn't.

THIRD CITIZEN: But he's all wrong; they said so in the *People's Messenger*.

SECOND CITIZEN: Yes, he must be wrong this time, for neither the Householders' Association nor the Citizens' Club would let him have a hall.

FIRST CITIZEN: They wouldn't even let him have a hall at the Baths.

SECOND CITIZEN: No, you may be sure they wouldn't.

A MAN (*in another group*): Now, whom are we to go with in this affair? H'm!

73

ANOTHER MAN: You just stick to Printer Aslaksen, and do what he does.

BILLING (*with a portfolio writing-case under his arm, makes his way through the crowd*): Excuse me, gentlemen. Will you allow me to pass? I am going to report for the *Messenger*. A thousand thanks.

A WORKINGMAN: Who's he?

ANOTHER WORKINGMAN: Don't you know him? That's Billing, who writes for Aslaksen's paper.

[CAPTAIN HORSTER *enters, leading in* MRS. STOCKMANN *and* PETRA *by the right-hand door.* EJLIF *and* MORTEN *follow them.*]

HORSTER: I think you'll all be comfortable here. You can easily slip out if anything should happen.

MRS. STOCKMANN: Do you think there will be any trouble?

HORSTER: One can never tell—with such a crowd. But do sit down, and don't be anxious.

MRS. STOCKMANN: Ah! it was good of you to let Stockmann have this room.

HORSTER: Well, as no one else would, I——

PETRA: And it was brave too, Horster.

HORSTER: Shouldn't think it needed much courage.

[HOVSTAD *and* ASLAKSEN *enter at the same moment, but make their way through the crowd separately.*]

ASLAKSEN: Hasn't the doctor come yet?

HORSTER: He's waiting in there. [*Movement at the door in the background.*]

HOVSTAD (*to* BILLING): There's the Burgomaster, look!

BILLING: Yes, God bless me, if he hasn't come to the fore after all.

[BURGOMASTER STOCKMANN *makes his way blandly through the meeting, bows politely and stands by the wall* L. *Immediately after,* DR. STOCKMANN *enters from first* R. *Entrance. He is carefully dressed in frock-coat and white waist-coat. Faint applause, met by a subdued hiss. Then silence.*]

DR. STOCKMANN (*in a low tone*): Well, how do you feel, Katrine?

MRS. STOCKMANN: Oh! I'm all right. Now do, for once, keep your temper, Thomas.

DR. STOCKMANN: Oh! I can control myself well enough, dear. (*Looks at his watch, ascends the raised platform, and bows.*) It is a quarter past the time, so I will begin.

[*Takes out his MS.*]

ASLAKSEN: But I suppose a chairman must be elected first.

DR. STOCKMANN: No; there's not the least necessity for that.

SEVERAL GENTLEMEN (*shouting*): Yes, yes.

74

BURGOMASTER: I am also of opinion that a chairman should be elected.

DR. STOCKMANN: But I have called this meeting to give a lecture, Peter!

BURGOMASTER: A lecture concerning the Baths may very possibly lead to divergence of opinion.

SEVERAL VOICES IN THE CROWD: A chairman! A chairman.

DR. STOCKMANN (*controlling himself*): Very well, then; let the meeting have its will.

ASLAKSEN: Will not the Burgomaster take the chair?

THREE GENTLEMEN: Bravo! Bravo!

BURGOMASTER: For several reasons, which I am sure you will understand, I must decline. But, fortunately, we have here in our midst one whom I think we all can accept. I allude to the president of the Householders' Association, Mr. Aslaksen.

MANY VOICES: Yes, yes! Long live Aslaksen! Three cheers for Aslaksen.

[DR. STOCKMANN *takes his MS. and descends from the platform.*]

ASLAKSEN: If I am called upon by the confidence of my fellow-citizens, I shall not be unwilling to——

[*Applause and cheers.* ASLAKSEN *ascends the platform.*]

BILLING (*writing*): So—"Mr.

Aslaksen was elected by acclamation——"

ASLAKSEN: And now, as I have been called to the chair, I take the liberty of saying a few brief words. I am a quiet, peace-loving man; I am in favor of discreet moderation and of—and of moderate discretion. That everyone who knows me, knows.

MANY VOICES: Yes, yes, Aslaksen!

ASLAKSEN: I have learnt in the school of life and of experience that moderation is the virtue which best becomes a citizen——

BURGOMASTER: Hear, hear!

ASLAKSEN: ——and it is discretion and moderation, too, that best serve the community. I will therefore beg our respected fellow-citizen who has called this meeting to reflect upon this and to keep within the bounds of moderation.

A MAN: Three cheers for the Moderation Society.

A VOICE: Go to the devil!

VOICES: Hush! hush!

ASLAKSEN: No interruptions, gentlemen! Does anyone wish to offer any observations?

BURGOMASTER: Mr. Chairman!

ASLAKSEN: Burgomaster Stockmann will address the meeting.

BURGOMASTER: In consideration of my close relationship—of which you are probably aware—to the gentleman who is at present medical officer to the Baths, I should very much have preferred not to speak here this evening. But the position I hold at the Baths, and my anxiety with regard to matters of the utmost importance to the town, force me to move a resolution. I may, no doubt, assume that not a single citizen here present thinks it desirable that unreliable and exaggerated statements, as to the sanitary condition of the Baths and the town, should be disseminated over a wider area.

MANY VOICES: No, no, certainly not. We protest.

BURGOMASTER: I therefore beg to move, "That this meeting refuses to hear the medical officer of the Baths either lecture or speak upon the subject."

DR. STOCKMANN (*flaming up*): Refuses to hear—what nonsense!

MRS. STOCKMANN (*coughing*): H'm! h'm!

DR. STOCKMANN (*controlling himself*): Then I'm not to be heard.

BURGOMASTER: In my statement in the *People's Messenger* I have made the public acquainted with the most essential facts, so that all well-disposed citizens can easily draw their own conclusions. You will see from this that the medical officer's proposal—besides being a vote of censure against the leading men of the town—at bottom only means saddling the rate-paying inhabitants of the town with an unnecessary expense of at least a hundred thousand crowns.

[*Noise and some hissing.*]

ASLAKSEN (*ringing the bell*): Order, gentlemen! I must take the liberty of supporting the Burgomaster's resolution. It is also *my* opinion there is something beneath the surface of the doctor's agitation. He speaks of the Baths, but it is a revolution he is trying to bring about; he wants to place the municipal government of the town in other hands. No one doubts the intentions of Dr. Stockmann—God forbid! there can't be two opinions as to that. I, too, am in favor of self-government by the people, if only the cost do not fall too heavily upon the ratepayers. But in this case it would do so, and for this reason I—damn it all—I beg your pardon—I can not go with Dr. Stockmann upon this occasion. You can buy even gold at too high a price; that's my opinion.

[*Loud applause on all sides.*]

HOVSTAD: I also feel bound to explain my attitude. In the beginning, Dr. Stockmann's agitation found favor in several quarters, and I supported it as impartially as I could. But when we found we had allowed ourselves to be misled by a false statement——

DR. STOCKMANN: False!

HOVSTAD: Well, then, a somewhat unreliable statement. The Burgomaster's report has proved this. I trust no one here present doubts my liberal principles; the attitude of the *Messenger* on all great political questions is well known to you all. But I have learned from experience and thoughtful men that in purely local matters a man must observe a certain amount of caution.

ASLAKSEN: I quite agree with the speaker.

HOVSTAD: And in the matter under discussion it is evident that Dr. Stockmann has public opinion against him. But, gentlemen, what is the first and foremost duty of an editor? Is it not to work in harmony with his readers? Has he not in some sort received a silent mandate to further assiduously and unweariedly the well-being of his constituents? or am I mistaken in this?

MANY VOICES: No, no, no! Hovstad is right.

HOVSTAD: It has cost me a bitter struggle to break with a man in whose house I have of late been a frequent guest—with a man who up to this day has enjoyed the universal good-will of his fellow-citizens—with a man whose only, or at any rate, whose chief fault is that he consults his heart rather than his head.

A FEW SCATTERED VOICES: That's true! Three cheers for Dr. Stockmann.

HOVSTAD: But my duty towards the community has forced me to break with him. Then, too, there is another consideration that compels me to oppose him, to stay him if possible from the fatal descent upon which he is entering: consideration for his family——

DR. STOCKMANN: Keep to the water-works and the sewers!

HOVSTAD: ——consideration for his wife and his unprovided-for children.

MORTEN: Is that us, mother?

MRS. STOCKMANN: Hush!

ASLAKSEN: I will now put the Burgomaster's resolution to the vote.

DR. STOCKMANN: It is not necessary. I haven't the slightest intention of speaking of all the filth at the Baths. No! You shall hear something quite different.

BURGOMASTER (*aside*): What nonsense has he got hold of now?

A DRUNKEN MAN: I'm a duly qualified ratepayer! And so I've a right to my opinion! My full, firm opinion is that——

SEVERAL VOICES: Silence, up there.

OTHERS: He's drunk! Turn him out!

[*The drunken man is put out.*]

DR. STOCKMANN: Can I speak?

ASLAKSEN (*ringing the bell*): Dr. Stockmann will address the meeting.

DR. STOCKMANN: I should have liked to see any one, but a few days ago, dare to make such an attempt to gag me as has been made here to-night! I would then have fought like a lion in defense of my holiest rights as a man. But now all this is quite indifferent to me, for now I have more important things to speak of. (*The people crowd closer round him.*) During the last few days I have thought, reflected much, have pondered upon so many things, till, at last, my head seemed to be in a whirl——

BURGOMASTER (*coughing*): H'm!

DR. STOCKMANN: ——but then I began to see things clearly; then I saw to the very bottom of the whole matter. And that is why I stand here this evening. I am about to make a great revelation to you, fellow-citizens! I am going to disclose that to you which is of infinitely more moment than the unimportant fact that our water-works are poisonous, and that our Hygienic Baths are built upon soil teeming with pestilence.

MANY VOICES (*shouting*): Don't speak about the Baths! We won't listen to that! Shut up about that!

DR. STOCKMANN: I have said I should speak of the great discovery I have made within the last few days—the discovery that all our spiritual sources of life are poisoned, and that our whole bourgeois society rests upon a soil teeming with the pestilence of lies.

SEVERAL VOICES: What is he saying?

BURGOMASTER: Such an insinuation——

ASLAKSEN (*with hand on bell*): I must call upon the speaker to moderate his expressions.

DR. STOCKMANN: I have loved my native town as dearly as man could love the home of his childhood. I was not old when I left our town, and distance, privations, and memory threw, as it were, a strange glamor over the town and its people. (*Some clapping and cheers of approval.*) Then for years I found myself stranded in an out-of-the-way corner in the north. Whenever I met any of the poor folk who lived there, hemmed in by rocks, it seemed to me, many a time, that it would have been better for those poor degraded creatures if they had had a cattle doctor to attend them than a man like me. (*Murmurs in the room.*)

BILLING (*laying down his pen*): God bless me! But I've never heard——

HOVSTAD: It is an insult to an estimable peasantry.

DR. STOCKMANN: One moment! I do not think anyone can reproach me with forgetting my native town up there. I brooded over my eggs like an eider duck, and what I hatched—were plans for the Baths here. (*Applause and interruptions.*) And when, at last,

78

after a long time, fate arranged all things so well and happily for me that I could come home again— then, fellow-citizens, it seems to me that I hadn't another wish upon earth. Yes; I had the one ardent, constant, burning desire to be useful to the place of my birth, and to the people here.

BURGOMASTER: The method is rather extraordinary—h'm!

DR. STOCKMANN: And when I came here I rejoiced blindly in my happy illusions. But yesterday morning—no, it was really two evenings ago—the eyes of my mind were opened wide, and the first thing I saw was the extraordinary stupidity of the authorities. [*Noise, cries and laughter.* MRS. STOCKMANN *coughs zealously.*]

BURGOMASTER: Mr. Chairman!

ASLAKSEN (*ringing bell*): In virtue of my office——!

DR. STOCKMANN: It is mean to catch me up on a word, Mr. Aslaksen. I only meant that I became aware of the extraordinary muddling of which the leading men have been guilty down there at the Baths. I detest leading men— I've seen enough of these gentry in my time. They are like goats in a young plantation; they do harm everywhere; they stand in the path of a free man wherever he turns— and I should be glad if we could exterminate them like other nox-

ious animals——

[*Uproar in the room.*]

BURGOMASTER: Mr. Chairman, can such an expression be permitted?

ASLAKSEN: Doctor Stockmann ——!

DR. STOCKMANN: I can't conceive how it is that I only now have seen through these gentry; for haven't I had a magnificent example before my eyes daily here in the town—my brother Peter—slow in grasping new ideas, tenacious in prejudice——

[*Laughter, noise and whistling.* MRS. STOCKMANN *coughs.* ASLAKSEN *rings violently.*]

THE DRUNKEN MAN (*who has come in again*): Do you mean me? Sure enough, my name is Petersen, but damn me if——

ANGRY VOICES: Out with that drunken man. Turn him out.

[*The man is again turned out.*]

BURGOMASTER: Who is that person?

A BYSTANDER: I don't know him, Burgomaster.

ANOTHER: He doesn't belong to this town.

A THIRD: Probably he's a loafer from——(*The rest is inaudible.*)

ASLAKSEN: The man was evidently intoxicated with Bavarian beer. Continue, Dr. Stockmann, but do strive to be moderate.

DR. STOCKMANN: Well, fellow-citizens, I will say no more about our leading men. If any one imagines, from what I have said here, that I want to exterminate these gentlemen to-night, he is mistaken —altogether mistaken. For I cherish the comforting belief that these laggards, these old remnants of a decaying world of thought, are doing this admirably for themselves. They need no doctor's help to hasten their end. Nor, indeed, is it this sort of people that are the most serious danger of society; it is not they who are the most effective in poisoning our spiritual life or making pestilential the ground beneath our feet; it is not they who are the most dangerous enemies of truth and freedom in our society.

CRIES FROM ALL SIDES: Who, then? Who is it? Name, name.

DR. STOCKMANN: Yes, you may be sure I will name them. For *this* is the great discovery I made yesterday. (*In a louder tone.*) The most dangerous enemies of truth and freedom in our midst are the compact majority. Yes, the damned, compact, liberal majority—they it is! Now you know it. [*Immense noise in the room. Most are shouting, stamping and whistling. Several elderly gentlemen exchange stolen glances and seem amused.* MRS. STOCKMANN *rises nervously.* EJLIF *and* MORTEN *advance threateningly towards*

the school-boys, who are making a noise.* ASLAKSEN *rings the bell and calls for order.* HOVSTAD *and* BILLING *both speak, but nothing can be heard. At last quiet is restored.*]

ASLAKSEN: The chairman expects the speaker to withdraw his thoughtless remarks.

DR. STOCKMANN: Never, Mr. Aslaksen. For it is this great majority of our society that robs me of my freedom, and wants to forbid me to speak the truth.

HOVSTAD: Right is always on the side of the majority.

BILLING: Yes, and the truth too, God bless me!

DR. STOCKMANN: The majority is never right. Never, I say. That is one of those conventional lies against which a free, thoughtful man must rebel. Who are they that make up the majority of a country? Is it the wise men or the foolish? I think we must agree that the foolish folk are, at present, in a terribly overwhelming majority all around and about us the wide world over. But, devil take it, it can surely never be right that the foolish should rule over the wise! (*Noise and shouts.*) Yes, yes, you can shout me down, but you can not gainsay me. The majority has might—unhappily— but right it has not. I and a few others are right. The minority is always right.

[*Much noise again.*]

HOVSTAD: Ha! ha! So Dr. Stockmann has turned aristocrat since the day before yesterday!

DR. STOCKMANN: I have said that I will not waste a word on the little, narrow-chested, short-winded crew that lie behind us. Pulsating life has nothing more to do with them. But I do think of the few individuals among us who have made all the new, germinating truths their own. These men stand, as it were, at the outposts, so far in advance that the compact majority has not yet reached them —and *there* they fight for truths that are too lately borne into the world's consciousness to have won over the majority.

HOVSTAD: So the doctor is a revolutionist now.

DR. STOCKMANN: Yes, by Heaven, I am, Mr. Hovstad! For I am going to revolt against the lie that truth resides in the majority. What sort of truths are those that the majority is wont to take up? Truths so full of years that they are decrepit. When a truth is as old as that, it is in a fair way to become a lie, gentlemen. (*Laughter and interruption.*) Yes, yes, you may believe me or not; but truths are by no means wiry Methuselahs, as some people think. A normally-constituted truth lives —let me say—as a rule, seventeen

or eighteen years, at the outside twenty years, seldom longer. But truths so stricken in years are always shockingly thin. And yet it is only then that a majority takes them up and recommends them to society as wholesome food. But I can assure you there is not much nutritious matter in this sort of fare; and as a doctor I know something about it. All these majority-truths are like last year's salt pork; they are like rancid, moldy ham, producing all the moral scrofula that devastates society.

ASLAKSEN: It seems to me that the honorable speaker is wandering very considerably from the subject.

BURGOMASTER: I quite agree with the chairman.

DR. STOCKMANN: I really think you quite mad, Peter! I am keeping as closely to the subject as I possibly can, for what I am speaking of is only this—that the masses, the majority, that damned compact majority—it is they, I say, who are poisoning our spiritual life, and making pestilential the ground beneath our feet.

HOVSTAD: And this the great, independent majority of the people do, just because they are sensible enough to reverence only assured and acknowledged truths?

DR. STOCKMANN: Ah! my dear Mr. Hovstad, don't talk so glibly about assured truths! The truths

81

acknowledged by the masses, the multitude, are truths that the advanced guard thought assured in the days of our grandfathers. We, the fighters at the outposts now-a-days, we no longer acknowledge them, and I don't believe that there is any other assured truth but this—that society can not live, and live wholesomely, upon such old, marrowless, lifeless truths as these.

HOVSTAD: But instead of all this vague talk, it would be more interesting to learn what are these old, lifeless truths which we are living upon.

[*Approving applause generally.*]

DR. STOCKMANN: Ah! I couldn't go over the whole heap of abominations; but to begin with, I'll just keep to one acknowledged truth, which at bottom is a hideous lie, but which, all the same, Mr. Hovstad, and the *Messenger*, and all adherents of the *Messenger* live upon.

HOVSTAD: And that is——?

DR. STOCKMANN: That is the doctrine that you have inherited from our forefathers, and that you heedlessly proclaim far and wide —the doctrine that the multitude, the vulgar herd, the masses, are the pith of the people—that, indeed, they are the people—that the common man, that this ignorant, undeveloped member of society has the same right to con-

demn or to sanction, to govern and to rule, as the few people of intellectual power.

BILLING: Now really, God bless me——

HOVSTAD (*shouting at the same time*): Citizens, please note that!

ANGRY VOICES: Ho, ho! Aren't we the people? Is it only the grand folk who're to govern?

A WORKINGMAN: Turn out the fellow who stands there talking such twaddle.

OTHERS: Turn him out!

A CITIZEN (*shouting*): Blow your horn, Evensen.

[*Loud hooting, whistling, and terrific noise in the room.*]

DR. STOCKMANN (*when the noise has somewhat subsided*): Now do be reasonable! Can't you bear to hear the voice of truth for once? Why, I don't ask you all to agree with me straight away. But I did certainly expect that Mr. Hovstad would be on my side, if he would but be true to himself. For Mr. Hovstad claims to be a free-thinker——

SEVERAL VOICES (*ask wondering, in a low voice*): Free-thinker, did he say. What? Editor Hovstad a free-thinker?

HOVSTAD (*shouting*): Prove it, Dr. Stockmann! When have I said that in print?

DR. STOCKMANN (*reflecting*): No; by Heaven, you're right there. You've never had the frankness to do that. Well, I won't get you into a scrape, Mr. Hovstad. Let me be the free-thinker then. For now I'll prove, and on scientific grounds, that the *Messenger* is leading you all by the nose shamefully, when it tells you that you, that the masses, the vulgar herd, are the true pith of the people. You see that is only a newspaper lie. The masses are nothing but the raw material that must be fashioned into the people. (*Murmurs, laughter, and noise in the room.*) Is it not so with all other living creatures on earth? How great the difference between a cultivated and an uncultivated breed of animals! Only look at a common barn hen. What sort of meat do you get from such a skinny animal? Nothing to boast of! And what sort of eggs does it lay? A fairly decent crow or raven can lay eggs nearly as good. Then take a cultivated Spanish or Japanese hen, or take a fine pheasant or turkey—ah! then you see the difference. And then I take the dog, man's closest ally. Think first of an ordinary common cur— I mean one of those loathsome, ragged, low mongrels, that haunt the streets, and are a nuisance to everybody. And place such a mongrel by the side of a poodle dog, who for many generations has been bred from a well-known strain, who has lived on delicate food, and has heard harmonious voices and music. Don't you believe that the brain of a poodle has developed quite differently from that of a mongrel? Yes, you may depend upon that! It is educated poodles like this that jugglers train to perform the most extraordinary tricks. A common peasant-cur could never learn anything of the sort—not if he tried till Doomsday.

[*Laughing and chaffing are heard all around.*]

A CITIZEN (*shouting*): Do you want to make dogs of us now?

ANOTHER MAN: We are not animals, doctor.

DR. STOCKMANN: Yes, on my soul, but we are animals, old fellow! We're one and all of us as much animals as one could wish. But, truly, there aren't many distinguished animals among us. Ah! there is a terrible difference between men—poodles and men-mongrels. And the ridiculous part of it is, that Editor Hovstad quite agrees with me so long as we speak of four-footed animals——

HOVSTAD: Oh! do drop them!

DR. STOCKMANN: All right! but so soon as I apply the law to the two-legged, Mr. Hovstad is up in arms; then he no longer dares to stick to his own opinions, he does not dare to think out his own thoughts to their logical end; then he turns his whole doctrines up-side down, and proclaims in the *People's Messenger* that barn-yard hens and gutter mongrels are precisely the finest specimens in the menagerie. But it is always thus so long as you haven't work'd the vulgarity out of your system, and fought your way up to spiritual distinction.

HOVSTAD: I make no kind of pretensions to any sort of distinction. I come from simple peasants, and I am proud that my root lies deep among the masses, who are being jeered at now.

SEVERAL WORKMEN: Three cheers for Hovstad! Hurrah! hurrah!

DR. STOCKMANN: The sort of people I am speaking of you don't find only in the lower classes; they crawl and swarm all around us—up to the very highest classes of society. Why, only look at your own smug, smart Burgomaster! Truly, my brother Peter is as much one of the vulgar herd as any man walking on two legs.

[*Laughter and hisses.*]

BURGOMASTER: I beg to protest against such personal allusions.

DR. STOCKMANN (*imperturbably*): ——and that not because he — like myself — is descended from a good-for-nothing old pirate of Pomerania, or somewhere thereabouts—yes, for that we are so——

BURGOMASTER: Absurd tradition! Has been refuted!

DR. STOCKMANN: ——but he is so because he thinks the thoughts of his forefathers, and holds the opinions of his forefathers. The people who do this, *they* belong to the unintellectual mob;—see—that's why my pretentious brother Peter is at bottom so utterly without refinement—and consequently so illiberal.

BURGOMASTER: Mr. Chairman——

HOVSTAD: So that the distinguished persons in this country are liberals? That's quite a new theory.

DR. STOCKMANN: Yes, that too is part of my new discovery. And you shall hear *this* also; that free thought is almost precisely the same thing as morality. And therefore I say that it is altogether unpardonable of the *Messenger* to proclaim day after day the false doctrine that it is the masses and the multitude, the compact majority, that monopolize free thought and morality, and that vice and depravity and all spiritual filth are only the oozings from education, as all the filth down there by the Baths oozes out from the Mill Dale Tan-works! (*Noise and interruptions.* DR. STOCKMANN *goes on imperturbably smiling in his eagerness.*) And yet this same *Messenger* can still preach about the masses and the many being raised to a higher level of life! But, in the devil's name—if the doctrine of the *Messenger* holds good, why, then, this raising up of the masses would be synonymous with hurling them into destruction! But, happily, it is only an old hereditary lie that education demoralizes. No, it is stupidity, poverty, the ugliness of life, that do this devil's work! In a house that isn't aired, and whose floors are not swept every day— my wife Katrine maintains that the floors ought to be scrubbed too, but we can't discuss that now; —well,—in such a house, I say, within two or three years, people lose the power of thinking or acting morally. A deficiency of oxygen enervates the conscience. And it would seem there's precious little oxygen in many and many a house here in the town, since the whole compact majority is unscrupulous enough to be willing to build up the prosperity of the town upon a quagmire of lies and fraud.

ASLAKSEN: I can not allow so gross an insult, leveled at all the citizens here present.

A GENTLEMAN: I move that the chairman order the speaker to sit down.

EAGER VOICES: Yes, yes, that's right! Sit down! Sit down!

DR. STOCKMANN (*flaring up*):

Then I will proclaim the truth from the house-tops! I'll write to other newspapers outside the town! The whole land shall know how matters are ordered here.

HOVSTAD: It would almost seem as if the doctor wanted to ruin the town.

DR. STOCKMANN: Yes, I love my native town so well I would rather ruin it than see it flourishing upon a lie.

ASLAKSEN: That is speaking strongly.

[*Noise and whistling.* MRS. STOCK-MANN *coughs in vain; the doctor no longer heeds her.*]

HOVSTAD (*shouting amid the tumult*): The man who would ruin a whole community must be an enemy of the people!

DR. STOCKMANN (*with growing excitement*): It doesn't matter if a lying community is ruined! It must be leveled to the ground, I say! All men who live upon lies must be exterminated like vermin! You'll poison the whole country in time; you'll bring it to such a pass that the whole country will deserve to perish. And should it come to this, I say, from the bottom of my heart: Perish the country! Perish all its people!

A MAN (*in the crowd*): Why, he talks like a regular enemy of the people!

BILLING: There, God bless me! spoke the voice of the people!

85

MANY SHOUTING: Yes! yes! yes! He's an enemy of the people! He hates the country! He hates the people!

ASLAKSEN: Both as a citizen of this town and as a man, I am deeply shocked at what I have been obliged to listen to here. Dr. Stockmann has unmasked himself in a manner I should never have dreamt of. I am reluctantly forced to subscribe to the opinion just expressed by a worthy citizen, and I think we ought to give expression to this opinion. I therefore beg to propose, "That this meeting is of opinion that the medical officer of the Bath, Dr. Thomas Stockmann, is an enemy of the people."

[*Thunders of applause and cheers. Many form a circle round the doctor and hoot at him.* MRS. STOCKMANN *and* PETRA *have risen.* MORTEN *and* EJLIF *fight the other school-boys who have also been hooting. Some grown-up persons separate them.*]

DR. STOCKMANN (*to the people hooting*): Ah! fools, that you are! I tell you that——

ASLAKSEN (*ringing*): The doctor is out of order in speaking. A regular vote must be taken, and out of consideration for the feeling of those present the vote will be taken in writing and without names. Have you any blank paper, Mr. Billing?

BILLING: Here's both blue and white paper——

ASLAKSEN: That'll do. We shall manage more quickly this way. Tear it up. That's it. (*To the meeting.*) Blue means no, white means yes. I will myself go round and collect the votes.

[*The* BURGOMASTER *leaves the room.* ASLAKSEN *and a few citizens go round with pieces of paper in hats.*]

A GENTLEMAN (*to* HOVSTAD): Whatever is up with the doctor? What does it all mean?

HOVSTAD: Why, you know how irrepressible he is.

ANOTHER GENTLEMAN (*to* BILLING): I say, you're intimate with him. Have you ever noticed if he drinks?

BILLING: God bless me! I really don't know what to say. Toddy is always on the table whenever anyone calls.

THIRD GENTLEMAN: No, I rather think he's not always right in his head.

FIRST GENTLEMAN: Yes—I wonder if madness is hereditary in the family?

BILLING: I shouldn't wonder.

FOURTH GENTLEMAN: No, it's pure jealousy. He wants to be over the heads of the rest.

BILLING: A few days ago he certainly was talking about a rise in his salary, but he did not get it.

ALL THE GENTLEMEN (*together*): Ah! that explains everything.

THE DRUNKEN MAN: I want a blue one, I do! And I'll have a white one too!

PEOPLE CALL OUT: There's the drunken man again! turn him out!

MORTEN KIIL: Well, Stockmann, do you see now what this tomfoolery leads to?

DR. STOCKMANN: I have done my duty.

MORTEN KIIL: What was that you said about the Mill Dale Tanneries?

DR. STOCKMANN: Why, you heard what I said; that all the filth comes from them.

MORTEN KIIL: From my tannery as well?

DR. STOCKMANN: Unfortunately, your tannery is the worst of all.

MORTEN KIIL: Will you put that in the papers too?

DR. STOCKMANN: I never keep anything back.

MORTEN KIIL: That may cost you dear, Stockmann!

[*Exit.*]

A FAT GENTLEMAN (*goes up to* HORSTER *without bowing to the ladies*): Well, Captain, so you lend your house to an enemy of the people.

HORSTER: I suppose I can do as I please with my own, sir.

THE MERCHANT: Then, of course, you can have no objection if I do the same with mine?

HORSTER: What do you mean, sir?

THE MERCHANT: You shall hear from me to-morrow.

[*Turns away, and exit.*]

PETRA: Wasn't that the shipowner?

HORSTER: Yes, that was Merchant Vik.

ASLAKSEN (*with the voting papers in his hands, ascends the platform and rings*): Gentlemen! I have to acquaint you with the result of the vote. All, with one exception——

A YOUNG GENTLEMAN: That's the drunken man?

ASLAKSEN: With one exception —a tipsy man—this meeting of citizens declares the medical officer of the Baths, Dr. Thomas Stockmann, an enemy of the people. (*Cheers and applause.*) Three cheers for our honorable old community of citizens! (*Applause.*) Three cheers for our able and energetic Burgomaster, who has so loyally put on one side the claims of kindred! (*Cheers.*) The meeting is dissolved.

BILLING: Three cheers for the chairman!

ALL: Hurrah for Printer Aslaksen!

DR. STOCKMANN: My hat and coat, Petra! Captain, have you room for passengers to the new world?

HORSTER: For you and yours,

doctor, we'll make room.

DR. STOCKMANN: Good! Come Katrine! come, boys!

[*He gives his wife his arm.*]

MRS. STOCKMANN (*in a low voice*): Dear Thomas, let us go out by the back way.

DR. STOCKMANN: No back ways, Katrine! (*In a louder voice.*) You shall hear of the enemy of the people before he shakes the dust from his feet! I'm not so forgiving as a certain person: I don't say I forgive you, for you know not what you do.

ASLAKSEN (*shouting*): That is a blasphemous comparison, Dr. Stockmann.

BILLING: It is, God bl—— A serious man can't stand that!

A COARSE VOICE: And he threatens us into the bargain!

ANGRY CRIES: Let's smash the windows in his house! Let's give him a ducking!

A MAN (*in the crowd*): Blow your horn, Evensen! Ta-rata ra-ra! [*Horn-blowing, whistling and wild shouting. The doctor, with his family, goes towards the door.* HORSTER *makes way for them.*]

ALL (*shouting after them as they go out*): Enemy of the people! Enemy of the people! Enemy of the people!

BILLING: Well, God bless me if I'd drink toddy at Dr. Stockmann's to-night!

[*The people throng towards the door; the noise is heard without from the street beyond; cries of "Enemy of the people! Enemy of the people!"*]

ACT V

DR. STOCKMANN's *study. Bookcases and various preparations along the walls. In the background, a door leading to the ante-room; to the left first entrance, a door to the sitting-room. In wall right are two windows, all the panes of which are smashed. In the middle of the room is the doctor's writing-table, covered with books and papers. The room is in disorder. It is morning.* DR. STOCKMANN *in dressing-gown, slippers and skull-cap, is bending down and raking with an umbrella under one of the cabinets; at last he rakes out a stone.*

DR. STOCKMANN: Katrine, I've found another one.

MRS. STOCKMANN: Ah! you're sure to find lots more.

DR. STOCKMANN (*placing the stone on a pile of others on the table*): I shall keep these stones as sacred relics. Ejlif and Morten shall see them every day, and when they are grown men they shall inherit them from me. (*Poking under the bookcase.*) Hasn't

—what the devil's her name?—
the girl—hasn't she been for the
glazier yet?

MRS. STOCKMANN: Yes, but he
said he didn't know whether he'd
be able to come to-day.

DR. STOCKMANN: You'll see he
daren't come.

MRS. STOCKMANN: Well, Rudine
also thought he didn't dare to
come, because of the neighbors.
What is it, Rudine?—All right.
Here's a letter for you, Thomas.

DR. STOCKMANN: Let's see.
(*Opens letter and reads.*) Ah, ha!

MRS. STOCKMANN: Whom is it
from?

DR. STOCKMANN: From the land-
lord. He gives us notice.

MRS. STOCKMANN: Is it possible?
Such a pleasantly-behaved man.

DR. STOCKMANN: He daren't do
otherwise, he says. He is very
loath to do it; but he daren't do
otherwise on account of his fellow-citizens, out of respect for
public opinion—is in a dependent
position—does not dare to offend
certain influential men——

MRS. STOCKMANN: There, you
can see now, Thomas.

DR. STOCKMANN: Yes, yes, I see
well enough; they are cowards,
every one of them cowards in this
town; no one dares do anything
for fear of all the rest. But that's
all the same to us, Katrine. Now
we're journeying to the new
world, and so——

MRS. STOCKMANN: Yes, but,
Thomas, is that idea of the journey
really well-advised?

DR. STOCKMANN: Perhaps you'd
have me stay here where they
have gibbeted me as an enemy of
the people, branded me, and
smashed my windows to atoms?
And look here, Katrine, they have
torn a hole in my black trousers.

MRS. STOCKMANN: Oh, dear, and
they're the best you've got.

DR. STOCKMANN: One ought
never to put on one's best trousers
when one goes fighting for liberty
and truth. Of course, you know
I don't care so much about the
trousers; you can always patch
them up for me. But it is that the
mob should dare to attack me as
if they were my equals—*that's*
what, for the life of me, I can't
stomach.

MRS. STOCKMANN: Yes, they've
been very insolent to you here,
Thomas; but must we leave the
country altogether on that account?

DR. STOCKMANN: Don't you think
the plebeians are just as imperti-
nent in other towns as here? Ah,
yes, they are, my dear; they're
pretty much of a muchness everywhere. Well, never mind, let the
curs snap; *that* is not the worst;
the worst is that all men are party
slaves all the land over. Nor is it
that—perhaps that's no better in
the free west either; there, too, the

89

compact majority thrives, and enlightened public opinion and all the other devil's trash flourishes. But you see the conditions are on a larger scale there than here; they may lynch you, but they don't torture you; they don't put the screw on a free soul there as they do at home here. And then, if need be, you can live apart. (*Walks up and down.*) If I only knew whether there were any primeval forest, any little South Sea island to be bought cheap——

MRS. STOCKMANN: Yes, but the boys, Thomas.

DR. STOCKMANN (*standing still*): What an extraordinary woman you are, Katrine! Would you prefer the boys to grow up amid such a society as ours? Why, you saw yourself yesterday evening that one-half of the population is quite mad, and if the other half hasn't lost its reason, that's because they're hounds who haven't any reason to lose.

MRS. STOCKMANN: But really, dear Thomas, you do say such imprudent things!

DR. STOCKMANN: Well! But isn't what I say the truth? Don't they turn all ideas upside down? Don't they stir up right and wrong in one mess of pottage? Don't they call lies what I know to be truth? But the maddest thing of all is that there are a whole mass of grown men, Liberals, who go

about persuading themselves and others that they are free! Did you ever hear anything like it, Katrine?

MRS. STOCKMANN: Yes, yes, it is certainly quite mad. But—— (PETRA *enters from sitting-room.*) Back from school already?

PETRA: Yes, I've been dismissed.

MRS. STOCKMANN: Dismissed?

DR. STOCKMANN: You, too!

PETRA: Mrs. Busk gave me notice, and so I thought it best to leave there and then.

DR. STOCKMANN: On my soul, you did right!

MRS. STOCKMANN: Who could have thought Mrs. Busk was such a bad woman?

PETRA: Oh! Mother, Mrs. Busk isn't really so bad; I saw clearly how much it pained her. But she didn't dare to do otherwise, she said; and so I'm dismissed.

DR. STOCKMANN (*laughing and rubbing his hands*): She dared not do otherwise, she too! Ah! that's delicious.

MRS. STOCKMANN: Ah! well! after the dreadful uproar last night——

PETRA: It wasn't only that. Now you shall hear, father!

DR. STOCKMANN: Well?

PETRA: Mrs. Busk showed me no less than three letters she had received this morning.

DR. STOCKMANN: Anonymous, of course?

PETRA: Yes.

DR. STOCKMANN: They didn't dare to give their names, Katrine——!

PETRA: And two of them wrote that a gentleman who frequently visits our house, said at the club last night that I had such extremely advanced opinions upon various matters.

DR. STOCKMANN: And, of course, you didn't deny that?

PETRA: Of course not. You know Mrs. Busk herself has pretty advanced opinions when we are alone together; but now this has come out about me she didn't dare keep me on.

MRS. STOCKMANN: And to think —it was one who came to our house! There, now, you see, Thomas, what comes of all your hospitality.

DR. STOCKMANN: We won't live any longer amid such foulness. Pack up as quickly as you can, Katrine; let us get away—the sooner the better.

MRS. STOCKMANN: Hush! I think there's some one outside in the passage. Just see, Petra.

PETRA (opening door): Ah! is it you, Captain Horster? Please come in.

HORSTER: Good morning. I thought I must just look in and see how you're getting on.

DR. STOCKMANN: Thanks; that's very beautiful of you.

MRS. STOCKMANN: And thanks for seeing us home, Captain Horster.

PETRA: But, however did you get back again?

HORSTER: Oh! that was all right. You know I'm pretty strong, and these folk's bark is worse than their bite.

DR. STOCKMANN: Isn't it marvelous, this piggish cowardice? Come here, I want to show you something! See, here are all the stones they threw in at us. Only look at them! Upon my soul there aren't more than two decent big fighting stones in the whole lot; the rest are nothing but pebbles —mere nothings. And yet they stood down there, and yelled, and swore they'd slay me—the corrupt one;—but for deeds, for deeds— there's not much of that in this town!

HORSTER: Well, that was a good thing for you this time, anyhow, doctor.

DR. STOCKMANN: Of course it was. But it's vexatious all the same; for should it ever come to a serious, really important struggle, you'll see, Captain Horster, that public opinion will take to its heels, and the compact majority will make for the sea like a herd of swine. It is *this* that is so sad to think of; it grieves me to the very heart. No, deuce take it— at the bottom all this is folly.

91

They've said I am an enemy of the people; well, then, I'll be an enemy of the people.

MRS. STOCKMANN: You will never be that, Thomas.

DR. STOCKMANN: You'd better not take your oath of it, Katrine. A bad name may work like a pin's prick in the lungs. And that damned word—I can't get rid of it; it has sunk into my diaphragm —there it lies and gnaws, and sucks like some acid. And magnesia is no good against that.

PETRA: Pshaw! You should only laugh at them, father.

HORSTER: The people will think differently yet, doctor.

MRS. STOCKMANN: Yes, Thomas, you may be as sure of that as you're standing here.

DR. STOCKMANN: Yes—perhaps when it is too late. Well, much good may it do them! Let them go on wallowing here in the mire, and repent that they have driven a patriot into exile. When do you sail, Captain Horster?

HORSTER: H'm!—it was really that I came to speak to you about ——

DR. STOCKMANN: Has anything gone wrong with the ship?

HORSTER: No; but it's like this, I'm not going with it.

PETRA: Surely you have not been dismissed?

HORSTER (smiling): Yes, I have.

PETRA: You too!

MRS. STOCKMANN: There you see, Thomas.

DR. STOCKMANN: And for truth's sake! Ah! had I thought such a thing——

HORSTER: You mustn't take it to heart; I shall soon get a berth with some other company.

DR. STOCKMANN: And this Merchant Vik! A wealthy man, independent of anyone! Good Heavens——

HORSTER: In other matters he is a thoroughly fair man, and he says himself he would gladly have kept me on if only he dared.

DR. STOCKMANN: But he didn't dare—that goes without saying.

HORSTER: It wasn't easy, he said, when you belong to a party——

DR. STOCKMANN: That was a true saying of the honorable man's! A party is like a sausage-machine; it grinds all the heads together in one mash; and that's why there are so many blockheads and fatheads all seething together!

MRS. STOCKMANN: Now really, Thomas!

PETRA (to HORSTER): If only you hadn't seen us home perhaps it would not have come to this.

HORSTER: I don't regret it.

PETRA (holding out her hands): Thank you for that!

HORSTER (to DR. STOCKMANN): And so what I wanted to say to you was this: that if you really want to leave I have thought of another way——

DR. STOCKMANN: That is good— only if we can get off——

MRS. STOCKMANN: Sh! Isn't that a knock?

PETRA: I'm sure that's uncle.

DR. STOCKMANN: Aha! (*Calls.*) Come in.

MRS. STOCKMANN: Dear Thomas, now do for once promise me—— [*Enter Burgomaster from ante- room.*]

BURGOMASTER: Oh! you're en- gaged. Then I'd better——

DR. STOCKMANN: No, no; come in.

BURGOMASTER: But I wanted to speak with you alone.

MRS. STOCKMANN: We'll go into the sitting-room.

HORSTER: And I'll look in again presently.

DR. STOCKMANN: No, no, go with them, Captain Horster, I must have further information——

HORSTER: All right, then I'll wait.

[*He follows* MRS. STOCKMANN *and* PETRA *into the sitting-room. The* BURGOMASTER *says noth- ing, but casts glances at the windows.*]

DR. STOCKMANN: Perhaps you find it rather drafty here to-day? Put your hat on.

BURGOMASTER: Thanks, if I may (*puts on hat*). I fancy I caught cold yesterday evening. I stood there shivering.

DR. STOCKMANN: Really? I should have said it was pretty warm.

BURGOMASTER: I regret that it was not in my power to prevent these nocturnal excesses.

DR. STOCKMANN: Have you noth- ing else to say to me?

BURGOMASTER (*producing a large letter*): I've this document for you from the Directors of the Baths.

DR. STOCKMANN: I am dis- missed?

BURGOMASTER: Yes; from to-day. (*Places letter on table.*) We are very sorry—but frankly, we dared not do otherwise on account of public opinion.

DR. STOCKMANN (*smiling*): Dared not? I've heard that word already to-day.

BURGOMASTER: I beg of you to understand your position clearly. You must not, for the future, count upon any sort of practice in the town here.

DR. STOCKMANN: Deuce take the practice! But are you so sure of this?

BURGOMASTER: The Household- ers' Association is sending round a circular from house to house, in which all well-disposed citizens are called upon not to employ you, and I dare swear that not a single father of a family will venture to refuse his signature; he simply *dare* not.

93

DR. STOCKMANN: Well, well; I don't doubt that. But what then?

BURGOMASTER: If I might give you a piece of advice, it would be this—to go away for a time.

DR. STOCKMANN: Yes, I've had some thought of leaving this place.

BURGOMASTER: Good. When you've done so, and have had six months of reflection, then if, after mature consideration, you could make up your mind to acknowledge your error in a few words of regret——

DR. STOCKMANN: I might perhaps be reinstated, you think.

BURGOMASTER: Perhaps; it is not absolutely impossible.

DR. STOCKMANN: Yes, but how about public opinion? You daren't on account of public opinion.

BURGOMASTER: Opinions are extremely variable things. And, to speak candidly, it is of the greatest importance for us to have such an admission from you.

DR. STOCKMANN: Then you may whistle for it! You remember well enough, damn it, what I've said to you before about these foxes' tricks!

BURGOMASTER: At that time your position was infinitely more favorable; at that time you might have supposed you had the whole town at your back——

DR. STOCKMANN: Yes, and now I feel I've the whole town on my back. (*Flaring up.*) But no— not if I had the devil himself and his grandmother on my back— never—never, I tell you!

BURGOMASTER: The father of a family must not act as you are doing; you must not, Thomas.

DR. STOCKMANN: Must not! There is but one thing on earth that a free man must not do, and do you know what that is?

BURGOMASTER: No.

DR. STOCKMANN: Of course not; but I will tell you. A free man must not behave like a blackguard; he must not so act that he would spit in his own face.

BURGOMASTER: That really sounds extremely plausible; and if there were not another explanation of your mulish obstinacy— but we know well enough there ——

DR. STOCKMANN: What do you mean by that?

BURGOMASTER: I'm sure you understand. But as your brother, and as a man of common sense, I give you this advice: don't build too confidently upon prospects and expectations that perhaps may fail you utterly.

DR. STOCKMANN: But what on earth are you driving at?

BURGOMASTER: Do you really want to make me believe that you are ignorant of the provisions Master Tanner Kiil has made in his will?

DR. STOCKMANN: I know that the little he has is to go to a home for old indigent working-men. But what's that got to do with me?

BURGOMASTER: To begin with, it is not a "little" we're speaking of. Tanner Kiil is a fairly wealthy man.

DR. STOCKMANN: I've never had any idea of that!

BURGOMASTER: H'm! Really? Then you hadn't any idea either that a not inconsiderable portion of his fortune is to go to your children, and that you and your wife are to enjoy the interest on it for life. Hasn't he told you that?

DR. STOCKMANN: No, on my soul! On the contrary, he was constantly grumbling because he was so preposterously over-taxed. But are you really so sure of this, Peter?

BURGOMASTER: I had it from a thoroughly reliable source.

DR. STOCKMANN: But, good Heavens! Why, then, Katrine is all right—and the children too! Oh! I must tell her—— (*Calls.*) Katrine, Katrine!

BURGOMASTER (*restraining him*): Hush! don't say anything about it yet.

MRS. STOCKMANN (*opening the door*): What is it?

DR. STOCKMANN: Nothing, my dear, go in again. (MRS. STOCKMANN *closes the door. He walks up and down.*) Provided for! Only think—all of them provided

for! And that for life! After all it is a pleasant sensation to feel yourself secure!

BURGOMASTER: Yes, but it is not exactly so—you are not. Tanner Kiil can annul his testament at any day or hour he chooses.

DR. STOCKMANN: But he won't do that, my good Peter. The badger is immensely delighted that I've attacked you and your wiseacre friends.

BURGOMASTER (*stops and looks searchingly at him*): Aha! that throws a new light upon a good many matters. .

DR. STOCKMANN: What matters?

BURGOMASTER: So the whole affair has been a combined manœuvre. These violent, restless attacks which you, in the name of truth, have launched against the leading men of the town.

DR. STOCKMANN: What, what?

BURGOMASTER: So this was nothing but a preconcerted return for that vindictive old Morten Kiil's will.

DR. STOCKMANN (*almost speechless*): Peter—you're the most abominable plebeian I've ever known in my life.

BURGOMASTER: Everything is over between us. Your dismissal is irrevocable—for now we have a weapon against you.

[*Exit.*]

DR. STOCKMANN: Shame! shame! shame! (*Calls.*) Katrine! The

floor must be scrubbed after him!
Tell her to come here with a pail
—what's her name?—confound it
—the girl with the sooty nose——

MRS. STOCKMANN (*in the sitting
room*): Hush! hush! Thomas!

PETRA (*also in the doorway*):
Father, here's grandfather, and he
wants to know if he can speak to
you alone.

DR. STOCKMANN: Yes, of course
he can. Come in, father-in-law.
(*Enters* MORTEN KIIL.) Well,
what is it? Sit you down.

MORTEN KIIL: I'll not sit down.
(*Looking about him.*) It looks
cheerful here to-day, Stockmann.

DR. STOCKMANN: Yes, doesn't it?

MORTEN KIIL: Sure enough it
does; and you've plenty of fresh
air, too; I should think you'd have
enough of that oxygen you chat-
tered about so much yesterday.
You must have an awfully good
conscience to-day, I should think.

DR. STOCKMANN: Yes, I have.

MORTEN KIIL: So I should suppose. (*Striking himself upon the
heart.*) But do you know what
I've got here?

DR. STOCKMANN: Well, a good
conscience, too, I hope.

MORTEN KIIL: Pshaw! No,
something far better than that.
[*Takes out a large pocket-book,
opens it and shows a mass of
papers.*]

DR. STOCKMANN (*looking at him
in astonishment*): Shares in the

Baths.

MORTEN KIIL: They weren't difficult to get to-day.

DR. STOCKMANN: And you've
been and bought these up——?

MORTEN KIIL: All I'd got the
money to pay for.

DR. STOCKMANN: But, my dear
father-in-law—just now, when the
Baths are in such straits.

MORTEN KIIL: If you behave like
a reasonable creature you can set
the Baths going again.

DR. STOCKMANN: Aye, why you
can see for yourself that I'm doing
all I can. But the people of this
town are mad!

MORTEN KIIL: You said yesterday that the worst filth came from
my tannery. Now, if that's really
the truth, then my grandfather,
and my father before me, and I
myself have all these years been
littering the town like three destroying angels. Do you think I'll
let such a stain remain upon me?

DR. STOCKMANN: Unfortunately,
you can't help yourself now.

MORTEN KIIL: No, thanks. I stand
for my good name and my rights.
I have heard that the people call
me "badger." Well, the badger is
a swinish sort of animal, but they
shall never be able to say that of
me. I will live and die a clean
man.

DR. STOCKMANN: And how will
you manage *that?*

MORTEN KIIL: You shall make

me clean, Stockmann.

DR. STOCKMANN: I!

MORTEN KIIL: Do you know with what money I've bought these shares? No, you can't know, but now I'll tell you. It's the money Katrine and Petra and the little lads will have after me. Yes, for you see, I've invested my little all to the best advantage anyhow.

DR. STOCKMANN (*flaring up*): And you've thrown away Katrine's money like this!

MORTEN KIIL: O, yes; the whole of the money is entirely invested in the Baths now. And now I shall really see if you're so possessed — demented — mad, Stockmann. Now, if you go on letting this dirt and filth result from my tannery, it'll be just the same as if you were to flay Katrine with a whip—and Petra, too, and the little lads. But no decent father of a family would ever do that—unless, indeed, he were a madman.

DR. STOCKMANN (*walking up and down*): Yes, but I *am* a madman; I *am* a madman!

MORTEN KIIL: But I suppose you're not so stark mad where your wife and bairns are concerned.

DR. STOCKMANN: Why on earth didn't you speak to me before you went and bought all that rubbish?

MORTEN KIIL: What's done can't be undone.

DR. STOCKMANN (*walking about uneasily*): If only I weren't so certain about the affair! But I'm thoroughly convinced that I'm right!

MORTEN KIIL (*weighing the pocketbook in his hand*): If you stick to your madness these aren't worth much.

DR. STOCKMANN: But, deuce take it! surely science will be able to find some remedy, some antidote.

MORTEN KIIL: Do you mean something to kill the animals?

DR. STOCKMANN: Yes, or at least to make them innocuous.

MORTEN KIIL: Can't you try rat's-bane?

DR. STOCKMANN: Tush! Tush! But all the people say it is nothing but fancy! Let them have their own way, then! Haven't the ignorant, narrow-hearted curs reviled me for an enemy of the people; and did not they try to tear the clothes from off my back!

MORTEN KIIL: And they've smashed all the windows for you, too!

DR. STOCKMANN: Then, too, one's duty to one's family. I must talk it over with Katrine; she is such a stickler in matters of this sort.

MORTEN KIIL: That's right. You just follow the advice of a sensible woman.

DR. STOCKMANN (*going to him angrily*): How could you act so perversely! Staking Katrine's money and getting me into this

97

horribly painful dilemma! I tell you that when I look at you I seem to see the devil himself——

MORTEN KIIL: Then I'd better be off. But you must let me know your decision by 2 o'clock. If it's *no*, all the shares go to the charity —and that this very day.

DR. STOCKMANN: And what does Katrine get?

MORTEN KIIL: Not a brass farthing. (*The door of the anteroom opens.* MR. HOVSTAD *and* ASLAKSEN *are seen outside of it.*) Do you see these two there?

DR. STOCKMANN: What! And they actually dare to come to me here!

HOVSTAD: Why, of course we do.

ASLAKSEN: You see there is something we want to talk to you about.

MORTEN KIIL (*whispers*): Yes or no—by 2 o'clock.

ASLAKSEN (*with a glance at* HOVSTAD): Aha!

[*Exit* MORTEN KIIL.]

DR. STOCKMANN: Well, what is it you want with me? Be brief.

HOVSTAD: I can very well understand that you resent our conduct at the meeting yesterday——

DR. STOCKMANN: And that's what you call conduct! Yes, it was charming conduct! I call it misconduct—disgraceful. Shame upon you!

HOVSTAD: Call it what you will; but we *could* not do otherwise.

DR. STOCKMANN: You *dared* not, I suppose? Is not that so?

HOVSTAD: Yes, if you will have it.

ASLAKSEN: But why didn't you drop a word beforehand? Just the merest hint to Mr. Hovstad or to me?

DR. STOCKMANN: A hint? What about?

ASLAKSEN: About what was at the bottom of it.

DR. STOCKMANN: I don't in the least understand you.

ASLAKSEN: Oh! yes, you do, Dr. Stockmann.

HOVSTAD: It's no good concealing it any longer now.

DR. STOCKMANN (*looking from one to the other*): Yes; but in the devil's own name——!

ASLAKSEN: May I ask—isn't your father-in-law going about the town and buying up all the shares in the Baths?

DR. STOCKMANN: Yes, he has bought shares in the Baths to-day, but——

ASLAKSEN: It would have been wiser if you'd set somebody else to do that—some one not so closely connected with you.

HOVSTAD: And then you ought not to have appeared under your own name. No one need have known that the attack on the Baths came from you. You should have taken me into your counsels, Dr. Stockmann.

DR. STOCKMANN (*stares straight*

in front of him; a light seems to break upon him, and he looks thunder-stricken): Are such things possible? Can such things be?

HOVSTAD (*smiling*): Well, we've seen they can. But you see it ought all to have been managed with *finesse*. And then, too, you ought to have had several in it; for you know the responsibility is less for the individual when it is shared by others.

DR. STOCKMANN (*calmly*): In one word, gentlemen, what is it you want?

ASLAKSEN: Mr. Hovstad can best——

HOVSTAD: No, you explain, Aslaksen.

ASLAKSEN: Well, it's this; now that we know how the whole matter stands, we believe we shall be able to place the *People's Messenger* at your disposal.

DR. STOCKMANN: You dare do so, now? But how about public opinion? Aren't you afraid that a storm will burst out against us?

HOVSTAD: We must strive to ride out the storm.

ASLAKSEN: And the doctor try to manage his face-about with dexterity. As soon as your attack has produced its effect——

DR. STOCKMANN: As soon as my father-in-law and I have bought up the shares at a low price, you mean.

HOVSTAD: No doubt it is scientific reasons principally that have impelled you to take over the direction of the Baths.

DR. STOCKMANN: Of course; it was for scientific reasons that I made the old Badger go and buy up these shares. And then we'll tinker up the water-works a bit, and then dig about a bit by the shore down there, without it costing the town a half-crown. Don't you think that can be done? H'm?

HOVSTAD: I think so—if you have the *Messenger* to back you up.

ASLAKSEN: In a free society the press is a power, doctor.

DR. STOCKMANN: Yes, indeed, and so is public opinion; and you, Mr. Aslaksen—I suppose you'll be answerable for the Householders' Association?

ASLAKSEN: Both for the Association and the Moderation Society. You may rely upon that.

DR. STOCKMANN: But, gentlemen —really I am quite ashamed to mention such a thing—but—what return?

HOVSTAD: Of course, you know we should be best pleased to give you our support for nothing. But the *Messenger* is not very firmly established; it is not getting on as it ought; and just now, that there is so much to be done in general politics, I should be very sorry to have to stop the paper.

DR. STOCKMANN: Naturally; that

would be very hard for a friend of the people like you. (*Flaring up.*) But I—I am an enemy of the people! (*Walking about the room.*) Wherever is my stick? Where the devil's my stick?

HOVSTAD: What do you mean?

ASLAKSEN: Surely you would not——

DR. STOCKMANN (*standing still*): And now, suppose I don't give you a single farthing out of all my shares? You must remember that we rich folk don't like parting with our money.

HOVSTAD: And *you* must remember that this business of the shares can be represented in two ways.

DR. STOCKMANN: Yes, you're the man for that; if I don't come to the rescue of the *Messenger,* you'll certainly see the affair in an evil light; you'll hunt me down, I suppose—bait me, try to strangle me as the dog does the hare.

HOVSTAD: That is a law of nature—every animal wishes to live.

ASLAKSEN: And must take its food where he can find it, you know.

DR. STOCKMANN: Then, go and see if you can't find some out there in the gutter (*rushes about the room*); for now, by Heaven! we'll see which is the strongest animal of us three. (*Finds umbrella and swings it.*) Now, look here——

HOVSTAD: You surely don't mean to use violence to us!

ASLAKSEN: I say, take care of that umbrella!

DR. STOCKMANN: Out at the window with you, Mr. Hovstad!

HOVSTAD (*by the door of the ante-room*): Are you quite mad?

DR. STOCKMANN: Out at the window, Mr. Aslaksen! Jump, I tell you! As well first as last.

ASLAKSEN (*running round the writing-table*): Be moderate, doctor. I'm a delicate man; I can stand so little. (*Screams.*) Help! help!

[MRS. STOCKMANN, PETRA *and* HORSTER *enter from sitting-room.*]

MRS. STOCKMANN: Good Heavens! Thomas, whatever is the matter?

DR. STOCKMANN (*brandishing the umbrella*): Jump out, I tell you. Out into the gutter.

HOVSTAD: An assault upon a defenseless man! I call you to witness, Captain Horster.

[*Rushes off through the sitting-room.*]

ASLAKSEN (*at his wit's end*): If only I knew the local conditions——

[*He slinks out through the sitting-room door.*]

MRS. STOCKMANN (*holding back the doctor*): Now, do restrain yourself, Thomas!

DR. STOCKMANN (*throwing down umbrella*): On my soul, they've got off after all.

MRS. STOCKMANN: But what do

they want with you?

DR. STOCKMANN: You shall hear that later; I've other matters to think of now. (*Goes to table and writes on a card.*) Look here, Katrine, what's written here?

MRS. STOCKMANN: Three big *Noes;* what is that?

DR. STOCKMANN: That, too, you shall learn later. (*Handing card.*) There, Petra; let the girl run to the Badger's with this as fast as she can. Be quick!

[PETRA *goes with the card.*]

DR. STOCKMANN: Well, if I haven't had visits to-day from all the emissaries of the devil, I don't know! But now I'll sharpen my pen against them till it is a dagger; I will dip it into venom and gall; I'll hurl my inkstand straight at their skulls.

MRS. STOCKMANN: Yes, but we're to go away, Thomas!

[PETRA *returns.*]

DR. STOCKMANN: Well!

PETRA: All right.

DR. STOCKMANN: Good. Go away, do you say? No, I'll be damned if we do; we stay where we are, Katrine.

PETRA: Stay!

MRS. STOCKMANN: Here in the town?

DR. STOCKMANN: Yes, here is the field of battle; here it shall be fought; here I will conquer! Now, as soon as my trousers are sewn up I'll go out into the town and look after a house, for we must have a roof over our heads for the winter.

HORSTER: That you can have with me.

DR. STOCKMANN: Can I?

HORSTER: Yes, indeed, you can. I've room enough, and, besides, I'm hardly ever at home.

MRS. STOCKMANN: Ah! How good it is of you, Horster.

PETRA: Thank you.

DR. STOCKMANN (*holding out hand*): Thanks, thanks! So that trouble, too, is over. And this very day I shall start on my work in earnest. Ah! there is so much to root out here, Katrine! But it's a good thing I've all my time at my disposal now; yes, for you know I've had notice from the Baths.

MRS. STOCKMANN (*sighing*): Ah, yes! I was expecting that.

DR. STOCKMANN: ——And now they want to take my practice in the bargain. But let them! The poor I shall keep anyhow—those who can't pay anything; and, good Lord! it's they who have the most need of me. But, by Heaven! I swear they shall hear me; I will preach to them in season and out of season, as it is written somewhere.

MRS. STOCKMANN: Dear Thomas, I fancy you've seen what good preaching does.

DR. STOCKMANN: You really are ridiculous, Katrine. Should I let

101

myself be beaten off the field by public opinion, and the compact majority, and such deviltry? No, thanks. Besides, what I want is so simple, so clear and straight-forward. I only want to drive into the heads of these curs that the Liberals are the worst foes of free men; that party-programmes wring the necks of all young living truths; that considerations of expediency turn morality and righteousness upside down, until life is simply hideous. Yes, Captain Horster, don't you think I shall be able to make the people understand that?

HORSTER: Maybe; I don't know much about such matters myself.

DR. STOCKMANN: Well, you see—now you shall hear! It is the party-leaders who must be got rid of. For you see, a party-leader is just like a wolf—like a starving wolf; if he is to exist at all he needs so many small beasts a year. Just look at Hovstad and Aslaksen! How many small beasts do not they devour; or else they mangle them and knock them about, so that they're fit for nothing else but householders and subscribers to the *People's Messenger*. (*Sits on edge of table.*) Now, Katrine, just come here; see how bravely the sun shines to-day. And the blessed fresh spring air, too, blowing in upon me.

MRS. STOCKMANN: Yes, if only we could live on sunshine and spring air, Thomas!

DR. STOCKMANN: Well, you'll have to pinch and save where you can—then it'll be all right. That's my least concern. Now what does trouble me is, that I don't see any man free and brave enough to dare to take up my work after me.

PETRA: Ah! don't think of that, father. You have time before you. Why, see, there are the boys already.

[EJLIF *and* MORTEN *enter from the sitting-room.*]

MRS. STOCKMANN: Have you had a holiday to-day?

MORTEN: No; but we had a fight with the other fellows in the play-time——

EJLIF: That's not true; it was the other fellows who fought us.

MORTEN: Yes, and so Mr. Rör-lund said it would be best if we stayed at home for a few days.

DR. STOCKMANN (*snapping his fingers and springing down from the table*): Now I have it, now I have it, on my soul! Never shall you set foot in school again!

THE BOYS: Never go to school!

MRS. STOCKMANN: But really, Thomas——

DR. STOCKMANN: Never, I say. I'll teach you myself—that is to say, I'll not teach you any blessed thing.

MORTEN: Hurrah!

DR. STOCKMANN: —— —— but

I'll make free, noble-minded men of you. Look here, you'll have to help me, Petra.

PETRA: Yes, father, you may be sure I will.

DR. STOCKMANN: And we'll have our school in the room where they reviled me as an enemy of the people. But we must have more pupils. I must have at least twelve boys to begin with.

MRS. STOCKMANN: You'll never get them here in this town.

DR. STOCKMANN: We shall see that. (*To the boys.*) Don't you know any street-boys—some regular ragamuffins——?

MORTEN: Yes, father, I know lots!

DR. STOCKMANN: That's all right; bring me a few specimens of them. I want to experiment with the good-for-nothings for once—there may be some good heads amongst them.

MORTEN: But what are we to do when we've become free and noble-minded men?

DR. STOCKMANN: Drive all the wolves out to the far west, boys. [EJLIF *looks rather doubtful;* MOR- TEN *jumps about, shouting hurrah!*]

MRS. STOCKMANN: If only the wolves don't drive you out, Thomas.

DR. STOCKMANN: You are quite mad, Katrine! Drive me away! now that I'm the strongest man in the town.

MRS. STOCKMANN: The strongest now?

DR. STOCKMANN: Yes, I dare to say so bold a word; that now I'm one of the strongest men upon earth.

MORTEN: I say, father!

DR. STOCKMANN (*in a subdued voice*): Hush! you must not speak about it yet; but I have made a great discovery.

MRS. STOCKMANN: What, again?

DR. STOCKMANN: Assuredly. (*Gathers them about him, and speaks confidently.*) You see, the fact is that the strongest man upon earth is he who stands most alone.

MRS. STOCKMANN (*shakes her head smiling*): Ah! Thomas——!

PETRA (*taking his hands trustfully*): Father!

ANTON CHEKHOV

1860 *Born, January 17, in port of Ta-*
ganrod on Black Sea. Father,
who had been born a serf, was an
unsuccessful merchant. Anton
worked hard during youth to help
support his poverty-stricken fam-
ily.

1876 *Father failed in business and*
moved with family to Moscow.
Anton remained at Taganrod, sup-
porting himself by tutoring, until
he finished high school in 1879.
Noted as a teller of humorous
stories.

1879 *Entered University of Moscow as*
student of medicine.

1880 *While studying medicine, wrote*
amusing stories and sketches of
Russian life for humorous papers.
These trifles, written rapidly in
crowded rooms where there was
"no light and less air," were the
to *major means of support of himself*
and his family. Published under
the name of Antosha Tchekhonte,
they gained him reputation as
an outstanding humorist. Re-
belled against necessity of writing
1885 *"unliterary work" for money.*

1884 *Took degree as doctor of medi-*
cine, and began practice of medi-
cine. Continued writing. Suc-
cessful at both professions.

1886 *Began to write for reputable daily*
paper, using own name. Symp-
toms of tuberculosis appeared.
Journeyed to southern Russia for
his health. Wrote first play,
IVANOV. *Somber note replaced*
lighter one in his writing.

1888 *Chekhov awarded Pushkin prize*
for "The Steppe."

1889 THE WOOD DEMON, *rewritten later*
as UNCLE VANYA.

1890 *Went to the Island of Saghalien*
"to write afterwards a book upon
our penal colony and prisons
there." Thereafter failure of
health caused him to spend most
of his time in the Crimea; from
there he made numerous trips to
Moscow to superintend production
of his later plays.

1891 *Traveled in Europe.*

1892 *Volunteered medical services to*
help fight cholera epidemic,
though in bad health. Refused
government remuneration for
these medical services because he
wanted to feel free in his literary
work. Recognized for excellence
of short stories.

1896 THE SEA-GULL.

1899 UNCLE VANYA *revised.*

1901 THE THREE SISTERS. *Married*
actress, Olga Knipper.

1904 THE CHERRY ORCHARD. *Died,*
July 2.

෴

THE SUBDUED *and subtle magic of Anton Chekhov's plays was first revealed to this country in the early 1920's by the Moscow Art Theatre, which Chekhov himself had helped inaugurate. Since their introduction, his major dramas have been presented to enchanted audiences by many of the ablest actors on the American stage. Today Chekhov is regarded as one of the great modern dramatists, and his fame seems increasing.*

Neither the source nor nature of Chekhov's unique power is adequately revealed by the diverse labels of orthodox critics. Some tell us that Chekhov is "The Voice of Twilight Russia," speaking for his time and country; some, that he depicts the "tragedy of the Russian intelligentsia." Some declare him to have been a hopeful prophet of the revolution; others, a discouraged member of the older order, preaching futility. Some have called him naturalist; some, symbolist. The best of these labels have an incidental value. It is well to know, for instance, that Chekhov lived during a stagnant period of Russian history, among a despairing, inert people and an impotent intelligentsia. But the frequent attempt to explain his peculiar power by this fact is futile. It is not his portrayal of Russian society that has captivated audiences in Europe and America, but his matchless revelation of humanity.

In his analysis of human nature Chekhov was naturalistic. Man he believed to be part of the material universe, and a knowledge of man's nature to be obtainable only by means of objective and disciplined observation. His own long practice of medicine, he thought, had given him a knowledge of human nature invaluable for his work as a writer. "Familiarity with the natural sciences and with scientific method has always kept me on my guard, and I have always . . . tried to be consistent with the facts of science. . . ." No naturalist, not even de Maupassant, whom Chekhov greatly admired, has surpassed the dispassionate objectivity with which the Russian dramatist portrayed his characters. It was his purpose "to show people people," and he would not vitiate his picture by a moral or a thesis. He advised a writer: "When you depict sad or unlucky people, and want to touch the reader's heart, try to be colder—it gives their grief a background, against which it stands out in greater relief." When critics misinterpreted his cultivated indifference as cynicism, Chekhov replied:

107

"*You abuse me for objectivity, calling it indifference to good and evil, lack of ideals and ideas, and so on. You would have me, when I describe horse-stealers, say 'Stealing horses is an evil.' But that has been known for ages. . . .*"

And he would no more prophesy than preach. A succession of tenderminded critics, reaching to the present time, have conceived it a merit to make Chekhov a sentimental optimist, who with a gently inane smile justifies present suffering as a preparation for future happiness. Mainly they support their opinion by imputing to him the sentiments expressed by some of his characters. This is to forget his dramatic objectivity. It is the most enervated and helpless of his dreamers who solace present pain by contemplation of a vague new day; their hopes and visions reveal only their own psychology. "Looking toward the future I call nothing but cowardice," Chekhov wrote to his close friend Suvorin; and in another of his letters he said: "I am not a liberal, not a conservative, not a believer in gradual progress, not a monk, not an indifferentist. I should like to be a free artist and nothing more."

And so, to become an artist, Chekhov renounced the tyranny of names. He renounced the trademarks and labels of the intellectuals as he previously had renounced the generalizations of the people. "Pharisaism, stupidity and despotism reign not in merchants' houses and prisons alone. I see them in science, in literature, in the younger generation. . . . I regard trademarks and labels as a superstition." In particular, he rejected the common naturalistic practice of explaining human personality by reference to facile abstract concepts—such as environment and heredity—supplied by some of the sciences. His characters, he said, were born neither out of vague notions nor "out of preconceived 'intellectual' ideas. They are the result of observing and studying life." All preconceived labels he abjured, because he saw people, not as classes or types, but as individuals. And the quality that distinguishes the individual he regarded as the hidden world of the mind—a world overshadowed by the subconscious, influenced by secret motives, and stirred by strange thoughts. Above all, it is an individual world, lonely and unique, which his characters themselves often do not understand and can never consciously reveal to others.

But Chekhov allows them to reveal this world to the audience by giving them complete freedom. He sets them free from labels; and each character acts and talks according to a scheme of values peculiar to himself. Moreover, Chekhov sets his characters free from the conventions of formal drama. He does not constrain their acts or words to fit into the development of a coherent theme or symmetrical plot; in fact, his plays have no such theme or plot. "The dramatic dialogue disappears, to give place to a peculiar form of speech built along parallel lines that never meet," writes Princess Toumanova. Thus Chekhov sets each person free to be himself, so that each speech or act appears to be a psychological disclosure and to have no other purpose. The result is surprising. For we are not used to seeing unconventionalized characters on the stage, and the very freedom which allows them to seem natural makes them seem strange. At first this combined effect of novelty and naturalness disturbs and puzzles us. Then suddenly we begin to feel that the unconventional word and act are the true ones; that for the first time we are seeing people rightly.

The development of art is always showing more subtle methods of "fitting the convention to life," says Arnold Bennett. In fitting conventions to the secret life of the human spirit no modern writer has done better than Chekhov. Though his plays dispense with the form of conventional drama, they are distinguished by a form of their own. At first the characters, by their insulated acts and speeches, seem detached from the play as a whole. But without losing their individuality they gradually achieve a complete unity of impression—a unity which derives from their blending into a representation of common humanity. And at the end of the play we feel we have seen not only individuals. We have seen mankind as Chekhov sees it, and the unity of mood inherent in his attitude toward life imposes itself upon us.

What then is Chekhov's attitude toward life? He shows us the frustration of the human heart because of its own illusions. One illusion is the hope for happiness in material things—a hope that ignores the fact that man lives in a universe which is indifferent to human values, and which he can never understand or control well enough to secure the material conditions he desires. Another frustrating illusion is the false values man pursues. For were his wishes granted him, he would not be happy. Sometimes the things he sets his heart upon are vicious; more often they are trivial and contemptible. Endlessly through his work Chekhov satirizes smug and stupid pettiness. "There is nothing more vulgar than a petty bourgeois life with its halfpence, its victuals, its futile talk, and its useless conventional virtue."

But the mood that Chekhov creates is not a negative mood of despair. The best writers are realists, he once wrote, but "they are

109

*going towards something and are summoning you towards it too . . .
and you feel, besides life as it is, the life which ought to be, and that
captivates you." The generalization is true of Chekhov. His appeal
is positive. In contrast with the life that is, he makes us feel the life
that ought to be—life free from false hopes and from trivial false values.
That life he found expressed in the ideal of the humanist—the cultiva-
tion of the human spirit—and he welcomed all of life or art that contributed to it. He was neither stoic nor ascetic. "My Holy of Holies,"
he wrote, "is the human body, health, mind, talent, inspiration, love,
and the most absolute freedom—freedom from violence and falsehood,
in whatever they may be manifested. This is the program I would
follow if I were a great artist." That is the program that Chekhov was
working toward, and that program he achieved. He achieved it as an
artist. He gave to his view of life the harmony and mood of a work
of art; and he makes us feel, contrasted with the futility of life as it is,
the beauty of freedom and culture that might exist in the heart of man.*

*Said one of the directors of the Moscow Art Theatre: ". . . the
Chekhovian world perception seized upon the group which partici-
pated in his plays . . . and its members infected one another with the
Chekhovian sense of life." It is this Chekhovian world perception and
sense of life that we have tried to suggest; for it is that which we need
to feel if we are to understand what Chekhov wrote. It is not necessary to know much else. Whatever slight difference may exist in the
polish or effectiveness of the various plays is a matter of personal reaction. The creation of mood and revelation of character are essentially
the same in all of them. We are speaking, of course, of Chekhov's full-
length plays. Although some of his one-act comedies, particularly* THE
BEAR *and* THE PROPOSAL, *were popular, they pretend to no lasting merit.
Chekhov described them as "vaudeville pieces."*

UNCLE VANYA *dispenses with plot and action more than Chekhov's
other plays. What the people say, rather than what they do, is important. In the static scenes of country life the characters reveal themselves by disconnected bits of dialogue. Each one lives a "lonely
stranger" to those to whom he speaks; his values and motives are peculiar to himself, and are misinterpreted by the accustomed names
given them by conventional language. For instance, the seductive
Helena, who will not be unfaithful to her old and unloved husband,
attributes her propriety to her regard for his professional greatness and
to her own morality—reasons which her own mind approves because*

she has so often heard them approved in society. But we see that the true motives for her faithfulness—motives, it is true, which she herself does not clearly understand—are the "morality of her indolence," and the fear that her "conscience may torment her."

Each person thinks he has missed something that would make him happy. The professor believes he is unappreciated, that his long life of study has caused him to miss the joy of living. Without gratitude toward Uncle Vanya or Sonia, whose sacrifices have made possible his easy, worthless life, he casually assumes it their duty to continue sacrificing so that he can live a carefree life in Petersburg. Uncle Vanya, "one of the most touching figures in the gallery of Chekhov's portraits," also feels—and in his case correctly—that he has been unappreciated; that he has wasted his life supporting the professor, whose stolid volumes on art show his confirmed insensitiveness to the love of beauty that illuminates Vanya himself. Stanislavsky tells of Chekhov's objection to an actor who had played Uncle Vanya as a slovenly squire. Of course, said Stanislavsky, the point was, not in the clothes, "but in the main idea of the play. Astroff and the poetic Uncle Vanya run to seed in a remote provincial hole, and the stupid professor and his like are having a splendid time in Petersburg." For Dr. Astroff, too, is attracted to beauty. He too is aware of something lost—of the gradual blunting of his sensibilities by the drab surroundings in which he toils. Helena allures him, but he is inwardly aware that his love-making is only a tribute to her transient beauty. And Sonia, unselfish, refined, physically unattractive, is entirely unnoticed by Astroff, whom she loves —Astroff, who professes to love in the abstract all the qualities that Sonia has. Toward the close of the third act, the professor precipitates the climax of the slight action by attempting to sell the estate, an action which would leave Uncle Vanya and Sonia without a home. Infuriated, Uncle Vanya shoots at the professor, only to miss him. But Uncle Vanya cannot keep up his struggle; he resigns himself to his fate. Then the professor gives up his plan, and decides to leave for Petersburg, with the understanding that Vanya and Sonia will continue to support him as in the past.

The fourth act sees no action—only the departure of the disturbing Helena, the professor, and Astroff. But the pathetic loneliness and mutual unintelligibility of the characters as they leave one another never to meet again create a final mood of futility that is one of the most impressive of Chekhov's achievements. Chekhov himself has indicated the mood he intended to create in that act.   In a letter to one of the players, he warned that Astroff should not be interpreted as being in love with Helena; he likes her because of her beauty, but he knows that nothing will come of it; "and he talks to her in that scene in the same tone as of the heat in Africa, and kisses her quite casually, to pass the time.   If Astroff takes that scene violently, the whole mood of the fourth act—quiet and despondent—is lost."   Stanislavsky, who first took the part of Dr. Astroff, tells us that Chekhov insisted that he should whistle during the last scene to show his indifference.   The departure of the disturbing characters is a relief to all.   Hope and desire leave with them—and peace comes to those whom they leave behind as each resigns himself again to the life from which he has been shaken. To Uncle Vanya comes the opportunity to work again; to Sonia, the dream of a heaven shining with jewels; to Marina, the old nurse, the vision of noodles once more.   And Astroff, tired and resigned, looks at the map of Africa with jaded interest: "I suppose it is roasting hot in Africa now."   The feeble little Telegin plays softly and aimlessly on his guitar; and the watchman's rattle reminds us of the passing of the days that never come again.   And the pathos and loneliness of the Chekhovian world achieve, as in all Chekhov's major plays, the beauty of a work of art.

After the first performance of UNCLE VANYA, *Maxim Gorky hastened to express to Chekhov his reaction to the play: "[I] returned home stunned. . . .   Watching its heroes, I felt as if I were sawed by a blunt saw. . . .   It seems to me that in this play you are colder toward mankind than the devil himself. . . .   Maupassant is excellent. . . .   You I like better."*

~⚓~

BIBLIOGRAPHICAL NOTE

Satisfactory working bibliographies of Chekhov may be found in B. H. Clark, A STUDY OF THE MODERN DRAMA, *Second Revised Edition (New York: D. Appleton-Century Company, Inc., 1938); and in Princess Nina A. Toumanova,* ANTON CHEKHOV: THE VOICE OF TWILIGHT RUSSIA *(New York: Columbia University Press, 1937).   The latter book is a valuable full-length study of* Chekhov.   *Other good criticism is contained in the following: Arnold Bennett,* BOOKS AND PERSONS *(New York: George H. Doran Company, 1917); Edward Garnett,* FRIDAY NIGHTS: LITERARY CRITICISMS AND APPRECIATIONS, *First Series (New York: Alfred A. Knopf, Inc., 1922); William Gerhardi, "Anton Chekhov: The Secret of His Literary Power,"* The Forum, *LXX, No. 5 (November,*

1923), 2144-2148; *Maxim Gorky* et al., REMINISCENCES OF ANTON CHEKHOV (*New York: The Viking Press,* 1921); *Alexander Kaun, "Chekhov's Smile,"* The Bookman, *LVII* (*March,* 1923), 93-95; *J. Middleton Murry,* ASPECTS OF LITERATURE (*London: Jonathan Cape,* 1934); *Vladimir Nemirovitch-Dant-* chenko, MY LIFE IN THE RUSSIAN THEATRE (*Boston: Little, Brown & Company,* 1936); *Stuart Sherman,* CRITICAL WOOD CUTS (*New York: Charles Scribner's Sons,* 1926); *Constantine Stanislavsky,* MY LIFE IN ART (*Boston: Little, Brown & Company,* 1924).

Uncle Vanya

CHARACTERS

ALEXANDER SEREBRAKOFF, *a retired professor.*

HELENA, *his wife, twenty-seven years old.*

SONIA, *his daughter by a former marriage.*

MME. VOITSKAYA, *widow of a privy councilor, and mother of* SEREB-RAKOFF'S *first wife.*

IVAN (VANYA) VOITSKI, *her son.*

MICHAEL ASTROFF, *a doctor.*

ILIA (WAFFLES) TELEGIN, *an impoverished landowner.*

MARINA, *an old nurse.*

A WORKMAN.

The scene is laid on SEREBRAKOFF'S *country place.*

❧

ACT I

A country house on a terrace. In front of it a garden. In an avenue of trees, under an old poplar, stands a table set for tea, with a samovar, etc. Some benches and chairs stand near the table. On one of them is lying a guitar. A hammock is swung near the table. It is three o'clock in the afternoon of a cloudy day. MARINA, *a quiet, gray-haired, little old woman, is sitting at the table knitting a stocking.* ASTROFF *is walking up and down near her.*

MARINA (*pouring some tea into a glass*): Take a little tea, my son.

ASTROFF (*takes the glass from her unwillingly*): Somehow, I don't seem to want any.

MARINA: Then will you have a little vodka instead?

ASTROFF: No, I don't drink vodka every day, and besides, it is too hot now. (*A pause.*) Tell

Reprinted from FIVE FAMOUS PLAYS, by Anton Chekhov; translated from the Russian by Marian Fell. Copyright 1939 by Charles Scribner's Sons. Used by permission of the publishers, Charles Scribner's Sons.

me, nurse, how long have we known each other?

MARINA (*thoughtfully*): Let me see, how long is it? Lord—help me to remember. You first came here, into our parts—let me think —when was it? Sonia's mother was still alive—it was two winters before she died; that was eleven years ago—(*thoughtfully*) perhaps more.

ASTROFF: Have I changed much since then?

MARINA: Oh, yes. You were handsome and young then, and now you are an old man and not handsome any more. You drink, too.

ASTROFF: Yes, ten years have made me another man. And why? Because I am overworked. Nurse, I am on my feet from dawn till dusk. I know no rest; at night I tremble under my blankets for fear of being dragged out to visit some one who is sick; I have toiled without repose or a day's freedom since I have known you; could I help growing old? And then, existence is tedious, anyway; it is a senseless, dirty business, this life, and goes heavily. Every one about here is silly, and after living with them for two or three years one grows silly oneself. It is inevitable. (*Twisting his mustache.*) See what a long mustache I have grown. A foolish, long

116

mustache. Yes, I am as silly as the rest, nurse, but not as stupid; no, I have not grown stupid. Thank God, my brain is not addled yet, though my feelings have grown numb. I ask nothing, I need nothing, I love no one, unless it is yourself alone. (*He kisses her head.*) I had a nurse just like you when I was a child.

MARINA: Don't you want a bite of something to eat?

ASTROFF: No. During the third week of Lent I went to the epidemic at Malitskoi. It was eruptive typhoid. The peasants were all lying side by side in their huts, and the calves and pigs were running about the floor among the sick. Such dirt there was, and smoke! Unspeakable! I slaved among those people all day, not a crumb passed my lips, but when I got home there was still no rest for me; a switchman was carried in from the railroad; I laid him on the operating table and he went and died in my arms under chloroform, and then my feelings that should have been deadened awoke again, my conscience tortured me as if I had killed the man. I sat down and closed my eyes—like this—and thought: will our descendants two hundred years from now, for whom we are breaking the road, remember to give us a kind word? No, nurse, they will forget.

MARINA: Man is forgetful, but God remembers.

ASTROFF: Thank you for that. You have spoken the truth.

[*Enter* VOITSKI *from the house. He has been asleep after dinner and looks rather disheveled. He sits down on the bench and straightens his collar.*]

VOITSKI: H'm. Yes. (*A pause.*) Yes.

ASTROFF: Have you been asleep?

VOITSKI: Yes, very much so. (*He yawns.*) Ever since the Professor and his wife have come, our daily life seems to have jumped the track. I sleep at the wrong time, drink wine, and eat all sorts of messes for luncheon and dinner. It isn't wholesome. Sonia and I used to work together and never had an idle moment, but now Sonia works alone and I only eat and drink and sleep. Something is wrong.

MARINA (*shaking her head*): Such a confusion in the house! The Professor gets up at twelve, the samovar is kept boiling all the morning, and everything has to wait for him. Before they came we used to have dinner at one o'clock, like everybody else, but now we have it at seven. The Professor sits up all night writing and reading, and suddenly, at two

o'clock, there goes the bell! Heavens, what is that? The Professor wants some tea! Wake the servants, light the samovar! Lord, what disorder!

ASTROFF: Will they be here long?

VOITSKI: A hundred years! The Professor has decided to make his home here.

MARINA: Look at this now! The samovar has been on the table for two hours, and they are all out walking!

VOITSKI: All right, don't get excited; here they come.

[*Voices are heard approaching.* SEREBRAKOFF, HELENA, SONIA, *and* TELEGIN *come in from the depths of the garden, returning from their walk.*]

SEREBRAKOFF: Superb! Superb! What beautiful views!

TELEGIN: They are wonderful, your Excellency.

SONIA: To-morrow we shall go into the woods, shall we, papa?

VOITSKI: Ladies and gentlemen, tea is ready.

SEREBRAKOFF: Won't you please be good enough to send my tea into the library? I still have some work to finish.

SONIA: I am sure you will love the woods.

[HELENA, SEREBRAKOFF, *and* SONIA *go into the house.* TELEGIN *sits down at the table beside*

117

MARINA.]

VOITSKI: There goes our learned scholar on a hot, sultry day like this, in his overcoat and goloshes and carrying an umbrella!

ASTROFF: He is trying to take good care of his health.

VOITSKI: How lovely she is! How lovely! I have never in my life seen a more beautiful woman.

TELEGIN: Do you know, Marina, that as I walk in the fields or in the shady garden, as I look at this table here, my heart swells with unbounded happiness. The weather is enchanting, the birds are singing, we are all living in peace and contentment—what more could the soul desire? (*Takes a glass of tea.*)

VOITSKI (*dreaming*): Such eyes —a glorious woman!

ASTROFF: Come, Ivan, tell us something.

VOITSKI (*indolently*): What shall I tell you?

ASTROFF: Haven't you any news for us?

VOITSKI: No, it is all stale. I am just the same as usual, or perhaps worse, because I have become lazy. I don't do anything now but croak like an old raven. My mother, the old magpie, is still chattering about the emancipation of woman, with one eye on her grave and the other on her learned books, in which she is always looking for the dawn of a new life.

ASTROFF: And the Professor?

VOITSKI: The Professor sits in his library from morning till night, as usual—

"Straining the mind, wrinkling the brow,
We write, write, write,
Without respite
Or hope of praise in the future or now."

Poor paper! He ought to write his autobiography; he would make a really splendid subject for a book! Imagine it, the life of a retired professor, as stale as a piece of hardtack, tortured by gout, headaches, and rheumatism, his liver bursting with jealousy and envy, living on the estate of his first wife, although he hates it, because he can't afford to live in town. He is everlastingly whining about his hard lot, though, as a matter of fact, he is extraordinarily lucky. He is the son of a common deacon and has attained the professor's chair, become the son-in-law of a senator, is called "your Excellency," and so on. But I'll tell you something; the man has been writing on art for twenty-five years, and he doesn't know the very first thing about it. For twenty-five years he has been chewing on other men's thoughts about realism, naturalism, and all such foolishness; for twenty-five years he has been reading and writing things that clever men have long known and stupid ones are not interested in; for twenty-five years he has been making his imaginary mountains out of mole-hills. And just think of the man's self-conceit and presumption all this time! For twenty-five years he has been masquerading in false clothes and has now retired, absolutely unknown to any living soul; and yet see him! stalking across the earth like a demi-god!

ASTROFF: I believe you envy him.

VOITSKI: Yes, I do. Look at the success he has had with women! Don Juan himself was not more favored. His first wife, who was my sister, was a beautiful, gentle being, as pure as the blue heaven there above us, noble, great-hearted, with more admirers than he has pupils, and she loved him as only beings of angelic purity can love those who are as pure and beautiful as themselves. His mother-in-law, my mother, adores him to this day, and he still inspires a sort of worshipful awe in her. His second wife is, as you see, a brilliant beauty; she married him in his old age and has surrendered all the glory of her beauty and freedom to him. Why? What for?

ASTROFF: Is she faithful to him?

VOITSKI: Yes, unfortunately she is.

ASTROFF: Why "unfortunately"?

VOITSKI: Because such fidelity is false and unnatural, root and branch. It sounds well, but there is no logic in it. It is thought immoral for a woman to deceive an old husband whom she hates, but quite moral for her to strangle her poor youth in her breast and banish every vital desire from her heart.

TELEGIN (*in a tearful voice*): Vanya, I don't like to hear you talk so. Listen, Vanya; every one who betrays husband or wife is faithless, and could also betray his country.

VOITSKI (*crossly*): Turn off the tap, Waffles.

TELEGIN: No, allow me, Vanya. My wife ran away with a lover on the day after our wedding, because my exterior was unprepossessing. I have never failed in my duty since then. I love her and am true to her to this day. *I* help her all I can and have given my fortune to educate the daughter of herself and her lover. I have forfeited my happiness, but I have kept my pride. And she? Her youth has fled, her beauty has faded according to the laws of nature, and her lover is dead. What has she kept?

[HELENA *and* SONIA *come in; after them comes* MME. VOITSKAYA *carrying a book. She sits down and begins to read.*

119

*Some one hands her a glass
of tea which she drinks without looking up.*]

SONIA (*hurriedly, to the nurse*):
There are some peasants waiting
out there. Go and see what they
want. I shall pour the tea.
[*Pours out some glasses of tea.
MARINA goes out. HELENA
takes a glass and sits drinking
in the hammock.*]

ASTROFF: I have come to see
your husband. You wrote me that
he had rheumatism and I know
not what else, and that he was
very ill, but he appears to be as
lively as a cricket.

HELENA: He had a fit of the
blues yesterday evening and com-
plained of pains in his legs, but he
seems all right again to-day.

ASTROFF: And I galloped over
here twenty miles at breakneck
speed! No matter, though, it is
not the first time. Once here, however, I am going to stay until to-
morrow, and at any rate sleep
quantum satis.

SONIA: Oh, splendid! You so
seldom spend the night with us.
Have you had dinner yet?

ASTROFF: No.

SONIA: Good. So you will have
it with us. We dine at seven now.
(*Drinks her tea.*) This tea is cold!

TELEGIN: Yes, the samovar has
grown cold.

HELENA: Don't mind, Monsieur
Ivan, we will drink cold tea, then.

TELEGIN: I beg your pardon, my
name is not Ivan, but Ilia, ma'am
—Ilia Telegin, or Waffles, as I am
sometimes called on account of my
pock-marked face. I am Sonia's
godfather, and his Excellency,
your husband, knows me very
well. I now live with you, ma'am,
on this estate, and perhaps you
will be so good as to notice that
I dine with you every day.

SONIA: He is our great help, our
right-hand man. (*Tenderly.*)
Dear godfather, let me pour you
some tea.

MME. VOITSKAYA: Oh! Oh!

SONIA: What is it, grandmother?

MME. VOITSKAYA: I forgot to tell
Alexander—I have lost my memory—I received a letter to-day
from Paul Alexevitch in Kharkoff.
He has sent me a new pamphlet.

ASTROFF: Is it interesting?

MME. VOITSKAYA: Yes, but
strange. He refutes the very theories which he defended seven
years ago. It is appalling!

VOITSKI: There is nothing appalling about it. Drink your tea,
mamma.

MME. VOITSKAYA: It seems you
never want to listen to what I have
to say. Pardon me, Jean, but you
have changed so in the last year
that I hardly know you. You used
to be a man of settled convictions
and had an illuminating personality——

VOITSKI: Oh, yes. I had an il-

luminating personality, which illuminated no one. (*A pause.*)
I had an illuminating personality!
You couldn't say anything more
biting. I am forty-seven years old.
Until last year I endeavored, as
you do now, to blind my eyes by
your pedantry to the truths of life.
But now—— Oh, if you only
knew! If you knew how I lie
awake at night, heartsick and angry, to think how stupidly I have
wasted my time when I might
have been winning from life
everything which my old age now
forbids.

SONIA: Uncle Vanya, how
dreary!

MME. VOITSKAYA (*to her son*):
You speak as if your former convictions were somehow to blame,
but you yourself, not they, were at
fault. You have forgotten that a
conviction, in itself, is nothing but
a dead letter. You should have
done something.

VOITSKI: Done something! Not
every man is capable of being a
writer *perpetuum mobile* like your
Herr Professor.

MME. VOITSKAYA: What do you
mean by that?

SONIA (*imploringly*): Mother!
Uncle Vanya! I entreat you!

VOITSKI: I am silent. I apologize and am silent.
          [*A pause.*]

HELENA: What a fine day! Not
too hot.

[*A pause.*]

VOITSKI: A fine day to hang oneself.

[TELEGIN *tunes the guitar.* MARINA
    *appears near the house, call-
    ing the chickens.*]

MARINA: Chick, chick, chick!

SONIA: What did the peasants
want, nurse?

MARINA: The same old thing,
the same old nonsense. Chick,
chick, chick!

SONIA: Why are you calling the
chickens?

MARINA: The speckled hen has
disappeared with her chicks. I
am afraid the crows have got her.

[TELEGIN *plays a polka. All listen
    in silence. Enter* WORKMAN.]

WORKMAN: Is the doctor here?
(*To* ASTROFF.) Excuse me, sir, but
I have been sent to fetch you.

ASTROFF: Where are you from?

WORKMAN: The factory.

ASTROFF (*annoyed*): Thank you.
There is nothing for it, then, but
to go. (*Looking around him for
his cap.*) Damn it, this is annoy-
ing!

SONIA: Yes, it is too bad, really.
You must come back to dinner
from the factory.

ASTROFF: No, I won't be able to
do that. It will be too late. Now
where, where—— (*to the* WORK-
MAN.) Look here, my man, get
me a glass of vodka, will you?
(*The* WORKMAN *goes out.*) Where
—where—— (*Finds his cap.*)

121

One of the characters in Ostroff's plays is a man with a long mustache and short wits, like me. However, let me bid you good-bye, ladies and gentlemen. (*To* HELENA.) I should be really delighted if you would come to see me some day with Miss Sonia. My estate is small, but if you are interested in such things I should like to show you a nursery and seed-bed whose like you will not find within a thousand miles of here. My place is surrounded by government forests. The forester is old and always ailing, so I superintend almost all the work myself.

HELENA: I have always heard that you were very fond of the woods. Of course one can do a great deal of good by helping to preserve them, but does not that work interfere with your real calling?

ASTROFF: God alone knows what a man's real calling is.

HELENA: And do you find it interesting?

ASTROFF: Yes, very.

VOITSKI (*sarcastically*): Oh, extremely!

HELENA: You are still young, not over thirty-six or seven, I should say, and I suspect that the woods do not interest you as much as you say they do. I should think you would find them monotonous.

SONIA: No, the work is thrilling. Dr. Astroff watches over the old

woods and sets out new plantations every year, and he has already received a diploma and a bronze medal. If you will listen to what he can tell you, you will agree with him entirely. He says that forests are the ornaments of the earth, that they teach mankind to understand beauty and attune his mind to lofty sentiments. Forests temper a stern climate, and in countries where the climate is milder, less strength is wasted in the battle with nature, and the people are kind and gentle. The inhabitants of such countries are handsome, tractable, sensitive, graceful in speech and gesture. Their philosophy is joyous, art and science blossom among them, their treatment of women is full of exquisite nobility——

VOITSKI (*laughing*): Bravo! Bravo! All that is very pretty, but it is also unconvincing. So, my friend (*to* ASTROFF), you must let me go on burning firewood in my stoves and building my sheds of planks.

ASTROFF: You can burn peat in your stoves and build your sheds of stone. Oh, I don't object, of course, to cutting wood from necessity, but why destroy the forests? The woods of Russia are trembling under the blows of the axe. Millions of trees have perished. The homes of the wild animals and birds have been desolated; the rivers are shrinking, and many beautiful landscapes are gone forever. And why? Because men are too lazy and stupid to stoop down and pick up their fuel from the ground. (*To* HELENA.) Am I not right, Madame? Who but a stupid barbarian could burn so much beauty in his stove and destroy that which he cannot make? Man is endowed with reason and the power to create, so that he may increase that which has been given him, but until now he has not created, but demolished. The forests are disappearing, the rivers are running dry, the game is exterminated, the climate is spoiled, and the earth becomes poorer and uglier every day. (*To* VOITSKI.) I read irony in your eye; you do not take what I am saying seriously, and—and—after all, it may very well be nonsense. But when I pass peasant-forests that I have preserved from the axe, or hear the rustling of the young plantations set out with my own hands, I feel as if I had had some small share in improving the climate, and that if mankind is happy a thousand years from now I will have been a little bit responsible for their happiness. When I plant a little birch tree and then see it budding into young green and swaying in the wind, my heart swells with pride and I—— (*Sees the* WORKMAN,

who is bringing him a glass of vodka on a tray.) However—(*he drinks*) I must be off. Probably it is all nonsense, anyway. Goodbye.

[*He goes toward the house.* SONIA *takes his arm and goes with him.*]

SONIA: When are you coming to see us again?

ASTROFF: I can't say.

SONIA: In a month?

[ASTROFF *and* SONIA *go into the house.* HELENA *and* VOITSKI *walk over to the terrace.*]

HELENA: You have behaved shockingly again. Ivan, what sense was there in teasing your mother and talking about *perpetuum mobile?* And at breakfast you quarreled with Alexander again. Really, your behavior is too petty.

VOITSKI: But if I hate him?

HELENA: You hate Alexander without reason; he is like every one else, and no worse than you are.

VOITSKI: If you could only see your face, your gestures! Oh, how tedious your life must be.

HELENA: It is tedious, yes, and dreary! You all abuse my husband and look on me with compassion; you think, "Poor woman, she is married to an old man." How well I understand your compassion! As Astroff said just now, see how you thoughtlessly destroy

123

the forests, so that there will soon be none left. So you also destroy mankind, and soon fidelity and purity and self-sacrifice will have vanished with the woods. Why cannot you look calmly at a woman unless she is yours? Because, the doctor was right, you are all possessed by a devil of destruction; you have no mercy on the woods or the birds or on women or on one another.

VOITSKI: I don't like your philosophy.

HELENA: That doctor has a sensitive, weary face—an interesting face. Sonia evidently likes him, and she is in love with him, and I can understand it. This is the third time he has been here since I have come, and I have not had a real talk with him yet or made much of him. He thinks I am disagreeable. Do you know, Ivan, the reason you and I are such friends? I think it is because we are both lonely and unfortunate. Yes, unfortunate. Don't look at me in that way, I don't like it.

VOITSKI: How can I look at you otherwise when I love you? You are my joy, my life, and my youth. I know that my chances of being loved in return are infinitely small, do not exist, but I ask nothing of you. Only let me look at you, listen to your voice——

HELENA: Hush, some one will overhear you.

[*They go toward the house.*]

VOITSKI (*following her*): Let me speak to you of my love, do not drive me away, and this alone will be my greatest happiness!

HELENA: Ah! This is agony!

[TELEGIN *strikes the strings of his guitar and plays a polka.* MME. VOITSKAYA *writes something on the leaves of her pamphlet.*]

THE CURTAIN FALLS

ACT II

The dining-room of SEREBRAKOFF's *house. It is night. The tapping of the* WATCHMAN's *rattle is heard in the garden.* SEREBRAKOFF *is dozing in an arm-chair by an open window and* HELENA *is sitting beside him, also half asleep.*

SEREBRAKOFF (*rousing himself*): Who is here? Is it you, Sonia?

HELENA: It is I.

SEREBRAKOFF: Oh, it is you, Nelly. This pain is intolerable.

HELENA: Your shawl has slipped down. (*She wraps up his legs in the shawl.*) Let me shut the window.

SEREBRAKOFF: No, leave it open; I am suffocating. I dreamt just now that my left leg belonged to

124

some one else, and it hurt so that I woke. I don't believe this is gout, it is more like rheumatism. What time is it?

HELENA: Half-past twelve.

[*A pause.*]

SEREBRAKOFF: I want you to look for Batushka's works in the library to-morrow. I think we have him.

HELENA: What is that?

SEREBRAKOFF: Look for Batushka to-morrow morning; we used to have him, I remember. Why do I find it so hard to breathe?

HELENA: You are tired; this is the second night you have had no sleep.

SEREBRAKOFF: They say that Turgenieff got angina of the heart from gout. I am afraid I am getting angina too. Oh, damn this horrible, accursed old age! Ever since I have been old I have been hateful to myself, and I am sure, hateful to you all as well.

HELENA: You speak as if we were to blame for your being old.

SEREBRAKOFF: I am more hateful to you than to any one.

[HELENA *gets up and walks away from him, sitting down at a distance.*]

SEREBRAKOFF: You are quite right, of course. I am not an idiot; I can understand you. You are young and healthy and beautiful, and longing for life, and I am an old dotard, almost a dead man already. Don't I know it? Of course I see that it is foolish for me to live so long, but wait! I shall soon set you all free. My life cannot drag on much longer.

HELENA: You are overtaxing my powers of endurance. Be quiet, for God's sake!

SEREBRAKOFF: It appears that, thanks to me, everybody's power of endurance is being overtaxed; everybody is miserable, only I am blissfully triumphant. Oh, yes, of course!

HELENA: Be quiet! You are torturing me.

SEREBRAKOFF: I torture everybody. Of course.

HELENA (*weeping*): This is unbearable! Tell me, what is it you want me to do?

SEREBRAKOFF: Nothing.

HELENA: Then be quiet, please.

SEREBRAKOFF: It is funny that everybody listens to Ivan and his old idiot of a mother, but the moment I open my lips you all begin to feel ill-treated. You can't even stand the sound of my voice. Even if I am hateful, even if I am a selfish tyrant, haven't I the right to be one at my age? Haven't I deserved it? Haven't I, I ask you, the right to be respected, now that I am old?

HELENA: No one is disputing your rights. (*The window slams in the wind.*) The wind is rising,

125

I must shut the window. (*She shuts it.*) We shall have rain in a moment. Your rights have never been questioned by anybody.

[*The* WATCHMAN *in the garden sounds his rattle.*]

SEREBRAKOFF: I have spent my life working in the interests of learning. I am used to my library and the lecture hall and to the esteem and admiration of my colleagues. Now I suddenly find myself plunged in this wilderness, condemned to see the same stupid people from morning till night and listen to their futile conversation. I want to live; I long for success and fame and the stir of the world, and here I am in exile! Oh, it is dreadful to spend every moment grieving for the lost past, to see the success of others and sit here with nothing to do but to fear death. I cannot stand it! It is more than I can bear. And you will not even forgive me for being old!

HELENA: Wait, have patience; I shall be old myself in four or five years.

[SONIA *comes in.*]

SONIA: Father, you sent for Dr. Astroff, and now when he comes you refuse to see him. It is not nice to give a man so much trouble for nothing.

SEREBRAKOFF: What do I care about your Astroff? He understands medicine about as well as I

understand astronomy.

SONIA: We can't send for the whole medical faculty, can we, to treat your gout?

SEREBRAKOFF: I won't talk to that madman!

SONIA: Do as you please. It's all the same to me. (*She sits down.*)

SEREBRAKOFF: What time is it?

HELENA: One o'clock.

SEREBRAKOFF: It is stifling in here. Sonia, hand me that bottle on the table.

SONIA: Here it is. (*She hands him a bottle of medicine.*)

SEREBRAKOFF (*crossly*): No, not that one! Can't you understand me? Can't I ask you to do a thing?

SONIA: Please don't be captious with me. Some people may like it, but you must spare me, if you please, because I don't. Besides, I haven't the time; we are cutting the hay to-morrow and I must get up early.

[VOITSKI *comes in dressed in a long gown and carrying a candle.*]

VOITSKI: A thunderstorm is coming up. (*The lightning flashes.*) There it is! Go to bed, Helena and Sonia. I have come to take your place.

SEREBRAKOFF (*frightened*): No, no, no! Don't leave me alone with him! Oh, don't. He will begin to lecture me.

VOITSKI: But you must give them a little rest. They have not slept for two nights.

SEREBRAKOFF: Then let them go to bed, but you go away too! Thank you. I implore you to go. For the sake of our former friendship do not protest against going. We will talk some other time——

VOITSKI: Our former friendship! Our former——

SONIA: Hush, Uncle Vanya!

SEREBRAKOFF (*to his wife*): My darling, don't leave me alone with him. He will begin to lecture me.

VOITSKI: This is ridiculous.

[MARINA *comes in carrying a candle.*]

SONIA: You must go to bed, nurse, it is late.

MARINA: I haven't cleared away the tea things. Can't go to bed yet.

SEREBRAKOFF: No one can go to bed. They are all worn out, only I enjoy perfect happiness.

MARINA (*goes up to* SEREBRAKOFF *and speaks tenderly*): What's the matter, master? Does it hurt? My own legs are aching too, oh, so badly. (*Arranges his shawl about his legs.*) You have had this illness such a long time. Sonia's dead mother used to stay awake with you too, and wear herself out for you. She loved you dearly. (*A pause.*) Old people want to be pitied as much as young ones, but nobody cares

about them somehow. (*She kisses* SEREBRAKOFF's *shoulder.*) Come, master, let me give you some linden-tea and warm your poor feet for you. I shall pray to God for you.

SEREBRAKOFF (*touched*): Let us go, Marina.

MARINA: My own feet are aching so badly, oh, so badly! (*She and* SONIA *lead* SEREBRAKOFF *out.*) Sonia's mother used to wear herself out with sorrow and weeping. You were still little and foolish then, Sonia. Come, come, master. [SEREBRAKOFF, SONIA, *and* MARINA *go out.*]

HELENA: I am absolutely exhausted by him, and can hardly stand.

VOITSKI: You are exhausted by him, and I am exhausted by my own self. I have not slept for three nights.

HELENA: Something is wrong in this house. Your mother hates everything but her pamphlets and the professor; the professor is vexed, he won't trust me, and fears you; Sonia is angry with her father, and with me, and hasn't spoken to me for two weeks! I am at the end of my strength, and have come near bursting into tears at least twenty times to-day. Something is wrong in this house.

VOITSKI: Leave speculating alone.

HELENA: You are cultured and

127

intelligent, Ivan, and you surely understand that the world is not destroyed by villains and conflagrations, but by hate and malice and all this spiteful tattling. It is your duty to make peace, and not to growl at everything.

VOITSKI: Help me first to make peace with myself. My darling! (*Seizes her hand.*)

HELENA: Let go! (*She drags her hand away.*) Go away!

VOITSKI: Soon the rain will be over, and all nature will sigh and awake refreshed. Only I am not refreshed by the storm. Day and night the thought haunts me like a fiend, that my life is lost forever. My past does not count, because I frittered it away on trifles, and the present has so terribly miscarried! What shall I do with my life and my love? What is to become of them? This wonderful feeling of mine will be wasted and lost as a ray of sunlight is lost that falls into a dark chasm, and my life will go with it.

HELENA: I am as it were benumbed when you speak to me of your love, and I don't know how to answer you. Forgive me, I have nothing to say to you. (*She tries to go out.*) Good-night!

VOITSKI (*barring the way*): If you only knew how I am tortured by the thought that beside me in this house is another life that is being lost forever—it is yours!

What are you waiting for? What accursed philosophy stands in your way? Oh, understand, understand——

HELENA (*looking at him intently*): Ivan, you are drunk!

VOITSKI: Perhaps. Perhaps.

HELENA: Where is the doctor?

VOITSKI: In there, spending the night with me. Perhaps I am drunk, perhaps I am; nothing is impossible.

HELENA: Have you just been drinking together? Why do you do that?

VOITSKI: Because in that way I get a taste of life. Let me do it, Helena!

HELENA: You never used to drink, and you never used to talk so much. Go to bed, I am tired of you.

VOITSKI (*falling on his knees before her*): My sweetheart, my beautiful one——

HELENA (*angrily*): Leave me alone! Really, this has become too disagreeable.

[HELENA *goes out. A pause.*]

VOITSKI (*alone*): She is gone! I met her first ten years ago, at her sister's house, when she was seventeen and I was thirty-seven. Why did I not fall in love with her then and propose to her? It would have been so easy! And now she would have been my wife. Yes, we would both have been waked to-night by the thunderstorm, and

128

she would have been frightened, but I would have held her in my arms and whispered: "Don't be afraid! I am here." Oh, enchanting dream, so sweet that I laugh to think of it. (*He laughs.*) But my God! My head reels! Why am I so old? Why won't she understand me? I hate all that rhetoric of hers, that morality of indolence, that absurd talk about the destruction of the world—— (*A pause.*) Oh, how I have been deceived! For years I have worshipped that miserable gout-ridden professor. Sonia and I have squeezed this estate dry for his sake. We have bartered our butter and curds and peas like misers, and have never kept a morsel for ourselves, so that we could scrape enough pennies together to send to him. I was proud of him and of his learning; I received all his words and writings as inspired, and now? Now he has retired, and what is the total of his life? A blank! He is absolutely unknown, and his fame has burst like a soap-bubble. I have been deceived; I see that now, basely deceived.

[ASTROFF *comes in. He has his coat on, but is without his waistcoat or collar, and is slightly drunk.* TELEGIN *follows him, carrying a guitar.*]

ASTROFF: Play!

TELEGIN: But every one is asleep.

ASTROFF: Play!

[TELEGIN *begins to play softly.*]

ASTROFF: Are you alone here? No women about? (*Sings with his arms akimbo*):

"The hut is cold, the fire is
    dead;
Where shall the master lay
    his head?"

The thunderstorm woke me. It was a heavy shower. What time is it?

VOITSKI: The devil only knows.

ASTROFF: I thought I heard Helena's voice.

VOITSKI: She was here a moment ago.

ASTROFF: What a beautiful woman! (*Looking at the medicine bottles on the table.*) Medicine, is it? What a variety we have; prescriptions from Moscow, from Kharkoff, from Tula! Why, he has been pestering all the towns of Russia with his gout! Is he ill, or simply shamming?

VOITSKI: He is really ill.

ASTROFF: What is the matter with you to-night? You seem sad. Is it because you are sorry for the professor?

VOITSKI: Leave me alone.

ASTROFF: Or in love with the professor's wife?

VOITSKI: She is my friend.

ASTROFF: Already?

VOITSKI: What do you mean by "already"?

ASTROFF: A woman can only become a man's friend after having first been his acquaintance and then his beloved—then she becomes his friend.

VOITSKI: What vulgar philosophy!

ASTROFF: What do you mean? Yes, I must confess I am getting vulgar, but then, you see, I am drunk. I usually only drink like this once a month. At such times my audacity and temerity know no bounds. I feel capable of anything. I attempt the most difficult operations and do them magnificently. The most brilliant plans for the future take shape in my head. I am no longer a poor fool of a doctor, but mankind's greatest benefactor. I evolve my own system of philosophy and all of you seem to crawl at my feet like so many insects or microbes. (*To* TELEGIN.) Play, Waffles!

TELEGIN: My dear boy, I would with all my heart, but do listen to reason; everybody in the house is asleep.

ASTROFF: Play!

[TELEGIN *plays softly.*]

ASTROFF: I want a drink. Come, we still have some brandy left. And then, as soon as it is day, you will come home with me. (*He sees* SONIA, *who comes in at that moment.*)

ASTROFF: I beg your pardon, I have no collar on.

[*He goes out quickly, followed by* TELEGIN.]

SONIA: Uncle Vanya, you and the doctor have been drinking! The good fellows have been getting together! It is all very well for him, he has always done it, but why do you follow his example? It looks dreadfully at your age.

VOITSKI: Age has nothing to do with it. When real life is wanting one must create an illusion. It is better than nothing.

SONIA: Our hay is all cut and rotting in these daily rains, and here you are busy creating illusions! You have given up the farm altogether. I have done all the work alone until I am at the end of my strength—— (*Frightened.*) Uncle! Your eyes are full of tears!

VOITSKI: *Tears?* Nonsense, there are no tears in my eyes. You looked at me then just as your dead mother used to, my darling—— (*He eagerly kisses her face and hands.*) My sister, my dearest sister, where are you now? Ah, if you only knew, if you only knew!

SONIA: If she only knew what, Uncle?

VOITSKI: My heart is bursting. It is awful. No matter, though. I must go.

[*He goes out.*]

SONIA (*knocks at the door*): Dr. Astroff! Are you awake? Please

130

come here for a minute.

ASTROFF (*behind the door*): In a moment.

[*He appears in a few seconds. He has put on his collar and waistcoat.*]

ASTROFF: What do you want?

SONIA: Drink as much as you please yourself, if you don't find it revolting, but I implore you not to let my uncle do it. It is bad for him.

ASTROFF: Very well; we won't drink any more. I am going home at once. That is settled. It will be dawn by the time the horses are harnessed.

SONIA: It is still raining; wait till morning.

ASTROFF: The storm is blowing over. This is only the edge of it. I must go. And please don't ask me to come and see your father any more. I tell him he has gout, and he says it is rheumatism. I tell him to lie down, and he sits up. To-day he refused to see me at all.

SONIA: He . has been spoilt. (*She looks in the sideboard.*) Won't you have a bite to eat?

ASTROFF: Yes, please. I believe I will.

SONIA: I love to eat at night. I am sure we shall find something in here. They say that he has made a great many conquests in his life, and that the women have spoiled him. Here is some cheese for you.

[*They stand eating by the sideboard.*]

ASTROFF: I haven't eaten anything to-day. Your father has a very difficult nature. (*He takes a bottle out of the sideboard.*) May I? (*He pours himself a glass of vodka.*) We are alone here, and I can speak frankly. Do you know, I could not stand living in this house for even a month? This atmosphere would stifle me. There is your father, entirely absorbed in his books, and his gout; there is your Uncle Vanya with his hypochondria, your grandmother, and finally, your step-mother——

SONIA: What about her?

ASTROFF: A human being should be entirely beautiful: the face, the clothes, the mind, the thoughts. Your step-mother is, of course, beautiful to look at, but don't you see? She does nothing but sleep and eat and walk and bewitch us, and that is all. She has no responsibilities, everything is done for her—am I not right? And an idle life can never be a pure one. (*A pause.*) However, I may be judging her too severely. Like your Uncle Vanya, I am discontented, and so we are both grumblers.

SONIA: Aren't you satisfied with life?

ASTROFF: I like life as life, but I hate and despise it in a little Russian country village, and as far

131

as my own personal life goes, by heaven! there is absolutely no redeeming feature about it. Haven't you noticed if you are riding through a dark wood at night and see a little light shining ahead, how you forget your fatigue and the darkness and the sharp twigs that whip your face? I work, that you know—as no one else in the country works. Fate beats me on without rest; at times I suffer unendurably and I see no light ahead. I have no hope; I do not like people. It is long since I have loved any one.

SONIA: You love no one?

ASTROFF: Not a soul. I only feel a sort of tenderness for your old nurse for old-times' sake. The peasants are all alike; they are stupid and live in dirt, and the educated people are hard to get along with. One gets tired of them. All our good friends are petty and shallow and see no farther than their own noses; in one word, they are dull. Those that have brains are hysterical, devoured with a mania for self-analysis. They whine, they hate, they pick faults everywhere with unhealthy sharpness. They sneak up to me sideways, look at me out of a corner of the eye, and say: "That man is a lunatic," "That man is a wind-bag." Or, if they don't know what else to label me with, they say I am strange. I like

the woods; that is strange. I don't eat meat; that is strange, too. Simple, natural relations between man and man or man and nature do not exist.

[*He tries to go out;* SONIA *prevents him.*]

SONIA: I beg you, I implore you, not to drink any more!

ASTROFF: Why not?

SONIA: It is so unworthy of you. You are well-bred, your voice is sweet, you are even—more than any one I know—handsome. Why do you want to resemble the common people that drink and play cards? Oh, don't, I beg you! You always say that people do not create anything, but only destroy what heaven has given them. Why, oh, why, do you destroy yourself? Oh, don't, I implore you not to! I entreat you!

ASTROFF (*gives her his hand*): I won't drink any more.

SONIA: Promise me.

ASTROFF: I give you my word of honor.

SONIA (*squeezing his hand*): Thank you.

ASTROFF: I have done with it. You see, I am perfectly sober again, and so I shall stay till the end of my life. (*He looks at his watch.*) But, as I was saying, life holds nothing for me; my race is run. I am old, I am tired, I am trivial; my sensibilities are dead. I could never attach myself to any

one again. I love no one, and—
never shall! Beauty alone has the
power to touch me still. I am
deeply moved by it. Helena could
turn my head in a day if she
wanted to, but that is not love,
that is not affection—— (*He
shudders and covers his face with
his hands.*)

SONIA: What is it?

ASTROFF: Nothing. During Lent
one of my patients died under
chloroform.

SONIA: It is time to forget that.
(*A pause.*) Tell me, doctor, if I
had a friend or a younger sister,
and if you knew that she, well—
loved you, what would you do?

ASTROFF (*shrugging his shoulders*): I don't know. I don't think
I should do anything. I should
make her understand that I could
not return her love—however, my
mind is not bothered about those
things now. I must start at once
if I am ever to get off. Good-bye,
my dear girl. At this rate we shall
stand here talking till morning.
(*He shakes hands with her.*) I
shall go out through the sitting-
room, because I am afraid your
uncle might detain me.

[*He goes out.*]

SONIA (*alone*): Not a word!
His heart and soul are still locked
from me, and yet for some reason
I am strangely happy. I wonder
why? (*She laughs with pleasure.*)
I told him that he was well-bred

and handsome and that his voice
was sweet. Was that a mistake?
I can still feel his voice vibrating
in the air; it caresses me. (*Wring-
ing her hands.*) Oh! how terrible
it is to be plain! I am plain, I
know it. As I came out of church
last Sunday I overheard a woman
say, "She is a dear, noble girl, but
what a pity she is so ugly!" So
ugly!

[HELENA *comes in and throws
open the window.*]

HELENA: The storm is over.
What delicious air! (*A pause.*)
Where is the doctor?

SONIA: He has gone.

[*A pause.*]

HELENA: Sonia!

SONIA: Yes?

HELENA: How much longer are
you going to sulk at me? We have
not hurt each other. Why not be
friends? We have had enough of
this.

SONIA: I myself—— (*She embraces* HELENA.) Let us make
peace.

HELENA: With all my heart.
(*They are both moved.*)

SONIA: Has papa gone to bed?

HELENA: No, he is sitting up in
the drawing-room. Heaven knows
what reason you and I had for not
speaking to each other for weeks.
(*Sees the open sideboard.*) Who
left the sideboard open?

SONIA: Dr. Astroff has just had
supper.

133

HELENA: There is some wine. Let us seal our friendship.

SONIA: Yes, let us.

HELENA: Out of one glass. (*She fills a wine-glass.*) So, we are friends, are we?

SONIA: Yes. (*They drink and kiss each other.*) I have long wanted to make friends, but somehow, I was ashamed to. (*She weeps.*)

HELENA: Why are you crying?

SONIA: I don't know. It is nothing.

HELENA: There, there, don't cry. (*She weeps.*) Silly! Now I am crying too. (*A pause.*) You are angry with me because I seem to have married your father for his money, but don't believe the gossip you hear. I swear to you I married him for love. I was fascinated by his fame and learning. I know now that it was not real love, but it seemed real at the time. I am innocent, and yet your clever, suspicious eyes have been punishing me for an imaginary crime ever since my marriage.

SONIA: Peace, peace! Let us forget the past.

HELENA: You must not look so at people. It is not becoming to you. You must trust people, or life becomes impossible.

SONIA: Tell me truly, as a friend, are you happy?

HELENA: Truly, no.

SONIA: I knew it. One more question: do you wish your husband were young?

HELENA: What a child you are! Of course I do. Go on, ask something else.

SONIA: Do you like the doctor?

HELENA: Yes, very much indeed.

SONIA (*laughing*): I have a stupid face, haven't I? He has just gone out, and his voice is still in my ears; I hear his step; I see his face in the dark window. Let me say all I have in my heart! But no, I cannot speak of it so loudly. I am ashamed. Come to my room and let me tell you there. I seem foolish to you, don't I? Talk to me of him.

HELENA: What can I say?

SONIA: He is clever. He can do everything. He can cure the sick, and plant woods.

HELENA: It is not a question of medicine and woods, my dear, he is a man of genius. Do you know what that means? It means he is brave, profound, and of clear insight. He plants a tree and his mind travels a thousand years into the future, and he sees visions of the happiness of the human race. People like him are rare and should be loved. What if he does drink and act roughly at times? A man of genius cannot be a saint in Russia. There he lives, cut off from the world by cold and storm and endless roads of bottomless mud, surrounded by a rough people who are crushed by poverty and disease, his life one continuous struggle, with never a day's respite; how can a man live like that for forty years and keep himself sober and unspotted? (*Kissing* SONIA.) I wish you happiness with all my heart; you deserve it. (*She gets up.*) As for me, I am a worthless, futile woman. I have always been futile; in music, in love, in my husband's house—in a word, in everything. When you come to think of it, Sonia, I am really very, very unhappy. (*Walks excitedly up and down.*) Happiness can never exist for me in this world. Never. Why do you laugh?

SONIA (*laughing and covering her face with her hands*): I am so happy, so happy!

HELENA: I want to hear music. I might play a little.

SONIA: Oh, do, do! (*She em-*

braces her.) I could not possibly go to sleep now. Do play!

HELENA: Yes, I will. Your father is still awake. Music irritates him when he is ill, but if he says I may, then I shall play a little. Go, Sonia, and ask him.

SONIA: Very well.

[*She goes out. The* WATCHMAN's *rattle is heard in the garden.*]

HELENA: It is long since I have heard music. And now, I shall sit and play, and weep like a fool. (*Speaking out of the window.*) Is that you rattling out there, Ephim?

VOICE OF THE WATCHMAN: It is I.

HELENA: Don't make such a noise. Your master is ill.

VOICE OF THE WATCHMAN: I am going away this minute. (*Whistles a tune.*)

SONIA (*comes back*): He says, no.

THE CURTAIN FALLS

ACT III

The drawing-room of SEREBRAKOFF's *house. There are three doors: one to the right, one to the left, and one in the center of the room.* VOITSKI *and* SONIA *are sitting down.* HELENA *is walking up and down, absorbed in thought.*

VOITSKI: We were asked by the professor to be here at one o'clock. (*Looks at his watch.*) It is now a quarter to one. It seems he has some communication to make to the world.

HELENA: Probably a matter of business.

VOITSKI: He never had any business. He writes twaddle, grumbles, and eats his heart out with jealousy; that's all he does.

SONIA (*reproachfully*): Uncle!

VOITSKI: All right. I beg your pardon. (*He points to* HELENA.) Look at her. Wandering up and down from sheer idleness. A sweet picture, really.

HELENA: I wonder you are not bored, droning on in the same key from morning till night. (*Despairingly.*) I am dying of this tedium. What shall I do?

SONIA (*shrugging her shoulders*): There is plenty to do if you would.

HELENA: For instance?

SONIA: You could help run this place, teach the children, care for the sick—isn't that enough? Before you and papa came, Uncle Vanya and I used to go to market ourselves to deal in flour.

HELENA: I don't know anything about such things, and besides, they don't interest me. It is only in novels that women go out and teach and heal the peasants; how can I suddenly begin to do it?

SONIA: How can you live here and not do it? Wait awhile, you will get used to it all. (*Embraces her.*) Don't be sad, dearest. (*Laughing.*) You feel miserable and restless, and can't seem to fit into this life, and your restlessness is catching. Look at Uncle Vanya, he does nothing now but haunt you like a shadow, and I have left my work to-day to come here and talk with you. I am getting lazy,

and don't want to go on with it. Dr. Astroff hardly ever used to come here; it was all we could do to persuade him to visit us once a month, and now he has abandoned his forestry and his practice, and comes every day. You must be a witch.

VOITSKI: Why should you languish here? Come, my dearest, my beauty, be sensible! The blood of a Nixey runs in your veins. Oh, won't you let yourself be one? Give your nature the reins for once in your life; fall head over ears in love with some other water sprite and plunge down head first into a deep pool, so that the Herr Professor and all of us may have our hands free again.

HELENA (*angrily*): Leave me alone! How cruel you are! (*She tries to go out.*)

VOITSKI (*preventing her*): There, there, my beauty, I apologize. (*He kisses her hand.*) Forgive me.

HELENA: Confess that you would try the patience of an angel.

VOITSKI: As a peace offering I am going to fetch some flowers which I picked for you this morning: some autumn roses, beautiful, sorrowful roses.

[*He goes out.*]

SONIA: Autumn roses, beautiful, sorrowful roses!

[*She and* HELENA *stand looking out of the window.*]

HELENA: September already! How shall we live through the long winter here? (*A pause.*) Where is the doctor?

SONIA: He is writing in Uncle Vanya's room. I am glad Uncle Vanya has gone out, I want to talk to you about something.

HELENA: About what?

SONIA: About what? (*She lays her head on* HELENA'S *breast.*)

HELENA (*stroking her hair*): There, there, that will do. Don't, Sonia.

SONIA: I am ugly!

HELENA: You have lovely hair.

SONIA: Don't say that! (*She turns to look at herself in the glass.*) No, when a woman is ugly they always say she has beautiful hair or eyes. I have loved him now for six years; I have loved him more than one loves one's mother. I seem to hear him beside me every moment of the day. I feel the pressure of his hand on mine. If I look up, I seem to see him coming, and as you see, I run to you to talk of him. He is here every day now, but he never looks at me, he does not notice my presence. It is agony. I have absolutely no hope, no, no hope. Oh, my God! Give me strength to endure. I prayed all last night. I often go up to him and speak to him and look into his eyes. My pride is gone. I am not mistress of myself. Yesterday I told Uncle Vanya. I couldn't control myself, and all the servants know it. Every one knows that I love him.

HELENA: Does he?

SONIA: No, he never notices me.

HELENA (*thoughtfully*): He is a strange man. Listen, Sonia, will you allow me to speak to him? I shall be careful, only hint. (*A pause.*) Really, to be in uncertainty all these years! Let me do it!

[SONIA *nods an affirmative.*]

HELENA: Splendid! It will be easy to find out whether he loves you or not. Don't be ashamed, sweetheart, don't worry. I shall be careful; he will not notice a thing. We only want to find out whether it is yes or no, don't we? (*A pause.*) And if it is no, then he must keep away from here, is that so?

[SONIA *nods.*]

HELENA: It will be easier not to see him any more. We won't put off the examination an instant. He said he had a sketch to show me. Go and tell him at once that I want to see him.

SONIA (*in great excitement*): Will you tell me the whole truth?

HELENA: Of course I will. I am sure that no matter what it is, it will be easier for you to bear than this uncertainty. Trust to me, dearest.

137

SONIA: Yes, yes. I shall say that you want to see his sketch. (*She starts out, but stops near the door and looks back.*) No, it is better not to know—and yet—there may be hope.

HELENA: What do you say?

SONIA: Nothing.

[*She goes out.*]

HELENA (*alone*): There is no greater sorrow than to know another's secret when you cannot help them. (*In deep thought.*) He is obviously not in love with her, but why shouldn't he marry her? She is not pretty, but she is so clever and pure and good, she would make a splendid wife for a country doctor of his years. (*A pause.*) I can understand how the poor child feels. She lives here in this desperate loneliness with no one around her except these colorless shadows that go mooning about talking nonsense and knowing nothing except that they eat, drink, and sleep. Among them appears from time to time this Dr. Astroff, so different, so handsome, so interesting, so charming. It is like seeing the moon rise on a dark night. Oh, to surrender oneself to his embrace! To lose oneself in his arms! I am a little in love with him myself! Yes, I am lonely without him, and when I think of him I smile. That Uncle Vanya says I have the blood of a Nixey in

my veins: "Give rein to your nature for once in your life!" Perhaps it is right that I should. Oh, to be free as a bird, to fly away from all your sleepy faces and your talk and forget that you have existed at all! But I am a coward, I am afraid; my conscience torments me. He comes here every day now. I can guess why, and feel guilty already; I should like to fall on my knees at Sonia's feet and beg her forgiveness, and weep.

[ASTROFF *comes in carrying a portfolio.*]

ASTROFF: How do you do? (*Shakes hands with her.*) Do you want to see my sketch?

HELENA: Yes, you promised to show me what you had been doing. Have you time now?

ASTROFF: Of course I have!

[*He lays the portfolio on the table, takes out the sketch and fastens it to the table with thumb-tacks.*]

ASTROFF: Where were you born?

HELENA (*helping him*): In St. Petersburg.

ASTROFF: And educated?

HELENA: At the Conservatory there.

ASTROFF: You don't find this life very interesting, I dare say?

HELENA: Oh, why not? It is true I don't know the country very well, but I have read a great deal about it.

ASTROFF: I have my own desk there in Ivan's room. When I am absolutely too exhausted to go on I drop everything and rush over here to forget myself in this work for an hour or two. Ivan and Miss Sonia sit rattling at their counting-boards, the cricket chirps, and I sit beside them and paint, feeling warm and peaceful. But I don't permit myself this luxury very often, only once a month. (*Pointing to the picture.*) Look there! That is a map of our country as it was fifty years ago. The green tints, both dark and light, represent forests. Half the map, as you see, is covered with it. Where the green is striped with red the forests were inhabited by elk and wild goats. Here on this lake lived great flocks of swans and geese and ducks; as the old men say, there was a power of birds of every kind. Now they have vanished like a cloud. Beside the hamlets and villages, you see, I have dotted down here and there the various settlements, farms, hermit's caves, and water-mills. This country carried a great many cattle and horses, as you can see by the quantity of blue paint. For instance, see how thickly it lies in this part; there were great herds of them here, an average of three horses to every house. (*A pause.*) Now, look lower down. This is the country as it was twenty-five years ago. Only a third of the map is green now with forests. There are no goats left and no elk. The blue paint is lighter, and so on, and so on. Now we come to the third part; our country as it appears to-day. We still see spots of green, but not much. The elk, the swans, the black-cock have disappeared. It is, on the whole, the picture of a regular and slow decline which it will evidently only take about ten or fifteen more years to complete. You may perhaps object that it is the march of progress, that the old order must give place to the new, and you might be right if roads had been run through these ruined woods, or if factories and schools had taken their place. The people then would have become better educated and healthier and richer, but as it is, we have nothing of the sort. We have the same swamps and mosquitoes; the same disease and want; the typhoid, the diphtheria, the burning villages. We are confronted by the degradation of our country, brought on by the fierce struggle for existence of the human race. It is the consequence of the ignorance and unconsciousness of starving, shivering, sick humanity that, to save its children, instinctively snatches at everything that can warm it and still its hunger. So it destroys everything it can lay its hands on, without a thought for the morrow. And almost everything has gone, and nothing has been created to take its place. (*Coldly.*) But I see by your face that I am not interesting you.

HELENA: I know so little about such things!

ASTROFF: There is nothing to know. It simply isn't interesting, that's all.

HELENA: Frankly, my thoughts were elsewhere. Forgive me! I want to submit you to a little examination, but I am embarrassed and don't know how to begin.

ASTROFF: An examination?

HELENA: Yes, but quite an innocent one. Sit down. (*They sit down.*) It is about a certain young girl I know. Let us discuss it like honest people, like friends, and then forget what has passed between us, shall we?

ASTROFF: Very well.

HELENA: It is about my stepdaughter, Sonia. Do you like her?

ASTROFF: Yes, I respect her.

HELENA: Do you like her—as a woman?

ASTROFF (*slowly*): No.

HELENA: One more word, and that will be the last. You have not noticed anything?

ASTROFF: No, nothing.

HELENA (*taking his hand*): You do not love her. I see that in your eyes. She is suffering. You must realize that, and not come here any more.

ASTROFF: My sun has set, yes, and then I haven't the time. (*Shrugging his shoulders.*) Where shall I find time for such things? (*He is embarrassed.*)

HELENA: Bah! What an unpleasant conversation! I am as out of breath as if I had been running three miles uphill. Thank heaven, that is over! Now let us forget everything as if nothing had been said. You are sensible. You understand. (*A pause.*) I am actually blushing.

ASTROFF: If you had spoken a month ago I might perhaps have considered it, but now—— (*He shrugs his shoulders.*) Of course, if she is suffering—but I cannot understand why you had to put me through this examination. (*He searches her face with his eyes, and shakes his finger at her.*) Oho, you are wily!

HELENA: What does this mean?

ASTROFF (*laughing*): You are a wily one! I admit that Sonia is suffering, but what does this examination of yours mean? (*He prevents her from retorting, and goes on quickly.*) Please don't put on such a look of surprise; you know perfectly well why I come here every day. Yes, you know perfectly why and for whose sake I come! Oh, my sweet tigress! don't look at me in that way; I am an old bird!

HELENA (*perplexed*): A tigress? I don't understand you.

ASTROFF: Beautiful, sleek tigress, you must have your victims! For a whole month I have done nothing but seek you eagerly. I have thrown over everything for you, and you love to see it. Now then, I am sure you knew all this without putting me through your examination. (*Crossing his arms and bowing his head.*) I surrender. Here you have me—now, eat me.

HELENA: You have gone mad!

ASTROFF: You are afraid!

HELENA: I am a better and stronger woman than you think me. Good-bye. (*She tries to leave the room.*)

ASTROFF: Why good-bye? Don't say good-bye, don't waste words. Oh, how lovely you are—what hands! (*He kisses her hands.*)

HELENA: Enough of this! (*She frees her hands.*) Leave the room! You have forgotten yourself.

ASTROFF: Tell me, tell me, where can we meet to-morrow? (*He puts his arm around her.*) Don't you see that we must meet, that it is inevitable?

[*He kisses her.* VOITSKI *comes in carrying a bunch of roses, and stops in the doorway.*]

HELENA (*without seeing* VOITSKI): Have pity! Leave me. (*Lays her head on* ASTROFF'S *shoulder.*) Don't! (*She tries to* break away from him.*)

ASTROFF (*holding her by the waist*): Be in the forest to-morrow at two o'clock. Will you? Will you?

HELENA (*sees* VOITSKI): Let me go! (*Goes to the window deeply embarrassed.*) This is appalling!

VOITSKI (*throws the flowers on a chair, and speaks in great excitement, wiping his face with his handkerchief*): Nothing—yes, yes, nothing.

ASTROFF: The weather is fine to-day, my dear Ivan; the morning was overcast and looked like rain, but now the sun is shining again. Honestly, we have had a very fine autumn, and the wheat is looking fairly well. (*Puts his map back into the portfolio.*) But the days are growing short.

[*Exit.*]

HELENA (*goes quickly up to* VOITSKI): You must do your best; you must use all your power to get my husband and myself away from here to-day! Do you hear? I say, this very day!

VOITSKI (*wiping his face*): Oh! Ah! Oh! All right! I—Helena, I saw everything!

HELENA (*in great agitation*): Do you hear me? I must leave here this very day!

[SEREBRAKOFF, SONIA, MARINA, *and* TELEGIN *come in.*]

TELEGIN: I am not very well myself, your Excellency. I have been

141

limping for two days, and my head——

SEREBRAKOFF: Where are the others? I hate this house. It is a regular labyrinth. Every one is always scattered through the twenty-six enormous rooms; one never can find a soul. (*Rings.*) Ask my wife and Madame Voitskaya to come here!

HELENA: I am here already.

SEREBRAKOFF: Please, all of you, sit down.

SONIA (*goes up to* HELENA *and asks anxiously*): What did he say?

HELENA: I'll tell you later.

SONIA: You are moved. (*Looking quickly and inquiringly into her face.*) I understand; he said he would not come here any more. (*A pause.*) Tell me, did he?

[HELENA *nods.*]

SEREBRAKOFF (*to* TELEGIN): One can, after all, become reconciled to being an invalid, but not to this country life. The ways of it stick in my throat and I feel exactly as if I had been whirled off the earth and landed on a strange planet. Please be seated, ladies and gentlemen. Sonia! (SONIA *does not hear. She is standing with her head bowed sadly forward on her breast.*) Sonia! (*A pause.*) She does not hear me. (*To* MARINA.) Sit down too, nurse. (MARINA *sits down and begins to knit her stocking.*) I crave your indulgence, ladies and gentlemen; hang your

ears, if I may say so, on the peg of attention. (*He laughs.*)

VOITSKI (*agitated*): Perhaps you do not need me—may I be excused?

SEREBRAKOFF: No, you are needed now more than any one.

VOITSKI: What is it you want of me?

SEREBRAKOFF: You—but what are you angry about? If it is anything I have done, I ask you to forgive me.

VOITSKI: Oh, drop that and come to business; what do you want?

[MME. VOITSKAYA *comes in.*]

SEREBRAKOFF: Here is mother. Ladies and gentlemen, I shall begin. I have asked you to assemble here, my friends, in order to discuss a very important matter. I want to ask you for your assistance and advice, and knowing your unfailing amiability I think I can count on both. I am a book-worm and a scholar, and am unfamiliar with practical affairs. I cannot, I find, dispense with the help of well-informed people such as you, Ivan, and you, Telegin, and you, mother. The truth is, *manet omnes una nox*, that is to say, our lives are in the hands of God, and as I am old and ill, I realize that the time has come for me to dispose of my property in regard to the interests of my family. My life is nearly over, and I am not thinking of myself, but I have a young wife and daughter. (*A pause.*) I cannot continue to live in the country; we were not made for country life, and yet we cannot afford to live in town on the income derived from this estate. We might sell the woods, but that would be an expedient we could not resort to every year. We must find some means of guaranteeing to ourselves a certain more or less fixed yearly income. With this object in view, a plan has occurred to me which I now have the honor of presenting to you for your consideration. I shall only give you a rough outline, avoiding all details. Our estate does not pay on an average more than two per cent on the money invested in it. I propose to sell it. If we then invest our capital in bonds, it will earn us four to five per cent, and we should probably have a surplus over of several thousand roubles, with which we could buy a summer cottage in Finland——

VOITSKI: Hold on! Repeat what you just said; I don't think I heard you quite right.

SEREBRAKOFF: I said we would invest the money in bonds and buy a cottage in Finland with the surplus.

VOITSKI: No, not Finland—you said something else.

SEREBRAKOFF: I propose to sell this place.

VOITSKI: Aha! That was it! So you are going to sell the place? Splendid. The idea is a rich one. And what do you propose to do with my old mother and me and with Sonia here?

SEREBRAKOFF. That will be decided in due time. We can't do everything at once.

VOITSKI: Wait! It is clear that until this moment I have never had a grain of sense in my head. I have always been stupid enough to think that the estate belonged to Sonia. My father bought it as a wedding present for my sister, and I foolishly imagined that as our laws were made for Russians and not Turks, my sister's estate would come down to her child.

SEREBRAKOFF: Of course it is Sonia's. Has any one denied it? I don't want to sell it without Sonia's consent; on the contrary, what I am doing is for Sonia's good.

VOITSKI: This is absolutely incomprehensible. Either I have gone mad or—or——

MME. VOITSKAYA: Jean, don't contradict Alexander. Trust to him; he knows better than we do what is right and what is wrong.

VOITSKI: I shan't. Give me some water. (*He drinks.*) Go ahead! Say anything you please—anything!

SEREBRAKOFF: I can't imagine why you are so upset. I don't pretend that my scheme is an ideal one, and if you all object to it I shall not insist.

[*A pause.*]

TELEGIN (*with embarrassment*): I not only nourish feelings of respect toward learning, your Excellency, but I am also drawn to it by family ties. My brother Gregory's wife's brother, whom you may know; his name is Constantine Lakedemonoff, and he used to be a magistrate——

VOITSKI: Stop, Waffles. This is business; wait a bit, we will talk of that later. (*To* SEREBRAKOFF.) There now, ask him what he thinks; this estate was bought from his uncle.

SEREBRAKOFF: Ah! Why should I ask questions? What good would it do?

VOITSKI: The price was ninety-five thousand roubles. My father paid seventy and left a debt of twenty-five. Now listen! This place could never have been bought had I not renounced my inheritance in favor of my sister, whom I deeply loved—and what is more, I worked for ten years like an ox, and paid off the debt.

SEREBRAKOFF: I regret ever having started this conversation.

VOITSKI: Thanks entirely to my own personal efforts, the place is entirely clear of debts, and now, when I have grown old, you want to throw me out, neck and crop!

SEREBRAKOFF: I can't imagine what you are driving at.

VOITSKI: For twenty-five years I have managed this place, and have sent you the returns from it like the most honest of servants, and you have never given me one single word of thanks for my work, not one—neither in my youth nor now. You allowed me a meager salary of five hundred roubles a year, a beggar's pittance, and have never even thought of adding a rouble to it.

SEREBRAKOFF: What did I know about such things, Ivan? I am not a practical man and don't understand them. You might have helped yourself to all you wanted.

VOITSKI: Yes, why did I not steal? Don't you all despise me for not stealing, when it would have been only justice? And I should not now have been a beggar!

MME. VOITSKAYA (*sternly*): Jean!

TELEGIN (*agitated*): Vanya, old man, don't talk in that way. Why spoil such pleasant relations? (*He embraces him.*) Do stop!

VOITSKI: For twenty-five years I have been sitting here with my mother like a mole in a burrow. Our every thought and hope was yours and yours only. By day we talked with pride of you and your work, and spoke your name with veneration; our nights we wasted reading the books and papers

144

which my soul now loathes.

TELEGIN: Don't, Vanya, don't. I can't stand it.

SEREBRAKOFF (*wrathfully*): What under heaven do you want, anyway?

VOITSKI: We used to think of you as almost super-human, but now the scales have fallen from my eyes and I see you as you are! You write on art without knowing anything about it. Those books of yours which I used to admire are not worth one copper kopeck. You are a hoax!

SEREBRAKOFF: Can't any one make him stop? I am going!

HELENA: Ivan, I command you to stop this instant! Do you hear me?

VOITSKI: I refuse! (SEREBRAKOFF *tries to get out of the room, but* VOITSKI *bars the door.*) Wait! I have not done yet! You have wrecked my life. I have never lived. My best years have gone for nothing, have been ruined, thanks to you. You are my most bitter enemy!

TELEGIN: I can't stand it; I can't stand it. I am going.

[*He goes out in great excitement.*]

SEREBRAKOFF: But what do you want? What earthly right have you to use such language to me? Ruination! If this estate is yours, then take it, and let me be ruined!

HELENA: I am going away out of this hell this minute. (*Shrieks.*)

This is too much!

VOITSKI: My life has been a failure. I am clever and brave and strong. If I had lived a normal life I might have become another Schopenhauer or Dostoieffski. I am losing my head! I am going crazy! Mother, I am in despair! Oh, mother!

MME. VOITSKAYA (*sternly*): Listen, Alexander!

[SONIA *falls on her knees beside the nurse and nestles against her.*]

SONIA: Oh, nurse, nurse!

VOITSKI: Mother! What shall I do? But no, don't speak! I know what to do. (*To* SEREBRAKOFF.) And you will understand me!

[*He goes out through the door in the center of the room and* MME. VOITSKAYA *follows him.*]

SEREBRAKOFF: Tell me, what on earth is the matter? Take this lunatic out of my sight! I cannot possibly live under the same roof with him. His room (*He points to the center door*) is almost next door to mine. Let him take himself off into the village or into the wing of the house, or I shall leave here at once. I cannot stay in the same house with him.

HELENA (*to her husband*): We are leaving to-day; we must get ready at once for our departure.

SEREBRAKOFF: What a perfectly dreadful man!

SONIA (*on her knees beside the*

145

nurse and turning to her father. She speaks with emotion.) You must be kind to us, papa. Uncle Vanya and I are so unhappy! (*Controlling her despair.*) Have pity on us. Remember how Uncle Vanya and Granny used to copy and translate your books for you every night—every, every night. Uncle Vanya has toiled without rest; he would never spend a penny on us, we sent it all to you. We have not eaten the bread of idleness. I am not saying this as I should like to, but you must understand us, papa, you must be merciful to us.

HELENA (*very excited, to her husband*): For heaven's sake, Alexander, go and have a talk with him—explain!

SEREBRAKOFF: Very well, I shall have a talk with him, but I won't apologize for a thing. I am not angry with him, but you must confess that his behavior has been strange, to say the least. Excuse me, I shall go to him.

[*He goes out through the center door.*]

HELENA: Be gentle with him; try to quiet him.

[*She follows him out.*]

SONIA (*nestling nearer to MARINA*): Nurse, oh, nurse!

MARINA: It's all right, my baby. When the geese have cackled they will be still again. First they cackle and then they stop.

146

SONIA: Nurse!

MARINA: You are trembling all over, as if you were freezing. There, there, little orphan baby, God is merciful. A little linden-tea, and it will all pass away. Don't cry, my sweetest. (*Looking angrily at the door in the center of the room.*) See, the geese have all gone now. The devil take them!

[*A shot is heard.* HELENA *screams behind the scenes.* SONIA *shudders.*]

MARINA: Bang! What's that?

SEREBRAKOFF (*comes in reeling with terror*): Hold him! hold him! He has gone mad!

[HELENA *and* VOITSKI *are seen struggling in the doorway.*]

HELENA (*trying to wrest the revolver from him*): Give it to me; give it to me, I tell you!

VOITSKI: Let me go, Helena, let me go! (*He frees himself and rushes in, looking everywhere for* SEREBRAKOFF.) Where is he? Ah, there he is! (*He shoots at him. A pause.*) I didn't get him? I missed again? (*Furiously.*) Damnation! Damnation! To hell with him!

[*He flings the revolver on the floor, and drops helpless into a chair.* SEREBRAKOFF *stands as if stupefied.* HELENA *leans against the wall, almost fainting.*]

HELENA: Take me away! Take

me away! I can't stay here—I shall I do? What shall I do?
can't!   SONIA (*softly*): Oh, nurse,
VOITSKI (*in despair*): Oh, what nurse!

THE CURTAIN FALLS

ACT IV

VOITSKI's *bedroom, which is also his office. A table stands near the*
window; on it are ledgers, letter scales, and papers of every description.
Near by stands a smaller table belonging to ASTROFF, *with his paints*
and drawing materials. On the wall hangs a cage containing a star-
ling. There is also a map of Africa on the wall, obviously of no use to
anybody. There is a large sofa covered with buckram. A door to the
left leads into an inner room; one to the right leads into the front hall,
and before this door lies a mat for the peasants with their muddy boots
to stand on. It is an autumn evening. The silence is profound.
TELEGIN *and* MARINA *are sitting facing one another, winding wool.*

TELEGIN: Be quick, Marina, or
we shall be called away to say
good-bye before you have finished.
The carriage has already been ordered.

MARINA (*trying to wind more*
quickly): I am a little tired.

TELEGIN: They are going to
Kharkoff to live.

MARINA: They do well to go.

TELEGIN: They have been frightened. The professor's wife won't
stay here an hour longer. "If we
are going at all, let's be off," says
she, "we shall go to Kharkoff and
look about us, and then we can
send for our things." They are
traveling light. It seems, Marina,
that fate has decreed for them not
to live here.

MARINA: And quite rightly.
What a storm they have just

raised! It was shameful!

TELEGIN: It was indeed. The
scene was worthy of the brush of
Aibazofski.

MARINA: I wish I'd never laid
eyes on them. (*A pause.*) Now
we shall have things as they were
again: tea at eight, dinner at one,
and supper in the evening; everything in order as decent folks, as
Christians like to have it. (*Sighs.*)
It is a long time since I have eaten
noodles.

TELEGIN: Yes, we haven't had
noodles for ages. (*A pause.*) Not
for ages. As I was going through
the village this morning, Marina,
one of the shop-keepers called
after me, "Hi! you hanger-on!" I
felt it bitterly.

MARINA: Don't pay the least attention to them, master; we are all

147

dependents on God. You and Sonia and all of us. Every one must work, no one can sit idle. Where is Sonia?

TELEGIN: In the garden with the doctor, looking for Ivan. They fear he may lay violent hands on himself.

MARINA: Where is his pistol?

TELEGIN (*whispers*): I hid it in the cellar.

[VOITSKI *and* ASTROFF *come in.*]

VOITSKI: Leave me alone! (*To* MARINA *and* TELEGIN.) Go away! Go away and leave me to myself, if but for an hour. I won't have you watching me like this!

TELEGIN: Yes, yes, Vanya.

[*He goes out on tiptoe.*]

MARINA: The gander cackles; ho! ho! ho!

[*She gathers up her wool and goes out.*]

VOITSKI: Leave me by myself!

ASTROFF: I would, with the greatest pleasure. I ought to have gone long ago, but I shan't leave you until you have returned what you took from me.

VOITSKI: I took nothing from you.

ASTROFF: I am not jesting, don't detain me, I really must go.

VOITSKI: I took nothing of yours.

ASTROFF: You didn't? Very well, I shall have to wait a little longer, and then you will have to forgive me if I resort to force. We shall have to bind you and search you.

I mean what I say.

VOITSKI: Do as you please. (*A pause.*) Oh, to make such a fool of myself! To shoot twice and miss him both times! I shall never forgive myself.

ASTROFF: When the impulse came to shoot, it would have been as well had you put a bullet through your own head.

VOITSKI (*shrugging his shoulders*): Strange! I attempted murder, and am not going to be arrested or brought to trial. That means they think me mad. (*With a bitter laugh.*) Me! I am mad, and those who hide their worthlessness, their dullness, their crying heartlessness behind a professor's mask, are sane! Those who marry old men and then deceive them under the noses of all, are sane! I saw you kiss her; I saw you in each other's arms!

ASTROFF: Yes, sir, I did kiss her; so there. (*He puts his thumb to his nose.*)

VOITSKI (*his eyes on the door*): No, it is the earth that is mad, because she still bears us on her breast.

ASTROFF: That is nonsense.

VOITSKI: Well? Am I not a madman, and therefore irresponsible? Haven't I the right to talk nonsense?

ASTROFF: This is a farce! You are not mad; you are simply a ridiculous fool. I used to think every fool was out of his senses, but now I see that lack of sense is a man's normal state, and you are perfectly normal.

VOITSKI (*covers his face with his hands*): Oh! If you knew how ashamed I am! These piercing pangs of shame are like nothing on earth. (*In an agonized voice.*) I can't endure them! (*He leans against the table.*) What can I do? What can I do?

ASTROFF: Nothing.

VOITSKI: You must tell me something! Oh, my God! I am forty-seven years old. I may live to sixty; I still have thirteen years before me; an eternity! How shall I be able to endure life for thirteen years? What shall I do? How can I fill them? Oh, don't you see? (*He presses* ASTROFF's *hand convulsively.*) Don't you see, if only I could live the rest of my life in some new way! If I could only wake some still, bright morning and feel that life had begun again; that the past was forgotten and had vanished like smoke. (*He weeps.*) Oh, to begin life anew! Tell me, tell me how to begin.

ASTROFF (*crossly*): What nonsense! What sort of a new life can you and I look forward to? We can have no hope.

VOITSKI: None?

ASTROFF: None. Of that I am convinced.

VOITSKI: Tell me what to do. (*He puts his hand to his heart.*) I feel such a burning pain here.

ASTROFF (*shouts angrily*): Stop! (*Then, more gently.*) It may be that posterity, which will despise us for our blind and stupid lives, will find some road to happiness; but we—you and I—have but one hope, the hope that we may be visited by visions, perhaps by pleasant ones, as we lie resting in our graves. (*Sighing.*) Yes, brother, there were only two respectable, intelligent men in this county, you and I. Ten years or so of this life of ours, this miserable life, have sucked us under, and we have become as contemptible and petty as the rest. But don't try to talk me out of my purpose! Give me what you took from me, will you?

VOITSKI: I took nothing from you.

ASTROFF: You took a little bottle of morphine out of my medicine-case. (*A pause.*) Listen! If you are positively determined to make an end to yourself, go into the woods and shoot yourself there. Give up the morphine, or there will be a lot of talk and guesswork; people will think I gave it to you. I don't fancy having to perform a post-mortem on you. Do you think I should find it interesting?

[SONIA *comes in.*]

VOITSKI: Leave me alone.

149

ASTROFF (*to* SONIA): Sonia, your uncle has stolen a bottle of morphine out of my medicine-case and won't give it up. Tell him that his behavior is—well, unwise. I haven't time, I must be going.

SONIA: Uncle Vanya, did you take the morphine?

ASTROFF: Yes, he took it. (*A pause.*) I am absolutely sure.

SONIA: Give it up! Why do you want to frighten us? (*Tenderly.*) Give it up, Uncle Vanya! My misfortune is perhaps even greater than yours, but I am not plunged in despair. I endure my sorrow, and shall endure it until my life comes to a natural end. You must endure yours, too. (*A pause.*) Give it up! Dear, darling Uncle Vanya. Give it up! (*She weeps.*) You are so good, I am sure you will have pity on us and give it up. You must endure your sorrow, Uncle Vanya; you must endure it. [VOITSKI *takes a bottle from the drawer of the table and hands it to* ASTROFF.]

VOITSKI: There it is! (*To* SONIA.) And now, we must get to work at once; we must do something, or else I shall not be able to endure it.

SONIA: Yes, yes, to work! As soon as we have seen them off we shall go to work. (*She nervously straightens out the papers on the table.*) Everything is in a muddle!

ASTROFF (*putting the bottle in his case, which he straps together*): Now I can be off.

[HELENA *comes in.*]

HELENA: Are you here, Ivan? We are starting in a moment. Go to Alexander, he wants to speak to you.

SONIA: Go, Uncle Vanya. (*She takes* VOITSKI's *arm.*) Come, you and papa must make peace; that is absolutely necessary.

[SONIA *and* VOITSKI *go out.*]

HELENA: I am going away. (*She gives* ASTROFF *her hand.*) Good-bye.

ASTROFF: So soon?

HELENA: The carriage is waiting.

ASTROFF: Good-bye.

HELENA: You promised me you would go away yourself to-day.

ASTROFF: I have not forgotten. I am going at once. (*A pause.*) Were you frightened? Was it so terrible?

HELENA: Yes.

ASTROFF: Couldn't you stay? Couldn't you? To-morrow—in the forest——

HELENA: No. It is all settled, and that is why I can look you so bravely in the face. Our departure is fixed. One thing I must ask of you: don't think too badly of me; I should like you to respect me.

ASTROFF: Ah! (*With an impatient gesture.*) Stay, I implore

you! Confess that there is nothing for you to do in this world. You have no object in life; there is nothing to occupy your attention, and sooner or later your feelings must master you. It is inevitable. It would be better if it happened not in Kharkoff or in Kursk, but here, in nature's lap. It would then at least be poetical, even beautiful. Here you have the forests, the houses half in ruins that Turgenieff writes of.

HELENA: How comical you are! I am angry with you and yet I shall always remember you with pleasure. You are interesting and original. You and I will never meet again, and so I shall tell you —why should I conceal it?—that I am just a little in love with you. Come, one more last pressure of our hands, and then let us part good friends. Let us not bear each other any ill will.

ASTROFF (*pressing her hand*): Yes, go. (*Thoughtfully.*) You seem to be sincere and good, and yet there is something strangely disquieting about all your personality. No sooner did you arrive here with your husband than every one whom you found busy and actively creating something was forced to drop his work and give himself up for the whole summer to your husband's gout and yourself. You and he have infected us with your idleness. I

have been swept off my feet; I have not put my hand to a thing for weeks, during which sickness has been running its course unchecked among the people, and the peasants have been pasturing their cattle in my woods and young plantations. Go where you will, you and your husband will always carry destruction in your train. I am joking of course, and yet I am strangely sure that had you stayed here we should have been overtaken by the most immense desolation. I would have gone to my ruin, and you—you would not have prospered. So go! É finita la commèdia!

HELENA (*snatching a pencil off* ASTROFF's *table, and hiding it with a quick movement*): I shall take this pencil for memory!

ASTROFF: How strange it is. We meet, and then suddenly it seems that we must part forever. That is the way in this world. As long as we are alone, before Uncle Vanya comes in with a bouquet— allow me—to kiss you good-bye— may I? (*He kisses her on the cheek.*) So! Splendid!

HELENA: I wish you every happiness. (*She glances about her.*) For once in my life, I shall! and scorn the consequences! (*She kisses him impetuously, and they quickly part.*) I must go.

ASTROFF: Yes, go. If the carriage is there, then start at once.

(*They stand listening.*)

ASTROFF: É finita!

[VOITSKI, SEREBRAKOFF, MME. VOIT-
SKAYA *with her book,* TELE-
GIN, *and* SONIA *come in.*]

SEREBRAKOFF (*to* VOITSKI):
Shame on him who bears malice
for the past. I have gone through
so much in the last few hours that
I feel capable of writing a whole
treatise on the conduct of life for
the instruction of posterity. I
gladly accept your apology, and
myself ask your forgiveness.

[*He kisses* VOITSKI *three times.*
HELENA *embraces* SONIA.]

SEREBRAKOFF (*kissing* MME.
VOITSKAYA's *hand*): Mother!

MME. VOITSKAYA (*kissing him*):
Have your picture taken, Alexander, and send me one. You know
how dear you are to me.

TELEGIN: Good-bye, your Excellency. Don't forget us.

SEREBRAKOFF (*kissing his daughter*): Good-bye, good-bye all.
(*Shaking hands with* ASTROFF.)
Many thanks for your pleasant
company. I have a deep regard
for your opinions and your enthusiasm, but let me, as an old man,
give one word of advice at parting: do something, my friend!
Work! Do something! (*They all
bow.*) Good luck to you all.

[*He goes out followed by* MME.
VOITSKAYA *and* SONIA.]

VOITSKI (*kissing* HELENA's *hand
fervently*): Good-bye — forgive

me. I shall never see you again!

HELENA (*touched*): Good-bye,
dear boy.

[*She lightly kisses his head as he
bends over her hand, and
goes out.*]

ASTROFF: Tell them to bring my
carriage around too, Waffles.

TELEGIN: All right, old man.

[ASTROFF *and* VOITSKI *are left behind alone.* ASTROFF *collects
his paints and drawing materials on the table and packs
them away in a box.*]

ASTROFF: Why don't you go to
see them off?

VOITSKI: Let them go! I—I can't
go out there. I feel too sad. I
must go to work on something at
once. To work! To work!

[*He rummages through his papers
on the table. A pause. The
tinkling of bells is heard as
the horses trot away.*]

ASTROFF: They have gone! The
professor, I suppose, is glad to go.
He couldn't be tempted back now
by a fortune.

[MARINA *comes in.*]

MARINA: They have gone.

[*She sits down in an arm-chair
and knits her stocking.* SONIA
comes in wiping her eyes.]

SONIA: They have gone. God
be with them. (*To her uncle.*)
And now, Uncle Vanya, let us do
something!

VOITSKI: To work! To work!

SONIA: It is long, long, since you

and I have sat together at this table. (*She lights a lamp on the table.*) No ink! (*She takes the inkstand to the cupboard and fills it from an inkbottle.*) How sad it is to see them go!

[MME. VOITSKAYA *comes slowly in.*]

MME. VOITSKAYA: They have gone.

[*She sits down and at once becomes absorbed in her book.* SONIA *sits down at the table and looks through an account book.*]

SONIA: First, Uncle Vanya, let us write up the accounts. They are in a dreadful state. Come, begin. You take one and I will take the other.

VOITSKI: In account with——

[*They sit silently writing.*]

MARINA (*yawning*): The sandman has come.

ASTROFF: How still it is. Their pens scratch, the cricket sings; it is so warm and comfortable. I hate to go.

[*The tinkling of bells is heard.*]

ASTROFF: My carriage has come. There now remains but to say good-bye to you, my friends, and to my table here, and then—away! [*He puts the map into the portfolio.*]

MARINA: Don't hurry away; sit a little longer with us.

ASTROFF: Impossible.

VOITSKI (*writing*): And carry forward from the old debt two seventy-five——

[WORKMAN *comes in.*]

WORKMAN: Your carriage is waiting, sir.

ASTROFF: All right. (*He hands the* WORKMAN *his medicine-case, portfolio, and box.*) Look out, don't crush the portfolio!

WORKMAN: Very well, sir.

SONIA: When shall we see you again?

ASTROFF: Hardly before next summer. Probably not this winter, though, of course, if anything should happen you will let me know. (*He shakes hands with them.*) Thank you for your kindness, for your hospitality, for everything! (*He goes up to* MARINA *and kisses her head.*) Goodbye, old nurse!

MARINA: Are you going without your tea?

ASTROFF: I don't want any, nurse.

MARINA: Won't you have a drop of vodka?

ASTROFF (*hesitatingly*): Yes, I might.

[MARINA *goes out.*]

ASTROFF (*after a pause*): My off-wheeler has gone lame for some reason. I noticed it yesterday when Peter was taking him to water.

VOITSKI: You should have him re-shod.

ASTROFF: I shall have to go

153

around by the blacksmith's on my way home. It can't be avoided. (*He stands looking up at the map of Africa hanging on the wall.*) I suppose it is roasting hot in Africa now.

VOITSKI: Yes, I suppose it is.

[MARINA *comes back carrying a tray on which are a glass of vodka and a piece of bread.*]

MARINA: Help yourself. (AS-TROFF *drinks.*) •

MARINA: To your good health! (*She bows deeply.*) Eat your bread with it.

ASTROFF: No, I like it so. And now, good-bye. (*To* MARINA.) You needn't come out to see me off, nurse.

[*He goes out.* SONIA *follows him with a candle to light him to the carriage.* MARINA *sits down in her arm-chair.*]

VOITSKI (*writing*): On the 2d of February, twenty pounds of butter; on the 16th, twenty pounds of butter again. Buckwheat flour

——

[*A pause. Bells are heard tinkling.*]

MARINA: He has gone.

[*A pause.*]

[SONIA *comes in and sets the candle-stick on the table.*]

SONIA: He has gone.

VOITSKI (*adding and writing*): Total, fifteen—twenty-five——

[SONIA *sits down and begins to write.*]

MARINA (*yawning*): Oh, ho! The Lord have mercy.

[TELEGIN *comes in on tiptoe, sits down near the door, and begins to tune his guitar.*]

VOITSKI (*to* SONIA, *stroking her hair*): Oh, my child, I am so miserable; if you only knew how miserable I am!

SONIA: What can we do? We must live our lives. (*A pause.*) Yes, we shall live, Uncle Vanya. We shall live through the long procession of days before us, and through the long evenings; we shall patiently bear the trials that fate imposes on us; we shall work for others without rest, both now and when we are old; and when our last hour comes we shall meet it humbly, and there, beyond the grave, we shall say that we have suffered and wept, that our life was bitter, and God will have pity on us. Ah, then, dear, dear Uncle, we shall see that bright and beautiful life; we shall rejoice and look back upon our sorrow here; a tender smile—and—we shall rest. I have faith, Uncle, fervent, passionate faith. (SONIA *kneels down before her uncle and lays her head on his hands. She speaks in a weary voice.*) We shall rest. (TELEGIN *plays softly on the guitar.*) We shall rest. We shall hear the angels. We shall see heaven shining like a jewel. We shall see all evil and all our pain sink away in the

154

great compassion that shall enfold the world. Our life will be as peaceful and tender and sweet as a caress. I have faith; I have faith. (*She wipes away her tears.*) My poor, poor Uncle Vanya, you are crying! (*Weeping.*) You have never known what happiness was, but wait, Uncle Vanya, wait! We shall rest. (*She embraces him.*) We shall rest. (*The* WATCHMAN's *rattle is heard in the garden;* TELEGIN *plays softly;* MME. VOITSKAYA *writes something on the margin of her pamphlet;* MARINA *knits her stocking.*) We shall rest.

THE CURTAIN SLOWLY FALLS

JOHN GALSWORTHY

1867 *Born at Parkfield, Kingston Hill, Surrey. Eldest son of prominent and wealthy London lawyer.*

1881 *Attended Harrow, where he was*
to *an enthusiastic athlete and a*
1886 *"good scholar."*

1886 *Entered New College, Oxford.*

1889 *Took honor degree in law.*

1890 *Received call to bar, but practiced very little.*

1891 *Travel: Canada, Australia, and the South Seas. Met Joseph Conrad,*
to *then first mate aboard the sailing ship* Torrens. *Beginning of a*
1893 *long and warm friendship.*

1899 *Published* JOCELYN, *his first novel, under the pseudonym of John Sinjohn.*

1904 *Published* THE ISLAND PHARISEES, *first novel under his own name.*

1905 *Married Ada Cooper Galsworthy.*

1906 *Galsworthy's annus mirabilis. Attained sudden fame with* THE

MAN OF PROPERTY. THE SILVER BOX *produced at the Court Theatre with great success. Double triumph as novelist and playwright.*

1909 FRATERNITY *published.* STRIFE *produced.*

1912 *Published* THE INN OF TRANQUILLITY, *a volume of essays expounding his aesthetic views and his philosophy. Production of* THE PIGEON.

1922 THE FORSYTE SAGA *published as a single volume. Production of* LOYALTIES, *perhaps Galsworthy's greatest box-office success. This year is another high-water mark in Galsworthy's fame.*

1929 *Accepted the Order of Merit, after having refused knighthood.*

1932 *Awarded the Nobel Prize for Literature.*

1933 *Died, age 66, at Grove Lodge, Hampstead.*

❧

So FAMILIAR *today is the dramatic technique employed by Galsworthy in most of his plays that one rarely thinks of him as an innovator. Nevertheless, the production of* THE SILVER BOX *in 1906 at the Court Theatre, then under the management of H. Granville-Barker and J. E. Vedrenne, was one of the bold ventures of a pioneering theatrical organization. Moreover, the success of the play gave marked impetus to the writing of plays dealing with social problems and to the spread of the influence of naturalism, a movement in the drama not yet se-*

158

curely established in England, in spite of the fact that the theatergoers had for two decades seen productions of Ibsen and Shaw.

The story of Galsworthy's development as a playwright is as remarkable as it is simple for the reason that this first play established him as a mature artist and struck the keynote of most of his future writing for the stage. Although his ideas of structure underwent some change late in his life—as in ESCAPE (1929), in which a cinematic technique is used without complete success—and although his plays are by no means of uniform excellence, throughout his dramatic work he makes little divergence from a course that he charted for himself from the start. Three years after the appearance of THE SILVER BOX, he wrote an essay, called "Some Platitudes Concerning the Drama," in which he set forth a "platform" for the naturalistic drama. Whereas the essay by no means offers a completely satisfactory statement for the whole movement, it has the virtues of simplicity and lucidity; and it is indispensable in evaluating the excellencies and the limitations of Galsworthy's own approach.

From the first, Galsworthy regarded the drama as an instrument of social development and reform. At the same time—like Chekhov, by whom he was plainly influenced—he abhorred the idea of mounting a soap box, wishing rather to be a scientist in gathering his material and an artist in presenting it. A drama, he explained, should have a "spire of meaning," a moral inherent in the purposeful presentation of a cross section or "grouping" of life and characters—not a cut-and-dried code of a platform moralist, but the phenomena of life, selected, "but not distorted," and set down without "fear, favour, or prejudice," leaving the public to draw its own moral. Since the moral of the "natural action" of men was his aim, he regarded a human being with perfect logic as "the best plot there is," and he insisted upon the austerity of dramatic dialogue, completely excluding jokes or epigrams severed from the characters themselves and avoiding any humor or pathos apart from "the fun and tears of life." "Take care of character," he exclaimed; "action and dialogue will take care of themselves!" Indeed, he saw the dramatist's task as merely that of rounding up characters and facts "within the ring fence of a dominant idea" and, from that point, letting the characters live their own lives.

From his plays it is obvious that his primary concern was the struggle of the individual with society. Everywhere he perceived the ironic and tragic enmeshment of the individual personality in established *social institutions. At least in theory, he insisted upon the dramatist's detachment in viewing the struggle, though not upon a lack of sympathy with "things for their own sake"; and he regarded the artist's task complete with the presentation of the problem involved, not with the solution of it.*

In such plays as THE SILVER BOX *(1906),* JUSTICE *(1916),* THE ELDEST SON *(1912), and* ESCAPE *(1929), he is concerned with problems of social, legal, and penal systems that maintain one moral standard for the rich and another for the poor and that exist rather for making the punishment fit the crime than for redeeming the criminal.* STRIFE *(1909) presents the age-old struggle between capital and labor in what is the most successful attempt of the dramatist to be strictly fair to both sides of the argument. The rich, hard though they are, are not denied some traces of human kindness; the poor do not escape the judgment that their misery has at least as a contributory cause their own pride and stubbornness.* THE MOB *(1914), like Ibsen's* AN ENEMY OF THE PEOPLE, *shows the idealist pitted against and crushed by the majority opinion.* THE SKIN GAME *(1920) deals with the struggle between the aristocratic old families and the new rich, in which neither side comes off with credit.* LOYALTIES *(1922) presents various forms of caste feeling in conflict with one another.*

*THE PIGEON *(1912), "a fantasy in conception and a realistic play in execution," is less poignant than* THE SILVER BOX *or* JUSTICE *and less dramatic than* STRIFE; *but its clever construction, its vivid characterization, and its ironic humor make it one of the brightest of the plays. In it, Galsworthy's technique is seen in its most delightful form, achieving excellent "theater" with complete absence of theatricality and "big scenes." The theme is the perennially baffling one of human charity. Around the sentimentalist Wellwyn revolve the human derelicts, who incarnate the problem, and the three reformers, who represent solutions offered by the Church, scientific philanthropy, and the police court. The theorists come to loggerheads. Wellwyn's realistic daughter Ann, who wants to solve the immediate problem by getting her father out of the reach of his lame ducks, is foiled. The play ends with characteristic inconclusion. But there is no doubt about its salient moral: namely, that abstract theories of philanthropy leaving the individual out of consideration can never meet the issue. There is also the final irony that those who have theories for solving the problem lack humanity and that those who have humanity lack judgment.*

During Galsworthy's lifetime the best of his plays engaged the talent of the greatest names in the English and American theater: Ethel Barrymore played in THE SILVER BOX, John Barrymore in JUSTICE, George Arliss in OLD ENGLISH, and Leslie Howard in ESCAPE. Since his death there have been no really important revivals. Even at the height of his dramatic fame, the critic Clayton Hamilton accused him of ineptness in handling of his dramatic material and saw him as a patrician concerning himself somewhat too self-consciously with the oppressed and downtrodden. A recent literary historian denies him the detachment and scientific impartiality that he himself insisted upon, and regards him throughout his plays as a blood brother to Wellwyn, "sentimentalizing sheer unsuccess and abject failure" and "clinging to the bad for its mere badness." He charges that Galsworthy's fairness is illusory and that in reality his plays are carefully prepared cases of social distress for which no satisfying artistic solution is possible.

Galsworthy's neglect in the theater of the thirties may be largely attributable to the war of ideologies that at the time of his death had already begun to pre-empt the field of the problem play. Obviously, Galsworthy's plays are very different from those of dramatists like Clifford Odets and Lillian Hellman. His own theory of the drama ruled out the sensational and the obviously theatrical. THE PIGEON is one of the best evidences that he has a redeeming sense of humor and the power of self-criticism. It is perfectly fair to look upon Wellwyn as Galsworthy's humorously exaggerated comment on himself. But an honest admission of the difficulties of living up to an almost impossible ideal of the artist-scientist may be regarded as an evidence of strength rather than one of weakness. Plays of social criticism dealing with problems and institutions that are in a constant state of change run the danger of being forgotten when the problems themselves are no longer vital. Galsworthy's permanence in the drama rests on the fact that his deepest concern is with fundamental weaknesses of human nature, the perennial problems of human behavior.

❧

BIBLIOGRAPHICAL NOTE

Galsworthy's plays are discussed in all comprehensive books on the modern drama. A full-dress biography has been published by H. V. Marrot (New York: Charles Scribner's Sons, 1936). The following special studies, all bearing the title JOHN GALSWORTHY, *are valuable: Sheila Kaye-Smith (London: Nisbet,* 1916); *Robert H. Coats (London: Duckworth,* 1926); *Leon Schalit (London: Heinemann,* 1929); *Herman Ould (London: Chapman and Hall,* 1934). *Dorothy Martin's "Mr. Galsworthy as Artist and Reformer,"* Yale Review, *XIV* (1924), 126-139, *is a stimulating brief summary.* Joseph Conrad's LAST ESSAYS *(London: Dent,* 1935) *contains a well-*known *"appreciation."*

Important to all students will be Galsworthy's own statements on the drama in "Some Platitudes Concerning Drama," from THE INN OF TRANQUILLITY *(New York: Charles Scribner's Sons,* 1912, 1916); *in "Anglo-American Drama and Its Future," from* ANOTHER SHEAF *(New York: Charles Scribner's Sons,* 1919); *and in* GLIMPSES AND REFLECTIONS *(London: Heinemann,* 1937).

The Pigeon

CHARACTERS

CHRISTOPHER WELLWYN, *an artist.*   FERRAND, *an alien.*

ANN, *his daughter.*   TIMSON, *once a cabman.*

GUINEVERE MEGAN, *a flower-seller.*   EDWARD BERTLEY, *a Canon.*

RORY MEGAN, *her husband.*   ALFRED CALWAY, *a Professor.*

SIR THOMAS HOXTON, *a Justice of the Peace.*

Also a police constable, three humble-men, and some curious persons.

The action passes in WELLWYN'S *Studio, and the street outside.*

ACT I: *Christmas Eve.* ACT II: *New Year's Day.* ACT III: *The First of April.*

❧

ACT I

It is the night of Christmas Eve, the scene is a Studio, flush with the street, having a skylight darkened by a fall of snow. There is no one in the room, the walls of which are whitewashed, above a floor of bare dark boards. A fire is cheerfully burning. On a model's platform stands an easel and canvas. There are busts and pictures; a screen, a little stool, two armchairs, and a long old-fashioned settle under the window. A door in one wall leads to the house, a door in the opposite wall to the model's dressing-room, and the street door is in the centre of the wall between. On a low table a Russian samovar is hissing, and beside it on a tray stands a teapot, with glasses, lemon, sugar, and a decanter of rum. Through a huge uncurtained window close to the street door the snowy lamplit street can be seen, and beyond it the river and a night of stars.

Reprinted from THE PIGEON by John Galsworthy. Copyright 1912 by Charles Scribner's Sons, 1940 by Ada Galsworthy. Used by permission of the publishers, Charles Scribner's Sons.

The sound of a latchkey turned in the lock of the street door, and ANN WELLWYN *enters, a girl of seventeen, with hair tied in a ribbon and covered by a scarf. Leaving the door open, she turns up the electric light and goes to the fire. She throws off her scarf and long red cloak. She is dressed in a high evening frock of some soft white material. Her movements are quick and substantial. Her face, full of no nonsense, is decided and sincere, with deep-set eyes, and a capable, well-shaped forehead. Shredding off her gloves she warms her hands.*

In the doorway appear the figures of two men. The first is rather short and slight, with a soft short beard, bright soft eyes, and a crumply face. Under his squash hat his hair is rather plentiful and rather grey. He wears an old brown ulster and woollen gloves, and is puffing at a hand-made cigarette. He is ANN's *father,* WELLWYN, *the artist. His companion is a well-wrapped clergyman of medium height and stoutish build, with a pleasant, rosy face, rather shining eyes, and rather chubby clean-shaped lips; in appearance, indeed, a grown-up boy. He is the Vicar of the parish—*CANON BERTLEY.

BERTLEY: My dear Wellwyn, the whole question of reform is full of difficulty. When you have two men like Professor Calway and Sir Thomas Hoxton taking diametrically opposite points of view, as we've seen to-night, I confess, I——

WELLWYN: Come in, Vicar, and have some grog.

BERTLEY: Not to-night, thanks! Christmas to-morrow! Great temptation, though, this room! Good-night, Wellwyn; good-night, Ann!

ANN (*coming from the fire towards the tea-table*): Good-night, Canon Bertley.

[*He goes out, and* WELLWYN, *shut-ting the door after him, approaches the fire.*]

ANN (*sitting on the little stool, with her back to the fire, and making tea*): Daddy!

WELLWYN: My dear?

ANN: You say you liked Professor Calway's lecture. Is it going to do you any good, that's the question?

WELLWYN: I—I hope so, Ann.

ANN: I took you on purpose. Your charity's getting simply awful. Those two this morning cleared out all my housekeeping money.

WELLWYN: Um! Um! I quite understand your feeling.

ANN: They both had your card,

so I couldn't refuse—didn't know what you'd said to them. Why don't you make it a rule never to give your card to anyone except really decent people, and—picture dealers, of course.

WELLWYN: My dear, I have—often.

ANN: Then why don't you keep it? It's a frightful habit. You *are* naughty, Daddy. One of these days you'll get yourself into most fearful complications.

WELLWYN: My dear, when they—when they look at you?

ANN: You know the house wants all sorts of things. Why do you speak to them at all?

WELLWYN: I don't—they speak to me.

[*He takes off his ulster and hangs it over the back of an arm-chair.*]

ANN: They see you coming. Anybody can see *you* coming, Daddy. That's why you ought to be so careful. I shall make you wear a hard hat. Those squashy hats of yours are hopelessly inefficient.

WELLWYN (*gazing at his hat*): Calway wears one.

ANN: As if anyone would beg of Professor Calway.

WELLWYN: Well—perhaps not. You know, Ann, I admire that fellow. Wonderful power of—of—

theory! How a man can be so absolutely tidy in his mind! It's most exciting.

ANN: Has any one begged of you to-day?

WELLWYN (*doubtfully*): No—no.

ANN (*after a long, severe look*): Will you have rum in your tea?

WELLWYN (*crestfallen*): Yes, my dear—a good deal.

ANN (*pouring out the rum, and handing him the glass*): Well, who was it?

WELLWYN: He didn't beg of me. (*Losing himself in recollection.*) Interesting old creature, Ann—real type. Old cabman.

ANN: Where?

WELLWYN: Just on the Embankment.

ANN: Of course! Daddy, you know the Embankment ones are *always* rotters.

WELLWYN: Yes, my dear; but this wasn't.

ANN: Did you give him your card?

WELLWYN: I—I—don't——

ANN: *Did* you, Daddy?

WELLWYN: I'm rather afraid I may have!

ANN: May have! It's simply immoral.

WELLWYN: Well, the old fellow was so awfully human, Ann. Besides, I didn't give him any money

165

—hadn't got any.

ANN: Look here, Daddy! Did you ever ask anybody for anything? You know you never did, you'd starve first. So would anybody decent. Then, why won't you see that people who beg are rotters?

WELLWYN: But, my dear, we're not all the same. They wouldn't do it if it wasn't natural to them. One likes to be friendly. What's the use of being alive if one isn't?

ANN: Daddy, you're hopeless.

WELLWYN: But, look here, Ann, the whole thing's so jolly complicated. According to Calway, we're to give the State all we can spare, to make the undeserving deserving. He's a Professor; he ought to know. But old Hoxton's always dinning it into me that we ought to support private organisations for helping the deserving, and damn the undeserving. Well, that's just the opposite. And he's a J.P. Tremendous experience. And the Vicar seems to be for a · little bit of both. Well, what the devil—? My trouble is, whichever I'm with, he always converts me. (*Ruefully.*) And there's no fun in any of them.

ANN (*rising*): Oh! Daddy, you are so—don't you know that you're the despair of all social reformers? (*She envelops him.*) There's a tear in the left knee of your trousers. You're not to wear them

again.

WELLWYN: Am I likely to?

ANN: I shouldn't be a bit surprised if it isn't your only pair. D'you know what I live in terror of?

[WELLWYN *gives her a queer and apprehensive look.*]

ANN: That you'll take them off some day, and give them away in the street. Have you got any money? (*She feels in his coat, and he in his trousers—they find nothing.*) Do you know that your pockets are one enormous hole?

WELLWYN: No!

ANN: Spiritually.

WELLWYN: Oh! Ah! H'm!

ANN (*severely*): Now, look here, Daddy! (*She takes him by his lapels.*) Don't imagine that it isn't the most disgusting luxury on your part to go on giving away things as you do! You know what you really are, I suppose—a sickly sentimentalist!

WELLWYN (*breaking away from her, disturbed*): It isn't sentiment. It's simply that they seem to me so —so—jolly. If I'm to give up feeling sort of—nice in here (*he touches his chest*) about people— it doesn't matter *who* they are— then I don't know what I'm to do. I shall have to sit with my head in a bag.

ANN: I think you ought to.

WELLWYN: I suppose they see I like them—then they tell me

things. After that, of course, you can't help doing what you can.

ANN: Well, if you *will* love them up!

WELLWYN: My dear, I don't want to. It isn't *them* especially —why, I feel it even with old Calway sometimes. It's only Providence that he doesn't want anything of me—except to make me like himself—confound him!

ANN (*moving towards the door into the house—impressively*): What you don't see is that other people aren't a bit like *you.*

WELLWYN: Well, thank God!

ANN: It's so old-fashioned too! I'm going to bed—I just leave you to your conscience.

WELLWYN: Oh!

ANN (*opening the door—severely*): Good-night—(*with a certain weakening*) you old—Daddy!

[*She jumps at him, gives him a hug, and goes out.* WELL-WYN *stands perfectly still. He first gazes up at the skylight, then down at the floor. Slowly he begins to shake his head, and mutter, as he moves towards the fire.*]

WELLWYN: Bad lot. . . . Low type—no backbone, no stability!

[*There comes a fluttering knock on the outer door. As the sound slowly enters his consciousness, he begins to wince, as though he knew, but would not admit its significance.*

Then he sits down, covering his ears. The knocking does not cease. WELLWYN *drops first one, then both hands, rises, and begins to sidle towards the door. The knocking becomes louder.*]

WELLWYN: Ah dear! Tt! Tt! Tt!

[*After a look in the direction of* ANN's *disappearance, he opens the street door a very little way. By the light of the lamp there can be seen a young girl in dark clothes, huddled in a shawl to which the snow is clinging. She has on her arm a basket covered with a bit of sacking.*]

WELLWYN: I can't, you know; it's impossible.

[*The girl says nothing, but looks at him with dark eyes.*]

WELLWYN (*wincing*): Let's see —I don't know you—do I?

[*The girl, speaking in a soft, hoarse voice, with a faint accent of reproach:* "Mrs. Megan—you give me this—" *She holds out a dirty visiting card.*]

WELLWYN (*recoiling from the card*): Oh! Did I? Ah! When?

MRS. MEGAN: You 'ad some vi'lets off of me larst spring. You give me 'arf a crown.

[*A smile tries to visit her face.*]

WELLWYN (*looking stealthily round*): Ah! Well, come in—just

167

for a minute—it's very cold—and tell us what it is.

[*She comes in stolidly, a sphinx-like figure, with her pretty tragic little face.*]

WELLWYN: I don't remember you. (*Looking closer.*) Yes, I do. Only—you weren't the same —were you?

MRS. MEGAN (*dully*): I seen trouble since.

WELLWYN: Trouble! Have some tea?

[*He looks anxiously at the door into the house, then goes quickly to the table, and pours out a glass of tea, putting rum into it.*]

WELLWYN (*handing her the tea*): Keeps the cold out! Drink it off!

[MRS. MEGAN *drinks it off, chokes a little, and almost immediately seems to get a size larger.* WELLWYN *watches her with his head held on one side, and a smile broadening on his face.*]

WELLWYN: Cure for all evils, um?

MRS. MEGAN: It warms you. (*She smiles.*)

WELLWYN (*smiling back, and catching himself out*): Well! You know, I oughtn't.

MRS. MEGAN (*conscious of the disruption of his personality, and withdrawing into her tragic abyss*): I wouldn't 'a come, but

you told me if I wanted an 'and——

WELLWYN (*gradually losing himself in his own nature*): Let me see—corner of Flight Street, wasn't it?

MRS. MEGAN (*with faint eagerness*): Yes, sir, an' I told you about me vi'lets—it was a luvly spring day.

WELLWYN: Beautiful! Beautiful! Birds singing, and the trees, &c.! We had quite a talk. You had a baby with you.

MRS. MEGAN: I got married since then.

WELLWYN: Oh! Ah! Yes! (*Cheerfully.*) And how's the baby?

MRS. MEGAN (*turning to stone*): I lost her.

WELLWYN: Oh! poor— Um!

MRS. MEGAN (*impassive*): You said something abaht makin' a picture of me. (*With faint eagerness.*) So I thought I might come, in case you'd forgotten.

WELLWYN (*looking at her intently*): Things going badly?

MRS. MEGAN (*stripping the sacking off her basket*): I keep 'em covered up, but the cold gets to 'em. Thruppence—that's all I've took.

WELLWYN: Ho! Tt! Tt! (*He looks into the basket.*) Christmas, too!

MRS. MEGAN: They're dead.

WELLWYN (*drawing in his*

168

breath): Got a good husband?

MRS. MEGAN: He plays cards.

WELLWYN: Oh, Lord! And what are you doing out—with a cold like that? (*He taps his chest.*)

MRS. MEGAN: We was sold up this morning—he's gone off with 'is mates. Haven't took enough yet for a night's lodgin'.

WELLWYN (*correcting a spasmodic dive into his pockets*): But who buys *flowers* at this time of night?

[MRS. MEGAN *looks at him, and faintly smiles.*]

WELLWYN (*rumpling his hair*): Saints above us! Here! Come to the fire!

[*She follows him to the fire. He shuts the street door.*]

WELLWYN: Are your feet wet? (*She nods.*) Well, sit down here, and take them off. That's right.

[*She sits on the stool. And after a slow look up at him, which has in it a deeper knowledge than belongs of right to her years, begins taking off her shoes and stockings.* WELLWYN *goes to the door into the house, opens it, and listens with a sort of stealthy casualness. He returns whistling, but not out loud. The girl has finished taking off her stockings, and turned her bare toes to the flames. She shuffles them back under her*

skirt.]

WELLWYN: How old are you, my child?

MRS. MEGAN: Nineteen, come Candlemas.

WELLWYN: And what's your name?

MRS. MEGAN: Guinevere.

WELLWYN: What? Welsh?

MRS. MEGAN: Yes—from Battersea.

WELLWYN: And your husband?

MRS. MEGAN: No. Irish, 'e is. Notting Dale, 'e comes from.

WELLWYN: Roman Catholic?

MRS. MEGAN: Yes. My 'usband's an atheist as well.

WELLWYN: I see. (*Abstractedly.*) How jolly! And how old is he—this young man of yours?

MRS. MEGAN: 'E'll be twenty soon.

WELLWYN: Babes in the wood! Does he treat you badly?

MRS. MEGAN: No.

WELLWYN: Nor drink?

MRS. MEGAN: No. He's not a bad one. Only he gets playin' cards—then 'e'll fly the kite.

WELLWYN: I see. And when he's not flying it, what does he do?

MRS. MEGAN (*touching her basket*): Same as me. Other jobs tires 'im.

WELLWYN: That's very nice! (*He checks himself.*) Well, what am I to do with you?

MRS. MEGAN: Of course, I could get me night's lodging if I like to

169

do—the same as some of them.

WELLWYN: No! no! Never, my child! Never!

MRS. MEGAN: It's easy that way.

WELLWYN: Heavens! But your husband! Um?

MRS. MEGAN (*with stoical vindictiveness*): He's after one I know of.

WELLWYN: Tt! What a pickle!

MRS. MEGAN: I'll 'ave to walk about the streets.

WELLWYN (*to himself*): Now how can I?

[MRS. MEGAN *looks up and smiles at him, as if she had already discovered that he is peculiar.*]

WELLWYN: You see, the fact is, I mustn't give you anything—because—well, for one thing I haven't got it. There are other reasons, but that's the—real one. But, now, there's a little room where my models dress. I wonder if you could sleep there. Come, and see.

[*The Girl gets up lingeringly, loth to leave the warmth. She takes up her wet stockings.*]

MRS. MEGAN: Shall I put them on again?

WELLWYN: No, no; there's a nice warm pair of slippers. (*Seeing the steam rising from her.*) Why, you're wet all over. Here, wait a little!

[*He crosses to the door into the house, and after stealthy lis-*

tening, steps through. The Girl, like a cat, steals back to the warmth of the fire. WELLWYN *returns with a candle, a canary-coloured bath gown, and two blankets.*]

WELLWYN: Now then! (*He precedes her towards the door of the model's room.*) Hsssh! (*He opens the door and holds up the candle to show her the room.*) Will it do? There's a couch. You'll find some washing things. Make yourself quite at home. See!

[*The Girl, perfectly dumb, passes through with her basket—and her shoes and stockings.* WELLWYN *hands her the candle, blankets, and bath gown.*]

WELLWYN: Have a good sleep, child! Forget that you're alive! (*He closes the door, mournfully.*) Done it again! (*He goes to the table, cuts a large slice of cake, knocks on the door, and hands it in.*) Chow-chow! (*Then, as he walks away, he sights the opposite door.*) Well—damn it, what could I have done? Not a farthing on me! (*He goes to the street door to shut it, but first opens it wide to confirm himself in his hospitality.*) Night like this!

[*A sputter of snow is blown in his face. A voice says: "Monsieur, pardon!"* WELLWYN *re-*

170

coils spasmodically. A figure moves from the lamp-post to the doorway. He is seen to be young and to have ragged clothes. He speaks again: "You do not remember me, Monsieur? My name is Ferrand—it was in Paris, in the Champs-Elysées—by the fountain. . . . When you came to the door, Monsieur —I am not made of iron. . . . Tenez, here is your card—I have never lost it." *He holds out to* WELLWYN *an old and dirty visiting card. As inch by inch he has advanced into the doorway, the light from within falls on him, a tall gaunt young pagan with fair hair and reddish golden stubble of beard, a long ironical nose a little to one side, and large, grey, rather prominent eyes. There is a certain grace in his figure and movements; his clothes are nearly dropping off him.*]

WELLWYN (*yielding to a pleasant memory*): Ah! yes. By the fountain. I was sitting there, and you came and ate a roll, and drank the water.

FERRAND (*with faint eagerness*): My breakfast. I was in poverty —veree bad off. You gave me ten francs. I thought I had a little the right (WELLWYN *makes a movement of disconcertion*), see-

ing you said that if I came to Eng-land——

WELLWYN: Um! And so you've come?

FERRAND: It was time that I con-solidated my fortunes, Monsieur.

WELLWYN: And you—have—— (*He stops embarrassed.*)

FERRAND (*shrugging his ragged shoulders*): One is not yet Roths-child.

WELLWYN (*sympathetically*): No. (*Yielding to memory.*) We talked philosophy.

FERRAND: I have not yet changed my opinion. We other vagabonds, we are exploited by the bourgeois. This is always my idea, Monsieur.

WELLWYN: Yes—not quite the general view, perhaps! Well— (*Heartily.*) Come in! Very glad to see you again.

FERRAND (*brushing his arms over his eyes*): Pardon, Monsieur —your goodness—I am a little weak. (*He opens his coat, and shows a belt drawn very tight over his ragged shirt.*) I tighten him one hole for each meal, during two days now. That gives you cour-age.

WELLWYN (*with cooing sounds, pouring out tea, and adding rum*): Have some of this. It'll buck you up. (*He watches the young man drink.*)

FERRAND (*becoming a size larger*): Sometimes I think that I

171

will never succeed to dominate my life, Monsieur—though I have no vices, except that I guard always the aspiration to achieve success. But I will not roll myself under the machine of existence to gain a nothing every day. I must find with what to fly a little.

WELLWYN (*delicately*): Yes; yes —I remember, you found it difficult to stay long in any particular —yes.

FERRAND (*proudly*): In one little corner? No—Monsieur— never! That is not in my character. I must see life.

WELLWYN: Quite, quite! Have some cake? (*He cuts cake.*)

FERRAND: In your country they say you cannot eat the cake and have it. But one must always try, Monsieur; one must never be content. (*Refusing the cake.*) *Grand merci*, but for the moment I have no stomach—I have lost my stomach now for two days. If I could smoke, Monsieur! (*He makes the gesture of smoking.*)

WELLWYN: Rather! (*Handing his tobacco pouch.*) Roll yourself one.

FERRAND (*rapidly rolling a cigarette*): If I had not found you, Monsieur—I would have been a little hole in the river to-night— I was so discouraged. (*He inhales and puffs a long luxurious whiff of smoke. Very bitterly.*) Life! (*He disperses the puff of smoke with his finger, and stares before him.*) And to think that in a few minutes HE will be born! Monsieur! (*He gazes intently at* WELLWYN.) The world would reproach you for your goodness to me.

WELLWYN (*looking uneasily at the door into the house*): You think so? Ah!

FERRAND: Monsieur, if HE himself were on earth now, there would be a little heap of gentlemen writing to the journals every day to call Him sloppee sentimentalist! And what is veree funny, these gentlemen they would all be most strong Christians. (*He regards* WELLWYN *deeply.*) But that will not trouble you, Monsieur; I saw well from the first that you are no Christian. You have so kind a face.

WELLWYN: Oh! Indeed!

FERRAND: You have not enough the Pharisee in your character. You do not judge, and you are judged. (*He stretches his limbs as if in pain.*)

WELLWYN: Are you in pain?

FERRAND: I 'ave a little the rheumatism.

WELLWYN: Wet through, of course! (*Glancing towards the house.*) Wait a bit! I wonder if you'd like these trousers; they've —er—they're not quite——

[*He passes through the door into the house.* FERRAND *stands at*

*the fire, with his limbs spread
as it were to embrace it,
smoking with abandonment.*
WELLWYN *returns stealthily,
dressed in a Jaeger dressing-
gown, and bearing a pair of
drawers, his trousers, a pair
of slippers, and a sweater.*]
WELLWYN (*speaking in a low
voice, for the door is still open*):
Can you make these do for the
moment?

FERRAND: *Je vous remercie,
Monsieur.* (*Pointing to the
screen.*) May I retire?

WELLWYN: Yes, yes.

[FERRAND *goes behind the screen.*
WELLWYN *closes the door into
the house, then goes to the
window to draw the curtains.
He suddenly recoils and
stands petrified with doubt.*]

WELLWYN: Good Lord!

[*There is the sound of tapping on
glass. Against the window-
pane is pressed the face of a
man.* WELLWYN *motions to
him to go away. He does not
go, but continues tapping.*
WELLWYN *opens the door.
There enters a square old
man, with a red, pendulous-
jawed, shaking face under a
snow besprinkled bowler hat.
He is holding out a visiting
card with tremulous hand.*]

WELLWYN: Who's that? Who
are you?

TIMSON (*in a thick, hoarse, shaking voice*): 'Appy to see you, sir;
we 'ad a talk this morning. Timson—I give you me name. You
invited of me, if ye remember.

WELLWYN: It's a little late,
really.

TIMSON: Well, ye see, I never
expected to 'ave to call on yer. I
was 'itched up all right when I
spoke to yer this mornin', but bein'
Christmas, things 'ave took a turn
with me to-day. (*He speaks with
increasing thickness.*) I'm reg'lar
disgusted—not got the price of a
bed abaht me. Thought you
wouldn't like me to be delicate—
not at my age.

WELLWYN (*with a mechanical
and distracted dive of his hands
into his pockets*): The fact is, it so
happens I haven't a copper on me.

TIMSON (*evidently taking this
for professional refusal*): Wouldn't
arsk you if I could 'elp it. 'Ad to
do with 'orses all me life. It's this
'ere cold I'm frightened of. I'm
afraid I'll go to sleep.

WELLWYN: Well, really, I——

TIMSON: To be froze to death—
I mean—it's awkward.

WELLWYN (*puzzled and un-
happy*): Well—come in a moment, and let's—think it out.
Have some tea!

[*He pours out the remains of the
tea, and finding there is not
very much, adds rum rather
liberally.* TIMSON, *who walks
a little wide at the knees,*

173

*steadying his gait, has fol-
lowed.*]

TIMSON (*receiving the drink*):
Yer 'ealth. 'Ere's—soberiety! (*He
applies the drink to his lips with
shaking hand. Agreeably surprised.*) Blimey! Thish yer tea's
foreign, ain't it?

FERRAND (*reappearing from behind the screen in his new clothes
of which the trousers stop too
soon.*) With a needle, Monsieur,
I would soon have with what to
make face against the world.

WELLWYN: Too short! Ah!

[*He goes to the dais on which
stands* ANN's *work-basket, and
takes from it a needle and
cotton. While he is so engaged* FERRAND *is sizing up
old* TIMSON, *as one dog will
another. The old man, glass
in hand, seems to have lapsed
into coma.*]

FERRAND (*indicating* TIMSON):
Monsieur! (*He makes the gesture of one drinking, and shakes
his head.*)

WELLWYN (*handing him the
needle and cotton*): Um! Afraid
so!

[*They approach* TIMSON, *who
takes no notice.*]

FERRAND (*gently*): It is an old
cabby, is it not, Monsieur? *Ceux
sont tous des buveurs.*

WELLWYN (*concerned at the old
man's stupefaction*): Now, my
old friend, sit down a moment.

(*They manœuvre* TIMSON *to the
settle.*) Will you smoke?

TIMSON (*in a drowsy voice*):
Thank 'ee—smoke pipe of 'baccer.
Old 'orse—standin' abaht in th'
cold. (*He relapses into coma.*)

FERRAND (*with a click of his
tongue*): *Il est parti.*

WELLWYN (*doubtfully*): He
hasn't really left a horse outside,
do you think?

FERRAND: *Non, non, Monsieur*—
no 'orse. He is dreaming. I know
very well that state of him—that
catches you sometimes. It is the
warmth sudden on the stomach.
He will speak no more sense to-
night. At the most, drink, and fly
a little in his past.

WELLWYN: Poor old buffer!

FERRAND: Touching, is it not,
Monsieur? There are many brave
gents among the old cabbies—
they have philosophy—that comes
from 'orses, and from sitting still.

WELLWYN (*touching* TIMSON's
shoulder*): Drenched!

FERRAND: That will do 'im no
'arm, Monsieur—no 'arm at all.
He is well wet inside, remember
—it is Christmas to-morrow. Put
him a rug, if you will, he will soon
steam.

[WELLWYN *takes up* ANN's *long
red cloak, and wraps it round
the old man.*]

TIMSON (*faintly roused*): Tha's
right. Put—the rug on th' old
'orse. (*He makes a strange noise,*

and works his head and tongue.)

WELLWYN (*alarmed*): What's the matter with him?

FERRAND: It is nothing, Monsieur; for the moment he thinks 'imself a 'orse. *Il joue "cache-cache,"* 'ide and seek, with what you call—'is bitt.

WELLWYN: But what's to be done with him? One can't turn him out in this state.

FERRAND: If you wish to leave him 'ere, Monsieur, have no fear. I charge myself with him.

WELLWYN: Oh! (*Dubiously.*) You—er—I really don't know, I hadn't contemplated—You think you could manage if I—if I went to bed?

FERRAND: But certainly, Monsieur.

WELLWYN (*still dubiously*): You —you're sure you've everything you want?

FERRAND (*bowing*): Mais oui, Monsieur.

WELLWYN: I don't know what I can do by staying.

FERRAND: There is nothing you can do, Monsieur. Have confidence in me.

WELLWYN: Well—keep the fire up quietly—very quietly. You'd better take this coat of mine, too. You'll find it precious cold, I expect, about three o'clock. (*He hands* FERRAND *his ulster.*)

FERRAND (*taking it*): I shall sleep in praying for you, Monsieur.

WELLWYN: Ah! Yes! Thanks! Well—good-night! By the way, I shall be down rather early. Have to think of my household a bit, you know.

FERRAND: *Très bien, Monsieur.* I comprehend. One must well be regular in this life.

WELLWYN (*with a start*): Lord! (*He looks at the door of the model's room.*) I'd forgotten——

FERRAND: Can I undertake anything, Monsieur?

WELLWYN: No, no! (*He goes to the electric light switch by the outer door.*) You won't want this, will you?

FERRAND: Merci, Monsieur.

[WELLWYN *switches off the light.*]

FERRAND: *Bon soir, Monsieur!*

WELLWYN: The devil! Er— good-night!

[*He hesitates, rumples his hair, and passes rather suddenly away.*]

FERRAND (*to himself*): Poor pigeon! (*Looking long at old* TIMSON.) *Espèce de type anglais!* [*He sits down in the firelight, curls up a foot on his knee, and taking out a knife, rips the stitching of a turned-up end of trouser, pinches the cloth double, and puts in the preliminary stitch of a new hem—all with the swiftness of one well-accustomed. Then, as if hearing a sound*

175

behind him, he gets up quickly and slips behind the screen. MRS. MEGAN, *attracted by the cessation of voices, has opened the door, and is creeping from the model's room towards the fire. She has almost reached it before she takes in the torpid crimson figure of old* TIMSON. *She halts and puts her hand to her chest—a queer figure in the firelight, garbed in the canary-coloured bath gown and rabbit's-wool slippers, her black matted hair straggling down on her neck. Having quite digested the fact that the old man is in a sort of stupor,* MRS. MEGAN *goes close to the fire, and sits on the little stool, smiling sideways at old* TIMSON. FERRAND, *coming quietly up behind, examines her from above, drooping his long nose as if enquiring with it as to her condition in life; then he steps back a yard or two.*]

FERRAND   (*gently*):   Pardon, Ma'moiselle.

MRS. MEGAN (*springing to her feet*): Oh!

FERRAND: All right, all right! We are brave gents!

TIMSON (*faintly roused*): 'Old up, there!

FERRAND: Trust in me, Ma'moiselle!

[MRS. MEGAN *responds by drawing away.*]

FERRAND (*gently*): We must be good comrades. This asylum—it is better than a doss-'ouse.

[*He pushes the stool over towards her, and seats himself. Somewhat reassured,* MRS. MEGAN *again sits down.*]

MRS. MEGAN: You frightened me.

TIMSON (*unexpectedly—in a drowsy tone*): Purple foreigners!

FERRAND: Pay no attention, Ma'moiselle. He is a philosopher.

MRS. MEGAN: Oh! I thought 'e was boozed.

[*They both look at* TIMSON.]

FERRAND: It is the same—veree 'armless.

MRS. MEGAN: What's that he's got on 'im?

FERRAND: It is a coronation robe. Have no fear, Ma'moiselle. Veree docile potentate.

MRS. MEGAN: I wouldn't be afraid of him. (*Challenging* FERRAND.) I'm afraid o' you.

FERRAND: It is because you do not know me, Ma'moiselle. You are wrong, it is always the unknown you should love.

MRS. MEGAN: I don't like the way you—speaks to me.

FERRAND: Ah! You are a Princess in disguise?

MRS. MEGAN: No fear!

FERRAND: No? What is it then you do to make face against the necessities of life? A living?

MRS. MEGAN: Sells flowers.

FERRAND (*rolling his eyes*): It is not a career.

MRS. MEGAN (*with a touch of devilry*): You don't know what I do.

FERRAND: Ma'moiselle, whatever you do is charming.

[MRS. MEGAN *looks at him, and slowly smiles.*]

MRS. MEGAN: You're a foreigner.

FERRAND: It is true.

MRS. MEGAN: What do *you* do for a livin'?

FERRAND: I am an interpreter.

MRS. MEGAN: You ain't very busy, are you?

FERRAND (*with dignity*): At present I am resting.

MRS. MEGAN (*looking at him and smiling*): How did you and 'im come here?

FERRAND: Ma'moiselle, we would ask you the same question.

MRS. MEGAN: The gentleman let me. 'E's funny.

FERRAND: *C'est un ange!* (*At* MRS. MEGAN's *blank stare he interprets.*) An angel!

MRS. MEGAN: Me luck's out—that's why I come.

FERRAND (*rising*): Ah! Ma'moiselle! Luck! There is the little God who dominates us all. Look at this old! (*He points to* TIMSON.) He is finished. In his day that old would be doing good business. He could afford himself —(*He makes a sign of drinking.*) Then come the motor cars. All goes—he has nothing left, only 'is 'abits of a cocher! Luck!

TIMSON (*with a vague gesture —drowsily*): Kick the foreign beggars out.

FERRAND: A real Englishman. . . . And look at me! My father was merchant of ostrich feathers in Brussels. If I had been content to go in his business, I would 'ave been rich. But I was born to roll —"rolling stone"—to voyage is stronger than myself. Luck! . . . And you, Ma'moiselle, shall I tell your fortune? (*He looks in her face.*) You were born for *la joie de vivre*—to drink the wines of life. *Et vous voilà!* Luck!

[*Though she does not in the least understand what he has said, her expression changes to a sort of glee.*]

FERRAND: Yes. You were born loving pleasure. Is it not? You see, you cannot say, No. All of us, we have our fates. Give me your hand. (*He kneels down and takes her hand.*) In each of us there is that against which we cannot struggle. Yes, yes!

[*He holds her hand, and turns it over between his own.* MRS. MEGAN *remains stolid, half-fascinated, half-reluctant.*]

TIMSON (*flickering into consciousness*): Be'ave yourselves! Yer crimson canary birds!

[MRS. MEGAN *would withdraw her hand, but cannot.*]

FERRAND: Pay no attention, Ma'moiselle. He is a Puritan.

[TIMSON *relapses into comatosity, upsetting his glass, which falls with a crash.*]

MRS. MEGAN: Let go my hand, please!

FERRAND (*relinquishing it, and staring into the fire gravely*): There is one thing I have never done—'urt a woman—that is hardly in my character. (*Then, drawing a little closer, he looks into her face.*) Tell me, Ma'moiselle, what is it you think of all day long?

MRS. MEGAN: I dunno—lots, I thinks of.

FERRAND: Shall I tell you? (*Her eyes remain fixed on his, the strangeness of him preventing her from telling him to "get along." He goes on in his ironic voice.*) It is of the streets—the lights—the faces—it is of all which moves, and is warm—it is of colour—it is (*he brings his face quite close to hers*) of Love. That is for you what the road is for me. That is for you what the rum is for that old—(*He jerks his thumb back at* TIMSON. *Then bending swiftly forward to the girl.*) See! I kiss you—Ah!

[*He draws her forward off the stool. There is a little struggle, then she resigns her lips. The little stool, overturned, falls with a clatter. They* spring up, and move apart. The door opens and ANN enters from the house in a blue dressing-gown, with her hair loose, and a candle held high above her head. Taking in the strange half-circle round the stove, she recoils. Then, standing her ground, calls in a voice sharpened by fright: "Daddy—Daddy!"]

TIMSON (*stirring uneasily, and struggling to his feet*): All ri——! I'm comin'!

FERRAND: Have no fear, Madame!

[*In the silence that follows, a clock begins loudly striking twelve.* ANN *remains, as if carved in stone, her eyes fastened on the strangers. There is the sound of someone falling downstairs, and* WELLWYN *appears, also holding a candle above his head.*]

ANN: Look!

WELLWYN: Yes, yes, my dear! It—it happened.

ANN (*with a sort of groan*): Oh! Daddy!

[*In the renewed silence, the church clock ceases to chime.*]

FERRAND (*softly, in his ironic voice*): HE is come, Monsieur! 'Appy Christmas! Bon Noël!

[*There is a sudden chime of bells. The stage is blotted dark.*]

CURTAIN

ACT II

It is four o'clock in the afternoon of New Year's Day. On the raised dais MRS. MEGAN *is standing, in her rags; with bare feet and ankles, her dark hair as if blown about, her lips parted, holding out a dishevelled bunch of violets. Before his easel,* WELLWYN *is painting her. Behind him, at a table between the cupboard and the door to the model's room,* TIMSON *is washing brushes, with the movements of one employed upon relief works. The samovar is hissing on the table by the stove, the tea things are set out.*

WELLWYN: Open your mouth.

[MRS. MEGAN *opens her mouth.*]

ANN (*in hat and coat, entering from the house*): Daddy!

[WELLWYN *goes to her; and, released from restraint,* MRS. MEGAN *looks round at* TIMSON *and grimaces.*]

WELLWYN: Well, my dear?

[*They speak in low voices.*]

ANN (*holding out a note*): This note from Canon Bertley. He's going to bring her husband here this afternoon. (*She looks at* MRS. MEGAN.)

WELLWYN: Oh! (*He also looks at* MRS. MEGAN.)

ANN: And I met Sir Thomas Hoxton at church this morning, and spoke to him about Timson.

WELLWYN: Um!

[*They look at* TIMSON. *Then* ANN *goes back to the door, and* WELLWYN *follows her.*]

ANN (*turning*): I'm going round now, Daddy, to ask Professor Calway what we're to do with that Ferrand.

WELLWYN: Oh! One each! I wonder if they'll like it.

ANN: They'll have to lump it. (*She goes out into the house.*)

WELLWYN (*back at his easel*): You can shut your mouth now.

[MRS. MEGAN *shuts her mouth, but opens it immediately to smile.*]

WELLWYN (*spasmodically*): Ah! Now that's what I want. (*He dabs furiously at the canvas. Then standing back, runs his hands through his hair and turns a painter's glance towards the skylight.*) Dash! Light's gone! Off you get, child—don't tempt me!

[MRS. MEGAN *descends. Passing towards the door of the model's room she stops, and stealthily looks at the picture.*]

TIMSON: Ah! Would yer!

WELLWYN (*wheeling round*): Want to have a look? Well—come on!

[*He takes her by the arm, and they stand before the canvas.*

179

After a stolid moment, she giggles.]

WELLWYN: Oh! You think so?

MRS. MEGAN (*who has lost her hoarseness*): It's not like my picture that I had on the pier.

WELLWYN: No—it wouldn't be.

MRS. MEGAN (*timidly*): If I had an 'at on, I'd look better.

WELLWYN: With feathers?

MRS. MEGAN: Yes.

WELLWYN: Well, you can't! I don't like hats, and I don't like feathers.

[MRS. MEGAN *timidly tugs his sleeve.* TIMSON, *screened as he thinks by the picture, has drawn from his bulky pocket a bottle and is taking a stealthy swig.*]

WELLWYN (*to* MRS. MEGAN, *affecting not to notice*): How much do I owe you?

MRS. MEGAN (*a little surprised*): You paid me for to-day—all 'cept a penny.

WELLWYN: Well! Here it is. (*He gives her a coin.*) Go and get your feet on!

MRS. MEGAN: You've give me 'arf a crown.

WELLWYN: Cut away now!

[MRS. MEGAN, *smiling at the coin, goes towards the model's room. She looks back at* WELLWYN, *as if to draw his eyes to her, but he is gazing at the picture; then, catching old* TIMSON's *sour glance, she grimaces at him, kicking up her feet with a little squeal. But when* WELLWYN *turns to the sound, she is demurely passing through the doorway.*]

TIMSON (*in his voice of dubious sobriety*): I've finished these yer brushes, sir. It's not a man's work. I've been thinkin' if you'd keep an 'orse, I could give yer satisfaction.

WELLWYN: Would the horse, Timson?

TIMSON (*looking him up and down*): I knows of one that would just suit yer. Reel 'orse, you'd like 'im.

WELLWYN (*shaking his head*): Afraid not, Timson! Awfully sorry, though, to have nothing better for you than this, at present.

TIMSON (*faintly waving the brushes*): Of course, if you can't afford it, I don't press you—it's only that I feel I'm not doing meself justice. (*Confidentially.*) There's just one thing, sir; I can't bear to see a gen'leman imposed on. That foreigner—'e's not the sort to 'ave about the place. Talk? Oh! ah! But 'e'll never do any good with 'imself. He's a alien.

WELLWYN: Terrible misfortune to a fellow, Timson.

TIMSON: Don't you believe it, sir; it's his *fault* I says to the young lady yesterday: Miss Ann, your father's a gen'leman (*with a sudden accent of hoarse sincerity*), and so you are—I don't mind sayin' it—*but,* I said, he's too easy-goin'.

WELLWYN: Indeed!

TIMSON: Well, see that girl now! (*He shakes his head.*) I never did believe in goin' behind a person's back—I'm an Englishman—but (*lowering his voice*) she's a bad hat, sir. Why, look at the street she comes from!

WELLWYN: Oh! you know it.

TIMSON: Lived there meself larst three years. See the difference a few days' corn's made in her. She's that saucy you can't touch 'er head.

WELLWYN: Is there any necessity, Timson?

TIMSON: Artful too. Full o' vice, I call 'er. Where's 'er 'usband?

WELLWYN (*gravely*): Come, Timson! You wouldn't like *her* to——

TIMSON (*with dignity, so that the bottle in his pocket is plainly visible*): I'm a man as always beared inspection.

WELLWYN (*with a well-directed smile*): So I see.

TIMSON (*curving himself round the bottle*): It's not for me to say nothing—but I can tell a gen'le-man as quick as ever I can tell an 'orse.

WELLWYN (*painting*): I find it safest to assume that every man is a gentleman, and every woman a lady. Saves no end of self-con-tempt. Give me the little brush.

TIMSON (*handing him the brush—after a considerable introspec-tive pause*): Would yer like me to stay and wash it for yer again? (*With great resolution.*) I will—I'll do it for you—never grudged workin' for a gen'leman.

WELLWYN (*with sincerity.*) Thank you, Timson—very good of you, I'm sure. (*He hands him back the brush.*) Just lend us a hand with this. (*Assisted by* TIM-SON *he pushes back the dais.*) Let's see! What do I owe you?

TIMSON (*reluctantly*): It so 'ap-pens, you advanced me to-day's yesterday.

WELLWYN: Then I suppose you want to-morrow's?

TIMSON: Well, I 'ad to spend it, lookin' for a permanent job. When you've got to do with 'orses, you can't neglect the publics, or you might as well be dead.

WELLWYN: Quite so!

TIMSON: It mounts up in the course o' the year.

WELLWYN: It would. (*Passing him a coin.*) This is for an ex-ceptional purpose—Timson—see. Not——

TIMSON (*touching his fore-head*): Certainly, sir. I quite un-derstand. I'm not that sort, as I think I've proved to yer, comin' here regular day after day, all the week. There's one thing, I ought to warn you perhaps—I might

181

ave to give this job up any day.
[*He makes a faint demonstration
with the little brush, then
puts it, absent-mindedly, into
his pocket.*]

WELLWYN (*gravely*): I'd never
stand in the way of your bettering
yourself, Timson. And, by the
way, my daughter spoke to a
friend about you to-day. I think
something may come of it.

TIMSON: Oh! Oh! She did!
Well, it might do me a bit o' good.
(*He makes for the outer door, but
stops.*) That foreigner! 'E sticks
in my gizzard. It's not as if there
wasn't plenty o' pigeons for 'im to
pluck in 'is own Gawd-forsaken
country. Reg-lar jay, that's what
I calls 'im. I could tell yer something——

[*He has opened the door, and
suddenly sees that* FERRAND
*himself is standing there.
Sticking out his lower lip,*
TIMSON *gives a roll of his jaw
and lurches forth into the
street. Owing to a slight
miscalculation, his face and
raised arms are plainly visible through the window, as
he fortifies himself for his
battle against the cold.* FER-
RAND, *having closed the door,
stands with his thumb acting
as pointer towards this spectacle. He is now remarkably
dressed in an artist's squashy
green hat, a frock coat too*

*small for him, a bright blue
tie of knitted silk, the grey
trousers that were torn, well-
worn brown boots, and a tan
waistcoat.*]

WELLWYN: What luck to-day?

FERRAND (*with a shrug*): Again
I have beaten all London, Monsieur—not one bite. (*Contemplating himself.*) I think perhaps,
that, for the bourgeoisie, there is
a little too much colour in my costume.

WELLWYN (*contemplating him*):
Let's see—I believe I've an old top
hat somewhere.

FERRAND: Ah! Monsieur, *merci*,
but *that* I could not. It is scarcely
in my character.

WELLWYN: True!

FERRAND: I have been to merchants of wine, of *tabac*, to hotels,
to Leicester Square. I have been
to a—Society for spreading Christian knowledge—I thought there
I would have a chance perhaps as
interpreter. *Toujours même chose*
—we regret, we have no situation
for you—same thing everywhere.
It seems there is nothing doing in
this town.

WELLWYN: I've noticed, there
never is.

FERRAND: I was thinking, Monsieur, that in aviation there might
be a career for me—but it seems
one must be trained.

WELLWYN: Afraid so, Ferrand.

FERRAND (*approaching the pic-*

182

ture): Ah! You are always working at this. You will have something of very good there, Monsieur. You wish to fix the type of wild savage existing ever amongst our high civilisation. *C'est très chic ça!* (WELLWYN *manifests the quiet delight of an English artist actually understood.*) In the figures of these good citizens, to whom she offers her flower, you would give the idea of all the cage doors open to catch and make tame the wild bird, that will surely die within. *Très gentil!* Believe me, Monsieur, you have there the greatest comedy of life! How anxious are the tame birds to do the wild birds good. (*His voice changes.*) For the wild birds it is not funny. There is in some human souls, Monsieur, what cannot be made tame.

WELLWYN: I believe you, Ferrand.

[*The face of a young man appears at the window, unseen. Suddenly* ANN *opens the door leading to the house.*]

ANN: Daddy—I want you.

WELLWYN (*to* FERRAND): Excuse me a minute! (*He goes to his daughter, and they pass out.*) [FERRAND *remains at the picture.* MRS. MEGAN *dressed in some of* ANN's *discarded garments, has come out of the model's room. She steals up behind*

FERRAND *like a cat, reaches an arm up, and curls it round his mouth. He turns, and tries to seize her; she disingenuously slips away. He follows. The chase circles the tea table. He catches her, lifts her up, swings round with her, so that her feet fly out; kisses her bent-back face, and sets her down. She stands there smiling. The face at the window darkens.*]

FERRAND: La Valse!

[*He takes her with both hands by the waist, she puts her hands against his shoulders to push him off—and suddenly they are whirling. As they whirl, they bob together once or twice, and kiss. Then, with a warning motion towards the door, she wrenches herself free, and stops beside the picture, trying desperately to appear demure.* WELLWYN *and* ANN *have entered. The face has vanished.*]

FERRAND (*pointing to the picture*): One does not comprehend all this, Monsieur, without well studying. I was in train to interpret for Ma'moiselle the chiaroscuro.

WELLWYN (*with a queer look*): Don't take it *too* seriously, Ferrand.

FERRAND: It is a masterpiece.

WELLWYN: My daughter's just

spoken to a friend, Professor Calway. He'd like to meet you. Could you come back a little later?

FERRAND: Certainly, Ma'moiselle. That will be an opening for me, I trust. (*He goes to the street door.*)

ANN (*paying no attention to him*): Mrs. Megan, will you too come back in half an hour?

FERRAND: *Très bien, Ma'moiselle!* I will see that she does. We will take a little promenade together. That will do us good.

[*He motions towards the door;* MRS. MEGAN, *all eyes, follows him out.*]

ANN: Oh! Daddy, they *are* rotters. Couldn't you *see* they were having the most high jinks?

WELLWYN (*at his picture*): I seemed to have noticed something.

ANN (*preparing for tea*): They were kissing.

WELLWYN: Tt! Tt!

ANN: They're hopeless, all three —especially her. Wish I hadn't given her my clothes now.

WELLWYN (*absorbed*): Something of wild-savage.

ANN: Thank goodness it's the Vicar's business to see that married people live together in his parish.

WELLWYN: Oh! (*Dubiously.*) The Megans are Roman Catholic-Atheists, Ann.

ANN (*with heat*): Then they're all the more bound.

[WELLWYN *gives a sudden and alarmed whistle.*]

ANN: What's the matter?

WELLWYN: Didn't you say you spoke to Sir Thomas, too. Suppose he comes in while the Professor's here. They're cat and dog.

ANN (*blankly*): Oh! (*As* WELLWYN *strikes a match.*) The samovar *is* lighted. (*Taking up the nearly empty decanter of rum and going to the cupboard.*) It's all right. He won't.

WELLWYN: We'll hope not. (*He turns back to his picture.*)

ANN (*at the cupboard*): Daddy!

WELLWYN: Hi!

ANN: There were *three* bottles.

WELLWYN: Oh!

ANN: Well! Now there aren't any.

WELLWYN (*abstracted*): That'll be Timson.

ANN (*with real horror*): But it's awful!

WELLWYN: It is, my dear.

ANN: In seven days. To say nothing of the stealing.

WELLWYN (*vexed*): I blame myself—very much. Ought to have kept it locked up.

ANN: You ought to keep *him* locked up!

[*There is heard a mild but authoritative knock.*]

WELLWYN: Here's the Vicar!

ANN: What are you going to do

about the rum?

WELLWYN (*opening the door to* CANON BERTLEY): Come in, Vicar! Happy New Year!

BERTLEY: Same to you! Ah! Ann! I've got into touch with her young husband — he's coming round.

ANN (*still a little out of her plate*): Thank Go——Moses!

BERTLEY (*faintly surprised*): From what I hear he's not really a bad youth. Afraid he bets on horses. The great thing, Wellwyn, with those poor fellows is to put your finger on the weak spot.

ANN (*to herself — gloomily*): That's not difficult. What would you do, Canon Bertley, with a man who's been drinking father's rum?

BERTLEY: Remove the temptation, of course.

WELLWYN: He's done that.

BERTLEY: Ah! Then—(WELLWYN *and* ANN *hang on his words*) then I should—er——

ANN (*abruptly*): Remove *him*.

BERTLEY: Before I say that, Ann, I must certainly see the individual.

WELLWYN (*pointing to the window*): There he is!

[*In the failing light* TIMSON's *face is indeed to be seen pressed against the window pane.*]

ANN: Daddy, I do wish you'd have thick glass put in. It's so disgusting to be spied at! (WELLWYN *going quickly to the door,*

has opened it.) What do you want?

[TIMSON *enters with dignity. He is fuddled.*]

TIMSON (*slowly*): Arskin' yer pardon—thought it me duty to come back—found thish yer little brishel on me. (*He produces the little paint brush.*)

ANN (*in a deadly voice*): Nothing else?

[TIMSON *accords her a glassy stare.*]

WELLWYN (*taking the brush hastily*): That'll do, Timson, thanks!

TIMSON: As I am 'ere, can I do anything for yer?

ANN: Yes, you can sweep out that little room. (*She points to the model's room.*) There's a broom in there.

TIMSON (*disagreeably surprised*): Certainly; never make bones about a little extra—never 'ave in all me life. Do it at onsh, I will. (*He moves across to the model's room at that peculiar broad gait so perfectly adjusted to his habits.*) You quite understand me—couldn't bear to 'ave anything on me that wasn't mine. (*He passes out.*)

ANN: Old fraud!

WELLWYN: "In" and "on." Mark my words, he'll restore the—bottles.

BERTLEY: But, my dear Wellwyn, that *is* stealing

185

WELLWYN: We all have our discrepancies, Vicar.

ANN: Daddy! Discrepancies!

WELLWYN: Well, Ann, my theory is that as regards solids Timson's an Individualist, but as regards liquids he's a Socialist . . . or *vice versâ*, according to taste.

BERTLEY: No, no, we mustn't joke about it. (*Gravely.*) I do think he should be spoken to.

WELLWYN: Yes, but not by me.

BERTLEY: Surely you're the proper person.

WELLWYN (*shaking his head*): It was my rum, Vicar. Looks so personal.

[*There sound a number of little tat-tat knocks.*]

WELLWYN: Isn't that the Professor's knock?

[*While* ANN *sits down to make tea, he goes to the door and opens it. There, dressed in an ulster, stands a thin, clean-shaved man, with a little hollow sucked into either cheek, who, taking off a grey squash hat, discloses a majestically bald forehead, which completely dominates all that comes below it.*]

WELLWYN: Come in, Professor! So awfully good of you! You know Canon Bertley, I think?

CALWAY: Ah! How d'you do?

WELLWYN: Your opinion will be invaluable, Professor.

ANN: Tea, Professor Calway?

[*They have assembled round the tea table.*]

CALWAY: Thank you; no tea; milk.

WELLWYN: Rum?

[*He pours rum into* CALWAY'S *milk.*]

CALWAY: A little — thanks! (*Turning to* ANN.) You were going to show me some one you're trying to rescue, or something, I think.

ANN: Oh! Yes. He'll be here directly—simply perfect rotter.

CALWAY (*smiling*): Really! Ah! I think you said he was a congenital?

WELLWYN (*with great interest*): What!

ANN (*low*): Daddy! (*To* CALWAY.) Yes; I think that's what you call him.

CALWAY: Not old?

ANN: No; and quite healthy—a vagabond.

CALWAY (*sipping*): I see! Yes. Is it, do you think chronic unemployment with a vagrant tendency? Or would it be nearer the mark to say: Vagrancy——

WELLWYN: Pure! Oh! pure! Professor. Awfully human.

CALWAY (*with a smile of knowledge*): Quite! And—er——

ANN (*breaking in*): Before he comes, there's another——

BERTLEY (*blandly*): Yes, when you came in, we were discussing what should be done with a

186

man who drinks rum—(CALWAY *pauses in the act of drinking*) that doesn't belong to him.

CALWAY: Really! Dipsomaniac?

BERTLEY: Well—perhaps you could tell us—drink certainly changing thine to mine. The Professor could see him, Wellwyn?

ANN (*rising*): Yes, do come and look at him, Professor Calway. He's in there.

[*She points towards the model's room.* CALWAY *smiles deprecatingly.*]

ANN: No, *really;* we needn't open the door. You can see him through the glass. He's more than half——

CALWAY: Well, I hardly——

ANN: Oh! Do! Come on, Professor Calway! We *must* know what to do with him. (CALWAY *rises.*) You can stand on a chair. It's all science.

[*She draws* CALWAY *to the model's room, which is lighted by a glass panel in the top of the high door.* CANON BERTLEY *also rises and stands watching.* WELLWYN *hovers, torn between respect for science and dislike of espionage.*]

ANN (*drawing up a chair*): Come on!

CALWAY: Do you seriously wish me to?

ANN: Rather! It's quite safe; he can't see you.

CALWAY: But he might come out.

[ANN *puts her back against the door.* CALWAY *mounts the chair dubiously, and raises his head cautiously, bending it more and more downwards.*]

ANN: Well?

CALWAY: He appears to be—sitting on the floor.

WELLWYN: Yes, that's all right!

[BERTLEY *covers his lips.*]

CALWAY (*to* ANN—*descending*): By the look of his face, as far as one can see it, I should say there was a leaning towards mania. I know the treatment.

[*There come three loud knocks on the door.* WELLWYN *and* ANN *exchange a glance of consternation.*]

ANN: Who's that?

WELLWYN: It sounds like Sir Thomas.

CALWAY: Sir Thomas Hoxton?

WELLWYN (*nodding*): Awfully sorry, Professor. You see, we——

CALWAY: Not at all. Only, I must decline to be involved in argument with him, please.

BERTLEY: He has experience. We might get his opinion, don't you think?

CALWAY: On a point of reform? A J.P.!

BERTLEY (*deprecating*): My dear Sir—we needn't take it.

[*The three knocks resound with extraordinary fury.*]

ANN: You'd better open the

187

door, Daddy.

[WELLWYN *opens the door.* SIR THOMAS HOXTON *is disclosed in a fur overcoat and top hat. His square, well-coloured face is remarkable for a massive jaw, dominating all that comes above it. His voice is resolute.*]

HOXTON: Afraid I didn't make myself heard.

WELLWYN: So good of you to come, Sir Thomas. Canon Bertley! (*They greet.*) Professor Calway you know, I think.

HOXTON (*ominously*): I do.

[*They almost greet. An awkward pause.*]

ANN (*blurting it out*): That old cabman I told you of's been drinking father's rum.

BERTLEY: We were just discussing what's to be done with him, Sir Thomas. One wants to do the very best, of course. The question of reform is always delicate.

CALWAY: I beg your pardon. There *is* no question here.

HOXTON (*abruptly*): Oh! Is he in the house?

ANN: In there.

HOXTON: Works for you, eh?

WELLWYN: Er—yes.

HOXTON: Let's have a look at him!

[*An embarrassed pause.*]

BERTLEY: Well—the fact is, Sir Thomas——

CALWAY: When last under observation——

ANN: He was sitting on the floor.

WELLWYN: I don't want the old fellow to feel he's being made a show of. Disgusting to be spied at, Ann.

ANN: You can't, Daddy! He's drunk.

HOXTON: Never mind, Miss Wellwyn. Hundreds of these fellows before me in my time. (*At* CALWAY.) The only thing is a sharp lesson!

CALWAY: I disagree. I've seen the man; what he requires is steady control, and the Dobbins treatment.

[WELLWYN *approaches them with fearful interest.*]

HOXTON: Not a bit of it! He wants one for his knob! Brace 'em up! It's the only thing.

BERTLEY: Personally, I think that if he were spoken to seriously——

CALWAY: I cannot walk arm in arm with a crab!

HOXTON (*approaching* CALWAY): I beg your pardon?

CALWAY (*moving back a little*): You're moving backwards, Sir Thomas. I've told you before, convinced reactionaryism, in these days——

[*There comes a single knock on the street door.*]

BERTLEY (*looking at his watch*): D'you know, I'm rather afraid this may be our young husband, Wellwyn. I told him half-past four.

WELLWYN: Oh! Ah! Yes. (*Going towards the two reformers.*) Shall we go into the house, Professor, and settle the question quietly while the Vicar sees a young man?

CALWAY (*pale with uncompleted statement, and gravitating insensibly in the direction indicated*): The merest sense of continuity—a simple instinct for order——

HOXTON (*following*): The only way to get order, sir, is to bring the disorderly up with a round turn. (CALWAY *turns to him in the doorway.*) You people without practical experience——

CALWAY: If you'll listen to me a minute.

HOXTON: I can show you in a mo——

[*They vanish through the door.*]

WELLWYN: I was afraid of it.

BERTLEY: The two points of view. Pleasant to see such keenness. I may want you, Wellwyn. And Ann perhaps had better not be present.

WELLWYN (*relieved*): Quite so! My dear!

[ANN *goes reluctantly.* WELLWYN *opens the street door. The lamp outside has just been lighted, and, by its gleam, is seen the figure of* RORY MEGAN, *thin, pale, youthful.* ANN *turning at the door into the house gives him a long, inquisitive look, then goes.*]

WELLWYN: Is that Megan?

MEGAN: Yus.

WELLWYN: Come in.

[MEGAN *comes in. There follows an awkward silence, during which* WELLWYN *turns up the light, then goes to the tea table and pours out a glass of tea and rum.*]

BERTLEY (*kindly*): Now, my boy, how is it that you and your wife are living apart like this?

MEGAN: I dunno.

BERTLEY: Well, if *you* don't, none of us are very likely to, are we?

MEGAN: That's what I thought, as I was comin' along.

WELLWYN (*twinkling*): Have some tea, Megan? (*Handing him the glass.*) What d'you think of her picture? 'Tisn't quite finished.

MEGAN (*after scrutiny*): I seen her look like it—once.

WELLWYN: Good! When was that?

MEGAN (*stoically*): When she 'ad the measles. (*He drinks.*)

WELLWYN (*ruminating*): I see —yes. I quite see—feverish!

BERTLEY: My dear Wellwyn, let me——(*To* MEGAN.) Now, I hope you're willing to come together again, and to maintain her?

MEGAN: If she'll maintain me.

BERTLEY: Oh! but—— I see, you mean you're in the same line of business?

189

MEGAN: Yus.

BERTLEY: And lean on each other. Quite so!

MEGAN: I leans on 'er mostly—with 'er looks.

BERTLEY: Indeed! Very interesting—that!

MEGAN: Yus. Sometimes she'll take 'arf a crown off of a toff. (*He looks at* WELLWYN.)

WELLWYN (*twinkling*): I apologise to you, Megan.

MEGAN (*with a faint smile*): I could do with a bit more of it.

BERTLEY (*dubiously*): Yes! Yes! Now, my boy, I've heard you bet on horses.

MEGAN: No, I don't.

BERTLEY: Play cards, then? Come! Don't be afraid to acknowledge it.

MEGAN: When I'm 'ard up—yus.

BERTLEY: But don't you know that's ruination?

MEGAN: Depends. Sometimes I wins a lot.

BERTLEY: You know that's not at all what I mean. Come, promise me to give it up.

MEGAN: I dunno abaht that.

BERTLEY: Now, there's a good fellow. Make a big effort and throw the habit off!

MEGAN: Comes over me—same as it might over you.

BERTLEY: Over me! How do you mean, my boy?

MEGAN (*with a look up*): To tork!

[WELLWYN, *turning to the picture, makes a funny little noise.*]

BERTLEY (*maintaining his good humour*): A hit! But you forget, you know, to talk's my business. It's not yours to gamble.

MEGAN: You try sellin' flowers. If that ain't a—gamble——

BERTLEY: I'm afraid we're wandering a little from the point. Husband and wife should be together. You were brought up to that. Your father and mother——

MEGAN: Never was.

WELLWYN (*turning from the picture*): The question is, Megan: Will you take your wife home? She's a good little soul.

MEGAN: She never let me know it.

[*There is a feeble knock on the door.*]

WELLWYN: Well, now come. Here she is!

[*He points to the door, and stands regarding* MEGAN *with his friendly smile.*]

MEGAN (*with a gleam of responsiveness*): I might, perhaps, to please *you,* sir.

BERTLEY (*appropriating the gesture*): Capital, I thought we should get on in time.

MEGAN: Yus.

[WELLWYN *opens the door.* MRS. MEGAN *and* FERRAND *are revealed. They are about to enter, but catching sight of* MEGAN, *hesitate.*]

BERTLEY: Come in! Come in!

[MRS. MEGAN *enters stolidly.* FER-
RAND, *following, stands apart
with an air of extreme detachment.* MEGAN, *after a quick
glance at them both, remains
unmoved. No one has no-
ticed that the door of the
model's, room has been
opened, and that the un-
steady figure of old* TIMSON
is standing there.]

BERTLEY (*a little awkward in
the presence of* FERRAND—*to the*
MEGANS): This begins a new
chapter. We won't improve the
occasion. No need.

[MEGAN, *turning towards his wife,
makes her a gesture as if to
say:* "Here! let's get out of
this!"]

BERTLEY: Yes, yes, you'll like to
get home at once—I know. (*He
holds up his hand mechanically.*)

TIMSON: I forbids the banns.

BERTLEY (*startled*): Gracious!

TIMSON (*extremely unsteady*):
Just cause and impejiment. There
'e stands. (*He points to* FER-
RAND.) The crimson foreigner!
The mockin' jay!

WELLWYN: Timson!

TIMSON: You're a gen'leman—
I'm aweer o' that—but I must
speak the truth—(*he waves his
hand*) an' shame the devil!

BERTLEY: Is this the rum——?

TIMSON (*struck by the word*):
I'm a teetotaler.

WELLWYN: Timson, Timson!

TIMSON: Seein' as there's ladies
present, I won't be conspicuous.
(*Moving away, and making for
the door, he strikes against the
dais, and mounts upon it.*) But
what I do say, is: He's no better
than 'er and she's worse.

BERTLEY: This is distressing.

FERRAND (*calmly*): On my honour, Monsieur!

[TIMSON *growls.*]

WELLWYN: Now, now, Timson!

TIMSON: That's all right. You're
a gen'leman, an' I'm a gen'leman,
but he ain't an' she ain't.

WELLWYN: We shall not believe
you.

BERTLEY: No, no; we shall not
believe you.

TIMSON (*heavily*): Very well,
you doubts my word. Will it
make any difference, Guv'nor, if
I speaks the truth?

BERTLEY: No, certainly not—
that is—of course, it will.

TIMSON: Well, then, I see 'em
plainer than I see (*pointing at*
BERTLEY) the two of you.

WELLWYN: Be quiet, Timson!

BERTLEY: Not even her husband
believes you.

MEGAN (*suddenly*): Don't I!

WELLWYN: Come, Megan, you
can see the old fellow's in Paradise.

BERTLEY: Do you credit such a
—such an object?

[*He points at* TIMSON, *who seems*

191

falling asleep.]

MEGAN: Naow!

[*Unseen by anybody,* ANN *has returned.*]

BERTLEY: Well, then, my boy?

MEGAN: I seen 'em meself.

BERTLEY: Gracious! But just now you were willing——

MEGAN (*sardonically*): There wasn't nothing against me honour, then. Now you've took it away between you, comin' aht with it like this. I don't want no more of 'er, and I'll want a good deal more of 'im; as 'e'll soon find.

[*He jerks his chin at* FERRAND, *turns slowly on his heel, and goes out into the street. There follows a profound silence.*]

ANN: What did I say, Daddy? Utter! All three.

[*Suddenly alive to her presence, they all turn.*]

TIMSON (*waking up and looking round him*): Well, p'raps I'd better go.

[*Assisted by* WELLWYN *he lurches gingerly off the dais towards the door, which* WELLWYN *holds open for him.*]

TIMSON (*mechanically*): Where to, sir?

[*Receiving no answer he passes out, touching his hat; and the door is closed.*]

WELLWYN: Ann!

[ANN *goes back whence she came.*

BERTLEY, *steadily regarding*

MRS. MEGAN, *who has put her arm up in front of her face, beckons to* FERRAND, *and the young man comes gravely forward.*]

BERTLEY: Young people, this is very dreadful. (MRS. MEGAN *lowers her arm a little, and looks at him over it.*) Very sad!

MRS. MEGAN (*dropping her arm*): Megan's no better than what I am.

BERTLEY: Come, come! Here's your home broken up! (MRS. MEGAN *smiles. Shaking his head gravely.*) Surely — surely — you mustn't smile. (MRS. MEGAN *becomes tragic.*) That's better. Now, what is to be done?

FERRAND: Believe me, Monsieur, I greatly regret.

BERTLEY: I'm glad to hear it.

FERRAND: If I had foreseen this disaster.

BERTLEY: Is that your only reason for regret?

FERRAND (*with a little bow*): Any reason that you wish, Monsieur. I will do my possible.

MRS. MEGAN: I could get an unfurnished room if (*she slides her eyes round at* WELLWYN) I 'ad the money to furnish it.

BERTLEY: But suppose I can induce your husband to forgive you, and take you back?

MRS. MEGAN (*shaking her head*): 'E'd 'it me.

BERTLEY: I said to forgive.

MRS. MEGAN: That wouldn't make no difference. (*With a flash at* BERTLEY.) An' I ain't forgiven him!

BERTLEY: That is sinful.

MRS. MEGAN: *I'm* a Catholic.

BERTLEY: My good child, what difference does that make?

FERRAND: Monsieur, if I might interpret for her.

[BERTLEY *silences him with a gesture.*]

MRS. MEGAN (*sliding her eyes towards* WELLWYN): If I 'ad the money to buy some fresh stock.

BERTLEY: Yes; yes; never mind the money. What I want to find in you both is repentance.

MRS. MEGAN (*with a flash up at him*): I can't get me livin' off of repentin'.

BERTLEY: Now, now! Never say what you know to be wrong.

FERRAND: Monsieur, her soul is very simple.

BERTLEY (*severely*): I do not know, sir, that we shall get any great assistance from your views. In fact, one thing is clear to me, she must discontinue your acquaintanceship at once.

FERRAND: Certainly, Monsieur. We have no serious intentions.

BERTLEY: All the more shame to you, then!

FERRAND: Monsieur, I see perfectly your point of view. It is very natural. (*He bows and is silent.*)

MRS. MEGAN: I don't want 'im hurt 'cos o' me. Megan'll get his mates to belt him—bein' foreign like he is.

BERTLEY: Yes, never mind that. It's *you* I'm thinking of.

MRS. MEGAN: I'd sooner they'd hit *me*.

WELLWYN (*suddenly*): Well said, my child!

MRS. MEGAN: 'Twasn't his fault.

FERRAND (*without irony—to* WELLWYN): I cannot accept that Monsieur. The blame—it is all mine.

ANN (*entering suddenly from the house*): Daddy, they're having an awful——!

[*The voices of* PROFESSOR CALWAY *and* SIR THOMAS HOXTON *are distinctly heard.*]

CALWAY: The question is a much wider one, Sir Thomas.

HOXTON: As wide as you like, you'll never——

[WELLWYN *pushes* ANN *back into the house and closes the door behind her. The voices are still faintly heard arguing on the threshold.*]

BERTLEY: Let me go in here a minute, Wellwyn. I must finish speaking to her. (*He motions* MRS. MEGAN *towards the model's room.*) We can't leave the matter thus.

FERRAND (*suavely*): Do you desire my company, Monsieur?

[BERTLEY, *with a prohibitive ges-*

*ture of his hand, shepherds
the reluctant* MRS. MEGAN *into
the model's room.*]

WELLWYN (*sorrowfully*): You
shouldn't have done this, Ferrand.
It wasn't the square thing.

FERRAND (*with dignity*): Monsieur, I feel that I am in the wrong.
It was stronger than me.

[*As he speaks,* SIR THOMAS HOXTON
and PROFESSOR CALWAY *enter
from the house. In the dim
light, and the full cry of argument, they do not notice the
figures at the fire.* SIR THOMAS
HOXTON *leads towards the
street door.*]

HOXTON: No, sir, I repeat, if the
country once commits itself to
your views of reform, it's as good
as doomed.

CALWAY: I seem to have heard
that before, Sir Thomas. And let
me say at once that your hitty-
missy cart-load of bricks *régime*
——

HOXTON: Is a deuced sight better, sir, than your grand-motherly
methods. What the old fellow
wants is a shock! With all this
socialistic molly-coddling, you're
losing sight of the individual.

CALWAY (*swiftly*): You, sir,
with your "devil take the hindmost," have never even seen him.

[SIR THOMAS HOXTON, *throwing
back a gesture of disgust,
steps out into the night, and
falls heavily.* PROFESSOR CAL-

WAY, *hastening to his rescue,
falls more heavily still.* TIMSON, *momentarily roused from
slumber on the doorstep, sits
up.*]

HOXTON (*struggling to his
knees*): Damnation!

CALWAY (*sitting*): How simultaneous!

[WELLWYN *and* FERRAND *approach
hastily.*]

FERRAND (*pointing to* TIMSON):
Monsieur, it was true, it seems.
They had lost sight of the individual.

[*A Policeman has appeared under
the street lamp. He picks up*
HOXTON's *hat.*]

CONSTABLE: Anything wrong,
sir?

HOXTON (*recovering his feet*):
Wrong? Great Scott! Constable!
Why do you let things lie about in
the street like this? Look here,
Wellwyn!

[*They all scrutinize* TIMSON.]

WELLWYN: It's only the old fellow whose reform you were discussing.

HOXTON: How did he come
here?

CONSTABLE: Drunk, sir. (*Ascertaining* TIMSON *to be in the street.*)
Just off the premises, by good
luck. Come along, father.

TIMSON (*assisted to his feet—
drowsily*): Cert'nly, by no means;
take my arm.

[*They move from the doorway.*

HOXTON *and* CALWAY *re-enter, and go towards the fire.*]

ANN (*entering from the house*): What's happened?

CALWAY: Might we have a brush?

HOXTON (*testily*): Let it dry!

[*He moves to the fire and stands before it.* PROFESSOR CALWAY *following stands a little behind him.* ANN *returning begins to brush the* PROFESSOR'S *sleeve.*]

WELLWYN (*turning from the door, where he has stood looking after the receding* TIMSON): Poor old Timson!

FERRAND (*softly*): Must be philosopher, Monsieur! They will but run him in a little.

[*From the model's room* MRS. MEGAN *has come out, shepherded by* CANON BERTLEY.]

BERTLEY: Let's see, your Christian name is——.

MRS. MEGAN: Guinevere.

BERTLEY: Oh! Ah! Ah! Ann, take Gui—— take our little friend into the study a minute: I am going to put her into service. We shall make a new woman of her, yet.

ANN (*handing* CANON BERTLEY *the brush, and turning to* MRS. MEGAN): Come on!

[*She leads into the house, and* MRS. MEGAN *follows stolidly.*]

BERTLEY (*brushing* CALWAY'S *back*): Have you fallen?

CALWAY: Yes.

BERTLEY: Dear me! How was that?

HOXTON: That old ruffian drunk on the doorstep. Hope they'll give him a sharp dose! These ragtags!

[*He looks round, and his angry eyes light by chance on* FERRAND.]

FERRAND (*with his eyes on* HOXTON—*softly*): Monsieur, something tells me it is time I took the road again.

WELLWYN (*fumbling out a sovereign*): Take this, then!

FERRAND (*refusing the coin*): Non, Monsieur. To abuse 'ospitality is not in my character.

BERTLEY: We must not despair of anyone.

HOXTON: Who talked of despairing? Treat him, as I say, and you'll see!

CALWAY: The interest of the State——

HOXTON: The interest of the individual citizen, sir——

BERTLEY: Come! A little of both, a little of both!

[*They resume their brushing.*]

FERRAND: You are now debarrassed of us three, Monsieur. I leave you instead—these sirs. (*He points.*) Au revoir, Monsieur! (*Motioning towards the fire.*) 'Appy New Year!

[*He slips quietly out.* WELLWYN, *turning, contemplates the three reformers. They are all now brushing away, scratching each other's backs, and gravely hissing. As he approaches them, they speak with a certain unanimity.*]

HOXTON: My theory——!

CALWAY: My theory——!

BERTLEY: My theory——!

[*They stop surprised.* WELLWYN *makes a gesture of discomfort, as they speak again with still more unanimity.*]

HOXTON: My——!

CALWAY: My——!

BERTLEY: My——!

[*They stop in greater surprise. The stage is blotted dark.*]

CURTAIN

ACT III

It is the first of April—a white spring day of gleams and driving showers. The street door of WELLWYN'S *studio stands wide open, and, past it, in the street, the wind is whirling bits of straw and paper bags. Through the door can be seen the butt end of a stationary furniture van with its flap let down. To this van three humble-men in shirt sleeves and aprons are carrying out the contents of the studio. The hissing samovar, the tea-pot, the sugar, and the nearly empty decanter of rum stand on the low round table in the fast-being-gutted room.* WELLWYN *in his ulster and soft hat, is squatting on the little stool in front of the blazing fire, staring into it, and smoking a hand-made cigarette. He has a moulting air. Behind him the humble-men pass, embracing busts and other articles of vertu.*

CHIEF H'MAN (*stopping, and standing in the attitude of expectation*): We've about pinched this little lot, sir. Shall we take the—reservoir?

[*He indicates the samovar.*]

WELLWYN: Ah! (*Abstractedly feeling in his pockets, and finding coins.*) Thanks — thanks — heavy work, I'm afraid.

H'MAN (*receiving the coins—a little surprised and a good deal pleased*): Thank'ee, sir. Much obliged, I'm sure. We'll 'ave to come back for this. (*He gives the dais a vigorous push with his foot.*) Not a fixture, as I understand. Perhaps you'd like us to leave these 'ere for a bit. (*He indicates the tea things.*)

WELLWYN: Ah! do.

[*The humble-men go out. There is the sound of horses being started, and the butt end of the van disappears.* WELLWYN *stays on his stool, smoking and brooding over the fire. The open doorway is dark-*

ened by a figure. CANON
BERTLEY *is standing there.*]

BERTLEY: Wellwyn! (WELLWYN
turns and rises.) It's ages since
I saw you. No idea you were
moving. This is very dreadful.

WELLWYN: Yes, Ann found this
—too exposed. That tall house in
Flight Street—we're going there.
Seventh floor.

BERTLEY: Lift?

[WELLWYN *shakes his head.*]

BERTLEY: Dear me! No lift?
Fine view, no doubt. (WELLWYN
nods.) You'll be greatly missed.

WELLWYN: So Ann thinks.
Vicar, what's become of that little
flower-seller I was painting at
Christmas? You took her into
service.

BERTLEY: Not we—exactly!
Some dear friends of ours. Painful subject!

WELLWYN: Oh!

BERTLEY: Yes. She got the foot-
man into trouble.

WELLWYN: Did she, now?

BERTLEY: Disappointing. I consulted with Calway, and he advised me to try a certain institution. We got her safely in—excellent place; but, d'you know, she
broke out three weeks ago. And
since—I've heard—(*he holds his
hands up*) hopeless, I'm afraid—
quite!

WELLWYN: I *thought* I saw her
last night. You can't tell me her
address, I suppose?

BERTLEY (*shaking his head*):
The husband too has quite passed
out of my ken. He betted on
horses, you remember. I'm sometimes tempted to believe there's
nothing for some of these poor
folk but to pray for death.

[ANN *has entered from the house.
Her hair hangs from under a
knitted cap. She wears a
white wool jersey, and a loose
silk scarf.*]

BERTLEY: Ah! Ann. I was telling your father of that poor little
Mrs. Megan.

ANN: Is she dead?

BERTLEY: Worse I fear. By the
way—what became of her accom-
plice?

ANN: We haven't seen him since.
(*She looks searchingly at* WELL-
WYN.) At least—have *you*—
Daddy?

WELLWYN (*rather hurt*): No,
my dear; I have not.

BERTLEY: And the—old gentleman who drank the rum?

ANN: He got fourteen days. It
was the fifth time.

BERTLEY: Dear me!

ANN: When he came out he got
more drunk than ever. Rather a
score for Professor Calway, wasn't
it?

BERTLEY: I remember. He and
Sir Thomas took a kindly interest
in the old fellow.

ANN: Yes, they fell over him.
The Professor got him into an In-

197

stitution.

BERTLEY: Indeed!

ANN: He was perfectly sober all the time he was there.

WELLWYN: My dear, they only allow them milk.

ANN: Well, anyway, he was reformed.

WELLWYN: Ye—yes!

ANN (*terribly*): Daddy! You've been seeing him!

WELLWYN (*with dignity*): My dear, I have not.

ANN: How do you know, then?

WELLWYN: Came across Sir Thomas on the Embankment yesterday; told me old Timson had been had up again for sitting down in front of a brewer's dray.

ANN: Why?

WELLWYN: Well, you see, as soon as he came out of the what d'you call 'em, he got drunk for a week, and it left him in low spirits.

BERTLEY: Do you mean he deliberately sat down, with the intention—of—er?

WELLWYN: Said he was tired of life, but they didn't believe him.

ANN: Rather a score for Sir Thomas! I suppose he'd told the Professor? What did *he* say?

WELLWYN: Well, the Professor said (*with a quick glance at* BERTLEY) he felt there was nothing for some of these poor devils but a lethal chamber.

BERTLEY (*shocked*): Did he really!

[*He has not yet caught* WELLWYN'S *glance.*]

WELLWYN: And Sir Thomas agreed. Historic occasion. And you, Vicar—H'm!

[BERTLEY *winces.*]

ANN (*to herself*): Well, there isn't.

BERTLEY: And yet! Some good in the old fellow, no doubt, if one could put one's finger on it. (*Preparing to go.*) You'll let us know, then, when you're settled. What was the address? (WELLWYN *takes out and hands him a card.*) Ah! yes. Good-bye, Ann. Goodbye, Wellwyn. (*The wind blows his hat along the street.*) What a wind! (*He goes, pursuing.*)

ANN (*who has eyed the card askance*): Daddy, have you told those other two where we're going?

WELLWYN: Which other two, my dear?

ANN: The Professor and Sir Thomas.

WELLWYN: Well, Ann, naturally I——

ANN (*jumping on to the dais with disgust*): Oh, dear! When I'm trying to get you away from all this atmosphere. I don't so much mind the Vicar knowing, because he's got a weak heart—— (*She jumps off again.*)

WELLWYN (*to himself*): Seventh floor! I felt there was something.

ANN (*preparing to go*): I'm going round now. But you must stay here till the van comes back. And don't forget you tipped the men after the first load.

WELLWYN: Oh! yes, yes. (*Uneasily.*) Good sorts they look, those fellows!

ANN (*scrutinising him*): What have you done?

WELLWYN: Nothing, my dear, really——!

ANN: What?

WELLWYN: I—I rather think I may have tipped them twice.

ANN (*drily*): Daddy! If it *is* the first of April, it's not necessary to make a fool of *oneself*. That's the last time you ever do these ridiculous things. (WELLWYN *eyes her askance.*) I'm going to see that you spend your money on yourself. You needn't look at me like that! I *mean* to. As soon as I've got you away from here, and all—these——

WELLWYN: Don't rub it in, Ann!

ANN (*giving him a sudden hug —then going to the door—with a sort of triumph*): Deeds, not words, Daddy!

[*She goes out, and the wind catching her scarf blows it out beneath her firm young chin.* WELLWYN *returning to the fire, stands brooding, and gazing at his extinct cigarette.*]

WELLWYN (*to himself*): Bad lot —low type! No method! No

theory!

[*In the open doorway appear* FERRAND *and* MRS. MEGAN. *They stand, unseen, looking at him.* FERRAND *is more ragged, if possible, than on Christmas Eve. His chin and cheeks are clothed in a reddish golden beard.* MRS. MEGAN'S *dress is not so woebegone, but her face is white, her eyes dark-circled. They whisper. She slips back into the shadow of the doorway.* WELLWYN *turns at the sound, and stares at* FERRAND *in amazement.*]

FERRAND (*advancing*): Enchanted to see you, Monsieur. (*He looks round the empty room.*) You are leaving?

WELLWYN (*nodding—then taking the young man's hand*): How goes it?

FERRAND (*displaying himself, simply*): As you see, Monsieur. I have done of my best. It still flies from me.

WELLWYN (*sadly—as if against his will*): Ferrand, it will always fly.

[*The young foreigner shivers suddenly from head to foot; then controls himself with a great effort.*]

FERRAND: Don't say that, Monsieur! It is too much the echo of my heart.

WELLWYN: Forgive me! I didn't

199

mean to pain you.

FERRAND (*drawing nearer the fire*): That old cabby, Monsieur, you remember—they tell me, he nearly succeeded to gain happiness the other day.

[WELLWYN *nods.*]

FERRAND: And those Sirs, so interested in him, with their theories? He has worn them out? (WELLWYN *nods.*) That goes without saying. And now they wish for him the lethal chamber.

WELLWYN (*startled*): How did you know that?

[*There is silence.*]

FERRAND (*staring into the fire*): Monsieur, while I was on the road this time I fell ill of a fever. It seemed to me in my illness that I saw the truth—how I was wasting in this world—I would never be good for any one—nor any one for me—all would go by, and I never of it—fame, and fortune, and peace, even the necessities of life, ever mocking me.

[*He draws closer to the fire, spreading his fingers to the flame. And while he is speaking, through the doorway* MRS. MEGAN *creeps in to listen.*]

FERRAND (*speaking on into the fire*): And I saw, Monsieur, so plain, that I should be vagabond all my days, and my days short, I dying in the end the death of a dog. I saw it all in my fever—

clear as that flame—there was nothing for us others, but the herb of death. (WELLWYN *takes his arm and presses it.*) And so, Monsieur, I *wished* to die. I told no one of my fever. I lay out on the ground—it was verree cold. But they would not let me die on the roads of their parishes—they took me to an Institution, Monsieur, I looked in their eyes while I lay there, and I saw more clear than the blue heaven that they thought it best that I should die, although they would not let me. Then Monsieur, naturally my spirit rose, and I said: "So much the worse for you. I will live a little more." One is made like that! Life is sweet, Monsieur.

WELLWYN: Yes, Ferrand; Life is sweet.

FERRAND: That little girl you had here, Monsieur—(WELLWYN *nods*) in her too there is something of wild-savage. She must have joy of life. I have seen her since I came back. She has embraced the life of joy. It is not quite the same thing. (*He lowers his voice.*) She is lost, Monsieur, as a stone that sinks in water. I can see, if she cannot. (*As* WELLWYN *makes a movement of distress.*) Oh! I am not to blame for that, Monsieur. It had well begun before I knew her.

WELLWYN: Yes, yes—I was afraid of it, at the time.

[MRS. MEGAN *turns silently, and slips away.*]

FERRAND: I do my best for her, Monsieur, but look at me! Besides, I am not good for her—it is not good for simple souls to be with those who see things clear. For the great part of mankind, to see anything—is fatal.

WELLWYN: Even for you, it seems.

FERRAND: No, Monsieur. To be so near to death has done me good; I shall not lack courage any more till the wind blows on my grave. Since I saw you, Monsieur, I have been in three Institutions. They are palaces. One may eat upon the floor—though it is true—for Kings—they eat too much of skilly there. One little thing they lack—those palaces. It is understanding of the 'uman heart. In them tame birds pluck wild birds naked.

WELLWYN: They mean well.

FERRAND: Ah! Monsieur, I am loafer, waster—what you like—for all that (*bitterly*) poverty is my only crime. If I were rich, should I not be simply veree original, 'ighly respected, with soul above commerce, travelling to see the world? And that young girl, would she not be "that charming ladee," "veree *chic*, you know!" And the old Tims—good old-fashioned gentleman — drinking his liquor well. *Eh! bien*—what

are we now? Dark beasts, despised by all. That is life, Monsieur. (*He stares into the fire.*)

WELLWYN: We're our own enemies, Ferrand. I can afford it—you can't. Quite true!

FERRAND (*earnestly*): Monsieur, do you know this? You are the sole being that can do us good—we hopeless ones.

WELLWYN (*shaking his head*): Not a bit of it; I'm hopeless too.

FERRAND (*eagerly*): Monsieur, it is just that. You *understand*. When we are with you we feel something—here—(*he touches his heart.*) If I had one prayer to make, it would be, Good God, give me to understand! Those sirs, with their theories, they can clean our skins and chain our 'abits—that soothes for them the æsthetic sense; it gives them too their good little importance. But our spirits they cannot touch, for they nevare understand. Without that, Monsieur, all is dry as a parched skin of orange.

WELLWYN: Don't be so bitter. Think of all the work they do!

FERRAND: Monsieur, of their industry I say nothing. They do a good work while they attend with their theories to the sick and the tame old, and the good unfortunate deserving. Above all to the little children. But, Monsieur, when all is done, there are always us hopeless ones. What can they

201

do with me, Monsieur, with that girl, or with that old man? Ah! Monsieur, we, too, 'ave our qualities, we others—it wants you courage to undertake a career like mine, or like that young girl's. We wild ones—we know a thousand times more of life than ever will those sirs. They waste their time trying to make rooks white. Be kind to us if you will, or let us alone like Mees Ann, but do not try to change our skins. Leave us to live, or leave us to die when we like in the free air. If you do not wish of us, you have but to shut your pockets and your doors—we shall die the faster.

WELLWYN (*with agitation*): But that, you know—we can't do—now can we?

FERRAND: If you cannot, how is it our fault? The harm we do to others—is it so much? If I am criminal, dangerous—shut me up! I would not pity myself—nevare. But we in whom something moves —like that flame, Monsieur, that *cannot* keep still—we others—we are not many—that must have motion in our lives, do not let them make us prisoners, with their theories, because we are not like them—it is life itself they would enclose! (*He draws up his tattered figure, then bending over the fire again*) I ask your pardon; I am talking. If I could smoke, Monsieur!

[WELLWYN *hands him a tobacco pouch; and he rolls a cigarette with his yellow-stained fingers.*]

FERRAND: The good God made me so that I would rather walk a whole month of nights, hungry, with the stars, than sit one single day making round business on an office stool! It is not to my advantage. I cannot help it that I am a vagabond. What would you have? It is stronger than me. (*He looks suddenly at* WELLWYN.) Monsieur, I say to you things I have never said.

WELLWYN (*quietly*): Go on, go on. (*There is silence.*)

FERRAND (*suddenly*): Monsieur! Are you really English? The English are so civilised.

WELLWYN: And am I not?

FERRAND: You treat me like a brother.

[WELLWYN *has turned towards the street door at a sound of feet, and the clamour of voices.*]

TIMSON (*from the street*): Take her in 'ere. I knows 'im.

[*Through the open doorway come a* POLICE CONSTABLE *and a* LOAFER, *bearing between them the limp white-faced form of* MRS. MEGAN, *hatless and with drowned hair, enveloped in the policeman's waterproof. Some curious persons bring up the rear, jostling in the doorway, among whom is* TIMSON *carrying in his hands the policeman's dripping waterproof leg pieces.*]

FERRAND (*starting forward*): Monsieur, it is that little girl!

WELLWYN: What's happened? Constable! What's happened!

[*The* CONSTABLE *and* LOAFER *have laid the body down on the dais; with* WELLWYN *and* FERRAND *they stand bending over her.*]

CONSTABLE: 'Tempted sooicide, sir; but she hadn't been in the water 'arf a minute when I got hold of her. (*He bends lower.*) Can't understand her collapsin' like this.

WELLWYN (*feeling her heart*): I don't feel anything.

FERRAND (*in a voice sharpened by emotion*): Let me try, Monsieur.

CONSTABLE (*touching his arm*): You keep off, my lad.

WELLWYN: No, constable—let him. He's her friend.

CONSTABLE (*releasing* FERRAND —*to the* LOAFER): Here you! Cut off for a doctor—sharp now! (*He pushes back the curious persons.*) Now then, stand away there, please—we can't have you round the body. Keep back—Clear out, now!

[*He slowly moves them back, and at last shepherds them through the door and shuts it*

on them, TIMSON *being last.*]

FERRAND: The rum!

[WELLWYN *fetches the decanter. With the little there is left* FERRAND *chafes the girl's hands and forehead, and pours some between her lips. But there is no response from the inert body.*]

FERRAND: Her soul is still away, Monsieur!

[WELLWYN, *seizing the decanter, pours into it tea and boiling water.*]

CONSTABLE: It's never drownin', sir—her head was hardly under; I was on to her like a knife.

FERRAND (*rubbing her feet*): She has not yet her philosophy, Monsieur; at the beginning they often try. If she is dead! (*In a voice of awed rapture.*) What fortune!

CONSTABLE (*with puzzled sadness*): True enough, sir—that! We'd just begun to know 'er. If she 'as been taken—her best friends couldn't wish 'er better.

WELLWYN (*applying the decanter to her lips*): Poor little thing! I'll try this hot tea.

FERRAND (*whispering*): La mort —le grand ami!

WELLWYN: Look! Look at her! She's coming round!

[*A faint tremor passes over* MRS. MEGAN's *body. He again applies the hot drink to her mouth. She stirs and gulps.*]

CONSTABLE (*with intense relief*): That's brave! Good lass! She'll pick up now, sir.

[*Then, seeing that* TIMSON *and the curious persons have again opened the door, he drives them out, and stands with his back against it.* MRS. MEGAN *comes to herself.*]

WELLWYN (*sitting on the dais and supporting her—as if to a child*): There you are, my dear. There, there—better now! That's right. Drink a little more of this tea.

[MRS. MEGAN *drinks from the decanter.*]

FERRAND (*rising*): Bring her to the fire, Monsieur.

[*They take her to the fire and seat her on the little stool. From the moment of her restored animation* FERRAND *has resumed his air of cynical detachment, and now stands apart with arms folded, watching.*]

WELLWYN: Feeling better, my child?

MRS. MEGAN: Yes.

WELLWYN: That's good. That's good. Now, how was it? Um?

MRS. MEGAN: I dunno. (*She shivers.*) I was standin' here just now when you was talkin', and when I heard 'im, it cam' over me to do it—like.

WELLWYN: Ah, yes I know.

MRS. MEGAN: I didn't seem no

good to meself nor any one. But when I got in the water, I didn't want to any more. It was cold in there.

WELLWYN: Have you been having such a bad time of it?

MRS. MEGAN: Yes. And listenin' to him upset me. (*She signs with her head at* FERRAND.) I feel better now I've been in the water. (*She smiles and shivers.*)

WELLWYN: There, there! Shivery? Like to walk up and down a little?

[*They begin walking together up and down.*]

WELLWYN: Beastly when your head goes under?

MRS. MEGAN: Yes. It frightened me. I thought I wouldn't come up again.

WELLWYN: I know—sort of world without end, wasn't it? What did you think of, um?

MRS. MEGAN: I wished I 'adn't jumped—an' I thought of my baby —that died—and—(*in a rather surprised voice*) and I thought of d-dancin'.

[*Her mouth quivers, her face puckers, she gives a choke and a little sob.*]

WELLWYN (*stopping and stroking her*): There, there—there!

[*For a moment her face is buried in his sleeve, then she recovers herself.*]

MRS. MEGAN: Then 'e got hold o' me, an' pulled me out.

WELLWYN: Ah! what a comfort —um?

MRS. MEGAN: Yes. The water got into me mouth. (*They walk again.*) I wouldn't have gone to do it but for *him.* (*She looks towards* FERRAND.) His talk made me feel all funny, as if people wanted me to.

WELLWYN: My dear child! Don't think such things! As if anyone would——!

MRS. MEGAN (*stolidly*): I thought they did. They used to look at me so sometimes, where I was before I ran away—I couldn't stop there, you know.

WELLWYN: Too cooped-up?

MRS. MEGAN: Yes. No life at all, it wasn't—not after sellin' flowers, I'd rather be doin' what I am.

WELLWYN: Ah! Well—it's all over, now! How d'you feel—eh? Better?

MRS. MEGAN: Yes. I feels all right now. (*She sits up again on the little stool before the fire.*)

WELLWYN: No shivers, and no aches; quite comfy?

MRS. MEGAN: Yes.

WELLWYN: That's a blessing. All well, now, Constable—thank you!

CONSTABLE (*who has remained discreetly apart at the door—cordially*): First rate, sir! That's capital! (*He approaches and scrutinises* MRS. MEGAN.) Right as rain, eh, my girl?

MRS. MEGAN (*shrinking a little*): Yes.

CONSTABLE: That's fine. Then I think perhaps, for 'er sake, sir, the sooner we move on and get her a change o' clothin', the better.

WELLWYN: Oh! don't bother about that—I'll send round for my daughter—we'll manage for her here.

CONSTABLE: Very kind of you, I'm sure, sir. But (*with embarrassment*) she seems all right. She'll get every attention at the station.

WELLWYN: But I assure you, we don't mind at all; we'll take the greatest care of her.

CONSTABLE (*still more embarrassed*): Well, sir, of course, I'm thinkin' of—— I'm afraid I can't depart from the usual course.

WELLWYN (*sharply*): What! But—oh! No! No! That'll be all right, Constable! That'll be all right! I assure you.

CONSTABLE (*with more decision*): I'll have to charge her, sir.

WELLWYN: Good God! You don't mean to say the poor little thing has got to be——

CONSTABLE (*consulting with him*): Well, sir, we can't get over the facts, can we? There it is! You know what sooicide amounts to—it's an awkward job.

WELLWYN (*calming himself with an effort*): But look here, Constable, as a reasonable man

205

—— This poor wretched little girl—*you* know what that life means better than anyone! Why! It's to her credit to try and jump out of it!

[*The* CONSTABLE *shakes his head.*]

WELLWYN: You said yourself her best friends couldn't wish her better! (*Dropping his voice still more.*) Everybody feels it! The Vicar was here a few minutes ago saying the very same thing—the Vicar, Constable! (*The* CONSTABLE *shakes his head.*) Ah! now, look here, I know something of her. Nothing can be done with her. We all admit it. Don't you see? Well, then hang it—you needn't go and make fools of us all by——

FERRAND: Monsieur, it is the first of April.

CONSTABLE (*with a sharp glance at him*): Can't neglect me duty, sir; that's impossible.

WELLWYN: Look here! She—slipped. She's been telling me. Come, Constable, there's a good fellow. May be the making of her, this.

CONSTABLE: I quite appreciate your good 'eart, sir, an' you make it very 'ard for me—but, come now! I put it to you as a gentleman, would you go back on yer duty if you was me?

[WELLWYN *raises his hat, and plunges his fingers through and through his hair.*]

206

WELLWYN: Well! God in heaven! Of all the d——d topsy-turvy——! Not a soul in the world wants her alive—and now she's to be prosecuted for trying to be where everyone wishes her.

CONSTABLE: Come, sir, come! Be a man!

[*Throughout all this* MRS. MEGAN *has sat stolidly before the fire, but as* FERRAND *suddenly steps forward she looks up at him.*]

FERRAND: Do not grieve, Monsieur! This will give her courage. There is nothing that gives more courage than to see the irony of things. (*He touches* MRS. MEGAN's *shoulder.*) Go, my child; it will do you good.

[MRS. MEGAN *rises, and looks at him dazedly.*]

CONSTABLE (*coming forward, and taking her by the hand*): That's my good lass. Come along! We won't hurt you.

MRS. MEGAN: I don't want to go. They'll stare at me.

CONSTABLE (*comforting*): Not they! I'll see to that.

WELLWYN (*very upset*): Take her in a cab, Constable, if you must—for God's sake! (*He pulls out a shilling.*) Here!

CONSTABLE (*taking the shilling*): I will, sir, certainly. Don't think I want to——

WELLWYN: No, no, I know. You're a good sort.

CONSTABLE (*comfortable*): Don't you take on, sir. It's her first try; they won't be hard on 'er. Like as not only bind 'er over in her own recogs not to do it again. Come, my dear.

MRS. MEGAN (*trying to free herself from the policeman's cloak*): I want to take this off. It looks so funny.

[*As she speaks the door is opened by* ANN; *behind whom is dimly seen the form of old* TIMSON, *still heading the curious persons.*]

ANN (*looking from one to the other in amaze*): What is it? What's happened? Daddy!

FERRAND (*out of the silence*): It is nothing, Ma'moiselle! She has failed to drown herself. They run her in a little.

WELLWYN: Lend her your jacket, my dear; she'll catch her death.

[ANN, *feeling* MRS. MEGAN'S *arm, strips off her jacket, and helps her into it without a word.*]

CONSTABLE (*donning his cloak*): Thank you, Miss—very good of you, I'm sure.

MRS. MEGAN (*mazed*): It's warm!

[*She gives them all a last half-smiling look, and passes with the* CONSTABLE *through the doorway.*]

FERRAND: That makes the third of us, Monsieur. We are not in luck. To wish us dead, it seems, is easier than to let us die.

[*He looks at* ANN, *who is standing with her eyes fixed on her father.* WELLWYN *has taken from his pocket a visiting card.*]

WELLWYN (*to* FERRAND): Here quick; take this, run after her! When they've done with her tell her to come to us.

FERRAND (*taking the card, and reading the address*): "No. 7, Haven House, Flight Street!" Rely on me, Monsieur—I will bring her myself to call on you. *Au revoir, mon bon Monsieur!*

[*He bends over* WELLWYN'S *hand; then, with a bow to* ANN *goes out; his tattered figure can be seen through the window, passing in the wind.* WELLWYN *turns back to the fire. The figure of* TIMSON *advances into the doorway, no longer holding in either hand a waterproof leg-piece.*]

TIMSON (*in a croaky voice*): Sir!

WELLWYN: What—you, Timson?

TIMSON: On me larst legs, sir. 'Ere! You can see 'em for yerself! Shawn't trouble yer long.

WELLWYN (*after a long and desperate stare*): Not now—Timson—not now! Take this! (*He takes out another card, and hands it to* TIMSON.) Some other time.

TIMSON (*taking the card*): Yer

new address! You *are* a gen'leman. (*He lurches slowly away.*)
[ANN *shuts the street door and sets
her back against it. The rum-
ble of the approaching van is
heard outside. It ceases.*]
ANN (*in a fateful voice*):
Daddy! (*They stare at each
other.*) Do you know what
you've done? Given your card to
those six rotters.
WELLWYN (*with a blank stare*):
Six?
ANN ' (*staring round the naked
room*): What was the good of
this?
WELLWYN (*following her eyes
—very gravely*): Ann! It is
stronger than me.
[*Without a word* ANN *opens the
door, and walks straight out.
With a heavy sigh,* WELLWYN
*sinks down on the little stool
before the fire. The three
humble-men come in.*]
CHIEF HUMBLE-MAN (*in an attitude of expectation*): This is the
larst of it, sir.
WELLWYN: Oh! Ah! yes!
[*He gives them money; then
something seems to strike
him, and he exhibits certain*

*signs of vexation. Suddenly
he recovers, looks from one
to the other, and then at the
tea things. A faint smile
comes on his face.*]
WELLWYN: You can finish the
decanter. (*He goes out in haste.*)
CHIEF HUMBLE-MAN (*clinking
the coins*): Third time of arskin'!
April fool! Not 'arf! Good old
pigeon!
SECOND HUMBLE-MAN: 'Uman
being, *I* call 'im.
CHIEF HUMBLE-MAN (*taking the
three glasses from the last pack-
ing-case, and pouring very equally
into them*): That's right. Tell you
wot, I'd never 'a touched this unless 'e'd told me to, I wouldn't—
not with 'im.
SECOND HUMBLE-MAN: Ditto to
that! This is a bit of orl right!
(*Raising his glass.*) Good luck!
THIRD HUMBLE-MAN: Same 'ere!
[*Simultaneously they place their
lips smartly against the liquor, and at once let fall their
faces and their glasses.*]
CHIEF HUMBLE-MAN (*with great
solemnity*): Crikey! Bill! *Tea!*
. . . 'E's *got* us!
[*The stage is blotted dark.*]

CURTAIN

EUGENE O'NEILL

1888 Born, October 16, at Broadway and Forty-third Street, New York City, son of the actor James O'Neill.

1894 Began seven years' experience in boarding schools.

1906 Matriculated at Princeton. Suspended for misconduct after a few months.

1909 Married Kathleen Jenkins. Marriage outside Catholic faith alienated his father. Went to Spanish Honduras as gold prospector. Invalided home eight months later with tropical fever.

1910 Shipped on a Norwegian windjammer for a sixty-five-day trip to Buenos Aires. When out of job and money, shipped on a British vessel to Durban, South Africa. Refused admission as undesirable alien, he shipped on another British vessel to Buenos Aires, where he became a beachcomber. Returning to New York, he lived at "Jimmy the Priest's," a waterfront dive, for seventy-five cents a week. Birth of son Eugene O'Neill, Jr.

1911 Shipped to Southampton as an able seaman. Upon return to New York, joined his father's touring "Monte Cristo" company in New Orleans and played a part. Took a job as reporter on his hometown paper, the New London, Connecticut, Telegraph. Contributed verse.

1912 Lungs affected. Spent six months in sanatorium. Divorced.

1913 Spent year reading and recuperat-
to ing. During this time he wrote
1914 several short plays.

1914 Student in Professor Baker's famous drama workshop at Harvard. His father financed publi-
to cation of his first collection of plays, THIRST AND OTHER ONE-ACT PLAYS, since recalled. Spent next
1915 year in Greenwich Village.

1916 Provincetown Players produced his first play, BOUND EAST FOR CARDIFF, at Wharf Theater, Provincetown.

1918 Married Agnes Boulton; had son Shane and daughter Oona. Lived next few years on New England coast, in Ridgefield, Connecticut, in Bermuda, in Touraine, in the Canaries, in Switzerland, and at Sea Island Beach, Georgia.

1920 BEYOND THE HORIZON won the Pulitzer Prize. THE EMPEROR JONES produced by Provincetown Players.

1921 ANNA CHRISTIE, produced by Arthur Hopkins in this year, was awarded Pulitzer Prize in 1922. O'Neill received gold medal of the National Institute of Arts and Letters for ANNA CHRISTIE and BEYOND THE HORIZON.

1922 THE HAIRY APE produced by Provincetown Players.

1924 ALL GOD'S CHILLUN GOT WINGS and DESIRE UNDER THE ELMS produced by Provincetown Players.

210

1926 THE GREAT GOD BROWN *produced, with O'Neill as co-producer. Honorary Litt. D. conferred upon him by Yale.*

1928 STRANGE INTERLUDE *won the third Pulitzer Prize for O'Neill. First of his successful productions in the Theatre Guild.*

1929 DYNAMO, *produced by Theatre Guild, a failure. Divorced. Married actress, Carlotta Monterey.*

1931 MOURNING BECOMES ELECTRA *produced by the Theatre Guild.*

1933 AH, WILDERNESS! *produced by the Theatre Guild.*

1936 *Received Nobel Prize.*

1936 *Lived at Sea Island Beach and Contra Costa County, California. Working on a cycle of nine plays.*
to *A play not belonging to the cycle,* THE ICEMAN COMETH, *produced by the Theatre Guild in October,*
1946 *1946.*

1947 MOON OF THE MISBEGOTTEN *produced in Columbus, Ohio.*

❧

W HATEVER *his absolute merit, Eugene O'Neill stands as the foremost American dramatist; besides, he is better known both in America and Europe than any other living dramatist except Shaw. Three times during the 1920's the Pulitzer award was given him—for* BEYOND THE HORIZON, ANNA CHRISTIE, *and* STRANGE INTERLUDE—*and in 1936 he received the Nobel Prize. The recent production, in 1946, of* THE ICEMAN COMETH, *his first play since 1934, absorbed the attention of the theatrical world.*

O'Neill began his work at a fortunate time. A vogue of rebellion against existent conventions had sought expression in the drama as in other forms of art. The "little theatre" movement, led by noncommercial groups like the Provincetown Players, was avid for native drama that would defy established dramatic forms and conventional interpretations of character. O'Neill delighted it with a succession of one-act plays beginning in 1916 with BOUND EAST FOR CARDIFF. *The best of this so-called "fo'c'sle group" were gathered together and published three years later under the title* THE MOON OF THE CARIBBEES AND SIX OTHER PLAYS OF THE SEA. *Experimental in form, these short plays introduced sailors, derelicts, and prostitutes, speaking the language of the sea and the gutter, gripped in violent action and meeting sudden death. And these characters struggled and died without reference to the logic of any conventional standard of ethics. Not only were they not punished or rewarded; they were not even judged. They dramatized, not the*

211

usual conflict between good and evil, but the struggle of elemental human beings to survive in a savage world.

But O'Neill was ambitious to succeed with the full-length play. After destroying five attempts, he completed BEYOND THE HORIZON *and* THE EMPEROR JONES, *both of which appeared in 1920. The latter gained him wide distinction. His subsequent work has been characterized by ceaseless experimentation with many forms and with many kinds of material. To Arthur Hobson Quinn he wrote: "I've tried to make myself a melting pot for all these methods, seeing some virtues for my ends in each of them, and thereby, if there is enough real fire in me, boil down to my own technique." But he has never found a single technique. As a result, his manifold forms forbid classification, and the merit and nature of the whole body of his plays cannot be adequately illustrated by any one of them. He is revealed only in his complete work.*

Yet through O'Neill's diverse forms and groups runs the unifying quality of his view of life. To George Jean Nathan he wrote: "The playwright of today must dig at the roots of the sickness of today as he feels it—the death of the old God and the failure of science and materialism to give any satisfactory new one. . . ." Upon that conviction is based the task O'Neill set himself: to reveal the frustration of the human heart in its search for happiness in the modern world. In some of his plays, the revelation is enough. But often he tries to solve the problem—to show the cause of frustration and to proclaim the remedy.

Man is frustrated, he believes, by the false morality imposed upon him by an outworn tradition and religion. It is a morality distinguished by ignorance and fear—by ignorance, because it rejects or is unaware of the teaching of science concerning man's own nature and his relation to the world he lives in; by fear, because it sees in nature a hostile power in conflict with the spirit of man, and holds that spiritual excellence, in this and in a future existence, is attainable only by renunciation of natural life. Because of this doctrine, life loses all positive value; and living becomes but a fear, and a long preparation for dying. Time and again O'Neill has created counterparts of the Mannons in MOURNING BECOMES ELECTRA—*people who "went to the white meetinghouse on Sabbaths and meditated on death. Life was a dying. Being born was starting to die."*

Sometimes the fear and ignorance by which man is frustrated exist

212

in his own mind; sometimes they exert their power through others, living or dead—through individuals, a social group, or a racial inheritance. Persistently O'Neill has sought in them a substitute for the classic fates—a source of tragedy acceptable to the modern mind, by which he can reveal in the form of art the defeat of the human spirit in his own age. Early in the twenties he wrote of THE HAIRY APE: "The subject here is . . . man and his struggle with his own fate. The struggle used to be with the gods, but is now with himself, his own past, his attempt 'to belong'." And a decade later he described MOURNING BECOMES ELECTRA as "a modern tragic interpretation of classic fate without benefit of gods—for it must . . . remain modern psychological play —fate springing out of the family—"

But though in some of his plays O'Neill records only man's tragic defeat, in others he shows that defeat is not inevitable. For man may free himself from the ignorance and fear that subdue him by achieving a new evaluation of life. To satisfy his intellect he must accept the teaching of science regarding his destiny and nature; he must recognize that traditional ethics is false; that a future life is uncertain; that the repression of emotion and instinct is harmful. Yet to be happy he must have a faith that satisfies not only his intellect but his spirit. He must believe in his heart in some positive value that makes life worth living.

That value O'Neill finds in the pagan sublimation of life itself. It is the conception of Nietzsche, who has been his most influential teacher. Let man establish himself in harmony with nature. Let him exult in the health and strength of his emotions and senses; exult not only in joy, but as well in sorrow—in the experience and spectacle of life as a fascinating, vivid, often terrible adventure of the human spirit, in which tragedy and death are but tense and exciting episodes. Thus can he free himself from his fear of life and his fear of death. "I've loved, lusted, won and lost, sung and wept," rejoices Dion in THE GREAT GOD BROWN. And Kublai urges, in MARCO MILLIONS: "Know . . . that the living of life can be noble! . . . Possess life as a lover—then sleep requited in the arms of death! If you awake, love again! If you sleep on, rest in peace! Who knows which? . . . It is nobler not to know." And man must exult not only in sorrow and joy; he must exult also in struggle. "Life is struggle," said O'Neill, "often, if not usually, unsuccessful struggle." Exultation in life: in life as desire and strength and struggle—this is the new vital value that O'Neill repeat-

*edly brings into dramatic conflict with the old doctrine of renuncia-
tion—explicitly, in* LAZARUS LAUGHED, *in* THE GREAT GOD BROWN, *in*
MARCO MILLIONS—*implicitly, in every play he has written.*

*O'Neill's experiments in dramatic form have been more distin-
guished by their novelty than by their effectiveness. Rapid shifting
of scene, regressive visions, varied sound effects, double speeches, simultaneous scenes in different rooms of a house, the use of puppets,
and his favorite device of masks—these are only a part of his technical
innovations. Mrs. Edith Isaacs has pointed out that none of them has
been a significant contribution to theatrical technique. Few of them,
moreover, have contributed essentially to the success of O'Neill's
work. "One can admire and applaud his experimental boldness," observes Bonamy Dobrée, "but one must insist that the things in which
he has experimented are merely subsidiary. . . . The only originality
that counts is that of the mind."*

*O'Neill's work is uneven. Some of it has been condemned even
by his admirers. But in his total work he has given us a serious and
powerful representation of human nature in terms amenable to modern
thought. Above all he has expressed the restless search for new values
and new artistic techniques that distinguishes his age. Says Barrett
Clark: "He is destined to go on striving, failing, seeking; the quest
alone is what matters to him."*

THE EMPEROR JONES *has been one of the most theatrically effective
of O'Neill's plays. Excellently acted by Charles Gilpin, it achieved
wide popularity in 1920, and has been successfully revived both with
Gilpin and Paul Robeson. It was put into operatic form, and with
Lawrence Tibbett in the feature role, was sung in 1933 at the Metro-
politan in New York. Some have commented on its indebtedness to*
THE DRUMS OF OUDE, *by Austin Strong. Here is O'Neill's story:*

"The idea of THE EMPEROR JONES *came from an old circus man I
knew. This man told me a story current in Hayti concerning the
late President Sam. This was to the effect that Sam had said they'd
never get him with a lead bullet; that he would get himself first with
a silver one. . . . This notion about the silver bullet struck me, and
I made a note of the story. About six months later I got the idea of
the woods, but I couldn't see how it could be done on the stage,
and I passed it up again. A year elapsed. One day I was reading
of the religious feasts in the Congo and the uses to which the drum*

214

is put there: how it starts at a normal pulse and is slowly intensified until the heartbeat of everyone present corresponds to the frenzied beat of the drum. There was an idea and an experiment. How would this sort of thing work on an audience in a theater? The effect of the tropical forest on the human imagination was honestly come by. It was the result of my own experience while prospecting for gold in Spanish Honduras."

The play is fundamentally naturalistic in its attempt to represent man's psychological nature as being determined by natural law; for the fears that develop in the mind of the Emperor, and mark the progress of the play, have their basic origin in his atavistic mentality—a mentality which, derived from his ancestors in the jungle, needs only his return to the jungle, and the sense of being pursued, to strip from him the tinsel of civilization and submerge him in the primitive savagery of his race. But though naturalistic in his interpretation of character, O'Neill forsakes the dramatic technique of the older naturalists for one which, in his own words, "we loosely call 'expressionism.'" Widely used in dramatic criticism, the term deserves consideration.

First, we may remark on its looseness, for critics have sometimes attempted to define Expressionism with an exactness which it does not permit. Expressionism is not a distinct genre, nor is it distinguished by the employment of any single technique. Historically, the term Expressionist has been applied to various dramatists since Ibsen, who came to regard the prevailing naturalistic technique as inadequate; for that technique, they believed, did not permit the representation of intangible forces that give direction and meaning to human life, nor did it allow revelation of complex and subconscious psychological states which are not expressed by natural words or acts. "The old 'naturalism'—or 'realism,' if you prefer—no longer applies," wrote O'Neill, in a tribute to Strindberg. "We have endured too much of the banality of surfaces." Because this criticism of "the old naturalism" has been the chief quality which the so-called Expressionists have had in common, as able a critic as Kenneth Macgowan has defined Expressionism as "the whole tendency against Realism, just as Romanticism is applied to the whole tendency against Classicism."

But the Expressionists were not mere negative critics of an older form. They sought methods for expressing what O'Neill has called the "behind-life"—the intangible and subconscious life which photo-

215

graphic naturalism had neglected.   Since they believed they could not express that life by natural speech or action, they usually tried to express it by symbolism—symbolism that sometimes appears in the speech or conduct of characters, sometimes in theatrical effects springing from scenery and lighting.   But their search has not discovered any one adequate technique.   Each of their successful plays has been distinguished by its own peculiar novelty, suitable to that play alone. This experimental and individualistic quality of their work prohibits any rigid definition of Expressionism.   In fact, Barrett H. Clark has said that although the term apparently originated in Germany, some of the Germans who have been considered leading Expressionists told him "either that there was no such thing as 'Expressionism,' or that they did not know what it was."   We may recognize, however, the generally accepted usage of the term: it has come to signify a recognizable trend in modern drama—a trend that has produced a number of plays which attempt to represent inarticulate qualities of life by symbolic, unrealistic methods.   In some of these plays the use of symbolism is so slight, or so far subordinate to other elements in the play, that it has been generally ignored; but plays in which symbolism is employed in a noticeable and effective manner are generally referred to as Expressionistic.

Such a play is THE EMPEROR JONES.   *The modern intellectual concept of the play—the determination of human fate by heredity and environment—O'Neill dramatizes by a succession of striking symbols. Particularly effective is his use of the drums, which, by the steady acceleration of their beat, create and intensify the dominant mood of the play—a mood that produces an emotional conviction of the power of the jungle over the human heart that belongs to it.   By no device has O'Neill better achieved what he has often sought: "a modern psychological approximation of the classic fates"—an emotional sense of a source of tragedy acceptable to modern thought.*

But the sound of the drums is not his only symbol.   Each of the scenes is a symbolic revelation of a mental state of the Negro.   Some scenes—for instance, the recessive visions of the murdered gambler and the convict gang—are apparitions derived from his personal experience, and may therefore be regarded as possible hallucinations. Even so, they create an impression of superstitious fear that ordinary realism cannot convey.   Other scenes, particularly those involving the slave ship and the witch doctor, indicate the way Expressionistic drama sometimes rejects completely the technique of realism in attempting to suggest some obscure truth. For these scenes are outside the Negro's personal experience, and therefore his seeing them, even as illusions, is impossible. Yet for the audience they have psychological validity, for they symbolize the Negro's racial heritage, and explain his conduct by relating it to a past with which he himself is unacquainted. None of the scenes, except the first, are episodes in the chronological development of a plot. In fact, they cannot be; for their only relation springs from the relation of the mental states they successively reveal; and in expressing that relation they reverse time, depicting in vivid symbols the psychological degeneration of the Negro as his augmenting fear returns him from pseudocivilization to jungle savagery. And so the effect of the culminating visions blends with that of the sound of the drums to intensify the mood that gives unity and meaning to the play—a feeling of fear and of the dark power of the jungle over the soul of the Negro who had called himself the Emperor Jones.

~

BIBLIOGRAPHICAL NOTE

Because O'Neill has arraigned the conventional values of his time, much of the criticism of his work has been animated by the emotional attitude of the critic toward those values, rather than by a consideration of O'Neill's attempt to represent them in dramatic art. Certain of these biased critics, it is true, have sometimes made discerning comments. But we need be suspicious of partial admirers—though there are impressive names among them—who compare O'Neill advantageously with Sophocles and Shakespeare; and on the other hand, we may ignore prejudiced detractors, some of whom have attempted to dismiss O'Neill as a "fake philosopher" and "wind machine." Some critics of O'Neill have had poise and detachment, however, and during the last decade their number has increased. Consider, for instance, the dis-criminating reviews in 1946 of THE ICEMAN COMETH: by Brooks Atkinson, in the New York Times, October 20; by Richard Watts, in the New York Post, October 10; by Louis Kronenberger, in PM, October 11; by Howard Barnes, in the New York Herald-Tribune, October 11. Full-length studies are: B. H. Clark, EUGENE O'NEILL: THE MAN AND HIS PLAYS, Revised Edition (New York: Dover Publications, 1947); S. K. Winther, EUGENE O'NEILL: A CRITICAL STUDY (New York: Random House, Inc., 1934) —a personal appreciation, rather than a critical study. The following contain valuable material: J. W. Krutch, THE AMERICAN DRAMA SINCE 1918 (New York: Random House, Inc., 1939); B. H. Clark, A STUDY OF THE MODERN DRAMA, Second Revised Edition (New York: D. Appleton Century Company, Inc., 1938); George Jean Nathan, THE INTI-

MATE NOTEBOOKS (*New York: Alfred A. Knopf, Inc.*, 1932). *Of marked acumen is an article by Hugo von Hofmannsthal, "Eugene O'Neill,"* The Freeman, VII, No. 157 (*March 21, 1923*), 39-41. *Other worth-while articles: Bonamy Dobrée, "Plays of Eugene O'Neill,"* The Southern Review, *II, No. 3 (Winter,* 1937), 435-446; *Edith J. R. Isaacs,* "Meet Eugene O'Neill," Theatre Arts, *XXI, No.* 10 (*October, 1946*), 576-587; *Mary B. Mullett, "The Extraordinary Story of Eugene O'Neill,"* The American Magazine, *XCIV, No.* 5 (*November 1,* 1922), 34 *et seq. For further bibliography, see F. B. Millett,* CONTEMPORARY AMERICAN AUTHORS (*New York: Harcourt, Brace & Company, Inc.,* 1940).

The Emperor Jones

CHARACTERS

BRUTUS JONES, *Emperor.*

HENRY SMITHERS, *a cockney trader.*

SOLDIERS, *adherents of Lem.*

AN OLD NATIVE WOMAN

LEM, *a native chief.*

The Little Formless Fears; Jeff; The Negro Convicts; The Prison Guard; The Planters; The Auctioneer; The Slaves; The Congo Witch-Doctor; The Crocodile God.

The action of the play takes place on an island in the West Indies as yet not self-determined by white Marines. The form of native government is, for the time being, an empire.

❧

SCENE I

SCENE—*The audience chamber in the palace of the Emperor—a spacious, high-ceilinged room with bare, white-washed walls. The floor is of white tiles. In the rear, to the left of center, a wide archway giving out on a portico with white pillars. The palace is evidently situated on high ground, for beyond the portico nothing can be seen but a vista of distant hills, their summits crowned with thick groves of palm trees. In the right wall, center, a smaller arched doorway leading to the living quarters of the palace. The room is bare of furniture with the exception of one huge chair made of uncut wood which stands at center, its back to rear. This is very apparently the Emperor's throne. It is painted a dazzling, eye-smiting scarlet. There is a brilliant orange cushion on the seat and another smaller one is placed on the floor to serve as a footstool. Strips of matting, dyed scarlet, lead from the foot of the throne to the two entrances.*

THE EMPEROR JONES. Copyright 1921–1948 by Eugene O'Neill.

219

It is late afternoon but the sunlight still blazes yellowly beyond the portico and there is an oppressive burden of exhausting heat in the air.

As the curtain rises, a native Negro woman sneaks in cautiously from the entrance on the right. She is very old, dressed in cheap calico, bare-footed, a red bandana handkerchief covering all but a few stray wisps of white hair. A bundle bound in colored cloth is carried over her shoulder on the end of a stick. She hesitates beside the doorway, peering back as if in extreme dread of being discovered. Then she begins to glide noiselessly, a step at a time, toward the doorway in the rear. At this moment, SMITHERS *appears beneath the portico.*

SMITHERS *is a tall, stoop-shouldered man about forty. His bald head, perched on a long neck with an enormous Adam's apple, looks like an egg. The tropics have tanned his naturally pasty face with its small, sharp features to a sickly yellow, and native rum has painted his pointed nose to a startling red. His little, washy-blue eyes are red-rimmed and dart about him like a ferret's. His expression is one of unscrupulous meanness, cowardly and dangerous. He is dressed in a worn riding suit of dirty white drill, puttees, spurs, and wears a white cork helmet. A cartridge belt with an automatic revolver is around his waist. He carries a riding whip in his hand. He sees the woman and stops to watch her suspiciously. Then, making up his mind, he steps quickly on tiptoe into the room. The woman, looking back over her shoulder continually, does not see him until it is too late. When she does* SMITHERS *springs forward and grabs her firmly by the shoulder. She struggles to get away, fiercely but silently.*

SMITHERS (*tightening his grasp —roughly*): Easy! None o' that, me birdie. You can't wriggle out now. I got me 'ooks on yer.

WOMAN (*seeing the uselessness of struggling, gives way to frantic terror, and sinks to the ground, embracing his knees supplicatingly*): No tell him! No tell him, Mister!

SMITHERS (*with great curiosity*): Tell 'im? (*Then scornfully.*) Oh, you mean 'is bloomin' Majesty. What's the gaime, any 'ow? What are you sneakin' away for? Been stealin' a bit, I s'pose. (*He taps her bundle with his riding whip significantly.*)

WOMAN (*shaking her head vehemently*): No, me no steal.

SMITHERS: Bloody liar! But tell me what's up. There's somethin'

220

funny goin' on. I smelled it in the air first thing I got up this mornin'. You blacks are up to some devilment. This palace of 'is is like a bleedin' tomb. Where's all the 'ands? (*The woman keeps sullenly silent.* SMITHERS *raises his whip threateningly.*) Ow, yer won't, won't yer? I'll show yer what's what.

WOMAN (*coweringly*): I tell, Mister. You no hit. They go— all go. (*She makes a sweeping gesture toward the hills in the distance.*)

SMITHERS: Run away—to the 'ills?

WOMAN: Yes, Mister. Him Emperor—Great Father. (*She touches her forehead to the floor with a quick mechanical jerk.*) Him sleep after eat. Then they go—all go. Me old woman. Me left only. Now me go too.

SMITHERS (*his astonishment giving way to an immense, mean satisfaction*): Ow! So that's the ticket! Well, I know bloody well wot's in the air—when they runs orf to the 'ills. The tom-tom 'll be thumping out there bloomin' soon. (*With extreme vindictiveness.*) And I'm bloody glad of it, for one! Serve 'im right! Puttin' on airs, the stinkin' nigger! 'Is Majesty! Gawd blimey! I only 'opes I'm there when they takes 'im out to

shoot 'im. (*Suddenly.*) 'E's still 'ere all right, ain't 'e?

WOMAN: Yes. Him sleep.

SMITHERS: 'E's bound to find out soon as 'e wakes up. 'E's cunnin' enough to know when 'is time's come. (*He goes to the doorway on right and whistles shrilly with his fingers in his mouth. The old woman springs to her feet and runs out of the doorway, rear.* SMITHERS *goes after her, reaching for his revolver.*) Stop or I'll shoot! (*Then stopping—indifferently.*) Pop orf then, if yer like, yer black cow. (*He stands in the doorway, looking after her.*)

[JONES *enters from the right. He is a tall, powerfully built, full-blooded Negro of middle age. His features are typically negroid, yet there is something decidedly distinctive about his face—an underlying strength of will, a hardy, self-reliant confidence in himself that inspires respect. His eyes are alive with a keen, cunning intelligence. In manner he is shrewd, suspicious, evasive. He wears a light blue uniform coat, sprayed with brass buttons, heavy gold chevrons on his shoulders, gold braid on the collar, cuffs, etc. His pants are bright red with a*

221

light blue stripe down the side. Patent-leather laced boots with brass spurs, and a belt with a long-barreled, pearl-handled revolver in a holster complete his make up. Yet there is something not altogether ridiculous about his grandeur. He has a way of carrying it off.]

JONES (*not seeing anyone—greatly irritated and blinking sleepily—shouts*): Who dare whistle dat way in my palace? Who dare wake up de Emperor? I'll git de hide frayled off some o' you niggers sho'!

SMITHERS (*showing himself—in a manner half-afraid and half-defiant*): It was me whistled to yer. (*As* JONES *frowns angrily.*) I got news for yer.

JONES (*putting on his suavest manner, which fails to cover up his contempt for the white man*): Oh, it's you, Mister Smithers. (*He sits down on his throne with easy dignity.*) What news you got to tell me?

SMITHERS (*coming close to enjoy his discomfiture*): Don't yer notice nothin' funny today?

JONES (*coldly*): Funny? No. I ain't perceived nothin' of de kind!

SMITHERS: Then yer ain't so foxy as I thought yer was. Where's all your court? (*Sarcastically.*) The Generals and the Cabinet Ministers and all?

JONES (*imperturbably*): Where dey mostly runs de minute I closes my eyes—drinkin' rum and talkin' big down in de town. (*Sarcastically.*) How come you don't know dat? Ain't you sousin' with 'em most every day?

SMITHERS (*stung but pretending indifference—with a wink*): That's part of the day's work. I got ter—ain't I—in my business?

JONES (*contemptuously*): Yo' business!

SMITHERS (*imprudently enraged*): Gawd blimey, you was glad enough for me ter take yer in on it when you landed here first. You didn' 'ave no 'igh and mighty airs in them days!

JONES (*his hand going to his revolver like a flash—menacingly*): Talk polite, white man! Talk polite, you heah me! I'm boss heah now, is you fergettin'? (*The Cockney seems about to challenge this last statement with the facts but something in the other's eyes holds and cows him.*)

SMITHERS (*in a cowardly whine*): No 'arm meant, old top.

JONES (*condescendingly*): I accepts yo' apology. (*Lets his hand fall from his revolver.*) No use'n you rakin' up ole times. What I was den is one thing. What I is now 's another. You didn't let me in on yo' crooked work out o' no kind feelin's dat time. I done de dirty work fo' you—and most o'

222

de brain work, too, fo' dat matter —and I was wu'th money to you, dat's de reason.

SMITHERS: Well, blimey, I give yer a start, didn't I—when no one else would. I wasn't afraid to 'ire yer like the rest was—'count of the story about your breakin' jail back in the States.

JONES: No, you didn't have no s'cuse to look down on me fo' dat. You been in jail you'self more'n once.

SMITHERS (*furiously*): It's a lie! (*Then trying to pass it off by an attempt at scorn.*) Garn! Who told yer that fairy tale?

JONES: Dey's some tings I ain't got to be tole. I kin see 'em in folk's eyes. (*Then after a pause —meditatively.*) Yes, you sho' give me a start. And it didn't take long from dat time to git dese fool, woods' niggers right where I wanted dem. (*With pride.*) From stowaway to Emperor in two years! Dat's goin' some!

SMITHERS (*with curiosity*): And I bet you got yer pile o' money 'id safe some place.

JONES (*with satisfaction*): I sho' has! And it's in a foreign bank where no pusson don't ever git it out but me no matter what come. You didn't s'pose I was holdin' down dis Emperor job for de glory in it, did you? Sho'! De fuss and glory part of it, dat's only to turn de heads o' de low-flung, bush niggers dat's here. Dey wants de big circus show for deir money. I gives it to 'em an' I gits de money. (*With a grin.*) De long green, dat's me every time! (*Then rebukingly.*) But you ain't got no kick agin me, Smithers. I'se paid you back all you done for me many times. Ain't I pertected you and winked at all de crooked tradin' you been doin' right out in de broad day? Sho' I has—and me makin' laws to stop it at de same time! (*He chuckles.*)

SMITHERS (*grinning*): But, meanin' no 'arm, you been grabbin' right and left yourself, ain't yer? Look at the taxes you've put on 'em! Blimey! You've squeezed 'em dry!

JONES (*chuckling*): No, dey ain't *all* dry yet. I'se still heah, ain't I?

SMITHERS (*smiling at his secret thought*): They're dry right now, you'll find out. (*Changing the subject abruptly.*) And as for me breakin' laws, you've broke 'em all yerself just as fast as yer made 'em.

JONES: Ain't I de Emperor? De laws don't go for him. (*Judicially.*) You heah what I tells you, Smithers. Dere's little stealin' like you does, and dere's big stealin' like I does. For de little stealin' dey gits you in jail soon or late. For de big stealin' dey makes you Emperor and puts you in de Hall o' Fame when you croaks. (*Reminiscently.*) If dey's one thing I learns in ten years on de Pullman ca's listenin' to de white quality talk, it's dat same fact. And when I gits a chance to use it I winds up Emperor in two years.

SMITHERS (*unable to repress the genuine admiration of the small fry for the large*): Yes, yer turned the bleedin' trick, all right. Blimey, I never seen a bloke 'as 'ad the bloomin' luck you 'as.

JONES (*severely*): Luck? What you mean—luck?

SMITHERS: I suppose you'll say as that swank about the silver bullet ain't luck—and that was what first got the fool blacks on yer side the time of the revolution, wasn't it?

JONES (*with a laugh*): Oh, dat silver bullet! Sho' was luck! But I makes dat luck, you heah? I loads de dice! Yessuh! When dat murderin' nigger ole Lem hired to kill me takes aim ten feet away and his gun misses fire and I shoots him dead, what you heah me say?

SMITHERS: You said yer'd got a charm so's no lead bullet'd kill yer. You was so strong only a silver bullet could kill yer, you told 'em. Blimey, wasn't that swank for yer —and plain, fat-'eaded luck?

JONES (*proudly*): I got brains and I uses 'em quick. Dat ain't luck.

SMITHERS: Yer know they wasn't 'ardly liable to get no silver bullets. And it was luck 'e didn't 'it you that time.

JONES (*laughing*): And dere all dem fool, bush niggers was kneelin' down and bumpin' deir heads on de ground like I was a miracle out o' de Bible. Oh Lawd, from dat time on I has dem all eatin' out of my hand. I cracks de whip and dey jumps through.

SMITHERS (*with a sniff*): Yankee bluff done it.

JONES: Ain't a man's talkin' big what makes him big—long as he makes folks believe it? Sho', I talks large when I ain't got nothin' to back it up, but I ain't talkin' wild just de same. I knows I kin fool 'em—I *knows* it—and dat's backin' enough fo' my game. And ain't I got to learn deir lingo and teach some of dem English befo' I kin talk to 'em? Ain't dat wuk? You ain't never learned ary word er it, Smithers, in de ten years you been heah, dough yo' knows it's money in yo' pocket tradin' wid 'em if you does. But you'se too shiftless to take de trouble.

SMITHERS: (*flushing*): Never mind about me. What's this I've 'eard about yer really 'avin' a silver bullet moulded for yourself?

JONES: It's playin' out my bluff. I has de silver bullet moulded and I tells 'em when de time comes I kills myself wid it. I tells 'em

224

dat's 'cause I'm de on'y man in de world big enuff to git me. No use'n deir tryin'. And dey falls down and bumps deir heads. (*He laughs.*) I does dat so's I kin take a walk in peace widout no jealous nigger gunnin' at me from behind de trees.

SMITHERS (*astonished*): Then you 'ad it made—'onest?

JONES: Sho' did. Heah she be. (*He takes out his revolver, breaks it, and takes the silver bullet out of one chamber.*) Five lead an' dis silver baby at de last. Don't she shine pretty? (*He holds it in his hand, looking at it admiringly, as if strangely fascinated.*)

SMITHERS: Let me see. (*Reaches out his hand for it.*)

JONES (*harshly*): Keep yo' hands whar dey b'long, white man. (*He replaces it in the chamber and puts the revolver back on his hip.*)

SMITHERS (*snarling*): Gawd blimey! Think I'm a bleedin' thief, you would.

JONES: No, 'tain't dat. I knows you'se scared to steal from me. On'y I ain't 'lowin' nary body to touch dis baby. She's my rabbit's foot.

SMITHERS (*sneering*): A bloomin' charm, wot? (*Venomously.*) Well, you'll need all the bloody charms you 'as before long, s' 'elp me!

JONES (*judicially*): Oh, I'se good for six months yit 'fore dey

gits sick o' my game. Den, when I sees trouble comin', I makes my getaway.

SMITHERS: Ho! You got it all planned, ain't yer?

JONES: I ain't no fool. I knows dis Emperor's time is sho't. Dat why I make hay when de sun shine. Was you thinkin' I'se aimin' to hold down dis job for life? No, suh! What good is gittin' money if you stays back in dis raggedy country? I wants action when I spends. And when I sees dese niggers gittin' up deir nerve to tu'n me out, and I'se got all de money in sight, I resigns on de spot and beats it quick.

SMITHERS: Where to?

JONES: None o' yo' business.

SMITHERS: Not back to the bloody States, I'll lay my oath.

JONES (*suspiciously*): Why don't I? (*Then with an easy laugh.*) You mean 'count of dat story 'bout me breakin' from jail back dere? Dat's all talk.

SMITHERS (*skeptically*): Ho, yes!

JONES (*sharply*): You ain't 'sinuatin' I'se a liar, is you?

SMITHERS (*hastily*): No, Gawd strike me! I was only thinkin' o' the bloody lies you told the blacks 'ere about killin' white men in the States.

JONES (*angered*): How come dey're lies?

SMITHERS: You'd 'ave been in

jail if you 'ad, wouldn't yer then? (*With venom.*) And from what I've 'eard, it ain't 'ealthy for a black to kill a white man in the States. They burns 'em in oil, don't they?

JONES (*with cool deadliness*): You mean lynchin' 'd scare me? Well, I tells you, Smithers, maybe I does kill one white man back dere. Maybe I does. And maybe I kills another right heah 'fore long if he don't look out.

SMITHERS (*trying to force a laugh*): I was on'y spoofin' yer. Can't yer take a joke? And you was just sayin' you'd never been in jail.

JONES (*in the same tone— slightly boastful*): Maybe I goes to jail dere for gettin' in an argument wid razors ovah a crap game. Maybe I gits twenty years when dat colored man die. Maybe I gits in 'nother argument wid de prison guard was overseer ovah us when we're wukin' de roads. Maybe he hits me wid a whip and I splits his head wid a shovel and runs away and files de chain off my leg and gits away safe. Maybe I does all dat an' maybe I don't. It's a story I tells you so's you knows I'se de kind of man dat if you evah repeats one word of it, I ends yo' stealin' on dis yearth mighty damn quick!

SMITHERS (*terrified*): Think I'd peach on yer? Not me! Ain't I always been yer friend?

JONES (*suddenly relaxing*): Sho' you has—and you better be.

SMITHERS (*recovering his composure—and with it his malice*): And just to show yer I'm yer friend, I'll tell yer that bit o' news I was goin' to.

JONES: Go ahead! Shoot de piece. Must be bad news from de happy way you look.

SMITHERS (*warningly*): Maybe it's gettin' time for you to resign —with that bloomin' silver bullet, wot? (*He finishes with a mocking grin.*)

JONES (*puzzled*): What's dat you say? Talk plain.

SMITHERS: Ain't noticed any of the guards or servants about the place today, I 'aven't.

JONES (*carelessly*): Dey're all out in de garden sleepin' under de trees. When I sleeps, dey sneaks a sleep, too, and I pretends I never suspicions it. All I got to do is to ring de bell and dey come flyin', makin' a bluff dey was wukin' all de time.

SMITHERS (*in the same mocking tone*): Ring the bell now an' you'll bloody well see what I means.

JONES (*startled to alertness, but preserving the same careless tone*): Sho' I rings. (*He reaches below the throne and pulls out a big, common dinner bell which is painted the same vivid scarlet as the throne. He rings this vigor-*

ously—then stops to listen. Then he goes to both doors, rings again, and looks out.)

SMITHERS (*watching him with malicious satisfaction, after a pause—mockingly*): The bloody ship is sinkin' an' the bleedin' rats 'as slung their 'ooks.

JONES (*in a sudden fit of anger flings the bell clattering into a corner*): Low-flung, woods' niggers! (*Then catching* SMITHERS' *eye on him, he controls himself and suddenly bursts into a low chuckling laugh.*) Reckon I overplays my hand dis once! A man can't take de pot on a bob-tailed flush all de time. Was I sayin' I'd sit in six months mo'? Well, I'se changed my mind den. I cashes in and resigns de job of Emperor right dis minute.

SMITHERS (*with real admiration*): Blimey, but you're a cool bird, and no mistake.

JONES: No use'n fussin'. When I knows de game's up I kisses it good-bye widout no long waits. Dey've all run off to de hills, ain't dey?

SMITHERS: Yes—every bleedin' man jack of 'em.

JONES: Den de revolution is at de post. And de Emperor better git his feet smokin' up de trail. (*He starts for the door in rear.*)

SMITHERS: Goin' out to look for your 'orse? Yer won't find any. They steals the 'orses first thing.

Mine was gone when I went for 'im this mornin'. That's wot first give me a suspicion of wot was up.

JONES (*alarmed for a second, scratches his head, then philosophically*): Well, den I hoofs it. Feet, do yo' duty! (*He pulls out a gold watch and looks at it.*) Three-thuty. Sundown's at six-thuty or dereabouts. (*Puts his watch back—with cool confidence.*) I got plenty o' time to make it easy.

SMITHERS: Don't be so bloomin' sure of it. They'll be after you 'ot and 'eavy. Ole Lem is at the bottom o' this business an' 'e 'ates you like 'ell. 'E'd rather do for you than eat 'is dinner, 'e would!

JONES (*scornfully*): Dat fool no-count nigger! Does you think I'se scared o' him? I stands him on his thick head more'n once befo' dis, and I does it again if he come in my way . . . (*Fiercely.*) And dis time I leave him a dead nigger fo' sho'!

SMITHERS: You'll 'ave to cut through the big forest—an' these blacks 'ere can sniff and follow a trail in the dark like 'ounds. You'd 'ave to 'ustle to get through that forest in twelve hours even if you knew all the bloomin' trails like a native.

JONES (*with indignant scorn*): Look-a-heah, white man! Does you think I'se a natural bo'n fool? Give me credit fo' havin' some sense, fo' Lawd's sake! Don't you s'pose I'se looked ahead and made sho' of all de chances? I'se gone out in dat big forest, pretendin' to hunt, so many times dat I knows it high an' low like a book. I could go through on dem trails wid my eyes shut. (*With great contempt.*) Think dese ign'rent bush niggers dat ain't got brains enuff to know deir own names even can catch Brutus Jones? Huh, I s'pects not! Not on yo' life! Why, man, de white men went after me wid bloodhounds where I come from an' I jes' laughs at 'em. It's a shame to fool dese black trash around heah, dey're so easy. You watch me, man! I'll make dem look sick, I will. I'll be 'cross de plain to de edge of de forest by time dark comes. Once in de woods in de night, dey got a swell chance o' findin' dis baby! Dawn tomorrow I'll be out at de oder side and on de coast whar dat French gunboat is stayin'. She picks me up, take me to Martinique when she go dar, and dere I is safe wid a mighty big bankroll in my jeans. It's easy as rollin' off a log.

SMITHERS (*maliciously*): But s'posin' somethin' 'appens wrong an' they do nab yer?

JONES (*decisively*): Dey don't—dat's de answer.

SMITHERS: But, just for argyment's sake—what'd you do?

JONES (*frowning*): I'se got five lead bullets in dis gun good enuff fo' common bush niggers—and after dat I got de silver bullet left to cheat 'em out o' gittin' me.

SMITHERS (*jeeringly*): Ho, I was fergettin' that silver bullet. You'll bump yourself orf in style, won't yer? Blimey!

JONES (*gloomily*): You kin bet yo' whole roll on one thing, white man. Dis baby plays out his string to de end and when he quits, he quits wid a bang de way he ought. Silver bullet ain't none too good for him when he go, dat's a fac'! (*Then shaking off his nervousness—with a confident laugh.*) Sho'! What is I talkin' about? Ain't come to dat yit and I never will—not wid trash niggers like dese yere. (*Boastfully.*) Silver bullet bring me luck anyway. I kin outguess, outrun, outfight, an' outplay de whole lot o' dem all ovah de board any time o' de day er night! You watch me! [*From the distant hills comes the faint, steady thump of a tomtom, low and vibrating. It starts at a rate exactly corresponding to normal pulse beat—72 to the minute—and continues at a gradually accelerating rate from this point uninterruptedly to the very end of the play.*]

[JONES *starts at the sound. A strange look of apprehension creeps into his face for a moment as he listens. Then he asks, with an attempt to regain his most casual manner.]*

What's dat drum beatin' fo'?

SMITHERS (*with a mean grin*): For you. That means the bleedin' ceremony 'as started. I've 'eard it before and I knows.

JONES: Cer'mony? What cer'mony?

SMITHERS: The blacks is 'oldin' a bloody meetin', 'avin' a war dance, gettin' their courage worked up b'fore they starts after you.

JONES: Let dem! Dey'll sho' need it!

SMITHERS: And they're there 'oldin' their 'eathen religious service—makin' no end of devil spells and charms to 'elp 'em against your silver bullet. (*He guffaws loudly.*) Blimey, but they're balmy as 'ell!

JONES (*a tiny bit awed and shaken in spite of himself*): Huh! Takes more'n dat to scare dis chicken!

SMITHERS (*scenting the other's feeling—maliciously*): Ternight when it's pitch black in the forest, they'll 'ave their pet devils and ghosts 'oundin' after you. You'll find yer bloody 'air 'll be standin' on end before termorrow mornin'. (*Seriously.*) It's a bleedin' queer place, that stinkin' forest, even in daylight. Yer don't know what might 'appen in there, it's that rotten still. Always sends the cold shivers down my back minute I gets in it.

JONES (*with a contemptuous sniff*): I ain't no chicken-liver like you is. Trees an' me, we'se friends, and dar's a full moon comin' bring me light. And let dem po' niggers make all de fool spells dey'se a min' to. Does yo' s'pect I'se silly enuff to b'lieve in ghosts an' ha'nts an' all dat ole woman's talk? G'long, white man! You ain't talkin' to me. (*With a chuckle.*) Doesn't you know dey's got to do wid a man was member in good standin' o' de Baptist Church? Sho' I was dat when I was porter on de Pullmans, befo' I gits into my little trouble. Let dem try deir heathen tricks. De Baptist Church done pertect me and land dem all in hell. (*Then with more confident satisfaction.*) And I'se got little silver bullet o' my own, don't forgit.

SMITHERS: Ho! You 'aven't give much 'eed to your Baptist Church since you been down 'ere. I've 'eard myself you 'ad turned yer coat an' was takin' up with their blarsted witch-doctors, or whatever the 'ell yer calls the swine.

JONES (*vehemently*): I pretends to! Sho' I pretends! Dat's part o' my game from de fust. If I finds out dem niggers believes dat black is white, den I yells it out

229

louder 'n deir loudest. It don't git me nothin' to do missionary work for de Baptist Church. I'se after de coin, an' I lays my Jesus on de shelf for de time bein'. (*Stops abruptly to look at his watch— alertly.*) But I ain't got de time to waste no more fool talk wid you. I'se gwine away from heah dis secon'. (*He reaches in under the throne and pulls out an expensive Panama hat with a bright multi-colored band and sets it jauntily on his head.*) So long, white man! (*With a grin.*) See you in jail sometime, maybe!

SMITHERS: Not me, you won't. Well, I wouldn't be in yer bloody boots for no bloomin' money, but 'ere's wishin' yer luck just the same.

JONES (*contemptuously*): You're de frightenedest man evah I see! I tells you I'se safe's 'f I was in New York City. It takes dem niggers from now to dark to git up de nerve to start somethin'. By dat time, I'se got a head start dey never kotch up wid.

SMITHERS (*maliciously*): Give my regards to any ghosts yer meets up with.

JONES (*grinning*): If dat ghost got money, I'll tell him never ha'nt you less'n he wants to lose it.

SMITHERS (*flattered*): Garn! (*Then curiously.*) Ain't yer takin' no luggage with yer?

JONES: I travels light when I wants to move fast. And I got tinned grub buried on de edge o' de forest. (*Boastfully.*) Now say dat I don't look ahead an' use my brains! (*With a wide, liberal gesture.*) I will all dat's left in de palace to you—and you better grab all you kin sneak away wid befo' dey gits here.

SMITHERS (*gratefully*): Righto —and thanks ter yer. (*As* JONES *walks toward the door in rear— cautioningly.*) Say! Look 'ere, you ain't goin' out that way, are yer?

JONES: Does you think I'd slink out de back door like a common nigger? I'se Emperor yit, ain't I? And de Emperor Jones leaves de way he comes, and dat black trash don't dare stop him—not yit, leastways. (*He stops for a moment in the doorway, listening to the far-off but insistent beat of the tom-tom.*) Listen to dat roll-call, will you? Must be mighty big drum carry dat far. (*Then with a laugh.*) Well, if dey ain't no whole brass band to see me off, I sho' got de drum part of it. So long, white man. (*He puts his hands in his pockets and with studied carelessness, whistling a tune, he saunters out of the doorway and off to the left.*)

SMITHERS (*looks after him with a puzzled admiration*): 'E's got 'is bloomin' nerve with 'im, s'elp me! (*Then angrily.*) Ho—the bleedin'

230

nigger—puttin' on 'is bloody airs!
I 'opes they nabs 'im an' gives 'im
what's what! (*Then putting business before the pleasure of this
thought, looking around him with*

cupidity.) A bloke ought to find
a 'ole lot in this palace that'd go
for a bit of cash. Let's take a look,
'Arry, me lad. (*He starts for the
doorway on right as*

THE CURTAIN FALLS

SCENE II

SCENE—*Nightfall. The end of the plain where the Great Forest
begins. The foreground is sandy, level ground dotted by a few stones
and clumps of stunted bushes cowering close against the earth to
escape the buffeting of the trade wind. In the rear the forest is a wall
of darkness dividing the world. Only when the eye becomes accustomed to the gloom can the outlines of separate trunks of the nearest
trees be made out, enormous pillars of deeper blackness. A somber
monotone of wind lost in the leaves moans in the air. Yet this sound
serves but to intensify the impression of the forest's relentless immo-
bility, to form a background throwing into relief its brooding, implacable silence.*

    JONES *enters from the left, walking rapidly. He stops as he nears
the edge of the forest, looks around him quickly, peering into the dark
as if searching for some familiar landmark. Then, apparently satisfied
that he is where he ought to be, he throws himself on the ground, dog-
tired.*

    JONES: Well, heah I is. In de
nick o' time, too! Little mo' an'
it'd be blacker'n de ace of spades
heahabouts. (*He pulls a bandana
handkerchief from his hip pocket
and mops off his perspiring face.*)
Sho'! Gimme air! I'se tuckered
out sho' 'nuff. Dat soft Emperor
job ain't no trainin' fo' a long hike
ovah dat plain in de brilin' sun.
(*Then with a chuckle.*) Cheah
up, nigger, de worst is yet to come.
(*He lifts his head and stares at the
forest. His chuckle peters out

abruptly. In a tone of awe.*) My
goodness, look at dem woods, will
you? Dat no-count Smithers said
dey'd be black an' he sho' called
de turn. (*Turning away from
them quickly and looking down
at his feet, he snatches at a chance
to change the subject—solici-
tously.*) Feet, you is holdin' up
yo' end fine an' I sutinly hopes you
ain't blisterin' none. It's time you
git a rest. (*He takes off his shoes,
his eyes studiously avoiding the
forest. He feels of the soles of his

231

feet gingerly.) You is still in de pink—on'y a little mite feverish. Cool yo'selfs. Remember you done got a long journey yit befo' you. (*He sits in a weary attitude, listening to the rhythmic beating of the tom-tom. He grumbles in a loud tone to cover up a growing uneasiness.*) Bush niggers! Wonder dey wouldn' git sick o' beatin' dat drum. Sound louder, seem like. I wonder if dey's startin' after me? (*He scrambles to his feet, looking back across the plain.*) Couldn't see dem now, nohow, if dey was hundred feet away. (*Then shaking himself like a wet dog to get rid of these depressing thoughts.*) Sho', dey's miles an' miles behind. What you gittin' fidgety about? (*But he sits down and begins to lace up his shoes in great haste, all the time muttering reassuringly.*) You know what? Yo' belly is empty, dat's what's de matter wid you. Come time to eat! Wid nothin' but wind on yo' stumach, o' course you feels jiggedy. Well, we eats right heah an' now soon's I gits dese pesky shoes laced up! (*He finishes lacing up his shoes.*) Dere! Now le's see. (*Gets on his hands and knees and searches the ground around him with his eyes.*) White stone, white stone, where is you? (*He sees the first white stone and crawls to it—with satisfaction.*) Heah you is! I knowed

dis was de right place. Box of grub, come to me. (*He turns over the stone and feels in under it— in a tone of dismay.*) Ain't heah! Gorry, is I in de right place or isn't I? Dere's 'nother stone. Guess dat's it. (*He scrambles to the next stone and turns it over.*) Ain't heah, neither! Grub, whar is you? Ain't heah. Gorry, has I got to go hungry into dem woods —all de night? (*While he is talking he scrambles from one stone to another, turning them over in frantic haste. Finally, he jumps to his feet excitedly.*) Is I lost de place? Must have! But how dat happen when I was followin' de trail across de plain in broad daylight? (*Almost plaintively.*) I'se hungry, I is! I gotta git my feed. Whar's my strength gonna come from if I doesn't? Gorry, I gotta find dat grub high an' low somehow! Why it come dark so quick like dat? Can't see nothin'. (*He scratches a match on his trousers and peers about him. The rate of the beat of the far-off tom-tom increases perceptibly as he does so. He mutters in a bewildered voice.*) How come all dese white stones come heah when I only remembers one? (*Suddenly, with a frightened gasp, he flings the match on the ground and stamps on it.*) Nigger, is you gone crazy mad? Is you lightin' matches to show dem whar you is? Fo'

Lawd's sake, use yo' haid. Gorry, I'se got to be careful! (*He stares at the plain behind him apprehensively, his hand on his revolver.*) But how come all dese white stones? And whar's dat tin box o' grub I had all wrapped up in oil cloth?

[*While his back is turned, the* LITTLE FORMLESS FEARS *creep out from the deeper blackness of the forest. They are black, shapeless, only their glittering little eyes can be seen. If they have any describable form at all it is that of a grubworm about the size of a creeping child. They move noiselessly, but with deliberate, painful effort, striving to raise themselves on end, failing and sinking prone again.* JONES *turns about to face the forest. He stares up at the tops of the trees, seeking vainly to discover his whereabout by their conformation.*]

Can't tell nothin' from dem trees! Gorry, nothin' 'round heah look like I evah seed it befo'. I'se done lost de place sho' 'nuff! (*With mournful foreboding.*) It's mighty queer! It's mighty queer! (*With sudden forced defiance— in an angry tone.*) Woods, is you tryin' to put somethin' ovah on me?

[*From the formless creatures on the ground in front of him*

comes a tiny gale of low mocking laughter like a rustling of leaves. They squirm upward toward him in twisted attitudes. JONES *looks down, leaps backward with a yell of terror, yanking out his revolver as he does so—in a quavering voice.*]

What's dat? Who's dar? What is you? Git away from me befo' I shoots you up! You don't? . . .

[*He fires. There is a flash, a loud report, then silence broken only by the far-off, quickened throb of the tom-tom. The formless creatures have scurried back into the forest.* JONES *remains fixed in his position, listening intently. The sound of the shot, the reassuring feel of the revolver in his hand, have somewhat restored his shaken nerve. He addresses himself with renewed confidence.*]

Dey're gone. Dat shot fix 'em. Dey was only little animals—little wild pigs, I reckon. Dey've maybe rooted out yo' grub an' eat it. Sho', you fool nigger, what you think dey is—ha'nts? (*Excitedly.*) Gorry, you give de game away when you fire dat shot. Dem niggers heah dat fo' su'tin! Time you beat it in de woods widout no long waits. (*He starts for the forest— hesitates before the plunge—then*

233

urging himself in with manful | *but de trees! Git in! (He*
resolution.) Git in, nigger! What | *plunges boldly into the forest.)*
you skeered at? Ain't nothin' dere

SCENE III

SCENE—*Nine o'clock. In the forest. The moon has just risen. Its beams, drifting through the canopy of leaves, make a barely perceptible, suffused, eerie glow. A dense low wall of underbrush and creepers is in the nearer foreground, fencing in a small triangular clearing. Beyond this is the massed blackness of the forest like an encompassing barrier. A path is dimly discerned leading down to the clearing from left, rear, and winding away from it again toward the right. As the scene opens nothing can be distinctly made out. Except for the beating of the tom-tom, which is a trifle louder and quicker than in the previous scene, there is silence, broken every few seconds by a queer, clicking sound. Then gradually the figure of the Negro, JEFF, can be discerned crouching on his haunches at the rear of the triangle. He is middle-aged, thin, brown in color, is dressed in a Pullman porter's uniform, cap, etc. He is throwing a pair of dice on the ground before him, picking them up, shaking them, casting them out with the regular, rigid, mechanical movements of an automaton. The heavy, plodding footsteps of someone approaching along the trail from the left are heard and JONES' voice, pitched in a slightly higher key and strained in a cheering effort to overcome its own tremors.*

JONES: De moon's rizen. Does you heah dat, nigger? You gits more light from dis out. No mo' buttin' yo' fool head agin' de trunks an' scratchin' de hide off yo' legs in de bushes. Now you sees whar yo'se gwine. So cheer up! From now on you has a snap. *He steps just to the rear of the triangular clearing and mops off his face on his sleeve. He has lost his Panama hat. His face is scratched, his brilliant uniform shows several large rents.)* What time's it gittin' to be, I wonder? I dassent light no match to find out. Phoo'. It's wa'm an' dat's a fac'! *(Wearily.)* How long I been makin' tracks in dese woods? Must be hours an' hours. Seems like fo'evah! Yit can't be, when de moon's jes' riz. Dis am a long night fo' yo', yo' Majesty! *(With a mournful chuckle.)* Majesty! Der ain't much majesty 'bout dis baby now. *(With attempted cheerfulness.)* Never min'. It's all part o' de game. Dis night

234

come to an end like everything else. And when you gits dar safe and has dat bankroll in yo' hands you laughs at all dis. (*He starts to whistle but checks himself abruptly.*) What yo' whistlin' for, you po' dope! Want all de worl' to heah you? (*He stops talking to listen.*) Heah dat ole drum! Sho' gits nearer from de sound. Dey're packin' it along wid 'em. Time fo' me to move. (*He takes a step forward, then stops—worriedly.*) What's dat odder queer clickety sound I heah? Dere it is! Sound close! Sound like—sound like— Fo' God sake, sound like some nigger was shootin' crap! (*Frightenedly.*) I better beat it quick when I gits dem notions. (*He walks quickly into the clear space—then stands transfixed as he sees JEFF—in a terrified gasp.*) Who dar? Who dat? Is dat you, Jeff? (*Starting toward the other, forgetful for a moment of his surroundings and really believing it is a living man that he sees—in a tone of happy relief.*) Jeff! I'se sho' mighty glad to see you! Dey tol' me you done died from dat razor cut I gives you. (*Stopping suddenly, bewilderedly.*) But how you come to be heah, nigger? (*He stares fascinatedly at the other who continues his mechanical play with the dice. JONES' eyes begin to roll wildly. He stutters.*) Ain't you gwine—look up—can't you speak to me? Is you—is you —a ha'nt? (*He jerks out his revolver in a frenzy of terrified rage.*) Nigger, I kills you dead once. Has I got to kill you again? You take it den. (*He fires. When the smoke clears away JEFF has disappeared. JONES stands trembling—then with a certain reassurance.*) He's gone, anyway. Ha'nt or no ha'nt, dat shot fix him. (*The beat of the far-off tom-tom is perceptibly louder and more rapid. JONES becomes conscious of it—with a start, looking back over his shoulder.*) Dey's gittin' near! Dey's comin' fast! And heah I is shootin' shots to let 'em know jes' whar I is. Oh, Gorry, I'se got to run. (*Forgetting the path he plunges wildly into the underbrush in the rear and disappears in the shadow.*)

SCENE IV

SCENE—*Eleven o'clock. In the forest. A wide dirt road runs diagonally from right, front, to left, rear. Rising sheer on both sides the forest walls it in. The moon is now up. Under its light the road glimmers ghastly and unreal. It is as if the forest had stood aside momentarily to let the road pass through and accomplish its veiled pur-*

pose. This done, the forest will fold in upon itself again and the road will be no more. JONES *stumbles in from the forest on the right. His uniform is ragged and torn. He looks about him with numbed surprise when he sees the road, his eyes blinking in the bright moonlight. He flops down exhaustedly and pants heavily for a while. Then with sudden anger.*

JONES: I'm meltin' wid heat! Runnin' an' runnin' an' runnin'! Damn dis heah coat! Like a strait-jacket! (*He tears off his coat and flings it away from him, revealing himself stripped to the waist.*) Dere! Dat's better! Now I kin breathe! (*Looking down at his feet, the spurs catch his eye.*) And to hell wid dese high-fangled spurs. Dey're what's been a-trip-pin' me up an' breakin' my neck. (*He unstraps them and flings them away disgustedly.*) Dere! I gits rid o' dem frippety Emperor trappin's an' I travels lighter. Lawd! I'se tired! (*After a pause, listening to the insistent beat of the tom-tom in the distance.*) I must 'a put some distance be-tween myself an' dem—runnin' like dat—and yit—dat damn drum sound jes' de same—nearer, even. Well, I guess I a'most holds my lead anyhow. Dey won't never catch up. (*With a sigh.*) If on'y my fool legs stands up. Oh, I'se sorry I evah went in for dis. Dat Emperor job is sho' hard to shake. (*He looks around him suspi-ciously.*) How'd dis road evah git heah? Good level road, too.

I never remembers seein' it befo'. (*Shaking his head apprehen-sively.*) Dese woods is sho' full o' de queerest things at night. (*With a sudden terror.*) Lawd God, don't let me see no more o' dem ha'nts! Dey gits my goat! (*Then trying to talk himself into confidence.*) Ha'nts! You fool nigger, dey ain't no such things! Don't de Baptist parson tell you dat many time? Is you civilized, or is you like dese ign'rent black niggers heah? Sho'! Dat was all in yo' own head. Wasn't nothin' dere. Wasn't no Jeff! Know what? You jus' get seein' dem things 'cause yo' belly's empty and you's sick wid hunger inside. Hunger 'fects yo' head and yo' eyes. Any fool know dat. (*Then pleading fervently.*) But bless God, I don't come across no more o' dem, whatever dey is! (*Then cautiously.*) Rest! Don't talk! Rest! You needs it. Den you gits on yo' way again. (*Looking at the moon.*) Night's half gone a'most. You hits de coast in de mawning! Den you'se all safe. [*From the right forward a small gang of Negroes enter. They*

236

are dressed in striped convict suits, their heads are shaven, one leg drags limpingly, shackled to a heavy ball and chain. .Some carry picks, the others shovels. They are followed by a white man dressed in the uniform of a prison guard. A Winchester rifle is slung across his shoulders and he carries a heavy whip. At a signal from the GUARD *they stop on the road opposite where* JONES *is sitting.* JONES, *who has been staring up at the sky, unmindful of their noiseless approach, suddenly looks down and sees them. His eyes pop out, he tries to get to his feet and fly, but sinks back, too numbed by fright to move. His voice catches in a choking prayer.*]

Lawd Jesus!

[*The* PRISON GUARD *cracks his whip —noiselessly—and at that signal all the convicts start to work on the road. They swing their picks, they shovel, but not a sound comes from their labor. Their movements, like those of* JEFF *in the preceding scene, are those of automatons,—rigid, slow, and mechanical. The* PRISON GUARD *points sternly at* JONES *with his whip, motions him to take his place among the other shovelers.* JONES *gets*

to his feet in a hypnotized stupor. He mumbles subserviently.]

Yes, suh! Yes, suh! I'se comin'.

[*As he shuffles, dragging one foot, over to his place, he curses under his breath with rage and hatred.*]

God damn yo' soul, I gits even wid you yit, sometime.

[*As if there were a shovel in his hands he goes through weary, mechanical gestures of digging up dirt, and throwing it to the roadside. Suddenly the* GUARD *approaches him angrily, threateningly. He raises his whip and lashes* JONES *viciously across the shoulders with it.* JONES *winces with pain and cowers abjectly. The* GUARD *turns his back on him and walks away contemptuously. Instantly* JONES *straightens up. With arms upraised as if his shovel were a club in his hands he springs murderously at the unsuspecting* GUARD. *In the act of crashing down his shovel on the white man's skull,* JONES *suddenly becomes aware that his hands are empty. He cries despairingly.*]

Whar's my shovel? Gimme my shovel till I splits his damn head! (*Appealing to his fellow convicts.*) Gimme a shovel, one o'

237

you, fo' God's sake!

[*They stand fixed in motionless attitudes, their eyes on the ground. The* GUARD *seems to wait expectantly, his back turned to the attacker.* JONES *bellows with baffled, terrified rage, tugging frantically at his revolver.*]

I kills you, you white debil, if it's de last thing I evah does! Ghost or debil, I kill you again!

[*He frees the revolver and fires point blank at the* GUARD's back. *Instantly the walls of the forest close in from both sides, the road and the figures of the convict gang are blotted out in an enshrouding darkness. The only sounds are a crashing in the underbrush as* JONES *leaps away in mad flight and the throbbing of the tom-tom, still far distant, but increased in volume of sound and rapidity of beat.*]

SCENE V

SCENE—*One o'clock. A large circular clearing, enclosed by the serried ranks of gigantic trunks of tall trees whose tops are lost to view. In the center is a big dead stump worn by time into a curious resemblance to an auction block. The moon floods the clearing with a clear light.* JONES *forces his way in through the forest on the left. He looks wildly about the clearing with hunted, fearful glances. His pants are in tatters, his shoes cut and misshapen, flapping about his feet. He slinks cautiously to the stump in the center and sits down in a tense position, ready for instant flight. Then he holds his head in his hands and rocks back and forth, moaning to himself miserably.*

JONES: Oh Lawd, Lawd! Oh Lawd, Lawd! (*Suddenly he throws himself on his knees and raises his clasped hands to the sky—in a voice of agonized pleading.*) Lawd Jesus, heah my prayer! I'se a po' sinner, a po' sinner! I knows I done wrong, I knows it! When I cotches Jeff cheatin' wid loaded dice my anger overcomes me and I kills him dead! Lawd, I done wrong! When dat guard hits me wid de whip, my anger overcomes me, and I kills him dead. Lawd, I done wrong! And down heah whar dese fool bush niggers raises me up to the seat o' de mighty, I steals all I could grab. Lawd, I done wrong! I knows it! I'se sorry! Forgive me, Lawd! Forgive dis po' sinner! (*Then beseeching terrifiedly.*) And keep dem away, Lawd! Keep dem

238

away from me! And stop dat
drum soundin' in my ears! Dat
begin to sound ha'nted, too.
(*He gets to his feet, evidently
slightly reassured by his prayer—
with attempted confidence.*) De
Lawd'll preserve me from dem
ha'nts after dis. (*Sits down on
the stump again.*) I ain't skeered
o' real men. Let dem come. But
dem odders . . . (*He shudders
—then looks down at his feet,
working his toes inside the shoes
—with a groan.*) Oh, my po' feet!
Dem shoes ain't no use no more
'ceptin' to hurt. I'se better off
widout dem. (*He unlaces them
and pulls them off—holds the
wrecks of the shoes in his hands
and regards them mournfully.*)
You was real, A-one patin' leather,
too. Look at you now. Emperor,
you'se gittin' mighty low!

[*He sits dejectedly and remains
with bowed shoulders, staring down at the shoes in his
hands as if reluctant to throw
them away. While his attention is thus occupied, a crowd
of figures silently enter the
clearing from all sides. All
are dressed in Southern cos-
tumes of the period of the
fifties of the last century.
There are middle-aged men
who are evidently well-to-do
planters. There is one spruce,
authoritative individual—the
*AUCTIONEER.   *There is a
crowd of curious spectators,
chiefly young belles and dandies who have come to the
slave-market for diversion.
All exchange courtly greet-
ings in dumb show and chat
silently together. There is
something stiff, rigid, unreal, marionettish about their
movements. They group
themselves about the stump.
Finally a batch of slaves are
led in from the left by an attendant—three men of different ages, two women, one
with a baby in her arms, nurs-
ing. They are placed to the
left of the stump, beside
JONES.*

*The white planters look them over
appraisingly as if they were
cattle, and exchange judgments on each. The dandies
point with their fingers and
make witty remarks. The
belles titter bewitchingly.
All this in silence save for the
ominous throb of the tom-
tom. The *AUCTIONEER* holds
up his hand, taking his place
at the stump. The group
strain forward attentively.
He touches *JONES* on the
shoulder peremptorily, motioning for him to stand on
the stump—the auction block.
JONES looks up, sees the figures on
all sides, looks wildly for
some opening to escape, sees*

239

none, screams and leaps madly to the top of the stump to get as far away from them as possible. He stands there, cowering, paralyzed with horror. The AUCTIONEER *begins his silent spiel. He points to* JONES, *appeals to the planters to see for themselves. Here is a good field hand, sound in wind and limb as they can see. Very strong still in spite of his being middle-aged. Look at that back. Look at those shoulders. Look at the muscles in his arms and his sturdy legs. Capable of any amount of hard labor. Moreover, of a good disposition, intelligent and tractable. Will any gentleman start the bidding? The* PLANTERS *raise their fingers, make their bids. They are apparently all eager to possess* JONES. *The bidding is lively, the crowd interested. While this has been going on,* JONES *has been seized by the courage of desperation. He*

dares to look down and around him. Over his face abject terror gives way to mystification, to gradual realization—stutteringly.]

What you all doin', white folks? What's all dis? What you all lookin' at me fo'? What you doin' wid me, anyhow? (*Suddenly convulsed with raging hatred and fear.*) Is dis a auction? Is you sellin' me like dey uster befo' de war? (*Jerking out his revolver just as the* AUCTIONEER *knocks him down to one of the planters— glaring from him to the purchaser.*) And *you* sells me? And *you* buys me? I shows you I'se a free nigger, damn yo' souls! (*He fires at the* AUCTIONEER *and at the* PLANTER *with such rapidity that the two shots are almost simultaneous. As if this were a signal the walls of the forest fold in. Only blackness remains and silence broken by* JONES *as he rushes off, crying with fear—and by the quickened, ever louder beat of the tom-tom.*)

SCENE VI

SCENE—*Three o'clock. A cleared space in the forest. The limbs of the trees meet over it forming a low ceiling about five feet from the ground. The interlocked ropes of creepers reaching upward to entwine the tree trunks give an arched appearance to the sides. The space thus enclosed is like the dark, noisome hold of some ancient vessel. The moonlight is almost completely shut out and only a vague, wan light filters through.   There is the noise of someone approaching from the left, stumbling and crawling through the undergrowth.   JONES' voice is heard between chattering moans.*

Oh, Lawd, what I gwine do now? Ain't got no bullet left on'y de silver one. If mo' o' dem ha'nts come after me, how I gwine skeer dem away? Oh, Lawd, on'y de silver one left—an' I gotta save dat fo' luck. If I shoots dat one I'm a goner sho'! Lawd, it's black heah! Whar's de moon? Oh, Lawd, don't dis night evah come to an end? (*By the sounds, he is feeling his way cautiously forward.*) Dere! Dis feels like a clear space. I gotta lie down an' rest. I don't care if dem niggers does cotch me. I gotta rest.

[*He is well forward now where his figure can be dimly made out. His pants have been so torn away that what is left of them is no better than a breech cloth. He flings himself full length, face downward on the ground, panting with exhaustion. Gradually it seems to grow lighter in the enclosed space and two rows of seated figures can be seen behind* JONES. *They are sitting in crumpled, despairing attitudes, hunched, facing one another with their backs touching the forest walls as if they were shackled to them. All are Negroes, naked save*

for loin cloths. At first they are silent and motionless. Then they begin to sway slowly forward toward each other and back again in unison, as if they were laxly letting themselves follow the long roll of a ship at sea. At the same time, a low, melancholy murmur rises among them, increasing gradually by rhythmic degrees which seem to be directed and controlled by the throb of the tom-tom in the distance, to a long, tremulous wail of despair that reaches a certain pitch, unbearably acute, then falls by slow gradations of tone into silence and is taken up again. JONES *starts, looks up, sees the figures, and throws himself down again to shut out the sight. A shudder of terror shakes his whole body as the wail rises up about him again. But the next time, his voice, as if under some uncanny compulsion, starts with the others. As their chorus lifts he rises to a sitting posture similar to the others, swaying back and forth. His voice reaches the highest pitch of sorrow, of desolation. The*

241

*light fades out, the other
voices cease, and only darkness is left.* JONES *can be
heard scrambling to his feet
and running off, his voice
sinking down the scale and*

*receding as he moves farther
and farther away in the
forest. The tom-tom beats
louder, quicker, with a more
insistent, triumphant pulsa-
tion.*]

SCENE VII

SCENE—*Five o'clock. The foot of a gigantic tree by the edge of
a great river. A rough structure of boulders, like an altar, is by the
tree. The raised river bank is in the nearer background. Beyond this
the surface of the river spreads out, brilliant and unruffled in the moonlight, blotted out and merged into a veil of bluish mist in the distance.*
JONES' *voice is heard from the left rising and falling in the long, despairing wail of the chained slaves, to the rhythmic beat of the tom-tom. As
his voice sinks into silence, he enters the open space. The expression
of his face is fixed and stony, his eyes have an obsessed glare, he moves
with a strange deliberation like a sleepwalker or one in a trance. He
looks around at the tree, the rough stone altar, the moonlit surface of
the river beyond, and passes his hand over his head with a vague gesture of puzzled bewilderment. Then, as if in obedience to some obscure impulse, he sinks into a kneeling, devotional posture before the
altar. Then he seems to come to himself partly, to have an uncertain
realization of what he is doing, for he straightens up and stares about
him horrifiedly—in an incoherent mumble.*

JONES: What—what is I doin'?
What is—dis place? Seems like
—seems like I know dat tree—an'
dem stones—an' de river. I remember—seems like I been heah
befo'. (*Tremblingly.*) Oh, Gorry,
I'se skeered in dis' place! I'se
skeered! Oh, Lawd, pertect dis
sinner!

[*Crawling away from the altar,
he cowers close to the ground,
his face hidden, his shoulders
heaving with sobs of hysteri-*

*cal fright. From behind the
trunk of the tree, as if he had
sprung out of it, the figure of
the* CONGO WITCH-DOCTOR *appears. He is wizened and
old, naked except for the fur
of some small animal tied
about his waist, its bushy tail
hanging down in front. His
body is stained all over a
bright red. Antelope horns
are on each side of his head,
branching upward. In one*

242

hand he carries a bone rattle, in the other a charm stick with a bunch of white cockatoo feathers tied to the end. A great number of glass beads and bone ornaments are about his neck, ears, wrists, and ankles. He struts noiselessly with a queer prancing step to a position in the clear ground between JONES and the altar. Then with a preliminary, summoning stamp of his foot on the earth, he begins to dance and to chant. As if in response to his summons the beating of the tom-tom grows to a fierce, exultant boom whose throbs seem to fill the air with vibrating rhythm. JONES looks up, starts to spring to his feet, reaches a half-kneeling, half-squatting position and remains rigidly fixed there, paralyzed with awed fascination by this new apparition. The WITCH-DOCTOR sways, stamping with his foot, his bone rattle clicking the time. His voice rises and falls in a weird, monotonous croon, without articulate word divisions. Gradually his dance becomes clearly one of a narrative in pantomime, his croon is an incantation, a charm to allay the fierceness of some implacable deity demanding sacrifice. He flees,

he is pursued by devils, he hides, he flees again. Ever wilder and wilder becomes his flight, nearer and nearer draws the pursuing evil, more and more the spirit of terror gains possession of him. His croon, rising to intensity, is punctuated by shrill cries. JONES has become completely hypnotized. His voice joins in the incantation, in the cries, he beats time with his hands and sways his body to and fro from the waist. The whole spirit and meaning of the dance has entered into him, has become his spirit. Finally the theme of the pantomime halts on a howl of despair, and is taken up again in a note of savage hope. There is a salvation. The forces of evil demand sacrifice. They must be appeased. The WITCH-DOCTOR points with his wand to the sacred tree, to the river beyond, to the altar, and finally to JONES with a ferocious command. JONES seems to sense the meaning of this. It is he who must offer himself for sacrifice. He beats his forehead abjectly to the ground, moaning hysterically.]

Mercy, Oh Lawd! Mercy! Mercy on dis po' sinner.

[The WITCH-DOCTOR springs to the

river bank. He stretches out his arms and calls to some god within its depths. Then he starts backward slowly, his arms remaining out. A huge head of a crocodile appears over the bank and its eyes, glittering greenly, fasten up-on JONES. *He stares into them fascinatedly. The* WITCH-DOCTOR *prances up to him, touches him with his wand, motions with hideous command toward the waiting monster.* JONES *squirms on his belly nearer and nearer, moaning continually.*]

Mercy, Lawd! Mercy!

[*The crocodile heaves more of his enormous hulk onto the land.* JONES *squirms toward him. The* WITCH-DOCTOR'S *voice shrills out in furious exulta-tion, the tom-tom beats mad-ly.* JONES *cries out in a fierce,*

exhausted spasm of anguished pleading.]

Lawd, save me! Lawd Jesus, heah my prayer!

[*Immediately, in answer to his prayer, comes the thought of the one bullet left him. He snatches at his hip, shouting defiantly.*]

De silver bullet! You don't git me yit!

[*He fires at the green eyes in front of him. The head of the croc-odile sinks back behind the river bank, the* WITCH-DOCTOR *springs behind the sacred tree and disappears.* JONES *lies with his face to the ground, his arms outstretched, whim-pering with fear as the throb of the tom-tom fills the silence about him with a somber pul-sation, a baffled but revenge-ful power.*]

SCENE VIII

SCENE—*Dawn. Same as Scene Two, the dividing line of forest and plain. The nearest tree trunks are dimly revealed but the forest behind them is still a mass of glooming shadows. The tom-tom seems on the very spot, so loud and continuously vibrating are its beats.* LEM *enters from the left, followed by a small squad of his soldiers, and by the Cockney trader,* SMITHERS. LEM *is a heavy-set, ape-faced old savage of the extreme African type, dressed only in a loin cloth. A re-volver and cartridge belt are about his waist. His soldiers are in dif-ferent degrees of rag-concealed nakedness. All wear broad palm-leaf hats. Each one carries a rifle.* SMITHERS *is the same as in Scene One. One of the soldiers, evidently a tracker, is peering about keenly on the*

244

ground. He grunts and points to the spot where JONES *entered the forest.* LEM *and* SMITHERS *come to look.*

SMITHERS (*after a glance, turns away in disgust*): That's where 'e went in right enough. Much good it'll do yer. 'E's miles orf by this an' safe to the Coast, damn 'is 'ide! I tole yer yer'd lose 'im, didn't I?—wastin' the 'ole bloomin' night beatin' yer bloody drum and castin' yer silly spells! Gawd blimey, wot a pack!

LEM (*gutturally*): We cotch him. You see. (*He makes a motion to his soldiers who squat down on their haunches in a semi-circle.*)

SMITHERS (*exasperatedly*): Well, ain't yer goin' in an' 'unt 'im in the woods? What the 'ell's the good of waitin'?

LEM (*imperturbably—squatting down himself*): We cotch him.

SMITHERS (*turning away from him contemptuously*): Aw! Garn! 'E's a better man than the lot o' you put together. I 'ates the sight o' 'im but I'll say that for 'im. (*A sound of snapping twigs comes from the forest. The soldiers jump to their feet, cocking their rifles alertly.* LEM *remains sitting with an imperturbable expression, but listening intently. The sound from the woods is repeated.* LEM *makes a quick signal with his hand. His followers creep quickly but noiselessly into the forest,*

scattering so that each enters at a different spot.)

SMITHERS (*in the silence that follows—in a contemptuous whisper*): You ain't thinkin' that would be 'im, I 'ope?

LEM (*calmly*): We cotch him.

SMITHERS: Blarsted fat eads! (*Then after a second's thought—wonderingly.*) Still an' all, it might 'appen. If 'e lost 'is bloody way in these stinkin' woods 'e'd likely turn in a circle without 'is knowin' it. They all does.

LEM (*peremptorily*): Sssh! (*The reports of several rifles sound from the forest, followed a second later by savage, exultant yells. The beating of the tom-tom abruptly ceases.* LEM *looks up at the white man with a grin of satisfaction.*) We cotch him. Him dead.

SMITHERS (*with a snarl*): 'Ow d'yer know it's 'im an' 'ow d'yer know 'e's dead?

LEM: My mens dey got 'um silver bullets. Dey kill him shore.

SMITHERS (*astonished*): They got silver bullets?

LEM: Lead bullet no kill him. He got um strong charm. I cook um money, make um silver bullet, make um strong charm, too.

SMITHERS (*light breaking upon him*): So that's wot you was up to

245

all night, wot? You was scared to put after 'im till you'd moulded silver bullets, eh?

LEM (*simply stating a fact*): Yes. Him got strong charm. Lead no good.

SMITHERS (*slapping his thigh and guffawing*): Haw-haw! If yer don't beat all 'ell! (*Then recovering himself—scornfully.*) I'll bet yer it ain't 'im they shot at all, yer bleedin' looney!

LEM (*calmly*): Dey come bring him now. (*The soldiers come out of the forest, carrying* JONES' *limp body. There is a little reddish-purple hole under his left breast. He is dead. They carry him to* LEM, *who examines his body with great satisfaction.* SMITHERS *leans over his shoulder—in a tone of frightened awe.*) Well, they did for yer right enough, Jonsey, me lad! Dead as a 'erring! (*Mockingly.*) Where's yer 'igh an' mighty airs now, yer bloomin' Majesty? (*Then with a grin.*) Silver bullets! Gawd blimey, but yer died in the 'eighth o' style, any'ow! (LEM *makes a motion to the soldiers to carry the body out left.* SMITHERS *speaks to him sneeringly.*)

SMITHERS: And I s'pose you think it's yer bleedin' charms and yer silly beatin' the drum that made 'im run in a circle when 'e'd lost 'imself, don't yer? (*But* LEM *makes no reply, does not seem to hear the question, walks out left after his men.* SMITHERS *looks after him with contemptuous scorn.*) Stupid as 'ogs, the lot of 'em! Blarsted niggers!

CURTAIN FALLS

GEORGE KELLY

1887 *Born in Philadelphia. Educated in public schools.*

1912 *Began career as an actor in New York on Keith and Orpheum circuits in sketches of his own composition.*

1922 *The production in this year of* THE TORCHBEARERS, *a satire on the "little theatre" movement, established Kelly as a successful dramatist.*

1924 *Repeated his success with* THE SHOW OFF.

1925 CRAIG'S WIFE *produced.*

1931 *Left New York for Hollywood because he felt that the commercial stage did not want serious studies of character. Has since lived mainly in California.*

1936 REFLECTED GLORY *produced first in San Francisco, later in New York.*

1946 *Moderate success with two draw-*
to *ing-room comedies,* THE DEEP MRS.
1947 SYKES *and* THE FATAL WEAKNESS, *the latter starring Ina Claire.*

1947 *Successful revival in New York of* CRAIG'S WIFE.

G<small>EORGE KELLY'S</small> *first full-length play,* THE TORCHBEARERS, *was successfully produced in New York in 1922. In its obvious aspect the play is a comic satire on the pretentious egotism and on the ignorance of dramatic art that have persistently marred the "little theatre" movement. Less obviously, it is a satire on the deep-seated vanity and vulgarity which amateur theatricals are an effective means of revealing.* THE SHOW OFF, *which appeared the following year, is another good-natured satire, this time of a likable braggart in whom are embodied many of the country-club values familiar in American civilization. Upon its production Heywood Broun called it the best comedy yet written by an American. Recommended for the Pulitzer prize by a subcommittee on play selection, its rejection by a majority of the main committee in favor of Hatcher Hughes's* HELL BENT FOR HEAVEN *caused the resignation of several members of the committee.*

In 1925 the Pulitzer award went to Kelly for his most successful work, CRAIG'S WIFE. *The play lacks the good humor of its predecessors. It is a devastating satire on a coldly calculating middle-class woman whose only values are material security, seclusion, conventional respectability, and—above all—domination. The symbol of all these*

248

values is the house she calls her home—an immaculate house kept in repellent order by her discouragement of outside acquaintances who might disarrange it and by her nagging discipline of members of her family. To realize her cold egotism by means of her home she disregards every consideration of humanity; she resorts to cool trickery, deceit, and lying. Even her sister and niece are victims of her callousness. Her husband she considers an unfortunately necessary means for the maintenance of the position she esteems. Dominating him is essential in order that she may dominate her household. When finally he leaves her, she regrets his departure only as a practical inconvenience and a commercial loss.

Yet it is significant that, though motivated by contemptible vices, and without any redeeming humanity, Mrs. Craig has not impressed the public as an exaggerated character. She seems real. The reason is that she is able to express her mean and shallow egotism through an attitude toward her home which is not only conventionally approved but applauded. For, after all, Mrs. Craig is a woman who desires above all else a good home; and as middle-class America knows, of such is the kingdom of heaven. Mrs. Craig has an exalted opinion of a wife's position in a home, and thinks she should dominate it; her opinion is widely upheld. Mrs. Craig assumes the right to be supported in safety and luxury by a man for whose happiness she has no concern, and to whom she owes no duty save not to be "unfaithful." For, after all, asks Mrs. Craig, he married her, didn't he? The ethics implied by the question has satisfied many besides Mrs. Craig.

In short, the play is not so much a revelation of a highly individualized character as a criticism of the sentimentalized American attitude toward home and toward woman's position in it. For it strips the pretense of sanctity from the orthodox values of material security and possessive domination—values conventionally acclaimed as the foundation of the home—and shows that they have no essential virtue; that their idealization may, in fact, lead to stultifying pettiness and debasement of character; that they may become an easy and fraudulent disguise by means of which woman obtains rights without duties, matriarchal power without humanity or wisdom, leisure without the responsibility of charm or culture.

That women like Mrs. Craig are numerous enough is shown by the fact that she gained such recognition as a type that the term "Craig's wife," like "Babbitt," has passed into the American language with the

249

significance of a common noun. When the play was revived in New York in 1947, it was even more popular than it had been when it first appeared. A critic declared that it was successful because everyone knows at least one Mrs. Craig. A true remark, but it misses something of her significance because, as a type, Mrs. Craig is a satire not only on those noxious women who are altogether like her, but also on the meaner qualities of ordinary women who resemble her solely in part. Perhaps we know only one Mrs. Craig; but we know many women of whom Mrs. Craig in some way reminds us.

Since CRAIG'S WIFE, *Kelly has disappointed those who expected his work to show continued improvement. He has attempted a serious interpretation of life by means of a technique which he has not effectively mastered. "A plot formula," he said, "is a good prop, but more than this it never could be. Following this idea I believe that 'The Three Sisters,' by Chekhov, is the finest play I have ever seen. It is my idea of the theatre." It is this ideal that Kelly seems to have set for himself—to reveal the meaning of human life by the difficult art of Chekhov. He has not been successful. The four plays which rapidly followed* CRAIG'S WIFE *are conspicuous for their lack of plot, their realistic dialogue, and their attempted suggestion of some philosophical interpretation of life. They contain some excellent scenes and characters, and their psychological analyses are acute. But they fail to create the unity of mood or meaning necessary to make such plays dramatically effective. Particularly inadequate is their use of realistic dialogue. With photographic accuracy Kelly reveals the littleness of little people. But his little people neither reveal nor suggest a meaning beyond their own unimportant acts—much less a world-outlook like Chekhov's.*

The plays that followed CRAIG'S WIFE *were received without enthusiasm. Friends and critics urged the author to return to light comedy, for which they felt he had undoubted talent. This Kelly refused to do, and after the failure of* PHILIP GOES FORTH, *probably the weakest of all his work, he abjured the taste of the theatergoing public and went to Hollywood. During fourteen years he wrote only one play,* REFLECTED GLORY. *Written for Tallulah Bankhead, it is the only play Kelly ever designed for merely popular theatrical success. Very recently he has returned to Broadway with* THE DEEP MRS. SYKES *and* FATAL WEAKNESS, *plays that resemble his work of the late 1920's. In his determination to write significant drama or none at all, Kelly has generally fallen just short of the high excellence necessary for success. In 1947 he had two plays on Broadway. The first of these,* THE FATAL WEAKNESS, *was well received; the other, a highly successful revival of* CRAIG'S WIFE, *indicates that his best work has lasting significance. This recent success gives reason to hope that in the future the dramatist will satisfy the expectations of his friends who have steadily believed in his ability. Says Mr. Burns Mantle: "Mr. Kelly continues to be potentially a leader among American writers for the stage, with a background second to few and a gift for the sane direction and balanced casting of his own plays that is quite notable."*

∾

BIBLIOGRAPHICAL NOTE

The best critical comment on Kelly's work may be found in the review of his several plays, reference to which is obtainable in THE READER'S GUIDE. Three of the ablest reviews are by Joseph W. Krutch in The Nation, CLXIV (Jan. 18, 1947), 81; by John Mason Brown in The Saturday Review of Literature, Vol. XXX, No. 10 (March 8, 1947), 32-34; by Stark Young in The New Republic, LX (Nov. 6, 1929), 323. Valuable also are John Van Druten, "Small Souls and Great Plays," Theatre Arts Monthly, XI (July, 1927), 493-498; and Burns Mantle, CONTEMPORARY AMERICAN PLAYWRIGHTS (New York: Dodd, Mead & Co., Inc., 1938). For other bibliography see F. B. Millett, CONTEMPORARY AMERICAN AUTHORS (New York: Harcourt, Brace & Company, Inc., 1940).

Craig's Wife

CHARACTERS

MISS AUSTEN   WALTER CRAIG

MRS. HAROLD   MRS. FRAZIER

MAZIE   BILLY BIRKMIRE

MRS. CRAIG   JOSEPH CATELLE

ETHEL LANDRETH   HARRY

EUGENE FREDERICKS

ACT I

*The entire action of the play transpires between five-thirty in the
evening and nine o'clock the following morning, in the living room in
the home of* MR. WALTER CRAIG. *This room, like all the other rooms in
the house, reflects the very excellent taste and fanatical orderliness of
its mistress. It is a kind of frozen grandeur, in dark, highly polished
wood—strewn with gorgeous, gold-colored rugs and draped in rich
brocaded satins. The piano scarf and the scarf on the oblong center
table are canary-colored, and the draperies on the bay window at the
left, and on the curving window on the stair landing at the back, are
dark green. This curving window has a beautiful built-in window
seat, with lovely cushions, and there is another built-in seat at the right
of the staircase, from which the balustrade curves upwards. On the
right, at the back, there is a wide door hung with brown velvet portières; and the rest of the room at the right is taken up with an ornamental mantelpiece, fancy mirror and fireplace. In front of this fire-*

place there is a beautiful high-backed chair. There is another big chair at the left of the center table, a small fancy chair beside the piano, and a chair at either side of the room, forward. There are two fancy benches, one immediately above the center table, and one in front of the center table. There is sufficient room between the table and this forward bench to permit of the business of passing between them. Up at the left there is a glass vestibule, one door of which opens into the room and the other out on to the front porch. As MRS. *CRAIG enters, she appears to have been dressed for this particular room. She wears an extremely fashionable fawn-colored ensemble suit, brown slippers and stockings, and a small, dark brown velvet toque. She carries a brown leather pocket-book and a brown silk umbrella.*

MISS AUSTEN *hurries down the stairs and out through the portières at the right.* MRS. HAROLD *comes in through the door up at the left, carrying the evening newspaper and some tabourette doilies, and moves down towards the center table.*

MRS. HAROLD: Is there something you wanted, Miss Austen?

MISS AUSTEN: No, thanks, dear, I'm just looking for that pattern that I sent for the other day: I wanted to show it to Mrs. Frazier.

MRS. HAROLD: Lift up the lid of that worktable there, Miss Austen; I think I saw a pattern of some kind in there this morning.

MISS AUSTEN: Yes, here it is, I have it. I knew I left it right here somewhere.

[*She hurries in through the portières and up the stairs.*]

MRS. HAROLD: I gave those roses she brought to Mazie to put in some water.

MISS AUSTEN: Oh, did you— thanks ever so much.

MRS. HAROLD: She's gettin' a

vase for them.

MISS AUSTEN: They're lovely, aren't they?

MRS. HAROLD: Yes, they're handsome.

[*She goes out onto the porch again, and* MAZIE *comes in through the portières, carrying a vase of pink roses, which she puts on the upper corner of the small grand piano at the left.*]

MAZIE (*calling out through the French windows to* MRS. HAROLD): Did the paper come yet, Mrs. Harold?

MRS. HAROLD: Yes, I just brought it in,—it's there on the table.

[MAZIE *picks up the paper, and strolls forward.*]

MAZIE: More rain again to-mor-

254

row.

MRS. HAROLD: Does it say so?

MAZIE: Unsettled to-night and Friday—probably thunder showers. Slightly cooler, with moderate winds.

MRS. HAROLD (*coming in*): I don't know where all the rain is comin' from.

MAZIE: It isn't very nice weather for Mrs. Craig, is it?

MRS. HAROLD: You can't tell; it might not be rainin' in Albany. Aren't these roses beautiful?

MAZIE: Yes, they're lovely.

MRS. HAROLD: I heard her telling Miss Austen she's got over two hundred rose bushes in her garden.

MAZIE (*turning and looking at* MRS. HAROLD): Is she still upstairs?

MRS. HAROLD: Yeh. I guess she's talkin' poor Miss Austen to death. (MAZIE *laughs and resumes her paper, and* MRS. HAROLD *gives an eye around the room.*) Bring that paper out with you when you're comin', Mazie; don't leave it layin' around in here.

MAZIE: All right.

MRS. HAROLD: It'ud be just like the lady to walk in on us.

[MAZIE *turns sharply and looks at her.*]

MAZIE: Mrs. Craig, do you mean?

MRS. HAROLD: She might, you can't tell.

MAZIE: I thought you said she wouldn't be back before Saturday.

MRS. HAROLD (*coming back to the table and picking up the doilies*): That's what she told me when she was goin' away. But it's just as well to keep a day or two ahead of a woman like Mrs. Craig, Mazie (*she flicks the dust from the table with the doilies*); if she gets an idea up there that there's a pin out of place around here,— she'll take the first train out of Albany. (MAZIE *makes a sound of amusement and resumes her paper and* MRS. HAROLD *starts for the door at the right.*) Oh, there's plenty like her—I've worked for three of them; you'd think their houses were God Almighty. (*She goes into the other room.*)

MAZIE: Didn't you tell me, Mrs. Harold, that you worked out on Willows Avenue one time?

MRS. HAROLD (*calling from the other room*): Yes, I worked out there for two years, at Doctor Nicholson's.

MAZIE: Did you know any people out that way by the name of Passmore?

MRS. HAROLD (*appearing between the portières*): By the name of what?

MAZIE: Passmore. Capital P-a-double s-m-o-r-e. Mr. J. Fergus Passmore and wife.

255

MRS. HAROLD: No, I don't remember anybody by that name; why?

MAZIE: Nothing.—It says here they were both found dead this morning in their home on Willows Avenue.

MRS. HAROLD: Oh, Lord have mercy on them! What happened to them?

MAZIE (*reading*): Why, it sez: "Fashionable Willows Avenue Residence Scene of Double Tragedy—Bodies of J. Fergus Passmore and Wife, Socially Prominent in This City, Found Dead in Library from Bullet Wounds—Empty Revolver Near Fireplace —Cause of Death Shrouded in Mystery—Police Working upon Identity of Gentleman Visitor Seen Leaving Premises in Automobile Shortly After Midnight." (MAZIE *looks fearfully at* MRS. HAROLD, *who shakes her head dolefully.*) "About eight o'clock this morning upon entering the library in the home of Mr. J. Fergus Passmore of 2214 Willows Avenue, Miss Selma Coates, a colored maid—"

MRS. HAROLD: Twenty-two fourteen must be out near the lake. (*The front doorbell rings incisively.*) See who that is, Mazie. [MRS. HAROLD *disappears into the other room and* MAZIE *crosses up to the door at the left, putting down the newspaper on*

256

the table as she passes.]

MRS. CRAIG (*out on the porch*): We can leave these right here, Ethel,—Mazie'll bring them in.

MAZIE: Oh, how do you do, Mrs. Craig.

MRS. CRAIG: Hello, Mazie.

MAZIE (*going out*): You're back a little ahead of time.

[MRS. HAROLD *comes in through the portières, peering out toward the front porch.*]

MRS. CRAIG: Yes, a little. Will you take these things, Mazie?

MAZIE: Yes, Ma'm.

[MRS. HAROLD *sees that it is* MRS. CRAIG, *gives a quick glance around the room, snatches up the paper from the table, and, with another glance over her right shoulder toward the front door, vanishes into the other room.*]

MRS. CRAIG: And will you see that that catch is on that screen door, Mazie—

MAZIE: Yes, Ma'm.

MRS. CRAIG (*appearing in the door*): It was half open when I came in. (*She comes into the room, sweeping it with a narrow eye, and crosses to the table to put down her handbag and umbrella.* ETHEL *wanders in after her and stands at the upper corner of the piano.*) Take your things off, dear, and sit down; you look tired. (*She moves across to the mirror over the mantelpiece at the right, and* ETHEL *puts her handbag on the piano and commences to remove her coat and hat.*) I think there's nothing in the world so exhausting as train riding. (MAZIE *comes in, carrying a lady's satchel and a suitcase.*) You may as well take those things right upstairs, Mazie.

MAZIE: Yes, Ma'm.

MRS. CRAIG (*crossing up and over to* ETHEL): Put that suitcase in the corner room, Mazie—Miss Landreth'll occupy that room for the next few days.

MAZIE (*going up the stairs*): Yes, Ma'm.

MRS. CRAIG (*taking* ETHEL's *hat and coat*): I'll take them, dear.

ETHEL: Thanks.

MRS. CRAIG: I'll have Mazie take them right up to your room.

[*She puts them down on the table carefully and* ETHEL *crosses down towards the mirror, settling her hair.*]

ETHEL: I suppose I look terrible, don't I?

MRS. CRAIG (*crossing and taking* ETHEL's *bag from the piano*): No, dear, you look quite all right. Would you like a drink of something?

ETHEL: I would like a drink of water, yes, if you don't mind.

[MRS. HAROLD *appears between the portières.*]

MRS. CRAIG: Hello, Mrs. Harold.

MRS. HAROLD: I see you're back again.

MRS. CRAIG: This is Mrs. Harold, Ethel.

ETHEL: How do you do.

[MRS. HAROLD *bows and* ETHEL *moves back again to the roses on the piano.*]

MRS. CRAIG: Miss Landreth will be staying here with us for a week or two, Mrs. Harold, so I wish you'd see that everything is all right in that corner room.

MRS. HAROLD: All right, I will.

[MAZIE *comes down the stairs.*]

MRS. CRAIG (*moving down to the mirror, removing her coat*): And will you bring a glass of water, please, Mrs. Harold.

MRS. HAROLD: Yes, Ma'm. Just one glass?

MRS. CRAIG: Yes, I don't want any.

[MRS. HAROLD *goes out again.*]

ETHEL: Aren't these roses beautiful. (MRS. CRAIG *shifts her eyes from* MAZIE, *who is gathering* ETHEL's *things up from the table, and looks steadily at the roses.*) I don't think I've ever seen such lovely roses.

MRS. CRAIG: Yes, they're very nice. Take those things upstairs, Mazie.

MAZIE (*starting up the stairs*): Yes, Ma'm.

MRS. CRAIG: And I wish you'd use that back way when you go up and down stairs, Mazie.

MAZIE (*coming down again*):

257

I always keep forgettin' that.

[ETHEL *turns and looks at* MAZIE, *and* MRS. CRAIG, *laying her coat across* MAZIE'S *arm as she passes her, moves up to look at the stairs closely.* MAZIE *goes out at the right.*]

MRS. CRAIG: This stairway'll soon look the way it did before, with everybody tramping up and down it every five minutes. (*She turns to* ETHEL *with a kind of apologetic smile, and commences to remove her gloves.*) It doesn't seem ever to occur to anybody in the house, Ethel, to use the back stairway. It's the funniest thing you've ever seen in your life, really. We might just as well not have one. No matter how many times they have to go up or down stairs, they must go tramping up and down this front way. And you know what stairs look like after they've been tramped up and down a few times. (MRS. HAROLD *comes in with a glass of water on a small silver tray.*) Thanks, Mrs. Harold.

ETHEL (*picking up a framed photograph from the piano*): Isn't this Mother's picture, Aunt Harriet?

[MRS. HAROLD *goes out.*]

MRS. CRAIG: Yes, that's your mother.

ETHEL: I thought it looked something like her.

MRS. CRAIG: She had it taken at Lakewood one summer, and I al-

ways liked it. I like that dress; it never seemed to get old-fashioned.

ETHEL (*starting to cry*): It doesn't look much like her now, does it?

MRS. CRAIG (*putting the picture back on the piano*): Now, Ethel dear, you mustn't start that. Your mother's been through this very same kind of thing many times before.

ETHEL: But, I should *be* there, Aunt Harriet. Supposing something should happen.

MRS. CRAIG: But, nothing is going to happen, dear child. I haven't the slightest doubt but that your mother will come through this little spell just as she's come through all the others.

ETHEL: I don't think the others have been as serious as this, though.

MRS. CRAIG: Listen, Ethel dear, I've seen your mother at least a dozen times at what I was perfectly sure was the point of death, and she's always come around all right.

ETHEL: Well, why did Doctor Wood send for me, if he didn't think it was serious?

MRS. CRAIG: Because your mother asked him to, I suppose, dear; just as she asked him to send for me. But he certainly couldn't have thought it was so very serious when he suggested you come away with me.

ETHEL: It wasn't the doctor that suggested that, Aunt Harriet, it was the night nurse,—I heard her tell him so. She said it upset Mother too much to see me, and if I were there she'd want to see me.

MRS. CRAIG: Well, that's very true, dear; but you know how she cried when you came in. And there's nothing in the world so upsetting to the heart as crying.

ETHEL: But, I should be there; it seems terrible to me now to have walked away and left Mother in that condition.

MRS. CRAIG: But, what could you do if you'd stayed, dear?

ETHEL (*with a touch of desperation*): I'd at least know what was going on.

MRS. CRAIG (*handing her the glass of water, and putting her arm around her shoulder*): Now, don't upset yourself, Ethel. Here, take a sip of this water. I'm perfectly sure you're magnifying the seriousness of your mother's condition, dear. And I most certainly should never have come away myself only that I've seen this same thing over and over again. (*She turns and settles the photograph on the piano.*) Besides, there isn't a solitary thing we could do if we'd stayed; those nurses won't allow it. And the doctor said I was upsetting your mother,—sim-

ply because I told her a few things I thought she should be told.

ETHEL: There was something I wanted to tell her, too, but he said he thought I'd better wait.

MRS. CRAIG: Well, I'd have told her anyway, if I'd been you.

ETHEL: I'm rather sorry now I didn't,—I think it would have made her easier in her mind.

MRS. CRAIG: Was it something important?

ETHEL: It was about Professor Fredericks, at school. Mother met him last year when she was up there at Commencement, and she liked him very much. And when we got home she said if he ever said anything to me, she'd be glad if I could like him well enough to marry him. She said she'd feel easier about me, in case anything ever happened to *her*. And I wanted to tell her.

MRS. CRAIG: You mean he *had* said something?

ETHEL: Yes, he asked me to marry him right after Easter. But I didn't write anything about it to Mother; I thought I'd wait until she'd be up there in June for my Commencement, and then I'd tell her.

MRS. CRAIG: I don't know why your mother should be so panicky about your future, Ethel; you're only nineteen.

ETHEL: She said she'd like to feel that I'd *have* somebody.

259

MRS. CRAIG: Why does a person need anybody, dear, if he has money enough to get along on? (*She turns and crosses to the mirror to remove her hat.*) And, as a matter of fact, you wouldn't be left absolutely desolate even if something *did* happen to your mother. You'd always have me— I'm your mother's sister. So that, really, I think you're a very foolish girl, Ethel, if you allow your mother's apprehensions to rush you into marriage. Unless, of course, it were an advantageous marriage.

ETHEL: She didn't want to rush me into it—she simply said she thought it would be better for me to be settled.

MRS. CRAIG (*bringing her hat back to the table, and taking a powder puff from her bag*): Well, naturally, I can understand that, of course. But, after all, simply being settled isn't everything, Ethel—a girl can be a great deal worse off being settled than when she was unsettled. And, personally, I can't conceive of being very much worse off than married to a college professor—stuck away in some dreadful place like Poughkeepsie or Northampton—with not a ten-cent piece to bless yourself with—unless you used your own money. I'm constantly reading agitations in the newspapers about the poor pay of college professors. And your marrying one

of them will hardly improve the situation. (*She flips the bag back onto the table, and moves forward to a small ornamental bench in front of the center table, where she kneels.*) Did you accept this man when he asked you?

ETHEL: Practically, yes. We'd rather thought of being married sometime during the summer.

MRS. CRAIG: Then, you mean you're engaged to him?

ETHEL: Yes. I knew Mother liked him, for she said so. The only thing was, she wanted me to be sure that *I* liked him.

MRS. CRAIG: Well, that's all very nice, Ethel, but simply liking a man isn't going to go very far toward keeping things going, is it?

ETHEL: Well, I have money of my own, Aunt Harriet.

MRS. CRAIG: I know that, dear child, but surely he isn't marrying you because of that?

ETHEL: No, of course not; he doesn't know anything about that.

MRS. CRAIG: Well, I hope not— he surely wouldn't expect you to use your own money to keep *his* house going. If a man marries a girl he certainly must expect to support her, at least.

ETHEL: Well, he does expect to support me, naturally.

MRS. CRAIG: How, dear—on a professor's salary?

ETHEL: Why, lots of professors are married, Aunt Harriet.

MRS. CRAIG: But their wives are not living the way you've been accustomed to living, Ethel: not the wives of young professors, at least. And I suppose this man is young, isn't he?

ETHEL: He's twenty-seven.

MRS. CRAIG: Well, there you are. He's very lucky if he's getting two hundred dollars a month: unless he's some very extraordinary kind of professor; and he can scarcely be that at twenty-seven years of age.

ETHEL: He's professor of the Romance Languages.

MRS. CRAIG: Naturally. And I suppose he's told you he loves you in all of them.

ETHEL: Well, I certainly shouldn't care to think about marriage at all, Aunt Harriet, unless I were at least in love with the man. [MRS. CRAIG *gives a little smile of pained amusement, and moves towards* ETHEL.]

MRS. CRAIG: That is your age, Ethel darling: we all pass through that. It's the snare of romance,—that the later experience of life shows us to have been nothing more than the most impractical sentimentality. (*She arranges the piano scarf more precisely.*) Only the majority of women are caught with the spell of it, unfortunately; and then they are obliged to revert right back to the almost primitive feminine dependence and

subjection that they've been trying to emancipate themselves from for centuries.

[*She crosses to the big chair at the left of the center table and straightens it.*]

ETHEL: Well, *you* married, Aunt Harriet.

MRS. CRAIG (*leaning on the back of the chair*): But not with any romantic illusions, dear. I saw to it that my marriage should be a way toward emancipation for *me*. I had no private fortune like you, Ethel; and no special equipment, —outside of a few more or less inapplicable college theories. So the only road to independence for *me*, that *I* could see, was through the man I married. I know that must sound extremely materialistic to *you*, after listening to the professor of romantic languages; —but it isn't really; because it isn't financial independence that I speak of particularly. I knew that would come—as the result of *another* kind of independence; and that is the independence of authority—*over* the man I married. And that doesn't necessarily imply any dishonesty of attitude toward that man, either. I have a full appreciation of Mr. Craig— he's a very good man; but he's a husband—a lord and master—*my* master. And I married to be independent.

ETHEL: Independent of your

husband too, do you mean?

MRS. CRAIG: Independent of everybody. I lived with a step-mother, Ethel, for nearly twelve years, and with your mother after she was married for over five; I know what it is to be on someone else's floor. And I married to be on my own—in every sense of the word. I haven't entirely achieved the condition yet—but I know it can be done.

[*She turns and glances up the stairs and out through the portières, to assure herself that no one is listening.*]

ETHEL: I don't understand what you mean, exactly, Aunt Harriet.

MRS. CRAIG (*turning to* ETHEL *again*): I mean that I'm simply exacting my share of a bargain. Mr. Craig wanted a wife and a home; and he has them. And he can be perfectly sure of them, be-cause the wife that he got hap-pens to be one of the kind that regards her husband and home as more or less ultimate conditions. And my share of the bargain was the security and protection that those conditions imply. And I have *them*. But, unlike Mr. Craig, I can't be absolutely sure of them; because I know that, to a very great extent, they are at the mercy of the *mood* of a *man*. (*She smiles knowingly.*) And I sup-pose I'm too practical-minded to accept that as a sufficient guaran-tee of their permanence. So I must secure their permanence for myself.

ETHEL: How?

MRS. CRAIG: By securing into my own hands the control of the man upon which they are founded.

ETHEL: How are you ever going to do a thing like that, Aunt Har-riet?

MRS. CRAIG: Haven't you ever made Mr. Fredericks do some-thing you wanted him to do?

ETHEL: Yes, but I always told him that I wanted him to do it.

MRS. CRAIG (*half-sitting on the arm of the big chair*): But there are certain things that men can't be told, Ethel; they don't under-stand them; particularly romantic men; and Mr. Craig is inveterately idealistic.

ETHEL: But, supposing he were to find out sometime?

MRS. CRAIG: Find out what?

ETHEL: What you've just been telling me—that you wanted to control him.

MRS. CRAIG: One never compre-hends, dear, what it is not in one's nature to comprehend. And even if it were possible, what about it? It's such an absolutely unprovable thing; that is, I mean to say, it isn't a thing that one does or says, spe-cifically; it's a matter of—interpre-tation. (*She is amused.*) And that's where women have such a tremendous advantage over men;

so few men are capable of interpreting them. But, they can always interpret themselves, if they're so disposed. And if the interpretation is for the instruction of a romantic husband, a woman can always keep it safely within the exigencies of the moment. (*She laughs a little, and moves over to* ETHEL, *resting her hand on* ETHEL's *shoulder.*) I know you're mentally deploring my lack of nobility.

ETHEL: No, I'm not at all, Aunt Harriet.

MRS. CRAIG: Yes, you are, I see it in your face. You think I'm a very sordid woman.

ETHEL: No, I don't think anything of the kind.

MRS. CRAIG: Well, what *do* you think?

ETHEL: Well, frankly, Aunt Harriet, I don't think it's quite honest.

MRS. CRAIG: But it's very much safer, dear—for everybody. Because, as I say, if a woman is the right kind of a woman, it's better that the destiny of her home should be in *her* hands—than in any man's. (MRS. HAROLD *appears between the portières.*) Did you want to see me about something, Mrs. Harold?

MRS. HAROLD: It'll do after a while, Mrs. Craig; I thought the young lady had gone upstairs.

MRS. CRAIG: No, not yet, she's going up immediately. That's

what I want you to do, Ethel—go upstairs and lie down for an hour or so; you'll feel ever so much better. I'll call you in time for dinner.

[ETHEL *rises and moves towards the stairs.*]

ETHEL: I don't think I'll be able to eat any dinner, Aunt Harriet.

MRS. CRAIG: Well, now, you might feel very different after you've had a bit of a rest.

ETHEL: I'm so terribly worried, Aunt Harriet.

MRS. CRAIG: I know, dear child, it's very trying; but it's one of the things we've got to go through with, I suppose. Besides, worrying can't possibly help her, dear.

[MRS. CRAIG *continues with* ETHEL *up to the landing, and* ETHEL *goes on up the stairs.*]

ETHEL: Oh, how can I help worrying.

MRS. CRAIG: You can't help it, of course, dear; that's the reason I want you to lie down for a while. I'll be up in a few minutes—just as soon as I've seen to a few things down here. It's the room straight down the hall, to the right. Mazie's very likely in there now. And don't worry, dear. (ETHEL *disappears at the head of the stairs, and* MRS. CRAIG *looks closely at the landing, to see if she can discover any fresh scratches upon it.* MRS. HAROLD *comes in at the right.*) What was it you wanted to see me about, Mrs. Harold?

[*She comes down into the room again.*]

MRS. HAROLD: Why, I wanted to tell you, Mrs. Craig, that the cook left on Thursday. She went away and didn't come back.

MRS. CRAIG: Did she get her wages?

MRS. HAROLD: I paid her up till Tuesday.

MRS. CRAIG: Did she take her things with her?

MRS. HAROLD: Why, she only had a suitcase and a small graphophone; she took *them*. But I didn't think anything about it, because she took *them* every Thursday.

MRS. CRAIG: Have you been doing the cooking since, Mrs. Harold?

MRS. HAROLD: Yes, we've been managin' between us. Mazie's a pretty good cook. I called up the Camac Agency on Saturday to send somebody out, but Miss Hewlitt said she wanted to see you first. She sez she's sent so many, she wants to find out what's the matter before she sends any more.

MRS. CRAIG (*crossing to the piano*): She ought to have a few of them cook for her; she'd *know* what was the matter. Where did these roses come from, Mrs. Harold?

MRS. HAROLD: Why, that woman across the street brought them over to Miss Austen.

MRS. CRAIG: Mrs. Frazier, you mean?

MRS. HAROLD: Yes, Ma'm, she brought them over to the porch —Miss Austen was sitting out there sewing.

MRS. CRAIG: Well, you'd better take them out of here, Mrs. Harold: the petals'll be all over the room.

[MRS. HAROLD *moves across to the roses, and* MRS. CRAIG *busies herself with the draperies in the bay window beyond the piano.*]

MRS. HAROLD: You didn't have to stay away as long as you thought, did you?

MRS. CRAIG: Well, I suppose I *could* have stayed away indefinitely, if I had allowed myself to become sentimental. But I'm afraid I haven't very much patience with sick people, Mrs. Harold.

[MRS. HAROLD *takes the vase of roses and starts back across towards the portières.*]

MRS. HAROLD: Well, I suppose it takes all kinds to make a world.

MRS. CRAIG: I suppose so.

MRS. HAROLD (*stopping, and turning*): Where do you want these roses put, Mrs. Craig?

MRS. CRAIG: I don't care where you put them, Mrs. Harold, as long as they're not in the rooms; I don't want to be picking up petals every two minutes.

MRS. HAROLD: Maybe Miss Austen 'ud like them in her room.

MRS. CRAIG (*moving down to examine the spot where the vase stood*): Maybe she would; you can ask her. Is she up there now?

MRS. HAROLD: Yes, Ma'm; Mrs. Frazier is showing her something about a pattern that she has.

[MRS. CRAIG *looks at her.*]

MRS. CRAIG: Do you mean to tell me that Mrs. Frazier is upstairs, Mrs. Harold?

MRS. HAROLD: Yes, Ma'm, she's up there.

MRS. CRAIG: And how did she happen to *get* up there?

MRS. HAROLD: Well, I don't know, I'm sure, Mrs. Craig, unless Miss Austen asked her.

MRS. CRAIG: All right. (*She crosses to the foot of the stairs and looks up, and* MRS. HAROLD *goes out through the portières.*) Have there been any letters or messages for me, Mrs. Harold, since I've been away?

MRS. HAROLD: Why, there were two letters, yes; I left them in your room. (*Coming into the room again.*) One came this morning, and one came Tuesday. And there was a gentleman called Mr. Craig last night about eight o'clock, but he'd gone out. So I gave him the telephone number that Mr. Craig gave me in case anybody called him.

MRS. CRAIG: Who was the gentleman? Did you get his name?

MRS. HAROLD: Yes, Ma'm, he said his name was Birkmire.

MRS. CRAIG: Do you know if he got Mr. Craig all right?

MRS. HAROLD: Yes, Ma'm, he did; because when I told Mr. Craig this morning about him calling, he said it was all right, that he'd talked to him last night. And then he called again this afternoon about half-past four.

[MRS. CRAIG *turns and looks at her.*]

MRS. CRAIG: Mr. Birkmire did?

MRS. HAROLD: Yes, Ma'm; he said he wanted Mr. Craig to get in touch with him as soon as he came in.

MRS. CRAIG: What number was it Mr. Craig gave you last night, Mrs. Harold, to have Mr. Birkmire call him at?

MRS. HAROLD: Why, it was Levering three, one hundred. I wrote it down on a piece of paper, so I wouldn't forget it.

MRS. CRAIG: All right, Mrs. Harold, I'll tell him when he comes. (MRS. HAROLD *goes out.*) And will you get another vase for those roses, Mrs. Harold, before you take them up—

MRS. HAROLD: All right, I will.

MRS. CRAIG: That one belongs down here. (*She stands and thinks quietly for a second; then, with a glance up the stairs and out after* MRS. HAROLD, *she moves to the telephone and picks it up.*) Give me Information, please. (*She waits, glancing toward the other room and up the stairs.* MAZIE *comes down the stairs.*)

MAZIE: Miss Landreth sent me down for her bag.

MRS. CRAIG: It's there on the table. Take that glass out, too, Mazie.

MAZIE (*picking up the glass from the table as she goes*): Yes, Ma'm.

MRS. CRAIG (*into the telephone*): Information? Why, could you give me the address of the telephone number, Levering three, one hundred? Oh, don't you?—All right, it isn't important —thank you very much.

[*She stands thinking for a second. Then the screen door outside bangs, and she sets down the telephone and moves towards the door.* MR. CRAIG *comes in briskly, wearing a Panama hat and carrying a newspaper.*]

CRAIG: Well, look who's here, bright and smiling!

[*He advances, removing his hat, and she moves a step or two towards him.*]

MRS. CRAIG: You almost beat me home.

CRAIG: How did this happen? (*He kisses her affectionately.*) When did you get in, Harriet?

MRS. CRAIG (*taking his hat and the newspaper from him and putting them on the table*): A few minutes ago. I left Albany at noon.

CRAIG (*tossing his gloves on the piano*): And how is it you didn't wire or something?

MRS. CRAIG (*picking up her own gloves from the table and straightening out the fingers*): I never thought of it, to tell the truth; there was so much to be done around there — getting Ethel's things together, and one thing and another.

CRAIG: Was Ethel there?

MRS. CRAIG: Yes, Estelle insisted that she be sent for last Saturday. And for the life of me I don't know why she did such a thing; for it upset her terribly. So the doctor said he thought the best thing to do would be to get Ethel out of her sight for a few days: so I brought her back with me. She's upstairs, lying down.

CRAIG: How *is* Estelle?

MRS. CRAIG: Why, I couldn't see that there was anything the matter with her—any more than usual. But you'd think from her letter she was dying. And then I have to walk out, and leave my house for a whole week, and go racing up to Albany.

CRAIG: Has she a trained nurse?

MRS. CRAIG (*picking up his hat from the table*): My dear, she's

266

had two of them, for over six weeks. But you know what trained nurses are.

CRAIG: Well, I'm sorry to hear Estelle is so bad.

MRS. CRAIG (*handing him his hat*): Here, take this, Walter.

CRAIG (*drawing her back into his arms*): But I'm glad to have you back again.

MRS. CRAIG (*laughing lightly*): Stop it, Walter.

CRAIG: Seems you've been away a month instead of a week.

[*He kisses the side of her head.*]

MRS. CRAIG: Don't break my bones, Walter!

CRAIG: That's what I think I'd like to do sometimes.

MRS. CRAIG (*laughing*): Now, stop it. (*He releases her and she straightens up, touching her hair.*) Stop. Here, take this hat and put it out where it belongs. (*He takes the hat and crosses above her towards the portières.*) And take this paper out of here too; this room's a sight. (*He steps back and takes the paper, then goes on out into the other room.*) Your aunt's company will be scandalized.

CRAIG: Has Auntie Austen got some company?

MRS. CRAIG (*moving up to arrange the pillows on the fancy seat at the right of the stairway*): So Mrs. Harold says. She's upstairs with her.

CRAIG: Who is it?

MRS. CRAIG: The lady of the roses, across the street there.

CRAIG: Mrs. Frazier?

MRS. CRAIG: Yes. She's getting very sociable.

CRAIG: She certainly has some beautiful roses over there, hasn't she?

MRS. CRAIG: She ought to have; she has nothing to do but look after them.

CRAIG: Those ramblers make a pretty effect, down at the side there, don't they?

MRS. CRAIG: Wait till you see them a week from now.

CRAIG (*turning to her*): Why?

MRS. CRAIG: Why, there'll be petals all over the place over there.

CRAIG: That ought to be prettier than the way it is now.

MRS. CRAIG: Well, you might not think it was so pretty if you had to sweep them up.

CRAIG (*taking some papers from his inside pocket, and moving to the chair beside the piano*): I wouldn't sweep them up. (MRS. CRAIG *makes a sound of vast amusement.*) I can't think of anything much prettier than to have rose petals scattered all over the lawn. (*He sits down.*)

MRS. CRAIG (*straightening the big chair in front of the fireplace*): You'd have a nice looking place, I must say.

267

CRAIG: It's a wonder she wouldn't bring a few of those roses over here to Auntie Austen.

MRS. CRAIG: I guess she has sense enough to know that if we wanted roses we could plant some. Listen; she's apt to be down here any minute, Walter, and if I were you I wouldn't be sitting there when she comes; for if she sees you you'll never get away till she's told you her entire history. I've just escaped it twice.

CRAIG: I've talked to her a couple of times on the way up from the garage.

MRS. CRAIG: You mean she's talked to you.

CRAIG: No, she was out there fixing the roses when I came by.

MRS. CRAIG: Of course she was. That's where she is most of the time. (*Becoming confidential, and moving towards him, below the table.*) And the funny part of it is, Walter, I don't think she realizes that people know exactly why she does it. Really, it's the most transparently obvious thing I've ever seen in my life.

CRAIG: Well, why do you think she does it?

MRS. CRAIG: Why do I think she does it?

CRAIG: Yes.

[MRS. CRAIG *laughs, with a shade of amused impatience.*]

MRS. CRAIG: Well now, Walter —why do certain women go about

all the time with a child by the hand, or a dog on a leash. To ᵢacilitate the—approach. (*She returns to the table and puts her gloves in her pocketbook; and* CRAIG *sits looking at her, mystified.*) Only the lady upstairs uses roses. So, really, I wouldn't be sitting there when she comes down, if I were you, Walter; you know there *is* a danger in propinquity.

CRAIG (*resuming his letters*): I guess she could have gotten plenty of men if she'd wanted them.

MRS. CRAIG: But she may not have been able to get the kind she wanted. And *you* may be the kind. (*He looks at her and laughs.*) And this little visit this afternoon, laden with flowers, may be simply the initial attack in a very highly premeditated campaign.

CRAIG: Did you say she brought some flowers over this afternoon?

MRS. CRAIG: I said, "highly premeditated." I believe you told me you'd stopped a number of times to talk to her.

CRAIG: I've stopped twice, as a matter of fact.

MRS. CRAIG: And admired her roses?

CRAIG: There was nothing much else to talk about.

MRS. CRAIG: Of course there wasn't; that's the point. And if there hadn't been any roses, there wouldn't have been anything at all to talk about. And you wouldn't have stopped, and talked. (*She looks at him directly and smiles.*) But since you did, why—it isn't at all inconceivable that she should conclude that you probably liked roses. And that you might regard it as a very charming little gesture if she were to just bring a few over sometime—to your aunt—when your wife was out of the city.

CRAIG (*leaning back against the piano and looking at his letters*): What are you trying to do, kid me, Harriet?

MRS. CRAIG: Not at all. Don't lean back against that piano that way, Walter, you might scratch it.

CRAIG: My coat won't scratch it.

MRS. CRAIG (*crossing hurriedly*): Well, there might be something in your pocket that will. (*She pushes him away from the piano.*) Now, sit up. (*She gives him a little slap on the back.*) Sit over there.

[*She indicates the big chair at the left of the center table, and he rises good-naturedly and crosses to it. Then she busies herself examining the spot on the piano where he leaned, and settling the piano scarf carefully.*]

CRAIG: Yes, sir, I think that's what you're trying to do, Harriet, just kid me.

MRS. CRAIG: Well now, do you think what I've been saying is at all improbable?

CRAIG: No, it isn't improbable; it's just funny.

MRS. CRAIG: The flowers were on the piano when I came in.

CRAIG: Well, if they were they were for Auntie Austen.

MRS. CRAIG: Maybe they were. I sent them up to her room, anyway. So Mrs. Frazier probably thinks I *thought* they were for Auntie Austen. (*She starts for the portières at the right, and he looks after her and laughs. She turns and looks at him.*) What are you laughing at?

CRAIG: You.

MRS. CRAIG: Really?

CRAIG: You're very amusing to-night.

MRS. CRAIG (*coming forward at the right of the table*): And I think you're just a little bit reckless, Walter—sitting there tempting the temptress.

CRAIG: You know, I think you're getting jealous of me, Harriet.

MRS. CRAIG (*amused*): Not at all, dear boy; I'm simply suspicious of rich, middle-aged divorcees, who specialize in wayside roses.

CRAIG: Mrs. Frazier isn't a divorcee.

MRS. CRAIG: Isn't she?

CRAIG: No, her husband was killed in an automobile accident

269

in 1915. She told me so herself. She was in the car with him.

MRS. CRAIG: And how is it she wasn't killed?

CRAIG (*laughing a little*): Well now, does everybody have to be killed in automobile accidents?

MRS. CRAIG: No, there's always the Galveston Flood, for husbands. You're a very guileless young man, Walter; and I'm sorry your mind doesn't work just a little bit more rapidly.

CRAIG: It works pretty thoroughly, though, when it sees the point.

MRS. CRAIG: But, that's a very slight advantage, Walter, if the point is made before you see it.

CRAIG: Do you know, I'd like to be able to see just what's going on in your mind to-night.

MRS. CRAIG: Well, if you could, I daresay you'd find something very similar to what's going on in the minds of most of our neighbors these days.

CRAIG: Now, just what do you mean by that?

MRS. CRAIG: They have eyes, Walter; and they use them. And I wish you'd use yours. And I also wish you'd tell me whose telephone number Levering three, one hundred is.

CRAIG: Fergus Passmore, why?

MRS. CRAIG: Nothing, I was just wondering. Mrs. Harold told me you gave her that number last night in case anybody wanted you, and I was wondering where it was.

[*She moves towards the door again.*]

CRAIG: Fergus Passmore's. I was playing cards out there last night. I ran into him yesterday in front of the First National, and he asked me to come out there last night and play a little poker.

MRS. CRAIG: What did Billy Birkmire want you for?

CRAIG: Why, a—

MRS. CRAIG: Mrs. Harold said he called you up.

CRAIG: Yes, Fergus told me to get hold of him, too, and bring him out there; so I did; but he called me up later to tell me that his father had just come in from St. Paul, and he wouldn't be able to make it. I wasn't here when he called, so I talked to him from there.

MRS. CRAIG: I hope you're not going to get into card-playing again, Walter.

CRAIG: Why, I never gave up card-playing.

MRS. CRAIG: Well, you haven't played in nearly a year.

CRAIG: Well, I suppose that's because *you* don't play. And most of the folks know that, so they don't ask *me*. I don't suppose Fergus would have asked me yesterday, only that I happened to mention that *you* were away.

MRS. CRAIG: Was his wife there?

CRAIG: She was for a while, but she didn't play; she was going out somewhere.

MRS. CRAIG: I suppose that's the reason Fergus asked you, wasn't it?

CRAIG: What do you mean?

MRS. CRAIG: Why, you know how insanely jealous of her he used to be.

CRAIG: Well, I'm sure he was never jealous of me.

MRS. CRAIG: He was jealous of everybody, from what I could see.

CRAIG: Oh, don't be silly, Harriet.

MRS. CRAIG: Well, you wouldn't know it, Walter, even if he were.

CRAIG: Well, I'm glad I wouldn't.

MRS. CRAIG: And you come to find out, I'll bet that's just the reason Billy Birkmire dodged it. I'll bet that's just what he called you up to tell you.

CRAIG: He didn't call me up to tell me anything of the kind, now, Harriet; he simply called me to tell me that his father had come in unexpectedly from—

MRS. CRAIG: I don't mean last night; I mean when he called you to-day.

CRAIG: He didn't call me to-day.

MRS. CRAIG: He did, this afternoon, around four o'clock.

CRAIG: Here?

MRS. CRAIG: So Mrs. Harold told me. Said he wanted you to get in touch with him as soon as you came in.

CRAIG (*rising, and crossing to the telephone*): Wonder why he didn't call the office.

MRS. CRAIG (*moving towards the portières*): Probably he did, and you'd gone.

CRAIG: What's Birkmire's number, do you know?

MRS. CRAIG: Park 840, isn't it? Unless they've changed it.

CRAIG: I think it is.

MRS. CRAIG (*lowering her voice*): And I'm really serious, Walter, about that woman upstairs.

CRAIG (*into the telephone*): Park 840.

[*There is a laugh from Mrs. Frazier, at the head of the stairs.*]

MRS. CRAIG: So if I were you I wouldn't be here when she comes down.

[*He silences her with a gesture; and, with a glance towards the head of the stairs, she goes out at the right.*]

MRS. FRAZIER: I used to have considerable difficulty myself, when I first started to use them.

CRAIG: Hello—Park 840?

MISS AUSTEN (*at the head of the stairs*): Well, I think I understand it now.

CRAIG: Is Mr. Birkmire there? (*Mrs. Frazier and Miss Austen come down the stairs.*) Oh, that's

271

too bad; I just missed him, didn't
I?

MRS. FRAZIER: Well now, please
don't hesitate to call me, Miss
Austen, if there's anything you
don't understand,—

CRAIG: Yes, this is Mr. Craig
speaking.

MISS AUSTEN: I will, I'll let you
know.

MRS. FRAZIER: Because I haven't
a solitary thing to do.

[*She sees* MR. CRAIG *at the telephone, and turns to* MISS AUS-
TEN, *laying her finger on her
lips.*]

CRAIG: Then, he'll probably be
here pretty soon. (MRS. FRAZIER
comes down into the room, and
MISS AUSTEN *stops on the landing,
looking at* MR. CRAIG.) Thanks—
that's fine. Thank you very much.
(*He hangs up.*)

MISS AUSTEN: Hello, Walter.

CRAIG: Hello, Auntie. How are
you?

MISS AUSTEN (*coming down
from the landing*): I didn't know
you were home.

CRAIG: Just got in this minute.
How do you do, Mrs. Frazier.

MRS. FRAZIER: How do you do,
Mr. Craig.

MISS AUSTEN: Mrs. Frazier was
kind enough to come up and show
me something about a new pattern
that I just bought.

CRAIG: That so?

MISS AUSTEN: Mrs. Harold tells

me that Harriet is home.

CRAIG: Yes, she just got in ahead
of me.

MISS AUSTEN: Did she say how
Mrs. Landreth was?

CRAIG: Pretty bad shape, I imagine, from what she says.

MISS AUSTEN: Where is Harriet,
upstairs?

CRAIG: Yes, she's just taken her
things up.

MRS. FRAZIER: Miss Austen was
telling me that Mrs. Craig's sister
has heart trouble.

CRAIG: Yes, she's had it a long
time.

MRS. FRAZIER: Poor woman.

MISS AUSTEN: Nearly ten years.

MRS. FRAZIER: How unfortunate.
I suppose Mrs. Craig is very much
upset, isn't she?

CRAIG: Yes, I suppose she is.

MRS. FRAZIER: Is she her only
sister?

CRAIG: Yes, there are just the
two of them.

MRS. FRAZIER: Too bad. But,
that's the way it seems to go as a
rule, doesn't it?

CRAIG: Yes, that's true.

MISS AUSTEN: Walter, you should
see all the wonderful roses Mrs.
Frazier just brought me over.

[MRS. FRAZIER *gives a little deprecating laugh and moves
towards the piano at the left.*]

CRAIG: Oh, yes?

MISS AUSTEN: They're perfectly
beautiful.

MRS. FRAZIER: Not a very generous giving, I'm afraid, when there are so many of them.

CRAIG AND MISS AUSTEN (*speaking together*):

CRAIG: Well, I'm sure we appreciate it very much.

MISS AUSTEN: I think it's very charming of you to remember us at all.

MRS. FRAZIER: Sometimes I think perhaps I am a bit foolish to have so many of them, because it *is* a lot of work.

MISS AUSTEN: It must be; I often say that to Walter.

MRS. FRAZIER: Yes, it is. But, you see, they were more or less of a hobby with my husband when he was alive; and I suppose I tend them out of sentiment, really, more than anything else.

MISS AUSTEN: How long has your husband been dead, Mrs. Frazier?

MRS. FRAZIER: He'll be dead ten years this coming November. Yes. Yes, he died the twenty-third of November, 1915. He was injured on the second, in an automobile accident at Pride's Crossing, Massachusetts: we were on our way back from Bar Harbor—I was telling Mr. Craig about it. And he lingered from that until the twenty-third. So, you see, the melancholy days have really a very literal significance for me.

MISS AUSTEN: I should say so, indeed.

MRS. FRAZIER: Yes, that is the one month I must get away. I don't care where I go, but I must go somewhere; I couldn't stand it here; I have too many memories. So every year, as soon as ever November comes around, I just pack up my things and go out to Dayton, Ohio. I have a married daughter living out there; her husband is connected with the National Cash Register Company. And, of course, she makes all manner of fun of my annual pilgrimages to Dayton. She says instead of being in England now that April's there, with me it's in Dayton now that November's there. (*She laughs faintly.*) We have great fun about it. But, of course, her husband's business is there. And I think sometimes perhaps I should spend more time with her; I think it would help us both. But the trouble is, when I go out there, it's so very difficult for me to get away again. She has the most adorable baby — just fifteen months old; and he thinks there's nobody in the world like his grandmother. And, of course, *I* think there's nobody in the world like *him*. Although, to tell the truth, I did resent him terrifically when he was born—to think that he'd made me a grandmother. But he's quite won me over; and I suppose I'm as foolish now as all

273

the other grandmothers.

MISS AUSTEN: Is she your only daughter, Mrs. Frazier?

MRS. FRAZIER: Yes, she was my only child.

CRAIG: Then, you live alone over here, Mrs. Frazier?

MRS. FRAZIER: All alone, yes.

MISS AUSTEN: Is that so?

MRS. FRAZIER: Yes, I've lived alone now for nearly four years— ever since my daughter was married. Alone at fifty. (*She laughs lightly.*) Rather a premature desolation, isn't it?

CRAIG: Certainly is.

MISS AUSTEN: I should say so.

MRS. FRAZIER: I remember reading a story by that name one time, a number of years ago; and I remember thinking then, how dreadful that would be—to be left alone —especially for a woman. And yet the very same thing happened to me before I was fifty.

MISS AUSTEN: Well, didn't you ever think of going out and living with your daughter, Mrs. Frazier?

MRS. FRAZIER: Well, of course, she has never given up trying to persuade me to do that; but I always say to her, "No, darling, I will live out my days in your father's house—even though he isn't there." I say, "I have my memories, at least; and nobody can take those from me." Of course, she says I'm sentimental; (*she laughs*) but I'm not, really—not the least

bit. Because if I were, I should have probably married again; but I feel that—

CRAIG: I should think you would have married again, Mrs. Frazier.

MRS. FRAZIER: Well, I suppose that would have been the logical thing to do, Mr. Craig; but, I don't know—I suppose perhaps I'm one of those one-man women. There are such women, you know.

MISS AUSTEN: Yes, indeed there are.

MRS. FRAZIER: Just as there are one-woman men. And I think it's particularly unfortunate when anything happens to the attachment of a person of that kind— whether it's death, or disillusionment, or whatever it is—because the impairment is always so absolutely irreparable. A person of that type can never care very greatly again, about anything.

MISS AUSTEN (*looking away off*): That's very true, Mrs. Frazier.

MRS. FRAZIER (*falling into a mood*): Never. (*She shakes her head slowly from side to side; then starts.*) Well, I think I'd better go, or you'll be agreeing with my daughter that I'm sentimental.

MISS AUSTEN AND CRAIG (*speaking together*):

MISS AUSTEN: Oh, not at all, Mrs. Frazier; I agree with you perfectly.

CRAIG: I think a little bit of

sentiment is a very nice thing sometimes.

MRS. FRAZIER: And I do hope you'll tell Mrs. Craig that I was inquiring about her sister.

CRAIG: I will, Mrs. Frazier, thank you very much.

MRS. FRAZIER: I hope she'll be better soon. Good afternoon, Mr. Craig.

[*She goes out.*]

CRAIG: Good afternoon, Mrs. Frazier. I hope you'll come over again very soon.

MRS. FRAZIER (*calling back*): Thanks ever so much, I shall be delighted to.

MISS AUSTEN (*following her out*): And thanks again for the roses.

[CRAIG *turns away from the door and goes up the stairs.* MRS. CRAIG *appears between the portières, looking darkly towards the bay window at the left, where* MRS. FRAZIER *can be seen passing across the lawn.*]

MRS. FRAZIER: Oh, don't mention it, dear child, I should have brought you twice as many.

MISS AUSTEN: And I'll let you know if there's anything I don't understand as I go along.

MRS. FRAZIER: Please do, now, Miss Austen; don't hesitate to call me.

MISS AUSTEN: I will, I'll let you know.

MRS. FRAZIER: Good-by.

MISS AUSTEN: Good-by, Mrs. Frazier.

[*The screen door slams. Mrs. Craig moves forward to the mirror over the mantelpiece at the right.*]

MRS. CRAIG: The silly creature.

[*She stands looking in the mirror, touching her hair. Miss Austen comes in.*]

MISS AUSTEN: Oh, Harriet, I was just going up to your room. How did you find your sister? Mrs. Harold told me a moment ago that you were back.

MRS. CRAIG (*without turning*): Yes, I'm back. (*Turning, with a touch of challenge in her manner.*) And I think it's about time I came back, don't you?

MISS AUSTEN: Why, dear?

MRS. CRAIG: Why?

MISS AUSTEN: Yes, I don't understand what you mean.

MRS. CRAIG: Well, from the looks of things, if I'd stayed away much longer, I should have probably come back to find my house a thoroughfare for the entire neighborhood.

MISS AUSTEN: You mean Mrs. Frazier being here?

MRS. CRAIG: You know perfectly well what I mean, Auntie Austen; please don't try to appear so innocent. (*She moves up to the foot of the stairs, to assure herself that* MR. CRAIG *is not within hearing distance.* MISS AUSTEN *gives her a long, narrow look and moves forward at the right of the piano. There is a pause; then* MRS. CRAIG *comes forward to the center table in a perfect fury.*) That's exactly what that woman's been trying to do ever since we've been here; and the minute you get my back turned you let her succeed—just for the sake of a lot of small talk. How did she happen to get in here?

MISS AUSTEN: Why, I asked her in, of course; you don't suppose she walked in of her own accord.

MRS. CRAIG: I wouldn't put it past her, if she knew I was away. (MISS AUSTEN *looks at her.*) I know Mrs. Frazier's type better than you do. (*She settles the things on the table.*) What did you do; go over after her?

MISS AUSTEN: No, I did not. I was sewing on the porch there, and she brought me some roses over, which I think was very thoughtful of her.

MRS. CRAIG: Very thoughtful.

MISS AUSTEN: And I happened to mention the dress that I was making, and that the pattern that I'd bought for it wasn't quite clear to me. And she seemed to know from my description just what pattern it was, and very kindly offered to help me.

MRS. CRAIG: Of course; and you walked right into the trap.

MISS AUSTEN: Well, why do you think she should be so anxious to get in *here,* Harriet?

MRS. CRAIG: For the same reason that a lot of other women in this neighborhood want to get in here —to satisfy their vulgar curiosity; and see what they can see.

MISS AUSTEN: And, why should you care if they do see?

MRS. CRAIG: I wouldn't gratify them—I don't want a lot of idle neighbors on visiting terms. Let them tend to their houses, and they'll have plenty to do: instead of wasting their time with a lot of silly roses. (*She crosses down to the mirror again.*) Mrs. Frazier is very likely one of those housekeepers that hides the dirt in the corners with a bunch of roses.

MISS AUSTEN: You know nothing about her house, Harriet.

MRS. CRAIG: I know what her lawn looks like,—that's enough for me. And you had to bring her upstairs, too, for fear she wouldn't see enough down here.

MISS AUSTEN: I don't suppose the woman knows what you've got in your house, Harriet.

MRS. CRAIG: Oh, Auntie Austen! Really, I wish you were as guileless in certain other respects as you seem to be in the matter of visiting neighbors.

MISS AUSTEN: A good neighbor is a very good thing sometimes, Harriet.

MRS. CRAIG: Well, you may have them; I don't want them running in and out to me.

MISS AUSTEN: None of them has ever run in and out to you so far that I remember.

MRS. CRAIG: One of them has just left.

MISS AUSTEN: She wasn't here to see you.

MRS. CRAIG: She was in my house, wasn't she?

MISS AUSTEN: And in your husband's house.

MRS. CRAIG: Oh—(*She gives a little laugh of mirthless amusement.*) Well, she was hardly here to see my husband, was she? [*Miss Austen holds her eye for a second.*]

MISS AUSTEN: No, she was not; although I've no doubt you'd attempt such an interpretation if you thought there was any possibility of Walter's believing it. I don't think any extremity would be too great for you, Harriet, as long as it kept people out of the Temple of the Lord. This Holy of Holies. It's a great wonder to me you haven't asked us to take off our shoes, when we walk across the carpet. (MR. CRAIG *coughs, somewhere upstairs, and* MRS. CRAIG *moves suddenly to the foot of the stairs and looks up.*) Mrs. Frazier was here to see *me,* your husband's aunt. And I made her welcome; and so did he. And

asked her to come back again. And I don't think you'd find him very much in accord with your attitude, if he knew about it.

MRS. CRAIG: Well, you'll probably tell him.

MISS AUSTEN: Oh, I've got a lot of things to tell him, Harriet.

MRS. CRAIG: I've no doubt you have.

MISS AUSTEN: I've had plenty of time to think about them during the past two years, up there in my room. And they've been particularly clear to me this past week that you've been away. That's why I've decided to tell Walter; (MRS. CRAIG *turns sharply and looks at her*) because I think he should be told. Only I want you to be here when I tell him, so that you won't be able to *twist* what I say.

MRS. CRAIG: You have a very good opinion of me, haven't you, Auntie Austen?

MISS AUSTEN: It isn't an opinion I have of you at all, Harriet; it's *you* that I have.

MRS. CRAIG: Well, whatever it is, I'm not at all interested in hearing about it. And I want you to know that I resent intensely your having brought Mrs. Frazier in here.

MISS AUSTEN: Oh, be honest about it, at least, Harriet!

MRS. CRAIG: What do you mean?

MISS AUSTEN: Why particularize on Mrs. Frazier?

277

MRS. CRAIG: Because I don't want her here.

MISS AUSTEN: You don't want anybody here.

MRS. CRAIG: I don't want *her.*
[*She strikes the table with her knuckles.*]

MISS AUSTEN (*looking directly at her*): You don't want your husband—(*Mrs. Craig starts slightly and then stands rigid.*) only that he's necessary to the upkeep here. But if you could see how that could be managed without him, his position here wouldn't be as secure as the position of one of those pillows there.

MRS. CRAIG: Well, I must say, Miss Austen, that's a very nice thing for you to say to me.

MISS AUSTEN: It's the truth, whether you like to hear it or not. You want your house, Harriet, and that's all you do want. And that's all you'll have, at the finish, unless you change your way. People who live to themselves, Harriet, are generally left to themselves; for other people will not go on being made miserable indefinitely for the sake of your ridiculous idolatry of house furnishings.

MRS. CRAIG: You seem to have borne it rather successfully.

MISS AUSTEN: I did it for Walter's sake; because I knew he wanted to have me here; and I didn't want to make it difficult. But I've been practically a recluse

in that room of mine upstairs ever since we've been here; just to avoid scratching that holy stairway, or leaving a footprint on one of these sacred rugs. I'm not used to that kind of stupidity. I'm accustomed to *living* in rooms; (MR. CRAIG *comes quietly down the stairs and stands on the landing, looking inquiringly from one to the other.* MRS. CRAIG *sees him out of the corner of her eye, and drifts forward to the mirror at the right.*) and I think too much of myself to consider their appearance where my comfort is concerned. So I've decided to make a change. Only I want my reasons to be made perfectly clear to Walter before I go—I think I owe it to him; for his own sake as well as mine.

[MISS AUSTEN *becomes aware of* CRAIG'S *presence on the stairway and turns and looks at him. There is a dead pause. Then she turns away, and* CRAIG *comes down into the room and forward at the left of the table.*]

CRAIG: What's the matter?

MRS. CRAIG (*turning*): I haven't the faintest idea, I'm sure. But from what Auntie Austen has just been saying, she seems to think there are quite a few things the matter.

CRAIG: What is it, Auntie?

MRS. CRAIG: She tells me she's

going to leave us.

[*He looks at his wife, then at his aunt.*]

MISS AUSTEN: It's nothing very new, Walter.

CRAIG (*to his wife*): Going to leave the house, you mean?

MRS. CRAIG: So she says.

[*He looks at Auntie Austen again.*]

CRAIG: You didn't say that, did you, Auntie?

MRS. CRAIG: Haven't I just told you she said it?

MISS AUSTEN: I am leaving to-morrow, Walter.

CRAIG: But, why? What's happened?

MRS. CRAIG: She says she finds my conduct of affairs here unendurable.

MISS AUSTEN: I'll be obliged to you, Harriet, if you'll allow me to explain the reasons for my going; I know them better than you do.

MRS. CRAIG (*turning to the large chair in front of the fireplace and sitting down*): You haven't any reasons that I can see; except the usual jealous reasons that women have—of the wives of men they've brought up.

MISS AUSTEN: You'll have plenty of time to give your version of my leaving after I've gone.

MRS. CRAIG: Well, sit down, then, and let us hear *your* version of it.

MISS AUSTEN: I prefer to stand, thank you.

MRS. CRAIG: Just as you please.

MISS AUSTEN (*glancing at the chair at the left, below the piano*): I doubt if I'd know quite *how* to sit in one of these chairs.

CRAIG: Why, what do you mean, Auntie? I can't believe that you've had any difficulty with any one; and especially with Harriet —who thinks the world of you. (MISS AUSTEN *smiles dryly.*) Now, you know she does, Auntie. Harriet is just as fond of you as I am. (*Turning to his wife.*) Why, it's incredible, positively.

MRS. CRAIG: I'm glad you're here —to hear some of this.

CRAIG: I suppose there *are* little irritations come up around a house occasionally, just as there are in any other business; but I'm sure you're too sensible, Auntie, to allow them to affect you to the extent of making you want to leave the house. Why, what would we do around here without you. It wouldn't seem to me that we had any house at all. What was it you said to Auntie, Harriet?

MRS. CRAIG: I haven't said anything to her, of course; she's simply using her imagination.

CRAIG: Then, it isn't anything that Harriet has said to you, Auntie?

MISS AUSTEN: Oh, no—Harriet never *says* anything. She simply acts; and leaves you to interpret

279

—if you're able. And it takes a long time to be able—until you find the key. And then it's all very simple—and very ridiculous, and incredibly selfish. So much so, Walter, that I rather despair of ever convincing you of my justification for leaving your house.

CRAIG: Well, what has Harriet done, Auntie?

MRS. CRAIG: I'll tell you what I did, Walter—I objected to Auntie Austen's having brought that woman across the street there in here while I was away.

CRAIG: You mean Mrs. Frazier?

MRS. CRAIG: Yes, I mean Mrs. Frazier.

CRAIG: Why, what's the matter with Mrs. Frazier?

MRS. CRAIG: She's a vulgar old busybody, that's what's the matter with her—that's been trying to get in here ever since we've been here.

CRAIG: What do you mean, she's been trying to get *in* here?

MRS. CRAIG: You wouldn't understand if I told you, Walter. It's a form of curiosity that women have about other women's houses that men can't appreciate.

MISS AUSTEN: Harriet is chiefly provoked, Walter, because she has allowed herself to be tempted off form for a moment. She would much prefer to have excluded Mrs. Frazier by the usual method —that has been employed in the exclusion of every other man and

woman that has ever visited here. But since she's blundered, she must attempt to justify herself now by arraigning Mrs. Frazier as everything from a vulgarian to a busybody—and even to insinuating that her visit here this afternoon was inspired by an interest in you.

MRS. CRAIG: I insinuated nothing of the kind. I simply asked a question in answer to an insinuation of yours.

MISS AUSTEN: The details are unimportant, Harriet; I know the principle.

MRS. CRAIG: Well, tell the truth about it, at least.

MISS AUSTEN: That is exactly what I am going to do—even at the risk of Walter's disfavor.

CRAIG: I don't think you could very well incur that, Auntie.

MISS AUSTEN: You're a man, Walter; and you're in love with your wife. And I am perfectly familiar with the usual result of interference under those circumstances.

CRAIG: Well, I hope I'm open to conviction, Auntie, if you have a grievance.

MISS AUSTEN: It isn't my own cause I'm about to plead; it doesn't matter about me. I sha'n't be here. But I don't want to be witness to the undoing of a man that was by way of becoming a very important citizen, without warning him of the danger.

CRAIG: I don't understand what you mean, Auntie.

MISS AUSTEN: That is probably the greater part of the danger, Walter—that you *don't* understand. If you did it would be scarcely necessary to warn you.

CRAIG: Of what?

[*There is a pause; and Miss Austen looks right into his eyes.*]

MISS AUSTEN: Your wife.

[MRS. CRAIG *breaks into a mirthless laugh, at the absurdity of* MISS AUSTEN'S *implication. Craig turns and looks at her.*]

CRAIG: What are you laughing at, Harriet?

MRS. CRAIG: Why, don't you think that's very amusing?

CRAIG: I don't know that I think it's so very amusing.

MRS. CRAIG: Well, wait till you've heard the rest of it; you'll probably change your mind.

MISS AUSTEN (*looking steadily at* MRS. CRAIG): Harriet isn't really laughing, Walter.

MRS. CRAIG: What *am* I doing, crying?

MISS AUSTEN: You are whistling in the dark.

MRS. CRAIG (*vastly amused, and rising*): Oh, dear! (*She touches her hair before the mirror.*)

MISS AUSTEN: You're terrified that your secret has been discovered.

[MRS. CRAIG *turns sharply and faces her.*]

MRS. CRAIG: Really? And what *is* my secret?

MISS AUSTEN: I think it's hardly necessary to tell you that, Harriet.

MRS. CRAIG: But, I'm interested in hearing it.

MISS AUSTEN: Well, you can listen while I tell it to Walter.

MRS. CRAIG: Very well.

MISS AUSTEN: But, I want you to know before I tell him that it didn't remain for your outburst against Mrs. Frazier here a few minutes ago to reveal it to me; I knew it almost as soon as Walter's mother knew it.

[*There is a pause: then Mrs. Craig moves a few steps towards her husband.*]

MRS. CRAIG (*with a touch of mock mysteriousness*): She means that I've been trying to poison you, secretly, Walter.

MISS AUSTEN: Not so secretly, either, Harriet.

[MRS. CRAIG *laughs lightly.*]

MRS. CRAIG (*going up towards the portières*): Well, I'm sorry I must go, for I'm sure this is going to be very amusing.

MISS AUSTEN: I've asked Harriet to stay here, Walter.

[MRS. CRAIG *turns sharply at the portières.*]

MRS. CRAIG: Well, I don't intend to stay.

MISS AUSTEN: I didn't think you would.

281

CRAIG: Why not, Harriet?

MRS. CRAIG: Because I have something more important to do than listen to a lot of absurdities.

MISS AUSTEN: Then I shall have to regard your going as an admission of the truth of those absurdities.

MRS. CRAIG: Well, you may regard it as you please: only I hope when you've finished discussing me, you'll be as frank in letting Walter know something of what *I've* been putting up with during the past two years. (*She goes out through the portières.*)

MISS AUSTEN: Playing the martyr as usual. (*Craig takes a step or two towards the portières, and they stand for a second looking after her. Then he turns and looks at his aunt.*) I could have almost spoken those last words *for* her, Walter; I know her so well.

CRAIG: I wish you'd tell me what's happened here, Auntie.

MISS AUSTEN: That isn't so easy to tell to a man, Walter; it requires a bit of elucidation.

CRAIG: What is it?

MISS AUSTEN: Walter—why do you suppose your mother asked you to promise her, when she was dying, that you'd take me with you when you married?

CRAIG: Why, I think that was a perfectly natural request, Auntie, considering what you'd been to both of us during her illness.

MISS AUSTEN: But, it wasn't as though I should *need* a home—for she knew I preferred to travel, —that that's what I was preparing to do when she was first stricken. And I never told you, Walter, but she asked *me* to promise her that I should accept your invitation when you made it. You see, she knew her woman, Walter, —the woman you were going to marry.

CRAIG: You mean that Mother didn't like Harriet?

MISS AUSTEN: Nobody could like Harriet, Walter; she doesn't want them to.

CRAIG: I like her.

MISS AUSTEN: You're blinded by a pretty face, son, as many another man has been blinded.

CRAIG: Well, what has Harriet done?

MISS AUSTEN: She's left *you* practically friendless, for one thing; because the visits of your friends imply an importance to you that is at variance with her plan: so she's made it perfectly clear to them, by a thousand little gestures, that they are not welcome in her house. Because this *is* her house, you know, Walter; it isn't yours—don't make any mistake about that. This house is what Harriet married—she didn't marry you. You simply went with the house—as a more or less regrettable necessity. And you must not obtrude; for she wants the house all to herself. So she has set about reducing you to as negligible a factor as possible in the scheme of things here.

CRAIG: You don't really believe that, Auntie, do you?

MISS AUSTEN: That is her plan concerning you, Walter, I'm telling you. That is why the visits of your friends have been discouraged.

CRAIG: I can't think that Harriet would discourage my friends, Auntie.

MISS AUSTIN: Does any of them come here?

CRAIG: Why, most of them have been here at one time or another, yes.

MISS AUSTEN: Not within the last eighteen months; and you've only been married two years.

CRAIG: Well, why shouldn't Harriet want my friends here?

MISS AUSTEN: For the same reason that she doesn't want anybody else here. Because she's a supremely selfish woman; and with the arrogance of the selfish mind, she wants to exclude the whole world—because she cannot impose her narrow little order upon it. And these four walls are the symbol of that selfish exclusion.

CRAIG (*turning away*), I can't believe that, Auntie.

MISS AUSTEN (*extending her arms towards the front door*):

Can you remember when any one has darkened that door—until here to-day, when Mrs. Frazier came over?—And you see the result of that. And why do you suppose that people have so suddenly *stopped* visiting you? They always visited you at home. It can hardly be that you've changed so radically in two years. And I daresay all those charming young men and women that used to have such pleasant times at home, thought that when you married your house would be quite a rendezvous. But they reckoned without their—hostess, Walter—just as they are beginning to reckon without you. (*He turns and looks at her.*) You never go out any more. —Nobody ever asks you.—They're afraid you might bring her; and they don't want her.—Because she's made it perfectly clear to them that she doesn't want *them*. (*Craig turns away again slowly.*) And just as your friends are beginning to reckon without you in their social life, so it is only a question of time till they begin to reckon without you in their *business* life. (*He looks at her again, and she moves across towards him.*) Walter—why do you suppose your appointment as one of the directors of the local bank never materialized?

CRAIG: Why, I think Littlefield had something to do with that;

he's been high-hatting me a bit lately.

MISS AUSTEN: Because Harriet insulted his wife here; I saw her do it.

CRAIG: When?

MISS AUSTEN: The week after New Year's, when Mrs. Littlefield called.

CRAIG: What did Harriet do?

MISS AUSTEN: Nothing—what Harriet always does. It was a little feline subtlety—that would sound too incredible in the ears of a man. But Mrs. Littlefield appreciated it, for all her stupidity. I *saw* her appreciate it—and you were not appointed. (*Craig looks away.*) And I want to tell you something else that I saw the other day in the city, or rather heard. I was having luncheon at the Colonnade, and two of your old Thursday-night poker crowd came in, and sat at a table within hearing distance of me. And presently a man and his wife came in and sat down at another table. And the wife immediately proceeded to tell the man how he should have sat down; and how he should sit now that he *was* down, and so on. And I distinctly heard one of your friends say to the other, "Listen to Craig's wife over here." (*Craig turns his head and looks right into Miss Austen's eyes. There is a slight pause.*) That is a little straw, Walter, that

should show you the way the wind is blowing. Your friends resent being told where they shall sit, and how; so they are avoiding the occasion of it—just as I am going to avoid it. But you cannot avoid it, so you must deal with it.

CRAIG: How? How should I deal with it?

MISS AUSTEN: By impressing your wife with the realization that there is a *man* of the house here, as well as a woman; and that *you* are that man. And if you don't, Walter, you are going to go the way of every other man that has ever allowed himself to be dominated by a selfish woman.—Become a pallid little echo of her distorted opinions; believing finally that every friend you ever had before you met her was trying to lead you into perdition— and that she rescued you, and made a man of you. (*She makes a little sound of bitter amusement, and turns away towards the foot of the stairs.*) The irony of it. And yet they can do it.

CRAIG: Harriet could never turn me against my friends.

MISS AUSTEN (*turning at the foot of the stairs, and speaking with level conviction*): Walter— they can make men believe that the mothers that nursed them— are their arch enemies. That's why I'm warning you. For you're fighting for the life of your manhood, Walter; and I cannot in conscience leave this house without at least turning on the light here, and letting you see what it is that you're fighting against.

[*She starts for the stairs, and* CRAIG *turns suddenly and follows her.*]

CRAIG: Auntie, I can't see you leave this house!

MISS AUSTEN (*stopping on the second step*): But, if I'm not happy here.

CRAIG: Well, why have I been so blind that I haven't seen that you were not happy, and fixed it so that you would be!

MISS AUSTEN (*quietly*): Because you haven't *seen* your wife, Walter.

CRAIG: Oh, I can't be convinced that there isn't an enormous element of misunderstanding between you and Harriet. (MISS AUSTEN *closes her eyes and shakes her head from side to side.*) Oh, I'm not disputing that she has a peculiar disposition—she may be all that you say of her;—but I really can't see the necessity of your leaving the house; the thing must be susceptible of some sort of adjustment.

MISS AUSTEN: No house is big enough, Walter, for two women who are interested in the same man.

CRAIG: I'll never have a minute's peace if you leave here; I'll reproach myself.

MISS AUSTEN: You have nothing to reproach yourself with, Walter; you've always been very kind and very good to me.

CRAIG: What will you do if you leave here?

MISS AUSTEN: What I've always wanted to do—travel—all over the world—far and wide: so that I shan't become—little. I have such a deadly fear of that after these past two years.

CRAIG: But, I promised Mother that you'd always have a home with me, and if you go, I'll feel somehow that I'm breaking that promise.

MISS AUSTEN: You haven't a home to offer me, Walter. (*He looks at her.*) You have a house —with furniture in it—that can only be used under highly specified conditions. I have the impression somehow or other, when I look at these rooms—that they are rooms that have died—and are laid out. (*She turns and starts up the stairs.*)

CRAIG: Well, whatever they are, they'll seem less if you leave them. I don't think I'd feel worse if it were Mother herself that were leaving.

[MISS AUSTEN *turns, with her hand on the balustrade.*]

MISS AUSTEN: Be glad that it isn't your mother, Walter; she would have left long ago.

[*She goes on up the stairs, and he stands looking after her. There is a ring at the front door. He turns and looks out through the French windows, then moves to the middle of the room and looks out through the portières. The bell rings again; then* MAZIE *comes down the stairs.*]

CRAIG: There's a little boy at the front door, Mazie.

MAZIE: Yes, sir, I heard the bell.

CRAIG: I'm expecting a gentleman, too, Mazie, in a few minutes; I'll be upstairs.

MAZIE: All right, Mr. Craig, I'll call you when he comes.

[MAZIE *goes out to answer the bell, and* CRAIG *goes up the stairs. He stops halfway up and thinks.*]

BOY'S VOICE (*at the front door*): Why, Christine, up at the corner, sez if you're goin' to the Society to-night, would you mind payin' her dues for her; she sez she can't go to-night.

[CRAIG *disappears.*]

MAZIE: Oh, sure, tell her I'll be glad to.

BOY'S VOICE: She sez the card's in the envelope there with the money.

[MRS. HAROLD *comes in through the portières and crosses towards the door, looking out keenly.*]

MAZIE: All right, dear, tell her

I'll tend to it.

[*The screen door slams and* MAZIE *comes in.*]

MRS. HAROLD: Did you answer that door, Mazie?

MAZIE: Yes, it was the tailor's little boy, up at the corner, with Christine's Society money. He sez Christine can't go to-night.

MRS. HAROLD: Is to-night Society night again already?

MAZIE (*putting an envelope back of the center ornament on the mantelpiece*): It's the third Friday.

MRS. HAROLD: I can never keep track of that old Society.

MAZIE: Do you want me to pay your dues for you?

MRS. HAROLD: No, dear, I'm paid up to the first of July. Where did Mr. Craig go—upstairs?

MAZIE: I guess so, unless he's out there somewhere.

MRS. HAROLD (*glancing towards the front porch, and taking a step or two towards* MAZIE): No, he's not out there.

MAZIE: Why, what's the matter?

MRS. HAROLD (*laying her hand on* MAZIE's *arm, and lowering her voice*): I think the old lady's goin' to leave.

MAZIE: Miss Austen?

[MRS. HAROLD *nods; and then looks out through the adjoining rooms.*]

MRS. HAROLD (*turning to* MAZIE): The lady made a row about

Mrs. Frazier being here.

MAZIE: Did she?

MRS. HAROLD: She was furious. I knew it was coming by the face on her when she told me to take the roses out of the room. So as soon as I heard Mrs. Frazier goin', I went right up to the library; you can hear every word up there, you know, over near the radiator.

MAZIE: Yes, I know you can. Was *he* here?

MRS. HAROLD: He wasn't at first, but I think he must have come down while they were at it. I heard *her* say she didn't want her house made a thoroughfare for the neighborhood.

MAZIE: Can you imagine it—as though anybody ever came *in* here.

MRS. HAROLD: That's what *I* felt like sayin'. But Miss Austen told her.

MAZIE: Did she?

MRS. HAROLD: I should say she did. It didn't take Mrs. Craig long to get out of the room once Miss Austen got started.

[*A door closes upstairs, and* MAZIE *darts to the center table and settles the table scarf.* MRS. HAROLD *steps to the big chair in front of the mantelpiece and feigns to be occupied in setting it straight.* MAZIE *glances over her right shoulder up the stairs, then steps up to the foot of the*

stairs and glances up. Then she hurries forward to MRS. HAROLD *again, glancing through the portières as she goes.*]

MAZIE: What did Mrs. Craig do, walk out of the room?

MRS. HAROLD: Yes. She said she had something else to do besides listenin' to a lot of silly talk. (MAZIE *raises her eyes to heaven.*) I felt like sayin' I'd like to know what it was she had to do.

MAZIE: So would I.

MRS. HAROLD: I've been here nearly a year now, and *I* have my first time to see her do anything— only a lot of snoopin'—after somebody else has finished.

MAZIE: It's too bad Miss Austen didn't tell her that while she was at it.

MRS. HAROLD: She told her enough.

MAZIE: Well, didn't *he* say anything?

MRS. HAROLD: Not very much; Miss Austen done most of the talkin'. (*She comes down to* MAZIE's *left, confidentially.*) She told him if he didn't do something very soon, his wife 'ud make him look like an echo.

MAZIE: She will, too.

MRS. HAROLD: He said she had a peculiar disposition — and that Miss Austen didn't understand her. Well, I felt like sayin' if Miss Austen don't understand her, I do.

And I'd soon tell her how well I understand her, too, only that she gives me a wide berth.

MAZIE: I feel kind of sorry for him sometimes, though.

MRS. HAROLD: Yes, it's a pity for *him*. (*Lowering her voice, and speaking with great conviction.*) She could build a nest in his ear, and he'd never know it. (*She turns to the table and settles the various ornaments.*)

MAZIE: She certainly is the hardest woman to please that I've ever worked for.

MRS. HAROLD: Well, I don't know whether she's hard to please or not, Mazie, for I've never tried to please her. I do my work, and if she don't like it she has a tongue in her head; she can soon tell me, and I can go somewhere else. I've worked in too many houses to be out of a place very long. Did I tell you about her wanting me to dust the leaves off that little tree in front of the dining-room window last week?

MAZIE: Dust the leaves?

MRS. HAROLD (*looking to heaven for witness*): That's the honest God's fact. And me with the rheumatism at the time.

MAZIE: Can you imagine such a thing?

MRS. HAROLD: Well, you know how I done it, don't you?

MAZIE: What'd you say to her?

MRS. HAROLD: I told her right up; I said, "I'll dust no tree for nobody."

MAZIE: You done right.

MRS. HAROLD: She sez, "You mean you refuse to dust it?"— "Yes," I sez, "I refuse, and," I sez, "what's more, I'm goin' to stay refuse." "Well," she sez, "it needs dusting, whether you dust it or not." "Well," I sez, "let it need it," I sez. I sez, "A little dust won't poison it." I sez, "We'll be dust ourselves some day, unless we get drownded."

MAZIE: You done right.

MRS. HAROLD: Oh, I told her. (*She glances out through the rooms.*)

MAZIE: I think the worst kind of woman a girl can work for is one that's crazy about her house.

MRS. HAROLD: I do, too; because I think they *are* crazy half the time. You know, you can go crazy over a house, Mazie, the same as you can over anything else.

MAZIE: Sure you can.

MRS. HAROLD: Doctor Nicholson's wife was one of them; although she wasn't as generous a woman as this one.

MAZIE: No, that's one thing you've got to say for Mrs. Craig; she's not stingy.

MRS. HAROLD: No, that's true, she isn't.

MAZIE: I don't think I've ever worked in a house where there was as good a table for the help.

MRS. HAROLD: That's right; you always get whatever they get.

MAZIE: And you never have to ask for your wages, neither.

[*The doorbell rings.*]

MRS. HAROLD: No, she's very good that way.

MAZIE (*going to answer the door, settling her cap and apron*): I guess that's that gentleman Mr. Craig's expectin'.

MRS. HAROLD: Come out when you come in, Mazie.

[*She goes out through the portières.* MR. CRAIG *comes down the stairs.*]

BIRKMIRE (*at the front door*): Good evening. Is Mr. Craig in?

MAZIE: Yes, sir, he's in.

[*The screen door is heard to close, and* BIRKMIRE *enters.*]

CRAIG (*coming in*): Hello, Billy, how are you?

BIRKMIRE (*shaking hands earnestly*): Hello, Walt. (*He looks right into* CRAIG'S *eyes.*)

CRAIG: I called your house a little while ago; (BIRKMIRE *turns to the piano with his raincoat and hat*) there was a message here for me when I got in, saying you'd called.

[MAZIE *comes in.*]

BIRKMIRE: Yes, I've been trying to get hold of you since four o'clock.

CRAIG: Let me take those things out of your way.

[MAZIE *stops near the portières and looks back, to see if they want her to take* BIRKMIRE'S *things.*]

BIRKMIRE: No, thanks, Walter, I've got to get right back to the house.

[MAZIE *goes out.*]

CRAIG: Your father still here?

BIRKMIRE: Yes, he'll be here for a day or two yet. (*He looks keenly out through the portières, stepping up towards the back of the room.*)

CRAIG (*watching him curiously*): What's the matter? (BIRKMIRE *makes a deft gesture, signifying that* MAZIE *may be within hearing distance.*) What is it?

BIRKMIRE (*stepping down close to Craig and laying his hand on his sleeve*): What about it, Walt?

CRAIG: About what?

BIRKMIRE: About Fergus and his wife. You were out there last night, weren't you?

CRAIG: Sure. That's where I talked to *you* from.

BIRKMIRE: Well, my God, what happened out there, Walter?

CRAIG: What do you mean?

BIRKMIRE: Haven't you seen the evening papers?

CRAIG: Not yet, no. Why?

BIRKMIRE (*smothering an exclamation, and stepping to the piano to get a newspaper out of his pocket*): Jesus, how did you miss it!

CRAIG: Why, what's happened?

BIRKMIRE: Fergus and his wife are dead.

CRAIG: What!

BIRKMIRE: Found them this morning in the library.

CRAIG: Passmore, you mean?

BIRKMIRE (*handing him the paper*): Here it is on the front page of the *Telegraph*.

CRAIG: What are you saying, Billy?

BIRKMIRE (*stepping over towards the portières and looking out*): It's in every paper in town.

CRAIG: Where is it?

BIRKMIRE (*coming forward at* CRAIG's *left and indicating a certain headline*): Fergus Passmore and wife found dead in library.

CRAIG: My God!

BIRKMIRE: I happened to see it over a man's shoulder coming down in the elevator in the Land Title Building about four o'clock, and I damned near had heart failure. (*He turns away to the left and takes a cigarette from a case.*) I've been trying to get you on the 'phone ever since. And I saw *her* myself at the Ritz last night at twelve o'clock. I was talking to her. I took the old man over there for a bit of supper after the show, and she was there with that military gent she's been stepping it with lately. (*Suddenly laying his hand on Craig's arm.*) That's my hunch on this thing, Walter. I

think she's been playing this soldier fellow a little too much lately and Fergus has heard of it and probably called it when she got in last night, and busted up the show. You know, he was always jealous as hell of her. (*He takes a step or two towards the back and glances through the portières.*)

CRAIG: There must be a catch in this thing somewhere, Billy.

BIRKMIRE (*coming forward again*): How could there be a catch in it, Walter? Do you think they'd print that kind of stuff for a joke?

CRAIG: Well, my God, I was out there last night till twelve o'clock.

BIRKMIRE (*tearing the cigarette between his fingers*): Well, evidently this thing happened after you got away from there. Did she get in before you left there last night?

CRAIG (*looking up from the paper*): What?

BIRKMIRE: I say, did Adelaide get in last night before you left out there?

CRAIG: No, but she was there when I got out there, about nine o'clock. She was going out somewhere.

BIRKMIRE: Yes, and I know who it was she was going out *with*, too; that's the third time I've run into her with that bird lately. And I want to find out what his name is right away quick, too, for he might be in on this thing.

CRAIG: Have you been out there yet?

BIRKMIRE: Out to Fergus', you mean?

CRAIG: Yes.

BIRKMIRE: Sure, I hopped right out there as soon as I read it; but you can't get near the place.

CRAIG: I think I ought to get in touch with Police Headquarters right away, Billy.

BIRKMIRE: Well, that's why I wanted to get hold of you. It says there they're looking for a man seen leaving the house after midnight.

CRAIG: Sure, that's me.

BIRKMIRE: Well, not necessarily you, Walter.

CRAIG: That's the time I got away from there.

BIRKMIRE: That doesn't mean anything. Only I think it 'ud be a good thing to let them know right away.

CRAIG (*turning suddenly and going up to the telephone*): Sure, I'll call up right away.

BIRKMIRE (*following him up*): Well, now, wait a minute, Walter, don't move too fast; you know a thing like this can take a thousand and one turns, and we don't want to make any false move. This kind of thing 'ud be pie for the newspapers, you know; and the fact that we were invited out there

to play cards wouldn't read any too well.

CRAIG: Well, *you* weren't out there.

BIRKMIRE: I know that; but I'm not sitting back in the corner in this thing, you know, Walter. It just so happened that I *wasn't* out there. But I talked to you on the telephone out there last night, from my house, and in a thing of this kind they trace telephone calls and everything else.

CRAIG (*looking at the paper again*): My God, this is a terrible thing, though, isn't it, Billy.

BIRKMIRE (*passing his hand across his brow*): I haven't got it myself yet.

CRAIG: Terrible.

BIRKMIRE: It'll be a jar to your wife when she hears it, won't it?

CRAIG: Awful.

BIRKMIRE: She'll very likely see it in the paper up there in Albany.

CRAIG: She's back from Albany.

BIRKMIRE: Is she?

CRAIG: She got in a while ago.

BIRKMIRE: Well, she doesn't know anything about this yet, does she?

CRAIG: I don't think so; unless she happened to see the paper I brought home. I suppose it's in it.

BIRKMIRE: Sure, it's in all of them.

CRAIG: I just took it from the boy and put it in my pocket.

BIRKMIRE: Where is Harriet?

291

CRAIG: She's upstairs.

BIRKMIRE (*lowering his voice*): Does she know you were out there last night?

CRAIG: I don't know, I guess she does. Yes, I think I mentioned it a while ago.

BIRKMIRE (*stepping to* CRAIG's *side, and laying his hand on his arm*): Well, now, listen, Walter— If she doesn't happen to see the paper, what she doesn't know won't bother her. And this thing is apt to clear itself up over night. It might be cleared up now, for all we know; for I suppose the police have been working on it all day. But, I think the wise move for us is just to hop out there and try to find out what's going on; and if they haven't found anything out yet, just get in touch with Police Headquarters and let them know where we're at.

CRAIG (*tossing the newspaper on to the seat beside the telephone table*): Yes, let's do that. Wait till I get my hat. (*He goes through the portières.*)

BIRKMIRE (*crossing to the piano for his things*): I've got my car out here; we can cut across the park and be out there in ten minutes. (*He throws his raincoat across his arm, picks up his hat, and steps quickly across to get the newspaper that* CRAIG *left on the seat. He glances up the stairs and out through the portières. Then*

he sees CRAIG *coming through the adjoining room, and starts for the front door.*)

CRAIG (*entering, wearing his hat, and carrying the newspaper he brought home*): I'll take this paper with me; keep it out of sight.

BIRKMIRE: I've got the other one here in my pocket.

[BIRKMIRE *goes out.*]

CRAIG (*glancing about the room as he crosses to the front door*): We take the *Globe* here in the afternoon, but I don't see it any-where around out there. (*He goes out.*)

BIRKMIRE (*outside*): I've got the car right out here.

CRAIG (*outside*): I guess across the park will be the quickest.

BIRKMIRE: Yes, we can be over there in ten minutes.

[*There is a dead pause. Then a clock somewhere out at the right strikes half-past six, with a soft gong. There is another slight pause, and then* MRS. CRAIG *sweeps through the portières, carrying an open newspaper. She sees that no one is in the room, and rushes to the forward window to see if she can see* MR. CRAIG *any-where about. Then she starts for the front door, but changes her mind and rushes up to the landing of the stairway.*]

MRS. CRAIG (*calling up the*

stairs): Walter! — Walter! — Are you up there, Walter? (*She hurries down into the room again and over to the portières.*) Mazie!— Mazie!

[*She runs across to the front door and out.* MAZIE *comes in through the portières and looks about, then starts towards the front door.* MRS. CRAIG *hurries in again.*]

MAZIE: Were you calling me, Mrs. Craig?

MRS. CRAIG: Yes, Mazie. Have you seen anything of Mr. Craig?

MAZIE: Why, he was here a few minutes ago, Mrs. Craig, with a gentleman.

MRS. CRAIG: What gentleman? Who was he?

MAZIE: I don't know who he was, Mrs. Craig; I never saw him before.

MRS. CRAIG: Didn't you catch his name?

MAZIE: No, Ma'm, I didn't. He came in an automobile.

MRS. CRAIG: Well, did Mr. Craig go away with him?

MAZIE: I don't know whether he did or not, Mrs. Craig. I didn't know he'd gone.

MRS. CRAIG (*turning* MAZIE *around quickly by the shoulder and urging her towards the portières*): See if Mr. Craig's hat's on the rack out there.

MAZIE (*hurrying out*): Isn't he up in his room?

MRS. CRAIG: No, he isn't. Oh, Lord! (*Turning to the portières again.*) Is it?

MAZIE (*from somewhere out at the right*): No, Ma'm, it isn't.

MRS. CRAIG: Well, listen, Mazie, run over to the garage there and see if he's there! No, no, come this way, it's quicker. (*She waits frantically until Mazie rushes through the portières and across towards the front door.*) And if he's there tell him to come over here immediately; I want to see him.

MAZIE: Yes, Ma'm. (*The screen door slams after her, and she hurries past the bay window at the left.*)

MRS. CRAIG: Hurry now, Mazie. Tell him I want him right away. (*She turns in the door and leans against the jamb, looking straight out, wide-eyed, and holding the newspaper against her bosom.*) Oh, my God! (*She hurries across above the center table and down to the window, forward, at the right.*) Oh, my God! (*She stands looking eagerly through the window as though watching* MAZIE *running down the street.*)

THE CURTAIN DESCENDS SLOWLY

ACT II

Ten minutes later. MRS. CRAIG *is standing at the window, forward, reading the newspaper. She stops reading, glances out the window, and then moves with a kind of controlled desperation to the bay window at the left, where she looks out again eagerly.* MRS. HAROLD *comes in from the right.*

MRS. HAROLD: Is Mazie here, Mrs. Craig?

[MRS. CRAIG *turns nervously.*]

MRS. CRAIG: No, she isn't, Mrs. Harold; I've sent her on an errand; she'll be back in a minute.

MRS. HAROLD (*turning to go out again*): I told her I thought I heard you calling her.

[*Telephone bell rings.*]

MRS. CRAIG: See who that is, Mrs. Harold, will you, please.

[MRS. HAROLD *comes back and picks up the telephone.*]

MRS. HAROLD: Hello?—Hello?

MRS. CRAIG: What's the matter; don't they answer?

MRS. HAROLD: No, Ma'm, they haven't answered yet. Hello!

MRS. CRAIG: Never mind it, Mrs. Harold; it's probably a mistake.

MRS. HAROLD (*hanging up the receiver*): It does that sometimes when it's a long-distance call.

[MRS. CRAIG *turns sharply.*]

MRS. CRAIG: They didn't say it was long distance, did they?

MRS. HAROLD: No, Ma'm, they didn't say anything; nobody answered at all.

MRS. CRAIG: Well, if they want us they'll ring again.

MRS. HAROLD: Will you tell Mazie I want her when she comes in, Mrs. Craig, please?

MRS. CRAIG: Yes, I'll send her out to you as soon as she comes back. (MRS. HAROLD *goes out through the portières, and* MRS. CRAIG *crosses over and down to the window, forward, and looks out. She sees* MAZIE *hurrying back from the garage, and steps quickly up to the door at the left.* MAZIE *can be seen running past the bay window. The screen door slams, and* MAZIE *rushes in.*) Isn't he over there, Mazie?

MAZIE: No, Ma'm, he isn't.

MRS. CRAIG: Are you sure?

MAZIE: Yes, Ma'm, I looked all around.

MRS. CRAIG: Did you go round to the back?

MAZIE: Yes, Ma'm, I looked everywhere. Old Mr. Foster was standin' over there; I ast him if he'd seen anything of Mr. Craig, but he said he hadn't.

MRS. CRAIG: Is the garage locked?

MAZIE: Yes, Ma'm, I tried the door.

MRS. CRAIG: Well, could you see

whether or not the car was in there?

MAZIE: Yes, Ma'm, they're both in there, the little one, too; I looked through the glass. (MRS. CRAIG *turns away to the right, with a troubled expression, and moves down towards the mirror, and* MAZIE *moves towards the door at the right.*) I guess maybe he musta went away with that gentleman that was here.

MRS. CRAIG: He probably did. You say that gentleman came in a car, Mazie?

MAZIE: Yes, Ma'm, I think it was his; it was standin' right in front of the house when I opened the door for him.

MRS. CRAIG: All right, Mazie. Mrs. Harold wants you for something.

MAZIE (*going out*): Oh, does she?

[MRS. CRAIG *leans against the mantelpiece and thinks hard. The telephone bell rings. She turns and looks at the telephone; it rings again. Then she moves to answer it.* MAZIE *comes in.*]

MRS. CRAIG: I'll answer it, Mazie.

MAZIE: Oh, all right.

[*She withdraws, and* MRS. CRAIG *picks up the telephone.*]

MRS. CRAIG (*in a subdued voice*): Mazie.

MAZIE: Yes, Ma'm?

MRS. CRAIG: Come here for a minute. (MAZIE *appears between the portières.*) Go up and see that Miss Landreth's door is closed.

MAZIE (*withdrawing*): Yes, Ma'm.

MRS. CRAIG: Be very quiet about it, now, Mazie, and don't disturb her if she's asleep.

MAZIE: All right.

[*Telephone bell rings again.*]

MRS. CRAIG: Hello?—Yes?—All right. (*She glances up the stairs, and then waits.*) Hello?—Yes— (*In a louder voice.*) Hello! Yes— this is *Mrs.* Craig at the telephone —Mr. Craig isn't here just now, if you wanted *Mr.* Craig. Oh— why-a- Miss Landreth is lying down just now. Who is this speaking, please?—Oh, I see. Why —not a thing in the world, Mr. Fredericks, except that she's very tired—We've only just now gotten in from Albany, and I suggested that she go upstairs and lie down for a while. Yes—Am I going to do what? No, I didn't understand what you said, Mr. Fredericks. Why, yes, of course, I'd go back with her if anything unforeseen developed—otherwise she can go back herself. We're simply waiting now to hear something from her mother's physician up there. —Yes, of course I'm sure. Why, why should you put yourself to that trouble, Mr. Fredericks?— There wouldn't be anything you

could do when you get here.—
Well, I'd much rather not call her,
if you don't mind, Mr. Fredericks;
she's lying down.—Well, can't you
tell me what it is you want to tell
her—and I can give her the message? Well, probably it would,
Mr. Fredericks;—it's very nice of
you to be so solicitous about her,
but I don't care to disturb her just
now. I'm very sorry.
[*She hangs up abruptly, and
glances toward the head of
the stairs.* MAZIE *appears between the portières.*]
MAZIE: The door was closed,
Mrs. Craig.
MRS. CRAIG: All right, Mazie.
(MAZIE *withdraws, and* MRS.
CRAIG *moves forward, thoughtfully. There is a tap at the front
door bell.* MAZIE *turns and crosses
to answer the door.* MRS. CRAIG
*is looking sharply toward the front
door.*) See what those gentlemen
want, Mazie.
MAZIE: Yes, Ma'm.
CATELLE (*at the front door*):
Mr. Craig in?
MAZIE: No, sir, he's not in just
now; he went out about twenty
minutes ago.
CATELLE: What time do you expect him back?
MAZIE: Why, I couldn't say for
certain; but I guess he'll be back
in time for dinner, about seven
o'clock.
CATELLE: Is his wife in?

MAZIE: Yes, sir, she's in.
CATELLE: I'd like to speak to her
for a minute if I could.
[MRS. CRAIG, *who has been standing very still, listening, vanishes through the portières,
looking over her shoulder
apprehensively towards the
front door.*]
MAZIE: Yes, sir. Will you just
step in? (*The screen door closes;
and immediately Mazie hurries
into the room.*) If you'll just take
a chair for a minute I'll call her.
[CATELLE *wanders in, removing
his hat, followed by* HARRY,
*who also removes his hat as
he enters.* CATELLE *moves
down to the center table, puts
his hat down, and takes a
small leather notebook from
his inside pocket; and* HARRY
*comes forward and sits in the
chair beside the piano. There
is a pause.*]
HARRY: They didn't get this
place with a pound of tea.
CATELLE: A lot of money. Phoe-
nix Fire Insurance people. This
lad's old man used to be the president of the Company. Died about
twelve years ago. I guess this
gent's in line for the old man's
job, if he lives.
[MRS. CRAIG *enters through the
portières.* HARRY *rises, and
CATELLE *turns to her.*]
MRS. CRAIG: Good evening.
HARRY: Good evening.

CATELLE: Good evening, Ma'm. I called to see Mr. Craig.

MRS. CRAIG: Mr. Craig isn't in just now, I'm sorry.

CATELLE: Are you Mrs. Craig?

MRS. CRAIG: Yes.

CATELLE: Have you any idea what time Mr. Craig'll *be* in?

MRS. CRAIG: Why, I'm expecting him any minute; he was here less than a half-hour ago, when I went upstairs; so he must be right here in the neighborhood somewhere.

CATELLE: I see.

MRS. CRAIG: He'll certainly be back for his dinner, at seven o'clock, if you'd care to call back.

CATELLE: Well, I've got to be over the other side of town at seven o'clock,—so it may be that you could give me the information I am looking for, as well as Mr. Craig. Would you sit down for a minute?

MRS. CRAIG: Yes, certainly.

[*She turns to the chair in front of the mantelpiece and sits down.* HARRY *resumes his chair beside the piano, and Catelle sits on the small bench immediately above the center table.*]

CATELLE: I thought I'd like to speak to *Mr.* Craig first, but I don't suppose it makes a great deal of difference.

MRS. CRAIG: I thought he might be over at the garage—I wanted him myself a few minutes ago; but the maid says he isn't over there.

CATELLE: Well, I'll tell you what it is I wanted to see him about, Mrs. Craig. I suppose you've seen in the evening paper about this unfortunate affair out here on Willows Avenue?

MRS. CRAIG: You mean that shooting affair?

CATELLE: Yes, at the Passmore home.

MRS. CRAIG: Yes, isn't that a dreadful thing!—I've just been reading it here.

CATELLE: Yes, it's a very sad affair.

MRS. CRAIG: They're *both* dead, aren't they?

CATELLE: Yes, they're both dead.

MRS. CRAIG: Isn't that terrible. That's what I wanted to see my husband for; I wanted to ask him if he knew that man.

CATELLE: He probably did; they're pretty well known people here in town.

MRS. CRAIG: Yes, they must be, according to the paper. I haven't had a chance to read it all yet, I've just gotten in from Albany.

CATELLE: It's a rather peculiar case.

MRS. CRAIG: Was it a robbery or something?

CATELLE: No, there wasn't anything taken. Of course, it could have been a foiled *attempt* at robbery, but that 'ud hardly explain certain other circumstances.

297

MRS. CRAIG: Are you gentlemen working on the case?

CATELLE: Yes, Ma'm, we're from Police Headquarters. But, that doesn't need to alarm *you*, Mrs. Craig; there's no particular connection between that and our visit *here*.

MRS. CRAIG: Well, I'm very glad to know that.

CATELLE: No, this Passmore affair looks to me pretty clearly a matter of jealousy motive. Of course, there are one or two attendant circumstances, as there usually are in cases of this kind, but they don't mean anything, as far as the actual shooting is concerned. There was a man seen leaving the house shortly after midnight in an automobile—One of the neighbors happened to see him; but it was too dark to establish any identification. Besides, that wouldn't account for the death of *Mrs.* Passmore; because she didn't get in until after three o'clock, and the man left there between twelve and one.

MRS. CRAIG: I see.

CATELLE: But, of course, as you understand, Mrs. Craig, it's part of our business to follow up any little outside clue that we happen to get hold of that might throw some additional light on a case.

MRS. CRAIG: Yes, of course.

CATELLE: And that's what I wanted to see Mr. Craig about.

MRS. CRAIG: You mean you think Mr. Craig might be the man that was seen leaving there last night.

CATELLE: No, that circumstance is really not being seriously considered; a house of that description might have had any number of visitors during the evening.

MRS. CRAIG: That's very true.

CATELLE: But, we've had a report late this afternoon, Mrs. Craig, from the Lynnebrooke Telephone Exchange, where your light comes in, that there was a call made on your telephone here at five-twenty-seven this evening, asking for the address of the telephone number Levering three, one hundred; and that happens to be the number of the telephone at Mr. Passmore's home.

MRS. CRAIG: You mean that somebody called from here?

CATELLE: On this telephone, yes, Ma'm. Oakdale, six, two, three. That's the number of your telephone here, isn't it?

MRS. CRAIG: Yes, that's our number.

CATELLE: That's what I've got here.

MRS. CRAIG: But I can't imagine who it would be that called.

CATELLE: The report says it was a woman's voice.

MRS. CRAIG: Who was it that reported it, do you know?

CATELLE: I couldn't tell you that, Mrs. Craig.

298

MRS. CRAIG: I mean to say, would it be possible that the person who reported it could have made a mistake in the number?

CATELLE: No, they're usually pretty careful in an affair of this kind.

MRS. CRAIG: And the call was made at five o'clock this evening, you say?

CATELLE: Five-twenty-seven, my report says. The operator didn't give the address, of course; it's against the telephone company's rules. And the party rang off.

MRS. CRAIG: Well, that's extraordinary. Although it might have been one of the servants—probably saw it in the evening paper and was curious to know where it was. (*Rising.*) I'll ask them.

CATELLE: Well, I could understand that curiosity if the address wasn't published; but it is; and the telephone number *isn't*. And I was interested in finding out why any one 'ud have that particular 'phone number to-day and not know the address—when it's been in all the newspapers since two o'clock this afternoon. And this call wasn't made till after five.

MRS. CRAIG: It does seem strange, doesn't it?

CATELLE: I haven't been able to figure it out.

MRS. CRAIG: But, I dare say there's some very simple explanation of it.

CATELLE: Has this telephone here been used at all, to your knowledge, Mrs. Craig, since five o'clock this afternoon?

MRS. CRAIG: Why, I *answered* a call, a few minutes ago, from Northampton, Massachusetts.

CATELLE: A long-distance call, you mean?

MRS. CRAIG: Yes. It was a Mr. Fredericks, at Smith College there, calling my niece, to inquire about her mother. Her mother is ill in Albany.

CATELLE: I see.

MRS. CRAIG: That's where we've just come from.

CATELLE: You don't know whether or not anybody from the outside has been in here since five o'clock?

MRS. CRAIG: Not to my knowledge; except a neighbor from across the avenue there, Mrs. Frazier. She brought some roses over to my husband's aunt. She was here when I got in; although I scarcely think she would have used the telephone. But, I'll ask Miss Austen if you like.

CATELLE: I wish you would, please, if you don't mind.

MRS. CRAIG (*going to the stairway landing*): Not at all. She's up in her room I believe.

CATELLE: Would you mind asking her to step down here for a few minutes?

MRS. CRAIG: Yes, certainly. (*Calling.*) Miss Austen!—Miss Austen!

MISS AUSTEN (*from upstairs*): Is some one calling me?

MRS. CRAIG: Yes,—it's me, Miss Austen. Would you mind coming down here for a minute or two, Miss Austen? I'd like to speak to you.

MISS AUSTEN: All right, I'll be down in a moment.

[MRS. CRAIG *turns to come down.*]

MRS. CRAIG: If you will, please. She'll be right down.

CATELLE: Thank you very much.

MRS. CRAIG: I suppose I'd better call the servants too, hadn't I? They'll probably know something about it.

CATELLE: Yes, I'd like to see them for a minute.

MRS. CRAIG (*going through the portières*): I'll call them right away.

[CATELLE *looks at his watch and rises.*]

CATELLE: What time have you got there, Harry?

[*He watches keenly through the portières.*]

MRS. CRAIG: Mazie!

HARRY: Just seven.

MAZIE (*out at the right*): Yes, Ma'm?

MRS. CRAIG: Would you come here for a minute?

CATELLE: Do you mind if I use this 'phone here, Mrs. Craig?

MRS. CRAIG: They'll be right in. (*She enters.*)

CATELLE: Do you mind if I use this 'phone here for a minute?

MRS. CRAIG: Not at all, go right ahead. I didn't hear what you said.

CATELLE: I've got a call to make at seven o'clock.

MRS. CRAIG: That's quite all right.

[*He stands holding the telephone, and* MRS. CRAIG *listens keenly.*]

CATELLE (*into the telephone*): Spring 4000.—Right.

[*There is a stillness: then the clock strikes seven, with a soft gong.* MAZIE *enters, on the third gong.*]

MAZIE: Did you want me, Mrs. Craig?

[MRS. CRAIG *motions to her to be silent;* MAZIE *stands looking from one to the other in a state of positive bewilderment.*]

CATELLE: Thielens? Catelle.— That so?—I got away from there before six. Period? Righto, Chuck. What are you trying to do, break Harry's heart? (*He gives a rather dry little laugh.*) All right, Chuck, I'll be right over. (*He hangs up and crosses to the table for his hat.*) We'd better get right out there, Harry. (*Harry rises and moves up to the door.*) I won't have to bother you any more right now, Mrs. Craig;

there's been a bit of additional information come in over at headquarters that'll hold things up temporarily.

MRS. CRAIG: Well, do you want me to have Mr. Craig get in touch with you when he comes in?

CATELLE: No, we'll get in touch with him if it's necessary.

MRS. CRAIG: And you don't want to question the rest of the people now, either?

[HARRY *goes out.*]

CATELLE: Not just now, Mrs. Craig, thank you very much. (*He starts for the door.*)

MRS. CRAIG: You're welcome, I'm sure. All right, Mazie.

[MAZIE *withdraws reluctantly, her eyes fastened upon* CATELLE.]

CATELLE: I'm sorry to have had to trouble you.

MRS. CRAIG (*following him to the door*): That's quite all right.

CATELLE (*turning at the door*): You can explain the circumstances to Mr. Craig, if you will.

MRS. CRAIG: Yes, I will. He'll probably know something about it.

CATELLE (*going out*): Very likely he will.

MRS. CRAIG: And if he doesn't, I'm sure one of the others will.

CATELLE: All right, thank you very much, Mrs. Craig.

MRS. CRAIG: You're very welcome, I'm sure.

CATELLE: Good evening.

MRS. CRAIG: Good evening.

[*The screen door closes, and* MRS. CRAIG *turns slowly and lifts her closed hands in a quiet panic. Then she hurries forward and across to the window and watches the two detectives going down the street.* MISS AUSTEN *comes down the stairs quietly, and stands on the landing, looking at her.*]

MISS AUSTEN: Did you want to see me about something, Harriet?

[MRS. CRAIG *starts slightly and turns.*]

MRS. CRAIG (*going out through the portières*): No, not now, Miss Austen; it isn't necessary. I'm sorry to have troubled you. (MISS AUSTEN *stands for a second looking after her; then she moves forward to the window, to see what it was that had so engaged* MRS. CRAIG'S *attention. Then she moves up towards the telephone, glancing through the portières.*)

MISS AUSTEN (*into the telephone*): Will you give me Clearfield, six, two,—six, two?—Please? (*She waits, glancing towards the portières and out the window.*) Hello? Is this the Mowers Express Office? Well, how early could I have some things taken away to-morrow morning? Six hundred and eighty Belmont Manor. Yes, just a square from the Park. Well, eight o'clock

301

would be time enough. Miss Irene Austen. That's right. Thank you. (*She hangs up, and goes up the stairs.* MRS. CRAIG *comes through the portières, glances towards the head of the stairs, and moves to the foot of the stairs to look up. Then she steps to the telephone table and settles everything precisely.* MAZIE *appears between the portières.*)

MRS. CRAIG: What is it, Mazie?

MAZIE: Why, Mrs. Harold wants to know if she'll serve the dinner now, Mrs. Craig.

MRS. CRAIG (*moving forward, thoughtfully*): Tell her not yet for a little while, till Mr. Craig gets here; I'm expecting him any minute.

MAZIE: Yes, Ma'm.

[*She goes out; and* MRS. CRAIG *stands thinking hard for a second. The screen door closes sharply, and she wheels round with a rapid movement.* CRAIG *enters, removing his hat.*]

MRS. CRAIG: Walter! Where have you been?

CRAIG: Out with Billy Birkmire. Why?

MRS. CRAIG (*indicating the outer door of the glass vestibule*): Shut that door.

[*He turns and shuts it, and she moves along the foot of the stairway, glancing up and out through the portières.*]

CRAIG (*coming into the room again*): What's the matter?

[MRS. CRAIG *turns and crosses back towards him.*]

MRS. CRAIG: My God, haven't you seen the evening paper about Fergus Passmore and his wife!

CRAIG: Yes, I've seen it.

MRS. CRAIG: Well, what about it, Walter?

CRAIG (*putting his hat down on the piano*): I don't know any more about it than you do, Harriet.

MRS. CRAIG: My God, isn't that a terrible thing! I've been nearly out of my mind for the last half-hour. I happened to see it in the paper there when I came downstairs, and I couldn't find you anywhere.

CRAIG: I went out with Birkmire.

MRS. CRAIG: Was that Birkmire that was here?

CRAIG: Yes, he wanted to see me about it.

MRS. CRAIG: I didn't even know whether you knew it or not; because you hadn't said anything about it when you came in this evening.

CRAIG: I didn't *know* it when I came in this evening.

MRS. CRAIG (*pointing at the paper on the table*): It's on the very front page of the paper there.

CRAIG: I didn't see the paper this evening till Birkmire showed it to me.

302

MRS. CRAIG: Well, why didn't you call me then, and not go rushing out of the house?

CRAIG: I didn't want to upset you.

MRS. CRAIG (*moving forward and across in front of the center table*): Well, I certainly couldn't have been any more upset than I have been. (*Turning to him.*) Mazie said there's been a man here, and that you'd gone away with him in an automobile—so, of course, I didn't know what to think. I thought probably you'd been arrested or something.

[*He looks at her sharply.*]

CRAIG: What would I be arrested for?

MRS. CRAIG: Why, in connection with this thing, of course. (*Taking a step towards him.*) The Police are looking for you; you know that, don't you?

CRAIG: Who says the Police are looking for me?

MRS. CRAIG: Two of them have just left here, not five minutes ago.

CRAIG: Policemen?

MRS. CRAIG: They said they were from Police Headquarters; that's all I know.

CRAIG: And what are they looking for me for?

MRS. CRAIG: Well, now, why do you suppose they're looking for you, Walter?

CRAIG: I don't know.

MRS. CRAIG: Doesn't it say in the paper there that you were seen leaving Passmore's at twelve o'clock last night?

CRAIG: It doesn't say that *I* was seen leaving there.

MRS. CRAIG: It says there was a man seen leaving there, and who else could it have been but you? You were out there, weren't you?

CRAIG: Yes.

MRS. CRAIG: Well, that's enough, isn't it? (*She turns away to her left, and crosses above the table towards the portières.*)

CRAIG: But *they* don't know that.

MRS. CRAIG: Oh, don't be absurd, Walter.

CRAIG: Who saw me?

MRS. CRAIG (*coming back towards him*): Somebody always sees in a case of this kind.

CRAIG: Who could it have been?

MRS. CRAIG: The butler saw you, didn't he?

CRAIG: What if he did?—he didn't know me from Adam. He says so there in the paper, doesn't he?

MRS. CRAIG: He could identify your picture, couldn't he?

CRAIG: Who's going to give him my picture?

MRS. CRAIG: Don't talk so loud. (*She steps back towards the portières, to assure herself that neither of the servants is listening.*)

CRAIG: Anyway, I don't believe he'd recognize my picture if he *did* see it; he only came into the

303

library for a couple of minutes to serve some drinks, and went right out again. And he didn't get my name, because Fergus was sitting on the lawn when I got there and took me in himself. And the butler was in bed when I left there.

MRS. CRAIG: Didn't any of the other servants see you?

CRAIG: Not that I know of.

MRS. CRAIG (*coming very close to him and lowering her voice*): Didn't you tell me that Billy Birkmire called you on the telephone out there last night?

CRAIG: Yes, I talked to him out there.

MRS. CRAIG: Well, didn't the butler get your name then?

CRAIG: No: Fergus answered the 'phone himself, on the extension in the library.

MRS. CRAIG: Well, those men have been here, anyway.

CRAIG: Well, what did they want?

MRS. CRAIG: Haven't I just told you want they wanted? They wanted to see *you.*

CRAIG: Did they say they knew it was I that was out there last night?

MRS. CRAIG: I don't remember *what* they said, exactly; I was too upset. But they wanted to know where you were, and, of course, I couldn't tell them; because you were here when I left the room, and then you suddenly disap-

304

peared. (*Turning away to the right.*) I was never placed in such a position in my life. I'm sure those men must have thought I was evading them. (*Turning back to him again.*) But I didn't know what to say to them—except that you'd probably taken a little walk around the neighborhood here; because I'd sent Mazie over to the garage to look for you as soon as I saw the paper, and she said both the cars were in there.

CRAIG: I went out in Birkmire's car.

MRS. CRAIG: Where did you go with him?

CRAIG: Over to Fergus' house.

MRS. CRAIG: And what in heaven's name did you do a thing like that for, Walter!

CRAIG: Why not?

MRS. CRAIG: Supposing you'd run into somebody out there?

CRAIG: And what if I did?

MRS. CRAIG: Do you want your name to be dragged into this thing?

CRAIG: My name'll be dragged into it anyway, won't it?

MRS. CRAIG: Why will it?

CRAIG: You say those men have been here already.

MRS. CRAIG: And what if they have? That doesn't mean anything.

CRAIG: It means that they must have associated my name with it already, doesn't it?

MRS. CRAIG: No, it doesn't mean anything of the kind; they were simply looking for information.

CRAIG: But it was to me they *came* for that information.

MRS. CRAIG: Because you were a friend of Passmore's.

CRAIG: Exactly. And they'll very likely come back here again.

MRS. CRAIG: But, you don't have to go out looking for them, do you?

CRAIG (*turning away and going up towards the door at the left*): You can't be playing any game in a thing like this, Harriet.

MRS. CRAIG (*following him up*): No, and you don't have to go rushing out to meet a lot of scandalous publicity, either. I should think your own common sense would show you what it would mean to have your name even mentioned in a thing of this kind. (*Turning away and down towards the center table.*) Why, it 'ud be in every newspaper in the country.

CRAIG (*coming forward at the right of the piano*): That wouldn't bother me in the least.

MRS. CRAIG (*aghast*): It wouldn't bother you!

CRAIG: Not the least bit—My conscience is clear.

MRS. CRAIG (*stepping to his side*): Oh, don't be so absurdly romantic, Walter!

CRAIG: It isn't a question of romanticism at all.

MRS. CRAIG: No, and it isn't a question of conscience, either. It's simply a matter of discretion. If you've had nothing to do with this thing, what's the use of becoming involved?

CRAIG: What do you mean, *if* I've had nothing to do with it?

MRS. CRAIG (*with sudden temper*): Oh, now don't start picking me up on every word! (*She turns away to the left and crosses above the center table towards the portières.*) I've had cross-examination enough in the last fifteen minutes. (CRAIG *takes a cigarette from a case and closes the case with a snap.* MRS. CRAIG *turns and sees that he is about to smoke.*) Now, don't smoke in this room, Walter. (*He throws the cigarette across the room to the fireplace.* MRS. CRAIG *looks at it in astonishment, and then at him.*) Well, that's a nice place to throw it, I must say. *She goes down to the fireplace and picks it up.*)

CRAIG (*sitting in the chair at the right of the piano*): Oh, what does it matter!

MRS. CRAIG: Don't you want it?

CRAIG: What good is it, if I can't smoke it?

MRS. CRAIG (*crossing above the table towards the front door, holding the cigarette away from her, between her thumb and finger*): There are plenty of other places in the house to smoke, if you want

305

to smoke.

CRAIG: I don't know where they are.

MRS. CRAIG (*going out the door*): You can smoke in your den, can't you?

CRAIG: If I shut the door. (*He sits thinking, deeply. The screen door slams, and* MRS. CRAIG *comes in again, looking keenly towards the portières.*) Did those men say when they'd be back here?

MRS. CRAIG: I don't remember whether they did or not!—I suppose they did. They said they'd get in touch with you if it was necessary. (*Coming forward to his side, and lowering her voice.*) But, if they *do* come back here, Walter, don't give them any more information than I did.

CRAIG: Well, I certainly won't deny that I was a friend of Fergus'.

MRS. CRAIG: You don't have to deny that you were a friend of his; but you certainly don't have to submit to a lot of cross-examination by detectives, either, simply because you happened to be a friend of his. (*She turns away and moves to the front of the center table.*) Let them go and cross-examine some of his other friends; you weren't the only friend he had.

CRAIG: Why did you submit to their cross-examination?

MRS. CRAIG (*turning to him*):

Because I didn't know at the time to what extent they were justified in questioning me. I thought probably they had some information about your having been out at Passmore's last night. And I was at my wit's end, trying to keep from saying something that would imply an admission of it. I told them right away that I'd just gotten in from Albany, so I suppose they assumed that I didn't know where you'd been last night.

CRAIG: How long did they stay here?

MRS. CRAIG: About fifteen minutes, I imagine; but it seemed like a year.

CRAIG: What were they talking about all that time?

MRS. CRAIG: About you, and Fergus Passmore, and where you were, and when you'd be back, and all kinds of questions. (*She goes to the piano and picks up his hat, settling the piano scarf.*)

CRAIG: Did they say they'd been to any other of Fergus' friends?

MRS. CRAIG: I don't remember, they may have. They said something about him being very well known here socially, so they probably have.

[CRAIG *thinks for a second, then rises abruptly and crosses below the center table and up to the telephone.*]

CRAIG: I think I'll call Birkmire up and see if they've been to see him.

MRS. CRAIG (*with a panicky movement towards him*): Now, wait a minute, Walter! (*She puts his hat on the table as she crosses above it.*) You're not going to do anything of the kind.

CRAIG: Why not?

MRS. CRAIG (*taking the telephone from him*): Now, go away from this 'phone. (*She draws him forward by the arm, away from the telephone.*) Let me tell you something.

CRAIG: What's the matter?

MRS. CRAIG: Don't you realize that that telephone is being watched—and that they are probably watching Birkmire's too?

CRAIG: Who is?

MRS. CRAIG: Why, the Police, of course. Haven't you any realization of your position in this affair?

CRAIG: I evidently haven't the same realization that you have.

MRS. CRAIG: Well, it's time you did have.

CRAIG: It is?

MRS. CRAIG: Yes, it is.

CRAIG: And what realization have you of my position?

MRS. CRAIG: Never mind what realization I have; that doesn't matter now. I simply know that the very first thing the Police do in a case of this kind is to watch the telephone calls to and from the house.

CRAIG: Not from this house.

MRS. CRAIG: I mean from Fergus' house.

CRAIG: I wasn't going to call Fergus' house.

MRS. CRAIG: You were going to call Billy Birkmire, weren't you?

CRAIG: At his own house, yes.

MRS. CRAIG: Well, what difference does it make, Walter. Do you think those detectives can't put two and two together? Birkmire called you last night at Passmore's, didn't he?

CRAIG: Yes.

MRS. CRAIG: And there's undoubtedly a record of the call.

CRAIG: That wouldn't involve my name, would it?

MRS. CRAIG: It would if the operator listened in.

CRAIG: And do you think she has nothing to do but listen in on calls?

MRS. CRAIG: She listened in on this one, didn't she?

CRAIG: On which one?

MRS. CRAIG: What? (*She steps back from him suddenly, and touches her hair, in an effort to appear casual.*) What did you say?

CRAIG: Which call do you say the operator listened in on?

MRS. CRAIG: I don't know which one she listened in on. But some one must have listened in on something or those men wouldn't have come here, would they?

CRAIG: Did they say the operator had reported on a call from here?

MRS. CRAIG: I don't remember what they said, distinctly. One of them kept rambling something about a telephone call, but I assumed it was the one that Birkmire made to you last night out at Fergus'.

CRAIG: Didn't they say when the call was made?

MRS. CRAIG: What does it matter when it was made, Walter?

CRAIG: It matters a lot.

MRS. CRAIG: The fact remains, doesn't it, that that telephone is undoubtedly being watched *now*.

CRAIG (*whirling round and picking up the telephone again*): Well, I want to know *why* it's being watched.

MRS. CRAIG (*springing to his side and seizing the telephone*): Now, listen to me, Walter Craig; you *must* not use that telephone. (*She looks him straight in the eyes, then moves back several steps and looks at him defiantly.*) I will not allow you to drag my name into a notorious scandal.

CRAIG (*whipping the receiver off and putting it to his ear*): I've got to find out where I'm at in this thing!

MRS. CRAIG (*raising her voice threateningly*): If you speak over that telephone I'll leave this house! (*He takes the receiver from his ear and looks at her*

steadily. *There is a pause.*) And you know what construction 'ud be put upon that, under the circumstances.

[*He slowly hangs up and sets the telephone back onto the little table, holding her eyes steadily. Then he moves slowly towards her.*]

CRAIG: What do you mean, you'll leave this house?

MRS. CRAIG (*stonily*): I mean exactly what I said. Do you think I could stay in this neighborhood twenty-four hours after my name had been associated with a thing of this kind?

CRAIG: And haven't you any appreciation of the necessity of my knowing what's happening in this case?

MRS. CRAIG: I have no appreciation of any necessity except the necessity of keeping still.

CRAIG: But supposing something developed that would reveal absolutely the fact that I had been out there last night—

MRS. CRAIG: What *can* develop, if you keep still?

CRAIG: But, supposing something did? Wouldn't it be very much better for me to have been open and aboveboard from the beginning, instead of having played a waiting game, and probably create an attitude of suspicion where there are no grounds for any?

MRS. CRAIG: There *are* grounds for suspicion, Walter; don't evade the issue.

CRAIG: What are they?

MRS. CRAIG: The fact that you were out there last night.

CRAIG: That doesn't mean a thing.

MRS. CRAIG: Evidently not, to you.

CRAIG: Does it to you?

MRS. CRAIG: What does it matter what it means to me? It isn't for me to determine the degree of your guilt or innocence. I'm not interested.

CRAIG: You're not interested!

MRS. CRAIG: I'm interested only in the impression on the popular mind,—and the respect of the community we've got to live in.

CRAIG: You mean you'd rather know I was involved in this thing and *keep* the respect of the community, than know I was a victim of circumstances, and lose it?

[MRS. HAROLD *appears between the portières.* MRS. CRAIG *sees her over* CRAIG'S *shoulder, and crosses quickly below him.*]

MRS. CRAIG: What is it, Mrs. Harold?

MRS. HAROLD: I'm sorry to bother you, Mrs. Craig, but I'm afraid the dinner'll be spoiled.

MRS. CRAIG (*going down to the mirror*): All right; Mrs. Harold, put it up; I'll be right out.

[CRAIG *moves forward to the up-per right-hand corner of the center table.*]

MRS. HAROLD (*withdrawing*): All right.

CRAIG: Mrs. Harold.

MRS. HAROLD (*stopping*): Yes, sir? (*She comes back a few steps towards him.*)

CRAIG: Mrs. Harold, do you know if anybody has called that number that I gave you last night here, to-day, on this telephone?

MRS. HAROLD: You mean the number you gave me to have Mr. Birkmire call you at?

CRAIG: Yes, Levering three one hundred.

MRS. HAROLD: No, sir, I don't know that anybody has. I only gave it to Mr. Birkmire over the telephone last night when he called.

CRAIG: *You* haven't had occasion to call that number to-day on this telephone, have you, Mrs. Harold?

MRS. HAROLD: No, sir, I haven't, Mr. Craig.

CRAIG: All right, Mrs. Harold, thanks very much.

[*She starts to go, then stops and turns again.*]

MRS. HAROLD: I never even thought about it to-day until Mrs. Craig asked me for it when she came in this evening.

[*There is a pause.* CRAIG *shifts his eyes to his wife, who raises her arm slowly and touches her hair before the mirror.*]

CRAIG: All right, Mrs. Harold, thank you very much. (MRS. HAROLD *withdraws, and* CRAIG *moves up slowly towards the portières and watches her out of hearing distance. Then he turns and looks at his wife. She stands very still. He moves a step or two slowly towards her.*) It was you that made that call. (*She turns and looks at him, with a touch of defiance.*) What were you doing, checking up on me?

MRS. CRAIG (*starting up towards the portières*): Don't flatter yourself, Walter.

CRAIG: That's what you were doing, wasn't it?

MRS. CRAIG: Don't flatter yourself. The man hasn't been born yet that I'd bother checking up on.

CRAIG: Why didn't you tell the truth?

MRS. CRAIG (*whirling upon him*): Because I anticipated an attack of your romantic conscience.

CRAIG: You were playing safe; that was it, wasn't it?

MRS. CRAIG: Exactly!

CRAIG: And at my expense!

MRS. CRAIG: I knew the necessity of it with you!

CRAIG: God!

MRS. CRAIG (*following him up*): I knew if I told you I made that call, you'd be on the telephone in five minutes telling the Police.

CRAIG (*turning sharply*): I intended doing that anyway.

MRS. CRAIG: You silly fool!

CRAIG: That's where I went this evening, with Birkmire, when I left here—to Police Headquarters.

MRS. CRAIG (*aghast*): Oh!

CRAIG: And the only reason I didn't tell them then was that the man in charge of the case had gone to his dinner and wouldn't be back till eight o'clock. But he'll be told *then!* (*He swings up to the front door.*)

MRS. CRAIG (*leaning across the center table, and speaking threateningly*): Well, if you do, you'll explain my leaving you, too.

CRAIG: That wouldn't worry me in the least, Harriet.

MRS. CRAIG: Well, it might worry *them.*

[*He turns sharply and looks at her, dismayed.*]

CRAIG (*coming back to the table*): Listen to me, Harriet. Why weren't you at least *honest* with me in this thing, and not try to make it appear that *I* was responsible for the visit of those detectives?

MRS. CRAIG: Because I knew exactly what you'd do if I told you. And that would mean an explanation of why I had called up; and the next thing would be an admission of the fact that you are the man the Police are looking for.

CRAIG: But it's *you* those detectives are looking for.

MRS. CRAIG: Oh, you needn't try to turn it on to me! They wouldn't be looking for either of us if you'd stayed at home last night, instead of being out card-playing with a lot of irregular people. (*She turns down to the mirror.*)

CRAIG: What was there irregular about Fergus Passmore?

MRS. CRAIG (*turning to him, in a wrath*): There must have been some irregularity, or this thing wouldn't have happened. Everybody that knew Fergus Passmore knew that he was insanely jealous of his wife; and then *you* have to go out visiting them. (*She crosses below the table to the piano.*) I felt in my bones up there in Albany that something 'ud happen while I was away; that was the reason I didn't stay up there any longer than I absolutely had to. I knew as soon as ever my back was turned you'd be out with your friends again.

[*He looks at her, under his brows; and there is a pause.*]

CRAIG: And what has your back being turned got to do with my visiting my friends?

MRS. CRAIG: Never mind what it has to do with it; only you wouldn't have *been* visiting them if I'd been here.

CRAIG: How would you have stopped me?

MRS. CRAIG: I'd have stopped you all right, one way or another.

CRAIG: What would you have done—locked the door on me?

MRS. CRAIG: It wouldn't have been necessary to lock the door on you. (*Turning and looking at him directly.*) You haven't *been* visiting them in the last eighteen months, have you?

CRAIG: No, I haven't.

MRS. CRAIG: And they haven't been visiting you, either?

CRAIG: No, they haven't.

MRS. CRAIG (*turning away*): Well—

CRAIG (*after a slight pause*): You mean you've kept them out of here?

MRS. CRAIG (*turning to him again and looking him straight in the eyes*): Well, if I did the end justified the means; you at least haven't been in the shadow of the law in the last eighteen months.

[*He holds her eye for a second, then moves forward to the front of the table.*]

CRAIG: You're certainly running true to form, Harriet.

MRS. CRAIG: Well, I'm glad of it if I am.

CRAIG: My aunt said here a while ago that you'd driven all my friends away from this house.

MRS. CRAIG (*with level significance*): There are ways of getting rid of people without driving them away from the house.

[CRAIG *makes a little sound of bit-*

311

ter amusement.]

CRAIG: And I thought she was imagining things at your expense.

MRS. CRAIG: Well, you see she probably had better perception than you'd given her credit for. [*He turns and looks at her darkly.*]

CRAIG: Probably she had; for she perceived something else, Harriet, that may be equally true.

MRS. CRAIG: Is that so?

CRAIG: She said you were trying to get rid of me too—(*She darts a look at him*) without actually driving me away from the house. (*She laughs derisively, and moves across towards the portières. He follows her up, raising his voice.*) And I believe that's true, too.

MRS. CRAIG: Keep your voice down! Do you want everybody in the house to hear you?

CRAIG: You've admitted it, by your attitude in this affair this evening.

MRS. CRAIG (*looking at him, and moving forward to the mantelpiece*): I don't know what you're talking about.

CRAIG (*coming forward and leaning on the table*): Very well you know what I'm talking about. And you knew what my aunt was going to talk about too, here a while ago; that's the reason you left the room before she started.

MRS. CRAIG: I'm sorry I didn't stay here now.

CRAIG: No danger of your staying here, Harriet; you couldn't bear it. (*She laughs, and he moves forward to the left.*) My God, how perfectly she knows you, Harriet! She couldn't have read you any better if you'd written it out for her. And I felt rather sorry listening to her, thinking she was probably getting a little old and suspicious; particularly when she said you had excluded my friends.

MRS. CRAIG: Do you think I wanted my house turned into a tavern?

CRAIG: My friends never turned my mother's house into a tavern.

MRS. CRAIG: They didn't play poker at your mother's house till all hours of the morning.

CRAIG: Every Thursday night for ten years; till two o'clock, if they felt like it.

MRS. CRAIG: Well, evidently, your mother and I had very different ideas of a house.

CRAIG: Very different indeed, Harriet; there was more actual home in one room of my mother's house than there'd be in all of this if we lived in it a thousand years.

MRS. CRAIG: Why didn't you stay in it, then, if you found it so attractive?

CRAIG: Now you're talking, Harriet; why didn't I do *just that.* (*He turns away to the left, then turns suddenly back.*) But, don't make any mistake that I think you didn't want my friends here simply because they played cards; you wouldn't have wanted them if they'd come here to hold prayer meetings. You didn't want them because, as my aunt says, their visits implied an importance to *me* that was at variance with your little campaign—the campaign that was to reduce me to one of those wife-ridden sheep that's afraid to buy a necktie for fear his wife might not approve of it. (*He goes up towards the front door.*)

MRS. CRAIG: Oh, don't try to make yourself out a martyr; you've had your share of this bargain.

[*He turns suddenly and looks at her, then comes forward again to the front of the table.*]

CRAIG: I never regarded this thing as a bargain.

MRS. CRAIG: Did you expect me to go into a thing as important as marriage with my eyes shut?

CRAIG: I wanted you to go into it honestly, as I went into it— fifty-fifty—And you've been playing safe right from the start. (*He turns away towards the piano.*)

MRS. CRAIG: I've been doing nothing of the kind.

CRAIG: Don't tell me what you've been doing; I see your game as clearly as my aunt sees it. (*He turns and comes back towards her.*) You've been *exploiting me,* consistently, in your shifty little business of personal safety. And you'd throw me right now to the suspicion of implication in this double murder—to preserve that safety. (*He goes back towards the piano again.*)

MRS. CRAIG (*almost crying*): I've been trying to preserve my home.

CRAIG: That's all I've heard from you since the day I married you.

MRS. CRAIG: Well, what else has a woman like me *but* her home?

CRAIG (*turning to her*): Hasn't she her husband?

MRS. CRAIG: She could lose her husband, couldn't she?—As many another woman has.

CRAIG: Couldn't she lose her home too?

MRS. CRAIG: She couldn't if she knew how to secure it.

CRAIG (*raising his finger solemnly*): That's the point in a nutshell, Harriet; if she knew how to *fix* it for herself. (*He turns away and rests his hands on the piano.*)

MRS. CRAIG: Well, what if I have fixed things for myself? You haven't lost anything by it, have you? If I've fixed them for myself I've fixed them for you too. Your home is here. And maybe if I hadn't played the game so consistently it wouldn't *be* here. And I wouldn't be the first woman that's lost her home, and her husband too, through letting the control of them get out of her hands.

313

(*She moves up towards the back of the room, in a crying temper.*) I saw what happened to my own mother, and I made up my mind it 'ud never happen to me. (*She turns and comes forward again.*) She was one of those "I will follow thee, my husband" women—that believed everything my father told her; and all the time he was mortgaging her home over her head for another woman. And when she found it out, she did the only thing that women like her *can* do, and that was to die of a broken heart—within six months; and leave the door open for the other woman to come in as stepmother over Estelle and me. (*She turns to the mantelpiece.*) And then get rid of us both as soon as Estelle was marriageable. (*Turning to him suddenly.*) But the house was never mortgaged over *her* head, I'll promise you that; for she saw to it that it was put in her name before ever she took him; and she kept it there, too, right to the finish. (*She sweeps up towards the back of the room again.*)

CRAIG: Why didn't you ask me to put this house in *your* name?

MRS. CRAIG (*whirling upon him*): Because I didn't *want* it in my name!

CRAIG: It would have been more honest.

MRS. CRAIG (*coming forward to*

the right end of the table*): I haven't done anything that wasn't honest!

CRAIG: How would you know, Harriet?

MRS. CRAIG: I've simply tried to be practical; but, with your usual romanticism, you want to make me appear like a criminal for it.

CRAIG: I'm not reproaching you at all.

MRS. CRAIG: Well, you shouldn't reproach me; for there's nothing to reproach me about.

CRAIG: You simply married the wrong man, Harriet.

MRS. CRAIG (*witheringly*): I married a romantic fool! (*He looks at her narrowly, and she holds his eye.*) That's what I married; (*she turns away and goes up to the portières to look out*) and I'm seeing it more every day I live.

[*There is a pause. Then Craig breaks into a hard little laugh.*]

CRAIG: How well we understand each other now, Harriet.

MRS. CRAIG (*coming forward to the mantelpiece again*): Well, I understand you, anyway, whether you understand me or not. (*Speaking directly to him.*) And you ought to thank your God that I do, for I don't know what 'ud become of you if I didn't.

[*She turns to the mantelpiece, and suddenly sees the card that*

MAZIE *left back of the center ornament. She picks up the little envelope deftly, takes the card out and reads it.* CRAIG *regards her icily; and after a pause, he speaks—in a level, rather dangerous tone.*]

CRAIG: The brass of you—and the presumption.

[*She looks at him.*]

MRS. CRAIG: What?

CRAIG: I'm just wondering how you *get* that way.

MRS. CRAIG: How I get what way?

CRAIG: So brazenly presumptuous, as to say such a thing to me.

MRS. CRAIG: What have I said? I don't know what you're talking about.

CRAIG (*moving slowly away a step or two from the piano*): What have you ever done, or a million others like you, that would warrant the assumption of such superiority over the men you're married to?

MRS. CRAIG: Nobody's assuming any superiority.

CRAIG: Doesn't your remark admit it?

MRS. CRAIG (*turning and moving up to the portières*): Don't get yourself into a temper.

CRAIG: That you don't know what 'ud become of me only that *you* understand me.

MRS. CRAIG (*glancing through* the portières): Neither I do.

CRAIG: The presumption of you.

MRS. CRAIG: What are you standing there for, Mazie?

MAZIE AND CRAIG (*speaking together*):

MAZIE: Why, Mrs. Harold sent me in to see if you were coming in to dinner.

CRAIG: That you should set yourself about to control the very destiny of a man,—

MRS. CRAIG: Yes, I'm coming right away.

MRS. CRAIG AND CRAIG (*speaking together*):

MRS. CRAIG: But I want to see you for a minute first, Mazie.

CRAIG: As though I were some mental incompetent.

MAZIE: Yes, Ma'm.

MRS. CRAIG (*turning and going towards Craig, lowering her voice, and trying to silence him with a gesture*): Don't make a show of yourself in front of Mazie. (MAZIE *comes through the portières, and* MRS. CRAIG *turns to her.*) Mazie, what is this card here?

MAZIE: Why, it's the Society card, Mrs. Craig, of the Mutual Benevolent.

MRS. CRAIG: And what is it doing here?

MAZIE: Why, Christine sent it down about an hour ago, with the tailor's little boy, to know if I'd pay her dues for her.

MRS. CRAIG: And couldn't you

315

find any place for it but back of that ornament?

MAZIE: Why, I was—

MRS. CRAIG: After all the times I've told you never to put anything on that mantelpiece.

MAZIE: Yes, you *have* told me, Mrs. Craig, but when I came in—

MRS. CRAIG: Then, why do you do it? Must I keep telling you the same thing indefinitely? You know perfectly well I never allow anybody even to *dust* that mantelpiece but myself. I even bought a special little brush for those ornaments, because I wouldn't trust them to anybody else. And yet the minute you get my back turned you must use them as a catchall for everything in the house.

MAZIE: Mrs. Harold asked me something when I came in, and—

MRS. CRAIG: I am not interested in what anybody asked you; that does not excuse you. (MAZIE *takes a handkerchief from the pocket of her apron and touches it to her eyes.*) I have told you over and over again *never* to put anything back of those ornaments; and you deliberately disobey me. You simply will *not* do as you are told. And when a girl will not do as she is told, the best thing for her to do is to go some place where she will be *made* to do it. So I want you to get your things together to-night and leave this

house to-morrow morning. (MAZIE *looks at her, then turns away to leave the room.*) Here's the card. And find some place for it besides back of an ornament. (MAZIE *takes the card and withdraws.*) And tell Mrs. Harold to put up the dinner, I'll be down in two minutes; (*She starts for the stairs.*) I'm going up to see what my niece wants for *her* dinner. (*She goes up the stairs haughtily. Halfway up she turns, but without stopping, and addresses Craig coldly.*) You'd better go out there and get your dinner, before it's cold.

[*She disappears at the head of the stairs, and* CRAIG *stands looking at the floor. His eyes wander up the stairs after her, and then down the right side of the room. They settle upon the ornament on the mantelpiece, and he looks at it hard; then crosses slowly and picks it up. He holds it in his hand, looking at it curiously: then suddenly lifts it in the air and smashes it on the bricks in front of the mantelpiece. He stands looking at the shattered pieces for a moment; then takes a cigarette from his case and strolls back across the room towards the piano. He taps the cigarette on the case, then takes out a match and lights it, tossing the burned match on to the floor. Then he leans against the piano and smokes, thoughtfully.* MRS. HAROLD *hurries in through the portières.*]

MRS. HAROLD: Did something get broke in here, Mr. Craig? (*He indicates the shattered ornament with a nod, and* MRS. HAROLD *looks towards the mantelpiece. She sees the pieces of the shattered ornament, and raising her hands and eyes to Heaven, takes a step or two towards them.*) Glory be to God this day and this night, how did that happen, Mr. Craig! Did it fall off the mantelpiece?

CRAIG (*without moving*): No, I smashed it, Mrs. Harold.

MRS. HAROLD (*puzzled*): On purpose, do you mean, Mr. Craig?

CRAIG: Yes.—I didn't like it.

MRS. HAROLD: I wish you'd tell Mrs. Craig it was you that done it, Mr. Craig; if she sees it she might think it was one of us that broke it.

CRAIG: I'll tell her all about it, Mrs. Harold; don't you worry about that. (*He straightens up and starts across slowly, towards the big chair in front of the mantelpiece, and* MRS. HAROLD *moves a step or two towards the portières.*)

MRS. HAROLD (*turning to him*): Will I get the dustpan and sweep that up, Mr. Craig?

CRAIG: No, don't bother about it now, Mrs. Harold; go out and get your dinner.

[*She moves towards the portières, then stops again.*]

MRS. HAROLD: Ain't you comin' to your dinner, Mr. Craig?

CRAIG (*sitting down*): No, I don't want any dinner to-night, Mrs. Harold.

MRS. HAROLD: Don't you want nothing at all?

CRAIG: Not a thing.

[*She withdraws; and he sits smoking and thinking.*]

MRS. CRAIG (*from the head of the stairs*): Are you down there, Walter?

CRAIG: Yes.

MRS. CRAIG: Listen—did something *fall* down there a minute ago?

CRAIG: No.

MRS. CRAIG: Are you sure?

CRAIG: Yes, I'm sure.

MRS. CRAIG: Well, it sounded up here as though the house fell down.

CRAIG (*after a slight pause*): Maybe it did, Harriet—I'm just sitting here wondering. (*He sits smoking. His gaze wanders up, and out, and away off.*)

THE CURTAIN DESCENDS SLOWLY

317

ACT III

SCENE: *Same as preceding act—the following morning, about eight-thirty.* CRAIG *is still sitting in the big chair before the fireplace, asleep. After a pause,* MRS. HAROLD *enters through the portières, carrying a dustpan and hand brush. She sees* CRAIG, *looks at him curiously, and also observes the pieces of the shattered ornament and the cigarette butts at his feet. She turns and puts the dustpan and brush down on the seat at the right of the stairway, and, with a glance up the stairs, crosses and unlocks the front door and goes out. The screen door slams after her and* CRAIG *wakes. He looks around, glances at his watch, gets up and settles himself before the mirror.* MRS. HAROLD *tiptoes in, bringing the morning paper.*

CRAIG: Good morning, Mrs. Harold.

MRS. HAROLD (*stopping above the center table*): Good morning, Mr. Craig.

CRAIG: I must have made a night of it sitting here.

MRS. HAROLD: Yes, I was wondering if you'd been there all night.

CRAIG: I must have fallen asleep.

MRS. HAROLD: You must feel pretty tired, don't you?

CRAIG (*turning to her*): No, I'm all right. Is that the morning paper you have there, Mrs. Harold?

MRS. HAROLD: Yes, sir, I was just bringing it in.

CRAIG: Let me see it, will you?

MRS. HAROLD: Yes, sir. (*He takes the paper; and, stepping to the window, forward, reads it eagerly.*) Would you like a cup of coffee, Mr. Craig?

CRAIG: Yes, I'll take a little coffee if you have it.

MRS. HAROLD (*starting for the portières*): It's all made;—I'll just turn on the percolator for a minute.

[*She goes out; and he stands reading. There is the sound of a door opening somewhere upstairs. He glances towards the head of the stairs, then crosses quickly up to the front door and out on to the porch.* MRS. HAROLD *comes in again; and, picking up the dustpan and brush, comes forward to the mantelpiece and starts to sweep up the ornament and cigarette butts.* MRS. CRAIG *appears on the stairway.*]

MRS. CRAIG: Mrs. Harold.

MRS. HAROLD (*straightening up*): Yes, Ma'm?

MRS. CRAIG: Has the morning paper come yet?

318

MRS. HAROLD: Yes, Ma'm, I just gave it to Mr. Craig; he's reading it there on the front porch.

MRS. CRAIG (*puzzled, and coming down the stairs*): What is *he* doing up so early?

MRS. HAROLD: I don't think he's been in bed at all, Mrs. Craig; he was sitting in this big chair here when I came in this morning, and he was sitting here last night when I locked up.

[MRS. CRAIG *crosses to the bay window at the left and looks out on to the porch; and* MRS. HAROLD *resumes her sweeping.* MRS. CRAIG *becomes aware of what* MRS. HAROLD *is doing, and turns to her.*]

MRS. CRAIG: What is that you're sweeping up there, Mrs. Harold?

MRS. HAROLD (*straightening up*): Why, it's that center ornament that was here, Mrs. Craig.

[MRS. CRAIG *crosses down in front of the center table, looking wide-eyed at the vacant place on the mantelpiece.*]

MRS. CRAIG: What!

MRS. HAROLD: It got broke last night.

MRS. CRAIG: Oh, my God, Mrs. Harold, don't tell me that that's that beautiful statuette!

MRS. HAROLD: Mr. Craig said that he broke it.

MRS. CRAIG (*looking at the shattered pieces in the dustpan, which* MRS. HAROLD *is holding*): Oh, my

God, look at the way it's broken!— It's smashed into a thousand pieces.

MRS. HAROLD: It must have fallen on the bricks here.

MRS. CRAIG: Oh, that never simply fell, Mrs. Harold; it's absolutely shattered—look at the size of the pieces. It's out of the question even to think of having it mended.

MRS. HAROLD: No, I don't think it could ever be mended now.

MRS. CRAIG (*almost crying*): That beautiful thing — that I wouldn't even allow anybody to go near; and look at it now.

MRS. HAROLD: It certainly is too bad.

MRS. CRAIG: And, of course, I might just as well throw those others away now, for they're absolutely meaningless without this one. (*She turns away, in a pang of grief, and moves a few steps towards the left, then suddenly turns again to* MRS. HAROLD.) How on earth did it ever happen, Mrs. Harold?

MRS. HAROLD: I don't know, I'm sure, Mrs. Craig.

MRS. CRAIG: I suppose Mazie broke it for spite, didn't she?— Because I reprimanded her last night for putting things back of it.

MRS. HAROLD: No, she didn't break it, Mrs. Craig, for she was out there in the kitchen with me when we heard it fall.

319

MRS. CRAIG (*turning away and crossing below the center table*): Well, send her in here to me now, I want to speak to her.

MRS. HAROLD: Mr. Craig said that *he* broke it; (MRS. CRAIG *turns and looks at her*) he said he didn't like that ornament.

MRS. CRAIG: Tell Mazie I want to see her.

MRS. HAROLD: She isn't here, Mrs. Craig; she's gone.

MRS. CRAIG: You mean she's left already?

MRS. HAROLD: Yes, Ma'm, she left right after she had her breakfast.

MRS. CRAIG: Of course she did, the contemptible little devil.

MRS. HAROLD: Mr. Craig said that he'd tell you all about it.

MRS. CRAIG: Where did Mazie go?

MRS. HAROLD: She said she was goin' to her married sister's for a while.

MRS. CRAIG: Did you pay her her wages?

MRS. HAROLD: Yes, Ma'm, I paid her last night.

MRS. CRAIG (*turning away towards the front door*): All right, Mrs. Harold. (MRS. HAROLD *goes out through the portières, taking the dustpan and brush with her.*) Walter, come in here for a minute, will you? (*She glances over her shoulder, to see that* MRS. HAROLD *is out of earshot, then turns and*

waits till CRAIG *comes in. He enters, carrying the newspaper.*) What does the paper say this morning about the Passmore thing?

CRAIG (*handing her the newspaper*): You're quite safe. (*He comes forward and across in front of the center table to the mirror, and straightens his tie.*)

MRS. CRAIG (*stepping forward to the piano and spreading the paper out eagerly*): What does it say?

CRAIG: His brother got in last night from Pittsburgh, with a letter that Fergus had written him, intimating his intentions.

MRS. CRAIG: Then, Fergus did it himself?

CRAIG: So it appears.

MRS. CRAIG: I always told you he was jealous of his wife.

[CRAIG *turns and looks at her.*]

CRAIG: He did it because she was dishonest.

MRS. CRAIG (*reading*): I suppose this telegram here from his brother about Fergus' letter was the additional information that that detective spoke about here last night. (*She straightens up and speaks directly to Craig.*) He called Police Headquarters from here about seven o'clock, and then he said it wouldn't be necessary to bother us any more for a while,—that there'd been some additional information come in on the case: so I suppose that's what it was; for it says here the telegram was received at Police Headquarters at six forty-five.

CRAIG (*moving with a wearied air towards the portières*): What does it matter now, Harriet?

MRS. CRAIG: It doesn't matter *now*, but it would have mattered —only that I kept my head last night, and didn't allow you to telephone, and make a show of us all. (*He laughs bitterly.*) You can laugh, as much as you like; but you can thank me that your name isn't in every paper in the city this morning. (*She resumes her reading.*)

CRAIG: Oh, I can thank you for more than that, Harriet.

MRS. CRAIG: Well, you can thank me for that, anyway.

CRAIG: I can thank you for having given me a new name last night—that fits me so perfectly that I've decided to continue its use. You called me a romantic fool.

MRS. CRAIG: Fergus must have known about this man that Adelaide's been going around with; for it says here he'd mentioned him once before in a letter to his brother.

[MRS. HAROLD *appears between the portières.*]

MRS. HAROLD: The coffee's ready, Mr. Craig.

CRAIG (*turning quietly toward the portières*): All right, Mrs.

Harold.

[*She withdraws, and he follows her.* MRS. CRAIG *looks up suddenly and crosses towards him.*]

MRS. CRAIG: Listen, Walter, come here for a minute.

[*He turns.*]

CRAIG: What?

MRS. CRAIG: Listen. (*She glances over his shoulder after* MRS. HAROLD, *then lowers her voice.*) Billy Birkmire 'ull very likely want you to go out there with him to Fergus' funeral; but don't you do it. And you'd better tell him not to go around there either; for one of you is apt to say something. And if that butler out there sees *you*, he might recognize you. And there's no use starting anything now, when the thing's all over.

[*He looks at her steadily.*]

CRAIG: Is that all you wanted to tell me?

MRS. CRAIG: Well, it's the thing to do, isn't it? It certainly wouldn't help matters *now* to say anything, would it? What are you smiling at?

CRAIG: At your wanting to help matters.

MRS. CRAIG: So I *have* wanted to help them.

CRAIG: Since when?

MRS. CRAIG (*turning away to the center table*): Well, don't let's go into all that again. I've been wanting to help *you* principally, but you don't seem to have sense enough to appreciate it.

CRAIG: Is that all you want me for?

MRS. CRAIG (*turning to him again*): No, it isn't all I want you for. I want to know about that ornament there that was broken here last night.

CRAIG: What about it?

MRS. CRAIG: I don't know *what* about it; that's the reason I'm asking you. Mrs. Harold tells me here this morning that you told her last night that you'd broken it.

CRAIG: So I did.

MRS. CRAIG: Well, you ought to be proud of yourself.

CRAIG: I was for a moment.

MRS. CRAIG: What were you doing—leaning against the mantelpiece again as usual?

CRAIG: No, it wasn't an accident; I did it deliberately.

MRS. CRAIG: What do you mean, you did it deliberately?

CRAIG: I mean that I smashed it purposely.

MRS. CRAIG: What for?

CRAIG: I became suddenly heroic.

MRS. CRAIG: I don't believe you.

CRAIG (*turning away*): Very well, that's that.

MRS. CRAIG: Why would you deliberately break a beautiful, expensive ornament like that?

CRAIG (*turning back*): I didn't

break it.

MRS. CRAIG: Well, you said you did.

CRAIG (*bitterly*): I said I smashed it—into a thousand little pieces, right here on these bricks here. And then I smoked one cigarette after another, till I had your sanctum sanctorum here absolutely littered with ashes and cigarette butts. I was positively a hell of a fellow around here for about an hour last night; you should have seen me.

MRS. CRAIG: What did you do, go out of your mind or something?

CRAIG: No, I was particularly clear in my mind, strange to say. You made a remark here last night, Harriet, that completely illuminated me; and illuminated you. And suddenly I saw—for the first time—everything—just as one sees an entire landscape at midnight in a flash of lightning. But, unfortunately, the lightning struck my house—and knocked it down; and I sat here all night wondering how I might build it up again.

MRS. CRAIG: What remark are you talking about?

CRAIG: You said that a woman might lose her husband but not her home, if she knew how to secure it.

MRS. CRAIG: Well, hasn't many a woman lost her husband?

CRAIG: And many a man has lost

his life too, Harriet, because his wife has never made a sufficiently illuminating remark. But you did make it. And that other remark —when you said there were ways of getting rid of people without driving them away from the house. (*He smiles bitterly.*) I saw your entire plan of life, Harriet, and its relationship to me. And my instinct of self-preservation suggested the need of immediate action—the inauguration of a new régime here: so I smashed the little ornament there—as a kind of opening gun. And I was going to smash all the other little ornaments—and Gods you had set up in the temple here, and been worshipping before me. I was going to put my house in order, including my wife; and rule it with a rod of iron. (MRS. CRAIG *turns away, faintly amused.*) I don't wonder that amuses you; it amused me; particularly when I suddenly remembered the truth of what you called me last night; and in view of that, the absurdity of my trying to sustain such a rôle indefinitely. It made me laugh— But I'm rather sorry you couldn't have seen me, anyway; I think you would at least have appreciated the sincerity of my *attempt* to continue here as your husband. (*He turns slowly and moves towards the portières.*)

MRS. CRAIG: What do you mean,

your attempt to continue here as my husband?

CRAIG: The rôle is not *for* me, Harriet; I can only play a romantic part.

[*She turns her head quietly and looks at him; and he holds her eye for a second, then goes out through the portières; and she stands looking after him. Then she moves slowly to the portières and stands, thinking. The doorbell rings, but evidently she doesn't hear it. She moves forward slowly, still thinking narrowly.* MRS. HAROLD *comes through the portières hurriedly.*]

MRS. CRAIG: There's some one at the door, Mrs. Harold.

[*The doorbell rings again.*]

MRS. HAROLD (*hurrying across to answer the door*): I guess maybe it's the man for Miss Austen's things.

MRS. CRAIG: Is Miss Austen leaving already?

MRS. HAROLD (*stopping near the door*): I think so; she said last night she was going first thing in the morning.

MRS. CRAIG: Is she up?

MRS. HAROLD: Yes, Ma'm, she asked me to call her at seven.

[*She goes out, and* MRS. CRAIG *crosses after her.*]

MRS. CRAIG: Well, if that's the man for her things, Mrs. Harold, have him go round to the side

323

door and bring her things down the back stairway; I don't want him dragging trunks down these front stairs. (*She steps to the bay window at the left and looks out at the expressman.*)

EXPRESSMAN (*at the front door*): Trunks ready?

MRS. HAROLD: Yes, they're ready. Would you mind going around to the side door; you can bring them down the back way.

EXPRESSMAN: Around this way?

MRS. HAROLD: Yes, up the steps; I'll open it for you.

[*The screen door slams, and she hurries in again, crossing towards the portières.*]

MRS. CRAIG: Are Miss Austen's things ready, Mrs. Harold?

MRS. HAROLD: Yes, Ma'm, I helped her pack last night.

MRS. CRAIG: Did she say where she was going?

MRS. HAROLD (*stopping*): Yes, Ma'm; she sez she's going to the Ritz-Carlton Hotel now, but after that she sez she's going to travel. (*Continuing to the portières.*) I must open the door for that man. [*She goes out, and* MRS. CRAIG *stands looking after her, thinking. She moves across towards the portières and stops again, looking out through the portières.* ETHEL *hurries down the stairs, with her hat and coat on.*]

MRS. CRAIG: Ethel, dear child,

what are you doing up so early?

ETHEL: I haven't been asleep all night. I've been waiting to hear some one else up.

MRS. CRAIG: You're not ill, are you, dear?

ETHEL: No, but I must go home immediately, Aunt Harriet; I'm too troubled in my mind to stay here any longer.

MRS. CRAIG: But you can't go immediately, dear.

ETHEL: I must go, Aunt Harriet.

MRS. CRAIG: But there's no train, dear, until the nine-seventeen.

ETHEL: Well, it's nearly that now, isn't it?

[MRS. CRAIG *looks at her watch.*]

MRS. CRAIG: It isn't a quarter of nine yet.

ETHEL: Well, it'll take that time to get to the station, won't it?

MRS. CRAIG: It doesn't take ten minutes, dear, in a taxicab; and I can have one here in five minutes.

ETHEL (*putting her bag on the table and crossing down to the mirror*): Well, will you call one, please?

MRS. CRAIG (*moving after her*): Certainly, dear; but there's no use calling it already, you'd only have to wait around the station there.

ETHEL: I'm so worried, Aunt Harriet.

MRS. CRAIG: I know, dear child; but I'm sure you're upsetting yourself unnecessarily; we certainly would have heard something if anything had happened.

ETHEL (*turning to* MRS. CRAIG): I really should call Mr. Fredericks on the long distance, Aunt Harriet; he'll be wondering what on earth is the matter. Because I rushed away as soon as ever I got Dr. Wood's wire, and simply left a note that Mother was very ill. And he's probably called me up at home by this time and found that I'm down here; and he won't know what to think of it.

MRS. CRAIG: Well, I wouldn't worry myself too much about what he'll think, dear.

ETHEL: But he'll think it's funny that I should be down here if Mother's so ill.

[*There is a sound upstairs of a trunk being moved.*]

MRS. CRAIG (*dashing towards the stairs and up on to the landing*): He probably hasn't given it a thought.

ETHEL (*moving across above the table and looking out the bay window*): Oh, don't say that, Aunt Harriet, I know he has.

[MRS. CRAIG *claps her hands briskly, to attract the expressman's attention.*]

MRS. CRAIG: Please be careful of that floor there, Mr. Expressman, will you?

EXPRESSMAN: This baby got away from me. I thought it was lighter than it is.

MRS. CRAIG: Well, please try to keep it away from that wall there; I don't want that wall all scratched up; I only had it painted in April. (*There is a sound of the trunk being dragged along the hallway to the back stairs, and then a heavy thud.* MRS. CRAIG *closes her eyes in an agony of suffering and leans heavily upon the banister to keep from fainting. Then she turns and comes down into the room again.*) Mr. Craig's aunt is sending some luggage away to be mended; and those expressmen are so careless they don't care if they tear down the house.

ETHEL: I haven't had a chance to speak to Miss Austen yet.

MRS. CRAIG: I suppose she's getting dressed.

ETHEL: I haven't seen Uncle Walter yet, either.

MRS. CRAIG: He's out there having some coffee, I believe. Don't you want to come out and have some too, dear?

ETHEL: I don't think I could touch a thing, Aunt Harriet.

MRS. CRAIG: You could take a sip of coffee.

ETHEL: I don't want Uncle Walter to see me looking so terrible.

MRS. CRAIG: What does it matter, darling; he understands the circumstances. And you really shouldn't start on that trip back home without something. And when you do go back, Ethel, I want you to consider seriously what I've been saying to you about Mr. Fredericks. You're not married to him yet; and if there's anything to be done, it's now that it must be done. You can't come back and undo a thing like marriage.

ETHEL: Oh, I don't know what to do, Aunt Harriet.

MRS. CRAIG: Well, there's no hurry about doing anything just now. And don't let him hurry you. Just think it over—for his sake as well as for your own. You don't want to be a burden to him, do you?

ETHEL: Certainly not.

MRS. CRAIG: Well, what else would you be to him, dear—unless you used your own money? And that isn't conducive to respect for a man. And, in any case, you'd find in time that he'd come to resent your independence of him.

MISS AUSTEN (*at the head of the stairs*): Yes, I have it here in my bag, Mrs. Harold.

MRS. CRAIG (*drawing* ETHEL *towards the portières*): So just think it over. And come on out to the breakfast room and let me get you something.

[*They go out through the portières.* MISS AUSTEN *comes down the stairs, dressed for the street. She glances through the portières and picks up the telephone.*]

MISS AUSTEN (*into the telephone*): Will you give me Market, three, three, three, three, please? Please. (MRS. HAROLD *comes down the stairs, dressed for the street, and carrying a suit case and a smaller bag.*) I think you might as well take those right out on to the porch, Mrs. Harold.

MRS. HAROLD (*going out*): Yes, Ma'm.

MISS AUSTEN: Have them ready when the cab comes. (*Into the telephone.*) Hello. — Will you please send a taxicab to six hundred and eighty Belmont Manor, right away, please? Yes. (*She sets the telephone down and* MRS. HAROLD *comes in.*) It'll be here in a few minutes, Mrs. Harold. Are you all ready?

MRS. HAROLD: Yes, Ma'm, I'm ready.

MISS AUSTEN: Hadn't you better speak to Mrs. Craig about your keys, Mrs. Harold?

MRS. HAROLD: I left them with yours up on her dressing table.

MISS AUSTEN: I think you'd better tell her, Mrs. Harold.

MRS. HAROLD: Do you want me to tell them *you're* going?

MISS AUSTEN (*going towards the door*): No, it isn't necessary, Mrs. Harold; I'll write to Mr. Craig. But, I think you'd better tell them that *you're* going.

MRS. HAROLD: I did tell Mr. Craig I was going; I told him this morning.

MISS AUSTEN: Well, I think you'd better tell Mrs. Craig, also.

MRS. HAROLD: Yes, Ma'm.

MISS AUSTEN: There might be something she'd want to ask you.

MRS. HAROLD: All right, I'll tell her.

MISS AUSTEN: I'll sit here on the porch till the taxi comes.

[*She goes out, and* MRS. HAR-OLD *goes to the mirror and straightens her funny hat.*]

MRS. CRAIG (*coming through the adjoining room*): Are you in there, Mrs. Harold? (MRS. HAR-OLD *moves up to the foot of the stairs and stands facing the portières.* MRS. CRAIG *comes in.*) Oh, I've been looking for you out there, Mrs. Harold; I wanted you to give my niece a little breakfast.

MRS. HAROLD: I've left everything ready out there, Mrs. Craig.

MRS. CRAIG: Where are you going, Mrs. Harold?

MRS. HAROLD: Why, I'm going with Miss Austen, Mrs. Craig.

MRS. CRAIG: Indeed?

MRS. HAROLD: She was tellin' me last night she was goin' to leave here, and I said I thought I'd be leavin' pretty soon myself; so she said if I was goin' anyway soon, she'd like very much to have me go with her.

MRS. CRAIG: And where are you going with her?

MRS. HAROLD: Why, we are goin'

to the Ritz-Carlton first, and after that she sez she's goin' to travel for a few years.

MRS. CRAIG: Well, that ought to be a very good experience for you.

MRS. HAROLD: Yes, I've never been many places outside of here and Long Branch, and I thought I'd better take the chance while I had it.

MRS. CRAIG: And do you think it's very considerate of you, Mrs. Harold, to walk away this way without giving me any notice?

MRS. HAROLD: You didn't give Mazie much notice last night, Mrs. Craig.

MRS. CRAIG: Mazie didn't deserve any notice; she was a very disobedient girl. She absolutely refused to do what I told her.

MRS. HAROLD: Well, I haven't done exactly what you told me to do, either, Mrs. Craig,—so maybe I deserve to go as well as Mazie.

MRS. CRAIG: Well, of course, you can suit yourself about going, Mrs. Harold, but you understand I shall have to tell Miss Hewlitt about your leaving without notice.

MRS. HAROLD: Miss Hewlitt knows all about my leaving, Mrs. Craig; she's surprised that I didn't leave long ago, to tell you the truth.

MRS. CRAIG: And why didn't you leave?

MRS. HAROLD: Well—there were no children—and it's near church.

327

But Miss Hewlitt told me when I came here that if I stayed a month I'd be the first out of seven that did.

MRS. CRAIG: Miss Hewlitt has sent some very unsatisfactory women here.

MRS. HAROLD: A lot of them have worked in some pretty fine places.

MRS. CRAIG (*turning away, and moving down to the mirror*): Well, of course, that depends upon what a person's idea of a fine place is. And I suppose the next *batch* she sends me won't be any more satisfactory than the rest.

MRS. HAROLD: I think you're very foolish to have her send any more, Mrs. Craig, if you ask me.

MRS. CRAIG: One person can't do everything.

MRS. HAROLD: I've heard you say yourself more than once that you had to do over again everything that any woman that ever worked for you did,—so why not save the money?

[MRS. CRAIG *turns from the mirror and comes towards her.*]

MRS. CRAIG: What about the keys?

MRS. HAROLD: I left them all on your dressin' table upstairs; and Miss Austen's, too.

MRS. CRAIG: Wasn't there anything else to be left?

MRS. HAROLD: Yes, Ma'm, I left the money that I had over with

the week's list in an envelope with the keys.

MRS. CRAIG (*turning to the portières*): All right.—I hope you enjoy your world tour.

MRS. HAROLD (*going towards the front door*): It'll be a change, anyway.

[MRS. CRAIG *turns at the portières.*]

MRS. CRAIG: And I hope when you come back, you'll be able to find a place that'll be as easy as this one has been.

MRS. HAROLD (*stopping at the door and turning*): Don't worry about me, Mrs. Craig; nobody belongin' to me ever died in the poorhouse.

[*She goes out on to the porch, and* MRS. CRAIG *looks after her stonily. The front doorbell rings incisively, and* MRS. CRAIG *steps forward at the right and looks keenly towards the front door.*]

FREDERICKS (*at the front door*): How do you do?

MRS. HAROLD: How do you do?

FREDERICKS: I should like to see Miss Landreth, if I could. My name is Fredericks.

[MRS. CRAIG *makes a rapid movement of consternation, then looks at the portières.* ETHEL *comes through the portières.*]

ETHEL AND MRS. HAROLD (*speaking together*):

ETHEL: I think I'd better get my things, Aunt Harriet; it must be nearly nine o'clock.

MRS. HAROLD: Oh, come in, please. I think Miss Landreth is just having her breakfast.

[*The screen door slams.*]

ETHEL AND FREDERICKS (*speaking together*):

ETHEL: Would you mind telephoning for a taxicab?

FREDERICKS: I suppose I am a bit early.

[ETHEL *hears his voice and stops at the foot of the stairs.* MRS. CRAIG *glides out through the portières.* MRS. HAROLD *comes in at the front door.*]

MRS. HAROLD: Oh, I was just comin' to call you, Miss Landreth; there's a Mr. Fredericks here to see you.

[*He comes in.*]

FREDERICKS: Hello, Ethel.

[MRS. HAROLD *passes to the door, back of him, and goes out again.*]

ETHEL: Gene, there isn't anything happened to Mother?

FREDERICKS: Not a thing in the world, dear, that I know of.

ETHEL: You're sure?

FREDERICKS: 'Pon my word, Ethel. I haven't been to your house.

ETHEL: Well, why did you come away down here, then, at this hour of the morning?

FREDERICKS (*taking a step to her*): I wanted to see *you*. (*She begins to cry, and he takes her in*

his arms.) I thought maybe you were ill or something. Don't cry, darling; I give you my word there isn't a thing wrong at home. I simply telephoned you as soon as I got your note, and they told me you'd left for here: so then I called you on the long distance. But I couldn't get any satisfaction on the long distance, and I didn't know what to think. So I just jumped on the night train and got in here at eight-twenty.

ETHEL (*straightening up and touching her hair*): I'm going back right away, Gene; there's a train at nine-seventeen from the station down town.

FREDERICKS: I'll go back with you.

ETHEL: I don't know why I ever came away in the first place.

FREDERICKS (*guiding her to the chair at the right of the piano*): Sit down here for a minute, dear; you look terribly pale.

[*He puts his hat on the piano.*]

ETHEL: I haven't closed my eyes since I've been here, I've been so worried.

FREDERICKS: I've been worried about *you*, too, ever since I got your note.

ETHEL: And then I told Aunt Harriet about our engagement, and that upset me more than ever.

FREDERICKS: Why?

ETHEL: Oh, she didn't seem to approve of it exactly.

329

FREDERICKS: Why not?

ETHEL (*rising*): Oh, for several reasons, Gene,—I'll tell you on the train. (*She starts for the foot of the stairs.*)

FREDERICKS (*taking her hand as she passes him*): I wish you'd tell me now, Ethel.

ETHEL (*turning to him*): There isn't time, dear.

FREDERICKS: But you make me uneasy.

ETHEL: It's nothing, Gene, particularly. She simply said she thought perhaps I hadn't considered the thing sufficiently.

FREDERICKS: What is there to consider, darling, in a thing of this kind—except that we love each other.

ETHEL: But she said a thing like marriage should be considered more practically.

FREDERICKS: I don't accept that argument, Ethel; I've seen too many carefully reasoned marriages turn out badly. It's simply a chance that one has to take, more or less. And I have a good way of getting along.

ETHEL: As a single man, yes.

FREDERICKS: And even as a married man.

ETHEL: You don't know that yet, Gene, whether you have or not.

FREDERICKS: But other fellows marry, darling, and get along, on a great deal less salary than I'm getting.

ETHEL: I know that, Gene; but, as Aunt Harriet says, their wives are not living the way I've been accustomed to living. Not that I'd mind that in the least, dear; only I wouldn't want you to feel that I was making any sacrifices. And she says you might feel that in your present circumstances.

FREDERICKS: But haven't you any faith in my ability to improve those circumstances?

ETHEL: Of course; but I wouldn't want to be a burden to you in the meantime.

FREDERICKS: But you're the kind of burden I need, Ethel. You know I've had three promotions since I've known you.

ETHEL: Yes, I know you have.

FREDERICKS: Well, I attribute it to nothing but the incentive that the thought of marrying you has given me. I've worked like a dog these past two years, with just that in mind; and if it were removed, —well, I just don't think beyond that, that's all.

[*He turns away to the left a few steps and stands looking straight out. She crosses and lays her hand on his arm.*]

ETHEL: I hadn't thought of not marrying you, Gene; I was just thinking whether or not it would be wise to postpone it.

FREDERICKS (*turning to her*): It *wouldn't* be wise, Ethel; it isn't a good thing to postpone a thing

330

like marriage—so many things can happen. (*He suddenly takes her in his arms.*) And I don't want anything to happen.

ETHEL: What else have I got, Gene, if anything happened to Mother? (*She buries her face in his shoulder and cries hard.*)

FREDERICKS: Nothing's going to happen to her, sweetheart. And if it did, you wouldn't feel any worse than I'd feel if anything happened to this.

[*She continues to cry for a second, then straightens up and presses her handkerchief to her eyes.*]

ETHEL: We'd better go, Gene, it must be nearly nine o'clock.

[*She starts across below the table towards the mirror, and* FREDERICKS *starts across above the table towards the telephone.* CRAIG *comes through the portières.*]

FREDERICKS: I'd better call a taxi, hadn't I?

ETHEL: Oh, Uncle Walter,—this is Mr. Fredericks.

[FREDERICKS *continues over to shake hands with* CRAIG, *and* ETHEL *moves up to* FREDERICKS' *left.*]

CRAIG (*shaking hands*): I'm glad to meet you, Mr. Fredericks.

FREDERICKS: How do you do, Mr. Craig?

ETHEL: Mr. Fredericks is the young man I'm engaged to be married to.

CRAIG: Well, I *am* glad to meet you.

FREDERICKS: Pretty lucky fellow, don't you think, Mr. Craig?

CRAIG: I'd say you were. And is it all set?

FREDERICKS: I hope so; although Ethel seems to feel a little nervous about it.

CRAIG: What are you nervous about, Ethel?

ETHEL: I'm not nervous—it isn't that. But I was telling Gene that I'd been discussing it with Aunt Harriet, and she seemed to think that probably I hadn't considered it enough.

[FREDERICKS *looks at* CRAIG.]

CRAIG: What did she want you to consider?

ETHEL: Well, she said on account of my age she didn't think I appreciated the practical side of marriage enough.

CRAIG: That's the one side of marriage that should not be appreciated too much, Ethel; it's a lack of faith in each other.

FREDERICKS: That's what I tell Ethel.

CRAIG: The only thing I think you need to consider really seriously—is whether or not you are both absolutely honest with each other. (FREDERICKS *looks at* ETHEL, *and* CRAIG *crosses below them towards the stairs.*) It doesn't seem to me that there's very much else

331

to worry about.

ETHEL: We're going back on that nine-seventeen, Uncle Walter; do you know the number of the taxicab company?

CRAIG (*starting up the stairs*): You won't need a taxi, I'm going right down past the station.

ETHEL: Are you going now?

CRAIG: Right away, yes. I'll get my hat. You have plenty of time; I can get you down there in less than ten minutes.

ETHEL: Uncle Walter, will you bring my satchel down when you're coming?

CRAIG: Yes, I'll get it.

ETHEL: It's on the chair there, right inside my door. (*Picking up her bag from the table and crossing down to the mirror to fix herself.*) We won't have to call a taxi.

[FREDERICKS *glances out through the portières, then comes forward, lowering his voice.*]

FREDERICKS: Did your aunt tell you I called you last night?

[ETHEL *turns and looks at him.*]

ETHEL: On the long distance, you mean?

FREDERICKS: Yes, I called you from Northampton as soon as I got your note. I called you at home first, of course, and they gave me this address.

ETHEL: And you called here?

FREDERICKS: Yes, about seven o'clock. Didn't she tell you?

ETHEL: No, she didn't, Gene.

FREDERICKS: I talked to her. She said you were asleep.

ETHEL: I couldn't have been asleep, Gene.

FREDERICKS: I asked her to call you to the telephone, but she didn't seem to want to do it. She said you'd just gotten in and you were tired out.

ETHEL: Well, I *was* tired, but she could have called me; she might have known I'd want to talk to you. Because I didn't know what you'd think of my being down here, after leaving word that I was going home.

FREDERICKS: Have you seen her this morning?

ETHEL: Yes, but she didn't say anything about it. And I was talking to her here this morning about you, too. I was saying that I ought to call *you* on the long distance, that you'd be wondering what was the matter.

CRAIG (*hurrying down the stairs with Ethel's satchel*): I'll run over and get the car.

FREDERICKS: Can I take that, Mr. Craig?

CRAIG: I'll leave it out here on the porch. I'll be back in two minutes. You have lots of time.

FREDERICKS (*going to the piano for his hat*): Are you ready, Ethel?

ETHEL: Yes, I'm ready, Gene. I'd better say good-by to Aunt Harriet.

FREDERICKS: Will I wait for you outside?

ETHEL: Don't you want to meet her, Gene?

FREDERICKS: I don't think she wants to meet me, Ethel.

ETHEL: Why not?

FREDERICKS: After what you've been telling me.

ETHEL: Oh, that's nothing, Gene.

FREDERICKS: She hung up on me last night.

ETHEL: Yes, I want to ask her about that call.

FREDERICKS (*going out*): I think I'd better wait for you outside.

[ETHEL *glances through the portières, then comes forward thoughtfully at the right. There is a slight pause. Then* MRS. CRAIG *glides through the portières and across to the bay window to look out.* ETHEL *watches her narrowly, then moves to the right end of the center table.*]

ETHEL: I'm just going, Aunt Harriet.

[MRS. CRAIG *turns, slightly startled.*]

MRS. CRAIG: Oh, I thought you'd gone. (*She comes back towards* ETHEL.) I didn't hear anybody in here, and I was wondering if you'd gone without telling me.

ETHEL: No, I'm just going.

MRS. CRAIG: Where are Mr. Craig and Mr. Fredericks?

ETHEL: Mr. Fredericks is there on the porch. (MRS. CRAIG *turns to the front door and glances out.*) Uncle Walter's gone over to get the car.

MRS. CRAIG: Oh, he's going to drive you in.

ETHEL: Yes.

MRS. CRAIG: Well, that'll be fine, —you won't have to bother calling a taxi. (*Coming forward to* ETHEL *again.*) Did Mr. Fredericks have any word about your mother?

ETHEL: No, he hadn't been home.

MRS. CRAIG: Why don't you call him in, Ethel; I should like to meet him.

ETHEL: He thought probably you wouldn't care to meet him.

MRS. CRAIG: Why, how absurd. Why not?

ETHEL: I was telling him about what you said last night, when I told you I was going to marry him.

MRS. CRAIG: Well, my dear child, I was simply talking in a general way. My remarks weren't directed against Mr. Fredericks particularly. I'm sure he'd appreciate the logic of what I said himself.

ETHEL: He doesn't, Aunt Harriet; I told him what you said, and he takes quite the opposite view.

MRS. CRAIG: Well, of course, he has considerable to gain by the

333

transaction, Ethel, you must remember that.

ETHEL: Well, Uncle Walter has nothing to gain by it, and he agrees with him.

MRS. CRAIG: Well, you remember I told you last night that Mr. Craig was extremely romantic.

ETHEL (*becoming very stony*): Why didn't you call me last night, Aunt Harriet, when Mr. Fredericks telephoned?

MRS. CRAIG: Because you were asleep, dear.

ETHEL: I couldn't have been asleep. I haven't closed my eyes since I've been here.

MRS. CRAIG: Well, I thought you were asleep, Ethel; I sent Mazie up to your room and she said your door was closed.

ETHEL: Well, she could have rapped.

MRS. CRAIG: Well, what was the sense of upsetting you, dear?

ETHEL: Because it was important to me.

MRS. CRAIG: I asked him if it was important, and if there was any message he wanted to leave, and he said no.

ETHEL: And you hung up on him.

MRS. CRAIG: Because he insisted upon talking to you; and you were not in any condition to be talked to. (*She turns and moves towards the bay window.*)

ETHEL: Why didn't you tell me

this morning that he'd called—when I said I should call him?

MRS. CRAIG (*turning coldly*): Now, please, Ethel dear—I shan't answer any more questions about Mr. Fredericks. (*She goes to the bay window to look out.*) I've had quite enough to worry me this morning without thinking about Mr. Fredericks. He's going back with you, I suppose?

ETHEL (*crossing up to the front door*): Yes.

MRS. CRAIG (*turning to her*): Well, I'm glad you won't have to make the trip alone. Good-by, dear. (*She kisses her.*) I hope you'll let me know right away how you find your mother.

ETHEL (*holding her hand*): Aunt Harriet—

MRS. CRAIG: What, dear?

ETHEL (*after a pause, and holding her eye*): Aunt Harriet, is Uncle Walter *leaving* you?

MRS. CRAIG: Why, what on earth ever put that into your head, Ethel?

ETHEL: Something he was saying when I came to the head of the stairs to come down this morning.

MRS. CRAIG: And what was he saying?

ETHEL: Something about your having made a remark that made it impossible for him to continue here as your husband.

MRS. CRAIG: I'm sure I haven't

the faintest idea what you're talking about, Ethel.

ETHEL: And then a while ago here, when I told him I was going to be married to Mr. Fredericks, he said the only thing we needed to consider seriously was whether or not we were absolutely honest with each other. And I was wondering if he'd found out.

MRS. CRAIG: Found out what?

ETHEL: That that you told me last night,—when I said I didn't think it was honest.

[*There is a movement on the front porch. The screen door slams, and* MRS. CRAIG *turns away quickly and looks out the bay window.*]

CRAIG (*outside*): All set?

FREDERICKS (*outside*): All set. Ethel's inside.

ETHEL (*going out*): Good-by Aunt Harriet.

MRS. CRAIG (*turning and following her to the door*): Good-by, dear.

ETHEL: I'll write you as soon as I get home.

MRS. CRAIG: Do, dear; let me know how your mother is.

ETHEL: Yes, I shall.

[*The screen door slams.*]

CRAIG: Ready, Ethel?

ETHEL: Yes, I'm coming, Uncle Walter.

[MRS. CRAIG *turns nervously and moves across and down to the mantelpiece.*]

CRAIG: Your satchel's in the car. I'll be with you in a minute. (*He comes in, taking a little leather key case from his pocket, and crosses to the portières.*)

MRS. CRAIG: Are you going to the office now?

CRAIG: Yes, it's nearly nine o'clock.

[*He goes through the portières, and* MRS. CRAIG *moves up to the portières.*]

MRS. CRAIG: Mrs. Harold says you haven't been in bed all night; you won't feel much like sitting at a desk all day.

CRAIG (*from the other room*): I'll have plenty of time to rest after a bit.

[MRS. CRAIG'S *eyes narrow, in an attempt to fathom this remark. She comes forward again at the right, slowly and thoughtfully. Craig enters, fastening the little key case, and crosses towards the front door, picking up his hat from the table as he passes.*]

MRS. CRAIG: Did you find what you were looking for?

CRAIG: I wasn't looking for anything—I was just leaving the key to your car and the garage, with some other things I've left there for you. (*He turns at the door.*) If you should want me for anything during the next week or two, Harriet, I'll be at the Ritz.

[*She turns suddenly and makes a*

335

rapid movement to the center table.]

MRS. CRAIG: Now, listen to me, Walter Craig, you're surely not serious about leaving this house.

CRAIG: Why, I should think that decision would please you very much.

MRS. CRAIG: Well, it doesn't please me at all; it's absolutely ridiculous.

CRAIG: But it's so absolutely practical.

MRS. CRAIG: Oh, don't try to be funny.

CRAIG: And you've been deploring my lack of practicality so long.

MRS. CRAIG: I'd like to know what's practical about a man walking out and leaving his wife and his home.

CRAIG: I have no wife to leave, —for you neither loved nor honored me.

MRS. CRAIG: Well, you married me, whether I did or not.

CRAIG: I never saw you before in my life, Harriet—until last night.

MRS. CRAIG: You married me, didn't you?

CRAIG: And you married a house; and if it's agreeable to you, I'll see that you have it; and that you can go on having it, just as though I were here.

MRS. CRAIG (*turning away towards the mantelpiece*): You'll be here; unless I'm very much mistaken.

CRAIG: You don't know your man, Harriet.

MRS. CRAIG: I know him well enough for that, anyway.

CRAIG: Oh, you knew me pretty well, I'll grant you that; particularly when you said my mind worked very slowly.

MRS. CRAIG: It's working pretty slowly now, when you don't appreciate the absurdity of a move of this kind.

CRAIG: But you failed to reckon with the thoroughness of my mind, Harriet, when it *does* work. And it appreciates this situation so thoroughly that it has no illusions about the impossibility of my continuance here.

MRS. CRAIG: What is there so impossible about it?

CRAIG: We've shown our hands, Harriet, and the game is up.

MRS. CRAIG: What did I do last night that was so terrible?

CRAIG: You simply showed your hand, that was all.

MRS. CRAIG: I simply kept you from making a fool of yourself; that was all I did.

CRAIG: But you also showed me how I could keep from making a fool of myself in the future.

MRS. CRAIG: Well, you're certainly not beginning very auspiciously, I can tell you that.

CRAIG: But I shall be at least a self-respecting fool; and that's something I could never be if I stayed here. There's something in a man, Harriet, that I suppose is his essential manhood; and you insulted that last night. And I should be too embarrassed here, under your eye, knowing that you had no respect for that manhood. I should remember my lover's ardors and enthusiasms for our future; and you bearing with me contemptuously, for the sake of *your* future. I couldn't stand it.

MRS. CRAIG: You're not telling the truth; I always respected you; and I never had anything but respect for your plans, either.

CRAIG: Don't try to soften the blow, Harriet; I assure you it isn't necessary.

[*He turns towards the door, and she makes a move towards him.*]

MRS. CRAIG: Where are you going when you leave here?

[*He turns and looks at her.*]

CRAIG: That'ud be rather interesting to know, Harriet—where a lot like me are going.—Out of fashion, possibly.

MRS. CRAIG: Well, what about your things?—Aren't you going to take anything with you?

CRAIG: You may send them to me if you like.

MRS. CRAIG (*turning away*): Well, I won't send them to you; for you'll very likely be back again within a week.

CRAIG: Perhaps it will be just as well if you don't send them to me, Harriet,—for I'm rather sentimental about things; and I might look back, and be turned into a romantic fool.

MRS. CRAIG: Oh, I suppose you'll never forgive me for calling you that.

CRAIG: No, there isn't a thing in the world I don't forgive you for, Harriet; that's the reason it won't be necessary for me to come back here any more; there's nothing to adjust. I guess possibly I'm just a bit of an old-fashioned man— I must be trusted—and you never trusted me.

MRS. CRAIG: I wouldn't trust any man after what I've seen.

CRAIG: I don't blame you. But I wonder that, with all your wisdom, it never occurred to you that one cannot play a dishonest game indefinitely.

MRS. CRAIG: I haven't played any dishonest game.

CRAIG: Possibly not, according to your standards; but I think you have. And I think you know you have. And that's the rock that you and I are splitting on, Harriet. If this affair at Passmores' hadn't revealed you, something else would: so my going may as well be to-day as to-morrow. Good-by, Harriet.

[*He goes out; she leans on the table. The screen door slams. She moves over to the bay*

337

window and watches him get into the automobile: then she comes forward to the window at the right and watches him down the street. After he has passed beyond her vision, her gaze wanders into the room again, and she becomes conscious of two tiny pieces of the broken ornament near the mantelpiece. She stoops and picks them up, flicking away with her foot any other invisible particles that may be about. Then she looks at the two remaining ornaments on the mantelpiece and tries to come to some conclusion about their arrangement. She places them equi-distant from each other and the ends of the mantelpiece, and stands off to observe the effect. The front doorbell rings sharply. She turns and crosses to answer it.]

BOY'S VOICE *(at the front door)*: Telegram for Mrs. Walter Craig. [*She signs for the telegram, the screen door slams and she comes in, opening the telegram. She reads the telegram, looks straight ahead for a second, thinking—looks at the wire again, and bursts into tears—sinking into the chair at the right of the piano. She cries hard for a moment, then smooths the telegram out and reads it again.* MRS.

FRAZIER *appears in the door, dressed in gray, and carrying an armload of white roses. She comes forward inquiringly.]*

MRS. FRAZIER: Good morning, Mrs. Craig. (MRS. CRAIG *doesn't hear her.*) Good morning. (MRS. CRAIG *looks at her, startled, gets up nervously and moves across to the front of the center table, touching her eyes and her hair.*) I do hope you'll pardon my walking in without ringing, but I thought Miss Austen 'ud be on the front porch, and I wanted to bring her these roses. (*She hands* MRS. CRAIG *the roses.*) I was telling her yesterday I'd bring her over some; she was saying she admired white roses so much; and I have so many of them over there just now.

MRS. CRAIG: I haven't seen her yet this morning.

MRS. FRAZIER (*preparing to go*): Well, if you'll just tell her I left them.

MRS. CRAIG: Yes, I shall; thanks ever so much.

MRS. FRAZIER (*turning back*): Oh, have you had any word about your sister this morning, Mrs. Craig? Miss Austen was telling me yesterday she was quite ill.

MRS. CRAIG (*starting to cry again*): She died this morning at six o'clock.

MRS. FRAZIER: Oh, dear me, how sad.

MRS. CRAIG: I just had this wire.

MRS. FRAZIER: Dear, dear, dear, isn't that too bad!

MRS. CRAIG: I had no idea she was so ill or I should never have come back.

MRS. FRAZIER: Dear, dear, dear, I'm so sorry. I shouldn't have bothered you at all.

MRS. CRAIG: That's quite all right.

MRS. FRAZIER: I'm sure you have my sympathy.

MRS. CRAIG: Thank you.

MRS. FRAZIER: I do hope you'll let me know, Mrs. Craig, if there's any way I can be of any service to you.

MRS. CRAIG: Thank you very much; I don't think there's anything anybody can do.

MRS. FRAZIER: I suppose you'll have to go right back up there again, won't you?

MRS. CRAIG: I don't know whether I shall be able to or not, to tell you the truth, Mrs. Frazier; it's been such a strain.

MRS. FRAZIER: Yes, those long illnesses are dreadful. But I hope you won't hesitate to let me know if there's anything I can do.

MRS. CRAIG: That's very kind of you. I'll give these roses to Miss Austen when I see her.

MRS. FRAZIER: If you will, please. (*She starts for the door.*) I'm terribly sorry. I'll run over again.

[*She goes out; and* MRS. CRAIG *stands very still until she hears the screen door close. Then she steps up to the door and clicks the latch. Then she turns, comes forward a few steps into the room again, and stands, holding the roses against her bosom and looking straight out. A clock out in one of the adjoining rooms strikes nine with a mournful gong. After the fourth gong her eyes wander in the direction of the clock and she moves slowly across towards the portières. Then she comes forward at the right, wandering, and crosses below the table to the piano. Several rose petals flutter to the floor. She stands at the piano for a moment, looking out through the bay window, then retraces her steps. She looks unseeingly at the scattered petals, continues up towards the portières, looks out through the deserted rooms, and finally stops. A few more petals drift to the floor. The curtain commences to descend, very, very slowly. She turns desolately and wanders back towards the piano again, clutching the roses close, her eyes wide and despairing.*]

THE END

JAMES THURBER

ELLIOT NUGENT

JAMES THURBER

1894 *Born in Columbus, Ohio, the son of an "honest politician."*

1913 *Attended Ohio State University,*
to *which he left without taking a*
1917 *degree.*

1918 *Code clerk in U. S. State Depart-*
to *ment in Washington and also in*
1920 *Paris.*

1920 *Took job on the Columbus Dis-*
patch. Later wrote for the Chi-
cago Tribune and the New York
Evening Post.

1926 *Began writing for the New Yorker.*

1929 *Published* IS SEX NECESSARY? *a*
highly successful collaboration
with E. B. White, parodying books
on sex education and containing
the famous line drawings as an
important feature.

1931 *Published two books,* THE OWL IN
to THE ATTIC *and* THE SEAL IN THE
1932 BEDROOM.

1934 *Published his "autobiography,"*
MY LIFE AND HARD TIMES.

1935 *Published* THE MIDDLE-AGED MAN
ON THE FLYING TRAPEZE.

1940 THE MALE ANIMAL *produced with*
great success.

1945 *Published* THE THURBER CARNIVAL,
selections from his work.

ELLIOT NUGENT

1899 *Born in Dover, Ohio. Parents were theatrical people.*

1919 *Received B.A. at Ohio State Uni-*
versity. For a time was an as-
sociate of Thurber on the college
literary magazine.

1921 *Played the juvenile in* DULCY, *his*
first role in New York. During
the run of the play, married
Norma Lee, also in the cast.

1922 *Produced* KEMPY, *in collaboration*
with his father, J. C. Nugent.

1923 *Produced* THE DUMB-BELL, *con-*
tining the collaboration that pro-
vided a play a year for the next
few years.

1925 *Produced* THE POOR NUT, *also a*
collaboration. The play was ex-
tremely successful.

1929 *In Hollywood, where his activi-*
to *ties included those of actor, writ-*
1940 *er, and director.*

1940 *Returned to Broadway as the star*
and collaborating playwright of
THE MALE ANIMAL.

1943 *Co-starred with Margaret Sullavan*
in John Van Druten's comedy THE
VOICE OF THE TURTLE *and won*
to *vote of New York dramatic critics*
for best acting of the 1943-44
1944 *season.*

342

THOUGH *James Thurber is still in his early fifties, he has already become an institution and a legend. Since his collaboration with E. B. White in an elaborate parody on books on sex education, IS SEX NECESSARY? (1929), his nonsense essays, his short stories, and his line drawings of "melancholy hounds" and "contentedly frustrated people" have made him one of the brightest ornaments of the consistently bright New Yorker and have earned for him a substantial reputation as a humorist and a satirist. The publication of THE THURBER CARNIVAL in 1945 brought forth a chorus of critical praise. William Rose Benét asserted that Thurber knew more about human nature than most psychiatrists. Thomas Sugrue called him "a satirist and a prophet, a Jeremiah in fool's cap, a mixture of laughing gas and deadly nightshade." D. S. Norton, writing in the New York Times, regarded him as ". . . not only a humorist, but . . . also a satirist who can toss a bomb while he appears to be tipping his hat." All agreed that Thurber had quietly and unobtrusively moved into a position of greatness.*

On the surface, Thurber's line drawings suggest the crudeness of a child's attempts to represent human and animal forms; but their artlessness is only temporarily deceptive. It does not take one long to discover that they embody the skill and the sophistication of an artist who moves unerringly to accomplish his purpose. Thurber's prose has some of the same surface ingenuousness and an equal amount of deadly efficacy.

The fact that Thurber's literary productions and his drawings are seldom raucously gay is explained by his assertion that "the damp hand of melancholy" has set in motion "the little wheels of their invention." The distinctive quality of his work is further explained by his definition of humor as "a kind of emotional chaos told about calmly and quietly in retrospect." One critic has remarked that "his fantastic people and animals, moving with sad persistence through incredible upsets, are all misshapen and repressed, the cynical products of a malignant fate." His bitterness has also been measured by his obsessive theme of the war of the sexes and his endless gallery of assertive, possessive, spiteful, malicious, and otherwise demoniac females. These are the women to whom the Thurber male inevitably must succumb in a contest hopelessly lost from the outset. Now and then he may develop the cunning of desperation, as he does in "The Catbird Seat." But more characteristically he makes a pitifully temporary escape from reality—as he does in "The Secret Life of Walter Mitty"—to a dream world, the only place where his dominance is possible. It is small wonder that Peter DeVries has attached to Thurber the epithet "the comic Prufrock," and that he sees in Thurber's work the humorous counterpart of T. S. Eliot's profound probing of human emptiness and frustration.

Whatever Thurber is, he is not a professional playwright. Thus, it is not surprising that THE MALE ANIMAL, *in many respects highly Thurberish in temper, is a product of collaboration. Actually, it is the result of the happiest sort of merging of two talents. Though the collaborator is a genius of a somewhat different order, he has decisively proved his brilliance as a playwright, a director, and an actor. Elliot Nugent was almost born on the stage. A member of an old-line theatrical family, he made his first public appearance at the age of four. In more recent years he has written (usually in collaboration with his father) a remarkable array of dramatic successes, in most of which he has also starred. He, therefore, possesses a natural sense of the theater. The fact that Thurber and Nugent were friends during their student days at Ohio State University gives their collaboration something of inevitability.*

Although an attempt to determine the exact division of labor in THE MALE ANIMAL *is in a measure defeated by the perfection of the collaboration, the relationship of the play to the work of both authors is perfectly clear. If the atmosphere and the characters are not actually the creation of Thurber, they undoubtedly bear the stamp of his humorously insane slant on life, in which "frustration is leavened by nonsense, indignation is alkalized by good nature." In the characters of the play one may detect some of the "grave lunacy combined with moronic God-like yearning" that permeates the drawings. The principal dramatic devices and not a little of the satire on college life are directly traceable to Mr. Nugent, who also contributed the prototypes of the most important characters.*

Actually, THE MALE ANIMAL *may be regarded as the lineal descendant of* THE POOR NUT, *a satire on college life with which Elliot Nugent and his father, J. C. Nugent, made a great success in 1925.* THE POOR NUT *has for its hero one John Miller, a bookish student at Ohio State University, who has an "inferiority complex" and who prefers the study of his beloved algae to achieving glories on the athletic* *field. Miller, having allowed himself to be overpersuaded to take part in a track meet in order to save dear old* alma mater, *loses what little nerve he has when he realizes that winning the race will commit him to an aggressive Wisconsin co-ed, "who knows Freud well, if not intimately," and who has taken a much too serious interest in his psychic development. Nevertheless, he wins the race and also the self-assertiveness to declare himself for the girl he really loves. Like* THE MALE ANIMAL, *the play is loosely constructed and fraily motivated. But its satire on the Freudian fad, fraternity life, and the religion of athletics, gives it significance. One of its high-water marks is the speech before the crucial race, in which the Coach, in a superbly handled crescendo of locker-room oratory, pictures the far-reaching consequences of failure: "[Your] grandchildren—how will they feel when the Gold Cup is mentioned? . . . They would have to say, 'My father didn't care for his University, or his friends, or his team, or his girl, or his* honor—*or his* Coach!' "*

The play ends on a note of delicious irony in Miller's reply to the college Babbitts of fraternity men and athletes: "You are all trying to make me amount to something, like you do—Well, I can't—I'm inferior —and doggone it, I'm gonna be *inferior. I'm going to be a professor, whether it's immoral or not."*

In THE MALE ANIMAL *John Miller has grown up and has changed his name and his field of study to appear as Tommy Turner, an English professor who, like his prototype, is a "worm" that finally turns to defy the dominance of athletics and the ideals of reactionary commercialism in university life. The Babbitts have grown up, too, but they are no less Babbitts. First, there is the "old grad" Joe Ferguson, former All-American, who has little else than the vestiges of brawn and sex-appeal and the memories of his physical prowess. Just as typical is the bumptious Ed Keller, the prosperous alumnus and trustee, whose sole educational aim is to produce winning football teams for* alma mater *and to keep the campus free from the taint of liberal thought. The campus radical, the cheerleader, and the football star are familiar campus figures, as also is the pretty co-ed who is faced with the usual choice between brawn and brains in a lover.*

The two dilemmas on which the play really turns are, if subjected to close analysis, both tenuous. Neither Turner's domestic situation nor his academic position need actually have been so seriously jeopardized by the circumstances. But the action engagingly wins our cre-

345

dence. Since the play is a farce and not a "problem" play or a play of social criticism, it presents no serious preachment on any subject. Yet in spite of its lightness it touches upon two perennial problems of American education: the proper place of athletics in college life and the more serious question of academic freedom. Perhaps even more pertinently, it reminds us of the persistent adolescence of the college-bred American.

❦

BIBLIOGRAPHICAL NOTE

Since Nugent's plays have had a greater appeal to playgoers than to serious students of the drama, there is no comprehensive critical discussion of his work. A stimulating review of THE POOR NUT *will be found in J. W. Krutch's "Freudian Farce," Nation, CXX (1925), 556-557. One of the most valuable discussions of Thurber's art in general is Peter DeVries' "James Thurber: The Comic Prufrock," Poetry, LXIII (1943), 150-159. A popular biographical article is C. Lester Walker's "The Legendary Mr. Thurber," Ladies' Home Journal, LXIII (July, 1946), 26-27, 119-125. Reviews of* THE MALE ANIMAL *in Newsweek, XV (January 23, 1940), 33, and Time, XXV (January 22, 1940), 49, are worth reading. Additional biographical material on James Thurber and Elliot Nugent may be found in Kunitz and Haycraft,* TWENTIETH CENTURY AUTHORS *(New York: H. W. Wilson Co., 1942) and* CURRENT BIOGRAPHY, *1944 (New York: H. W. Wilson Co., 1944).*

The Male Animal

CHARACTERS

CLEOTA	JOE FERGUSON
ELLEN TURNER	MRS. BLANCHE DAMON
TOMMY TURNER	ED KELLER
PATRICIA STANLEY	MYRTLE KELLER
WALLY MYERS	NUTSY MILLER
DEAN FREDERICK DAMON	NEWSPAPER REPORTER
MICHAEL BARNES	

Time: The present. The scene of the play is the living room of the Turners' house, in a Mid-Western college town. ACT ONE: *A Friday in late fall, evening.* ACT TWO: SCENE I. *The next day, after lunch.* SCENE II. *Three hours later.* ACT THREE: *Two days later.*

∽✒

ACT I

SCENE: *The living room of a pleasant, inexpensive little house. There is no distinction of architectural design, but someone with natural good taste has managed to make it look attractive and liveable on a very modest budget. There are some good prints on the walls. The hangings are cheerful, and the furniture, picked up through various bargains and inheritances, goes together to make a pleasing, informal atmosphere.*

The front door opens onto a porch. The wall is lined with bookshelves which continue around the corner to the fireplace. Below this fireplace is a stand with a radio-phonograph. In the center of the rear wall is a bay window with window seat. This corner is used by the Turner family as a casual depository for visitors' hats and coats, although they have also a coat-rail just inside the front door. In front of the bay window, a long table backs a comfortable couch. To the right of the bay window are more bookshelves, a small landing, and a stairway running up and off-stage. In the corner below the stair near the dining-room door a table has been prepared today to serve as a temporary bar, with a tray, cocktail shaker, and two or three bottles and glasses. On the right there are two doors, one leading to the dining room, the other to another porch and the back yard. Two small sofas, an armchair, a couple of small end or coffee tables, and one or two straight chairs complete the furnishings of the room. There are two or three vases of flowers, and the books and magazines which frequently litter this room have been put tidily away.

At the rise of the curtain, the phone on the table behind the sofa is ringing. CLEOTA, *a colored maid, enters from the dining room and answers it.*

CLEOTA: Professah Turner's res-i-dence. . . . Who? . . . You got de wrong numbah. . . . Who? . . . What you say? . . . Oh, Mistah *Turner!* No, he ain' heah. He jus' went out to buy some lik-kah. . . . Who is dis callin'? Yessuh. Yessuh. Ah doan get dat, but Ah'll tell him Doctah Damon. Ah say Ah'll tell him. (*She hangs up phone, starts for dining room.*)

ELLEN'S VOICE (*upstairs*): Who was it, Cleota?

CLEOTA: It was Doctah Damon. He say he comin' ovah to see Mistah Turner or Mistah Turner come over to see him, or sumpin'. (*She turns on lights from wall switch.*)

ELLEN (*coming downstairs*): What was that again, Cleota?

(*She is an extremely pretty young woman about twenty-nine or thirty. Quick of speech and movement, she has a ready smile and a sweetness of personality that warms the room. She is completely feminine and acts always from an emotional, not an intellectual stimulus.*)

CLEOTA: Doctah Damon doan talk up. He kinda muffles.

[ELLEN *begins to put finishing touches to the room with quick efficiency, putting away magazines and books.*]

ELLEN: I'm afraid it's you that kind of muffles.

CLEOTA: Yessum. Miz Turner, Ah'm fixin' dem hoar doves for the pahty. Did you say put dem black seed ones in de oven?

348

ELLEN: Black seed ones? Oh, heavens, Cleota, you're not heating the caviar?

CLEOTA: No'm, Ah ain' heatin' it, but taste lak' sumpin' oughtta be done to it.

ELLEN: It's to be served cold. Here, you pick up the rest of the magazines. I'll take a look at the canapés. (*Hurries off into dining room.*)

CLEOTA: Yessum. Ah ain' no hand at 'em. People where Ah worked last jus' drank without eatin' anything. (*There is the sound of whistling outside, and* TOMMY TURNER *enters. He is a young associate professor, thirty-three years old. He wears glasses, is rather more charming than handsome. His clothes are a little baggy. He has a way of disarranging his hair with his hands, so that he looks like a puzzled spaniel at times. He is carrying chrysanthemums and two bottles of liquor, wrapped in paper and tied with string.*) Oh, hello, Mr. Turner.

TOMMY: Hello, Cleota.

CLEOTA: You bettah not mess up dis room 'cause dey is guess comin'.

TOMMY: All right, Cleota. I'll be good.

[CLEOTA *gives him a doubting look and dawdles off to dining room. We see what she means when* TOMMY *unwraps*

his packages. In a moment, paper and string drop about him like falling leaves. Manfully, he sticks flowers in the vase among the other flowers. A book with a gay jacket catches his eye. He looks at it disapprovingly, throws it in wastebasket. ELLEN *enters from dining room.*]

ELLEN: Hello, dear.

TOMMY: Hello, Ellen. Those are for you. (*Indicates his flowers.*)

ELLEN: Oh, thank you, Tommy. They're lovely. (*Surveys the flowers.*)

TOMMY: The ones in the middle.

ELLEN: Yes . . .

TOMMY: I got the liquor, too.

ELLEN (*taking flowers out of vase*): Did you get the right kind?

TOMMY: I got both kinds.

[ELLEN *picks up the litter he has made.*]

ELLEN: Tommy, you're a housewrecker, but you're nice. (*Kisses him.*)

TOMMY: Did I do something right?

ELLEN: Cleota! Cleota, will you fill this vase with water, please? (*Hands vase to* CLEOTA *in doorway.* CLEOTA *goes out.*) What became of the book that was on this table?

TOMMY: That? Oh, I threw it

349

in the wastebasket. It's trash.

ELLEN (*rescuing book*): But you can't throw it away. Wally gave it to Patricia.

TOMMY: Oh, he did?

ELLEN: Besides, it's just the right color for this room.

[*Young voices are raised outside and* PATRICIA STANLEY, ELLEN'S *sister, opens the door and backs into the room. She is a pretty, lively girl of nineteen or twenty. She is followed by* WALLY MYERS, *who is six-feet-one, and weighs 190 pounds, mostly muscle.*]

PAT'S VOICE: Oh, Wally, quit arguing! I'm going to dinner with Mike, and then to the rally with you. You can't feed me at the training table.

WALLY: Aw, that guy Barnes! I don't see why you have to . . . Oh, how do you do, Mrs. Turner —Professor Turner?

TOMMY: Hello, Butch.

ELLEN: That's Wally Myers.

WALLY (*to* PATRICIA): Oh, has Butch been coming here, too?

PATRICIA: Go on, get out of here, half-back. I have to get dressed. (*As she sits down and inspects a run in her stocking.*) Hey, Ellen, excited about seeing the great Ferguson again? He just drove up to the Beta House in a Duesenberg!

[CLEOTA *re-enters with the vase;*

gives it to ELLEN *and leaves.*]

ELLEN (*arranging* TOMMY'S *flowers*): Did you see him?

PATRICIA: No, the kids were telling me. Has he still got his hair?

ELLEN: I haven't seen him in ten years. We'll soon find out.

WALLY: Say, is he coming here?

ELLEN: Yes. Why don't you come back and meet him, Wally? You can tell him all about the game tomorrow.

WALLY: Gee, thanks! But nobody could tell Joe Ferguson anything about a football game. He's all-time All-American, you know. Well, thanks, Mrs. Turner. I'll be back. See you later, Pat. (WALLY *goes out.*)

TOMMY: Does he mean that now Joe belongs to the ages, like Lincoln?

ELLEN: Um-hum, in a way.

TOMMY (*crossing to bookcase*): Well, I suppose he has passed into legend. I used to admire him myself—almost.

ELLEN: Pat, why don't you and Michael stay here for dinner? Supper, rather. It's just a bite. We're all going out to eat after the rally.

PATRICIA: No, thanks. You know Michael hates Mr. Keller. He'd spit in his eye.

TOMMY: Why do we have to have Ed Keller to this party?

(*Carrying three copies of* Harper's, *he sits on settee.*)

ELLEN: Oh, Joe has to have someone to talk football with. Besides, Ed's his closest friend here. He practically paid Joe's way through college. You can stand the Kellers one night.

TOMMY: Just barely. I don't know how to entertain trustees.

PATRICIA: You'd better be entertaining tonight with the great Ferguson coming. (*Rises.*) Weren't you engaged to him once, Ellen?

ELLEN: Not officially. Just for fun.

PATRICIA (*going upstairs*): Baby, that can be dangerous, too!

ELLEN: Oh, Dean Damon phoned, Tommy.

TOMMY: What'd he want?

ELLEN: I don't know. Cleota answered the phone.

TOMMY: Oh . . . I see. . . . Oh, I'll bet I know what it was. I saw him this morning. What do you think?

ELLEN: Oh, I don't know. . . . Oh, Tommy, you don't mean . . . ?

TOMMY: Yes, I do.

ELLEN: Oh, Tommy, that's wonderful! It's three hundred and fifty more a year, isn't it?

TOMMY: Five hundred! I'm no piker.

ELLEN: Well, you certainly deserve it. (*Gives him a little kiss.*)

TOMMY: Now I can get you that fur coat next February. People must think I let you freeze in the winter.

ELLEN (*crossing to table*): No, they don't. And, don't worry about me—you need some new things yourself. . . . I love the flowers, Tommy. And this promotion couldn't have come on a better day for me. Do you know what day it is?

TOMMY: Friday, isn't it? Why?

ELLEN: Oh, nothing — never mind. (*Glances around room.*) What became of all the match boxes? I had one in each ash tray. (*She returns and digs in his coat pocket.*)

TOMMY: I haven't seen any match boxes. What's going on here? Say, you look very pretty tonight. That's a new dress, isn't it?

ELLEN: No. It's my hair that's bothering you. It's done a new way.

TOMMY: Doesn't bother me. I like it.

ELLEN (*who has found two match boxes*): One more.

TOMMY: Oh, you exaggerate this match-box thing. Oh. (*Hands her one.*) I ought to take you out to dinner more and show you off.

ELLEN (*redistributing match boxes*): Well, we're going out tonight after the rally.

TOMMY: I mean just the two of

351

us. Tonight will be just like old times. Remember how Joe was always horning in on our dinner dates? I don't believe we ever had one that he didn't come over and diagram the Washington Monument play or something on the tablecloth with a pencil.

ELLEN: Statue of Liberty play, darling.

TOMMY: He was always coming. I never saw him going.

ELLEN: There's still one missing.

TOMMY: I haven't got it. (*He finds it.*) I'll bet Joe does something to get his wife down. Probably cleans his guns with doilies. Clumsy guy. Always knocking knives and forks on the floor.

ELLEN: He wasn't clumsy. He was very graceful. He was a swell dancer. (*She puts away some books.*)

TOMMY: I remember he got the first and the last dance with you the last time we all went to a dance together.

ELLEN: Phi Psi Christmas dance, wasn't it?

TOMMY: No, the May dance. Out at the Trowbridge Farm. Remember how it rained?

ELLEN: I remember I had the last dance with Joe because you disappeared somewhere.

TOMMY: No, I was watching— from behind some ferns.

ELLEN: They played "Three O'Clock in the Morning" and

"Who?" It was a lovely night, wasn't it?

TOMMY: No, it poured down. You and Joe were dancing out on the terrace when it started. You both got soaked, but you kept right on dancing. (*Having found what he wanted,* TOMMY *returns two magazines to shelves.*)

ELLEN: Oh, yes, I remember. My dress was ruined.

TOMMY: You were shining wet —like Venus and Triton.

ELLEN: Why didn't you cut in? (*Takes magazine* TOMMY *left on coffee table to bookcase.*)

TOMMY: I had a cold. Besides, my feet hurt. (*He starts toward stairs.*) I'll dress. (*Doorbell rings.*) Lord, I hope he isn't here already.

[ELLEN *admits* DAMON *and* MICHAEL. DAMON, *the head of the English department, is a tall, thin, distinguished-looking man of some sixty-five years. He has gray hair, eyes capable of twinkling through glasses whose rims he has a habit of peering over. He talks slowly, selecting his words, in a voice at once compelling and humorous. He often hesitates, peers over his glasses before saying the last word of a phrase or a sentence.* MICHAEL BARNES *is a senior in the Arts College, an intensely serious young man and a fine literary student. The older people who surround him find his youthful grimness about life's problems sometimes amusing, but more frequently alarming.*]

ELLEN: Oh, come in, Dr. Damon. Hello, Michael.

MICHAEL: How do you do?

TOMMY: How do you do, sir?

DAMON: Hello, Thomas.

ELLEN: Where's Mrs. Damon?

DAMON: I shall pick her up and bring her along shortly for the festivities. This is in the nature of an unofficial call.

TOMMY: Hello, Michael. You both look a little grim. Has anything happened?

DAMON: Michael has written another of his fiery editorials.

[PATRICIA *runs down the stairs.*]

PATRICIA: Ellen, did you see my— Oh! How do you do, Dr. Damon? Hi, Michael.

MICHAEL: H'lo.

DAMON: Sit down, my dear. I have here an editorial written by Michael for *The Lit*, which comes out tomorrow. Perhaps, to save time, one of us should read it aloud. . . .

"When this so-called University forces such men out of its faculty as Professor Kennedy, Professor Sykes, and Professor Chapman, because they have been ignorantly called Reds, it surrenders its right to be called a seat of learning. It admits that it is nothing more nor less than a training school"—(you will recognize the voice of our good friend, Hutchins, of Chicago)—"a training school for bond salesmen, farmers, real-estate dealers, and ambulance chasers. It announces to the world that its faculty is subservient. . . ." (DAMON *peers over glasses at* MICHAEL.)

MICHAEL: Oh, I didn't mean you, of course, Dr. Damon.

DAMON: ". . . that its faculty is subservient to its trustees, and that its trustees represent a political viewpoint which must finally emerge under its proper name, which is—Fascism."

PATRICIA: Oh, Michael! There you go again!

DAMON: Wait till you hear where he has actually gone.

PATRICIA: Isn't that all?

DAMON: Unhappily, there is more.

PATRICIA: Oh, Lord!

[TOMMY *sits down.*]

DAMON (*continuing*): "These professors were not Reds. They were distinguished liberals. Let us thank God that we still have one man left who is going ahead teaching what he believes should be taught."

TOMMY: Who's that?

DAMON: Sh! "He is not afraid to bring up even the Sacco-Vanzetti case. He has read to his

353

classes on the same day Vanzetti's last statement and Lincoln's letter to Mrs. Bixby." (I hope we are not alienating the many friends of Abraham Lincoln.) (TOMMY *rises and glances at* MICHAEL *questioningly.*) "The hounds of bigotry and reaction will, of course, be set upon the trail of this courageous teacher, but, if they think they are merely on the spoor of a lamb they are destined to the same disappointment as the hunters who, in chasing the wild boar, came accidentally upon a tigress and her cubs. Our hats are off to Professor Thomas Turner of the English Department." That's all.

ELLEN: Tommy?

TOMMY: Michael, I think you might have consulted me about this.

PATRICIA: Michael, you fool! They'll kick you out of school for this—and Tommy, too!

ELLEN: You never told me you had brought up the Sacco-Vanzetti case in your classes, Tommy.

DAMON: Yes, just what is this Vanzetti letter you have read?

TOMMY: I haven't read it yet.

MICHAEL: When you told me the other day you were going to read it, I thought you meant that day.

TOMMY: No, Michael, I just meant some day. But I was talking to you as a friend, I was not giving an interview to an editor.

ELLEN: But why were you going to read this letter, Tommy?

TOMMY: Because it's a fine piece of English composition, and I'm teaching a class in English composition. An obscure little class. I don't want any publicity, Michael. I just want to be let alone.

ELLEN: But, Tommy, nobody thinks of Vanzetti as a writer.

TOMMY: It happens that he developed into an extraordinary writer. I don't think you could help being interested in the letter yourself, Dr. Damon.

DAMON: You would be surprised at my strength of will in these matters, Thomas. What I am interested in is preserving some air of academic calm here at Midwestern—and also in retaining my chair in the English department.

PATRICIA: You don't want to get Tommy kicked out of school, do you, Michael?

MICHAEL: No. I didn't think of that. I thought Mr. Turner was about the only man we had left who would read whatever he wanted to to his classes. I thought he was the one man who would stand up to these stadium builders.

TOMMY: I'm not standing up to anyone, Michael. I'm not challenging anyone. This is just an innocent little piece I wanted to read.

[MICHAEL *turns away.*]

ELLEN (*rises*): I know it must be all right, Tommy, but you can't read it now. Keller and the other trustees kicked Don Chapman out last month for doing things just as harmless as this. (*Turning to* MICHAEL.) You'll have to change that editorial, Michael.

MICHAEL: I can't. The magazines were run off the presses last night. They've already been delivered to the newsstands.

DAMON: They go on sale in the morning. (*To* ELLEN.) I think that our—er—tigress here may have to issue a denial tomorrow. After all, he hasn't read it.

ELLEN (*to* TOMMY): Yes, and you mustn't read it now.

PATRICIA: Will Michael be kicked out of school, Dr. Damon?

DAMON: Sufficient unto the day is the evil thereof, my dear. (*He gets his hat.*)

PATRICIA (*to* MICHAEL): There! You see—

DAMON (*coming to* TOMMY *who has seated himself at the other side of the room*): I quite understand how you meant to present it, Thomas, but our good friend, Mr. Keller, would not. Do not underestimate Mr. Edward K. Keller. He rolls like the juggernaut over the careers of young professors.

TOMMY: I know.

DAMON (*starting to door*): Well —since he must be with us tonight let us confine our conversation to the woeful inadequacies of the Illinois team.

TOMMY (*rising*): Oh, it isn't Illinois we're playing—it's Michigan.

DAMON: Oh, I must remember that. (*Goes out.*)

PATRICIA (*to* MICHAEL): There, you see! You will be kicked out.

MICHAEL: He didn't say that.

PATRICIA: Yes, he did. Don't come back for me, Michael. I'm staying here for supper. (*Runs up the stairs.*)

MICHAEL: I see. . . . I'm sorry, Mr. Turner. I guess I got—well— carried away.

TOMMY (*crossing*): I know, Michael. Sometimes, when I see that light in your eye I wish I could be carried away too.

MICHAEL: Yes, sir. (*He goes out grimly. There is a slight pause.*)

TOMMY: Well—

ELLEN: I'm sorry, Tommy.

TOMMY: Oh, it's all right. Maybe I can read this thing later on, after all the fuss quiets down— say, next spring.

ELLEN: It would still be dangerous.

TOMMY: Yes, I guess it would. . . . I know I'm not a tiger, but I don't like to be thought of as a pussycat either.

ELLEN (*with an understanding smile*): It's getting late. You'd better go and put on that gray suit

355

I laid out for you.

TOMMY: Yeh, sure. (*Crosses to stairs.*)

ELLEN: And be sure your socks are right side out, and, Tommy— don't try to be a tiger in front of Ed Keller.

TOMMY (*at stair landing*): I won't. I'm scared of those Neanderthal men. I'll talk about football.

ELLEN: Thank you, darling. That's swell. You know how Joe is—always cheerful. And we do want it to be a good party.

TOMMY (*starting upstairs*): I'll be cheerful. I'll be merry and bright. I'll be the most cheerful son-of-a-gun in this part of the country. (*He disappears. We hear him singing a snatch of "Who's Afraid of the Big Bad Wolf?" The doorbell rings.*)

ELLEN: Hurry, Tommy! They're here! (*Crosses to the door and admits* JOE FERGUSON, *followed by* WALLY MYERS.) Hello, Joe!

JOE: Ellen! How are you, baby? God, you look great! Why, you're younger and prettier than ever! If I were a braver man, I'd kiss you. Doggone it, I will kiss you! (*Kisses her on cheek, hugs her, lifts her off the floor—whirls her around.* WALLY *closes door.* JOE *is all that we have been led to expect: big, dynamic, well dressed, prosperous. He is full of good nature and a boundless enthusiasm*

356

for everything.)

ELLEN (*catching something of his ebullience*): It's terribly nice to see you again, Joe. If I were a younger woman, I'd say it's been all of ten years.

JOE (*whipping off his coat, he puts down a small box on sofa*): Gosh, this is swell! Where's the great Thomas?

ELLEN: Tommy will be right down. I see Wally found you— so you've met?

JOE: Yeh. We joined forces outside.

[WALLY *hangs up* JOE's *coat.*]

ELLEN (*at settee*): Come on over here and sit down.

JOE: I forgot to ask you, Wally, who's going in at the other half tomorrow? Stalenkiwiecz?

WALLY: No, sir. Wierasocka.

JOE: Really?

WALLY: He's a Beta. From Oregon.

JOE: Oh, yeh—yeh, I know.

WALLY: Stalenkiwiecz is laid up. They think he's got whooping cough. (*He sits in center of settee beside* ELLEN.)

JOE: That's bad! I've got a thousand fish on that game. (*Sits on settee. It is very crowded.*)

WALLY: I think it's safe, all right, Mr. Ferguson, but I wish we had you. Stalenkiwiecz, Wierasocka, Myers and Whirling Joe Ferguson.

ELLEN: Do they still call you

Whirling Joe?

JOE: Oh, sure, remember how—

WALLY: Say, he was the greatest open-field runner there ever was.

ELLEN: Yes. Joe, why haven't you ever been—

WALLY: Why, you made Red Grange look like a cripple.

JOE: Well, they say you're not so bad yourself. Say, Ellen, how's—

WALLY: Aw, I'm just fair, that's all. (*Produces a clipping.*) This is what Grantland Rice said about me. (*Hands it to* JOE.)

JOE (*beginning to wish* WALLY *would go*): Yeh. Too bad this is Wally's last year. We're going to miss him—eh, Ellen?

ELLEN (*pointedly*): Have you got anything to do, Wally?

WALLY: Coach wants me to help him with the backfield next season. Not much money in it, of course.

JOE (*hands clipping back to* WALLY): Well, if you want my advice, don't go in for coaching. I had a sweet offer from Cincinnati in twenty-nine. Remember that, Ellen?

ELLEN: I remember very well. Do you remember when—

WALLY: Nineteen twenty-nine! I was only twelve years old then.

TOMMY (*coming downstairs*): Hello, Joe! It's nice to see you again!

JOE (*rises and shakes hands*): Tommy, old man, how are you? Ten years! Teaching must be good for you. And Ellen, here, looks like a million bucks! That reminds me—I came laden with gifts. (*Turns and almost runs into* WALLY. *He recovers and gets the small box.*) These are a few flowering weeds. . . .

ELLEN (*opening the box of orchids*): Oh, thank you, Joe. They're lovely. Tommy, will you call Cleota?

TOMMY: Sure. (*Goes to dining-room door, calls.*) Cleota!

ELLEN: It's fun to get flowers. Very festive.

JOE: Oh, it's nothing much, but I wanted you to know I remembered the great day. Think I'd forget it was your birthday?

ELLEN: You never used to. (TOMMY *has rejoined them.*) Tommy gave me some flowering weeds, too—for my birthday.

TOMMY: Yes, I got her some— for your—oh—yes. . . . Not such nice ones, I'm afraid. (*To* ELLEN.) I'm a lucky man.

[CLEOTA *enters.*]

ELLEN: Will you find something to put these in, Cleota?

CLEOTA: Ah'll hafta put 'em in de sink wit dat ice. (*Goes out with flowers.*)

JOE: Boy, it's sure great to be here!

TOMMY: It's nice to have you. . . . Staying long?

357

JOE: Got to be in Washington next week. Well, Tommy, I see you've still got a lot of books.

TOMMY: Oh, yes.

JOE: You know I never get a chance to read books. (*He sits on settee again.*)

WALLY: Say, you must have a swell job! (*He sits on bench before fireplace.*)

JOE: By the time I get through at night, I'm lucky if I can keep up with what's going on in the world. Way things are changing, you gotta do that. I take fifteen magazines. That keeps me busy.

ELLEN (*linking an arm through* TOMMY'S): Tommy's had several articles in *Harper's* and the *Atlantic*.

JOE: No! Say, that's fine! But you'll have to boil them down to *The Reader's Digest* to reach me, Tommy. You know, that's a great little magazine.

TOMMY: Do you like bullion cubes?

ELLEN (*hastily*): Tommy, you'd better make a drink.

TOMMY: Yes. We have a lot of celebrating to do. (*He goes out to dining room, calling* CLEOTA.)

ELLEN: How've you been, Joe? (*Sits next to* JOE.)

JOE: Fine, except for a little sinus trouble.

WALLY: You know, Mrs. Turner, I recognized him right away from that big picture in the gym.

[TOMMY *re-enters with bowl of ice, mixes drinks at table.*]

ELLEN: That's fine. How's Brenda? I meant to ask before.

JOE: Fine! Great! Little heavier, maybe. We're being divorced, you know.

ELLEN: But I didn't know. Oh, Joe, I'm sorry.

JOE: Nothing to be sorry about. It's just one of those things.

TOMMY: What's the matter?

ELLEN: Joe and his wife are breaking up.

TOMMY: Oh, that's too bad.

JOE: No, it's all fine. We're both taking it in our stride. Took her out to dinner last week—along with her new boy friend.

TOMMY: Wasn't that rather complicated?

ELLEN: Oh, you're not up to date, Tommy. That's the modern way of doing things.

JOE: Sure. Take it in your stride. Gosh, Ellen, I can't take my eyes off you. (*At* WALLY'S *chuckle*, JOE *rises and changes the subject.*) Nice little place you got here. Need any help, Tommy? I'm a demon on Manhattans. (*He is starting toward* TOMMY *when the doorbell rings.*)

TOMMY: I'm all right, thanks.

JOE: I hope that's Ed, the old scoundrel.

[ELLEN *admits the* DAMONS.]

ELLEN: I'm so glad— Hello, Mrs. Damon.

BLANCHE: Hello, Ellen, dear. How do you do, Mr. Turner?

ELLEN: You must know Joe Ferguson.

BLANCHE: Oh, of course. How do you do?

[JOE *bows, smiling.*]

ELLEN: This is Mrs. Damon, Joe. And you remember Dean Damon?

JOE: Yes, indeed. Nice to see you again, sir.

DAMON (*crossing to him and shaking hands*): Back for the slaughter of the—uh—Michigan innocents, eh?

JOE: That's right.

[ELLEN *and* BLANCHE *have turned to* WALLY.]

ELLEN: Mrs. Damon, may I present Mr. Myers?

[BLANCHE *shakes hands with him.*]

WALLY: How do you do?

BLANCHE: Oh, yes, of course we all know about our great full-back.

[TOMMY *gives* JOE *a cocktail.*]

ELLEN: Let me help you with your coat.

BLANCHE: Thank you, dear. (*To* WALLY.) Tell me, are you nervous about the game tomorrow?

WALLY: No, ma'am.

BLANCHE: Not the least little bit?

WALLY: No, ma'am.

BLANCHE: That's nice. (*Smiling at his surprise, she sits on settee.*)

DAMON (*to* JOE): I remember you not only from the gridiron but

from my Shakespeare class. You slept very quietly.

JOE: I never did finish reading *Hamlet.* I always wondered how that came out. (*He laughs heartily;* DAMON *laughs politely.*)

TOMMY: Does anybody mind a Manhattan?

BLANCHE: Oh, Ellen. Could we have sherry?

ELLEN: Certainly. Tommy . . .

[TOMMY, *who is bringing two cocktails to the* DAMONS, *pauses uncertainly.*]

TOMMY: Sherry coming right up. Here, Wally. (*Gives him cocktail.*)

WALLY: No, thanks. I'm in training.

TOMMY: Well, just hold it. Sherry for you, too, Dr. Damon?

DAMON (*disappointed*): When Mrs. Damon says we, she means me. Sherry, thanks.

[TOMMY *drinks the left-over cocktail.*]

BLANCHE: A little sherry is such fun. (WALLY *offers her a cigarette from the box on the coffee table.*) No, thanks, I'll smoke my Spuds.

[WALLY *lights* BLANCHE'S *cigarette.*]

PATRICIA (*coming downstairs*): Hello, everybody.

ELLEN (*presenting* PAT *to* JOE): This is my sister, Patricia.

PATRICIA: How do you do?

JOE (*admiring her*): How do

359

you *do?* My goodness! Why, you're as big and pretty as your sister. How about a drink?

PATRICIA: No, thanks. (*To* EL-LEN, *as she crosses to* WALLY.) Still has his hair. Hello, Wally. [TOMMY *serves sherry to the* DA-MONS.]

WALLY: Hi, Pat. Look, can I pick you up at Hennick's a little earlier?

PATRICIA: I'm not going to Hennick's. I'm eating here. That date's off.

WALLY: With Barnes? Say, that's swell. . . . I got to run along, Mrs. Turner. Nice party. (*Crosses to* JOE.) Glad I met you, Joe—I mean, Mr. Ferguson. (*They shake hands.*) I'll be seeing you. Good-bye, everybody. I'll go out the back way. (*He goes out the door which leads into the garden.*)

JOE: Take it easy, old man. Don't break a leg on me. Remember, I've got a thousand fish on that game. (*Follows* WALLY *out.*)

BLANCHE: He's a handsome boy, Patricia. (*Doorbell rings.*) And seems very healthy.

PATRICIA: I have to keep in training for him. (PATRICIA *and* DAMON *sit down on the bench before the fireplace.*)

TOMMY (*going to door*): I'll get it.

[ELLEN *joins* TOMMY *and greets the* KELLERS *as they come in.*]

ED KELLER *is a big, loud, slightly bald man of about thirty-eight, heavy around the middle. He is a prosperous real-estate man, owns the Keller Building, is a trustee and as such is the biggest voice and strongest hand on the board.* MYRTLE KELLER, *also in her late thirties, dresses well and is not bad looking, was once pretty, but is now a slightly faded blonde.*]

ED: Hello, Ellen! Hi, Turner! Where is he? (*He passes* TOMMY *fast, without a handshake, looking for* JOE *who reappears. The two men run to meet each other. This is a typical meeting between two old friends of the hale-and-hearty, back-slapping persuasion who haven't met for years.*) Hiya, you old rascal! Hahya, boy?

JOE (*as they clinch in the middle of the room, hugging, slapping backs, etc.*): Hello, you old son-of-a-gun! How are you, Ed? (*He goes to* MYRTLE.) Hello, Myrtle. Gosh, I'm glad to see you! (*He hugs her, lifting her off her feet.*)

MYRTLE (*screams*): Oh! I'm glad to see you, too! Ellen . . .

JOE (*returning to* ED): Gee, you're looking swell, Ed, old boy, old boy!

ED: Judas Priest, this is swell! How are you anyway, Joe?

[The men's voices predominate.]

JOE: Fine! Swell! Never better. You've put on a little weight, eh, Eddie? And what's happened to the crowning glory?

ED: Worry: real-estate, Roosevelt. Wonder I got any left.

MYRTLE: How do you do, Dr. Damon? How do you do, Mrs. Damon? Haven't seen you in a long, long time. Hello, Patricia. . . . *(She sits beside* MRS. DAMON.) Oh, quiet down! Ed! Are we late, Ellen?

ELLEN: Not at all. Just in time for the canapés.

JOE: How long's it been, Ed? Seven, eight years, isn't it?

ED: Eight, anyway.

ELLEN: Look, you two, break it up and say hello to people!

ED: All right, Ellen, but it sure is fine to see the Whirler again. How do you do, Dr. Damon? Not drinking straight Scotch, I hope?

DAMON: If I did that, my stomach—and Mrs. Damon—would punish me severely.

ELLEN: Won't you have a cocktail, Ed? *(Brings drink to* ED.)

ED: Thanks.

JOE: Say, this is Ellen's birthday. How about a little toast?

TOMMY: Well, fill 'em up. *(He pours drinks, including one for himself.)*

ED: Well, happy birthday, Ellen. *(He starts "Happy Birthday to You," and they all sing. It is* obvious TOMMY *is bored; he sits down, sips his drink, then noticing everybody standing, he rises and sings the last line very off key.* CLEOTA *enters, comes up behind* DAMON *with a plate of canapés.)*

CLEOTA *(after their song dies)*: Hoar doves?

DAMON *(startled)*: I beg your pardon—oh! Thank you.

JOE *(as* TOMMY *pours another round)*: Let's drink one toast to The Big Red Team. What do you say? *(*TOMMY *starts humming "The Big Bad Wolf.")*

ED: The Big Red Team!

TOMMY *(singing softly to himself)*:

"The Big Red Team—
Big Red Team.
Who's afraid of The Big Red
    Team . . ."

ED: What's that?

TOMMY: Huh? *(*ED *glares at him. To* ELLEN.) What did I do?

ELLEN: Tommy, you'd better eat something. Those cocktails are strong.

TOMMY: I'm doing all right, honey. How's everything in Detroit, Joe?

JOE: I don't know. All right, I guess. *(*ED *and* JOE *seat themselves on settee away from the women.)*

ELLEN: Tommy means Pittsburgh. The Bryson Steel Company is in Pittsburgh, Tommy. *(*CLEOTA *gives* ELLEN *the tray and*

361

goes out.)

TOMMY: Oh, yes, sure. Well, how's everything in Pittsburgh?

JOE: Well, it might be worse.

ED: Couldn't be much worse out here.

TOMMY: Have a drink.

ELLEN (*takes canapés to* MYRTLE): How are the kids, Myrtle?

MYRTLE: They're all right. The baby has some kind of rash on her little hips, but it's nothing, really. Makes her cross, though.

ED: Time sure does fly. Now Buster wants to go to Princeton. No matter how you watch 'em, they get in with the wrong kids. [*The women's voices predominate.*]

BLANCHE: How's your sister?

MYRTLE: They took a stone out of her as big as a walnut. She can't weigh more than ninety pounds.

JOE: I remember when I actually got along with only one car, and thought it was plenty. Now I've got three, and the bills are terrific. . . . Do you know what my gas bill was last month? . . . [DAMON *rises, bored, picks out a book and glances through it.*]

BLANCHE: They cut old Mrs. Wilmot open for the same trouble, and didn't find a thing!

MYRTLE: Ed, when was it I had that impacted tooth out?

ED: Seven years ago. Year the banks closed. Thirty-three.

TOMMY: Fill 'em up. (*Pours himself another.*)

ELLEN: Tommy! (*She takes shaker away from him.*) Dividend for the women folks. Give me your glass, Myrtle.

MYRTLE: Thanks.

BLANCHE: No more for us. Mercy, we'd be light-headed.

TOMMY (*following* ELLEN, *takes shaker from her, pours himself another*): But we're celebrating: the homecoming game, banks closing and everything.

JOE: How's building out here now, Ed?

TOMMY (*sauntering over to the men*): Yeh, how's building?

ED: Lousy. Whatta ya expect with that man in the White House? You know what *I* think? I think he's crazy.

JOE: You know what I heard? [*The women stop their talk to listen, but* JOE *whispers in* ED'S *ear.*]

ED: I wouldn't be a damn bit surprised!

[TOMMY *puts down shaker.*]

[ED'S *voice predominates in the following:*]

ED: Only hope for business I see is this war. And he'll probably do something to ruin that.

BLANCHE (*sotto voce*): Patricia, may I see the little girl's room?

MYRTLE: Me, too.

PATRICIA: Yes. I'll show you. [*They start toward stairs.*]

MYRTLE (*as they start upstairs*):
Is it serious?

BLANCHE: They took a pint of
pus out of her!

[*Men react to this. The women
go off, still chattering.*]

MYRTLE: Why, what's the matter with her?

BLANCHE: They don't know.
They just hold consultations.

[TOMMY *and* ELLEN *sit on the long
sofa to listen. She quietly
takes the drink from his
hand.*]

ED: Well, Dr. Damon, we men
on the Board of Trustees are certainly glad that this Red scare is
over.

DAMON: No doubt you are.

ED: Now maybe the new stadium project will get somewhere.

DAMON (*eagerly moving toward
*ED): And the Endowment Fund?

ED: Yeh, sure—that's important
too. I'm working to convince the
substantial alumni that we've got
all this Parlor-Pink business over
and done with. Got 'em all
weeded out.

JOE: Yeah—all that newspaper
stuff was pretty bad.

ED: Sure. Nobody felt like coming through for anything when
they read about men like Kennedy and Sykes and Chapman
being on the faculty. That Chapman was nothing but a damn Red.

[DAMON *covers his disgust and
turns to* ELLEN.]

TOMMY: No, he wasn't, Mr. Keller. Don Chapman was a humanist.

ELLEN (*laying a quieting hand
on* TOMMY's *arm*): We knew him
very well.

JOE: How do you know he
wasn't a Red, Tommy?

ED: He went to Soviet Russia
for his vacation once, didn't he?

TOMMY (*rising*): He just went
to see the Drama Festival.

ED (*suspiciously*): Well, it's a
mighty long way to go to see a
show.

CLEOTA (*who has just entered*):
Suppah is se'ved. (*Retires to dining room.*)

ELLEN (*rising*): Shall we go
into the dining room? It's only a
salad. We're going out to eat
afterwards. Come along, Ed, we
don't want to miss that rally.
(*She links her arm through* ED's,
and they go out to dining room.)

ED: Say, that's right. I haven't
missed a Michigan rally in seventeen years!

[ELLEN *re-enters, goes to stairs,
calls:*]

ELLEN: Supper's ready!

[PAT, BLANCHE, *and* MYRTLE *come
downstairs.*]

BLANCHE: Thank you. Come,
Frederick. (DAMON *and* BLANCHE
go into dining room.)

ELLEN: Patricia, you get a plate
for Mr. Ferguson. He's the guest
of honor, you know.

363

JOE: And I'll get a plate for you, Ellen. Come on. (JOE *and* PAT *follow the* DAMONS.)

MYRTLE (*as she goes into the dining room*): Oh, what a lovely table, Ellen!

[*During the following scene until* ED's *re-entrance, there is the general conversation in the dining room, as everybody is finding his supper and beginning to eat.*]

ELLEN (*crossing to* TOMMY): Tommy, don't say any more about Don Chapman tonight, please.

TOMMY: All right, I won't. Let's get something to eat. (EL-LEN *takes his arm. They start for dining room.*) Joe looks better, doesn't he?

ELLEN: Better?

TOMMY: Well, bigger anyway.

[*They exit.* CLEOTA *has entered with a clean-up tray. She clears away drinks and canapés, singing "I Can't Give You Anything But Love" softly. She finds one glass with some liquor in it. After a long scrutiny she raises it to her lips.*]

ED (*off-stage*): Come on, Myrtle. Hurry up. Joe's got to speak at this rally.

[CLEOTA *drinks and quickly puts glass on tray and resumes song as* ED *enters with plate of food. He plants himself in the center of a settee, and*

also takes possession of a cof-fee table.* BLANCHE *and* MYRTLE *enter, with* DAMON *following them and carrying two plates.*]

BLANCHE: Come, Myrtle, sit over here with me. Frederick, put it down over there on that table.

MYRTLE (*as they cross the room*): What makes you think there was something suspicious about it?

[*The women settle themselves on settee.*]

BLANCHE: Well, his family wouldn't allow a post-mortem. Thank you, Frederick, that's fine.

[ELLEN *and* JOE *come in.*]

ELLEN: I hope you can all find a place to sit.

JOE (*crossing to long sofa*): What's the matter with this? Come on, Ellen, give me a break.

[ELLEN *smiles and sits beside him, then speaks to* PATRICIA, *who appears in dining-room door.*]

ELLEN: Pat, is Tommy getting some food?

PATRICIA: Yeh, he's all right. (*She joins the women and* DAMON, *who is eating standing up at the mantel.*)

TOMMY (*entering*): Sure, I'm fine. (*He looks around for a place to settle.*)

ELLEN: Bring in the coffee, please, Cleota.

364

[CLEOTA *nods and goes out.*]

ED: There's room here for some-body.

TOMMY: No, thanks, I'll sit— (*Looks around for any place away from* ED; *the only vacant spot is a chair beside* ED's *settee.*)—here.

MYRTLE: Eat your vegetables, Ed.

ED: Aw, this is a party.

BLANCHE: Where's Michael Barnes this evening, Patricia? Frederick tells me he's written a remarkable editorial. (DAMON *drops his fork.*) Be careful, Frederick!

ED: Barnes? Barnes? I haven't read a decent editorial since Brisbane died.

PATRICIA: Michael couldn't come. He doesn't like Mr.—er—

MYRTLE: Doesn't like what?

PATRICIA: Doesn't like parties.

BLANCHE: I'm always so interested in *The Literary Magazine.* What was the editorial, Patricia?

DAMON: Eat your dinner, my dear. Remember, Mr. Keller— wants to get to the rally.

ED: Huh?

BLANCHE (*staring at him*): What's the matter with you? (*He shushes her. To* PAT.) I hope I haven't said anything, dear. (PAT *shakes her head.*)

[CLEOTA *enters with coffee and serves the guests.*]

ED: What's going on over there? Who is this Barnes?

TOMMY: One of Patricia's beaux.

ED: Some writer?

TOMMY: He's a student. Editor of *The Literary Magazine.*

ED: Oh, yeah, I've heard of him. What's he done now?

ELLEN: Oh, it's nothing, really.

TOMMY: Well, since it's come up, Ellen, we might as well tell Mr. Keller. He'll read about it to-morrow. . . . (ELLEN *rises.*) I told Michael I was going to read something to one of my English classes, and he got a mistaken idea about it and wrote a sort of—

ELLEN (*breaking in quickly*): Just a silly little editorial—that's all.

ED: I see.

PATRICIA: Because Tommy isn't really going to read it at all.

[MYRTLE *murmurs to* BLANCHE, *rises and goes to dining room.*]

ED: What was it this kid said you were going to read? Any-thing important?

TOMMY (*after a moment*): It's a short, but beautifully written piece of English by Bartolomeo Vanzetti.

ED: Never heard of him. (*Then, as the name registers.*) Hey, you don't mean Vanzetti of Sacco and Vanzetti?

TOMMY: Yes, the same man.

ED: You mean you're going to read something *he* wrote?

TOMMY: Yes, I was going to.

ELLEN (*quickly*): But now he's not—Michael didn't understand.

ED: Why would you ever think of such a dumb thing in the first place?

[TOMMY *has lost any appetite he may have had. He rises and puts his plate and cup on the table.*]

TOMMY: It's part of a series. I read many such letters to my class.

ED: You mean letters by anarchists?

TOMMY (*restrains himself*): No, letters by men who were not professional writers—like Lincoln, General Sherman . . .

ED: Well, it's a damn good thing you changed your mind. Putting Lincoln and General Sherman in a class with Vanzetti! Wouldn't look very good.

JOE: What's this?

ED: Wait a minute. (*To* TOMMY.) Is this thing going to be printed? This editorial?

DAMON: We discovered it too late to stop it.

ED: And this kid didn't submit it to the publications committee?

DAMON: Unfortunately, he did not. Ellen, dear, Mrs. Damon and I must be running along.

ELLEN: Oh, I'm sorry.

DAMON: I have a committee meeting.

BLANCHE (*astonished*): What committee?

DAMON: Come, Blanche.

BLANCHE (*rising*): Oh, yes, that little committee.

ED: Well, I hope this thing's not too bad. You better deny it quick, Turner. I tell you! I'll call the papers in the morning.

TOMMY: No, I'll take care of it.

JOE (*rises*): What's going on here?

MYRTLE (*enters from dining room with two dishes of sherbet*): Here's some sherbet, Ed.

ED: Put it down there. (*To* JOE.) I'm just telling Turner here we've had enough of this Red business among the students and the faculty. Don't want any more.

TOMMY (*returning to his chair*): This isn't Red, Mr. Keller.

ED: Maybe not, but it looks bad. We don't want anything Red—or even Pink—taught here.

TOMMY: But who's to decide what is Red and Pink?

ED: We are! Somebody's got to decide what's fit to teach. If we don't, who would?

DAMON: I thought that perhaps the faculty had . . .

ED: No, sir. You fellows are too wishy-washy. We saw that in the Chapman case. Americanism is what we want taught here.

JOE: Americanism is a fine thing.

TOMMY: Fine. But how would you define Americanism?

ED: Why—er—everybody knows what Americanism is! What do

366

you believe in?

TOMMY: I believe that a college should be concerned with ideas. Not just your ideas . . . or my ideas, but all ideas.

ED: No, sir! That's the *trouble* . . . too damn many ideas floating around. . . . You put ideas of any kind into young people's heads, and the first thing you know, they start believing them.

DAMON: On the contrary. I have been putting ideas into young people's heads for forty-two years with no—visible—results whatever.

[*There is a dubious laugh from* BLANCHE.]

BLANCHE: Come, Frederick. Good night, Ellen. Lovely party. (*She bustles* DAMON *out the door.*)

ED (*rises*): Turner, you better think twice before you read anything. I can promise you the trustees will clamp down on any professor who tries anything funny! I'm telling you that for your own good.

JOE: Say, I thought we were going to have some fun. Let's break this up. How about some music? (*He goes over to Victrola and puts on a record.*)

ED: That's right. We're celebrating tonight. Just wanted to get that out of my system. (*He picks up the dish of ice.*) Oh, I didn't want this—I wanted some

of that ice cream. (*He starts for the dining room.*)

MYRTLE: He means he wants both. Here, I'll show you. (*She follows him out.*)

[PATRICIA *starts to go, too;* ELLEN, *worried about* TOMMY, *stops her, whispering to her.* PAT *nods and turns to* JOE, *who is looking through the records.*]

PATRICIA: I'll bet you'd like some ice cream, too, Mr. Ferguson.

JOE: No, I . . . (PATRICIA *winks at him; he glances at* TOMMY.) Oh, sure. Sure, I would.

PATRICIA (*linking an arm through his*): Can you still skip?

JOE: No—not at my age. (*They go into the dining room,* PAT *closing the door softly.* TOMMY *pours himself a drink.*)

ELLEN: Tommy, have you had too much to drink?

TOMMY: No. Not enough.

ELLEN: Your eyes have that funny look.

TOMMY: Did you hear what Mr. Keller said to me? I don't like to be talked to like that.

ELLEN: Just because he was nasty and you've had a few drinks. . . . (*Goes to him.*) Tommy, you're not going to go ahead and read that letter?

TOMMY: Yes, Ellen, I think I have to.

ELLEN: Tommy, try to be prac-

367

tical for once. At least wait until you're not so mad. Try to think of this the way any other man would think of it.

TOMMY: I'm not any other man.

ELLEN: Well, try to be. Do you think Joe would do something that would get him into trouble just because somebody irritated him?

TOMMY: *Joe!* I don't see why you don't try to understand how *I* feel about this.

ELLEN: I'm simply trying to keep you out of a lot of trouble. I don't see why—

TOMMY: But you see how Joe would feel. That's very plain to you, isn't it?

ELLEN: Yes, it is. Joe wouldn't get all mixed up.

TOMMY: I'm not mixed up. I'm trying to understand what goes on in your mind. It *can't* be like Joe Ferguson's mind!

ELLEN: Oh, you and your mind! (*Turns away, exasperated.*) I have to go through such a lot with your mind!

TOMMY: Maybe you wouldn't if you understood it better.

ELLEN: Oh, I know, I know! I'm too dumb for you!

TOMMY: Now, Ellen, I didn't say that.

ELLEN: You said Joe and I were stupid.

TOMMY: I said he was.

ELLEN: But he isn't. He's a big man. In some ways he's smarter than you.

TOMMY: Well, you ought to know. (*He turns away from her.*)

ELLEN (*catching his arm*): Oh, look, Tommy—what are we fighting about?

TOMMY (*turns*): You said I was dumb.

ELLEN: Tommy, you've had too many drinks or you wouldn't say that.

TOMMY: No, I haven't, but I don't feel very well. I feel very unhappy and slightly sick.

ELLEN: I'll get you some bicarbonate of soda.

TOMMY (*crossing to the stairs*): No, you won't. I'll go upstairs and lie down for a few minutes, myself. I can do that. Let's not bring this down to the level of bicarbonate of soda. (*He starts up slowly, then suddenly feels squeamish and makes a mad dash for it.* ELLEN *hesitates for a minute at the foot of the stairs—calls after him.*)

ELLEN: Tommy. Tommy, I didn't—

[JOE *comes from the dining room with a dish of ice cream.*]

JOE: Anything the matter?

ELLEN: Oh—no. Tommy's not feeling well. He got sick once before at a party. He's not used to drinking, and he's very sensitive about it. (JOE *nods and goes to turn off the Victrola.* CLEOTA *comes in, starts clearing away sup-*

per plates. ELLEN *goes to her, speaks in a low voice.*) Cleota, will you get Mr. Turner some bicarbonate of soda from the kitchen? (CLEOTA *nods, retires to the dining room.*) Cleota will get him some bicarbonate of soda from the kitchen. He'd never find it upstairs.

JOE (*takes off the record and hunts for another one to his liking*): Why wouldn't he? Where do you keep it?

ELLEN: In the medicine chest.

JOE: What was that stuff between him and Ed?

ELLEN: Oh, it's nothing, really. I'll tell you about it tomorrow. (*Her mind is on* TOMMY, *upstairs.*)

JOE: Fine. . . . Say, look what I found! "Who?" Remember that, Ellen? (*He puts the record on, starts it.* ELLEN *moves closer to the Victrola and listens as it plays:*)

"Who-o-o stole my heart away?
Who-o-o makes me dream all day?
Dreams I know can never come true.
Seems as though I'd ever be blue.
Who-o-o means my happiness . . ."

(*As naturally as if they were always dancing to this song, they both begin to dance.*) Gee, this takes me back . . . the May dance. Remember?

ELLEN: Um-huh—it rained.

JOE: You said you didn't know it was raining. I know I didn't. (*Holds her closer.*)

ELLEN (*breaks away*): I'm a little rusty, Joe. I haven't danced in—oh, I don't remember when. Makes me feel young.

JOE: Then what are we stopping for? Come on.

ELLEN: Well—all right. (*They go back into the dance. Dreaming,* ELLEN *glances up at* JOE. *They slow down to a stop and stand looking at each other, he ardently, she caught up in the music.*)

JOE: I can answer all those questions. . . . No one but you. (*As the music goes into the instrumental reprise,* JOE *kisses her, and she kisses back for a long moment, then tries to pull away.*)

ELLEN (*as he tries to kiss her again*): Oh, no, Joe, please, I . . . Say, how many cocktails did I have? (*They stand for an instant, looking at each other.*)

[*Off-stage we hear:*]

MYRTLE: Ed, come away from that ice cream. You've had enough.

[JOE *and* ELLEN *quietly start dancing again, smiling.*]

ED: Oh—all right.

[TOMMY, *a little pale and disheveled, comes down the stairs and sees them dancing there; he stops;* MYRTLE *and* ED *en-*

369

ter.]

MYRTLE (*nudging* ED): Look, Ed! Just like the old days, isn't it? Seeing them dancing together?

ED: I'll say. (*Then, loudly.*) They make a darn' handsome couple, don't they?

[TOMMY, *although he has not seen the kiss, has sensed the whole intimacy of the scene and the meaning of* ED's *remark; he nods soberly.*]

JOE: She dances like a dream.

ED (*chuckling*): Like a "dream can never come true," eh, Joe? You look mighty sweet in there, boy.

[ELLEN *sees* TOMMY. *Following her glance,* ED, MYRTLE *and* JOE *turn and look at* TOMMY.]

ELLEN (*breaking away*): Oh— Tommy—are you all right?

TOMMY (*coming down*): Yes, thanks. . . . Don't—let me spoil the party.

ED: Party's breaking up anyway, Tommy.

[JOE *turns off Victrola.*]

TOMMY: I just thought I'd get some more air. . . . (*Crosses to the door which leads out to the garden.*)

ED: I don't want to miss any of that rally. (*A band is heard in the distance, approaching. Holds out* MYRTLE's *coat.*) Myrtle!

[MYRTLE *crosses to him.*]

[PATRICIA *enters from dining room with bicarbonate of soda in glass.*]

PATRICIA: Who's this for, Ellen?

ELLEN: Tommy. (*To* TOMMY, *as he stands with his back turned, breathing the fresh air.*) Tommy, will you take this bicarbonate?

TOMMY: Just—put it by for a moment. You go to the rally, Ellen. . . . I'm going to walk around out here—until I feel better. Good night, everybody. . . . You're coming to lunch tomorrow, aren't you, Joe?

JOE: Yes, sir!

TOMMY: That's what I thought. (*He goes out, closing the screen door.* PATRICIA *looks out the window; the band is heard louder.*)

PATRICIA: Ellen! It's the team and the band and a lot of the kids! They must be going in the Neil Avenue gate!

ED: Come on, let's step on it!

JOE: Yeh. (*Listens to music.*) Boy, that sounds good! God, doesn't that take you back?

MYRTLE: Where'll we go after the rally?

JOE: I'll take you all to the Dixie Club! Whatta ya say, Ellen?

ELLEN: Oh, I haven't been there in years! It would be fun. . . . But, no, I'm not going. (*Calls.*) I'm going to stay here with you, Tommy.

TOMMY (*off-stage*): No, I'd rather you didn't—really.

PATRICIA (*as music gets much louder*): Hey! They're stopping in front of the house!

[WALLY *runs in as the music*

stops.]

WALLY: Ready, Pat?

PATRICIA: Sure!

[*Breathless and excited,* WALLY *goes to* JOE.]

WALLY: Look, we brought the band over to escort you to the chapel, Mr. Ferguson! You're going to ride in the Axline Buggy!

ED: The Axline Buggy!

WALLY: We hauled it out of the trophy room! We got two horses —not the old black ones, but we got two horses! Whatta ya say?

ED: Fine! Fine!

[NUTSY *runs in, dressed in a band-leader's uniform and carrying his glistening baton.*]

NUTSY: Hey, come on! Let's get going! The carriage waits, Mr. Ferguson! (*Does drum major's salute and clicks heels.*)

WALLY: This is Nutsy Miller, the leader of the band.

JOE (*shaking hands*): Hiya, Nutsy?

NUTSY: Hiya, Joe?

JOE: Okay, fellas! Whatta ya say, Ellen—you ride with me. Some fun, huh?

ELLEN (*in the spirit of it*): Oh— all right. Hurray!

JOE: Hit her, Ed!

ED, JOE, WALLY, ELLEN, PATRICIA, NUTSY (*sing*):

"And if we win the game,
  We'll buy a keg of booze,
  And we'll drink to old Mid-
    western

Till we wobble in our shoes."

[*They all go out,* JOE *and* ELLEN *the center of the gay, excited group, arm in arm. A shout goes up as* JOE *appears outside. You hear a triple "rah-team" for* JOE.]

VOICES (*outside*):

Rah-rah-rah!

Rah-rah-rah!

Rah-rah-rah!

Ferguson! Ferguson! *Ferguson!*

[*The band starts another march.* TOMMY *has reappeared in the lower door a moment after the general exit. He crosses slowly and closes upper door. The cheers for* FERGUSON *and the band music slowly die away as* TOMMY *turns and sees the glass of soda. He picks it up, looks at it in distaste—distaste for himself.*]

TOMMY: Rah-rah-rah! (*He throws down the spoon, crosses to the Victrola and starts the record.*)

VICTROLA: ". . . Dreams I know can never come true. . . ."

[TOMMY *listens for a moment, then makes awkwardly, solemnly, a couple of dance steps, frowns, shakes his head, and drops onto settee, giving it up. He drinks the bitter cup of soda as the music ends and the*

CURTAIN FALLS

371

ACT II

SCENE I: *The Turners' living room—same as Act I. About one o'clock the following day. At rise:* JOE, *with coat off, is arranging plates, knives, saucers and forks on the floor in the form of a football formation. The end table has evidently been used for serving luncheon as it still holds a plate and cup.* ELLEN *is seated center, finishing her coffee and watching* JOE. PATRICIA *is down on her knees on the floor studying the array of dishes, napkins, salt cellars, and glasses which are ankle-deep around* JOE. CLEOTA *enters from the dining room, carrying an empty tray. She crosses to the end table, begins clearing away the dishes, keeping a suspicious eye on* JOE *and the black magic he is up to.*

JOE: Now here—it's a balanced line. Move those two men out a little more. (PAT *moves the men out.*) This is a wonderful play! The coach gave it to me in the strictest confidence.

ELLEN: Cleota, did you phone Mr. Turner's office again?

CLEOTA (*at end table, clearing away dishes*): Yessum. Dey ain' no answeh.

PATRICIA: I saw Tommy, Ellen —about an hour ago.

ELLEN: Where?

PATRICIA: He was walking out on the little road back of the Ag buildings. Just moping along. I yelled at him, but he didn't hear me.

ELLEN: I'm getting worried.

JOE (*intent on his own activity*): Everything's going to be okay. Nothing to worry about. . . . Now, study this play, girls, or you won't know it when you see

it this afternoon. This is Michigan. And this is Midwestern. . . . Now! From the balanced line, we shift. Hup! (*He executes a Notre Dame shift, grimaces a little as his right knee resents this activity.*) Wally takes the left-end's place, but he plays out a little. [PATRICIA *exchanges cup and cream pitcher.*]

PATRICIA: Isn't Wally going to carry the ball?

JOE: Shh. Michigan spreads out. They're watching that wide end, but it's too obvious. They're watching the other side of the line, too.

CLEOTA (*moving down, wide-eyed*): What's goin' on heah?

ELLEN: Football game!

JOE (*ignoring her*): The ball is snapped back. Now look, here we go! Both of us. . . . (*Carrying a plate and a napkin.*) Close together. Fading back, but threat-

372

ening a left-end run as well as a
pass.

PATRICIA: But who are you?

JOE: I'm both of them—Lindstrom and Wierasocka ... (*Comes
forward.*) Skolsky cuts down the
left side line deep and takes out
Wupperman—that's the jam pot.
(*He picks up "Wally."*) Wally
is running wide around right end
(*Runs around end.*) faking as
though he had the ball but hasn't
really got it—apparently! . . .
Now, then, just as Michigan is
charging in on Lindstrom and
Wierasocka, trying to decide
which one has the ball, Wally lets
himself out! *He's really got it!*

PATRICIA: Hooray!

JOE: It's a fake fake. It's an old
play, so corny only a football genius like Coach Sprague would use
it. With no interference at all,
Wally cuts over and goes straight
down the right side of the field!
He stiff-arms the safety man . . .
(*Running with the cream pitcher.*) Touchdown!

PATRICIA: Whoopee! (*She
knocks over the jam pot.*) Oh,
God, there goes Wupperman!

[*During* JOE'S *"touchdown,"*
TOMMY *has appeared quietly
in the door to the back yard.
He watches* JOE *with distaste.
No one notices him in the
confusion.*]

CLEOTA: Um-hm. You through
playin' now?

[PATRICIA *and* JOE *help her pick
up the dishes.*]

PATRICIA: I'm sorry, Ellen.

ELLEN: It's all right. You can
take the teams to the showers
now, Cleota. Can't she, Joe?

JOE: Sure. How do you like it?

ELLEN: I think it's nice.

JOE: Nice?! It's marvelous!
That play is going to put us in the
Rose Bowl. (*To* PATRICIA.) Did
I ever tell you about how we used
the Statue of Liberty play? (*He
uses a cream pitcher as a football.*) I would go back for a pass,
and Jonesy would take it out of
my hand and cut around to the
left . . . (*He loses himself in the
play, then suddenly realizes that
not the imaginary ball but the
cream pitcher has been taken out
of his hand and that there is no
Jonesy. He looks around slowly,
puzzled, too late to have seen
TOMMY quietly returning to the
outdoors with the pitcher which
he has snatched from* JOE'S *hand.
Doorbell rings.*)

ELLEN: I'll answer it. (*She goes
to the front door.* JOE *looks to see
where he might have dropped the
pitcher; he is vastly puzzled.*)

PATRICIA: It's a wonderful play,
Mr. Ferguson. If it works. (*She
runs upstairs.*)

JOE: The coach gave it to me in
strictest confidence. (*He gives
another look for the pitcher with
the expression of a prize blood-*

hound who has lost a scent. ELLEN *admits* DEAN DAMON.)

ELLEN: Can you come in and wait, Dr. Damon? Tommy is out somewhere, but I'm expecting him back.

[CLEOTA *goes out with the tray and dishes, leaving the coffee things on a table.*]

DAMON: I can't wait very long. (*Indicates the magazine in his pocket.*)

ELLEN: Is that *The Literary Magazine?*

DAMON: It's a powder magazine. The bombs are bursting all around. (*He sees* JOE, *who has been putting on his coat and looking in the door drapes for the lost pitcher.*) Oh—good afternoon.

JOE: How are you, Dr. Damon?

[*The phone rings.*]

ELLEN: Excuse me—I'll . . . (*She goes to the phone.*) Hello. . . . Yes, thank you. That was Ed Keller's office, Joe. He's on his way over here.

JOE: Oh, yeah. He called me this morning. He's fit to be tied about this literary magazine thing. Have you seen it?

DAMON: Yes. This is it.

JOE: May I take a look at it? Gosh, I didn't realize what this thing was—(*He takes the magazine and scans the editorial.*) Calls the trustees Fascists! This kid's dangerous—un-American.

DAMON: Oh, no.

ELLEN: Oh, no, not really. He's from an old Chillicothe family.

JOE: This is bad stuff for the university. I'm afraid all hell's going to break loose. Of course, it's none of my business, but . . .

DAMON (*taking the magazine out of* JOE'*s hand*): You take the words right out of my mouth. It's been a very trying morning. I haven't had such a day since poor Dr. Prendergast shot his secretary.

JOE: Well, I'm not a trustee, but I know how they feel.

ELLEN (*anxiously*): I know.

JOE: Tommy'd better deny this, pretty fast, and get himself out in the clear, I'm telling you. I'm sorry about this, Ellen. Where is Tommy?

ELLEN: I don't know.

JOE: You don't think—(*He lowers his voice.*) You don't think he may be a little sore about your going out with me last night?

ELLEN: I don't know. Oh, Joe, I'm all upset.

[*The doorbell rings.*]

JOE: Shall I open it? (*He does.*) Hi, Ed.

ED (*off-stage*): Turner here?

ELLEN: No, he isn't.

[ED *appears in the doorway.*]

ED (*sternly*): Well, I want to see him before the game. Tell him to call my office. Coming, Joe?

ELLEN (*quickly*): I don't know just when he'll . . . Won't you

374

come in? Dr. Damon is here.

ED: Oh. (*He comes into the room a few steps.* JOE *closes the door.*) Well, I'm glad somebody's here. How do you do, sir? Do you know where I could find President Cartwright?

DAMON: His secretary informed me that he is at the barber shop having his beard trimmed.

ED (*his anger going up fast*): That'll be a big help! I thought Turner was going to deny this story. Papers keep calling *me*—they say he hasn't. Here I am, bearing the brunt of this damn disgraceful attack. "Fascists!" You oughtta heard Si McMillan! And do you know Kressinger's in town from Detroit?

ELLEN: Is he a trustee, too?

DAMON: Oh, yes, young Michael has exploded his dynamite at a moment when the concentration of trustees is at its thickest.

ED: Yeh. There goes the new stadium. There goes your Endowment Fund! Unless something is done, and done quick! (*He turns on* ELLEN, *with a roar.*) Ellen, you tell your husband what I said!

JOE (*moving in*): Look, Ed, it isn't Ellen's fault.

ED (*between fury and tears*): It isn't my fault, either. I kept this whole week end free. I got my office full of eighteen-year-old Bourbon so we fellows could cut

loose a little. And look what happens! All we need now is for Wierasocka to fumble a punt! (*He stomps out of the house.*)

JOE: I'll—see you later. (*He goes out after* ED.)

DAMON: I didn't like the way Mr. Keller said "There goes your Endowment Fund." (*The phone rings.*) If that's the newspapers I'm not here.

ELLEN: Oh, I don't want to talk to them either. Cleota—

[*As the phone rings again,* PATRICIA *runs down the stairs.*]

PATRICIA (*angrily*): I'm going out to talk to Michael! I got him on the phone but he hung up on me! Good afternoon, Dr. Damon. I'll knock his ears off. (*She slams out the door. The phone rings on.*)

DAMON: Good afternoon, Patricia.

[CLEOTA *enters from the dining room.*]

ELLEN: Answer the phone, Cleota.

CLEOTA (*picking up the receiver cautiously*): Hello. . . . Says what? . . . Say, he *is?* . . . Ah didn' say you said he was, Ah say what is it? . . . No, he ain' heah. . . . No, dis ain' Miz Turner. (*She is getting a little surly.*)

ELLEN: *Who is calling, please!*

CLEOTA: Who's dis? . . . Wait a minute. . . . (*She puts her hand over the mouthpiece. To*

375

ELLEN.) It's de Daily sumpin'.

ELLEN: Hang up, Cleota.

CLEOTA (*brightly*): G'bye. (*She hangs up and exits.*)

ELLEN: Oh, Lord, see what's happened already! Dr. Damon, suppose Tommy *didn't* read this letter?

DAMON: Let us not take refuge in conditional clauses.

ELLEN: Would you read it if you were Tommy?

DAMON: Now we go into the subjunctive. My dear, for forty-two years I have read nothing to *my* classes which was written later than the first half of the seventeenth century.

ELLEN: There must be some way — some compromise — that wouldn't be too humiliating.

DAMON: The policy of appeasement? Yes, it has its merits. (*He rises.*) I can't wait any longer for Thomas. Tell him that if he decides not to read the letter, I shall feel easier in my mind. Much easier. (*He picks up his hat.*) And—slightly disappointed. . . . Good afternoon, my dear. . . . (*He opens the door, and in flies* PATRICIA. *They collide.*) Wup, wup, wup!

PATRICIA: Don't let Michael in! I don't want to talk to him any more!

DAMON: Did you—uh—knock his ears off?

PATRICIA (*loudly*): I got him

told! But he wants to tell me *his* side. He thinks *he* has a side.

DAMON (*quietly*): A common failing, my dear. . , . Good afternoon. (*He goes out and* PATRICIA *bolts the door after him, hotly.*)

PATRICIA: There, I've bolted that young genius out! Oh, Ellen! Give me a football player any time. (*She crosses to her sister for comfort.*) Give me a guy without so much intellect or whatever it is. Somebody that doesn't want to be bawling the world out all the time—always doing something brave or fine or something. (MICHAEL, *greatly upset, steps into the room from the back yard.*) Go away!

ELLEN: Quiet down, Patricia. . . . Come in, Michael.

MICHAEL (*to* PATRICIA): You're being very silly.

ELLEN (*noticing* MICHAEL'S *distraught look*): Can I give you a glass of milk?

MICHAEL: No, thank you. She won't listen to me, Mrs. Turner. I'm not trying to ruin your husband's life or my life or anybody's life. It's the principle of the thing she won't see.

PATRICIA: Oh, the principle! (*She stomps over to him.*) I'll bet nobody else would make a fool of himself and his friends and—my brother-in-law—over a principle. [ELLEN, *taking the dishes with her, quietly slips out to the kitch-*

en, unnoticed by MICHAEL.]

MICHAEL (*with the enormous gravity of the young man in love*): All right, Pat. I'm very glad to know the qualities you admire in a man. They are certainly the noble virtues, and I'm sure Wally is lousy with them.

PATRICIA: Oh, make up your mind who you're imitating, Ralph Waldo Emerson or Hemingway! You—you *writer!*

MICHAEL: *Now* who's imitating Hemingway?

PATRICIA: I wish you'd go away!

MICHAEL (*rushing to the front door*): I'm going! I'm going for good! I'm going out of your life! (*On the last word he jerks at the door to make a dramatic exit, but it won't open, since* PATRICIA *bolted it. The door-knob comes off in his hand.*)

PATRICIA (*going out the lower door to the porch*): It's bolted, you dope!

[MICHAEL *gets the door open finally and in walks an extremely puzzled* TOMMY *with the other door-knob in his hand. The two stand and look at each other.*]

MICHAEL (*a little guiltily*): Sorry, Mr. Turner!

TOMMY: What's going on here?

[MICHAEL *puts his knob in and* TOMMY *screws the other knob on.*]

MICHAEL: I was just going.

TOMMY: That's all right. Come in, if you want to.

MICHAEL (*noticing* TOMMY's *haggard look*): Say, you look terrible.

TOMMY: Me? Why, what's the matter?

MICHAEL (*his mind on his own woes*): I've got to get out of here.

TOMMY: Why? Did somebody do something to you?

MICHAEL: Patricia. She did plenty. I suppose it's just as well. I've found out what she wants in life: a handsome, half-witted halfback.

TOMMY: Yes, I know how that feels.

MICHAEL: Yes, sir. Well, you can't get anywhere with a woman who doesn't understand what you have to do.

TOMMY: No. No, you can't, Michael. You'd like to, but you can't. . . . Good-bye, Michael. . . . (*He shakes hands with* MICHAEL, *grimly.*) Come back in about an hour, will you? I want to give you a piece of my mind.

MICHAEL (*puzzled*): Yes, sir. (*He goes slowly out the front door, as* TOMMY *takes the pitcher he snatched from* JOE *out of his overcoat pocket.* TOMMY *sits sadly, and sighs as* ELLEN *enters.*)

ELLEN: Oh, hello, darling!

TOMMY: Hello.

ELLEN (*uneasily*): Well, I'm glad you remembered where you

377

live. I was beginning to be worried. We phoned your office three times, but nobody knew where you were.

TOMMY (*looking up slowly*): Huh?

ELLEN: I say nobody knew where you were—since early this morning.

TOMMY: I was walking.

ELLEN: Without any breakfast? All this time?

TOMMY: Well, I—came around to the back door a while ago, but Joe was doing the Statue of Liberty or something again, so I went away.

ELLEN: You were right here and you went away?

TOMMY: Yes, I couldn't face that right now. Not the Statue of Liberty.

ELLEN: Oh. Well, Dr. Damon's been here—and Ed Keller, and the newspapers have been calling up. There's going to be a lot of trouble if you don't hurry up and deny that story of Michael's—or have you done it?

TOMMY: No—I haven't denied it.

ELLEN (*troubled*): You mean you've made up your mind to read it? Is that what you've been—walking around for? Tommy, I don't know what to say to you.

TOMMY: I think maybe you've said enough already.

ELLEN: That isn't very kind.

TOMMY: None of this is going to sound very kind but I've figured out exactly what I want to say, and I have to get it out before I get all mixed up.

ELLEN: I don't see why you are being so mean.

TOMMY: It's just last night I began to see you, and myself, clearly for the first time.

ELLEN: If this is a story you're writing, and you're trying it out on me, it isn't very good.

TOMMY: Oh, I saw you and Joe clearly, too.

ELLEN (*relieved, crosses to* TOMMY): Oh, you saw him kiss me. . . . I thought that was it. . . .

TOMMY: No. . . . No, I didn't. . . . Did he kiss you? Well, that's fine. . . . I've been meaning to ask you, what became of Housman's "Last Poems"? (*He turns to the bookshelves.*)

ELLEN: Tommy (*She puts her hand on his shoulder.*), listen to me. . . . I wanted to have a good time last night, and you spoiled it. . . .

TOMMY: Didn't you enjoy it at all?

ELLEN (*piqued*): Yes, I did. I'm not a hundred years old—yet. I just decided to quit worrying about you and have a little fun. For about an hour I felt like a girl again — wearing flowers at a Spring dance—when I was young and silly. . . .

TOMMY: Young and happy.

ELLEN: All right, he . . . kissed me. I kissed him, too. We didn't go out in the dark to do it.

TOMMY (*piling the books he is taking from the bookshelves on the settee*): I hope you didn't lend that book to anybody; it was a first edition.

ELLEN: Did you *hear* what I said?

TOMMY: Sure, I heard you. I'm listening. . . . You said you went out in the dark and kissed Joe.

ELLEN: I said no such thing! and you know it.

TOMMY: I wish we had had separate bookplates.

ELLEN (*beginning to flame*): So that when you really make me mad and I get out of here, I can find my own books quickly?

TOMMY: I hate sentimental pawing over things by a couple breaking up. We're not living in the days of Henry James and Meredith. Look at Joe and his wife.

ELLEN: Tommy. (*She goes to him again.*) I want you to stop this. If you're going to be jealous *be* jealous, rave or throw things, but don't act like the lead in a senior-class play! (*This thrust gets home.*) •

TOMMY (*angrily*): I'm trying to tell you that I don't care what you and Joe do! I'm trying to tell you that it's fine! It's very lucky that he came back just now.

ELLEN: Why, what do you mean?

TOMMY: I mean on the money *I* make, I can go on fine alone, reading whatever I want to to my classes! That's what I want! And that's what I'm going to do.

ELLEN: Oh, that's what you want! Suddenly that's what you want. More than me?

TOMMY: It isn't so sudden. Not any more sudden than your feeling for Joe. It's logical. We get in each other's way. You wear yourself out picking up after me. Taking matches out of my pockets. Disarranging my whole way of life. (*She follows him as he moves away from her.*)

ELLEN: Why haven't you said all this before?

TOMMY: I couldn't very well.

ELLEN: Why couldn't you? If you felt this way?

TOMMY: Well, we hadn't split up on this letter issue, for one thing—and then there was no place for you to go. (*He sits on a sofa.*) I didn't want you to have to go back to Cleveland, or to work in some tea shoppe!

ELLEN: Oh, I see. Some tea shoppe! That's what you think I'd have to do! Well, you needn't have spared my feelings. I can make as much money as you!

TOMMY: You don't have to, now.

ELLEN (*whirling*): Oh, you

379

mean you waited to tell me all this till Joe came along! I thought you were jealous of Joe. I could understand that. You aren't the least bit aroused at the idea of his kissing me—*out in the dark—for hours!*

TOMMY: No, I'm not.

ELLEN (*full of exclamation points*): So that's why you've been wandering around! That's what you've been figuring out! How nice it would be if he would take me off your hands, so you could be left alone with your books and match boxes and *litter!* I suppose any man would do as well as Joe! (*She rushes up to him.*)

TOMMY (*rising to face her*): He's not just any man, and you know that! He's always been in love with you, and you've always been in love with him! (*He is angry and jealous now and brings up his own exclamation points.*)

ELLEN: That's ridiculous!

TOMMY (*moving toward her*): I felt it when I saw you dancing together. It was unmistakable. You've just admitted it.

ELLEN: Oh, you can't do that *now!* You can't be jealous *now,* just because you think I want you to be!

TOMMY (*rising to his big denunciation*): I saw you dancing together—like angels! I saw you go out in that goddamn carriage together! I saw you together

years ago, when I was young enough and dumb enough to believe that I really took you away from him. There's something that happens when you two dance together that doesn't happen when *we* dance together!

ELLEN (*worried, angry and tired*): All right—have it your way. If you want to be free, then I want to be free—and I've gone around for ten years mooning about Joe. . . . Well, maybe I have—maybe I have, because I'm certainly sick of you right now! (*She whirls away from him.*)

TOMMY (*deathly afraid of her being sick of him*): Ellen . . . Ellen, listen!

ELLEN: Never mind—all right— *all right—* ALL RIGHT! (*She is shouting as* JOE *enters brightly.*)

JOE: Oh, I'm sorry—if I . . . (*He stops in embarrassment. There is a pause. He has caught only the tone; but he sees and feels the tension. He is carrying a wrapped bottle and a newspaper.*)

TOMMY: Hello, Joe.

JOE: Hello. I brought the rum. (*He crosses to the coffee table, puts the bottle on the table; holds up the newspaper.*) Big picture of Wally all over the front page. (ELLEN *stares out the window,* TOMMY *stares at* JOE.) Good picture, isn't it?

TOMMY: You and Ellen have

some rum.

JOE: The rum's for the punch—later.

ELLEN: Could I have some—now?

[TOMMY *goes out to dining room.*]

JOE (*surprised*): Right now? Sure.

TOMMY (*yelling from dining room*): I'll get you some glasses. (*He reappears with two glasses.*)

JOE (*unscrewing the top of the rum bottle*): Tommy, old man, I just left Ed Keller and Si McMillan. This thing your young friend wrote in the magazine. (*Pours a drink.*) I read that piece over again. He's got you on a spot, Tommy. (*He gives* ELLEN *her drink.*)

ELLEN: Want to drink a toast, Joe? To Tommy's happiness?

[JOE *looks at both of them.*]

JOE (*puzzled*): Sure. . . . (*Pours himself a drink.*) Your happiness, Tommy. (*They drink amid a long silence,* JOE *nervously finishing his,* ELLEN *taking a long drink, grimacing as it burns her throat.* JOE *decides to dive in.*) What's the matter? What's it about? Maybe I could talk to Ed . . .

᾽ TOMMY: No. I don't want that. I'll run my own life my own way.

ELLEN: That's what it's about. Tommy wants to—live alone.

JOE: What?

ELLEN: He wants to be left

alone. . . .

JOE: I beg your pardon?

ELLEN (*almost shouting*): Us! Tommy and me! We're breaking up!

JOE (*awed*): *Just before the game?* You're both crazy! Maybe I better go.

TOMMY: Not at all. You're not exactly a stranger around here. You knew Ellen as long ago as I did.

JOE: I knew her a long time before you did . . . and this is a hell of a way to be treating her.

TOMMY (*baiting a hook*): Yes, I know. I was just saying I barged in and took her away from you.

[ELLEN *stares at* TOMMY.]

JOE (*taking the bait*): Oh, no, you didn't! You had nothing to do with it. She got sore at me on account of another girl.

TOMMY (*triumphantly*): Oh, *that's* where I came in?

JOE: Sure. If you think you took her away from me, you're crazy. Here, you better have some rum.

ELLEN (*the wife*): He can't drink this early.

TOMMY: *I* don't *need* any rum. Go on, Joe.

JOE (*sitting near* TOMMY): Well, Ellen and I had a fight. You weren't in on it. You came in later. . . .

ELLEN (*wearily, also warily*): Joe, do we have to . . .

381

TOMMY: It's all right. It's his turn.

JOE: She said she hated me and never wanted to see me again. She threw something at me. She thought I slept with this girl—I mean . . .

TOMMY (*coolly*): I know what you mean. . . .

ELLEN (*indignantly*): I never said you sl . . . I never said that.

JOE (*turning from* TOMMY *to* ELLEN): Oh, yes, you did—you intimated it.

ELLEN: No, that was *your* idea. I thought you were bragging about it!

JOE (*turning farther away from* TOMMY): Well, you got awfully mad. I thought you never did want to see me again. I guess I was dumb. Brenda says it shows you liked me. (*From* ELLEN's *expression,* JOE *is reminded of* TOMMY's *presence. He turns to* TOMMY, *a little sheepishly.*) Oh —sorry.

TOMMY (*the tolerant man of the world*): Oh, don't mind me. Who's Brenda? Another girl?

JOE: My wife.

TOMMY: Oh, sorry.

JOE: Ellen knows her. She's from Cleveland. Brenda's always been jealous of Ellen. She found a picture of you.

TOMMY (*not so tolerant*): What picture?

ELLEN: I gave him a picture.

He wouldn't give it back.

JOE: It's a swell picture. You were wearing that floppy hat. Red.

ELLEN: Blue.

JOE: It had ribbons. Made you look like you were sixteen.

TOMMY: *I've* never seen it.

ELLEN: It was a silly hat. That was ages ago.

TOMMY: I mean, I've never seen the picture.

ELLEN (*angrily*): I threw them all away.

JOE (*looking back over the years*): It kind of went down over one eye.

TOMMY (*remembering an old lovely hat*): She looks nice in hats like that.

[ELLEN *suddenly begins to cry and collapses on the sofa.*]

JOE (*rising*): *Now* look what you've done!

TOMMY (*rising*): Look what *you've* done! Bringing up old floppy blue hats! (JOE *moves to* ELLEN.) Don't touch her! She doesn't like to be touched when she's crying.

JOE: I've seen her cry. I know what to do.

TOMMY: Oh, you do?

JOE: She cried when we had that fight about the girl. She was lying on the floor and crying and kicking—on her stomach.

ELLEN: I was not!

TOMMY: Be careful what you

say!

JOE: Well, I mean I knew what to do. (*Crosses to other end of sofa.*) I picked her up that time.

TOMMY (*following him*): Well, you're not going to pick her up now.

ELLEN: Will you both please let me alone?! Will you please go away!

JOE (*getting sore*): She wants you to go away. And I don't blame her, if this is the way you treat her. I wouldn't have stood for it ten years ago, and I'm not going to stand for it now.

TOMMY: But what are you going to do?

JOE: I'm going to get her away from all this! It isn't *nice!*

TOMMY: It isn't exactly to my taste, either. I didn't want it to turn out this way, but it did. Ellen crying, me feeling like a cad, and you acting like a fool.

JOE: *Me* acting like a fool?

ELLEN (*sitting up*): Everybody's acting like a fool.

JOE: You've certainly messed things up, brother.

TOMMY: Don't call me brother! I can't stand that now.

JOE: If Ellen weren't here, I'd call you worse than brother!

ELLEN: Well, I'm not going to be here! Please, please stop— both of you! Nobody has said a word about what I want to do. You're going to settle that between yourselves. Bandying me back and forth!

TOMMY: Nobody's bandying you, Ellen.

ELLEN (*mad*): I know when I'm being bandied! (*On her feet.*) I don't want either of you! You can both go to hell! (*She runs upstairs, crying.*)

[*Both men follow and look after her.*]

TOMMY: She means me.

JOE: She said both of us.

TOMMY: She was looking at me.

JOE: How did we get into this, anyway?

TOMMY: You two-stepped into it. You kissed your way into it.

JOE: I'm sorry about that. Sorry it happened.

TOMMY: You're not sorry it happened. You're sorry I found it out. Do you know anything about women? Didn't you know what she was thinking about when she was dancing with you?

JOE: No. I don't think when I'm dancing.

TOMMY: I know. You think in your office. Well, you'll have to think in your home after this. She likes to be thought about.

JOE: I thought about her. I remembered her birthday. I brought her flowers.

TOMMY: Well, you'll have to keep on bringing her things whether it's her birthday or not. Fur coats and—things. She's still

383

young and pretty.

JOE (*narrowing his eyes*): I don't get you.

TOMMY: I'm being broad-minded. I'm taking things in my stride. It's the modern way of doing things. You ought to know that.

JOE (*shrewdly*): Um, hm. But what makes me think you're still crazy about her and are up to some goddamn something or other?

TOMMY (*a little taken aback*): Don't be acute. I couldn't stand you being acute.

JOE: I'm not dumb.

TOMMY: Yes, you are. It isn't what *I* feel that counts. It's what *she* feels. I think she's always been in love with you. Why, I don't know. It's supposed to be beyond reason. I guess it is.

JOE: You think that just because of last night?

TOMMY: No. Because of what lay behind last night. That wasn't just a kiss. That's nothing. This thing is too deep for jealousy or for anything but honesty. A woman must not go on living with a man when she dances better with another man.

JOE: That's silly! *That's the silliest* . . . ! Dancing doesn't mean everything!

TOMMY: The way *you* do it does. The thing that happens to you. The *light* you give off.

JOE: *Light?!*

TOMMY: Oh, these things are too subtle for you, Joe. I've made some study of them. (*Turns away.*)

JOE: Maybe all this studying's bad for you.

TOMMY (*pinning him down*): All I want to know is whether you felt the same thing she felt last night.

JOE: I felt fine. This is god-damn embarrassing! A man makes love to a woman. He doesn't talk it over with her husband!

TOMMY: I'm just trying to be honest.

JOE: You're a funny guy. Con-scientious. What does it get you? Like this letter you're going to read. . . . Say, is that what started the trouble?

TOMMY: Yes, it's an integral part of the trouble—things like that.

JOE: Well, what are we going to do? I mean now? I mean from now on?

TOMMY: From now on will work itself out. Right now you'd better go upstairs and comfort her. She'll be expecting you.

JOE: Oh, no. Not me! You ought to know more what to do right now. It's your house. She's your wife.

TOMMY: She doesn't want to talk to me. She's just done that.

But she oughtn't to be left alone right now.

JOE (rises): Well—(*He takes a few steps.*) What'll I say?

TOMMY: What did you say last night, when you were dancing?

JOE (*going to the foot of the stairs*): It doesn't seem right somehow for me to go upstairs.

TOMMY: This is not a moment for cheap moralizing!

JOE: Well—good God almighty! (*He goes upstairs.*)

[MICHAEL *has come in the front door in time to hear* JOE's *last expletive.*]

MICHAEL (*as* TOMMY *looks after* JOE): What's the matter?

TOMMY: Never mind. . . . (*He paces, glares upstairs, still has his glare when he turns back to* MICHAEL.)

MICHAEL: Well, I came back like you said. Before you start in on me, Mr. Turner, please remember that I've been through a lot today. I can't stand much more. (TOMMY *pats him on shoulder. Gloomily.*) They'll probably do something to you—especially if we lose to Michigan. You know what Keller did the last time they beat us in a Homecoming Game? He ran the flag on his office building down to half-mast.

TOMMY (*looking upstairs—distracted*): Don't worry about me.

MICHAEL: Well, I'm feeling better. I've put her out of my mind.

It's ended as simply as that. (*He drops into a chair.*) There's a girl who could sit with you and talk about Shelley. Well, I'm glad I found out about women. (*Crash upstairs.*) What was that?

TOMMY: I'm sure I don't know. What were you saying?

MICHAEL: I say Patricia knew things. She knew odd things like "A Sonnet on Political Greatness." She quoted that one night. Wouldn't you think a girl like that had some social consciousness?

TOMMY: That's the sonnet that ends:

"Quelling the anarchy of
     hopes and fears,
     Being himself alone."

MICHAEL: Yes, but when an issue comes up and a man has to be himself alone, she reveals the true stature of her character and goes off to Hennick's with that football player. I saw them—right in the front window—drinking Seven-Up. He uses a straw.

TOMMY: Yes, but he's handsome. What is more, he whirls. He's a hunter. He comes home at night with meat slung over his shoulders, and you sit there drawing pictures on the wall of your cave.

MICHAEL: I see. Maybe I ought to sock him with a ball-bat.

TOMMY: No. You are a civilized man, Michael. If the male animal in you doesn't like the full implications of that, he must neverthe-less be swayed by Reason. You are not living in the days of King Arthur when you fought for your woman. Nowadays, the man and his wife and the other man talk it over. Quietly and calmly. They all go out to dinner together. (*He sits on the sofa across the stage from* MICHAEL.)

MICHAEL: Intellectually, Patricia is sleeping with that guy. I feel like going out tonight with the Hot Garters.

TOMMY: With the what?

MICHAEL: It's a girl. They call her that. What if she was kicked out of the Pi Phi House? She's honest! She does what she be-lieves in! And—well, Hot Garters doesn't argue all the time anyway.

TOMMY (*removing his glasses*): Look, hasn't she got a name? You don't call her *that*, do you?

MICHAEL: Marcia Gardner. They just call her . . .

TOMMY: Yes, you told me what they call her.

[*Slight pause.*]

MICHAEL: Patricia's not coming to class when you read that letter. She's gone over to the Philistines. . . . Oh, God, Mr. Turner, I wish I were like you! Middle-aged, settled down, happily married—and through with all this hell you feel when you're young and in love.

TOMMY (*nettled*): Middle-

aged?

MICHAEL: Yes, you know what Rupert Brooke says:
"That time when all is over. . . .
(TOMMY *writhes, turns his back.*)
And love has turned to kindliness."
Is kindliness peaceful?

TOMMY: Don't ask *me*. (*Two quick crashes from upstairs bring* TOMMY *to his feet just as* JOE *hurries down the stairs, looking worn and worried, his hair slightly dis-arranged. Sharply.*) You look ruffled!

JOE (*just as sharply, but a bit absently*): What? (*The two men look each other over.*)

TOMMY: I say—what ruffled you?

JOE: Do we have to discuss these things in front of this boy?

MICHAEL (*rising*): I am not a boy.

TOMMY: This is Michael Barnes.

JOE: Oh, so you're the little boy that started all this! I want to tell you that you write too much, you have too much to say, you get too many people into too much trou-ble. You've not only got Tommy and Ellen involved, but me.

MICHAEL: I don't see how this concerns you, do you, Mr. Turner?

TOMMY: Yes.

MICHAEL: Oh, well, I'll go out and climb a tree, Mr. Turner. I'll come back when this blows over. (*Goes out into the garden.*)

JOE: Oh, God, I wish I was in Pittsburgh! (*He sits heavily in chair vacated by* MICHAEL.)

TOMMY (*eagerly*): What happened?

JOE: Well, old man, I guess you're right. She was pretty bitter—about you. She picked up something you'd given her and threw it against the wall and broke it into a thousand pieces.

TOMMY: What was it?

JOE: I didn't see it till after she threw it.

TOMMY: Oh.

JOE: Every time she mentioned your name, she threw something. Kept me ducking.

TOMMY (*sadly*): I see. (*He, too, sits heavily on the large sofa.*) You want to marry Ellen, don't you?

JOE: Well, I always liked her, but I don't like to go through so much. (*Pause.*) Are you sure you understand women?

TOMMY: Yes.

JOE: Well, when Ellen and I had that fight about the girl, she threw things on account of me, and Brenda thinks that meant she was in love with me. Now she throws things on account of *you*.

TOMMY (*after an instant of hope*): In both instances, she threw them at *you*, didn't she?

JOE (*glumly*): Yeh, I guess so.

TOMMY: Well, there you are. What did she say when you left? What was she doing?

JOE: She was in a terrible state. I don't think she'll be able to go to the game. She may have a sick headache for days. What do you do then?

TOMMY (*rises, and goes to dining room with sudden efficiency*): You get her a hot-water bottle. Cleota! Cleota!

CLEOTA (*off-stage*): Yes, suh?

TOMMY (*off-stage*): There's a hot-water bottle out there in the . . . somewhere. Fill it and bring it in, please.

CLEOTA (*off-stage*): Yes, *suh.*

[TOMMY *returns.* JOE *glances at his wrist watch, rises, and paces across stage.*]

JOE: I don't want to miss this game. I sort of wish Stalenkiwiecz wasn't laid up, don't you?

TOMMY (*sits on sofa again*): I haven't given it much thought one way or another.

JOE: Of course, Wierasocka's all right, but Stalenkiwiecz is a better pass receiver.

TOMMY: Is he? Why?

JOE: I don't know why. He just is. "Why!" (*His pacing has carried him to the door leading to the garden. He remembers the vanishing pitcher and takes one more look, then resumes his prowl.*) 'Course they may not give Brenda a divorce.

TOMMY: I think they will.

JOE: I don't know.

[CLEOTA *comes in with hot-water bottle and towel. She hands them to* TOMMY.]

CLEOTA: Is you gotta pain?

TOMMY: No. Oh, thank you.

[CLEOTA *retires.*]

JOE: I don't suppose we ought to go and leave her.

TOMMY (*going to him with bottle*): Oh, I'm not going. Here. (*Hands him bottle and towel.*)

JOE (*taking it as if it were a baby*): Ow!

TOMMY: Hold it by the end.

JOE: Won't this thing burn her?

TOMMY (*impatiently, showing him*): You wrap the towel around it.

JOE: You shouldn't stay here in the house alone with her, things being the way they are, should you?

TOMMY (*turning away*): Please don't worry about that!

JOE (*looking at the bottle*): I thought these things were different now than they used to be.

TOMMY: What do you mean, different?

JOE: I mean better looking . . . somehow. (*There is a pause during which* JOE *tries to wrap the towel around the hot-water bottle, but various parts of it insist on remaining exposed. Finally* TOMMY *crosses down to* JOE *angrily.*)

TOMMY: Well, why don't you take it up to her?

ELLEN (*coming down the stairs*): It's time to get started, isn't it? (*The two men turn and stare at her,* JOE *still holding the hot-water bottle.* ELLEN *is utterly serene, with no sign of tears or hysterics. Washed and powdered, with her hat on, she stands at the foot of the stairs, ready for the game.*) Do you realize what time it is? The Kellers will be waiting for us at Esther Baker's. We'll leave the car there and walk to the stadium. It's only a block. (*The men are still staring.*) What are you doing with that thing, Joe?

TOMMY: He was going to lie down with it for a while.

JOE: I was not! Here! (*Tries to hand it to* TOMMY.)

TOMMY: I don't want it.

ELLEN: We've got to hurry, Joe. (*Takes the bottle from* JOE *and puts it on the sofa.*) Have you got the tickets?

JOE: Yeh, I've got them. (*Goes to radio.*) Say, what number is the game on?

ELLEN: It's around 1210 on the dial. (*As* JOE *turns on radio and fiddles with dial,* ELLEN *turns to* TOMMY.) Sure you won't go to the game?

TOMMY. Oh, no. . . . (*With shy politeness.*) How are you?

ELLEN (*as if surprised at the question*): Me? I'm fine.

[As JOE *keeps fiddling with dials, dance music comes on, then band music.*]

TOMMY: That's good.

JOE: Well, it hasn't started yet —just music. Let's go. (*Gets* ELLEN'S *coat from hook.*) This yours?

ELLEN: Yes.

JOE: Well, is it warm enough?

ELLEN: Yes. Oh, it's very warm.

TOMMY (*angrily*): No, it isn't.

[CLEOTA *enters with the thermos, which she gives to* TOMMY.]

CLEOTA: Here's your thermos, Mr. Turner.

TOMMY: Thank you. (*Takes it.* CLEOTA *goes out.*)

ELLEN: It's a very warm day, anyway, and we'll have the lap robe from the car.

TOMMY: Ellen. (*She goes to him eagerly.*) You forgot your thermos bottle. . . . (*His tone is jocular, and he pretends to screw the cap on tighter to cover his hurt.*) You'd better make a note of this, Joe. It gets cold in stadiums late in the afternoon. Ellen gets chilly sometimes, so she likes hot coffee. . . . Well, here. (*He hands thermos to* ELLEN. JOE *nods, goes to the front door, and opens it.* ELLEN, *who has been staring at* TOMMY, *suddenly throws the thermos bottle on the floor, then rushes out, passing* JOE. JOE *looks after her, then comes back to face* TOMMY *threateningly.*)

JOE: Did you slap her?

TOMMY: No, I kicked her.

JOE: Well, you did something!

[*An* ANNOUNCER'S VOICE *breaks into the band music.*]

ANNOUNCER'S VOICE: Well, here we are on Midwestern's field on a mighty fine afternoon for a football game. . . . It looks like the Big Day of the year, folks. Neither one of these great teams has lost a game. The Michigan squad is out on the field warming up. They look even bigger than last year. . . .

JOE (*torn between interest in the announcement and his aroused chivalry*): Here I get her all calmed down and you make her cry again. I see now what kind of a life she has here. I'm going to take her away from this and keep her away!

TOMMY (*shouting*): All right! Why don't you get started?

JOE (*topping him*): Because I've got a few more things to say to you. First! (*As he takes a breath, the* ANNOUNCER'S VOICE *comes through clearly.*)

ANNOUNCER'S VOICE: Here comes the Scarlet Stampede now! (*There is a roar of cheering.*)

JOE: My God, they're coming out on the field! We'll miss the kick-off! *God damn it!!* (*He turns and dashes out the front door.* TOMMY *stands looking after him as the band blares, and the*

CURTAIN FALLS

SCENE II: *The Turner living room, two hours later. It is growing dark outside.* TOMMY *and* MICHAEL *are sitting in chairs wide apart, facing the audience, so that they have to turn their heads to see each other. Each has a glass in his hand, and they are sprawled in their chairs, silent, brooding. The room shows indications of quite a bout: a bottle here, a few magazines flung there, a cushion on the floor.* TOMMY *gets the Scotch bottle, pours a little into* MICHAEL'S *glass, emptying the bottle. He starts to pour some into his own glass, finds the bottle empty so pours some from* MICHAEL'S *glass into his own. Throws the bottle into the wastebasket. There is a pause.*

MICHAEL: He is probably still running with that ball. . . .

[*Pause.*]

TOMMY: Quiet — quiet! . . . What time is it?

MICHAEL (*looks at his wrist watch, has trouble seeing it*): It's getting dark.

[*Pause.*]

TOMMY: Do you know the first law of human nature?

MICHAEL: Yes. Self-propagation.

TOMMY: Not any more. That's gone with last year's nightingale.

MICHAEL: Gone with last year's rose.

[*Slight pause.*]

TOMMY: Yes. . . . Defense of the home. . . . Against prowlers and predatory — prowlers. . . . Do you know what the tiger does when the sanctity of his home is jeopardized?

MICHAEL: I know. You told me. He talks it over with the other man, quietly and calmly.

TOMMY: He does not. I am ashamed of you.

MICHAEL: I think we must have another drink—possibly.

TOMMY: All right. Hey! HEY! (*He is pleased with this shouting.*) That's the way to talk to 'em. (*He puts back his head and yells.*) HEYYY!!

[CLEOTA *enters, and turns on the lights.*]

CLEOTA: Mistah Turner, what is it?

TOMMY: What do you want? Oh, we should like to have something more to drink.

CLEOTA: They ain' any more to drink. I'll make you some black coffee. (*She goes out.*)

TOMMY (*pause*): What'd she say?

MICHAEL: Nothing.

TOMMY: Where was I?

MICHAEL: Let's see—you were talking about tigers.

TOMMY: Oh, yes. But let us take the wolf. What does he do? I mean, when they come for his mate. He tears 'em to pieces.

390

MICHAEL: But we are civilized men. Aren't we?

TOMMY: And so does the leopard, and the lion, and the hawk. They tear 'em to pieces. Without a word.

MICHAEL: You had it figured out the other way around a while ago. You said we should give up our women. (TOMMY *stands, falters.*) It's better sitting down. (TOMMY *sits.*)

TOMMY: Let us say that the tiger wakes up one morning and finds that the wolf has come down on the fold. What does he—? Before I tell you what he does, I will tell you what he does not do.

MICHAEL: Yes, sir.

TOMMY: He does not expose everyone to a humiliating intellectual analysis. He comes out of his corner like this—(*Rises, assuming an awkward fighting pose, fists up, then sits quickly again.*) The bull elephant in him is aroused.

MICHAEL (*plaintively*): Can't you stick to one animal?

TOMMY: No, that's my point. All animals are the same, including the human being. We are male animals, too. (MICHAEL *stares at him, bewildered.*)

MICHAEL: You said . . .

TOMMY: Even the penguin. (*His voice shows some emotion as he thinks of the penguin.*) He stands for no monkey-business where his mate is concerned. Swans have been known to drown scotties who threatened their nests.

MICHAEL: I don't think so.

TOMMY: There it is, in us always, though it may be asleep. The male animal. The mate. When you are married long enough, you become a mate. . . . Think of the sea-lion for a minute.

MICHAEL: All right.

TOMMY: His mate is lying there in a corner of the cave on a bed of tender boughs or something. (*Turns to* MICHAEL *for confirmation.*) Is that all right, "tender boughs"?

MICHAEL: Yeah!

TOMMY (*illustrating by a gesture, a great seal, or eel*): Now, who comes swimming quietly in through the early morning mist, sleek and powerful, dancing and whirling and throwing kisses?

MICHAEL: Joe Ferguson.

TOMMY: And what do I do?

MICHAEL: You say, "Hello."

TOMMY (*in self-disgust*): The sea-lion knows better. He snarls. He gores. He roars with his antlers. He knows that love is a thing you do something about. He knows it is a thing that words can kill. You do something. You don't just sit there. (MICHAEL *rises.*) I don't mean you. (MICHAEL *sits.*) A woman likes a man who does something. All the male animals fight for the female, from the land crab to the bird of paradise. They don't just sit and talk. They act. (*He removes his glasses and blinks owlishly around.*) I hope I have made all this clear to you. Are there any questions?

MICHAEL: No, sir.

[ELLEN *and* JOE *enter.* ELLEN *takes in the disordered room, the bottles on the floor,* TOMMY'S *and* MICHAEL'S *condition.* MICHAEL *and* TOMMY *rise.*]

ELLEN: Tommy! What in the world have you been doing?

TOMMY: Drinking.

ELLEN: What for?

TOMMY: I was celebrating. Ellen, I have found myself. (*Glances at* JOE.) I know now what I have to do.

ELLEN: Yes, I know. We've been through all that.

TOMMY: Perhaps you had better go away for a little while. (*Waves toward stairs.*)

ELLEN: I'm going. I'll be down in a minute, Joe. (*She slams upstairs.*)

JOE: Boy, wasn't that some football game? I'm running Wally Myers for President.

TOMMY (*beckoning to* MICHAEL): Come on. (*With drunken carefulness, he and* MIKE *begin moving furniture to the sides of the room.*)

JOE (*watches, slightly puzzled,*

making talk): Yes, sir, some game, wasn't it? What did you think of Michigan going into the lead like that? If Wally hadn't snared that pass . . .

MICHAEL: We didn't listen to the game.

JOE: You didn't listen to the game?

MICHAEL: No, we turned it off. (*He flips off an imaginary dial.*)

TOMMY: The game didn't last all this time. Where have you been?

JOE: Well, we stopped in at President Cartwright's house.

TOMMY: What for?

JOE: 'Cause Ellen and I were making one last effort to get you out of this mess.

TOMMY: Ellen and you. You would know exactly what to do, wouldn't you?

JOE: You guys are pie-eyed!

TOMMY (*to* MICHAEL): Did you hear that?

MICHAEL: Yes.

JOE: What's the idea of moving all the furniture around like this?

TOMMY: I don't want you to break anything when you fall.

JOE: I'm not going to fall.

TOMMY: Yes, you are. I am going to knock you cold. (*The furniture safe,* TOMMY *rolls up his sleeves, and* MICHAEL *sits on the arm of a settee, watching.*)

JOE (*kindly*): Let's sit down and talk this over.

TOMMY (*turning to* MICHAEL): Talk, he says, to a man of action. Sit down, he says, to a tigress and her cubs!

JOE: How the hell did you guys get so cockeyed? I wish Ellen'd hurry up. (*Goes to dining-room door.*) Cleota!

TOMMY: Don't call for help. I could take Cleota and you in the same ring!

JOE: Well, what's this all about?

TOMMY: You crept into this house to take Ellen away, didn't you? You thought it was the house of a professor who would talk and *talk* and TALK . . .

JOE: And by God you have! I came here to see a football game—

MICHAEL: That's a lie.

JOE: Why don't you go home?

MICHAEL: 'Cause I want to watch.

JOE: Well, there isn't going to be anything to watch.

TOMMY (*assuming a fighter's pose*): Come on, put up your fists.

JOE: Get away from me, Tommy. (*Pushes* TOMMY's *arm which pivots* TOMMY *around so he faces* MICHAEL.) I'd break you in two, and I don't want to do that.

TOMMY (*speaking first to* MIKE, *then, realizing he is facing the wrong way, turning to* JOE): Why don't you want to do that?

JOE: 'Cause how would it look if I came here and took Ellen and

knocked you down on the way out?

MICHAEL: Maybe he's right. That's a point of honor, Mr. Turner.

TOMMY: Is it?

MICHAEL: But we could fight him about something else.

TOMMY: About what?

MICHAEL: He doesn't want you to read that letter.

TOMMY: That's right. (MICHAEL *rises and slowly moves to a spot behind* JOE.) Going to the president's office. Trying to make me lose my job.

JOE: Why the hell should I?

TOMMY: So you could get Ellen.

JOE: Now, listen—

TOMMY: Yes! Now I'm going to have to knock you further than I had previously decided upon. Come out in the back yard. (*He tugs at* JOE, *but doesn't move him.* MICHAEL *helpfully gives* JOE *a good push.*)

JOE (*turns and strides back to* MICHAEL): Don't push me!

TOMMY: Hey! (*As* JOE *turns,* TOMMY *lunges at* JOE *with a badly aimed haymaker.* JOE *ducks and catches* TOMMY *to keep him from falling.*)

JOE: Now look, if you do ever get in a fight, Tommy, don't lead with your right. It leaves you wide open.

TOMMY: Oh, does it?

[ELLEN *comes down the stairs with*

a suitcase which she drops when she sees the odd positions of the belligerents.]

ELLEN: What's happened? Tommy, what are you doing now?

TOMMY: Fighting.

[*The music of the band is heard in the distance. Through the following scene it grows louder to* ELLEN'*s exit, then dies away as the band goes around the corner, and comes up again for the end of the scene.*]

ELLEN (*hopefully*): Fighting! What about?

MICHAEL: Penguins.

ELLEN: What!

JOE (*trying to explain*): Oh, it was all mixed up—about that letter thing and a lot of tigers and a cub. Tommy doesn't care what you and I are trying to do! He wants us to stay out of it!

ELLEN (*disappointed bitterly*): Oh, I see. That's what you were fighting about.

TOMMY: It wasn't about you. Point of honor.

ELLEN: Oh, yes, I see. You don't want me mixed up in anything. All right. You can pull the house down on top of you with your damn birds and letters and whiskey. Just let me get out of—what is all that racket!!

JOE (*opens the door a crack, then closes it*): Oh, they're having a victory parade, and they want me to ride in that damn carriage with Wally Myers and the band.

TOMMY: You attract bands like flies, don't you?

ELLEN (*as she starts for the door*): Good-bye, Tommy! I'll be out in the car, Joe! Bring my bag, please! (*She slams out. The men look after her; then* JOE *gets* ELLEN'*s bag, and faces* TOMMY.)

JOE: You're getting me in deeper and deeper! I shoulda taken a poke at you when I had the chance!

TOMMY: Fine! Come out in the back yard! (*He walks to the garden door, holds it open.*)

JOE: I'm not coming out in the back yard! (MICHAEL *pushes him, and* TOMMY, *catching him, turns him around to the lower door.*) Don't push me. I said, I don't like to be pushed!

TOMMY: No . . . You said, Don't lead with your right." (*He hits* JOE *on the nose with his* left *hand.*)

JOE (*pinching bridge of nose*): Ow-w-w! Now you've started my sinus trouble! (*He flings down suitcase and spreads his hand easily across* TOMMY'*s face.*) By God, if you want a fight, you've got a fight! (*He pushes* TOMMY *outside, his arms flailing the air.*)

[MICHAEL *plants a chair in front of the door and sits watching the fight off-stage. He applauds its progress.*]

MICHAEL: Hit him! Hit him! (*Quotes softly:*)
"And all the summer after-
noon
They hunted us and slew!
But tomorrow—by the liv-
ing God!
We'll try the game again!"
Don't forget to lead with your right, Mr. Turner! . . . That's right! Right in the eye!
[CLEOTA *is attracted from the din-
ing room by the noise.* WALLY
and PATRICIA *come in the
front door, rush over to* MI-
CHAEL, *who bars the door
with outstretched arms.*]
PATRICIA: Michael!
WALLY: What's going on here?
CLEOTA (*peering at fight off-
scene*): Godamighty!
PATRICIA: Oh—Michael, stop them! Wally, stop them!
MICHAEL: No, don't stop them! Let Mr. Turner alone and he'll tear him to pieces!
[*Crash outside.*]
WALLY: Get away from that door! (*He hurls* MICHAEL *aside.*
PATRICIA *runs and kneels beside*

MICHAEL.)
PATRICIA: Michael! Michael!
[ELLEN *re-enters the front door,
calling:*]
ELLEN: Joe, are you coming? (*She sees* MICHAEL *and* PATRICIA *on the floor, and looks around the room for* TOMMY *and* JOE. MI-
CHAEL *continues to quote poetry dramatically.*)
MICHAEL (*with rapid fervor*):
"And many-a-broken heart is
here . . ."
ELLEN: What is it?
MICHAEL:
"And many-a-broken head,
But tomorrow—by the liv-
ing God!—
We'll try the game again!"
(*He tries to rise;* PATRICIA *drops
him in disgust.*)
PATRICIA: Oh, Michael!
[JOE *and* WALLY *carry in the
unconscious* TOMMY, *and de-
posit him on the sofa.*]
ELLEN (*screams*): Tommy!!
[*The phone rings insistently.*]
CLEOTA (*shouts imperturbably
into phone*): Professah Turner's res-i-dence!

THE CURTAIN FALLS SWIFTLY

ACT III

SCENE: *The Turner living room. Same as Acts One and Two.
About noon, Monday. The room is neat and orderly, but the flowers
and other signs of festivity have been removed. The stage is empty,
but the telephone bell is ringing. A moment later, the doorbell also
begins to sound insistently.* CLEOTA *enters from the dining room,*

wiping her hands on her apron, scuttles for an instant between the bells, picks up phone.

CLEOTA (*into phone*): Stop ringin' dis thing both at once . . . Who? . . . Ah cain' heah you foh de ringin'. Hol' on . . . (*Putting down the receiver, she hurries to the front door and opens it cautiously, bracing herself to prevent a forced entrance. She speaks through the crack of the door to the man standing there.*) Ah tol' you to stop ringin' eve'ything. Ah'm heah, ain' I?

REPORTER: I'd like to see Mr. Turner.

CLEOTA: Is you a newspapah?

REPORTER: Yeh, I'm from the *Daily Journal.*

CLEOTA: He cain' see nobody—he's sick.

REPORTER: I know—but will he be up today? Is he going to his class?

CLEOTA: He ain' goin' nowheah. His haid huhts him. He's sick. Go 'way. (*She forces the door shut, returns to the telephone.*) Professah Turner's res-i-dence. . . . Daily what? . . . You jus' *was* heah. . . . No, Professah Turner ain' talkin' to nobody. He's sick in bed with his haid. . . . No, he ain' goin' an' you ain' comin'. He ain' not talkin' 'cause he doan wanta talk. He jus' ain' talkin' 'cause he cain' talk. Goo'bye. (*The bolted door is rattled from*

outside, then the doorbell begins to ring insistently. CLEOTA *looks at the door angrily and starts for it. She looks back at the phone and mutters.*) What's goin' on heah? . . . I told you to go 'way. (*She opens the door and* PATRICIA *enters.*)

PATRICIA: What's the matter?

CLEOTA (*giggling in embarrassment*): Oh, it's you. I thought it was that newspapah again. He jus' went.

PATRICIA: He didn't go—he's outside picketing. Where's my sister, Cleota?

CLEOTA: Upstaihs . . . Miss Patricia, Ah wish Ah knew bettah what's goin' on heah.

PATRICIA: Never mind.

CLEOTA: Mr. Michael jus' left.

PATRICIA: Oh. Well, if Mr. Michael Barnes comes here again, *don't let him in!*

CLEOTA: No, ma'am. (CLEOTA *goes into the dining room just as* ELLEN, *looking very depressed, comes from upstairs.*)

PATRICIA: Hello, Ellen. How's Tommy? Is he still asleep?

ELLEN: Yes, but he tosses around and mutters. The doctor says he can get up this afternoon.

PATRICIA: No concussion, then?

ELLEN: Yes, a little.

PATRICIA (*seating herself on set-*

tee): I guess when anybody's as crazy as Tommy or Michael, a little concussion doesn't make any difference.

ELLEN: Did you get the butter?

PATRICIA: Oh, Lord, no. I'll go back.

ELLEN: Never mind. I need a little air.

PATRICIA: How's *your* head?

ELLEN: Oh, all right.

PATRICIA: Is it? Say, what is this second springtime you're all going through, anyway?

ELLEN: Tommy won't let me in on what he's really thinking about. He thinks I'm not smart enough to understand it—that's what it comes down to.

PATRICIA: Oh, a mental problem. I haven't been exactly listening at keyholes, but isn't there a Joe Something-or-other mixed up in this?

ELLEN: Oh, there's more to it than a fight about Joe.

PATRICIA: Pretty good one round here Saturday about Joe. (*Then, directly.*) You know Tommy was fighting for you in his mid-Victorian way, don't you?

ELLEN: Oh, but he was drunk. When he's sober he despises me. He thinks I'm a dim-wit.

PATRICIA: Oh, he wouldn't want you any other way than you are.

ELLEN: Thanks.

PATRICIA: I mean you're smart enough for Tommy, and you know

it, and he knows it.

ELLEN (*unhappily*): I'm all mixed up. I want to go away some place where I can think.

PATRICIA: Look: this is a new century. You're not Diana-of-the-Crossways or somebody.

ELLEN: Well, what do you want me to do—stay here when he doesn't want me?

PATRICIA (*vigorously*): No, but if you're going away, go away with Joe. Tommy's certainly been throwing you at him. Why don't you take him up on it? See what happens.

ELLEN: Is this advice to the lovelorn? Do you think he would come running after me?

PATRICIA: Well, you've got to quit moping around and do something. I thought we Stanley women were supposed to have some resources. (*Rises and faces* ELLEN.) Look, your great-grandmother chased her man all the way to Nebraska in a covered wagon.

ELLEN: Well, I'm not going to chase anybody anywhere! I'm going to talk this over with Tommy, fairly and squarely, face to face. (*Starts to front door.*)

PATRICIA: "Fairly and squarely!" How did your generation ever get through the 1920's?

ELLEN (*sadly*): We didn't. (*She goes out.*)

[PATRICIA *sighs in despair.*

397

TOMMY *comes slowly down-stairs. He wears a terry-cloth bathrobe, and has a wet turk-ish towel twisted about his head.*]

TOMMY: Hello, Pat.

PATRICIA: Tommy—you should-n't be up!

TOMMY: I'm all right. What day is this?

PATRICIA: Monday.

TOMMY: Cleota! Cleota! (*To* PATRICIA.) Can I take this thing off?

PATRICIA: You're not supposed to. You ought to lie down. (TOMMY *sinks in chair.*)

TOMMY: I'll just lean back. (*Winces as he tries it.*) No—I guess I won't.

[CLEOTA *appears in dining-room door.*]

CLEOTA: Mistah Turner—is you up?

TOMMY: Yes, I'm up. Cleota, don't let anyone in this house ex-cept Mr. Michael Barnes.

[PATRICIA *shakes her head "No" to* CLEOTA.]

CLEOTA (*nodding to both*): Yes-suh—Ah do de best Ah can. (*Backs out of room.*)

TOMMY: Where's Ellen?

PATRICIA: She went out to—to get the transfer man—for her trunk.

TOMMY: She's going away?

PATRICIA: Oh, no. She just likes to call on transfer men. Didn't

you know that?

TOMMY: I can't stand irony so early in the day, Patricia.

PATRICIA: You're all right now, you see. She wouldn't go before. I don't know why.

TOMMY: You ought to know why. Your sister wouldn't walk out on anybody when he's down —even when he's down with de-lirium tremens.

PATRICIA: You didn't have D.T.'s. You had concussion.

TOMMY: Seemed more like D.T.'s.

PATRICIA: You don't know very much about my little sister, do you?

TOMMY: I know a lot more than I did last Friday. I think I will lie down. (*Goes to sofa.*)

PATRICIA: Why do you have to make everything as hard as you can? (TOMMY *groans a little with pain.*) Do you want another cold towel?

TOMMY: No, thanks.

[*Phone rings.*]

PATRICIA (*answering phone*): Yes? . . . Who? No, Michael Barnes isn't here.

TOMMY (*lying down carefully*): He was here and he's coming back.

PATRICIA: This is Patricia Stan-ley. . . . Yes . . . Yes . . . I'll be very glad to tell him to call you—if I see him. Good-bye. (*Slams receiver down.*) That was

398

Hot Garters Gardner!

TOMMY: Oh. Why did she call here?

PATRICIA: She said they told her Michael was on his way here, but obviously she just called for my benefit . . . So that's where he went Saturday night! You had that Hot—that Miss Gardner in some of your classes; do you remember her?

TOMMY (reflectively): I don't know. What does she look like?

PATRICIA: Well, she—doesn't wear any . . . (Gestures a brassière.)

TOMMY: I only had her in Wordsworth.

PATRICIA: Calling up here! (There is a knock at the door; PATRICIA smiles grimly. She goes to the door and opens it. MICHAEL steps in; he is taken aback at seeing PATRICIA.) Good morning, Michael. Come in.

TOMMY (in warning, sepulchral tones): Yes, come in, Michael. (PATRICIA's back is turned so TOMMY pantomimes "telephone" for MICHAEL's benefit. MICHAEL peers at him nervously.)

MICHAEL: I got the car for you. . . . Feel better now that you're up? (Doesn't get the pantomime.)

TOMMY: Yes, much better. How do you feel?

MICHAEL: I feel all right.

TOMMY: That's good. (Mimics

PATRICIA's brassière gesture.)

PATRICIA (turning): If you'll excuse me . . .

MICHAEL: Oh, Pat, wait! I— could I talk to you for a minute? Couldn't we go outside there and . . .

PATRICIA: No, we couldn't go outside there! Is it anything you're ashamed to say in front of Tommy?

MICHAEL (stiffening): No. No, I'm not. Only— Well, I don't want to get off on the wrong foot again. I'm sorry I got so mad Saturday. I said things and did things that . . .

PATRICIA: You certainly did!

MICHAEL: Well, I'm sorry, and . . . Oh, Pat, you ought to be able to see this my way. We just lost our tempers and—well—Mr. Turner and I are in a jam. I think you ought to—well—make an effort to understand what we're trying to do and stand by us—that is, if you care anything about me at all.

PATRICIA (so sweetly): Oh, I certainly do. I've been standing by—taking messages for you— phone calls. I'm so glad we had this nice talk. (Shakes his hand.) And before you go, be sure to call Maple 4307! (She hurls the last at him furiously, then sweeps out the front door.)

MICHAEL (looking after her): Maple 430 . . . (Horrified, as he

399

realizes who the number belongs to.) Did The Garters call here?

TOMMY: That's what I was trying to tell you. Patricia answered the phone. The—elastics —snapped right in her face.

MICHAEL: And I didn't even *do* anything. (*Sits beside* TOMMY *on sofa.*) I hope.

TOMMY: Michael, you're making me nervous.

[*A pause.*]

MICHAEL: Will you be able to go to the faculty meeting tonight?

TOMMY: I'll be there.

MICHAEL: They'll be out to get you. . . . I know this is all my fault, Mr. Turner.

TOMMY: Yes, you're certainly the man that lighted the match.

MICHAEL: I just came from the president's office; he flayed me alive.

TOMMY: Are you kicked out?

MICHAEL: Suspended.

TOMMY: Michael, tell me . . . are you really a Communist?

MICHAEL: Me? No. I only know one guy who is. I'm—well, I guess I'm an unconfused liberal. . . . I think I'll go to Stringfellow Barr's School in Annapolis and read the classics.

TOMMY: I wonder where I'll go?

[ELLEN *enters front door with parcel.*]

MICHAEL (*rises*): Hello, Mrs. Turner.

ELLEN: Good morning. (*Sees*

TOMMY.) Good morning, Tommy. . . . (*Goes to dining-room door and calls.*) Cleota . . .

TOMMY: Good morning.

[CLEOTA *enters.*]

ELLEN: Here's the butter, Cleota. Will you make Mr. Turner a cup of tea? (*Turns back to him.*) Would you like a hard-boiled egg?

TOMMY: No, thanks. Nothing hard. My teeth hurt.

[CLEOTA *retires.*]

ELLEN: Are you waiting for Patricia, Michael?

MICHAEL: I saw her. I'm leaving town, Mrs. Turner.

ELLEN: I'm awfully sorry, Michael.

WALLY (*off-stage*): Pat! Oh, Pat!

ELLEN: Come in, Wally. (WALLY *comes in from the garden.*) Patricia's gone out somewhere.

WALLY: Oh, I see. (*To* MICHAEL.) You waiting for her?

MICHAEL: That's none of your business. Why? (*He strides over to* WALLY.)

WALLY (*lowers his voice*): I know what you did Saturday night, that's why. Well, thanks, Mrs. Turner. I just cut across the back way. I'll walk on down to the house. (*Starts out.*)

MICHAEL (*stops him*): I think I'll walk along down to the house. I want to talk to you.

WALLY: You don't have to.

MICHAEL: If I didn't have to, I wouldn't do it. I'm no masochist. (*Starts out.* 'WALLY *stares after him blankly, then follows.*)

WALLY: You don't have to use words like that in front of ladies!

MICHAEL: I'll be back in time to drive you to class, Mr. Turner.

[*Both boys go out.*]

TOMMY: Thanks.

[CLEOTA *enters, and* ELLEN *takes the tray from her.*]

ELLEN: Here's your tea.

[CLEOTA *goes out.*]

TOMMY: Thanks.

ELLEN (*with some constraint*): How do you feel?

TOMMY: Very strange.

ELLEN: Is everything clear to you now?

TOMMY: Clear in the center. It's kind of fuzzy around the edges.

[ELLEN *has made up her mind what she wants to say; she seats herself and begins.*]

ELLEN: I hope it's clear enough to give me a chance to say something, without your going off on one of your literary tangents.

TOMMY: I don't do that.

ELLEN: I know you think I'm not very bright or something (TOMMY *tries to demur, but she continues.*) but you must realize that you got me all mixed up Friday, and that you were even less helpful Saturday.

TOMMY: That wasn't me Saturday. That was a drunken sea-lion.

ELLEN: I rather liked you as a sea-lion.

TOMMY: Yes, I must have been very funny. Did you ever read Hodgson's poem, "The Bull"?

ELLEN: Oh, Tommy!

TOMMY: It's the story of the defeated male. There is no defeat that can be quite so complete.

ELLEN: You wouldn't admit that this defeat was on account of— No, it has to be something out of a book.

TOMMY: "When the bull's head is in the dust, life goes on and leaves him there"; it's a psychological fact. The poets understand these things.

ELLEN: And all the cows react the same way? As if they were reading instructions from a blackboard? Oh, Tommy, listen to me . . .

[*The doorbell rings.*]

TOMMY: The point is, I don't want any pity.

CLEOTA (*hurrying from dining room*): It's dat prize-fightah! I seen him from de windah!

[ELLEN *admits* JOE, *who comes in without his old bounce; he is worried and restless.*]

ELLEN: Hello, Joe.

JOE: Hello. Hello. (*Awkwardly, to* TOMMY.)

TOMMY: Hello.

401

JOE: I'm sorry, Tommy. I didn't hit you hard. You slipped and hit your head on a bench.

TOMMY: Yeh, I know. What's the matter with your hands?

JOE: You kinda bit me. . . . Ed's out in the car. We just chased a reporter away hanging around out there.

ELLEN: Well, don't let any reporters in, Cleota.

TOMMY: And don't let Keller in. [CLEOTA *nods and exits to kitchen.*]

JOE (*indicating wet towel*): Do you have to keep that thing on?

TOMMY: No, I just do it because I like it. (*Throws down towel.*)

JOE: Could I have a little slug of something? I . . .

ELLEN: Certainly. Scotch?

JOE: Yeh, fine. (ELLEN *goes to dining room.* JOE *paces.*) I got the galloping jumps. I can use a little drink. Haven't slept for two nights.

TOMMY: Worrying about something?

JOE: Yeh, worrying about something. And my cold's worse.

TOMMY: Want some Kleenex?

JOE (*irritated*): No, I don't want some Kleenex! Damn reporters been bothering me, too.

TOMMY: What do they want with you?

JOE: Oh, they wanted me to pick an All-American team.

TOMMY (*incredulously — al-*

most): Did you?

JOE: Yeh. Kinda took my mind off things.

TOMMY (*sarcastically*): Who'd you pick for right guard?

JOE: Shulig — Kansas State Teachers'. (*Faces* TOMMY.) Look, Tommy, where the hell do we all stand now? (TOMMY *picks up towel, presses it to his head again.*) Does that kinda throb?

TOMMY: No.

JOE: Well, I wanta know where we all stand.

TOMMY: Oh, let it alone, Joe. It'll work out. You and I can handle this. I don't want Ellen worried about details now. She's got enough trouble with me—sitting around the house looking like a hot-oil shampoo. . . .

[ELLEN *enters with bowl of ice. She fixes a drink.*]

ELLEN: There's been more drinking in this house in the last two days than we've done in ten years.

[JOE *sits on settee at far side of room.*]

TOMMY (*after a pause*): Ellen, Joe picked Shulig of Kansas State Teachers' for right guard, on his All-American. Isn't that nice?

[ELLEN *looks annoyed.*]

JOE (*reminiscently*): It was kinda hard choosing between him and Feldkamp of Western Reserve. Both big and fast.

ELLEN (*crossing with drink*):

Here you are, dear. (*She is coolly oblivious of* TOMMY's *hand which he puts out for the drink; goes on to* JOE, *who doesn't realize she means him.*) Dear. (*He looks up at her with a start, glances at* TOMMY, *then takes the drink.*)

TOMMY (*sulkily*): I don't want any.

JOE: Say, have you got a Pennsylvania timetable around?

ELLEN: Where are you going, Joe?

JOE: Well, I've got to be in Washington tomorrow.

ELLEN: That's going to rush me.

JOE: What do you mean?

ELLEN: Well, Joe, I thought you and I might start out by going up to that little inn at Granville tonight. Just for a few days. (*She sits close to* JOE *on settee.*)

TOMMY (*rises*): What did you say?

ELLEN (*to* JOE): I think it's the nicest place around here. Don't you?

JOE (*flopping on the hook*): I— I—eh— Could I have a little more Scotch? (*He hurries across the room, pours himself another drink.*)

ELLEN (*gaily*): I don't want you to get drunk, Joe.

JOE: I'll be all right—I'll be all right. What time is it?

TOMMY: Never mind what time it is. (*To* ELLEN.) Would you

mind explaining this a little better?

ELLEN: I'll try to make it as clear as I can for both of you. I simply have to make a fresh start now, Tommy. You understand women; you must see that. I can't stay here now. You've made your plans and now I have to make mine.

TOMMY: Yes—but not like this —not running off to Granville!

ELLEN: All right, if you're afraid of a scandal, we'll go farther away. Put Granville out of your mind, then. We'll go directly to Pittsburgh.

JOE: Huh?

ELLEN: It's a very big town. Nobody need know anything about it.

JOE: About what?

ELLEN: About us. About our living together.

[*Both men stop cold.*]

TOMMY: Ellen!

JOE (*desperately*): But you see —I don't live in Pittsburgh. (*He makes a large circular gesture with both hands.*) I live in Sewickly. (*The gesture is small and loving now.*) And my boss lives there, too. And my mother. My mother's not very well. My mother . . .

TOMMY: Oh, you and your mother!

JOE: Besides it's a Presbyterian town.

403

ELLEN: You're not being very gallant, Joe.

TOMMY: No. Are you trying to get out of this?

JOE: No, but I come from a long line of married people! And besides, I'm not going to Pittsburgh directly. I've got to go to Washington, and that's one place I couldn't take you, Ellen!

TOMMY: You'll take her any place she wants to go, but she's not going any place!

ELLEN: Oh, yes, I am!

[*There is a loud knock, and* ED KELLER *enters.*]

ED: I can't sit out in that car all day, you know.

JOE: Oh, I'm sorry, Ed, but —jees, I forgot all about you. (*Turns to* TOMMY.) I persuaded Ed to come over and talk to you before this thing gets too bad. (*He leads* ED *over to* TOMMY.)

TOMMY: It couldn't get any worse!

JOE: I mean about the trustees.

TOMMY: Let the trustees take care of themselves. We have troubles of our own.

ED: You'll find out this is your trouble. Is he able to talk?

JOE: God, yes!

ED (*to* TOMMY): Well, then, listen. We just had a trustees' meeting in the president's office. Michael Barnes is out, and you're on your way out. You'll be asked to resign tonight.

ELLEN (*rises*): Oh, Tommy!

JOE: Ed's trying to help him while there's still time. After tonight, it will be too late.

TOMMY: What do you care what happens tonight? You'll be in Granville or somewhere.

ED: What're you going to be doing in Granville?

TOMMY: Please don't ask personal questions!

ELLEN: Do you mind if I stay a little while, Tommy?

TOMMY (*angrily*): Why shouldn't you stay? It's your house.

ED: Sit down, Ellen. (*She sits. To* TOMMY.) There's just one thing you can do: come out with a statement to the papers, quick. Say you were sick. Say you didn't know anything about Barnes' editorial. You think it's an outrage. You're not going to read this Vanzetti thing, and you think Barnes is getting what he deserves. That's the only thing that'll save your neck.

ELLEN: Tommy wouldn't say that about Michael, Ed, and you shouldn't ask him to.

TOMMY: Thank you!

ED: All right, then. That's all I had to say. Good-bye. This is on your own head.

ELLEN: Ed. Just a minute, please. (*Faces* TOMMY.) I know that reading this letter must mean something to you, Tommy. Some-

404

thing none of us can quite understand. I wish I could. It might
help me to understand a lot of
other things, when I can get away
where I can think.

TOMMY: Such as what?

ELLEN: Such as what is important to you. What you've been
fighting for. Whether it's something you really believe in and
love, or just your own selfish pride.
I think you got into this just because you were mad at me. And
that's ridiculous, because now you
don't care what I do or say about
it. You're out of that.

ED (*to* JOE): I don't see what
she's talking about. (JOE *motions
him to be quiet.*)

TOMMY: All right, I'll try to
explain what it means to me.
Perhaps, originally, pride had
something to do with this. And
jealousy.

ELLEN: And stubbornness. . . .

TOMMY: And—please. I am
trying to say that—now—I am not
fighting about you and me at all.
This is bigger than you and me or
any of us.

ELLEN: Is it?

ED (*ironically*): It must be a
masterpiece. That letter must be
quite a nice piece of propaganda.

TOMMY: Why don't you read it
and find out?

ED: I don't read things like that.

TOMMY: My God, you don't
even know what you're objecting

to!

JOE: Well, Tommy, why don't
you read the letter to us, and let
us see what it is?

TOMMY: I'll be glad to read it to
you, but I'll read it to my class,
too. (*He goes to bookcase and
hunts for the book; not finding it,
he remembers it is upstairs and
goes up.*)

ED: You don't have to read it to
me. I know what kind of stuff it
is.

[*The front door bursts open, and
PATRICIA backs in, followed
by WALLY, leaving the door
open.*]

PATRICIA: But I can't go with
you now! I told you I've got to
wait here and see what Tommy's
going to do.

WALLY: But you're not going to
the class! You said you're not going!

PATRICIA: I'm not! I just want
to know!

WALLY: I'll bet you *are* going!
You're waiting here for Michael to
go with you!

PATRICIA: Oh, go away! (*Turning, she sees the others, who are
listening.*) Oh—I'm sorry. (*She
rushes across to the door leading
to the garden.*)

ED: What's this now?

JOE (*grinning*): Hey, Pat, you
better think twice before you
scrap with Wally here. He's coming in with me at Pittsburgh next

405

year.

WALLY: A lot she cares about Pittsburgh! I run sixty-two yards through Michigan, and all she wants is to listen to Mike Barnes talk about free love. (*He stalks over to* PATRICIA.)

ED: She does?

ELLEN (*trying to stop* WALLY): Uh—Wally, how's Stalenkiwiecz?

WALLY (*brushing past her*): He's much better. (*To* PATRICIA.) If you knew what I know about that guy Barnes . . .

PATRICIA: I know what you're hinting at! And what if he did? It only shows what an intense person Michael is! I know that no matter what he did, he was thinking of me!

WALLY: That's disgusting!

PATRICIA: And aren't you a little bit disgusting to mention it? I thought *men* had some loyalty! (*She goes out.*)

WALLY (*following her out*): Now, listen here . . . I want to tell you about that guy. Do you know what he did? . . .

ED (*sitting on sofa*): What kind of a house is this?

[*As* TOMMY *comes downstairs with an open book in his hand,* DAMON, *carrying his ever-present umbrella, walks quietly in the open front door and looks around.*]

TOMMY: All right, here it is. Now sit down—or stand up—but

listen! Oh, hello, Dr. Damon. You're just in time.

DAMON: In time for what? (*Sees* ED, *moves toward him.*) Oh, has the Inquisition moved its headquarters?

TOMMY: I'm just going to read the Inquisition a letter from one of its victims.

ED: That's about enough of that.

DAMON: Gentlemen, gentlemen. This may not be wise, Thomas.

TOMMY: It may not be wise, but it's necessary. I think you'll have to take a stand, too, Dr. Damon.

DAMON: I hope not. (*Sits on settee;* JOE *seats himself on the fireplace bench;* ELLEN *sits at opposite side of room.*)

TOMMY: So did I hope not. I didn't start out to lead a crusade. I simply mentioned one day that I meant to read to my class three letters by men whose profession was not literature, but who had something sincere to say. Once I had declared that very harmless intention, the world began to shake, great institutions trembled, and football players descended upon me and my wife! I realized then that I was doing something important.

ED (*sarcastically*): You make it sound mighty innocent. Reading Lincoln and General Sherman—and Vanzetti. What was the reason you gave for picking out Vanzetti?

TOMMY (*to* ED): *Originally* I chose him to show that what we call broken English can sometimes be very moving and eloquent, but now—

ED: We wouldn't object if this was just a case of broken English —it's more than that.

TOMMY: Yes, you've made it more than that.

ED: Vanzetti was an anarchist! He was executed for murder.

TOMMY: He was accused of murder, but thousands of people believe he was executed simply because of the ideas he believed in.

ED: That's a dangerous thing to bring up.

TOMMY (*getting really mad*): No, it's a dangerous thing to keep down. I'm fighting for a teacher's rights, but if you want to make it political, all right! You can't suppress ideas because you don't like them—not in this country—not yet. This is a university! (*To* DAMON.) It's our business to bring what light we can into this muddled world—to try to follow truth!

DAMON: You are quite right, Thomas, but I wish you would make an effort not to—uh—uh— intone.

TOMMY: I'm not intoning—I'm yelling! And for God's sake, sir, put away that umbrella! (DAMON *covers his umbrella with his hat.*)

Don't you see: this isn't about Vanzetti; this is about us! If I can't read this letter today, tomorrow none of us will be able to teach anything except what Mr. Keller here and the legislature permit us to teach. Can't you see what that leads to—what it has led to in other places? We're holding the last fortress of free thought, and if we surrender to prejudice and dictation, we're cowards! (*He strides across the room.*)

ELLEN: Tommy, no matter how deeply you feel about this, what can you *do?* What can any one man do? Except to lose everything . . .

TOMMY: Ellen, I have very little more to lose. And I can't tell you what I hope to gain. I can't answer that. I only know that I have to do it.

[PATRICIA *appears in the doorway, stops and listens.*]

DAMON: May we hear the letter —in a slightly calmer mood, perhaps?

TOMMY: Yes, sir . . . This may disappoint you a little, Mr. Keller. It isn't inflammatory, so it may make you feel a little silly. At least, I hope so. . . . (*He holds up the book, pauses.* ED *and* JOE *get set in their chairs.*) Vanzetti wrote this in April, 1927, after he was sentenced to die. It has been printed in many newspapers. It appears in this book. You could destroy every printed copy of it, but it would not die out of the language, because a great many people know it by heart. (*He reads, hardly referring to the book, watching them.*) "If it had not been for these thing, I might have live out my life talking at street corners to scorning men. I might have die, unmarked, unknown, a failure. Now we are not a failure. Never in our full life could we hope to do so much work for tolerance, for Justice, for man's understanding of man, as now we do by accident. Our words—our lives—our pain—nothing! The taking of our lives—the lives of a good shoe-maker and a poor fish-peddler—all! That last moment belongs to us—that agony is our triumph!" . . . Well, that's it! (*He closes the book and drops it on the table. There is silence for a moment;* KELLER *is puzzled;* ELLEN, *who has been moved by the letter, looks up in surprise, meets* TOMMY'S *eyes, then drops hers.*)

JOE (*uncomfortably*): Well, that isn't so bad! That isn't a bad letter.

ED: Is that all of it?

TOMMY: Yes, that's all!

JOE (*rises*): Maybe Tommy's right. I don't see that it would do so much harm.

ED (*slowly*): Yes, it will. If he reads this letter to his class he'll get a lot of those kids worried about that man. Make socialists out of 'em.

JOE: It's got me worried already.

ED (*rises, facing* TOMMY): No —I won't have it. You fellows are trying to defy the authority of the trustees. You say you're going to take a stand. Well, we've *taken* a stand. I wouldn't care if that letter were by Alexander Hamilton.

TOMMY (*measuring him*): Neither would I! The principle is exactly the same.

JOE (*speaking hopefully*): Well, then, read something else. Why can't you read Hoover?

ED: Yeah.

JOE: He writes a lot of stuff—a lot of good stuff in his book.

TOMMY (*his artistic ire is aroused*): Hoover can't *write* as well as Vanzetti.

ED (*winces*): That's a terrible thing to say. You'll get in trouble saying things like that.

TOMMY: Very likely! (*He strides to garden door.*)

JOE: Ed, look—can't we compromise somehow? Seems a shame that a little thing like this should . . .

ELLEN (*rises*): It isn't little! Joe, you have some influence around here.

TOMMY: I can fight my own battles, Ellen.

ELLEN: Can't I say anything any

more—even on your side?

ED: Turner, I've heard the letter and . . .

TOMMY (*answering* ELLEN): Not out of a sense of self-sacrifice or something!

ED: What?

ELLEN: Oh, yes, you always know . . .

ED (*to* JOE): Do we always have to have women butting into this?

JOE: Ellen isn't women. She's Tommy's wife.

ELLEN (*furiously*): No, I'm not!

ED: No. Turner, it comes to this. . . . (*Turns to* ELLEN.) You're not what? Do you mean to stand there and tell me you two are not—

TOMMY (*raging*): Will you please not ask personal questions?

ED (*to* TOMMY): No. *We can't have that in this school!*

ELLEN (*with a glance at* JOE): It's Joe and I who are going to live together!

ED: Yeh, will you let me— (*To* ELLEN.) You and Joe are going to what! (*Turns on* JOE.) What the hell is going on here anyway?

JOE: Now don't look at me!

ED: You can't live with Ellen!

JOE: I didn't say . . .

ELLEN (*twisting the knife in both men's backs*): We might as well tell him now. I'm going to Pittsburgh with Joe. (*Plants herself on settee.*)

ED (*turning back to* ELLEN):

Why, you can't do that! The newspapers would make Midwestern University look like some kind of honky-tonk or something! Why, this is worse than that goddamn letter!

TOMMY: Aren't you getting off the subject?

ED: No! What kind of a woman are you?

TOMMY (*advancing on* ED): Why don't you come out in the back yard?

JOE: Better be careful, Ed!

ELLEN: No more fights, please!

DAMON (*rises*): I think I shall get a breath of fresh air. (*Goes to front door and opens it.*)

ELLEN: Well, I can't stay *here* now!

JOE: Look, Ed, you don't understand. You get things all mixed up.

ED: Well, I've got this much straight—if we can keep sex out of this for a minute! I came here to say to you that if you read this letter today you're out of this university tomorrow! You take this stand and you stand alone!

DAMON (*turning, walks deliberately over to* ED): Mr. Keller, for forty-two years I have followed a policy of appeasement. I might say I have been kicked around in this institution by one Edward K. Keller after another. . . .

ED: There is only one Edward K. Keller.

409

DAMON: There has always been at least one. But there is an increasing element in the faculty which resents your attitude toward any teacher who raises his voice or so much as clears his throat. I warn you that if you persist in persecuting Thomas Turner, you will have a fight on your hands, my friend.

ED: Do you think that Bryson and Kressinger and I are afraid of a few dissatisfied book-worms who work for twenty-five hundred dollars a year?

DAMON (*with strong indignation*): These men are not malcontents! Some of them are distinguished scholars who have made this university what it is!

ED (*aghast*): They've made it what it is! What about me? Who's getting this new stadium? Who brought Coach Sprague here from Southern Methodist?

JOE: He means that this thing is bigger than stadiums and coaches, Ed.

ED: Nothing's bigger than the new stadium.

JOE: We've all had a bad week-end around here, Ed, and you're not helping any.

ED: Do you think I've had a good week-end!

[MICHAEL *and* NUTSY *come in the front door.*]

MICHAEL: Come in, Nutsy.

ED: Now what!?

MICHAEL: We're circulating petitions for Mr. Turner. Show 'em, Nutsy.

NUTSY (*whipping out some sheets full of signatures*): This one's just from 14th Avenue and the Athletic House. We've got 357 names.

DAMON: We want no student insurrections!

JOE: Let me see that thing. (*Takes petition from* NUTSY, *scans it hurriedly.*)

ED: You're wasting your time with that handful of names. Turner will be out tomorrow and Barnes is on his way home now.

MICHAEL: I'm not on my way home yet, sir.

ED: OHHH! So you're Barnes!!! So you're the little puppy that called me a Fascist!

[PATRICIA *comes between* ED *and* MICHAEL.]

PATRICIA (*to* ED): Well, the way you're treating everybody, I think you are a Fascist!

ELLEN: Patricia!

TOMMY: Let her alone!

ELLEN: Oh, she can stand up for Michael, but I can't stand up for you! Is that it?

TOMMY: It's not the same.

ED: Do I have to stand here and be insulted by every sixteen-year-old child that comes into this room?

PATRICIA: I'm not sixteen, I'm nineteen!

MICHAEL: She'll soon be twenty!

ED: Why don't *you* get packing?

MICHAEL: You don't need to worry about me. I'll be far away from here by tomorrow. Come on, Nutsy! (NUTSY *starts out,* MICHAEL *following.*)

PATRICIA: If you throw him out, I'm going with him! Wait, Michael! (*Starts after him.*)

ED: Are you married to that little radical?

PATRICIA: You don't have to be married to somebody to go away with him—*do you, Ellen?* (*She and* MICHAEL *go out.*)

DAMON (*who can't cope with any more*): I think I shall go home, have my Ovaltine and lie down. (*He goes out the front door.*)

ED: He'll need his Ovaltine.

JOE (*suddenly, awesomely*): Say, Ed, look. This thing has been signed by Stalenkiwiecz and Wierasocka.

ED: What! I don't believe it! (*Snatches petition, scans it, in all its terrible significance.*)

JOE: Ed, you ought to have some respect for men like Dean Damon and Stalenkiwiecz and Wierasocka.

ED (*stricken*): They can't do this to me! Two of the biggest men in the university signing the red petition! You, the greatest half-back we ever had, running away with a woman! Why—

they'll never ask us to the Rose Bowl now!

TOMMY: What is the Rose Bowl?

[ED *almost screams.*]

ED: I'm getting out of this house! Coming, Joe?

JOE: No.

ED: By God, you can't depend on anybody! I've a damn good notion to resign from the board of trustees. (*Stiffening.*) But I'll kick you out if it's the last thing I do.

TOMMY (*grimly*): Just to make things even—I'll kick you out. Here's your hat. (*Gives him* JOE's *derby.*)

ED: Very well! (*Puts on hat and leaves angrily.*)

JOE: Hey, that's *my* hat!

TOMMY: Well, get another one! (*He closes door.*) Well, that's that. (*They look at each other. Here they are again; the triangle.*)

JOE: Yeh, that's that. (*Pause. He eyes the others doubtfully.*) Well, I s'pose Ed will never speak to me again.

TOMMY: I have to go to class, I'll be late. (*Starts for stairs.*)

ELLEN (*appealingly, to* TOMMY): Tommy, I . . .

TOMMY: I know. I know.

ELLEN: You know what?

TOMMY: I know what you're going to say—but I don't want substitutes. I don't want *loyalty.*

[ELLEN *turns away.*]

411

JOE: What's the matter with that?

TOMMY: I just don't want Ellen standing by like a Red Cross nurse because she knows I'm in trouble!

JOE: I don't know whether you need a nurse or a psychoanalyst!

ELLEN: I think he's analyzed it very well himself. It isn't because you think I don't care, it's because you don't.

TOMMY (*almost bursting*): I thought we could settle this *quietly* and *calmly.*

ELLEN: Quietly and calmly! Oh, God! (*She picks up large ash tray from a table and smashes it on the floor.*)

TOMMY: Now, don't do that! I can throw things, too! (*He picks up his tea-cup.*)

ELLEN: No, you can't — you haven't got enough blood in you! [TOMMY *glares at her, puts cup down coldly, suddenly snatches it up, and hurls it into the fireplace, reaches for the saucer.*]

JOE (*leaps for* TOMMY, *grabs the saucer from him*): Now wait—let me handle this. I *don't throw things.* . . . I just want to say that I came to this city *to see a football game.* . . .

ELLEN (*right into* JOE's *face*): Oh, no, you didn't! You came for me. You haven't been here for a ball game in ten years. You wait till Brenda and you are separated,

then you come for me!

JOE: Oh, hell! (*Throws the saucer in fireplace, then wilts as he realizes this household has affected him, too.*)

TOMMY (*desperately insisting upon his doom*): That's very smart, Ellen. That's very penetrating. That's all I wanted to know. (*To* JOE.) Subconsciously, you came here for Ellen, so don't try to deny it.

JOE: I don't do things subconsciously! You're full of childish explanations of every goddamn thing that comes up!

TOMMY: And you're full of psychological evasions!

ELLEN (*screaming. It's a madhouse now*): Oh, shut up! I am not going to listen to any more of this! (*She runs upstairs.* TOMMY *sits limply on sofa and covers his face with his hands. There is a long pause.*)

JOE (*slowly, and with determination*): Well, I'll tell you one thing! I'm not going upstairs this time! If you'd explained what you were standing for on Saturday, things would have cleared up around here and I'd be in Washington now, talking to Ickes.

TOMMY (*in a low grim tone*): Are you still in love with Norma?

JOE: Norma who?

TOMMY: Your wife.

JOE: My wife's name is Brenda. And you're not going to talk her

412

over with me. I can't be alone with you two minutes and have any private life left!

ELLEN (*from upstairs*): Tommy! *What did you do with my nail file??!*

JOE: Oh, God—she sounds worse than last Saturday!

TOMMY: I haven't got it. (*He absently goes through a pocket, finds it, brings it out.*) Oh. Yeh, I've got it.

JOE: I've gone through more hell here in three days than I've had with Phyllis in three years.

TOMMY (*grimly rising*): Phyllis? Who is Phyllis? Are you living with some other woman in Pittsburgh? You can't do this.

JOE (*springing to his feet*): I'm not living with anybody! Phyllis is my secretary, and there's nothing between us!

TOMMY: *Then why did you say you've been going through hell for three years?*

JOE (*yelling*): 'Cause you get me all balled up!

[ELLEN *stomps downstairs with a suitcase and sets it down.*]

TOMMY: Here . . . here's your nail file. (*Hands it to her.*) You didn't pack anything!

ELLEN: I've been packed for three days!

TOMMY (*his voice threatens to break, but he holds out*): Well, you can't go with just one suitcase. . . . There isn't much here, but —there're the books. They're yours. Most of them I gave to you. (*He turns away.*)

ELLEN: Can I have *The Shropshire Lad?* Isn't that the one that has: "And now the fancy passes by . . ."

TOMMY: "And nothing will remain. . . ." (*He brings her the book from the bookcase. Everyone is miserable.* MICHAEL *sticks his head in the front door.*)

MICHAEL (*beaming*): You've just five minutes to get to your class, Mr. Turner. We'll wait for you in the car. (*He goes out.*)

TOMMY (*bravely*): Well, so long, Joe. I know you'll get her a place of her own for a while anyway. You can take that four-poster money with you, Ellen. I'll have one more check coming, too. (*He starts slowly upstairs.*)

JOE: What's "four-poster money"?

ELLEN (*her voice trembling pathetically*): We were saving up to buy a new bed. (*She cries, and collapses on settee.*)

JOE: Oh, God, here we go again!

TOMMY (*comes back again, desperately*): Why did you have to ask what four-poster money is? (*To* ELLEN.) Ellen, please.

ELLEN (*hysterically*): Oh, go on! Go on! Put on your coat. If you're going to be kicked out of school, you can't go over there looking like a tramp.

413

TOMMY (*balefully*): All right! (*He clumps upstairs like King Lear.*)

JOE: Look, Ellen, everything's gonna be all right.

ELLEN: Is it?

JOE (*looking after* TOMMY): I wouldn't worry about that guy.

ELLEN: I don't!

JOE: I mean he's sure to get another job. He's had more publicity than Wally Myers.

ELLEN: I don't care what becomes of him. (JOE *studies her drooping figure narrowly.*)

JOE: Come here. (*He pulls her to her feet, facing him.*) You're still crazy about that guy, aren't you?

ELLEN: I'm kind of scared of him. He used to be just—nice, but now he's wonderful!

[TOMMY *appears on stairs in time to catch the end of this. Very slowly light begins to dawn upon him.* JOE *sees him, but* ELLEN *doesn't.*]

JOE: I don't think he's so wonderful.

ELLEN: Yes, he is! That letter's wonderful. What he's trying to do is wonderful. He wouldn't let me or you or anyone stop him. Even Ed.

JOE: He's a scrapper, all right, but he can't dance. (*He crosses to the Victrola, pulling her along. He has an idea and does everything for* TOMMY's *benefit.* TOM-

MY *comes down slowly.* JOE *turns on the Victrola, which plays "Who?"*)

ELLEN: Oh, who wants to dance now?

[JOE *makes her dance, keeping her back to* TOMMY.]

JOE: This is important. It's all in the light you give off.

ELLEN: Light? What are you talking about?

JOE (*with intensity*): The important thing about dancing is that the man has got to lead. (*He beckons to* TOMMY; *with one stride,* TOMMY *turns her away from* JOE.)

TOMMY: May I cut in?

ELLEN: Tommy! Let me go!

TOMMY (*shouting*): No, I think you're wonderful, too!

ELLEN: You think I'm dumb! Were you listening?

TOMMY: No, I wasn't.

JOE (*up near door*): Hey—don't start that again!

TOMMY (*puts on his hat, still dancing feverishly*): Joe—why don't you go back to your wife? We can send her a wire.

JOE: Don't worry about me, brother. I sent her a wire this morning. (*He goes out into the fresh air, a happy man.* TOMMY *still dances with* ELLEN—*they are almost in tears.*)

TOMMY: Quit leading!

ELLEN: I'm not leading! You *were* listening!

TOMMY: You were yelling. Well, turn!

ELLEN: Make me turn. (*He does.*) Don't be so rough—and put your hat on straight! You look terrible! (*Half-crying, she throws her arms around* TOMMY. *They are kissing each other very, very hard as the*

CURTAIN FALLS

LILLIAN HELLMAN

1905 *Born, on June 20, in New Orleans, daughter of a shoe merchant.*

1910 *Moved to New York.*

1911 *Educated in New York public*
to *schools, at New York University (which she left after three years), and at Columbia University.*
1924

1924 *Began work as "general factotum" for a New York publisher.*

1925 *Married Arthur Kober, playwright and author, and began book reviewing for the New York* Herald-Tribune.

1927 *Employed as a play reader for several New York producers.*

1930 *Went to Hollywood, where she was a scenario reader.*

1932 *Returned to New York and began play reading for Herman Shumlin, the producer.*

1934 *Achieved great success with* THE CHILDREN'S HOUR *(later filmed as* THESE THREE*).*

1935 *Wrote scenario for* DARK ANGEL.

1936 DAYS TO COME *failed after one week. Trip to Europe, visiting Russia, France, and Spain.*

1937 *After undergoing bombardment by Franco forces in Spain, returned to America a militant anti-Fascist.*

1939 THE LITTLE FOXES *achieved another success, with Tallulah Bankhead as Regina Giddens. (The later film version starred Bette Davis.)*

1941 *Produced* WATCH ON THE RHINE, *anti-Fascist in theme.*

1944 *Produced* THE SEARCHING WIND.

1946 *Produced* ANOTHER PART OF THE FOREST.

❧

LILLIAN HELLMAN *is one of the most successful craftsmen in the contemporary theater. She knows how to construct a play filled with suspense, and she is a past master of hard, biting characterization. Her handling of dialogue is sensitive and acute, and her employment of irony is brilliantly skillful. Her themes are bold. All these elements have contributed to her great box-office success. Of six plays that she has written to date, only one has been a failure, a record that few playwrights have surpassed.*

Her first play, THE CHILDREN'S HOUR, *revealed a fully developed dramatic talent. The story of the way in which a demoniac little girl ruins, by her lying, the lives of a headmistress and a teacher in an Eastern school won immediate acclaim when it was staged in 1934. In choosing a theme involving sexual abnormality, the playwright was*

418

courageous. Fortunately, her skill in handling the delicate subject matched her courage. The play is relentlessly plotted to work out the complete destruction of the two leading characters; and up to the climax the action is searingly convincing. As brilliantly constructed as the play is, however, it is not perfect. On the very relentlessness of the plotting it founders at the end. Miss Hellman herself has stated that the play should conclude with the suicide of the headmistress and has agreed that the ruin of the friend is needless.

DAYS TO COME, Miss Hellman's next play, has for its theme the cruelty and stupidity of strikebreaking. The central character, Andrew Rodman, the owner of a brush-making factory long in the family, is forced by financial involvement to employ professional strikebreakers to settle a labor dispute in his plant. The act results in the death of the child of an employee and the complete loss of the respect and love that the inhabitants of the model factory village had had for the Rodman family. In the midst of a trying industrial situation, Andrew also discovers the infidelity of his wife, who is sympathetic with the strikers. The play as a whole is muddled and unconvincing; and at times it echoes Galsworthy's STRIFE, in contrast with which it undoubtedly suffers. Though the strikebreakers are caricatures and though most of the other characters in the play possess little interest, Cora, the spinster sister of Andrew, with her dwarfed, mean soul and her inability to comprehend anything beyond the dividends from the factory, embodies some of the basic traits that make the Hubbards of THE LITTLE FOXES so thoroughly despicable. Moreover, the play is important in introducing the playwright's interest in broad social forces.

As in DAYS TO COME, so also in THE LITTLE FOXES Miss Hellman sets out to examine an aspect of capitalism. Though the Rodmans started out by being benevolent capitalists, the Hubbards were never benevolent. Indeed, they are as predatory a family as ever trod the boards of a theater, each of them constantly poised to prey on society or on one of themselves. In fact, to call them "the little foxes that spoil the vines" is actually to make an ironic understatement. Motivated as they are by lust for power through wealth, they will stoop to anything from theft to murder to achieve their purposes; and they emerge as monstrous beasts of prey. In the play they are presented as belonging to the America of the early 1900's, but in actuality they serve as prototypes of the kind of individualists that a capitalistic society may continue to nourish.

419

The playwright intimates that she wishes to awake her audiences to the "hundreds of Hubbards sitting in rooms like this throughout the country" and to arouse them to the danger that the Hubbards may yet some day own the nation. But the social implications of the play have a tendency to become lost in the gripping melodrama. Almost everybody is willing to believe for the duration of the action that the Hubbards do exist; but few will be convinced by the play that the Hubbards still exist in menacing numbers outside the theater. Such is the strength and the weakness of Miss Hellman's art. She often tells her story too well and develops her characters too intensely. Thus she robs her dramatic presentation of much significance extending beyond the three walls of the stage itself.

The selection of setting and characters in THE LITTLE FOXES *is worth observing. Whereas the Hubbards are an Alabama family, they are not members of the old landed aristocracy of the "Deep South." Rather are they the "new rich," who have acquired wealth by "cheating niggers on a pound of bacon," and who seal their dominance of a community by building cotton mills and exploiting cheap labor. The symbolically named Birdie, a fluttery creature enslaved by a husband who is one of the most sadistic of the Hubbards, is from an entirely different social stratum. In her pitiful way she is "the embodiment of an idea and a point of view," representing the gentility and nobility of the old paternalistic landed gentry—which, though not admirable, is infinitely to be preferred (Miss Hellman would have us believe) to the capitalistic society that supplanted it.*

As deep-dyed in corruption as all the Hubbards are, they are sharply and deftly distinguished in characterization. Regina is seductive, ruthless, cool, dangerous—almost too steel-like to be human. Her calculating schemes to achieve power make her sister under the skin to Lady Macbeth. Ben is hard and shrewd. Oscar is cruel and flabby; his son, Leo, is weak and degenerate. In the father-son combination the degeneracy of the Hubbards is presented in its most revolting aspects. Though Oscar forbids his Negroes to hunt on his property, he himself kills game that he does not use. He browbeats his wife in the same way in which he is cruel to animals. Leo beats horses and steals from the bank. The only redemptive act by any member of the clan is the revolt of Alexandra, Regina's daughter; but the revolt is not made important enough to give to the whole play a redemptive turn. And in spite of the fact that we are given a hint of Regina's misgivings just before the final curtain falls, evil is really triumphant in the play.

Joseph Wood Krutch's review of the play in the Nation *was labelled, simply, "Unpleasant Play." From one point of view, the judgment is not unfair. Normally, one finds aesthetic pleasure in the presentation of evil on the stage only if that evil is appropriately punished or if the final solution of the problem of evil makes some sort of affirmation of moral order in the universe. One may leave a performance or a reading of* THE LITTLE FOXES *with a certain lack of satisfaction because the Hubbards were not visited by some violent fate befitting their flagitious behavior. Certainly, their badness was colossal enough to warrant their complete destruction; and one might have been particularly pleased with the kind of "poetic justice" that would have allowed them to bring down a final terrible destruction on themselves.*

But the failure of the play to provide a more definite sort of catharsis than it does, does not diminish its dramatic power. The playwright obviously knew what she was doing, and she constructed her play deliberately to achieve her effect. Beginning with an exciting first act, the action is appreciably retarded in the second and moves to a gripping climax in the third. None will leave the play unconvinced that Miss Hellman has written an impressive drama.

When she came to write WATCH ON THE RHINE *Miss Hellman had different subject matter and motivation. Written after her experience in Europe just before the past war, the play is a spirited attempt to portray the heroism necessary to carry on the fight against Fascism. The central character is a German engineer who escapes to this country, the homeland of his wife, in order to raise funds for the underground fight against Hitler in his native land. In a powerful climax he kills a would-be informer, bids his family farewell, and starts back on a perilous journey to Germany.*

In THE SEARCHING WIND *the playwright demonstrates how wealth and career diplomacy stupidly failed to see the implication of events in Europe between wars and how the democracies consequently sold out to the totalitarians through appeasement. Both plays lack some of the tautness of construction found in Miss Hellman's earlier work, but both have been effective on stage and screen. At times they attain eloquence and beauty. Rarely are they profound, and in the main their themes do not attain importance superior to their exciting action and their striking characterization.*

421

ANOTHER PART OF THE FOREST *returns to the Hubbards as they were twenty years before the time of* THE LITTLE FOXES. *Here one sees the paternal Hubbard, born in extreme poverty, forcing his way forward by corruption and trickery. Thoroughly hated by everybody, including his children, he had once barely escaped lynching. He had held his sons and his wife, a poor half-crazed creature, under his whip hand. Only Regina refused to cower. The play revolves about a struggle for power in this "kingdom of the damned" which Ben finally wins by revealing a surprising secret about his father.*

Though Miss Hellman regards herself as a "moral dramatist" concerned with the problem of good and evil, she has actually undertaken no real probing of human conscience or conduct and has made no illuminating comment on the moral order of the universe. For her, evil has been thus far essentially a surface manifestation, which she has been able to present in its persistently fiendish aspects after the manner of the Elizabethan dramatists. Little Mary Tilford, in THE CHILDREN'S HOUR, *is indeed "an Iago in pinafore," and the Hubbards of* THE LITTLE FOXES *and* ANOTHER PART OF THE FOREST *are as monstrous as any of the creations of Marlowe, Webster, or Tourneur. Into somewhat the same class might fall the Nazi house guest in* WATCH ON THE RHINE. *Miss Hellman has not achieved tragedy because, as Professor Krutch has suggested, her "fables are not really suitable vehicles for the emotion which they are intended to carry." It is also significant that her most ambitious attempt to write a "problem" play was a failure. On the other hand, her brilliant ability to handle violent and exciting action indicates that her genius up to the present time has been melodrama of a very high order. Her future development will be distinctly worth watching.*

BIBLIOGRAPHICAL NOTE

Comprehensive biographical and critical treatments of Miss Hellman are not yet available. The chief biographical facts are recorded in CURRENT BIOGRAPHY, 1941, *ed. Maxine Bloch (New York: The H. W. Wilson Company, 1941). An amusing, though not extremely astute, portrayal will be found in* Margaret Case Harriman's "Miss Lily of New Orleans," *New Yorker, XVII, No. 39 (November 8, 1941), 22-35. For reviews of the plays the student should consult the New York Times Index and the index of Theatre Arts for the years in which the plays were produced. Two stimulating reviews of* THE LITTLE FOXES are those by Otis Ferguson, "A Play, a Picture," New Republic, *XCVIII* (1939), 279, *and Joseph Wood Krutch,* "Unpleasant Play," Nation, *CXLVIII* (1939), 244-245. *Though Professor Krutch's comments on Miss Hellman in* THE AMERICAN DRAMA SINCE 1918 *(New* York: Random House, 1939) *cover only the first three plays, they are still pertinent. The student should read the playwright's own frank and modest comments in the introduction to her* FOUR PLAYS *(New York: Random House,* 1942).

The Little Foxes

CHARACTERS

ADDIE	REGINA GIDDENS
CAL	WILLIAM MARSHALL
BIRDIE HUBBARD	BENJAMIN HUBBARD
OSCAR HUBBARD	ALEXANDRA GIDDENS
LEO HUBBARD	HORACE GIDDENS

The scene of the play is in the living-room of the Giddens House, a small town in the South. ACT ONE: *The spring of 1900, evening.* ACT TWO: *A week later, early morning.* ACT THREE: *Two weeks later, late afternoon. There has been no attempt to write Southern dialect. It is to be understood that the accents are Southern.*

❧

ACT I

SCENE: *The living room of the Giddens house, a small town in the deep South, the spring of 1900. Upstage is a staircase leading to the second story. Upstage, right, are double doors to the dining room. When these doors are open we see a section of the dining room and the furniture. Upstage, left, is an entrance hall with a coat-rack and umbrella stand. There are large lace-curtained windows on the left wall. The room is lit by a center gas chandelier and painted china oil lamps on the tables. Against the wall is a large piano. Downstage, right, is a high couch, a large table, several chairs. Against the left back wall is a table and several chairs. Near the window there is a smaller couch and tables. The room is good-looking, the furniture expensive; but it reflects no particular taste. Everything is of the best, and that is all.*

AT RISE: ADDIE, *a tall, nice-looking Negro woman of about fifty-five, is closing the windows. From behind the closed dining room doors there is the sound of voices. After a second* CAL, *a middle-aged Negro, comes in from the entrance hall, carrying a tray with glasses and a bottle of port wine.* ADDIE *crosses, takes the tray from him, puts it on table, begins to arrange it.*

ADDIE (*pointing to the bottle*): You gone stark out of your head?

CAL: No, smart lady, I ain't. Miss Regina told me to get out that bottle, (*points to bottle*) that very bottle for the mighty honored guest. When Miss Regina changes orders like that you can bet your dime she got her reason.

ADDIE (*points to dining room*): Go on. You'll be needed.

CAL: Miss Zan she had two helpings frozen fruit cream and she tell that honored guest, she tell him that you make the best frozen fruit cream in all the South.

ADDIE (*smiles, pleased*): Did she? Well, see that Belle saves a little for her. She like it right before she go to bed. Save a few little cakes, too, she like——

[*The dining room doors are opened and quickly closed again by* BIRDIE HUBBARD. BIRDIE *is a woman of about forty, with a pretty, well-bred, faded face. Her movements are usually nervous and timid, but now, as she comes running into the room,*

she is gay and excited. CAL *turns to* BIRDIE.]

BIRDIE: Oh, Cal. (*Closes door.*) I want you to get one of the kitchen boys to run home for me. He's to look in my desk drawer and—— My, Addie. What a good supper. Just as good as good can be.

ADDIE: You look pretty this evening, Miss Birdie, and young.

BIRDIE (*laughing*): Me, young? Maybe you better find Simon and tell him to do it himself. He's to look in my desk, the left drawer, and bring my music album right away. Mr. Marshall is very anxious to see it because of his father and the opera in Chicago. (*To* ADDIE.) Mr. Marshall is such a polite man with his manners, and very educated and cultured, and I've told him all about how my Mama and Papa used to go to Europe for the music—— (*Laughs. To* ADDIE.) Imagine going all the way to Europe just to listen to music. Wouldn't that be nice, Addie? Just to sit there and listen and—— *Left* drawer,

Cal. Tell him that twice because he forgets. And tell him not to let any of the things drop out of the album and to bring it right in here when he comes back.

[*The dining room doors are opened and quickly closed by* OSCAR HUBBARD. *He is a man in his late forties.*]

CAL: Yes'm. But Simon he won't get it right. (*Crossing to door left.*) But I'll tell him.

BIRDIE: Left drawer, Cal, and tell him to bring the blue book and——

OSCAR (*sharply*): Birdie.

BIRDIE (*turning nervously*): Oh, Oscar. I was just sending Simon for my music album.

OSCAR (*to* CAL *who has stopped at door left to listen*): Never mind about the album. Miss Birdie has changed her mind.

BIRDIE: But, really, Oscar. Really I promised Mr. Marshall. I—— (CAL *looks at them and goes out.*)

OSCAR: Why do you leave the dinner table and go running about like a child? (ADDIE *crosses around sofa to window, closes windows.*)

BIRDIE (*trying to be gay*): But Oscar, Mr. Marshall said most specially he *wanted* to see my album. I told him about the time Mama met Wagner and Mrs. Wagner gave her the signed pro-

gram and the big picture. (OSCAR *moves away.*) Mr. Marshall wants to see that. (BIRDIE *moves to him.*) Very, very much. We had such a nice talk and——

OSCAR (*taking step to her*): You have been chattering to him like a magpie. You haven't let him be for a second. I can't think he came South to be bored with you. (*He turns away.*)

BIRDIE (*quickly, hurt*): He wasn't bored. I don't believe he was bored. He's a very educated, cultured gentleman. (*Her voice rises.*) I just don't believe it. You always talk like that when I'm having a nice time.

OSCAR (*turning to her, sharply*): You have had too much wine. Get yourself in hand now.

BIRDIE (*drawing back, about to cry, shrilly*): What am I doing? I am not doing anything. What am I doing?

OSCAR (*taking a step to her, tensely*): I said get yourself in hand. Stop acting like a fool. (ADDIE *closes windows.*)

BIRDIE (*moves up, then turns to him, quietly*): I don't believe he was bored. I just don't believe it. Some people like music and like to talk about it. (LEO *enters from dining room.* REGINA *in dining room rings bell.*) That's all I was doing.

[LEO HUBBARD *comes hurrying*

through the door. He is a young man of twenty, with a weak kind of good looks.]

LEO: Mama! (BIRDIE *turns sharply to him.*) Papa. They are coming in now.

OSCAR (*softly, stepping up to* BIRDIE): Sit down, Birdie. Sit down now. (BIRDIE *sits down in chair and bows her head as if to hide her face.*)

[*The dining room doors are opened by* CAL. *We see people beginning to rise from the table.* REGINA GIDDENS *comes in with* WILLIAM MARSHALL. REGINA *is a handsome woman of forty.* MARSHALL *is forty-five, pleasant looking, self possessed. Behind them comes* ALEXANDRA GIDDENS, *a very pretty, rather delicate looking girl of seventeen. She is followed by* BENJAMIN HUBBARD, *fifty-five, with a large jovial face and the light graceful movements that one often finds in large men.* REGINA *after a sharp look at* BIRDIE *and* OSCAR, *crosses to sofa right.* MARSHALL *crosses center to chair right center.* ALEXANDRA *sits on settee.*)

REGINA: Mr. Marshall, I think you're trying to console me. Chicago may be the noisiest, dirtiest city in the world but I should still prefer it to the sound of our horses and the smell of our azaleas. I should like crowds of people, and theaters, and lovely women——— (REGINA *sits on sofa, smiles at* MARSHALL *and indicates for him to sit next to her.*) Very lovely women, Mr. Marshall?

MARSHALL: In Chicago? Oh, I suppose so. But I can tell you this: I've never dined there with three *such* lovely ladies. (*He sits on sofa to right of* REGINA.)

[ADDIE *comes down to table, takes bottle off tray and serves wine.*]

BEN (*nods*): Our Southern women are well favored.

LEO (*laughs*): But one must go to Mobile for the ladies, sir. Very elegant worldly ladies, too.

[ADDIE *is serving* REGINA *who hands a glass to* MARSHALL, *then takes one for herself.*]

BEN (*looks at him very deliberately*): Worldly, eh? *Worldly*, did you say?

OSCAR (*hastily, to* LEO): Your Uncle Ben means that worldliness is not a mark of beauty in any woman.

LEO (*quickly*): Of course, Uncle Ben. I didn't mean———

[BEN *crosses to chair right center, sits.*]

MARSHALL: Your port is excellent, Mrs. Giddens.

[ADDIE *serves* BIRDIE, *who catches* OSCAR'S *look at her, and refuses the drink.*]

REGINA: Thank you Mr. Marshall. We had been saving that bottle, hoping we could open it just for you.

ALEXANDRA (*as* ADDIE *comes to her with tray*): Oh. May I *really*, Addie?

ADDIE: Better ask Mama.

ALEXANDRA: May I, Mama?

REGINA (*nods, smiles*): In Mr. Marshall's honor.

ALEXANDRA (*smiles*): Mr. Marshall, this will be the first taste of port I've ever had.

[ADDIE *serves* LEO.]

MARSHALL (*leaning forward*): No one ever had their first taste of a better port. (*He lifts his glass in a toast; she lifts hers, they both drink. Sits back. Looks around the room, smiles.*) Well, I suppose it is all true, Mrs. Giddens.

REGINA: What is true?

[ADDIE *crosses to table for bottle, takes the tray to table, places it there, then exits.*]

MARSHALL: That you Southerners occupy a unique position in America. You live better than the rest of us, you eat better, you drink better. I wonder you find time, or want to find time, to do business.

BEN (*laughs*): A great many Southerners don't.

MARSHALL: Do all of you live here together?

REGINA: Here with me? (*Laughs.*) Oh, no. My brother Ben lives next door. My brother

Oscar and his family live in the next square.

BEN (*sitting forward*): But we are a very close family. We've always *wanted* it that way.

MARSHALL: That is very pleasant. Keeping your family together to share each other's lives. My family moves around too much. My children seem never to come home. Away at school in the winter; in the summer, Europe with their mother——

REGINA (*eagerly*): Oh, yes. Even down here we read about Mrs. Marshall in the society pages.

MARSHALL: I dare say. She moves about a great deal. And all of you are part of the same business? Hubbard Sons?

BEN (*motions to* OSCAR): Oscar and me. (*Motions to* REGINA.) My sister's good husband is a banker.

MARSHALL (*looks at* REGINA, *surprised*): Oh.

REGINA: I am so sorry that my husband isn't here to meet you. He's been very ill. He is at Johns Hopkins. But he will be home soon. We think he is getting better now.

LEO: I work for Uncle Horace. (REGINA *looks at him.*) I mean I work for Uncle Horace at his bank. I keep an eye on things while he's away.

REGINA (*smiles*): Really, Leo?

BEN (*looks at him, then to* MAR-

429

SHALL): Modesty in the young is as excellent as it is rare. (*Looks at* LEO *again.*)

OSCAR (*to* LEO): Your Uncle means that a young man should speak more modestly.

LEO (*hastily*): Oh, I didn't mean, sir——

MARSHALL: Oh, Mrs. Hubbard. Where's that Wagner autograph you promised to let me see? My train will be leaving soon and—— [LEO *crosses to table and pours himself a drink.*]

BIRDIE: The autograph? Oh. Well. Really, Mr. Marshall, I didn't mean to chatter so about it. Really I——(*Nervously, looking at* OSCAR.) You must excuse me. I didn't get it because, well, because I had—I—I had a little headache and——

OSCAR: My wife is a miserable victim of headaches.

REGINA (*quickly*): Mr. Marshall said at supper that he would like you to play for him, Alexandra.

ALEXANDRA (*who has been looking at* BIRDIE): It's not I who play well, sir. It's my aunt. She plays just wonderfully. She's my teacher. (*Rises, eagerly.*) May we play a duet? May we, Mama?

BIRDIE (*taking* ALEXANDRA'S *hand*): Thank you, dear. But I have my headache now. I——

OSCAR (*sharply*): Don't be stubborn, Birdie. Mr. Marshall wants you to play.

MARSHALL: Indeed I do. If your headache isn't——

BIRDIE (*hesitates, then gets up, pleased*): But I'd like to, sir. Very much. (*She and* ALEXANDRA *go to piano.* ALEXANDRA *brings chair from upstage left corner to piano for herself.* BIRDIE *moves stool, then takes some music from top of piano. They talk about the music for a second, then study it.*)

MARSHALL: It's very remarkable how you Southern aristocrats have kept together. Kept together and kept what belonged to you.

BEN: You misunderstand, sir. Southern aristocrats have *not kept* together and have *not* kept what belonged to them.

MARSHALL (*laughs, indicates room*): You don't call this keeping what belongs to you?

BEN: But we are not aristocrats. (*Points to* BIRDIE *at piano.*) Our brother's wife is the only one of us who belongs to the Southern aristocracy.

[BIRDIE *selects a book of music. She opens it as* ALEXANDRA *sits down. She is stopped by "our brother's wife," looks toward* BEN. ALEXANDRA *looks up at her.*]

MARSHALL (*smiles*): My information is that you people have been here, and solidly here, for a long time.

[BIRDIE *turns back and goes through the pages.*]

OSCAR: And so we have. Since our great-grandfather.

BEN (*smiles*): Who was *not* an aristocrat, like Birdie's.

MARSHALL (*a little sharply*): You make great distinctions.

[BIRDIE *has found the page, and looks up again on "like* BIRDIE'S." ALEXANDRA *turns head a little to them.* BIRDIE *turns back to music.*]

BEN: Oh, they have been made for us. And maybe they are important distinctions. (*Leans forward, intimately.*) Now you take Birdie's family. When my great-grandfather came here they were the highest tone plantation owners in this state.

[BIRDIE *looks at them.* ALEXANDRA *looks back to her, takes her hand, pats it.*]

LEO (*steps to* MARSHALL. *Proudly*): My mother's grandfather was *governor* of the state before the war.

OSCAR: They owned the plantation, Lionnet. You may have heard of it, sir?

MARSHALL (*laughs*): No, I've never heard of anything but brick houses on a lake, and *cotton mills.*

BEN: Lionnet in its day was the best cotton land in the South. It still brings us in a fair crop. (*Sits back.*) Ah, they were great days for those people—even when I can remember. They had the best of everything. (BIRDIE *turns to*

them.) Clothes from Paris, trips to Europe, horses you can't raise any more, niggers to lift their fingers——

BIRDIE (*suddenly*): We were good to our people. Everybody knew that. We were better to them than——

[MARSHALL *looks up at* BIRDIE.]

REGINA (*a quick look at* MARSHALL, *then to* BIRDIE): Why, Birdie. You aren't playing.

[MARSHALL *has been looking curiously at* BIRDIE.]

BEN: But when the war comes these fine gentlemen ride off and leave the cotton, *and* the women, to rot.

BIRDIE: My father was killed in the war. He was a fine soldier, Mr. Marshall. A fine man.

REGINA: Oh, certainly, Birdie. A famous soldier.

BEN (*to* BIRDIE): But that isn't the tale I am telling Mr. Marshall. (*To* MARSHALL.) Well, sir, the war ends. (BIRDIE *goes back to piano, puts down music, sits and is ready to play.*) Lionnet is almost ruined, and the sons finish ruining it. And there were thousands like them. Why? (*Leans forward.*) Because the Southern aristocrat can adapt himself to nothing. Too high-toned to try.

MARSHALL: Sometimes it is difficult to learn new ways.

[BIRDIE *and* ALEXANDRA *begin to play.* MARSHALL *leans for-*

431

ward, listening.]

BEN: Perhaps, perhaps. (*All listen to music. He sees that* MAR-SHALL *is paying attention to the music. Irritated, he turns to* BIRDIE *and* ALEXANDRA *at piano, then back to* MARSHALL.) You're right, Mr. Marshall. It is difficult to learn new ways. But maybe that's why it's profitable. *Our* grandfather and *our* father learned the new ways and learned how to make them pay. They work. (*Smiles nastily.*) *They* are in trade. Hubbard Sons, Merchandise. Others, Birdie's family for example, look down on them. (*Settles back in chair.*) To make a long story short, Lionnet now belongs to *us*. (BIRDIE *stops playing and turns to them.*) Twenty years ago we took over their land, their cotton, and their daughter. [BIRDIE *rises and stands stiffly by piano.* MARSHALL, *who has been watching her, rises.*]

MARSHALL: May I bring you a glass of port, Mrs. Hubbard?

BIRDIE (*softly*): No thank you, sir. You are most polite.

[*She turns away and sits.* ALEX-ANDRA *tries to soothe her and asks her to play again. She pantomimes that she cannot, and for* ALEXANDRA *to play alone.*]

REGINA (*sharply, to* BEN): You are boring Mr. Marshall with these ancient family tales.

BEN: I hope not. I hope not. I am trying to make an important point——(*bows to* MARSHALL) for our future business partner.

OSCAR (*to* MARSHALL): My brother always says that it's folks like us who have struggled and fought to bring to our land some of the prosperity of your land.

BEN: Some people call that patriotism.

REGINA (*laughs gaily*): I hope you don't find my brothers too obvious, Mr. Marshall. I'm afraid they mean that this is the time for the ladies to leave the gentlemen to talk business.

MARSHALL (*hastily*): Not at all. We settled everything this afternoon. (ALEXANDRA *starts to play, alone.* MARSHALL *looks at his watch.*) I have only a few minutes before I must leave for the train. (*Smiles at her.*) And I insist they be spent with you.

REGINA: And with another glass of port.

MARSHALL: Thank you.

[REGINA *looks at him, smiles, gets up, takes his glass and crosses to table.* MARSHALL *rises when she does, then sits.*]

BEN (*to* REGINA *as she passes him*): My sister is right. (*To* MARSHALL.) I am a plain man and I am trying to say a plain thing. (*Sitting forward.*) A man ain't only in business for what he can get out of it. It's got to give

432

him something here. (*Puts hand to his breast.* REGINA *pours* MARSHALL'S *drink.*) That's every bit as true for the nigger picking cotton for a silver quarter, as it is for you and me. If it don't give him something here, then he don't pick the cotton right. Money isn't all. Not by three shots.

MARSHALL: Really? Well, I always thought it was a great deal.

REGINA: And so did I, Mr. Marshall.

MARSHALL (*leans forward. Pleasantly, but with meaning*): Now you don't have to convince me that you are the right people for the deal. I wouldn't be here if you hadn't convinced me six months ago. You want the mill here, and I want it here. It isn't my business to find out *why* you want it.

BEN: To bring the machine to the cotton, and not the cotton to the machine.

MARSHALL (*amused*): You have a turn for neat phrases, Hubbard. Well, however grand your reasons are, mine are simple: (LEO *crosses to table—pours drink.*) I want to make money and I believe I'll make it on you. (*As* BEN *starts to speak, he smiles.*) Mind you, I have no objections to more high minded reasons. They are mighty valuable in business. It's fine to have partners who so closely follow the teachings of Christ. (*Gets*

up.) And now I must leave for my train. (*Puts his glass on table. All except* BIRDIE *rise.* ALEXANDRA *stops playing.*)

REGINA: I'm sorry you won't stay over with us, Mr. Marshall, but you'll come again, any time you like.

BEN (*motions to* LEO, *indicating bottle*): Fill them up, boy, fill them up. (LEO *moves around, filling glasses as* BEN *speaks.*) Down here, sir, we have a strange custom. We drink the *last* drink for a toast. That's to prove that the Southerner is always still on his feet for the last drink. (*Picks up his glass.*) It was Henry Frick, your Mr. Henry Frick, who said, "Railroads are the Rembrandts of investments." Well, *I* say "Southern cotton mills *will* be the Rembrandts of investments." So I give you the firm of Hubbard Sons and Marshall, Cotton Mills, and to it a long and prosperous life.

[*They all pick up their glasses.* MARSHALL *looks at them, amused. Then he, too, lifts his glass, smiles.*]

OSCAR: The children will drive you to the depot. Leo! Alexandra! You will drive Mr. Marshall down.

LEO (*eagerly, looks at* BEN *who nods*): Yes, sir. (*To* MARSHALL.) Not often Uncle Ben lets *me* drive the horses. And a beautiful pair

433

they are. (*Starts for hall.*) Come on Zan. (*Exits.*)

ALEXANDRA (*crosses to* BEN): May I drive tonight, Uncle Ben, please? I'd like to and——

BEN (*shakes his head, laughs*): In your evening clothes? Oh, no, my dear.

ALEXANDRA: But Leo, always —— (*Stops, exits quickly.*)

REGINA: I don't like to say good-bye to you, Mr. Marshall.

MARSHALL: Then we won't say goodbye. You have promised that you would come and let me show you Chicago. Do I have to make you promise again?

REGINA (*looks at him as he presses her hand*): I promise again.

[BEN *crosses to hall.*]

MARSHALL (*touches her hand again, then moves to* BIRDIE): Goodbye, Mrs. Hubbard.

[BIRDIE *rises.*]

BIRDIE (*shyly, with sweetness and dignity*): Goodbye, sir.

[*He bows, starts toward entrance hall.* REGINA *crosses to center.*]

MARSHALL (*as he passes* RE-GINA): Remember.

REGINA: I will.

OSCAR: We'll see you to the carriage.

[MARSHALL *exits followed by* OS-CAR. *For a second* REGINA *and* BIRDIE *stand looking after them. Then* REGINA *throws*

up her arms, laughs happily.]

REGINA: And there, Birdie, goes the man who has opened the door to our future.

BIRDIE (*surprised at the unaccustomed friendliness*): What?

REGINA (*turning to her*): Our future. Yours and mine, Ben's and Oscar's, the children's—— (*Looks at* BIRDIE'S *puzzled face, laughs.*) Our future! You were charming at supper, Birdie. Mr. Marshall certainly thought so.

BIRDIE (*pleased*): Why, Regina. Do you think he did?

REGINA: Can't you tell when you're being admired?

BIRDIE: Oscar said I bored Mr. Marshall. (*Then quietly.*) But he admired *you.* He told me so.

REGINA: What did he say?

BIRDIE: He said to me, "I hope your sister-in-law will come to Chicago. Chicago will be at her feet." He said the ladies would bow to your manners and the gentlemen to your looks.

REGINA (*crossing to sofa*): Did he? He seems a lonely man. Imagine being lonely with all that money. I don't think he likes his wife.

BIRDIE: Not like his wife? What a thing to say.

REGINA (*sits on sofa*): She's away a great deal. He said that several times. And once he made fun of her being so social and high-toned. But that fits in all

434

right. (*Sits back, arms on back of sofa, stretches.*) Her being social, I mean. She can introduce me. It won't take long with an introduction from her.

BIRDIE (*bewildered*): Introduce you? In Chicago? You mean you really might go? (*Crosses to table.*) Oh, Regina, you can't leave here. What about Horace?

REGINA: Don't look so scared about everything, Birdie. I'm going to live in Chicago. I've always wanted to. And now there'll be plenty of money to go with.

BIRDIE (*sits*): But Horace won't be able to move around. You know what the doctor wrote.

REGINA: There'll be millions, Birdie, millions. You know what I've always said when people told me we were rich? I said I think you should either be a nigger or a millionaire. In between, like us, what for? (*Laughs. Looks at* BIRDIE.) But I'm not going away tomorrow, Birdie. (*Takes her arms down.*) There's plenty of time to worry about Horace when he comes home. If he ever decides to come home.

BIRDIE: Will we be going to Chicago? I mean, Oscar and Leo and me?

REGINA: You? I shouldn't think so. (*Laughs. Leaning forward.*) Well, we must remember tonight. It's a very important night and we mustn't forget it. We shall

plan all the things we'd like to have and then we'll really have them. Make a wish, Birdie, any wish. It's bound to come true now.

[BEN *and* OSCAR *enter.*]

BIRDIE (*laughs*): Well. Well, I don't know. Maybe. (REGINA *turns to look at* BEN.) Well, I guess I'd know right off what I wanted.

[BEN *crosses to above* REGINA. OSCAR *stands by the upper window, waves to the departing carriage.*]

REGINA (*looks up at* BEN, *smiles. He smiles back at her*): Well, you did it. (*Grasps his hand.*)

BEN: Looks like it might be we did.

REGINA (*springs up, laughs*): Looks like it! Don't pretend. (*Rises.*) You're like a cat who's been licking the cream. (*Crosses to wine bottle on table.*) Now we must all have a drink to celebrate.

OSCAR (*from window*): The children, Alexandra and Leo, make a very handsome couple, Regina. (REGINA *does not look at him.* BEN *and* REGINA *drink.* OSCAR *steps in.*) Marshall remarked himself what fine young folks they were. How well they looked together.

REGINA (*sharply*): Yes. You said that before, Oscar. (*She puts drink down, crosses to chair left center—sits.*)

BEN: Yes, sir. It's beginning to look as if the deal's all set. I may not be a subtle man—but—— Now somebody ask me how I know the deal is set.

OSCAR: What do you mean, Ben?

BEN: You remember I told him that down here we drink the *last* drink for a toast?

OSCAR (*thoughtfully*): Yes. I never heard that before.

BEN: Nobody's ever heard it before. (*Turns chair downstage, right, to face room. Stands in front of it.*) God forgives those who invent what they need. (*Holding up his glass.*) I already had his signature. But we've all done business with men whose word over a glass is better than a bond. Anyway it don't hurt to have both. (*He sits.*)

OSCAR (*turns to* REGINA): You understand what Ben means?

REGINA (*smiles*): Yes, Oscar. I understand. I understood immediately.

BEN (*looks at her admiringly*): Did you, Regina? Well, when he lifted his glass to drink, I closed my eyes and saw the bricks going into place.

REGINA: And *I* saw a lot more than that.

[OSCAR *sits on sofa, lights cigar, sits back to relax.*]

BEN: Slowly, slowly: As yet we have only our hopes.

REGINA: Birdie and I have just been planning what we want. I know what I want. What will you want, Ben?

BEN: Caution. Don't count the chickens. (*Leans back, laughs.* REGINA *laughs.*) Well, God would allow us a little day dreaming. Good for the soul when you've worked hard enough to deserve it. (*Pauses.*) I think I'll have a stable. For a long time I've had my good eyes on Carter's in Savannah. A rich man's pleasure, the sport of kings, why not the sport of Hubbards? Why not?

REGINA (*smiles*): Why not? What will you have, Oscar?

OSCAR: I don't know. (*Thoughtfully—leaning forward on table.*) The pleasure of seeing the bricks grow will be enough for me.

BEN: Oh, of course. Our *greatest* pleasure will be to see the bricks grow. But we are all entitled to a little side indulgence.

OSCAR (*looking front*): Yes, I suppose so. Well, then, I think we might take a few trips here and there, (*to* BIRDIE) eh, Birdie?

BIRDIE (*surprised at being consulted*): Yes, Oscar. I'd like that.

OSCAR (*looking front*): We might even make a regular trip to Jekyll Island. I've heard the Cornelly place is for sale. We might think about buying it. Make a

436

nice change. (*To* BIRDIE.) Do you good, Birdie, a change of climate. Fine shooting, on Jekyll, the best.

BIRDIE: I'd like——

OSCAR (*indulgently*): What would you like?

BIRDIE: *Two* things. Two things I'd like most.

REGINA: Two! I should like a thousand. You are modest, Birdie.

BIRDIE (*warmly, delighted with the unexpected interest*): I should like to have Lionnet back. I know you own it now, but I'd like to see it fixed up again, the way Mama and Papa had it. Every year it used to get a nice coat of paint—Papa was very particular about the paint—and the lawn was so smooth all the way down to the river, with the trims of zinnias and red-feather plush. And the figs and blue little plums and the scuppernongs—— (*Smiles. Turns to* REGINA.) The organ is still there and it wouldn't cost much to fix. We could have parties for Zan, (*rises, crosses to* REGINA) the way Mama used to have for me. (*Crosses upstage, center, moving about, dreamily.*)

BEN: That's a pretty picture, Birdie. Might be a most pleasant way to live. (*Dismissing* BIRDIE.) What do you want, Regina?

BIRDIE (*very happily, not noticing that they are no longer listening to her*): I could have a cutting garden. Just where Mama's used to be. Oh, I do think we could be happier there. Papa used to say that *nobody* had ever lost their temper at Lionnet, and *nobody* ever would. Papa would never let anybody be nasty spoken, or mean. No, sir. He just didn't like it.

BEN: What do you want, Regina?

REGINA: I'm going to Chicago. And when I'm settled there and know the right people and the right things to buy—because I certainly don't now—I shall go to *Paris* and buy them. (*Laughs.*) I'm going to leave you and Oscar to count the bricks.

BIRDIE (*turning to* OSCAR): Oscar. Please let me have Lionnet back.

OSCAR (*to* REGINA): You are serious about moving to Chicago? [BIRDIE *crosses to table, pours drink, drinks it fast.*]

BEN: She is going to see the great world and leave us in the little one. Well, we'll come and visit you and meet all the great and be proud to think you are our sister.

REGINA (*gaily*): Certainly. And you won't even have to learn to be subtle, Ben. Stay as you are. You will be rich and the rich don't have to be subtle.

OSCAR: But what about Alexandra? She's seventeen. Old enough to be thinking about marrying.

BIRDIE (*crosses to* OSCAR): And, Oscar, I have one more wish. Just one more wish.

OSCAR (*turns*): What is it, Birdie? What are you saying?

BIRDIE: I want you to stop shooting. I mean, so much. I don't like to see animals and birds killed just for the killing. You only throw them away——

BEN (*to* REGINA): It'll take a great deal of money to live as you're planning, Regina.

REGINA: Certainly. But there'll be plenty of money. You have estimated the profits very high.

BEN: I have——

BIRDIE (*does not notice that* OSCAR *is looking at her furiously*): And you never let anybody else shoot, and the niggers need it so much to keep from starving. It's wicked to shoot food just because you like to shoot, when poor people need it so——

BEN (*laughs*): I have estimated the profits very high—for myself.

REGINA: What did you say?

BIRDIE: I've always wanted to speak about it, Oscar.

OSCAR (*slowly, carefully*): What are you chattering about?

BIRDIE (*finally catches his tone, nervously*): I was talking about Lionnet and—and about your shooting——

OSCAR: You are exciting yourself.

REGINA (*to* BEN): I didn't hear you. There was so much talking.

OSCAR (*to* BIRDIE): You have been acting very childish, very excited, all evening.

BIRDIE: Regina asked me what I'd like——

REGINA: What did you say, Ben?

BIRDIE: ——now that we'll be so rich. Everybody was saying what they would like, so *I* said what *I* would like, too.

BEN: I said—— (*He is interrupted by* OSCAR.)

OSCAR (*to* BIRDIE): Very well. We've all heard you. That's enough now.

BEN: I am waiting! (*They stop. Irritated, to* OSCAR.) I am waiting for you to finish. You and Birdie. Four conversations are three too many. (BIRDIE *crosses, upstage, center, slowly, sits in chair right of table.* OSCAR *nods,* BEN *waits, sees that everything is quiet. Smiles, to* REGINA.) I said that I had, and I do, estimate the profits very high—for myself, and Oscar, of course.

REGINA (*slowly*): And what does that mean?

[BEN *shrugs, looks toward* OSCAR.]

OSCAR (*looks at* BEN, *clears throat*): Well, Regina, it's like this. For forty-nine per cent Marshall will put up four hundred thousand dollars. For fifty-one per cent—— (*Smiles archly.*) a controlling interest, mind you, we will put up two hundred and twenty-five thousand dollars besides offering him certain benefits that our (*looks at* BEN *to include him*) local position allows us to manage. Ben means that two hundred and twenty-five thousand dollars is a lot of money.

REGINA: I know the terms and I know it's a lot of money.

BEN (*nodding*): It is.

OSCAR: Ben means that we are ready with our two-thirds of the money. Your third, Horace's, I mean, doesn't seem to be ready. (*Raises his hand as* REGINA *starts to speak.*) Ben has written to Horace, I have written, and you have written. He answers. But he never mentions this business. Yet we have explained it to him in great detail, and told him the urgency. Still he never mentions it. Ben has been very patient, Regina. (*Sits back.*) Naturally, you are our sister and we want you to benefit from anything we do. (*Looks at* BEN.)

REGINA (*rises. To* OSCAR): And in addition to your concern for me, you do not want control to go out of the family. (*To* BEN.) That right, Ben?

BEN: That's cynical. (*Smiles.*) Cynicism is only an unpleasant way of saying the truth.

OSCAR (*rises*): No need to be cynical. We'd have no trouble raising the third share, the share that you want to take.

REGINA: I am sure you could get the third share, the share you were saving for me. But that would give you a strange partner. And strange partners sometimes want a great deal. (*Smiles unpleasantly.*) But perhaps it would be wise for you to find him.

OSCAR (*turns*): Now, now. Nobody says we *want* to do that. We would like to have you in and you would like to come in.

REGINA: Yes. I certainly would.

BEN (*laughs, puts up his hand*): But we haven't heard from Horace.

REGINA: I've given my word that Horace will put up the money. That should be enough. [OSCAR *crosses to table downstage, left—flicks ash off cigar.*]

BEN: Oh, it was enough. I took your word. But I've got to have more than your word now. The contracts will be signed this week, and Marshall will want to see our money soon after. Regina, Horace has been in Baltimore for five months. I know that you've written him to come home, and that he hasn't come.

OSCAR: It's beginning to look as if he doesn't want to come home.

REGINA: Of course, he wants to

come home. You can't move around with heart trouble at any moment you choose. You know what doctors are like once they get their hands on a case like this—

OSCAR: They can't very well keep him from answering letters, can they? They couldn't keep him from arranging for the money if he wanted to——

REGINA: Has it occurred to you that Horace is also a good business man?

BEN: Certainly. He is a shrewd trader. Always has been. The bank is proof of that.

REGINA: Then, possibly, he may be keeping silent because he doesn't think he is getting enough for his money. Seventy-five thousand he has to put up. That's a lot of money, too. (*She sits on sofa.*)

OSCAR: Nonsense. He knows a good thing when he hears it. He knows that we can make *twice* the profit on cotton goods manufactured *here* than can be made in the North.

BEN: That isn't what Regina means. (*Smiles.*) May I interpret you, Regina? (*To* OSCAR.) Regina is saying that Horace wants *more* than a third of our share.

OSCAR (*amazed, playing along*): But he's only putting up a third of the money. You put up a third

and you get a third. What else *could* he expect?

REGINA: Well, *I* don't know. I don't know about these things. It would seem that if you put up a third you should only get a third. But then again, there's no law about it, is there? I should think that if you knew your money was very badly needed, well, you just might say, I want more, I want a bigger share. You *boys* have done that. I've heard you say so.

BEN: So you believe he has deliberately held out? For a larger share? (*Leaning forward.*) Well, I *don't* believe it. But I *do* believe that's what *you* want. Am I right, Regina?

REGINA: Oh, I shouldn't like to be too definite. (OSCAR *sits. To* BEN.) But I *could* say that I wouldn't like to persuade Horace unless he did get a larger share. I must look after his interests. It seems only natural——

OSCAR: And where would the larger share come from?

REGINA: I don't know. That's not my business. (*Giggles.*) But perhaps it could come off your share, Oscar.

[REGINA *and* BEN *laugh.*]

OSCAR (*rises and wheels furiously on both of them as they laugh*): What kind of talk is this?

BEN: I haven't said a thing.

OSCAR: *You* are talking very big tonight.

REGINA (*stops laughing*): Am I? Well, you should know me well enough to know that I wouldn't be asking for things I didn't think I could get.

OSCAR: Listen. I don't believe you can even get Horace to come home, much less get money from him or talk quite so big about what you want.

REGINA: Oh, I can get him home.

OSCAR: Then why haven't you?

REGINA: I thought I should fight his battles for him, before he came home. Horace is a very sick man. And even if *you* don't care how sick he is, I do.

BEN: Stop this foolish squabbling. (OSCAR *turns.*) How *can* you get him home?

REGINA: I will send Alexandra to Baltimore. She will ask him to come home. She will say that she *wants* him to come home, and that *I* want him to come home.

BIRDIE (*suddenly*): Well, of course she wants him here, but he's sick and maybe he's happy where he is.

REGINA (*as if she had not heard* BIRDIE, *to* BEN): You agree that he will come home if she asks him to, if she says that I miss him and want him——

BEN (*looks at her, smiles*): I admire you, Regina. And I agree. That's settled now, and —— (*Starts to rise.*)

REGINA (*quickly stopping him*): But before she brings him home, I want to know what he's going to get.

BEN: What do you want?

REGINA: Twice what you offered.

BEN: Well, you won't get it.

OSCAR (*to* REGINA): I think you've gone crazy.

REGINA: I don't want to fight, Ben——

BEN: I don't either. You won't get it. There isn't any chance of that. (*Roguishly.*) You're holding us up, and that's not pretty, Regina, not pretty. (*Holds up his hand as he sees she is about to speak.*) But we need you, and I don't want to fight. Here's what I'll do: I'll give Horace forty per cent, instead of the thirty-three and a third he really should get. I'll do that provided he is home and his money is up within two weeks. How's that?

REGINA: All right.

OSCAR (*crossing center to* BEN): I've asked before: Where is this extra share coming from?

BEN (*pleasantly*): From you. From your share.

OSCAR (*furiously*): From me, is it? That's just fine and dandy. That's my reward. For thirty-five years I've worked my hands to the bone for you. For thirty-five years I've done all the things you didn't want to do. And this is what I——

BEN (*turns slowly to look at* OS-CAR. OSCAR *breaks off*): My, my. I am being attacked tonight on all sides. First by my sister, then by my brother. And I ain't a man who likes being attacked. I can't believe that God wants the strong to parade their strength, but I don't mind doing it, if it's got to be done. (OSCAR *turns, crosses to chair left center, facing left. Leans back in his chair.*) You ought to take these things better. Oscar. I've made you money in the past. I'm going to make you more money now. You'll be a very rich man. What's the difference to any of us if a little more goes here, a little less goes there —it's all in the family. And it will stay in the family. (ADDIE *enters, begins to gather the glasses from table upstage, center.* OSCAR *turns to* BEN.) So my money will go to Alexandra and Leo. They may even marry some day and—— (ADDIE *looks at* BEN, *crosses to table right, picks up glasses, then crosses to table upstage, center, picks up tray and exits.*)

BIRDIE (*rising*): Marry—Zan and Leo——

OSCAR (*carefully*): That would make a great difference in my feelings. If they married. (*Sits in chair left, center.* BIRDIE *sits in chair upstage, center.*)

BEN: Yes, that's what I mean. Of course it would make a difference.

OSCAR (*carefully*): Is that what *you* mean, Regina?

REGINA: Oh, it's too far away. We'll talk about it in a few years.

OSCAR: I want to talk about it now.

BEN (*nods*): Naturally.

REGINA: There's a lot of things to consider. They are first cousins, and——

OSCAR: That isn't unusual. Our grandmother and grandfather were first cousins.

REGINA (*giggles*): And look at us.

[BEN *giggles.*]

OSCAR (*angrily—rises*): You're both being very gay with my money. (OSCAR *pacing in front of piano.*)

BEN (*sighs*): These quarrels. I dislike them so. (*Leans forward to* REGINA. OSCAR *stops walking at table on left. Listens.*) A marriage might be a very wise arrangement, for several reasons. And then, Oscar has given up something for you. You should try to manage something for him.

REGINA: I haven't said I was opposed to it. But Leo is a wild boy. There were those times when he took a little money from the bank and——

OSCAR: That's all past history——

442

REGINA: Oh, I know. And I know all young men are wild. I'm only mentioning it to show you that there are considerations——

BEN (*irritated that she does not understand he is trying to keep* OSCAR *quiet*): All right, so there are. But please assure Oscar that you will think about it very seriously.

REGINA (*smiles, nods*): Very well. I assure Oscar that I will think about it seriously.

OSCAR (*sharply*): That is not an answer.

REGINA: My, (*rises*) you're in a bad humor and you shall put me in one. I have said all that I am willing to say now. After all, Horace has to give his consent, too.

OSCAR: Horace will do what you tell him to.

REGINA: Yes, I think he will.

OSCAR: And I have your word that you will try to——

REGINA (*patiently*): Yes, Oscar. You have my word that I will think about it. Now do leave me alone.

[*There is the sound of* ALEXANDRA *and* LEO *opening and closing the front door.*]

BIRDIE (*rising*): I——Alexandra is only seventeen. She——

REGINA (*calling, crossing in to hall*): Alexandra? Are you back?

[BIRDIE *sits.*]

ALEXANDRA: Yes, Mama.

LEO (*comes into room*): Mr. Marshall got off safe and sound. Weren't those fine clothes he had? You can always spot clothes made in a good place. Look like maybe they were done in England. (REGINA *and* ALEXANDRA *enter room.*) Lots of men in the North send all the way to England for their stuff.

BEN (*to* LEO): Were you careful driving the horses?

LEO (*turns to* BEN): Oh, yes sir. I was.

[ALEXANDRA *has come in on* BEN'S *question, hears the answer, looks angrily at* LEO.]

ALEXANDRA (*crosses to* BIRDIE): It's a lovely night. You should have come, Aunt Birdie.

REGINA: Were you gracious to Mr. Marshall?

ALEXANDRA: I think so, Mama. I liked him.

[LEO *crosses to settee on left.— Sits.*]

REGINA: Good. And now I have great news for you. (ADDIE *enters with tray with water pitcher and glasses. Crosses to table upstage, center.* ALEXANDRA *crosses to* REGINA.) You are going to Baltimore in the morning to bring your father home.

ALEXANDRA (*gasps, then delighted*): Me? Papa said I should come? That must mean—— (*Turns to* ADDIE.) Addie, he

443

must be well. (*Crosses to* ADDIE.) Think of it, he'll be back home again. We'll *bring* him home.

REGINA: You are going alone, Alexandra. (*Sits on sofa.*)

ADDIE (ALEXANDRA *has turned in surprise*): Going alone? Going by herself? A child that age! Mr. Horace ain't going to like Zan traipsing up there by herself.

REGINA (*sharply*): Go upstairs and lay out Alexandra's things.

ADDIE: He'd expect me to be along——

REGINA: I'll be up in a few minutes to tell you what to pack. (ADDIE *slowly begins to climb steps. To* ALEXANDRA.) I should think you'd like going alone. At your age it certainly would have delighted me. You're a strange girl, Alexandra. Addie has babied you so much.

ALEXANDRA: I only thought it would be more fun if Addie and I went together.

BIRDIE (*timidly*): Maybe I could go with her, Regina. I'd really like to.

REGINA: She is going alone. She is getting old enough to take some responsibilities.

OSCAR: She'd better learn now. She's almost old enough to get married. (*Jovially, to* LEO, *slapping him on shoulder.*) Eh, son?

LEO: Huh?

OSCAR (*annoyed with* LEO *for not understanding*): Old enough

to get married, you're thinking, eh?

LEO: Oh, yes, sir. (*Feebly.*) Lots of girls get married at Zan's age. Look at Mary Prester and Johanna and——

REGINA: Well, she's not getting married tomorrow. But she is going to Baltimore tomorrow, so let's talk about *that*. (*To* ALEXANDRA.) You'll be glad to have Papa home again.

ALEXANDRA: I wanted to go before, Mama. You remember that. But you said *you* couldn't go, and that *I* couldn't go alone.

REGINA: I've changed my mind. (*Too casually.*) You're to tell Papa how much you missed him, and that he must come home now —for your sake. Tell him that you *need* him home.

ALEXANDRA: Need him home? I don't understand.

REGINA: There is nothing for you to understand. You are simply to say what I have told you.

BIRDIE (*rises and makes a step toward* REGINA): He may be too sick. She couldn't do that——

ALEXANDRA: Yes. He may be too sick to travel. I couldn't make him think he had to come home for me, if he is too sick to——

REGINA (*looks at her, sharply, challengingly*): You *couldn't* do what I tell you to do, Alexandra?

ALEXANDRA (*looks at her,*

quietly): No. I couldn't. If I thought it would hurt him.

REGINA (*after a second's silence, smiles pleasantly*): But you are doing this for Papa's own good. (*Takes* ALEXANDRA's *hand.*) You must let me be the judge of his condition. It's the best possible cure for him to come home and be taken care of here. He mustn't stay there any longer and listen to those alarmist doctors. You are doing this entirely for his sake. Tell your Papa that I want him to come home, that I miss him very much.

ALEXANDRA (*slowly*): Yes, Mama.

REGINA (*to the rest—rises*): I must go and start getting Alexandra ready now. (*Crosses to stairs.*) Why don't you all go home?

BEN (*rises*): I'll attend to the railroad ticket. One of the boys will bring it over. Good night, everybody. Have a nice trip, Alexandra. The food on the train is very good. The celery is so crisp. Have a good time and act like a little lady. (*He exits.*)

REGINA (*on landing*): Good night, Ben. Good night, Oscar —— (*Playfully.*) Don't be so glum, Oscar. It makes you look as if you had chronic indigestion. (*He does not answer.*)

BIRDIE: Good night, Regina.

REGINA: Good night, Birdie.

(*Exit upstairs.*)

OSCAR (*starts for hall, to* BIRDIE *and* LEO): Come along.

LEO (*To* ALEXANDRA): Imagine your not wanting to go! What a little fool you are. Wish it were me. What I could do in a place like Baltimore!

ALEXANDRA (*angrily, looking away from him*): Mind your business. I can guess the kind of things *you* could do.

LEO (*laughs*): Oh, no, you couldn't. (*He exits.*)

REGINA (*calling from top of stairs*): Come on, Alexandra.

BIRDIE (*quickly, crossing downstage, left, to* ALEXANDRA, *softly*): Zan.

ALEXANDRA (*quietly*): I don't understand about my going, Aunt Birdie. (*Shrugs.*) But anyway, Papa will be home again. (*Pats* BIRDIE's *arm.*) Don't worry about me. I can take care of myself. Really I can.

BIRDIE (*shakes her head, softly*): That's not what I'm worried about, Zan——

ALEXANDRA (*comes close to her*): What's the matter?

BIRDIE: It's about Leo——

ALEXANDRA (*whispering*): He beat the horses. That's why we were late getting back. We had to wait until they cooled off. He always beats the horses as if——

BIRDIE (*whispering frantically, holding* ALEXANDRA's *hands*): He's my son. My own son. But you are more to me—more to me than my own child. I love you more than anybody else——

ALEXANDRA: Don't worry about the horses. I'm sorry I told you.

BIRDIE (*her voice rising*): *I am not worrying about the horses. I am worrying about you.* You are *not* going to marry Leo. I am not going to let them do that to you——

ALEXANDRA: Marry? To Leo? (*Laughs.*) I wouldn't marry, Aunt Birdie. I've never even thought about it——

BIRDIE: Hush! But they have thought about it. (*Wildly.*) Zan, I couldn't stand to think about such a thing. You and——

[OSCAR *has come into doorway on* ALEXANDRA'S *speech. He is standing quietly, listening.*]

ALEXANDRA (*laughs*): But I'm not going to marry. And I'm certainly not going to marry Leo.

[OSCAR *takes one step into the room.*]

BIRDIE: Don't you understand? They'll make you. They'll make you——

ALEXANDRA (*takes* BIRDIE'S *hands, quietly, firmly*): That's foolish, Aunt Birdie. I'm grown now. Nobody can make me do anything.

BIRDIE: I just couldn't stand——

OSCAR (*sharply*): Birdie.

(BIRDIE *looks up, draws quickly away from* ALEXANDRA. *She stands rigid, fearful. Quietly.*) Birdie, get your hat and coat.

ADDIE (*unseen, calls from upstairs hallway*): Come on, baby. Your Mama's waiting for you, and she ain't nobody to keep waiting.

ALEXANDRA: All right. (*Then softly, embracing* BIRDIE.) Good night, Aunt Birdie. (*Crosses upstairs. As she passes* OSCAR.) Good night, Uncle Oscar. (BIRDIE *begins to move slowly towards door as* ALEXANDRA *climbs the stairs.* ALEXANDRA *is almost out of view when* BIRDIE *reaches* OSCAR *in doorway. As* BIRDIE *quickly attempts to pass him, he slaps her hard, across the face.* BIRDIE *cries out, puts her hand to her face. On the cry,* ALEXANDRA *turns, begins to run down the stairs.*) Aunt Birdie! What happened? What happened? I——

BIRDIE (*softly, without turning*): Nothing, darling. Nothing happened. (*Quickly, as if anxious to keep* ALEXANDRA *from coming close.*) Now go to bed. (OSCAR *exits.*) Nothing happened. (*Turns to* ALEXANDRA, *who is holding her hand.*) I only —I only twisted my ankle. (*She goes out.* ALEXANDRA *stands on stairs looking after her as if she were puzzled and frightened.*)

MEDIUM CURTAIN

ACT II

scene: *Same as Act I.   A week later, morning.   At rise: The light comes from the open shutter of the right window; the other shutters are tightly closed.* addie *is standing at window, looking out.   Near the dining room doors are brooms, mops, rags, etc.   After a second* oscar *comes into entrance hall, looks in the room, shivers, decides not to take his hat and coat off, comes into the room.   At the sound of the door,* addie *turns to see who has come in.*

addie (*without interest*): Oh, it's you, Mr. Oscar. (addie *turns back to window, closes windows.*)

oscar: What is this?   It's not night.   What's the matter here? (*Shivers.*)   Fine thing at this time of the morning.   Blinds all closed. (addie *begins to open shutters.   The room lights up.*)   Where's Miss Regina?   It's cold in here.

addie: Miss Regina ain't down yet.

oscar: She had any word?

addie (*wearily picks up feather duster*): No sir.

oscar: Wouldn't you think a girl that age could get on a train at one place and have sense enough to get off at another? (*He sits on settee.*)

addie: Something must have happened.   If Zan say she was coming last night, she's coming last night.   Unless something happened.   Sure fire disgrace to let a baby like that go all that way alone to bring home a sick man without——

oscar: You do a lot of judging around here, Addie, eh?   Judging of your white folks, I mean.

addie (*looks at him, sighs*): I'm tired.   I been up all night watching for them.

regina (*who cannot be seen —speaking from upstairs hall*): Who's downstairs, Addie? (*She appears in a dressing gown, peers down from landing.* addie *picks up carpet sweeper, dustpan, and brush and goes out.*)   Oh, it's you, Oscar.   What are you doing here so early?   I haven't been down yet.   I'm not finished dressing.

oscar (*speaking up to her*): You had any word from them?

regina: No.

oscar: Then something certainly has happened.   People don't just say they are arriving on Thursday night, and they haven't come by Friday morning.

regina: Oh, nothing has happened.   Alexandra just hasn't got sense enough to send a message.

oscar: If nothing's happened, then why aren't they here?

447

REGINA: You asked me that ten times last night. My, you do fret so, Oscar. Anything might have happened. They may have missed connections in Atlanta, the train may have been delayed—oh, a hundred things could have kept them.

OSCAR: Where's Ben?

REGINA: Where should he be? At home, probably. Really, Oscar, I don't tuck him in his bed and I don't take him out of it. Have some coffee and don't worry so much.

OSCAR: Have some coffee? There isn't any coffee. (*Looks at his watch, shakes his head. After a second* CAL *enters with a large silver tray, coffee urn, small cups, newspaper. He puts tray on table upstage, center, begins to set out cups.*) Oh, there you are. Is everything in this house always late?

CAL (*looks at him surprised*): You ain't out shooting this morning, Mr. Oscar?

OSCAR: First day I missed since I had a head cold. First day I missed in eight years. (*Sits on settee.*)

CAL: Yes, sir. I bet you. Simon he say you had a mighty good day yesterday morning. That's what Simon say. (*Brings* OSCAR *small coffee and newspaper.*)

OSCAR: Pretty good, pretty good. (*Opens newspaper.*)

CAL (*laughs, slyly, puts coffee cup on table left of settee, moves table toward* OSCAR): Bet you got enough bob-white and squirrel to give every nigger in town a Jesus-party. Most of 'em ain't had no meat since the cotton picking was over. Bet they'd give anything for a little piece of that meat——

OSCAR (*turns his head to look at* CAL): Cal, if I catch a nigger in this town going shooting, you know what's going to happen.

[LEO *enters.*]

CAL (*hastily steps back*): Yes sir, Mr. Oscar. I didn't say nothing about nothing. It was Simon who told me and— Morning, Mr. Leo. You gentlemen having your breakfast with us here?

LEO (*comes immediately to* OSCAR): The boys in the bank don't know a thing. They haven't had any message.

[CAL *waits for an answer, gets none, shrugs, moves to door left, looks back at them, exits.*]

OSCAR (*peers at* LEO): What you doing here, son?

LEO: You told me to find out if the boys at the bank had any message from Uncle Horace or Zan——

OSCAR: I told you if they had a message to bring it here. I told you that if they didn't have a message to stay at the bank and do your work.

LEO: Oh, I guess I misunderstood.

OSCAR: You didn't misunderstand. You just were looking for any excuse to take an hour off. (LEO *crosses to table upstage, center, pours coffee.*) You got to stop that kind of thing. You got to start settling down. You going to be a married man one of these days.

LEO: Yes, sir.

OSCAR: You also got to stop with that woman in Mobile. (*As* LEO *is about to speak, he puts up a hand.* LEO *turns back for sugar.*) You're young and I haven't got no objections to outside women. That is, I haven't got no objections so long as they don't interfere with serious things. Outside women are all right in their place, but *now* isn't their place! You got to realize that.

LEO (*nods*): Yes, sir. I'll tell her. She'll act all right about it. (*He drinks his coffee.*)

OSCAR: Also, you got to start working harder at the bank. You got to convince your Uncle Horace you going to make a fit husband for Alexandra.

LEO: What do you think has happened to them? Supposed to be here last night—— (*Laughs.*) Bet you Uncle Ben's mighty worried. Seventy-five thousand dollars worried.

OSCAR (*smiles happily*): Ought to be worried. Damn well ought to be. First he don't answer the letters, then he don't come home —— (*Giggles.*)

LEO: What will happen if Uncle Horace don't come home or don't——?

OSCAR: Or don't put up the money? Oh, we'll get it from outside. Easy enough.

LEO (*surprised*): But *you* don't want outsiders. (*Sits.*)

OSCAR: What do I care who gets my share? I been shaved already. Serve Ben right if he had to give away some of his.

LEO: Damn shame what they did to you.

OSCAR (*looking up the stairs*): Don't talk so loud. (LEO *starts to speak.*) Don't you worry. When I die, you'll have as much as the rest. You might have yours *and* Alexandra's. I'm not so easily licked.

LEO (*smoothly*): I wasn't thinking of myself, Papa——

OSCAR: Well, you should be, you should be. It's every man's duty to think of himself.

LEO (*turns to* OSCAR): You think Uncle Horace don't want to go in on this?

OSCAR (*giggles*): That's my hunch. He hasn't showed any signs of *loving* it yet.

LEO (*laughs*): But he hasn't listened to Aunt Regina yet,

449

either. Oh, he'll go along. It's too good a thing. (*Rises.*) Why wouldn't he want to? (*Crosses to pour another coffee.*) He's got plenty and plenty to invest with. He don't even have to sell anything. Eighty-eight thousand worth of Union Pacific bonds sitting right in his safe deposit box. All he's got to do is open the box.

OSCAR (*after a pause—looks at his watch*): Mighty late breakfast in this fancy house. Yes, he's had those bonds for fifteen years. Bought them when they were low and just locked them up.

LEO (*nods*): Yeah. Just has to open the box and take them out. That's all. Easy as easy can be. (*Laughs.*) The things in that box! There's all those bonds, looking mighty fine. (OSCAR *slowly puts down his newspaper and turns to* LEO.) Then right next to them is a baby shoe of Zan's and a cheap old cameo on a string, and, *and*—nobody'd believe this—a piece of an old violin. Not even a whole violin. Just a piece of an old thing, a piece of a violin.

OSCAR (*very softly; as if he were trying to control his voice —looking at* LEO): A piece of a violin! What do you think of that!

LEO: Yes, siree. A lot of other crazy things, too. (*Turns to* OSCAR *who is staring at him.*) A

poem, I guess it is, signed with his mother's name, and two old school books with notes and—— (LEO *catches* OSCAR's *look. His voice trails off. He turns his head away.*)

OSCAR (*very softly*): How do you know what's in the box, son?

LEO (*stops, draws back, frightened, realizing what he has said. Then after a second, he manages to speak*): Oh, well. Well—er. (*Crossing left to chair left center.*) Well, one of the boys, sir. It was one of the boys at the bank. He took old Mander's keys. It was Joe Horns. He just up and took Manders' keys and, and— well, took the box out. (*Quickly.*) Then they all asked me if I wanted to see, too. So I looked a little, I guess, but then I made them close up the box quick and I told them never——

OSCAR (*looks at him*): Joe Horns, you say? He opened it?

LEO: Yes, sir, yes he did. My word of honor. (*Very nervously looking away.*) I suppose that don't excuse *me* for looking,— (*Looking at* OSCAR.) but I did make him close it up and put the keys back in Manders' drawer——

OSCAR (*leans forward, very softly*): Tell me the truth, Leo. I am not going to be angry with you. Did you open the box yourself?

LEO: *No sir, I didn't.* I told you

450

I didn't. No, I——

OSCAR (*irritated, patient*): I am *not* going to be angry with you. Sometimes a young fellow deserves credit for looking round him to see what's going on. Sometimes that's a good sign in a fellow your age. (LEO *turns head to listen.* OSCAR *rises.*) Many great men have made their fortune with their eyes.—Did you open the box?

LEO (*very puzzled*): No. I——

OSCAR (*taking a step to him*): Did you open the box? It may have been——well, it may have been a good thing if you had.

LEO (*after a long pause*): I opened it.

OSCAR (*quickly*): Is that the truth? (LEO *nods.*) Does anybody also know that you opened it? Come, Leo, don't be afraid of speaking the truth to me.

LEO: No. Nobody knew. Nobody was in the bank when I did it. But——

OSCAR: Did your Uncle Horace ever know you opened it?

LEO (*shakes his head*): He only looks in it once every six months when he cuts the coupons, and sometimes Mander even does that for him. Uncle Horace don't even have the keys. Mander keeps them for him. Imagine not looking at all that. You can bet if I had the bonds, I'd watch 'em like——

OSCAR: If you had them. *If* you had them. Then you could have the share in the mill, you and me. (*Turns to* LEO.) A fine, big share, too. (*Pauses—shrugs.*) Well, a man can't be shot for wanting to see his son get on in the world, can he, boy?

[OSCAR *sits on sofa.*]

LEO (*looks up, begins to understand*): No, he can't! Natural enough. (*Laughs.*) But I haven't got the bonds and Uncle Horace has. And now we can just sit back and wait to be a millionaire.

OSCAR (*innocently*): You think your Uncle Horace likes you well enough to lend *you* the bonds if he decides not to use them himself?

LEO: Papa, it must be that you haven't had your breakfast! (*Laughs loudly.*) Lend me the bonds! My God——

OSCAR (*disappointed*): No, I suppose not. Just a fancy of mine. A loan for three months, maybe four, easy enough for us to pay it back then. Anyway, this is only April—— (*Slowly counting the months on his fingers.*) and if he doesn't look at them until fall, he wouldn't even *miss* them out of the box.

LEO: That's it. He wouldn't even miss them. Ah, well——

OSCAR: No, sir. Wouldn't even miss them. How could he miss them if he never looks at them?

(*Sighs as* LEO *stares at him.*) Well, here we are sitting around waiting for him to come home and invest his money in something he hasn't lifted his hand to get. But I can't help thinking he's acting strange. You laugh when I say he could lend you the bonds if he's not going to use them himself. But would it hurt him?

LEO (*slowly looking at* OSCAR): No. No, it wouldn't.

OSCAR: People *ought* to help other people. But that's not always the way it happens. (BEN *enters, hangs his coat and hat on hall tree. Very carefully.*) And so sometimes you got to think of yourself. (*As* LEO *stares at him,* BEN *appears in doorway.*) Morning, Ben.

BEN (*coming in, carrying his newspaper*): Fine, sunny morning. Any news from the runaways? (BEN *sits in chair right center.*)

REGINA (*on landing*): There's no news or you would have heard it. (*Coming down stairs.*) Quite a convention so early in the morning, aren't you all? (*Goes to coffee urn.*)

OSCAR: You rising mighty late these days. Is that the way they do things in Chicago society?

BEN (*looking at his paper*): Old Carter died up in Senateville. Eighty-one is a good time for us all, eh? What do you think has really happened to Horace, Regina?

REGINA: Nothing.

BEN (*too casually, still reading*): You don't think maybe he never started from Baltimore and never intends to start?

REGINA (*irritated*): Of course they've started. Didn't I have a letter from Alexandra? What is so strange about people arriving late? (*Crosses to table—pours coffee.*) He has that cousin in Savannah he's so fond of. He may have stopped to see him. They'll be along today some time, very flattered that you and Oscar are so worried about them.

BEN: I'm a natural worrier. Especially when I am getting ready to close a business deal and one of my partners remains silent *and* invisible.

REGINA (*laughs*): Oh, is that it? I thought you were worried about Horace's *health.*

OSCAR: Oh, that too. Who could help but worry? *I'm* worried. This is the first day I haven't shot since my head cold.

REGINA (*starts toward dining room*): Then you haven't had your breakfast. Come along.

[OSCAR *and* LEO *follow her.* BEN *remains seated.*]

BEN: Regina. (*She turns at dining-room door.*) That cousin of Horace's has been dead for years and, in any case, the train does not go through Savannah.

REGINA (*laughs—then contin-ues into dining-room, seats her-self, motions to* LEO *and* OSCAR): Did he die? You're always re-membering about people dying. (BEN *rises, leaves newspaper on table, crosses upstage, left, to dining-room.*) Now I intend to eat my breakfast in peace, and read my newspaper. (*Rings bell.*)

BEN (*goes toward dining-room as he talks*): This is second break-fast for me. My first was bad. Celia ain't the cook she used to be. Too old to have taste any more. If she hadn't belonged to Mama, I'd send her off to the country.

[CAL *is putting two silver serving dishes on table.* OSCAR *and* LEO *start to eat.* BEN *seats himself.*]

LEO: Uncle Horace will have some tales to tell, I bet. Balti-more is a lively town.

REGINA (*to* CAL): The grits isn't hot enough. Take it back.

CAL: Oh, yes'm. (*Calling into kitchen as he exits off dining-room.*) Grits didn't hold the heat. Grits didn't hold the heat.

LEO: When I was at school three of the boys and myself took a train once and went over to Bal-timore. It was so big we thought we were in Europe. I was just a kid then——

REGINA (*looks up, helps herself from a dish*): I find it very pleas-ant to have breakfast alone. I hate chattering before I've had something hot. (CAL *has come back, closes dining-room doors.*) Do be still, Leo.

[ADDIE *comes into the room, be-gins gathering up cups, car-ries them to the large tray, then quickly she runs into the hall. Outside there are the sounds of* VOICES *and* PEO-PLE *moving about. A few seconds later* ADDIE *appears again in the doorway, her arm around the shoulders of* HORACE GIDDENS, *supporting him.* HORACE *is a tall man of about forty-five. He has been good-looking, but now his face is tired and ill. He walks stiffly, as if it were an enormous effort, and care-fully, as if he were unsure of his balance.* ADDIE *takes off his overcoat and hangs it on hall tree. She then helps him across to the chair left cen-ter.*)

HORACE (*as they are crossing*): How are you, Addie? How have you been?

ADDIE: I'm all right, Mr. Hor-ace. I've just been worried about you.

[HORACE *sits in chair.* ALEXAN-DRA *enters. She is flushed and excited, her hat awry,*

453

her face dirty. Her arms are full of packages, but she comes quickly to ADDIE.]

ALEXANDRA: Now don't tell me how worried you were. We couldn't help it and there was no way to send a message.

ADDIE (*to* HORACE, *begins to take packages from* ALEXANDRA): Yes, sir, I was mighty worried.

ALEXANDRA: We had to stop in Mobile over night. Papa— (*Looks at him.*) Papa didn't feel well. The trip was too much for him, and I made him stop and rest— (*As* ADDIE *takes last package.*) No, don't take that. That's father's medicine. (*Crosses to table right center.* ADDIE *puts the packages on the chair left of table upstage, center, then crosses to* ALEXANDRA.) I'll hold it. It mustn't break. Now, about the stuff outside. Papa must have his wheel chair. I'll get that and the valises— (ALEXANDRA *starts to go, but* ADDIE *stops her.*)

ADDIE (*very happy, holding* ALEXANDRA'S *arms*): Since when you got to carry your own valises? Since when I ain't old enough to hold a bottle of medicine? (HORACE *coughs.*) You feel all right, Mr. Horace!

HORACE (*nods*): Glad to be sitting down.

ALEXANDRA (*opening package of medicine on table*): He doesn't

feel all right. He just says that. The trip was very hard on him, and now he must go right to bed.

ADDIE (*looking at him carefully*): Them fancy doctors, they give you help?

HORACE: They did their best.

LEO (*in dining-room*): Papa, can I have your part of the paper?

ALEXANDRA (*has become conscious of the voices in dining-room*): I bet Mama was worried. I better tell her we're here now. (*She starts for door.*)

HORACE: Zan. (*She stops.*) Not for a minute, dear.

ALEXANDRA: Oh, Papa, you feel bad again. I knew you did. Do you want your medicine?

HORACE: No, I don't feel that way. I'm just tired, darling. Let me rest a little.

ALEXANDRA: Yes, but Mama will be mad if I don't tell her we're here.

ADDIE: They're all in there eating breakfast.

ALEXANDRA: Oh, are they all here? Why do they *always* have to be here? I was hoping Papa wouldn't have to see anybody, that it would be nice for him and quiet.

ADDIE (*patting* ALEXANDRA'S *arm*): Then let your Papa rest for a minute.

HORACE: Addie, I bet your coffee's as good as ever. They don't have such good coffee up North.

(*Looks hungrily at urn.*) Is it as good, Addie?

[ADDIE *starts for coffee urn.*]

ALEXANDRA: No. Dr. Reeves said not much coffee. Just now and then. (*Proudly to* ADDIE.) I'm the nurse now, Addie.

ADDIE: You'd be a better one if you didn't look so dirty. (*Taking* ALEXANDRA *to stairs.*) Now go and take a bath, Miss Grownup. Change your linens, get out a fresh dress and give your hair a good brushing—go on——

ALEXANDRA: Will you be all right, Papa?

ADDIE (*slapping her backside*): Go on.

ALEXANDRA (*on stairs, talks as she goes up*): The pills Papa must take once every four hours. (ADDIE *steps into room.*) And the bottle only when—only if he feels very bad. (*On landing.*) Now don't move until I come back and don't talk much and remember about his medicine, Addie——

ADDIE: Ring for Belle and have her help you and then I'll make you a fresh breakfast.

ALEXANDRA (*as she disappears up stairs*): How's Aunt Birdie? Is she here?

ADDIE: It ain't right for you to have coffee? It will hurt you?

HORACE (*slowly*): Nothing can make much difference now. Get me a cup, Addie. (*She looks at him, crosses to urn, pours a cup.*)

Funny. They can't make coffee up North. (ADDIE *brings him a cup.*) They don't like red pepper, either. (*He takes cup and gulps it greedily.*) God, that's good. You remember how I used to drink it? Ten, twelve cups a day. (*Slight laugh as he picks up cup again. He speaks more slowly.*) Addie, before I see anybody else, I want to know why Zan came to fetch me home. She's tried to tell me, but she doesn't seem to know herself. (*Drinks.*)

ADDIE (*turns away*): I don't know. (*Crosses right to table.*) All I know is big things are going on. (*To* HORACE.) Everybody going to be high-tone rich. Big rich. You too. (*Looks away —at table.*) All because smoke's going to start out of a building that ain't even up yet. (*She angrily creases the medicine bottle paper on the table.*)

HORACE: I've heard about it.

ADDIE: And er—— (*Hesitates.*) And—well, Zan, she going to marry Mr. Leo in a little while.

HORACE (*looks at her, then very slowly*): What are you talking about?

ADDIE: That's right. That's the talk, God help us.

HORACE (*angrily*): What's the talk?

ADDIE: I'm telling you. There's going to be a wedding—— (*An-*

455

grily clenches paper in her hand, turns head away.) Over my dead body there is.

HORACE (*he hands cup to* ADDIE, *not looking at her, after a second, quietly*): Go and tell them I'm home.

ADDIE (*hesitates*): Now you ain't to get excited. You're to be in your bed——

HORACE: Go on, Addie. Go and say I'm back.

[ADDIE *takes cup and paper to tray, looking at him as he is rising, then crosses left and opens dining-room doors. He rises with difficulty, stands stiff as if he were in pain, facing the dining-room.*]

ADDIE (*opens doors, then stands in corner upstage, left.*) Miss Regina. They're home. They got here——

[EVERYBODY *turns to look at her.*]

BEN: They are?

OSCAR: Good.

LEO: Just now?

REGINA: Horace.

[REGINA *quickly rises, runs into the room.* OTHERS *follow her.*]

REGINA (*warmly*): Horace! You've finally arrived. (*As she kisses him, the* OTHERS *come forward, all talking together.*)

BEN (*in doorway, carrying a napkin*): Well, sir, you had us all mighty worried. (*He steps for-*

ward. They shake hands. ADDIE watches them, then exits.)

OSCAR: You're a sight for sore eyes.

HORACE: Hello Ben.

[LEO *enters eating biscuit.*]

OSCAR: And how you feel? Tip-top, I bet, because that's the way you're looking.

HORACE (*coldly, irritated with* OSCAR's *lie*): Hello, Oscar. Hello Leo. (LEO *extends hand.*) How are you?

LEO (*shaking hands*): I'm fine, sir. But a lot better now that you're back.

REGINA (*steps to* HORACE): Now sit down. (LEO *backs away as* HORACE *sits.*) What did happen to you and where's Alexandra? I am so excited about seeing you that I almost forgot about her.

HORACE: I didn't feel good, a little weak, I guess, and we stopped overnight to rest. Zan's upstairs washing off the train dirt.

REGINA: Oh, I am so sorry the trip was hard on you. I didn't think that——

HORACE (*sarcastically, looking around at them*): Well, it's just as if I had never been away. All of you here——

BEN: Waiting to welcome you home.

[BIRDIE *bursts in. She is wearing a flannel kimono and her face is flushed and excited.* BEN *crosses to mantel.*]

BIRDIE (*runs to him, kisses him*): Horace!

HORACE (*warmly pressing her arm*): I was just wondering where you were, Birdie.

BIRDIE (*excited*): Oh, I would have been here. I didn't know you were back until Simon said he saw the buggy—— (*She draws back to look at him. Her face sobers.*) Oh, you don't look well, Horace. No you don't.

REGINA (*laughs*): Birdie, what a thing to say——

HORACE (*looking at* OSCAR): Oscar thinks I look very well.

OSCAR (*annoyed—turns on* LEO): Don't stand there holding that biscuit in your hand.

LEO: Oh. Well. I'll just finish my breakfast, Uncle Horace, and then I'll give you all the news about the bank—— (*He exits into dining-room, taking newspaper from settee.*)

OSCAR (*comes to* BIRDIE): And what is that costume you have on?

BIRDIE (*looking at* HORACE): Now that you're home, you'll feel better. Plenty of good rest and we'll take such fine care of you —— (*Stops.*) But where is Zan? (*Horace motions to staircase.*) I missed her so much.

OSCAR: I asked you what is that strange costume you're parading around in?

BIRDIE (*nervously, backing toward stairs*): Me? (*Looks at cos-tume—drops* HORACE's *hand.* Oh! It's my wrapper. I was so excited about Horace I just rushed out of the house——

OSCAR: Did you come across the square dressed that way? My dear Birdie, I——

HORACE (*to* REGINA, *wearily*): Yes, it's just like old times.

REGINA (*quickly to* OSCAR): Now no fights. This is a holiday.

BIRDIE (*runs quickly up stairs*): Zan! Zannie!

OSCAR: Birdie! (*She stops.*)

BIRDIE: Tell Zan I'll be back in a little while. (*Exits door on right.*)

REGINA (*to* OSCAR *and* BEN): Why don't you go finish your breakfast—— (*Looks at* OSCAR. *He looks at* BEN, *then crosses into dining-room.*) and let Horace rest for a minute?

BEN: Never leave a meal unfinished. There are too many poor people who need the food. Mighty glad to see you home, Horace. Fine to have you back. Fine to have you back.

OSCAR (*to* LEO *as* BEN *is closing dining-room doors*): Your mother has gone crazy. Running around the streets like a woman—— (*The moment* REGINA *and* HORACE *are alone, they become awkward and self-conscious.*)

REGINA (*laughs awkwardly*): Well. Here we are. It's been a long time. (*HORACE smiles.*)

457

Five months. You know, Horace, I wanted to come and be with you in the hospital, but I didn't know where my duty was. Here, or with you. But you know how much I *wanted* to come.

HORACE: That's kind of you, Regina. There was no need to come.

REGINA: Oh, but there was. Five months lying there all by yourself, no kin-folk, no friends. Don't try to tell me you didn't have a bad time of it.

HORACE: I didn't have a bad time. (*As she shakes her head, he becomes insistent.*) No, I didn't, Regina. Oh, at first when I—when I heard the news about myself—but after I got used to that, I liked it there.

REGINA: You *liked* it? (*Coldly.*) Isn't that strange! You liked it so well you didn't want to come home?

HORACE: That's not the way to put it. (*Then, kindly, as he sees her turn her head away.*) But there I was and I got kind of used to it, kind of to like lying there and thinking. (*Smiles.*) I never had much time to think before. And time's become valuable to me.

REGINA: It sounds almost like a holiday.

HORACE (*laughs*): It was, sort of. The first holiday I've had since I was a little kid.

REGINA: And here I was thinking you were in pain and—

HORACE (*quietly*): I *was* in pain.

REGINA: And instead you were having a holiday! (*She sits.*) A holiday of thinking. Couldn't you have done that here?

HORACE: I wanted to do it before I came here. I was thinking about us.

REGINA: About us? About you and me? Thinking about you and me after all these years? (*Unpleasantly. Rises, crosses downstage, right.*) You shall tell me everything you thought— some day.

HORACE (*there is silence for a minute*): Regina. (*She turns to him.*) Why did you send Zan to Baltimore?

REGINA: Why? Because I wanted you home. (*Crossing to him.*) You can't make anything suspicious out of that, can you?

HORACE: I didn't mean to make anything suspicious about it. (*Hesitantly, taking her hand.*) Zan said you wanted me to come home. I was so pleased at that and touched, it made me feel good.

REGINA (*taking away her hand, turns*): Touched that I should want you home?

HORACE (*sighs*): I'm saying all the wrong things, as usual. Let's try to get along better. There isn't so much more time. Regina, what's all this crazy talk I've been hearing about Zan and Leo? (*Slight laugh.*) Zan and Leo marrying?

REGINA (*turning to him, sharply*): Who gossips so much around here?

HORACE (*shocked*): Regina!

REGINA (*annoyed, anxious to quiet him*): It's some foolishness that Oscar thought up. I'll explain later. I have no intention of allowing any such arrangement. It was simply a way of keeping Oscar quiet in all this business I've been writing you about——

HORACE (*carefully*): What has Zan to do with any business of Oscar's? Whatever it is, you had better put it out of Oscar's head immediately. You know what I think of Leo.

REGINA: But there's no need to talk about it now.

HORACE: There is no need to talk about it ever. Not as long as I live. (REGINA *turns, crossing right.* HORACE *stops, slowly, turns to look at her.*) As long as I live. I've been in a hospital for five months. Yet since I've been here you have not once asked me about —about my health. (*Then gently.*) Well, I suppose they've written you. I can't live very long.

REGINA (*coldly*): I've never understood why people have to

talk about this kind of thing.

HORACE (*there is a silence— then he looks up at her, his face cold*): You misunderstand. I don't intend to gossip about my sickness. I thought it was only fair to tell you. I was not asking for your sympathy.

REGINA (*sharply, turns to him*): What do the doctors think caused your bad heart?

HORACE: What do you mean?

REGINA: They didn't think it possible, did they, that your fancy women may have——?

HORACE (*smiles, unpleasantly*): Caused my heart to be bad? I don't think that's the best scientific theory. You don't catch heart trouble in bed.

REGINA (*angrily*): I didn't think you did. I only thought you might catch a bad conscience—in bed, as you say.

HORACE: I didn't tell them about my bad conscience. Or about my *fancy women.* Nor did I tell them that my wife has not wanted me in bed with her for ——(*Sharply.*) How long is it, Regina? (REGINA *turns to him.*) Ten years? Did you bring me home for this, to make me feel guilty again? That means you want something. But you'll not make me feel guilty any more. My "thinking" has made a difference.

REGINA: I see that it has.

459

BEN (*in dining-room*): Put down that paper, Leo.

REGINA (*she looks toward dining-room door—then comes to him, her manner warm and friendly*): It's foolish for us to fight this way. I didn't mean to be unpleasant. I was stupid.

HORACE (*wearily*): God knows I didn't either. I came home wanting so much not to fight, and then all of a sudden there we were. I got hurt and——

REGINA (*hastily*): It's all my fault. I didn't ask about—your illness because I didn't want to remind you of it. Anyway I never believe doctors when they talk about—— (*Brightly.*) when they talk like that.

HORACE (*not looking at her*): Well, we'll try our best with each other. (*He rises, starts for stairs. REGINA stops him.*)

REGINA (*quickly, crossing with him*): I'll try. Honestly, I will. Horace, (*He stops, turns to her.*) Horace, I know you're tired but, but—couldn't you stay down here a few minutes longer? I want Ben to tell you something.

HORACE: Tomorrow.

REGINA: I'd like to now. It's very important to me. It's very important to all of us. (*Gaily, as she moves toward dining-room.*) Important to your beloved daughter. She'll be a very great heiress——

HORACE: Will she? That's nice.

REGINA (*opens doors*): Ben, are you finished breakfast?

HORACE: Is this the mill business I've had so many letters about?

REGINA (*to BEN*): Horace would like to talk to you now.

HORACE: Horace would not like to talk to you now. I am very tired, Regina—— (*He starts.*)

REGINA (*comes to him and stops him*): Please. You've said we'll try our best with each other. I'll try. Really, I will. But please do this for me now. (*Urging him into chair.*) You will see what I've done while you've been away. How I watched your interests. (*Laughs gaily.*) And I've done very well, too. But things can't be delayed any longer. Everything must be settled this week —— (HORACE *crosses—sits on chair right, center.* REGINA *crosses to* BEN *who is entering.* OSCAR *has stayed in the dining-room, his head turned to watch them.* LEO *is pretending to read newspaper.*) Now you must tell Horace all about it. Only be quick because he is very tired and must go to bed. (HORACE *is looking up at her as if he finally understood. His face hardens as she speaks.*) But I think your news will be better for him than all the medicine in the world.

BEN (*who is looking at* HOR-

ACE): It could wait. Horace may not feel like talking today.

REGINA: What an old faker you are! You know it can't wait. You know it must be finished this week. You've been just as anxious for Horace to get here as I've been.

BEN (*very jovial*): I suppose I have been. And why not? Horace has done Hubbard Sons many a good turn. Why shouldn't I be anxious to help him now?

REGINA (*laughs*): Help him! Help him when you need him, that's what you mean. (*Sits on sofa.*)

BEN: What a woman you married, Horace! (*Laughs awkwardly when* HORACE *does not answer.*) Well, then I'll make it quick. You know what I've been telling you for years. How I've always said that every one of us little Southern business men had great things—— (*Extends his arm, moves his fingers.*) —right beyond our finger-tips. It's been my dream: my dream to make those fingers grow longer. I'm a lucky man, Horace, a lucky man. To dream and to live to get what you've dreamed of. That's *my* idea of a lucky man. (*Looks at his fingers as his arm drops slowly.*) For thirty years I've cried, bring the cotton mills to the cotton! (HORACE *opens medicine bottle, pours dose into*

spoon.)   Well, finally I got up nerve to go to the Marshall Company in Chicago.

HORACE (*has finally taken his eyes from* REGINA): I know all this. (*He takes medicine.* REGINA *rises.*)

BEN: Can I get you something?

HORACE: Some water, please.

REGINA (*turns quickly*): Oh, I'm sorry. Let me. (*Crosses to tray on table upstage, center, brings him glass. He drinks as they wait in silence.*) You feel all right now?

HORACE: Yes. You wrote me. I know all that. (OSCAR *rises— crosses to dining-room doors.*)

REGINA (*triumphantly*): But you don't know that in the last few days Ben has agreed to give us—you, I mean—a much larger share.

HORACE: Really? That's very generous of him.

BEN (*laughs*): It wasn't so generous of me; it was smart of Regina.

REGINA (*as if she were signalling* HORACE): I explained to Ben that perhaps you hadn't answered his letters because you didn't think he was offering you enough, and that the time was getting short and you could guess how much he needed you——

HORACE (*smiles at her—nods*): And I could guess that he wants to keep control in the family?

461

REGINA (*to* BEN, *triumphantly*): Exactly. (*To* HORACE.) So I did a little bargaining for you and convinced my brothers they weren't the only Hubbards who had a business sense.

HORACE: Did you have to convince them of that? How little people know about each other! (OSCAR *laughs.*) But you'll know better about Regina next time, eh, Ben? (BEN, REGINA, HORACE *laugh together.* OSCAR's *face is angry.*) Now let's see. We're getting a bigger share. (*Looking at* OSCAR.) Who's getting less?

BEN: Oscar.

HORACE: Well, Oscar, you've grown very unselfish. What's happened to you?

[LEO *rises, crosses to dining-room doors.*]

BEN (*quickly, before* OSCAR *can answer*): Oscar doesn't mind. Not worth fighting about now, eh, Oscar?

OSCAR (*angrily*): I'll get mine in the end. You can be sure of that. I've got my son's future to think about.

HORACE (*sharply*): Leo? Oh, I see. (*Puts his head back, laughs.* REGINA *looks at him nervously.*) I am beginning to see. Everybody will get theirs.

BEN: I knew you'd see it. Seventy-five thousand, and that seventy-five thousand will make you a million.

REGINA (*steps to table, leaning forward*): It will, Horace, it will.

HORACE: I believe you. (REGINA *steps back, sits on sofa. After a second.*) Now I can understand Oscar's self-sacrifice, but what did you have to promise Marshall Company besides the money you're putting up?

BEN: They wouldn't take promises. They wanted guarantees.

HORACE: Of what?

BEN (*nods*): Water power. Free and plenty of it.

HORACE: You got them that, of course?

BEN: Cheap. You'd think the governor of a great State would make his price a little higher. From pride, you know. (HORACE *smiles.* BEN *smiles.*) Cheap wages. (*Sits.*) What do you mean by cheap wages, I say to Marshall? Less than Massachusetts, he says to me, and that averages eight a week. (*Leans back.*) Eight a week! By God, I tell him, I'd work for eight a week myself. Why, there ain't a mountain white or a town nigger but wouldn't give his right arm for three silver dollars every week, eh Horace?

HORACE: Sure. And they'll take less than that when you get around to playing them off against each other. You can save a little money *that* way, Ben. (*Angrily.*) And make them hate each other just a little more than they do now.

REGINA: What's all this about?

BEN (*laughs*): There'll be no trouble from anybody, white or black. Marshall said that to me. "What about strikes? That's all we've had in Massachusetts for the last three years." I say to him, "What's a strike? I never heard of one. Come South, Marshall. We got good folks and we don't stand for any fancy fooling."

HORACE: You're right. (*Slowly.*) Well, it looks like you made a good deal for yourselves, and for Marshall, too. (CAL *has come into dining-room and closes doors. To* BEN.) Your father used to say he made the thousands and you boys would make the millions. I think he was right. (*Rises.*)

REGINA (*they are all looking at* HORACE; *she laughs, nervously, leans forward*): Millions for *us*, too.

HORACE: Us? You and me? I don't think so. We've got enough money, Regina. We'll just sit by and watch the boys grow rich. (*Takes a step upstage, center, holding on to chair.* OSCAR *sits on piano stool. They watch him tensely, as he begins to move toward staircase. He passes* LEO, *looks at him for a second. Brightly.*) How's everything at the bank, Leo?

LEO: Fine, sir. Everything is fine.

HORACE: How are all the ladies in Mobile? (LEO *draws back.* HORACE *turns, a step to* REGINA, *sharply.*) Whatever made you think I'd let Zan marry——?

REGINA: Do you mean that you are turning this down? Is it possible that's what you mean?

BEN (*nervously, but speaking with good nature—gesturing* REGINA *to be quiet*): No, that's not what he means. Turning down a fortune! Horace is tired. He'd rather talk about it tomorrow——

REGINA: We can't keep putting it off this way. Oscar must be in Chicago by the end of the week with the money and contracts. (*Crosses to* HORACE.)

OSCAR (*giggles, pleased*): Yes, sir. Got to be there end of the week. No sense going without the money.

REGINA (*tensely*): I've waited long enough for your answer. I'm not going to wait any longer.

HORACE (*crossing to stairs, very deliberately*): I'm very tired now, Regina.

BEN (*hastily*): Now Horace probably has his reasons. Things he'd like explained. Tomorrow will do. I can——

REGINA (*turns to* BEN, *sharply*): I want to know his reasons now.

HORACE (*as he climbs the steps*): I don't know them all myself. Let's leave it at that.

REGINA (*crosses upstage to foot

463

of stairs): *We shall not leave it at that.* We have waited for you here like children. Waited for you to come home.

HORACE: So that you could invest my money. So this is why you wanted me home? Well, I had hoped—— (*Quietly.*) If you are disappointed, Regina, I'm sorry. But I must do what I think best. We'll talk about it another day.

REGINA: We'll talk about it now. Just you and me.

HORACE (*stops on landing, looks down at her; his voice is tense*): Please, Regina. It's been a hard trip. I don't feel well. Please leave me alone now.

REGINA (*quietly*): I want to talk to you, Horace. I'm coming up. (*He looks at her for a moment, then moves on again out of sight. She begins to climb stairs.*)

BEN (*softly; REGINA turns to him as he speaks*): Sometimes it is better to wait for the sun to rise again. (*She does not answer.*) And sometimes, as our mother used to tell you, (*REGINA starts up stairs*) it's unwise for a good-looking woman to frown. (*BEN rises, crosses upstage to landing.*) Softness and a smile do more to the heart of men—— (*She disappears. BEN stands looking up the stairs. A long silence. Then, suddenly, OSCAR giggles.*)

OSCAR: Let us hope she'll change his mind. Let us hope.

[*After a second BEN crosses to table, picks up his newspaper, continues to sofa, sits— begins to read. OSCAR looks at BEN. The silence makes LEO uncomfortable.*]

LEO: The paper says twenty-seven cases of Yellow Fever in New Orleans. Guess the flood waters caused it. (*Nobody pays attention.*) Thought they were building levees high enough. Like the niggers always say: a man born of woman can't build nothing high enough for the Mississippi. (*Gets no answer. Gives an embarrassed laugh.*)

[*Upstairs there is the sound of* VOICES. *The* VOICES *are not loud, but* BEN, OSCAR, LEO *become conscious of them.* LEO *crosses upstage to landing, looks up, listens.*]

REGINA: I can't understand what you mean. I can't believe that you mean to turn this down. This is what you've been waiting for, what all of us have been waiting for. You must be going crazy or you must have reasons that you are not telling us.

HORACE: I don't know my reasons. I just don't want it.

REGINA: You don't want it. But I do want it.

OSCAR (*pointing up*): Now just suppose she don't change his mind? Just suppose he keeps on refusing?

BEN (*without conviction*): He's tired. It was a mistake to talk to him today. He's a sick man but he isn't a crazy one.

OSCAR (*giggles*): But just suppose he is crazy. What then?

[LEO *crosses slowly to back of sofa.*]

BEN (*puts down his paper, peers at* OSCAR): Then we'll go outside for the money. There's plenty who would give it.

OSCAR: And plenty who will want a lot for what they give. The ones who are rich enough to give will be smart enough to want. That means we'd be working for them, don't it, Ben?

BEN: You don't have to tell me the things I told you six months ago.

OSCAR: Oh, you're right not to worry. She'll change his mind. She always has.

[*There is a silence.* Suddenly REGINA'S *voice becomes louder and sharper. All of them begin to listen now. Slowly* BEN *rises, goes to listen by the staircase.* OSCAR, *watching him, smiles. As they listen* REGINA'S *voice becomes very loud.* HORACE'S *voice is no longer heard.*]

REGINA: People don't pass up chances like this. I won't let you pass up chances like this. I won't let you pass up this one just be-

cause you've gone crazy!

OSCAR: Maybe.

REGINA: And if you change your mind in a week, it will be too late. It's got to be done now.

HORACE: I won't change my mind. I don't want it.

REGINA: You don't want it but I do want it. I'm your wife. I have a right to expect that you will take care of my future. Of your child's future.

OSCAR: But I don't believe it. I never did believe he was going in with us.

BEN (*turning on him*): What the hell do you expect me to do?

OSCAR (*mildly*): Nothing. You done your almighty best. Nobody could blame you if the whole thing just dripped away right through our fingers. (BEN *crosses to sofa for paper.*) You can't do a thing. But there may be something I could do for us. (OSCAR *rises.* BEN *starts to pick up paper but is stopped by* OSCAR'S *words.*) Or, I might better say, (*crossing to center*) Leo could do for us. (BEN *stops, turns, looks at* OSCAR. LEO *is staring at* OSCAR. *Turns to* LEO.) Ain't that true, son. (LEO *crosses downstage, left.*) Ain't it true you might be able to help your own kin-folks?

LEO (*nervously taking a step to him*): Papa, I——

BEN (*slowly*): How would he

465

help us, Oscar?

OSCAR: Leo's got a friend. Leo's friend owns eighty-eight thousand dollars in Union Pacific bonds. (BEN *turns to look at* LEO.) Leo's friend don't look at the bonds much, not for five or six months at a time.

BEN (*after a pause*): Union Pacific. Uh, huh. Let me understand. Leo's friend would—would lend him these bonds and he——?

OSCAR (*nods*): Would be kind enough to lend them to us.

BEN: Leo.

LEO (*excited, comes to him*): Yes, sir?

BEN: When would your friend be wanting the bonds back?

LEO (*very nervous*): I don't know. I—well, I——

OSCAR (*sharply—steps toward him*): You told me he won't look at them until fall——

LEO: Oh. That's right. But I —not till fall. Uncle Horace never——

BEN (*sharply*): Be still.

OSCAR (*smiles at* LEO): Your Uncle doesn't wish to know your friend's name.

LEO (*starts to laugh*): That's a good one. Not know his name.

———

OSCAR: Shut up, Leo! (LEO *turns away slowly, moves to table on left.* BEN *turns to* OSCAR.) He won't look at them again until

September. That gives us five months. Leo will return the bonds in three months. And we'll have no trouble raising the money once the mills are going up. Will Marshall accept bonds? [BEN *stops to listen to sudden sharp voices from above. The voices are now very angry and very loud.*]

REGINA: I have a right to expect that.

HORACE: Please go away and leave me alone.

REGINA: I won't leave you alone. I demand that you put up this money and I demand that you do it immediately.

BEN (*then smiling*): Why not? Why not? (*Laughs—to* OSCAR.) Good. We are lucky. We'll take the loan from Leo's friend—I think he will make a safer partner than our sister. (*Nods toward stairs. Turns to* LEO.) How soon can you get them?

LEO: Today. Right now. (*Steps to* BEN.) They're in the safe deposit box and——

BEN (*sharply*): I don't want to know where they are.

OSCAR (*laughs*): We will keep it secret from you. (*Pats* BEN's *arm.*)

BEN (*smiles*): Good. Draw a check for our part. You can take the night train for Chicago. (*To* OSCAR.) Well, Oscar, (*holds out his hand—*OSCAR *takes it, they* *shake hands*) good luck to us.

OSCAR (*turns to* BEN): Leo will be taken care of?

LEO: I'm entitled to Uncle Horace's share. I'd enjoy being a partner——

BEN (*turns to stare at him*): You would? You can go to hell, you little—— (*Starts toward* LEO.)

OSCAR (*nervously, stopping* BEN): Now, now. He didn't mean that. I only want to be sure he'll get something out of all this.

BEN: Of course. We'll take care of him. We won't have any trouble about that. I'll see you at the store.

OSCAR (*nods*): That's settled then. Come on, son. (*Starts for door.*)

LEO (*puts out his hand— crosses to* BEN): I didn't mean just that. I was only going to say what a great day this was for me and——

[BEN *ignores his hand.*]

BEN: Go on.

[LEO *looks at him, turns, follows* OSCAR *out.* BEN *stands where he is, thinking. Again the* VOICES UPSTAIRS *can be heard.* REGINA'S *is high and furious.* BEN *looks up, smiles, winces at the noise.*]

REGINA: Nobody would turn this down. You must have your reasons. You must have reasons you won't talk about.

[*The noise of fists pounding against a door is heard, and* ALEXANDRA'S *voice.*]

ALEXANDRA: Mama—Mama— don't——

[*The noise of running footsteps is heard, and* ALEXANDRA *comes running down the steps, speaking as she comes, together with the voices upstairs.*]

REGINA: What are they? What possible reasons could there be? I demand to know. All my life I've had to force you to make something out of yourself.

HORACE: Let me alone.

REGINA: I won't let you alone. If I'd let you alone you'd still be working for somebody else.

HORACE: So that's why you wanted me home?

REGINA: Yes, that's the reason.

HORACE: Then it's a bad one. Because it won't work.

REGINA: Did you think I wanted you home for yourself? Is that what you thought?

ALEXANDRA (*almost crying—on landing*): Uncle Ben! (*Coming down stairs.*) Uncle Ben! Please go up. Please make Mama stop. Uncle Ben, he's sick, he's so sick. How can Mama talk to him like that—please, make her stop. She'll——

BEN: Alexandra, you have a tender heart.

ALEXANDRA: Go on up, Uncle

467

Ben, please——

[*Suddenly the noise from above stops, and a second later there is the sound of a door opening and then being slammed.*]

BEN: Now you see. Everything is over. Don't worry. (*He starts for door.*) Alexandra, I want you to tell your mother how sorry I am that I had to leave. And don't worry so, my dear. Married folk frequently raise their voices, unfortunately. (*He starts to put on his hat and coat as* REGINA *appears on stairs. When she speaks to* BEN, *her voice is cold and calm.*)

ALEXANDRA (*furiously*): How can you treat Papa like this! He's sick. He's very sick. Don't you know that! I won't let you.

REGINA: Mind your business, Alexandra. (ALEXANDRA *turns. To* BEN.) How much longer can you wait for the money?

BEN: He has refused? My, that's too bad.

REGINA: He will change his mind. I'll find a way to make him. What's the longest you can wait now?

BEN: I could wait until next week. But I can't wait until next week. (*He giggles, pleased at the joke.*) I could but I can't. Could and can't. Well, I must go now. I'm very late—— (*He starts.*)

REGINA (*coming downstairs toward him*): You're not going. I want to talk to you.

BEN (*looks at her*): Oh, I was about to give Alexandra a message for you. I wanted to tell you that Oscar is going to Chicago tonight, so we can't be here for our usual Friday supper.

REGINA (*tensely*): Oscar is going to Chi—— (*Softly.*) What do you mean?

BEN: Just that. Everything is settled. He's going on to deliver to Marshall——

REGINA (*taking a step to him*): I demand to know what—you are lying. You are trying to scare me. *You haven't got the money.* How could you have it? You can't have—— (*Ben laughs.*) you will wait until I——

[HORACE *comes into view on landing.*]

BEN: You are getting out of hand. Since when do I take orders from you? (*He turns.*)

REGINA: Wait, you—— (BEN *stops.*) How *can* he go to Chicago? Did a ghost arrive with the money? (BEN *starts for hall.*) I don't believe you. Come back here. (REGINA *starts after him.*) Come back here, you——

[*The door slams. She stops in the doorway, staring, her fists clenched. After a pause she turns slowly and steps into the room.*]

HORACE (*standing on landing of*

the stairs, very quietly): It's a great day when you and Ben cross swords. I've been waiting for it for years.

ALEXANDRA: Papa, Papa, please go back! You will——

HORACE: And so they don't need you, and so you will not have your millions, after all?

REGINA (*turns slowly*): You hate to see anybody live now, don't you? You hate to think that I'm going to be alive and have what I want. (*Comes toward stairs, looking up at him.*)

HORACE: I should have known you'd think that was the reason.

REGINA: Because you're going to die and you know you're going to die.

ALEXANDRA (*shrilly*): Mama! Don't—Don't listen, Papa. Just don't listen. Go away——

HORACE: Not to keep you from getting what you want. Not even partly that. (*Steps down one step, holding on to rail, leaning over to look down at her.*) I'm sick of you, sick of this house, sick of my life here. I'm sick of your brothers and their dirty tricks to

make a dime. There must be better ways of getting rich than cheating niggers on a pound of bacon. Why should I give you the money? (*Very angrily.*) To pound the bones of this town to make dividends for you to spend? You wreck the town, you and your brothers, *you* wreck the town and live on it. Not me. Maybe it's easy for the dying to be honest. But it's not my fault I'm dying. (ADDIE *enters on left, stands at door quietly.*) I'll do no more harm now. I've done enough. I'll die my own way. And I'll do it without making the world any worse. I leave that to you.

REGINA (*looks up at him slowly, calmly*): I hope you die. I hope you die soon. (*Smiles.*) I'll be waiting for you to die.

ALEXANDRA (*shrieking*): Papa! Don't—don't listen—don't——

ADDIE: Come here, Zan. Come out of this room.

[ALEXANDRA *runs quickly to* ADDIE, *who holds her in her arms.* HORACE *turns slowly and starts upstairs.*]

MEDIUM CURTAIN

ACT III

SCENE: *Same as Act One.   Two weeks later.   It is late afternoon and it is raining.   At rise:* HORACE *is sitting near the window in a wheel chair.   On the table next to him is a safe deposit box, and one small bottle of medicine and spoon.* BIRDIE *and* ALEXANDRA *are playing the piano.   On the chair right of table upstage, center, is a large sewing-basket.   (A phrase of the song is played before the curtain rises.   As the curtain is going up the song is reaching its conclusion.)*

BIRDIE (*counting for* ALEXAN-DRA): One and two and three and four.   One and two and three and four.   (*They finish song and laugh.*   ALEXANDRA *repeats a phrase.   Nods—turns to* HORACE.) We used to play together, Horace.   Remember?

HORACE (*has been looking out of window*): What, Birdie?

BIRDIE: We played together. You and me.

ALEXANDRA (*stops playing, looks to* HORACE, *then* BIRDIE): Papa used to play?

BIRDIE: Indeed he did.   (ADDIE *appears at door on left in a large kitchen apron.   She is wiping her hands on a towel.*)   He played the fiddle and very well, too. (*Turns to piano and starts playing.*)

ALEXANDRA (*turns to smile at* HORACE): I never knew——

ADDIE: Where's your Mama?

ALEXANDRA: Gone to Miss Safronia's to fit her dresses.

[ADDIE *nods, starts to exit.*]

HORACE: Addie.

ADDIE: Yes, Mr. Horace.

HORACE (*speaks as if he had made a sudden decision*): Tell Cal to get on his things.   I want him to go an errand.

[ADDIE *nods, exits left.*   HORACE

moves nervously in his chair, looks out of window.]

ALEXANDRA (*who has been watching him*): It's too bad it's been raining all day, Papa.   But you can go out in the yard tomorrow.   Don't be restless.

HORACE: I'm not restless, darling.

[ALEXANDRA *turns to piano and joins* BIRDIE *in playing; after playing one measure together* BIRDIE *stops and turns to* HORACE.   ALEXANDRA *continues playing alone.*]

BIRDIE: I remember so well the time we played together, (*To* ALEXANDRA.) your Papa and me. (*To* HORACE.)   It was the first time Oscar brought me here to supper.   I had never seen all the Hubbards together before, (*to* ALEXANDRA) and you know what a ninny I am and how shy. (*Turns to look at* HORACE.)   You said you could play the fiddle (*rises and goes upstage, center*) and you'd be much obliged if I'd play with you.   (*Pouring glass of water.*)   *I* was obliged to *you*, all right, all right.   (*Laughs when he does not answer her.*)   Horace, (*steps to him, holding glass*) you haven't heard a word I've said.

HORACE: Birdie, when did Oscar get back from Chicago?

BIRDIE: Yesterday. Hasn't he been here yet?

ALEXANDRA (*stops playing*): No. Neither has Uncle Ben since —since that day.

BIRDIE: Oh. (*To* ALEXANDRA.) I didn't know it was *that* bad. (*Turns to* HORACE.) Oscar never tells *me* anything——

HORACE (*smiles, nods*): The Hubbards have had their great quarrel. I knew it would come some day. (*Laughs.*) It came.

ALEXANDRA: It came. It certainly came all right.

BIRDIE (*amazed*): But Oscar was in such a good humor when he got home, (ADDIE *enters.*) I didn't——

HORACE: Yes, I can understand that.

[ADDIE *is carrying a large tray with three water glasses, a carafe of elderberry wine and a plate of cookies, which she puts on the table downstage, left.* BIRDIE *hurries to* ADDIE, *leaving water glass on table upstage, center.*]

ALEXANDRA: Addie! A party! What for?

ADDIE (*pouring wine into the three glasses*): Nothing for. I had the fresh butter so I made the cakes, and a little elderberry does the stomach good in the rain. (ADDIE *looks at* HORACE, *then crosses to center, moves chair upstage, then crosses to him, moves him to center.*)

BIRDIE (*takes her glass and puts* ALEXANDRA's *on piano*): Isn't this nice! A party just for us. Let's play *party* music, Zan.

[ALEXANDRA *begins to play a gay piece.*]

ADDIE (*to* HORACE, *wheeling his chair to center*): Come over here, Mr. Horace, and don't be thinking so much. (*She crosses to table for* HORACE's *glass, brings it to him.* ALEXANDRA *stops playing, turns and watches him.*) A glass of elderberry will do more good.

[ALEXANDRA *reaches for another cake,* BIRDIE *pours herself another glass of wine.*]

ALEXANDRA (*her mouth full*): Good cakes, Addie. It's nice here. Just us. Be nice if it could always be this way.

BIRDIE (*nods, happily*): Quiet and restful. (*Drinks, then crosses to piano stool, sits.*)

ADDIE (*lights lamp on table upstage, center*): Well, it won't be that way long. Little while now, even sitting here, you'll hear the red bricks going into place. The next day the smoke'll be pushing out the chimneys (ALEXANDRA *goes to chair at piano, sits*) and by church time that Sunday every human born of woman will be living on chicken. (*Crossing right to mantel.*) That's how Mr.

Ben's been telling the story.

HORACE (*looks at her*): They believe it that way?

ADDIE: Believe it? (*Placing footstool so that she can reach upstage lamp on mantel.* BIRDIE *crosses to table, pours another drink.*) They use to believing what Mr. Ben orders. There ain't been so much talk around here since Sherman's army didn't come near. (*Lights upper mantel lamp.*)

HORACE (*softly*): They are fools.

ADDIE (*nods*): You ain't born in the South unless you're a fool. (ADDIE *moves footstool to downstage end of mantel, and lights lower mantel lamp.*)

BIRDIE (*has drunk another glass; she has been listening to the others*): But we didn't play together after that night. (*Goes to settee.*) Oscar said he didn't like me to play on the piano. (*Turns to* ALEXANDRA.) You know what he said that night?

[ADDIE *goes to chair upstage, center, gets sewing basket, crosses to chair downstage, right, turns it to face them, sits.*]

ALEXANDRA: Who?

BIRDIE: Oscar. He said that music made him nervous. He said he just sat and waited for the next note. (ALEXANDRA *laughs.*) He wasn't poking fun. He meant it. Ah, well—— (*She finishes

her glass, shakes her head.* HORACE *looks at her, smiles. Crossing to* HORACE.) Your Papa don't like to admit it, but he's been mighty kind to me all these years. (*Running the back of her hand along his sleeve.*) Often he'd step in when somebody said something and once—— (*She stops, turns away, her face still.*) Once he stopped Oscar from—— (*She stops, turns, steps upstage. Quickly.*) I'm sorry I said that. (*Crossing back of settee.*) Why, here I am so happy and yet I think about bad things. (*Laughs nervously.*) That's not right, now is it? (*Goes to table left, pours drink, crosses to upper end of piano.*)

[CAL *appears in the door left. He has on an old coat and is carrying a torn umbrella.*]

ALEXANDRA: Have a cake, Cal.

CAL (*comes in, takes a cake*): Yes'm. You want me, Mr. Horace?

HORACE: What time is it, Cal? (*Puts glass on table.*)

CAL: 'Bout ten minutes before it's five.

HORACE: All right. Now you walk yourself down to the bank. [ALEXANDRA *starts to play softly.*]

CAL: It'll be closed. Nobody'll be there but Mr. Mander, Mr. Joe Horns, Mr. Leo——

HORACE: Go in the back way. They'll be at the table, going over the day's business. (*Points to deposit box.*) See that box?

CAL (*nods*): Yes, sir.

HORACE: You tell Mander that Mr. Horace says he's much obliged to him for bringing the box; it arrived all right.

CAL (*bewildered*): He know you got the box. He bring it hisself Wednesday. I opened the door to him and he say, "Hello, Cal, coming on to summer weather"——

HORACE: You say just what I tell you. Understand?

[BIRDIE *crosses to table left, pours drink, stands at table.*]

CAL: No, sir. I ain't going to say I understand. I'm going down and tell a man he give you something he already know he give you, and you say "understand."

HORACE: Now, Cal——

CAL: Yes, sir. I just going to say you obliged for the box coming all right. I ain't going to understand it, but I'm going to say it——

HORACE: And tell him I want him to come over here after supper, and to bring Mr. Sol Fowler with him.

[ALEXANDRA *playing.*]

CAL (*nods*): He's to come after supper and bring Mr. Sol Fowler, your attorney-*at*-law, with him.

HORACE (*smiles*): That's right. Just walk right in the back room and say your piece. (*Slowly.*)

In front of everybody.

CAL: Yes, sir. (*Mumbles to himself as he exits on left.*)

ALEXANDRA (*who has been watching* HORACE): Is anything the matter, Papa?

HORACE: Oh, no. Nothing.

ADDIE (*watching* BIRDIE *take another glass of wine*): Miss Birdie, that elderberry going to give you a headache spell.

BIRDIE (*beginning to be drunk —gaily*): Oh, I don't think so. I don't think it will. (*Drinks.*)

ALEXANDRA (*as* HORACE *puts his hand to his throat—rises, crosses to his left*): Do you want your medicine, Papa?

HORACE: No, no. I'm all right, darling.

BIRDIE: Mama used to give me elderberry wine when I was a little girl. For hiccoughs. (*Laughs.*) You know, I don't think people get hiccoughs anymore. Isn't that funny? (BIRDIE *laughs.* HORACE *and* ALEXANDRA *laugh, too.*) I used to get hiccoughs just when I shouldn't have. (*Crosses to piano, sits, starts playing, drinks.*)

ADDIE (*nods*): And nobody get growing pains no more. That is funny. Just as if there was some style in what you get. One year an ailment's stylish (BIRDIE *stops playing*) and the next year, it ain't.

BIRDIE (*turns to them*): I re-

473

member. It was my first big party, at Lionnet I mean, and I was so excited—(*rises, crosses to table on left*) and there I was with hiccoughs and Mama laughing. (*Softly. Looking at carafe.*) Mama always laughed. (*Picks up carafe.*) A big party, a lovely dress from Mr. Worth in Paris, France, and hiccoughs. (*Pours drink.*) My brother pounding me on the back and Mama with the elderberry bottle, laughing at me. Everybody was on their way to come, and I was such a ninny, hiccoughing away. (*Drinks. Pauses.*) You know, that was the first day I ever saw Oscar Hubbard. The Ballongs were selling their hosses and he was going there to buy. He passed and lifted his hat—we could see him from the window—and my brother, to tease Mama, said maybe we should have invited the Hubbards to the party. He said Mama didn't like them because they kept a store, and he said that was old-fashioned of her. (*Her face lights up—looking out.*) And then, and *then*, I saw Mama angry for the first time in my life. She said that wasn't the reason. She said she was old-fashioned, but not that way. She said she was old-fashioned enough not to like people who killed animals they couldn't use, and who made their money charging awful in-

terest to poor, ignorant niggers and cheating them on what they bought. She was very angry, Mama was. I had never seen her face like that. And then suddenly she laughed and said, "Look, I've frightened Birdie out of the hiccoughs." (*Her head drops, then softly.*) And so she had. They were all gone. (*Moves up to sofa, sits.*)

ADDIE (*to her sewing*): Yeah, they got mighty well off cheating niggers. (*To them.*) Well, there are people who eat the earth and eat all the people on it like in the Bible with the locusts. Then, there are people who stand around and watch them eat it. (*Softly.*) Sometimes I think it ain't right to stand and watch them do it.

BIRDIE (*thoughtfully*): Like I say, if we could only go back to Lionnet. Everybody'd be better there They'd be good and kind. I like people to be kind. (*Pours drink.*) Don't you, Horace, don't you like people to be kind?

HORACE: Yes, Birdie.

BIRDIE (*very drunk now*): Yes, that was the first day I ever saw Oscar. Who would have thought ——? (*Drinks quickly—caressing the glass.*) You all want to know something? Well, I don't like Leo. My very own son, and I don't like him. (*Laughs, gaily.*) My, I guess, I even like Oscar

474

more. (*Drinks.*)

ALEXANDRA: Why did you marry Uncle Oscar?

ADDIE (*sharply*): That's no question for you to be asking.

HORACE (*sharply*): Why not? She's heard enough around here to ask anything.

ALEXANDRA: Aunt Birdie, why did you marry Uncle Oscar?

BIRDIE (*places glass on table— pleasantly*): I don't know. I thought I liked him. He was so kind to me and I thought it was because he liked me, too. But that wasn't the reason—— (*Wheels on* ALEXANDRA.) Ask why *he* married *me!* I can tell you that: he's told it to me often enough.

ADDIE (*leaning forward*): Miss Birdie, don't——

BIRDIE (*speaking very rapidly, tensely*): My family was good and the cotton on Lionnet's fields was better. Ben Hubbard wanted the cotton and (*rises*) Oscar Hubbard married it for him. He was kind to me, then. He used to smile at me. He hasn't smiled at me since. Everybody knew that's what he married me for. (AD-DIE *rises.*) Everybody but me. (*Turns away.*) Stupid, stupid me.

ALEXANDRA (*to* HORACE, *holding his hand, softly*): I see. (*Hesitates.*) Papa, I mean—when you feel better couldn't we go away?

I mean, by ourselves. Couldn't we find a way to go——

HORACE (*placing his hand over hers*): Yes, I know what you mean. We'll try to find a way. I promise you, darling.

ADDIE (*looks at them for a second, then goes to* BIRDIE): Rest a bit, Miss Birdie. You get talking like this you'll get a headache and——

BIRDIE (*sharply turning to her*): I've never had a headache in my life. (*Begins to cry; hysterically.*) You know it as well as I do. (*Turns to* ALEXANDRA.) I never had a headache, Zan. That's a lie they tell for me. *I drink.* All by myself, in my own room, by myself, *I drink.* Then, when they want to hide it, they say "Birdie's got a headache again"——

ALEXANDRA (*comes to her, quickly*): Aunt Birdie.

BIRDIE (*turning away*): Even you won't like me now. You won't like me, any more.

ALEXANDRA: I love you. I'll always love you.

BIRDIE (*furiously*): Well, don't. (*Turns to* ALEXANDRA.) Don't love me. Because in twenty years you'll just be like me. They'll do all the same things to you. (*Begins to laugh, hysterically.*) You know what? In twenty-two years I haven't had a whole day of happiness. Oh, a little, like today with you all. But never a single,

whole day. I say to myself, if
only I had one more *whole* day,
then—— (*The laugh stops.*)
And that's the way you'll be.
And you'll trail after them, just
like me, hoping they won't be so
mean that day or say something
to make you feel so bad—only
you'll be worse off because you
haven't got my Mama to remember—— (*Turns away, her head
drops. She stands quietly, swaying a little, holding onto sofa.*
ALEXANDRA *leans down, puts her
cheek on* BIRDIE'S *arm.*)

ALEXANDRA (*to* BIRDIE): I guess
we were all trying to make a
happy day. You know, we sit
around and try to pretend nothing's happened. We try to pretend we are not here. We make
believe we are just by ourselves,
some place else, and it doesn't
seem to work. (*Kisses* BIRDIE'S
*hand, which she has been hold-
ing.*) Come now, Aunt Birdie, I'll
walk you home. You and me.
(*She takes* BIRDIE'S *arm; they
move slowly out. In the hallway*
ALEXANDRA *places a raincoat over*
BIRDIE'S *shoulders. They go out.*
ADDIE *and* HORACE *are silent.*)

ADDIE: Well. (*Sighs.*) First
time I ever heard Miss Birdie say
a word. Maybe it's good for her.
(*Picks up glass.*) I'm just sorry
Zan had to hear it. (*Takes glass
to center table.* HORACE *moves
his head as if he were uncom-

fortable.) You feel bad, don't
you? (*He shrugs.*)

HORACE: So you didn't want
Zan to hear? It would be nice to
let her stay innocent, like Birdie
at her age. Let her listen now.
Let her see everything. How else
is she going to know that she's
got to get away? I'm trying to
show her that. I'm trying, but
I've only got a little time left.
She can even hate me when I'm
dead, if she'll only learn to hate
and fear this.

ADDIE: Mr. Horace——

HORACE: Pretty soon there'll be
nobody to help her but you.

ADDIE: What can I do?

HORACE: Take her away.

ADDIE: How can I do that? Do
you think they'd let me just go
away with her——?

HORACE: I'll fix it so they can't
stop you when you're ready to go.
You'll go, Addie?

ADDIE (*after a second, softly*):
Yes sir, I promise. (*He touches
her arm, nods.*)

HORACE (*after a second,
quietly*): I'm going to have Sol
Fowler make me a new will.
They'll make trouble, but you
make Zan stand firm and Fowler'll
do the rest. Addie, I'd like to
leave you something for yourself.
I always wanted to.

ADDIE (*laughs*): Don't you do
that, Mr. Horace. A nigger
woman in a white man's will! I'd

476

never get it nohow.

HORACE: I know. But upstairs in the armoire drawer there's seventeen hundred-dollar bills. It's money left from my trip. It's in an envelope with your name. It's for you.

ADDIE: Seventeen hundred-dollar bills! My God, Mr. Horace, I won't know how to count up that high. (*Shyly.*) It's mighty kind and good of you. I don't know what to *say* for thanks——

CAL (*appears in doorway*): I'm back. (*Stands umbrella in corner. No answer. Crossing to center.*) I'm back.

ADDIE (*crossing to chair downstage, right, sits*): So we see.

HORACE: Well?

CAL: Nothing. I just went down and spoke my piece. Just like you told me, I say Mr. Horace he thank you mightily for the safe box arriving in good shape and he say you come right after supper to his house and bring Mr. Attorney-at-law Sol Fowler with you. Then I wipe my hands on my coat. Every time I ever told a lie in my whole life, I wipe my hands right after. Can't help doing it. Well, while I'm wiping my hands, Mr. Leo jump up and say to me "What box! What you talking about?"

HORACE (*smiles*): Did he?

CAL: And Mr. Leo say he got to leave a little early 'cause he got

something to do. And then Mr. Mander say Mr. Leo should sit right down and finish up his work and stop acting like somebody made him Mr. President. So he sit down. Now, just like I told you, Mr. Mander was mighty surprised with the message because he knows right well he brought the box—— (*Pointing to box. Sighs.*) But he took it all right. Some men take everything easy and some do not.

HORACE (*puts his head back, laughs*): Mr. Leo was telling the truth: he *has* got something to do. I hope Mander don't keep him too long. (*Outside there is the sound of voices.* CAL *exits.* ADDIE *crosses quickly to* HORACE, *begins to wheel his chair toward the stairs. Sharply.*) No. Leave me where I am.

ADDIE: But that's Miss Regina coming back.

HORACE (*nods, looking at door*): Go away, Addie.

ADDIE (*hesitates*): Mr. Horace. Don't talk no more today. You don't feel well and it won't do no good——

HORACE: (*As he hears footsteps in hall*): Go on.

[*She looks at him for a second, then picks up her sewing from table and exits as* REGINA *comes in from hall.* HORACE'S *chair is now so placed that he is in front of*

477

table with the medicine. RE-
GINA *stands in the hall, shakes
umbrella, stands it in corner,
takes off her cloak and throws
it over bannister. She stares
at* HORACE.]

REGINA (*as she takes off her
gloves*): We had agreed that you
were to stay in your part of this
house and I in mine. This room
is *my* part of the house. Please
don't come down here again.

HORACE: I won't.

REGINA (*crosses toward bell-
cord below mantel*): I'll get Cal
to take you upstairs.

HORACE (*smiles*): Before you
do I want to tell you that after
all, we have invested our money
in Hubbard Sons and Marshall,
Cotton Manufacturers.

REGINA (*stops, turns, stares at
him*): What are you talking
about? You haven't seen Ben—
When did you change your mind?

HORACE: I didn't change my
mind. *I* didn't invest the money.
(*Smiles at the expression on her
face.*) It was invested for me.

REGINA (*angrily*): What——?

HORACE: I had eighty-eight thousand dollars' worth of Union Pacific bonds in that safe deposit
box. They are not there now.
Go and look. (*As she stares at
him. Points to box.*) Go and
look, Regina. (*She crosses quickly
to box, opens it. He speaks when
she is at table.*) Those bonds are

478

as negotiable as money. (*She
closes box.*)

REGINA (*turns back to him*):
What kind of joke are you playing now? Is this for my benefit?

HORACE: I don't look in that box
very often, but three days ago, on
Wednesday it was, because I had
made a decision——

REGINA: I want to know what
you are talking about.

HORACE (*sharply*): Don't inter-
rupt me again. (REGINA *stiffens.*)
Because I had made a decision, I
sent for the box. The bonds were
gone. Eighty-eight thousand dollars gone. (*He smiles at her.*)

REGINA (*after a moment's silence*): Do you think I'm crazy
enough to believe what you're
saying?

HORACE (*shrugs*): Believe anything you like.

REGINA (*stares at him, slowly*):
Where did they go to?

HORACE: They are in Chicago.
With Mr. Marshall, I should
guess.

REGINA: What did they do?
Walk to Chicago? Have you
really gone crazy?

HORACE: Leo took the bonds.

REGINA (*turns sharply then
speaks softly, without conviction*):
I don't believe it.

HORACE (*leans forward*): I
wasn't there but I can guess what
happened. (REGINA *sits.*) This
fine gentleman, to whom you

were willing to marry your daughter, took the keys and opened the box. You remember that the day of the fight, Oscar went to Chicago? Well, he went with my bonds that his son Leo had stolen for him. (*Pleasantly.*) And for Ben, of course, too.

REGINA (*slowly, nods*): When did you find out the bonds were gone?

HORACE: Wednesday night.

REGINA: I thought that's what you said. Why have you waited three days to do anything? (*Suddenly laughs.*) This *will* make a fine story.

HORACE (*nods*): Couldn't it?

REGINA (*still laughing—rises, crosses upstage left, takes off hat*): A fine story to hold over their heads. How could they be such fools? (*Turns to him back of settee.*)

HORACE: But I'm not going to hold it over their heads.

REGINA (*the laugh stops*): What?

HORACE (*turns his chair to face her*): I'm going to let them keep the bonds—as a loan from you. An eighty-eight thousand dollar loan; they should be grateful to you. They will be, I think.

REGINA (*slowly, smiles*): I see. You are punishing me. But I won't let you punish me. If you won't do anything, I will. Now. (*She starts for door.*)

HORACE: You won't do anything. Because you can't. (RE-GINA *stops.*) It won't do you any good to make trouble because I shall simply say that I lent them the bonds.

REGINA (*slowly*): You would do that?

HORACE: Yes. For once in your life I am tying your hands. There is nothing for you to do. (*There is silence. Then she sits down.*)

REGINA: I see. You are going to lend them the bonds and let them keep all the profit they make on them, and there is nothing I can do about it. Is that right?

HORACE: Yes.

REGINA (*softly*): Why did you say that I was making this gift?

HORACE: I was coming to that. I am going to make a new will, Regina, leaving you eighty-eight thousand dollars in Union Pacific bonds. The rest will go to Zan. It's true that your brothers have borrowed your share for a little while. After my death I advise you to talk to Ben and Oscar. They won't admit anything and Ben, I think, will be smart enough to see that he's *safe*. Because I knew about the theft and said nothing. Nor *will* I say anything as long as I live. Is that clear to you?

REGINA (*nods, softly, without looking at him*): You will not say anything as long as you live.

479

HORACE: That's right. And by that time they will probably have replaced your bonds, and then they'll belong to you and nobody but us will ever know what happened. (*Stops, smiles.*) They'll be around any minute to see what I am going to do. I took good care to see that word reached Leo. They'll be mighty relieved to know I'm going to do nothing and Ben will think it all a capital joke on you. And that will be the end of that. There's nothing you can do to them, nothing you can do to me.

REGINA: You hate me very much.

HORACE: No.

REGINA: Oh, I think you do. (*Puts her head back, sighs.*) Well, we haven't been very good together. Anyway, I don't hate you either. I have only contempt for you. I've always had.

HORACE: From the very first?

REGINA: I think so.

HORACE: I was in love with *you.* But why did *you* marry *me?*

REGINA: I was lonely when I was young.

HORACE: *You* were lonely?

REGINA: Not the way people usually mean. Lonely for all the things I wasn't going to get. Everything in this house was so busy and there was so little place for what I wanted. I wanted the world. Then, and then——

(*Smiles.*) Papa died and left the money to Ben and Oscar.

HORACE: And you married me?

REGINA: Yes, I thought—but I was wrong. You were a small-town clerk then. You haven't changed.

HORACE (*nods, smiles*): And that wasn't what you wanted.

REGINA: No. No, it wasn't what I wanted. (*Pauses, leans back, pleasantly.*) It took me a little while to find out I had made a mistake. As for you—I don't know. It was almost as if I couldn't stand the kind of man you were—— (*Smiles, softly.*) I used to lie there at night, praying you wouldn't come near——

HORACE: Really? It was as bad as that?

REGINA (*nods*): Remember when I went to Doctor Sloan and I told you he said there was something the matter with me and that you shouldn't touch me any more?

HORACE: I remember.

REGINA: But you believed it? I couldn't understand that. I couldn't understand that anybody could be such a soft fool. That was when I began to despise you.

HORACE (*puts his hand to his throat, glances around at bottle of medicine on table, then to her*): Why didn't you leave me?

REGINA: I told you I married you *for* something. It turned out it was only for this. (*Carefully.*) This wasn't what I wanted, but it was something. I never thought about it much, but if I had, (HORACE *puts his hand to his throat.*) I'd have known that you would die before I would. But I couldn't have known that you would get heart trouble so early and so bad. I'm lucky, Horace. I've always been lucky. (HORACE *turns slowly to medicine.*) I'll be lucky again. [HORACE *looks at her. Then he puts his hand to his throat. Because he cannot reach the bottle he moves the chair closer. He reaches for medicine, takes out cork, picks up spoon, tries to pour some in the spoon, the bottle slips out of his shaking fingers, and crashes on the table. He draws in his breath, gasps.*]

HORACE: Please. Tell Addie— the other bottle is upstairs.

[*She has not moved. She does not move now. He stares at her. Then, suddenly as if he understood, he raises his voice. It is a panic-stricken whisper, too small to be heard outside the room.*] Addie! Addie! Come—— (*Stops as he hears the softness of his voice. He makes a sudden, furious spring from the chair to the stairs, taking the first few steps as if he were a desperate runner. On* the fourth step he slips, gasps, grasps the rail, makes a great effort to reach the landing. When he reaches the landing, he is on his knees. His knees give way, he falls on the landing, out of view. REGINA *has not turned during his climb up the stairs. Now she waits a second. Then she goes below the landing, speaks up.*]

REGINA: Horace. (*When there is no answer, she turns, crosses to the left door, opens it, calls.*) Addie! Cal! Come in here. (*Starts up the steps. When she is on first step,* ADDIE *appears, followed by* CAL. *Both run toward stairs.*) He's had an attack. Come up here. (*They run up steps quickly, passing* REGINA.)

CAL: My God! Mr. Horace——

REGINA (*they cannot be seen now; her voice comes from the head of the stairs*): Be still, Cal. Bring him in here.

[*Before the footsteps and voices have completely died away,* ALEXANDRA *appears in hall door, in her raincloak and hood. She comes into the room, begins to unfasten the cloak, suddenly looks around, sees the empty wheel-chair, stares, begins to move swiftly as if to look in the dining-room. At the same moment,* ADDIE *runs down the stairs.*

481

She turns and stares up at ADDIE.]

ALEXANDRA: Addie! What?

ADDIE (*takes* ALEXANDRA *by the shoulders*): I'm going for the doctor. Go upstairs.

[ALEXANDRA *looks at her, then quickly breaks away and runs up the steps.* ADDIE *goes out on the left. The stage is empty for a minute. Then the front door bell begins to ring. When there is no answer it rings again. A second later* LEO *appears in the hall, talking as he comes in.*]

LEO (*very nervous*): Hello. (*Irritably.*) Never saw any use ringing a bell when a door was open. If you are going to ring a bell, then somebody should answer it. (*Gets in the room, looks around, puzzled, listens, hears no sound.*) Aunt Regina. (*Puts hat on sofa. No answer. He moves around restlessly.*) Addie—— Where the hell——? (*Crosses to bell cord, rings it impatiently, twice, waits and gets no answer; calls.*) Cal! (*Rings again, then calls.*) Cal—— (*After a second* CAL *appears on stair landing.*)

CAL (*his voice is soft, shaken*): Mr. Leo. Miss Regina says you stop that screaming noise.

LEO (*angrily*): Where is everybody?

CAL: Mr. Horace he got an attack. He's bad. Miss Regina says you stop that noise.

LEO: Uncle Horace—What—— What happened? (CAL *starts down stairs.* CAL *shakes his head, begins to move swiftly toward doorway.* LEO *looks around wildly.*) But when— You seen Mr. Oscar or Mr. Ben? (CAL *shakes his head. Moves on.* LEO *grabs him by the arm.*) Answer me, will you?

CAL: No ain't seen 'em. I ain't got time to answer you. (CAL *breaks* LEO's *hold.*) I got to get things. (CAL *exits.*)

LEO: But what's the matter with him? When did this happen——? (*Calling after* CAL.) You'd think Papa'd be some place where you could find him. I been chasing him all afternoon.

[OSCAR *and* BEN *come swiftly into the room, talking excitedly.*]

OSCAR: I hope it's not a bad attack.

BEN: It's the first one he's had since he come home.

[LEO *crosses to* OSCAR, *excitedly.*]

LEO: Papa, I've been looking all over town for you and Uncle Ben——

BEN: Where is he?

OSCAR: Addie said it was sudden.

BEN (*to* LEO): Where is he? When did it happen?

LEO: Upstairs. Will you listen to me, please? I been looking for you for——

OSCAR (*to* BEN): You think we should go up?

[BEN, *looking up the steps, shakes his head.*]

BEN: I don't know. I don't know.

OSCAR (*shakes his head*): But he was all right——

LEO (*almost yelling*): *Will you listen to me?*

OSCAR (*sharply to* LEO): What is the matter with you?

LEO (*coming to him*): I been trying to tell you. I been trying to find you for an hour——

OSCAR: Tell me what?

LEO: Uncle Horace knows about the bonds. He knows about them. He's had the box since Wednesday——

BEN (*sharply*): Stop shouting! What the hell are you talking about?

LEO (*furiously — crossing to* BEN): I'm telling you he knows about the bonds. Ain't that clear enough——?

OSCAR (*grabbing* LEO's *arm*): You God damn fool! Stop screaming!

BEN: Now what happened? Talk quietly.

LEO (*closes his eyes, angrily, attempting patience*): You heard me. Uncle Horace knows about the bonds. He's known since Wednesday.

BEN: How do you know that? (*After a second.* OSCAR *draws close to them.*)

LEO: Because Cal comes down to Mander and says the box came O. K. and——

OSCAR (*trembling, crosses to* BEN, *pushing* LEO *away*): That might not mean a thing——

LEO (*angrily*): No? It might not, huh? (*Takes* OSCAR's *arm.*) Then he says Mander should come here tonight and bring Sol Fowler with him. I guess that don't mean a thing either.

OSCAR (*panicky, to* BEN): Ben —What—Do you think he's seen the——

BEN (*motions to box*): There's the box. (*Both* OSCAR *and* LEO *turn sharply.* LEO *makes a leap to the box, picks it up.*) You ass. Put it down. What are you going to do with it, eat it?

LEO: I'm going to—— (*Starts.*)

BEN (*furiously*): Put it down. Don't touch it again. Now sit down and shut up for a minute.

[LEO *puts box down on table.*]

OSCAR: Since Wednesday. (*To* LEO.) You said he had it since Wednesday. Why didn't he say something—— (*To* BEN.) I don't understand——

LEO: I can put it back. I can put it back before anybody knows.

BEN (*softly*): He's had it since Wednesday. Yet he hasn't said a word to us.

OSCAR: *Why? Why?*

483

LEO: What's the difference why? He was getting ready to say plenty. He was going to say it to Fowler tonight——

OSCAR (*angrily*): Be still. (*Turns to* BEN, *looks at him, waits.*)

BEN (*after a moment*): I don't believe that.

LEO (*wildly, leaning toward* BEN *over table*): You don't believe it? What do I care what *you* believe? I do the dirty work and then——

BEN (*turning his head sharply to* LEO): I'm remembering that. I'm remembering that, Leo.

OSCAR: What do you mean?

LEO: You——

BEN (*to* OSCAR): If you don't shut that little fool up, I'll show you what I mean. (OSCAR *makes a gesture at* LEO. LEO *crosses upstage, center.*) For some reason he knows, but he don't say a word.

OSCAR (*crossing to* BEN): Maybe he didn't know that *we.*

BEN (*quickly*): That *Leo*——? He's no fool. (*Crossing up to* LEO.) Does Mander know the bonds are missing?

LEO: How could I tell? I was half crazy. I don't think so. Because Mander seemed kind of puzzled and——

OSCAR: But we got to find out——

[*He breaks off as* CAL *comes into the room carrying a kettle of*

hot water and clean cloths, leaving door open. They turn to CAL.]

BEN: How is he, Cal?

CAL: I don't know, Mr. Ben. He was bad. (*Going toward stairs.*)

OSCAR: But when did it happen?

CAL (*shrugs*): He wasn't feeling so bad early. (ADDIE *comes in quickly from hall.*) Then there he is next thing on the landing, fallen over, his eyes tight—— (*He hurries toward stairs.*)

ADDIE (*to* CAL): Dr. Sloan's over at the Ballongs. Hitch the buggy and go get him. (*She takes kettle and cloths from him, pushes him, runs up stairs.*) Go on. (*She disappears.*)

[CAL *goes out on left, picking up his umbrella as he goes.*]

BEN (*takes off coat and hat, places them on chair*): Never seen Sloan anywhere when you need him.

OSCAR (*softly*): Sounds bad.

LEO (*taking a step to* BEN): He would have told *her* about it. Aunt Regina. He would have told his own wife——

BEN (*turning to* LEO): Yes, he might have told her. (*Crossing, to front wheel-chair.*) But they weren't on such pretty terms and maybe he didn't. Maybe he didn't. (*Goes quickly to* LEO.) Now, listen to me. If she doesn't know, it may work out all right. (*Holding* LEO's *lapel.*) If she does know, you're to say he lent you the bonds.

LEO: Lent them to me! Who's going to believe that?

BEN: Nobody.

OSCAR (*to* LEO): Don't you understand? It can't do no harm to say it——

[BEN *releases grip on* LEO's *lapel.*]

LEO: Why should I say he lent them to me? Why not to you? (*Carefully.*) Why not to Uncle Ben?

BEN (*smiles*): Just because he didn't lend them to me. Remember that.

LEO: But all he has to do is say he didn't lend them to me——

BEN (*furiously*): But for some reason, he doesn't seem to be talking, does he?

[*There are footsteps above. They all stand looking at the stairs.* REGINA *begins to come slowly down.*]

BEN (*moving toward* REGINA): What happened?

REGINA: He's had a bad attack.

OSCAR: Too bad. I'm so sorry we weren't here when—when Horace needed us.

BEN: When *you* needed us.

REGINA: Yes.

BEN: How is he? Can we—can we go up?

REGINA (*shakes her head*): He's not conscious.

OSCAR (*pacing around*): It's that—it's that bad? Wouldn't you think Sloan could be found quickly, just once, just once?

REGINA: I don't think there is much for him to do.

BEN (*crossing to* REGINA): Oh, don't talk like that. He's come through attacks before. He will now.

[REGINA *sits down. After a second she speaks softly.*]

REGINA: Well. We haven't seen each other since the day of our fight.

BEN (*tenderly*): That was nothing. Why, you and Oscar and I used to fight when we were kids.

OSCAR (*hurriedly*): Don't you think we should go up? Is there anything we can do for Horace——

BEN: You don't feel well. Ah——

REGINA (*without looking at them*): No, I don't.—Horace told me about the bonds this afternoon.

[*There is an immediate shocked silence.*]

LEO (*taking several short steps*): The bonds. What do you mean? What bonds? What——?

OSCAR (*looks at him furiously— then to* REGINA): The Union Pacific bonds? *Horace's* Union Pacific bonds?

REGINA: Yes.

OSCAR (*steps to her, very nerv-*

485

ously): Well. Well what—what about them? What—what could he say?

REGINA: He said that Leo had stolen the bonds and given them to you.

OSCAR (*aghast, very loudly*): That's ridiculous, Regina, absolutely——

LEO: I don't know what you're talking about. What would I— why——

REGINA (*wearily to* BEN): Isn't it enough that he stole them from me? Do I have to listen to this in the bargain?

OSCAR: You are talking——

LEO: I didn't steal anything. I don't know why——

REGINA (*to* BEN): Would you ask them to stop that, please?

[*There is silence for a minute.* BEN *glowers at* OSCAR *and* LEO, LEO *looks at* OSCAR.]

BEN: Aren't we starting at the wrong end, Regina? What did Horace tell you?

REGINA (*smiles at him*): He told me that Leo had stolen the bonds.

LEO (*to* BEN): I didn't steal——

REGINA: Please. Let me finish. Then he told me that he was going to pretend that he had lent them to you (LEO *turns sharply to* REGINA, *then looks at* OSCAR, *then looks back at* REGINA.) as a present from me to my brothers. He said there was nothing I could do

about it. He said the rest of his money would go to Alexandra. That is all.

[*There is a silence.* OSCAR *coughs,* LEO *smiles slyly.*]

LEO (*taking a step to her*): I told you he had lent them—I could have told you——

REGINA (*ignores him, smiles sadly at* BEN): So I'm very badly off, you see. (*Carefully.*) But Horace said there was nothing I could do about it as long as he was alive to say he had lent you the bonds.

BEN: You shouldn't feel that way. It can all be explained, all be adjusted. It isn't as bad——

REGINA: So you, at least, are willing to admit that the bonds were stolen?

OSCAR (*laughs nervously*): I admit no such thing. It's possible that Horace made up that part of the story to tease you—— (*Looks at her.*) Or perhaps to punish you. Punish you.

REGINA (*sadly*): It's not a pleasant story. I feel bad, Ben, naturally. I hadn't thought——

BEN: Now you shall have the bonds safely back. That was the understanding, wasn't it, Oscar?

OSCAR: Yes.

REGINA: I'm glad to know that. (*Smiles.*) Ah, I had greater hopes——

BEN: Don't talk that way. That's foolish. (*Looks at his*

watch.) I think we ought to drive out for Sloan ourselves. (*Looks at* OSCAR.) If we can't find him we'll go over to Senateville for Doctor Morris. (*Looks at her.* OSCAR *crosses for hat,* LEO *crosses back of sofa to hall, picking up hat.*) And don't think I'm dismissing this other business. I'm not. We'll have it all out on a more appropriate day. (BEN *crosses to chair for coat and hat.*)

REGINA (*waits until they are near the door; looks up, quietly*): I don't think you had better go yet. I think you had better stay and sit down.

[OSCAR *crosses to hall.*]

BEN (*picking up coat and hat*): We'll be back with Sloan.

REGINA: Cal has gone for him. I don't want you to go.

[OSCAR *turns, looks at them.*]

BEN (*crossing upstage, center*): Now don't worry and——

REGINA: You will come back in this room and sit down. I have something more to say.

[LEO *steps back into view.*]

BEN (*turns, comes toward her*): Since when do I take orders from you?

REGINA (*smiles*): You don't— yet. (OSCAR *takes a step in. Sharply.*) Come back, Oscar. You too, Leo.

OSCAR (*takes another step in— sure of himself, laughs*): My dear Regina——

BEN (*crosses to her—softly, pats her hand*): Horace has already clipped your wings and very wittily. Do I have to clip them, too? (*Smiles at her.*) You'd get farther with a smile, Regina. I'm a soft man for a woman's smile.

REGINA: I'm smiling, Ben. I'm smiling because you are quite safe while Horace lives. But I don't think Horace will live. (LEO *looks at* OSCAR. *To* BEN.) And if he doesn't live I shall want seventy-five per cent in exchange for the bonds.

BEN (*steps back—whistles, laughs*): Greedy! What a greedy girl you are! You want so much of everything.

REGINA: Yes. And if I don't get what I want I am going to put all three of you in jail.

OSCAR (*furiously*): You're mighty crazy. Having just admitted——

BEN: And on what evidence would you put Oscar and Leo in jail?

REGINA (*laughs, gaily*): Oscar, listen to him. He's getting ready to swear that it was you and Leo! What do you say to that? (*As* OSCAR *turns furiously toward* BEN): Oh, don't be angry, Oscar. I'm going to see that he goes in with you.

BEN: Try anything you like, Regina. (*Sharply.*) And now we can stop all this and say goodbye

487

to you. (ALEXANDRA *comes into view on landing, moving slowly down steps.*) It's his money and he's obviously willing to let us borrow it. (*More pleasantly.*) Learn to make threats when you can carry them through: for how many years have I told you a good-looking woman gets more by being soft and appealing? Mama used to tell you that. (*Looks at his watch.*) Where the hell is Sloan? (*To* OSCAR.) Take the buggy and—— (*As* BEN *turns to* OSCAR, *he sees* ALEXANDRA *and stops.* OSCAR *turns to her.* ALEXANDRA *has come slowly down the steps. She walks stiffly. She comes down as if she did not see any of them. She goes slowly to lower window, her head bent. They all turn to look at her.*)

OSCAR (*after a second, moving toward her above sofa*): What? Alexandra——

[*She does not answer. After a second* ADDIE *comes slowly down the stairs, moving as if she were very tired. At foot of steps, she looks at* ALEXAN-DRA, *then turns and slowly crosses to left door and exits.* REGINA *rises. She sees* ADDIE. BEN *looks nervously at* ALEX-ANDRA, *at* REGINA.]

OSCAR (*as* ADDIE *passes him, irritably to* ALEXANDRA): Well, what is—— (*Turns into room—sees* ADDIE *at foot of steps.*)—

what's? (BEN *puts up a hand, shakes his head. His movements become nervous and fidgety, as if he were anxious to get out.* OSCAR *clears his throat, looks at* REGINA, *tries to fill the silence.* LEO *comes downstage.*) My God, I didn't know—who *could* have known—I didn't know he was that sick. Well, well—I——

[REGINA *stands quietly, her back to them.*]

BEN (*softly, sincerely*): Seems like yesterday when he first came here. (*Places coat and hat on chair above wheel-chair.*)

OSCAR (*sincerely, nervously*): Yes, that's true. (*Turns to* BEN.) The whole town loved him and respected him.

ALEXANDRA (*turns and crosses to sofa*): Did you love him, Uncle Oscar?

OSCAR: Certainly, I—What a strange thing to ask? I——

ALEXANDRA (*turns to look at* BEN): Did you love him, Uncle Ben?

BEN (*simply*): He had——

ALEXANDRA (*suddenly starts to laugh very loudly*): And you, Mama, did you love him, too?

REGINA: I know what you feel, Alexandra, but please try to control yourself.

ALEXANDRA (*still laughing*): I'm trying, Mama. I'm trying very hard.

BEN: Grief makes some people

laugh and some people cry. It's better to cry, Alexandra.

ALEXANDRA (*the laugh has stopped; tensely—moves toward* REGINA, *crossing to front sofa*): What was Papa doing on the staircase?

REGINA (*crossing to* ALEXANDRA. BEN *turns to look at* ALEXANDRA *with interest*): Please go and lie down, my dear. We all need time to get over shocks like this. (ALEXANDRA *does not move.* REGINA's *voice becomes softer, more insistent.*) Please go, Alexandra.

ALEXANDRA: No, Mama. I'll wait. I've got to talk to you.

REGINA: Later. Go and rest now.

ALEXANDRA (*quietly*): I'll wait, Mama. I've plenty of time. (*Sits down on sofa.*) All my life.

REGINA (*hesitates, stares, makes a half shrug, turns back to* BEN): As I was saying. Tomorrow morning I am going up to Judge Simmes. I shall tell him about Leo.

BEN (*motioning toward* ALEXANDRA): Not in front of the child, Regina. I——

REGINA (*turns to him—sharply*): I didn't ask her to stay. Tomorrow morning I go to Judge Simmes——

OSCAR: And what proof? What proof of all this——

REGINA (*turns, crosses to center between* BEN *and* OSCAR; *to* OSCAR *sharply*): None. I won't need any. The bonds are missing and they are with Marshall. That will be enough. If it isn't, I'll add what's necessary.

BEN: I'm sure of that.

REGINA: You can be quite sure.

OSCAR: We'll deny——

REGINA: Deny your heads off. You couldn't find a jury that wouldn't weep for a woman whose brothers steal from her. *And* you couldn't find twelve men in this State you haven't cheated and hate you for it.

OSCAR: What kind of talk is this? You couldn't do anything like that! We're your own brothers. How can you talk that way when upstairs not five minutes ago—— (*Points up stairs.*)

REGINA (*slowly*): There are people who can never go back, who must finish what they start. I am one of those people, Oscar. (*After a slight pause, turns back to* BEN, *almost teasingly.*) Where was I? (*Smiles at* BEN.) Well, they'll convict you. But I won't care much if they don't. (*Leans forward, pleasantly.*) Because by that time you'll be ruined. I shall also tell my story to Mr. Marshall, who likes me, I think, and who will not want to be involved in your scandal. A respectable firm like Marshall & Company! The deal would be off in an hour. (*Turns to them an-*

grily.) And you know it. Now I don't want to hear any more from any of you. *You'll do no more bargaining in this house.* I'll take my seventy-five per cent and we'll forget the story forever. That's one way of doing it, and the way I prefer. (*Crosses to settee.*) You know me well enough to know that I don't mind taking the other way. (*Sits down on settee.*)

BEN (*after a second, slowly*): None of us have ever known you well enough, Regina.

REGINA: You're getting old, Ben. Your tricks aren't as smart as they used to be. (*There is no answer. She waits, then smiles.*) All right. I take it that's settled and I get what I asked for.

OSCAR (*furiously to* BEN): Are you going to let her do this——?

BEN (*turns to look at him, slowly*): You have a suggestion?

REGINA (*puts her arms above her head, stretches, laughs*): No, he hasn't. All right. Now, Leo, I have forgotten that you ever saw the bonds. (*Archly, to* BEN *and* OSCAR.) And as long as you boys both behave yourselves, I've forgotten that we ever talked about them. You can draw up the necessary papers tomorrow.

[BEN *laughs.* LEO *stares at him, starts for door. Exits.* OSCAR *moves toward door, angrily.* REGINA *looks at* BEN, *nods,*

490

laughs with him. For a second, OSCAR *stands in the door, looking back at them. Then he exits.*]

REGINA: You're a good loser, Ben. I like that.

BEN (*he picks up his coat, then turns to her*): Well, I say to myself, what's the good? You and I aren't like Oscar. We're not sour people. I think that comes from a good digestion. (*Putting on coat.*) Then, too, one loses today and wins tomorrow. I say to myself, years of planning and I get what I want. Then I don't get it. But I'm not discouraged. The century's turning, the world is open. Open for people like you and me. Ready for us, waiting for us. After all, this is just the beginning. There are hundreds of Hubbards sitting in rooms like this throughout the country. All their names aren't Hubbard, but they are all Hubbards and they will own this country some day. We'll get along.

REGINA (*smiles*): I think so.

BEN (*crosses to chair, picks up hat*): Then, too, I say to myself, things may change. (*Looks at* ALEXANDRA.) I agree with Alexandra. (*Looks up at landing.*) What is a man in a wheel-chair doing on a staircase? I ask myself that.

REGINA (*looks up at him*): And what do you answer?

BEN: I have no answer. But maybe some day I will. Maybe never, but maybe some day. (*Smiles. Patting her arm.*) When I do, I'll let you know. (*Starts toward hall.*)

REGINA (*as he turns for door*): When you do, write me. I will be in Chicago. (*Gaily.*) Ah, Ben, if Papa had only left me his money.

BEN: I'll see you tomorrow.

REGINA: Oh, yes. Certainly. You'll be sort of working for me now.

BEN (*turns, crosses to sofa, looks at* ALEXANDRA, *smiles at her*): Alexandra, you're turning out to be a right interesting girl. (*Looks at* REGINA.) Well, good-night, all. (*He exits.*)

REGINA (*sits quietly for a second, stretches, turns to look at* ALEXANDRA): What do you want to talk to me about, Alexandra?

ALEXANDRA (*slowly*): I've changed my mind. I don't want to talk. There's nothing to talk about now.

REGINA: You're acting very strange. Not like yourself. You've had a bad shock today. I know that. And you loved Papa, but you must have expected this to come someday. You knew how sick he was.

ALEXANDRA: I knew. We all knew.

REGINA: It will be good for you to get away from here. Good for me, too. Time heals most wounds, Alexandra. You're young, you shall have all the things I wanted. I'll make the world for you the way I wanted it to be for me. (*Uncomfortably.*) Don't sit there staring. You've been around Birdie so much you're getting just like her.

ALEXANDRA (*nods*): Funny. That's what Aunt Birdie said today.

REGINA (*nods*): Be good for you to get away from all this.

[ADDIE *enters.*]

ADDIE: Cal is back, Miss Regina. He says Dr. Sloan will be coming in a few minutes.

REGINA: We'll go in a few weeks. A few weeks! That means two or three Saturdays, two or three Sundays. (*Sighs.*) Well, I'm very tired. I shall go to bed. I don't want any supper. Put the lights out and lock up. (ADDIE *moves to the piano lamp, turns it out.*) You go to your room, Alexandra Addie will bring you something hot. You look very tired. (*Rises, crosses upstage center. To* ADDIE.) Call me when Dr. Sloan gets here. I don't want to see anybody else. I don't want any condolence calls tonight. The whole town will be over.

ALEXANDRA: Mama, I'm not coming with you. I'm not going

491

to Chicago.

REGINA (*turns, to her*): You're very upset, Alexandra.

ALEXANDRA (*quietly*): I mean what I say. With all my heart.

REGINA (*quietly*): We'll talk about it tomorrow. The morning will make a difference.

ALEXANDRA: It won't make any difference. And there isn't anything to talk about. I am going away from you. Because I want to. Because I know Papa would want me to.

REGINA (*puzzled, careful, polite*): You *know* your Papa wanted you to go away from me?

ALEXANDRA: Yes.

REGINA (*softly*): And if I say no?

ALEXANDRA (*looks at her, firmly*): Say it, Mama, say it. And see what happens.

REGINA (*softly, after a pause*): And if I make you stay?

ALEXANDRA: That would be foolish. It wouldn't work in the end.

REGINA: You're very serious about it, aren't you? (*Crosses to steps—up two steps.*) Well, you'll change your mind in a few days.

ALEXANDRA: You only change your mind when you want to. And I won't want to.

REGINA (*going up steps*): Alexandra, I've come to the end of my rope. (*On fifth step.*) Some-

where there has to be what I want, too. Life goes too fast. Do what you want; think what you want; go where you want. I'd like to keep you with me, but I won't make you stay. Too many people used to make me do too many things. No. (*Going up to landing.*) I won't make you stay.

ALEXANDRA: You couldn't, Mama, because I want to leave here. As I've never wanted anything in my life before. Because I understand what Papa was trying to tell me. (*Pause.*) All in one day: Addie said there were people who ate the earth and other people who stood around and watched them do it. And just now Uncle Ben said the same thing. Really, he said the same thing. (*Tensely.*) Well, tell him for me, Mama, I'm not going to stand around and watch you do it. Tell him I'll be fighting as hard as he'll be fighting (*rises*) someplace where people don't just stand around and watch.

REGINA: Well, you have spirit, after all. I used to think you were all sugar water. We don't have to be bad friends. I don't want us to be bad friends Alexandra. (*Starts off, stops, turns to* ALEXANDRA.) Would you like to come and talk to me, Alexandra? Would you—would you like to sleep in my room tonight?

ALEXANDRA (*takes a step to-*

492

ward her): Are you afraid,
Mama?
[REGINA *does not answer, but
moves slowly out of sight.*

ADDIE *then comes to* ALEXAN-
DRA, *squeezes her arm with
affection and pride, then
starts for the other lamp, as*

THE CURTAIN FALLS

Brown, John Mason, BROADWAY IN REVIEW. New York: W. W. Norton & Company, Inc., 1940.

Chandler, Frank W., ASPECTS OF MODERN DRAMA. New York: The Macmillan Company, 1914.

Cheney, Sheldon, THE THEATRE. New York: Longmans, Green & Company, Inc., 1929.

Clark, Barrett H., and Freedley, George H., A HISTORY OF MODERN DRAMA. New York: D. Appleton-Century Company, Inc., 1947.

Clark, Barrett H., A STUDY OF MODERN DRAMA, Second Revised Edition. New York: D. Appleton-Century Company, Inc., 1938.

Clurman, Harold, THE FERVENT YEARS—THE STORY OF THE GROUP THEATRE AND THE THIRTIES. New York: Alfred A. Knopf, Inc., 1945.

Dickinson, Thomas H., ed., THE THEATRE IN A CHANGING EUROPE. New York: Henry Holt & Company, Inc., 1937.

Dobree, Bonamy, TIMOTHEUS: OR THE FUTURE OF THE THEATRE. New York: E. P. Dutton & Co., Inc., 1925.

Gassner, John, MASTERS OF THE DRAMA. New York: Dover Publications, 1945.

Huneker, James, ICONOCLASTS. New York: Charles Scribner's Sons, 1905.

Jones, Robert E., THE DRAMATIC IMAGINATION. New York: Duell, Sloan & Pearce, Inc., 1941.

Krutch, Joseph W., THE AMERICAN DRAMA SINCE 1918. New York: Random House, Inc., 1939.

Lewisohn, Ludwig, EXPRESSION IN AMERICA. New York: Harper & Brothers, 1932.

Macgowan, Kenneth, FOOTLIGHTS ACROSS AMERICA. New York: Harcourt, Brace & Company, Inc., 1929.

Mantle, Burns, THE BEST PLAYS OF 1919-20 (and subsequent years). New York: Dodd, Mead & Company, 1920 to date.

Mantle, Burns, CONTEMPORARY AMERICAN PLAYWRIGHTS. New York: Dodd, Mead & Company, 1938.

Peacock, Ronald, THE POET IN THE THEATRE. New York: Harcourt, Brace & Company, Inc., 1946.

Selden, Samuel, THE STAGE IN ACTION. New York: F. S. Crofts & Company, 1941.

Shaw, G. B., DRAMATIC OPINIONS AND ESSAYS, 2 vols. New York: Brentano's, 1907.

Thouless, Priscilla, MODERN POETIC DRAMA. New York: Peter Smith, 1934.